D1161212

ARGENTINA
1516-1982

ARGEN
1516-

TINA
1982

*From Spanish Colonization
to the Falklands War*

DAVID ROCK

UNIVERSITY OF CALIFORNIA PRESS
BERKELEY   LOS ANGELES

University of California Press
Berkeley and Los Angeles, California

© 1985 by
The Regents of the University of California

Library of Congress Cataloging in Publication Data

Rock, David, 1945–
  Argentina, 1516–1982.

  Bibliography: p.
  Includes index.
  1. Argentina—History. I. Title.
F2831.R68 1985 982 83-17948
ISBN 0-520-05189-0

Printed in the United States of America

1 2 3 4 5 6 7 8 9

For Rosalind, Edward, Charles, and our families at home

In Xanadu did Kubla Khan
    A stately pleasure-dome decree:
Where Alph, the sacred river, ran
Through caverns measureless to man
    Down to a sunless sea.
    So twice five miles of fertile ground
    With walls and towers were girdled round:
And there were gardens bright with sinuous rills
Where blossom'd many an incense-bearing tree;
And here were forests ancient as the hills,
Enfolding sunny spots of greenery.

But O, that deep romantic chasm which slanted
Down the green hill athwart a cedarn cover!
A savage place! as holy and enchanted
As e'er beneath a waning moon was haunted
By woman wailing for her demon-lover!
And from this chasm, with ceaseless turmoil seething,
As if this earth in fast thick pants were breathing,
A mighty fountain momently was forced;
Amid whose swift half-intermitted burst
Huge fragments vaulted like rebounding hail,
Or chaffy grain beneath the thresher's flail:
And 'mid these dancing rocks at once and ever
It flung up momently the sacred river.
Five miles meandering with a mazy motion
Through wood and dale the sacred river ran,
Then reach'd the caverns measureless to man,
And sank in tumult to a lifeless ocean:
And 'mid this tumult Kubla heard from far
Ancestral voices prophesying war!

Coleridge

Contents

List of Maps

List of Illustrations

FOLLOWING PAGE 190

FOLLOWING PAGE 376

List of Tables

Acknowledgments

I am grateful to John Lynch, Anthony MacFarlane, and Enrique Tandeter. In their company at the London University Institute of Latin American Studies this book had its inception in 1976. In California I thank W. Elliot and Mary Brownlee, Frank J. Frost, Tulio Halperín Donghi, C. Warren Hollister, Jeffrey B. Russell, and all my colleagues and students at the Department of History, University of California, Santa Barbara. In Argentina I thank David and Carlota Roberts for their generous and unfailing hospitality under sometimes difficult circumstances, and also numerous friends and colleagues who directly and indirectly have assisted my work. My thanks to the Fellows of St. Antony's College, Oxford, for an appointment as senior visiting member in 1982. Of course, none of my friends and colleagues bear any responsibility for my errors or misjudgments. I should also acknowledge financial assistance for my research from London University and the University of California at Santa Barbara. My thanks too to Mrs. Melva McClatchey for her patience and care in typing the final manuscript, to Amy Einsohn for her exceptional editing, and to the staff of the University of California Press in preparing the manuscript for publication.

Preface

The international community's perceptions of Argentina have changed profoundly during the past generation. Until about 1950 the prevailing opinion held Argentina to be a land of boundless natural riches and frontier wildernesses, and the stirring Colossus of the South, destined infallibly to become one of the world's greatest nations. Such judgments and expectations recur throughout the accounts of travelers and commentators in the nineteenth and early twentieth centuries. Among the best known of these observers are the British merchants, like the Robertson brothers, who seized the coming of independence to ply their goods in the remote communities of the interior; Charles Darwin, for whom the southern deserts of Patagonia inspired ideas that contributed to his theory of evolution; and the great French geographer, Jean Antoine Victor Martin de Moussy, whose multivolumed description of the country remains almost unsurpassed in breadth and detail. For the English novelist W. H. Hudson, the great pampas prairies evoked the romantic and nostalgic reminiscences of *Far Away and Long Ago*, while the Mulhalls captured the country's headlong economic expansion in their statistical yearbooks of the 1880s. Panegyrists of the early twentieth century include W. H. Koebel, Ernesto Tornquist, Alberto Martinez and Maurice Lewandowski, Lloyd's Bank of London, and the economist Colin Clark who predicted in his *The Economics of 1960*, published in 1942, that Argentina would soon enjoy standards of living second only to the United States.[1]

Indeed, for many decades many Europeans believed that Argentina offered an opportunity equal to, if not greater than, North America. The pampas *estancieros* enjoyed the reputation that Texas or Arab oil magnates have today, and the expression *riche comme un Argentin* remained a commonplace among the French until the 1930s. In 1907 Georges Clemenceau perceived the genesis of a great new national community originating from a spirit he equated with Manifest Destiny in the United States. "The real Argentino [*sic*]," he commented, "seems to me convinced there is a magic elixir of youth which springs from his soil and makes of him a new man, descendant of none, but ancestor of endless generations to come."[2] The Spanish philosopher José Ortega y Gasset issued a similar pronouncement in 1929. The Argentine people, he declared, "do not content themselves with being one nation among others: they hunger for an overarching destiny, they demand of themselves a proud future. They would not know a history without triumph."[3]

Such copious expectations and laudatory reflections form a stark and bitter contrast with more recent judgments. For at least the past two decades economists have classified Argentina in the under-developed or "third" world, and by the 1960s Argentina was becoming a byword for political instability, inflation, and labor unrest. During the 1970s a sudden procession of horror stories emanated from Argentina—unbridled popular riots, guerrilla warfare, assassinations, abductions, imprisonment of dissidents, institutionalized torture, and eventually mass murder. For a time Argentina elicited a single association: *los desaparecidos*, the thousands of students, workers, writers, lawyers, architects, and journalists, men and women alike, who had "disappeared," simply vanished without trace. At this time too, Rio de Janeiro, Mexico City, Los Angeles, Paris, New York, London, and Rome became refuges for a vast diaspora of political and economic exiles from Argentina.

Lastly, in 1982 Argentina suddenly invaded and took the British-held Falkland Islands. But here Argentina's so-called fascist generals met their nemesis, as a British counterattack repulsed the ruling junta's military forces. Compounding the ignominy of this military defeat and renewed political instability was an unprecedented economic collapse: at least a fifth of the population was unemployed; prices were rising two- or threefold annually; the peso was depreciating at a rate recalling the fate of the German mark during the early 1920s; the foreign debt exceeded $35 billion; and hunger plagued a country endowed with almost 200,000 square miles of the finest temperate farm land in the world. By late 1982 scarcely any country in the world exhibited more parlous and wretched conditions.

The central, compelling question about Argentina is simply, What went wrong? Why has Argentina failed to realize its promise? The most popular response blames Argentina's downfall on the economic consequences of Perón. Formidable critiques of Juan Perón, his movement, and his policies appeared in a United Nations report in 1959, and more recently in Carlos F. Diaz Alejandro's *Essays in the Economic History of the Argentine Republic*.[4] A vast array of data supports the conclusions of both these works; they are, in many ways, unassailable. Without doubt, many of Argentina's misfortunes originated in Perón's heyday during the 1940s and early 1950s.

But are explanations that blame Perón and Peronism alone fully satisfying? Such accounts often depict Argentine history from an unduly narrow partisan standpoint, and by personalizing history to the extent they do, the anti-Peronists render Perón a *diabulus ex machina* in a way that misleadingly inflates the political power he wielded. From such accounts we are often left with the intellectually and historically suspect impression that Argentina's decline was simply due to the actions of a political psychopath. *Anti-peronista* writing fails to examine fully or justly the content of Peronist programs and to evaluate the extent to which Perón enjoyed policy options. Nor does it examine adequately or persuasively the underlying issue: even if Perón did so much damage, what gave birth to Peronism?

Such were my instincts and preliminary questions when embarking on this study. My intent was in no sense to rehabilitate Perón but to create a wider historical picture and explanation for the events of the past thirty or forty years. Among the general arguments of this book is that long-term crises broadly similar to today's have occurred at earlier periods in Argentina's history: in the mid seventeenth and the early nineteenth centuries. One could no doubt unearth errors like those attributed to Perón that were committed by political leaders in earlier crises. But an account of the seventeenth century that blamed, say, Hernandarias, or one of the early nineteenth century pivoting on the failures of Rivadavia would satisfy no one. If we reject the notion of the *diabulus ex machina* during earlier crises, why accept such a narrow slant for the country's modern history?

Yet if this study departs from one orthodoxy, it is influenced—though I hope neither dictated nor overdetermined—by another. At a basic and broad level this book treats Argentina as a classically "colonial" society. It also views Argentine history as shaped

by long-established institutional structures, as well as by person-
alities, power, policies, and programs. Throughout its history Argentina has manifested several obvious colonial features: the country has·
always imported the bulk of its manufactured goods, and for long
periods much of its capital; and economic progress in Argentina has
largely stemmed from stable and complementary commercial and investment partnerships. Argentina also has a typically colonial physical structure: Buenos Aires, as the leading port-city and entrepôt, has
constantly dominated an inescapably fettered hinterland. By and
large "collaborating elites" with outside great powers have exercised
stable, enduring political leadership. Argentina's middle class is more
the *comprador* or "clientistic" type than a classical capitalist bour-
geoisie. We might also argue that Argentina has manifested classical
colonial cultural traits in that its society generally imitates foreign
examples rather than innovates.

Let me add to these conventional ideas the observation that Argentina is also colonial in that once an established system of complementary external linkages lies shattered—as a result of war abroad
and changes in the international order—Argentine society has invariably failed to revolutionize itself in a self-sustaining independent
direction. Instead, following such ruptures, society has turned in on
itself in fierce competition to monopolize static or diminishing resources. Such are the common general features of the seventeenth,
the early nineteenth and the later twentieth centuries. In each case,
although the competitors for dominance were different, external rupture was closely attended by severe political stress and usually by
political breakdown.

The recent history of countries like Canada or Australia (and perhaps in some measure Ireland, South Korea, Singapore, and even
Cuba), shows that "colonial" forms are not invariably incompatible
with economic expansion, high standards of living, or social and
political stability. Indeed colonial societies can flourish, as Argentina
once did. However, complementary external partnerships have always been a necessary condition for progress. Since World War II all
successful colonial societies have maintained or created links with one
or several of the the major industrial blocs: the United States, Japan,
the European Economic Community, or the Soviet Union. In this
sphere Argentina has failed. One of the major keys to its recent decline (if by no means the whole explanation), was its failure to con-
serve old links with Europe or create substitutes elsewhere.

The general aims of this study are to explore the impact of changing external partnerships and the development of colonial forms in successive stages of Argentine history. Commonly made analogies between Australia or Canada and Argentina that stem from their similarities in resources and from the temporary intersections in their respective developments in the late nineteenth and early twentieth centuries are in some important respects highly misleading. Such comparisons overlook contrasting historical origins and some quite different basic institutions. Unlike Canada or Australia, Argentina, of course, is "Latin American." The country was taken not by Britain in the eighteenth century, but by Spain in the sixteenth. Spaniards established in the River Plate region a standard microcosm of their American imperial system. The system's most basic principle was the exploitation of indigenous peoples by a white elite through tribute institutions. Remote as this early colonizing era is from the main currents of Argentine history—and neglected as it is by historians—it deserves closer attention as the origin of an enduring colonial tradition.

Tributary institutions prompted the emergence of a simple agro-pastoral economy but one inherently impeded from diversifying and developing. For tribute induced obstacles through the division of the social order into an indigenous mass close to subsistence and a small white ruling class. The latter desired a variety of manufactured goods, few of which could be produced locally under the existing social organization. To meet this demand the whites continually monopolized local resources, exploiting them to generate an inflow of imported manufactures. First they monopolized Indian labor, later cattle, and ultimately land.

In this way a colonial system based originally on tribute gradually evolved into one based on rent, as the sixteenth-century *encomendero* metamorphosed into the nineteenth-century *estanciero*. At the same time, demand for manufactured goods that the local economy remained unable to produce conferred parallel monopoly power on merchants who supplied such goods from abroad and on the mercantile urban centers that developed as import supply points. As a result a dualistic (and later pyramidal) social order, with its origin in tribute and resource monopoly, assumed an external physical form: elites controlled land and labor; the merchants and governing bodies of Buenos Aires captured resources from the interior elites; the city grew while the hinterland languished.

Argentina thus developed with basically the same features as the rest of Latin America. Colonialism had its roots in the mode of contact between Spaniards and the indigenous peoples, which by institutionalizing underconsumption and monopoly produced an uneven, underdeveloped, and soon largely inflexible economic structure. Argentina's beginnings made it fundamentally different from the United States, for example, though the two countries share some striking similarities in physical resources and economic potential. However, as early as the seventeenth century among the New England and Mid-Atlantic British colonies access to resources, particularly land, became increasingly open, and within less than a hundred years these British colonies had developed a substantial, expanding rural middle class that became a market for local manufacturers and the pillar of an evolving egalitarian political tradition. In the River Plate region not even the embryo of such a class appeared until the middle of the nineteenth century. Similarly, by the late seventeenth century the British colonies had developed shipbuilding, iron, textile, flour milling, rum distilling, hat making, glass, brick, and paper industries. In the River Plate region some small-scale manufacturing activities did appear, but they remained extremely fragile and insubstantial, largely dependent for their survival on nonwage, coercive labor systems.

In the River Plate the colonial economy created by the Spaniards persisted unchecked for some three hundred years—the period in which the region remained a formal dependency of Spain, and well after it had gained independence. Throughout society failed to develop metacolonial counterstructures. The region had a history of long cycles of ascent and regression. Following the tribute age of the sixteenth century came prolonged crisis and depression in the seventeenth century. Argentine society became increasingly isolated from European connections and retracted upon its existing foundations instead of undergoing internal change and development. The eighteenth century brought another long cycle of recovery, but numerous colonial forms persisted. The caste system, for example, simply updated ethnic-based relations of domination; monopoly reappeared in the burgeoning pampas cattle economy; and a succession of merchant cliques in Buenos Aires demonstrated a growing power to orchestrate the pace of economic growth and appropriate most of its fruits. Toward the outbreak of the struggle for independence, at the turn of the nineteenth century, came another long cycle of decline.

The Spanish colonial system fell into disarray, and external commercial partnerships collapsed. But in this period too, amid prolonged turmoil and breakdown, retrenchment rather than complete revolutionary change eventually predominated. Elites clung to power, adapting to new conditions and circumstances rather than being mastered or suppressed.

Thus for some three hundred years Argentina had repeatedly shown itself to be a society that could expand, under given conditions and within certain limits, but that lacked an autonomous drive toward development. One export commodity succeeded another as the economic leader; new regions were laid open to development; and social structures became more varied and sophisticated. But within such growing complexity, markedly atavistic features remained: colonial structures were invariably refashioned rather than transcended. During a celebrated congressional debate on protection in the 1870s, the historian Vicente Fidel López referred to the city of Buenos Aires as "an intermediary exposed to frequent crises, employed merely in sending abroad the products of the countryside and the provinces, and transporting foreign goods to the interior." López denounced the way in which "foreign manufacturers impose prices on our products. . . . We are the farmyard of foreigners, a piece of foreign territory, because we have no independence."[5] By this point, we may argue, colonial forms had become so deeply embedded as to be insuperable unless subject to a shattering, overwhelming, and prolonged external blow.

Forces launched to mount such a challenge in the late nineteenth and early twentieth centuries did so incompletely and eventually failed. Around 1860 Argentina's agrarian resources attracted a multitude of European immigrants and a massive infusion of foreign investment. Both settlers and investors encountered a society willing to afford them shares in its material bounties, but one that also checked their efforts to alter its course or modify its fundamental identity; rather, the host society deflected foreign influences to extend and deepen many of its own historic propensities.

On the surface, however, capital and immigration provoked enormous change, as suddenly Argentina became a famous showpiece of pioneer agrarianism. But although few overt signs remained to testify to tribute and race domination as the founding principles of Argentine society, change remained incomplete in several crucial spheres. Economic growth was still primed by foreign capital and access to foreign markets; land tenure patterns betrayed numerous legacies of monopoly; manufacturing remained weak and stunted; and Buenos Aires upheld its historic economic and political primacy.

The incompleteness of this late–nineteenth-century revolution exacted a severe toll in the 1930s, when Argentina entered another downward cycle. As the foreign stimulus to expansion waned and disappeared, society lurched into crisis. The depression of the 1930s resulted in the divisive and eventually abortive effort to achieve recovery under Perón, followed by progressive and by 1982 still unchecked, decline.

In endeavoring to cover so broad a span in this book, I have of necessity adopted an interpretative and synthetic approach. My chief concerns are with economic issues and politics, supplemented by brief discussions of the social order, as the data allow. Constraints of space and time have permitted only occasional, brief generalizations in the field of intellectual history and have precluded any discussion of Argentine cultural history or its notable literary tradition.

While acknowledging the importance of the early colonial period, much of the book deals with the twentieth century. This bias is partly a matter of personal preference and interest, but also a necessary response to constraints imposed by historiography and data. For the period before 1776 texts are few, and formal studies usually old. A fully documented history awaits the labors of battalions of future historians; until their work is forthcoming, our view of the sixteenth through eighteenth centuries is provisional and highly conditional. For the subsequent period, 1776–1852, several major monographs have recently become available, including Tulio Halperín Donghi's study of society at independence and John Lynch's account of Rosas.[6] But these studies and a handful of others are incandescent beacons in an otherwise all-encompassing veil of obscurity. In depicting the general features of this period, I have deliberately avoided undue reliance on this small corpus of historiographical landmarks, a decision that required the exhumation of an armory of traditional works. Such are more of the inevitable travails of an extensive study, which to meet its objectives must rely heavily on an incomplete and uneven body of research.

Other historirgraphical problems complicate research on the later nineteenth and early twentieth centuries. "Neoliberal" historians have for the past twenty years sought to demonstrate the revolutionary scope and depth of this period's transition, arguing in effect that this period marked a total rupture with all preceding it.[7] In developing such arguments, the same writers have assembled a mass of data that no historian following them can possibly overlook. On the other hand, "neoliberals" have sometimes depreciated evidence pointing in another direction—that the late nineteenth-century transition was less profound or complete than they would like to believe. Here, too, insufficient data hinder the attempt to launch a counter-argument drawing on the elements of continuity between the late nineteenth century and earlier periods in Argentine history.

Lastly, I must offer a *pro forma* but necessary caution concerning statistics. All scholars agree that the statistical data on Argentina are weak until the second half of the nineteenth century and that they are again unreliable (and often frustratingly contradictory) from the mid 1940s on, when the bureaucracy weakened and data became a tool of propaganda. Statistics and quantifications in Argentine history are thus better treated as illustrating trends or relationships.

I

THE SPANISH
SETTLEMENTS, 1516-1680

In the sixteenth and seventeenth centuries the River Plate territories—a vast region of more than a million square miles—were among the least developed in Spain's great American empire, remaining a remote, ignored outpost of the viceroyalty of Peru. European settlement was confined to isolated pockets, often quite far apart and sparsely populated in comparison with the centers of the empire, Mexico and Peru. Although some 250,000 Spaniards came to the New World in the sixteenth century, only about 3,000 ever set foot in the southern lands; and while the Indian population of central Mexico at the time of the Spanish conquest may have been as high as 25 million, no more than 750,000 Indians—and quite possibly only half that number—lived in what became Argentina. Thus at most the population density was only two persons for each three square miles.[1]

Despite its vast size, the Plate region has relatively simple general contours. In the far west stands the great Andean *cordillera*, a mountain mass formed from granite, basalt, crystalline limestone, obsidian, and pyrites, yet with an eastern flank poor in minerals and metals. In the south, where the mountains stretch out toward the Magellan Straits and Cape Horn, the Andes have only a modest elevation, but in the center and the north, they pose a towering barrier. There, the great peaks ascend beyond the clouds and decline precipitously into deep, glaciated valleys; the mean elevation is 13,000 feet, and the highest peaks top 20,000 feet. Except toward the south, the unforested

1

mountains stand as gaunt and bare sentinels over the lands below them.

East of the Andes lies a less forbidding *sierra* region, often several hundred miles in breadth. Elevations reach as high as 4,000 feet in the center, and in the north higher hills and plateaus run down from the Andean *altiplano*. The *sierras* are principally granite, but they also contain numerous intrusions of gneiss, mica, felspar, and limestone. Silver and copper are to be found in some parts, but only in small quantities.

Farther east still lies another wide-banded region where elevations rarely exceed 250 feet and are frequently as low as 25 feet near the coast. These plains fall into three quite distinct parts. South of the forty-second parallel are the windswept deserts of Patagonia. In the center, forming a near semicircle roughly five hundred miles in radius from the River Plate estuary, are the alluvial lands of the pampas. This region, which has become one of the world's great agricultural and grazing areas, was formed of sand, aeolian clay, and a mass of vegetal deposits during the Tertiary period. Its soils contain numerous fossilized remains of mammal life from remote, prehistoric eras, but its rich, almost uniformly flat landscape is largely treeless and stoneless. Finally, in the far north the pampas give way once more to desert, and beyond this to the hot forest and bushlands of the Chaco. From its edges at about the twenty-second parallel, this vast area, bounded on the west by the *sierras* and the *altiplano* and on the east by subtropical grasslands and forest, stretches far to the north into modern Paraguay and Brazil.

The part of the Plate territories that became Argentina is an area some 2,300 miles in length. Its northern borders lie beyond the Tropic of Capricorn and its southern extremes reach almost as far as fifty-five degrees south latitude (see Map 1).

Of Argentina's three great rivers, the largest is the Plate estuary, river basin for a quarter of the land mass of South America. Some 650 miles at its widest point, it is surpassed in size throughout the Americas by only the mouth of the Amazon. Second is the westerly tributary of the Plate, the Paraná-Paraguay, whose crocodile-infested source lies almost 2,500 miles due north of the Plate in the Mato Grosso region of Brazil, not far from the rivers pursuing an opposite northerly course to feed the Amazon. The Paraná, at its crossing of the border between Paraguay and Argentina, is one of the great natural waterways of the world. It flows southward toward the pampas, bounded by a low west bank and a higher, more undulating eastern

Map 1. Modern Argentina: physical features and oldest cities.

flank. Then, within a hundred miles of the River Plate, it becomes a great delta of shifting islands and thick vegetation. Some two hundred miles east of the Paraná, but eventually drawing closer to it as both approach the estuary, is the third great waterway, the river Uruguay. Only a third the size of the Paraná, it is nevertheless broad and capacious. No other rivers in the country compare with these three in size or ease of navigation. Nearly all the others flow easterly or southeasterly: the Pilcomayo (*Piscú-Moyú*, River of the Birds); the Bermejo to the far north in the Chaco; the Salado and the Dulce further south; and the major rivers of Patagonia: the Colorado, the Negro, the Chubut, and the Deseado.[2]

In the sixteenth and seventeenth centuries the main Spanish settlements lay along an arc toward the northeast between Buenos Aires on the Plate estuary and the silver mining city of Potosí in Upper Peru. Along this tenuous line of communication, about a thousand miles in length, were Santa Fe, Córdoba, Santiago del Estero, San Miguel del Tucumán, Salta, and Jujuy. Around Santiago and Córdoba the arc was broken by spurs to other westerly settlements among the *sierras*, chief among them La Rioja and a city known successively as Londres, San Bautista de la Rivera, and finally Catamarca. A second and still more slender ribbon of settlements stretched northward from Buenos Aires to Asunción del Paraguay along the Paraná. Here beyond Santa Fe was the city of Corrientes. Last, a small cluster of cities lay due west of Buenos Aires in the Cuyo region, east of the Andes: Mendoza, throughout the most prominent, San Juan to its north and San Luis to its east.

Beyond this was nothing. Vast areas—the barren, undulating deserts of Patagonia, the fertile valley of the Rio Negro, the grasslands of the pampas, the mesopotamian region between the Paraná and Uruguay, the arid northern regions of modern Santa Fe and Santiago del Estero, the wild bush curtain of the Chaco jungle—were traversed by the Spaniards in vain pursuit of bullion mines or captive Indian labor. But these areas remained unsettled and their few inhabitants free from white tutelage until a much later date; indeed, some areas remained relatively unexplored until the twentieth century.

The settlements between Buenos Aires and Jujuy stood along a trade route linking the silver mines of Potosí with the River Plate, from which ships sailed across the Atlantic to Europe. The volume of silver that flowed southward varied with the conditions in Potosí, which supplied a native labor force and the mercury used in refining silver ore; the demand for silver in Europe; international trading conditions, which determined the volume of shipping reaching Buenos Aires; and the Spanish crown's policies and the effectiveness of the colonial administration, since Spain banned exports of silver by way of Buenos Aires. Impediments to the supply and circulation of silver hindered development in the wider River Plate region, limiting its foreign trade, supplies of imports, internal intracity commerce, and the migration of Europeans.

The location of the early settlements mirrored different types of preconquest Indian society. Except for the two ports of Buenos Aires and Santa Fe, which furnished outlets to the Atlantic and connections along the Paraná, the cities lay in regions of sedentary, agrarian Indian cultures. Here, as throughout the Americas, the Spaniards set themselves as overlords to the native peoples, forcing them to provide tribute and labor. The resulting society was sharply divided along ethnic lines, with incomes and consumption highly unequal among the various ethnic groups. As elsewhere, Spanish tribute exactions disrupted the native economies, and in doing so contributed significantly to epidemics that decimated the Indian population soon after the creation of the colonial system. During the early colonial period, the economy developed in cycles of swift expansion closely followed by steep decline, the latter caused by falling supplies of silver and dwindling Indian population.

The tradable goods yielded by this economy—raw cotton, cereals, cattle, sheep, horses and mules, and animal derivatives such as wool and hides—were mostly marketed in Upper Peru in return for silver, which was then exchanged for imported manufactured goods: weapons, tools, European clothing, and a host of other everyday items. Imports were often in extreme short supply, in part by deliberate design. The trade monopoly enforced by the Crown, which limited supplies, enabled Spanish merchants to mark up prices and increase profits. Manipulation of the terms of trade enabled Spain to generate additional revenues from its imperial possessions. The commercial system also contributed to the further exploitation of the Indians by the white settlers, in their efforts to meet the prices of imports. Similarly the maintenance of monopoly trading continually undercut the Crown's professed adherence to the protection of its Indian vassals.[3]

For the River Plate territories, the Crown determined that imports were to be acquired by way of Peru: they were first sent from Spain to the Isthmus of Panama, and then on to Lima to be transported overland to consumers in the far south. By the time the goods reached their destination, having passed through numerous intermediaries, their already high prices were still more inflated. Thus the southern settlers had to control disproportionately large numbers of Indians to acquire a given quantity of imports; since the Indian population was small, the area could support only a smaller-still Spanish population.

For much of the early colonial period, contraband imports were also available from Atlantic suppliers, primarily the Portuguese. Coming by a much shorter route, they were invariably cheaper than Spanish goods brought from Lima. From an early date contraband trading weakened the economic ties between the Plate territories and Peru, and strengthened the territories' links with the Atlantic economy. The shift gave Buenos Aires, the point of access for foreign traders, a crucial role in the emergent economy. As exchange with the Portuguese increased, much of the silver garnered from trade with Potosí found its way to Buenos Aires instead of flowing back to Lima. By funneling contraband to consumers in its hinterland, the city developed as an entrepôt, carving out for itself a share of the wealth raised from Indian tribute and from internal trade with Upper Peru.

The first 170 years that followed the Spanish expeditions to the River Plate in 1516 may be discussed in three phases. The first, between 1516 and 1580, was that of exploration, conquest, and initial settlement. A second, between 1580 and 1630, embraced the development of internal and external commerce under an *encomienda* labor system. The third, between 1630 and 1680, was marked by slow growth and in some measure by regression.

EXPEDITIONS AND FOUNDATIONS, 1516–1580

The name *Argentina* is derived from a latinized rendering of the Spanish word for "silver," as it was used by Spanish poets from the Renaissance onward. The lure of bullion or of an empire rivaling that of the Aztecs or Incas drew the Spaniards into the territory. But they found neither, for the country was ill-named—its only exploitable natural resource was the native Indian population.

The northwest, a rectangle embracing the modern provinces of La Rioja, Catamarca, Córdoba, Santiago del Estero, Salta, and Jujuy, was the homeland of roughly two-thirds of the territory's Indian population. Although these maize-based cultures lacked by far the scale, luster, and grandeur of those in Peru or Mexico, they all shared several features. The introduction of irrigation and high-yield crops to the hilly terrain a millennium before the Spanish conquest made possible the efflorescence of native cultures and religions, and the formation of small towns and villages.[4]

The largest tribal entity of the region was the Diaguita. Their stronghold was the Calchaquí valley between La Rioja and Salta, but branches of this people were scattered throughout modern San Juan, La Rioja, Tucumán, and Salta. Although the Diaguita lacked a centralized political system, toward the end of the fifteenth century, three or four generations before the coming of the Spaniards, they were drawn into informal links with the Incan empire of Peru. By the mid sixteenth century their vestments, feather decorations, religion and language, their music, basketwork, and fortifications each betrayed Incan influences. Incan penetration was accompanied by the growth of trading relations and the construction of highways from Peru, which the Spaniards employed as they moved southward into the area.

The Diaguita dwelt in small, dispersed villages, and in shelters made from straw and twigs and sometimes stone. The villages furnished a collective labor force for the construction of irrigation dams and windwalls along the valley hillsides. The Diaguita used obsidian hand plows to cultivate maize, potatoes, beans, squash, and on the higher ground quinoa. Those living in the outlying areas were root and fruit collectors, and hunters of rhea, deer, wild pigs, and fish. For clothing they used llama, guanaco, and alpaca wool. The Diaguita had a rich ceramic and metallurgical tradition, and manufactured copper hatchets and a few gold and silver ornaments. Polygamy, another indicator of a relatively advanced culture, was similarly widespread.[5]

Other agricultural Indian peoples of the northwest were less advanced than the Diaguita, but for the most part their cultures were similarly maize-based. Among them were the Comechingone, a confederation of tribes around which the city of Córdoba was built. Elsewhere in the gray, saline flatlands between San Miguel del Tucumán and Santiago del Estero were the Juríes, known too as the Tonocotes, practitioners of flood farming, and the Sanavirones. Around La Rioja and Catamarca were the Sanagastas; around Salta, the Chicoanas and Vilelas; around San Miguel, the Lules; and around Jujuy, the Ocloyas and Omauacas.[6]

Another group of native agricultural peoples were the Guaraní across the Chaco in the northeast. They inhabited the eastern Paraguay region, segments of the lower Paraná, and a wide belt of territory northward into Brazil. The Guaraní belonged to a Bronze Age civilization. They too were organized in loose confederations. But here, where population was less dense and villages rudimentary, slash-

and-burn agriculture prevailed. On these shifting plots the Guaraní cultivated sweet potatoes, maize, manioc, and beans. They also produced cotton textiles and ceramics.[7]

Elsewhere were nomadic groups spread out thinly in all directions across the pampas (see Map 2). Living in small clusters of *toldos*, or tepees made from animal skins, were the Querandí, who subsisted mainly on guanaco and rhea, which they killed with bows and arrows, or trapped by weighted triangular thongs (*boleadoras*). Elsewhere, in the Chaco to the north and Patagonia to the south, were numerous other groups like them: the Pampa, the Chonik, and the Kaingang; in the Chaco, the Abipones, the Mocoví, the Toba, and Matacos; in the farthest south in Tierra del Fuego, the Onas, Yamanas, and the Alcalufes. All these primitive nomadic groups were to elude the Spaniards for generations, often centuries.[8]

European exploration of the region began with the discovery of its great Atlantic estuary. The River Plate was first investigated in 1516 by Juan Díaz de Solís, a Portuguese navigator in the employ of the Crown of Castile, who was seeking the southwestern route to the Far East and India. Solís landed with a handful of his crew on the east bank; there, he and his men were summarily butchered by a band of Querandí. In 1520 Ferdinand Magellan also explored the estuary in the course of his epochal voyage around the world. Seven years later another of the great navigators, Sebastian Cabot, made a full reconnaissance of the area for the Spanish crown. Having penetrated the Paraná delta, Cabot established a small fort upriver at Sancti Espiritus, not far from present-day Rosario. Succeeding expeditions helped chart the coasts of Brazil and Patagonia, but apart from the ruins of Cabot's fort and a handful of Spaniards stranded in the region, these early ventures left nothing permanent.[9]

Nevertheless by 1530 Europe showed growing interest in the estuary and the lands beyond. Cabot reembarked for Spain with a handful of silver trinkets gleaned from the Paraná Indians. He also returned with some alluring stories from Spaniards he had encountered there, who reported that beyond the rivers lay a great Indian kingdom, rich in precious metals. Fables of "Trapalanda" or the "Kingdom of the White Caesars" drew the Spaniards back to the "Silver River," sparking their resolve to embark on its conquest.

The same rumors reached Portugal, and the Portuguese too began to manifest interest in the area. In 1531 they sent an exploratory mission led by Affonso de Souza to the Plate. He also returned with reports of Indian kingdoms and gold and silver mines. A race then

Map 2. Spanish settlements and Indian societies in sixteenth-century Argentina.

began between the crowns of Castile and Portugal to equip an expedition of conquest. Each claimed that the area lay on its side of the Tordesillas line, 370 leagues west of the Azores, which divided Castile's sector (on the west) from Portugal's sector.

In 1534 Charles V of Castile issued a *capitulación* embracing the land between the twenty-fifth and thirty-sixth parallels, roughly between the modern cities of Bahía Blanca and Santos, and from there across the continent to the Pacific. The grant was made to a court aristocrat, Pedro de Mendoza, who was entrusted with forestalling the Portuguese and with the conquest of the legendary Indian kingdom of the interior. As was standard with grants of this kind, Mendoza was promised a generous share of any treasures found if he accomplished his task.

Financing the expedition in part by loans from Charles V's Flemish and Dutch bankers, Mendoza departed in 1535. In February 1536 the expedition arrived at the River Plate. Here on the west bank the *adelantado* established a temporary encampment, which he christened Puerto Nuestra Señora Santa María del Buen Aire. Within months Francisco Pizarro founded Lima on the Pacific. But the fates of the two expeditions were very different: Pizarro proceeded from Lima to the conquest of the Incan empire, while most of Mendoza's men fought, starved, and quickly died in their precarious foothold at the edge of the pampas.

Mendoza's expedition was large and highly organized in comparison with most early Spanish ventures to the Americas. His sixteen ships had a complement of sixteen hundred men, three times the number that accompanied Cortés in the conquest of Mexico some sixteen years previously. But the expedition's size was among the main reasons for the debacle that ensued. The men arrived at the end of the southern summer, when it was no longer possible to sow cereals, and had to rely heavily on fish from the estuary or the delta. Fish alone soon proved insufficient, and the severe food shortages worsened when a few Indians cajoled into gathering supplies rapidly tired of their impossible obligations and disappeared into the plains. Attempts by the Spaniards to round up more Indians prompted a war with the Querandí. By June 1536 bands of Indians were laying siege to the camp. The continuing Indian attacks, starvation, and disease reduced the expedition to a third of its original size within eighteen months of its arrival. According to their German chronicler, Ulrich Schmidel, the Spaniards first slaughtered most of their cattle and horses, and were ultimately driven to cannibalism:

Finally, there was such want and misery that there were neither rats, nor mice, nor snakes to still the great dreadful hunger and unspeakable poverty, and shoes and leather were resorted to for eating and everything else.

It happened that three Spaniards stole a horse, and ate it secretly, but when it was known, they were imprisoned and interrogated under the torture. Whereupon, as soon as they admitted their guilt, they were sentenced to death by the gallows, and all three were hanged.

Immediately afterwards, at night, three other Spaniards came to the gallows to the three hanging men, and hacked off their thighs and pieces of their flesh, and took them home to still their hunger.

A Spaniard also ate his brother, who died in the city of Buenos Aires.[10]

Early in 1537 a troop led by Mendoza's deputy, Pedro de Ayolas, set off northward along the Paraná in search of the fabled Indian kingdom in the interior. Ayolas and his men failed in this quest but did encounter a more congenial environment in which to recover from their privations. In the upper reaches of the Paraná they discovered the Guaraní, with whom they quickly established friendly relations. The decision was taken to build a second settlement, and in August 1537 the city of Asunción del Paraguay was born. Soon there was a stream of migration to Paraguay from the hard-pressed community on the estuary. In Paraguay, unlike the plains to the south, food was in great abundance, as the land yielded two maize crops each year. Here too lived an ample and cooperative Indian population. Profligate gifts of women, exotic foods, and Indian labor were bestowed on the Spaniards. Eventually, in May 1541, the encampment at the mouth of the Plate was abandoned. The settlers left behind a store of grains for future Spanish ships and a few horses, which immediately began multiplying on the pampas.

But the chief memorial of Mendoza's expedition was Asunción, a remote stronghold deep in the continent to which the remnants of his followers disappeared. There, for the next thirty years they were under the command of Domingo de Irala. In Paraguay, Irala succeeded Mendoza, who died on the high seas in 1537 seeking to return to Spain, and Ayolas, who perished in the Chaco in another forlorn search for the Indian empire.[11]

Preliminary explorations of other parts of the Argentine territories were already underway at the time of Mendoza's expedition to the River Plate. The northwest, known from the time of its discovery as Tucumán, was first traversed in 1535 by Diego de Almagro, the partner of the Pizarros in Peru, during his expedition of discovery to Chile. A second expedition came in 1547, once more inspired by rumors of Indian kingdoms in the south. Its leader was Diego de Rojas, who a generation before was with Cortés at the fall of Tenochtitlán. Following the Rio Dulce, Rojas's followers eventually reached the site of Cabot's fort on the Paraná, although they failed to make contact with Asunción. Both the Almagro and Rojas expeditions were offshoots from the conquest of Peru, assembled from among the losers in the division of the spoils from the Incan empire, men forced to seek their fortunes elsewhere.[12]

Permanent settlement in Tucumán started in the 1550s as Spaniards crossed the Andes from Chile with two chief aims: to create better links with Upper Peru than the existing maritime connections allowed and to find new stores of Indians. A *capitulación* granted to Juan Nuñez del Prado in Chile in 1549 stated in its preamble there was an "abundance of Indians" in Tucumán who would "serve the Spaniards," enabling them to "cultivate the goods of Castile" and extend "our Holy Catholic Faith."[13] After several failed efforts, in 1553 Francisco de Aguirre founded the city of Santiago del Estero; other settlements soon followed: Londres de la Nueva Inglaterra, Nieva, Córdoba del Calchaquí, and Del Barco. But except for Santiago, all were destroyed by Indian attacks in 1562. In 1565 a second permanent settlement was established north of Santiago del Estero at San Miguel del Tucumán.

In the early 1560s Chilean Spaniards also began erecting settlements in Cuyo. Their object once more was to capture Indians, but also to establish access to the River Plate enabling troop reinforcements from Spain for the wars against the Araucanian Indians in the south. From this eastward movement in 1561, on a site that was an eight-day trek from Santiago de Chile through the passes of the high Andes, arose the city of Mendoza. The following year San Juan was founded a little to the north.[14]

In 1563 Tucumán, which had originally been made a dependency of Chile, was placed under the direct rule of the viceroy of Peru, and the judicial authority of the Audiencia of Charcas in Upper Peru. Expansion into the Plate territories from Chile now largely ceased. Rather, new settlements accompanied the growth of Potosí. Silver had been discovered there in 1545, but output was fairly small until 1572, with the introduction of the mercury amalgamation process and the wider application of the *mita*, the drafting of forced labor in the mines. Silver production increased from less than 130,000 marks in the early

1570s to one million marks by 1592, by which time the mines were also employing between 13,000 and 17,000 *mitayo* laborers. The population of Potosí itself, barely 3,000 in the 1540s, rose to 120,000 by the 1580s and reached 160,000 by 1610, which made it for a time the largest Latin city in the world. Meanwhile Huancavélica, also situated on the *altiplano*, developed as a source of mercury and as a second center of population. At its peak toward 1600 Huancavélica produced two-thirds of the mercury used in Potosí. As the mining economy prospered, there was renewed expansion into Tucumán.[15]

In 1571 the viceroy of Peru, Francisco de Toledo, commissioned a new settlement in Tucumán by Jerónimo Luis de Cabrera. Toledo's intent was to create a garrison point immediately south of the *altiplano*. However, commercial interests in Potosí, supported by the Audiencia of Charcas, urged a move much further southward to develop outlets on the Atlantic for silver exports. Cabrera, following the aspiration "to open gateways to the land" (*abrir puertas a la tierra*) rather than Toledo's plan, pushed far to the south toward the River Plate. In 1573, on the edge of the *sierras* among the Comechingone, he founded the city of Córdoba. During the next twenty years three more-permanent settlements appeared in Tucumán, these in the more northerly areas originally favored by Toledo. In 1582 the city of Salta was founded in a fertile valley about two hundred miles south of the *altiplano;* in 1591 La Rioja appeared to the southwest, close to the largest concentrations of Diaguita; and in 1593, San Salvador de Jujuy, to the north of Salta. These three cities served to protect Potosí from the south, to secure the route between Upper Peru and Chile, and to provide supply points for the mines.[16]

The occupation of Tucumán was thus accomplished after several decades of exploration during which the Europeans had identified the main concentrations of friendly Indians and the possibilities of exploiting intertribal feuds. The silver miners of Potosí, as Cabrera's exploit had shown, were also interested in establishing contact with the Atlantic, an objective that was also accomplished by 1580.

As the line of settlements from Potosí became established, the Paraguayans turned once more to the rivers to the south, seizing their opportunity to end more than thirty years of isolation. In 1573, having gathered a retinue with promises to share out the herds of wild horses on the pampas, Juan de Garay led an expedition from Asunción to found Santa Fe on the lower reaches of the Paraná. This new base gave the Paraguayans access to Santiago del Estero. To increase contact with Córdoba and Chile, and to create another route north better sheltered from the Chaco Indians, the Paraguayans moved still further south. In 1580 Garay resettled the site on the estuary that Irala had abandoned thirty-nine years before.

This second settlement at Buenos Aires survived. During the initial stages of recolonization the city's sixty-six male founders, of whom ten were white Spaniards and the rest *mestizos*, were plentifully supplied with cattle, horses, and cereals from Asunción and Santa Fe. Relations with the plains Indians were thus more amicable, and Garay used his mestizo lancers to hold back the Indians when war threatened. In 1587 another settlement, which became Corrientes, was founded further north along the Paraná. From this settlement and those at Santa Fe and Buenos Aires, the Paraguayans hoped to obtain a share in the silver trade expected to flow from Potosí. They also intended to develop the export of cattle hides, in this way joining the intercontinental trade flow.[17]

In the sixteenth century the Spaniards founded twenty-five cities in what became Argentina, among which fifteen survived. This task was accomplished by a very small contingent—less than 2,000 Spaniards lived throughout the country in 1570 and perhaps 4,000 *mestizos*. In 1583 Córdoba, the largest settlement, had a white population of only 250; as late as 1600 there were no more than 700 Spaniards throughout the Tucumán region. Almost all of these were men of humble origins, for after the fate that befell Mendoza and the realization that little silver was to be found, few men of any pedigree ventured into these nether regions.[18]

Here in the extreme periphery, the colonial order was consolidated later and less completely than in more central areas of the empire. As was the custom of the Spaniards throughout the New World, the creation of settlements was conducted according to elaborate rituals. Locations were chosen with considerable care with an eye to the availability of Indians and the suitability of the land for farming and pasturing. Once the site was selected, proclamations were issued concerning the city's creation and the legal rights and authority upon which it was based. Officeholders were chosen for the city *cabildo*, the Church was formally established, and Indians were distributed in *encomienda*. Inhabitants of the city were divided into two groups: the white *vecinos*, who enjoyed full civic rights, and the usually nonwhite *moradores*, or simple "dwellers," who did not.[19]

Responsibilities of the *cabildos*, which included the regulation of food prices, supplies, and wage rates, were defined and codified by

Viceroy Toledo. Following late medieval practice in Spain, at first *cabildo* officials were elected. But later, from about 1610 onward, offices were put up for sale, and they fell into the hands of local settler oligarchies. *Cabildos abiertos*, the procedure used to convoke the *vecino* population to general deliberations on matters of common public interest, were relatively frequent, especially in Tucumán during the Indian wars of the seventeenth century.[20]

In 1563, when the northwest was removed from Chilean jurisdiction, two *gobernaciones* were created, Tucumán and Paraguay–Rio de la Plata (see Map 3). Cuyo was administered separately by a *corregidor*, who remained subject to the captain-general of Chile until 1776. In 1617 the River Plate and Paraguay were separated into two governorships. This arrangement also persisted into the eighteenth century, except that between 1663 and 1672 an *audiencia* was established at Buenos Aires in an effort to curb contraband trading.[21]

Until about 1600 the governorships were nominal jurisdictions. Among the bands of *conquistadores* infiltrating the region in the last half of the sixteenth century, authority rested less upon the grants of the Crown or viceroys than upon military prowess and natural cunning to outmaneuver competitors and opponents. None of the early *gobernadores* survived long enough to institutionalize his position. Most were overthrown by mutiny, to be returned to Peru in disgrace or, in some cases, to be murdered by rivals. Violent deposition was the fate of Aguirre and Cabrera, founders of Santiago del Estero and Córdoba, and Gonzalo de Abreu, who for a time controlled Tucumán during the 1570s.[22]

Only in the 1590s, with the arrival of Juan Ramírez de Velasco, founder of La Rioja and Jujuy, did such chronic factitiousness wane. Salaried officials gradually replaced the early plundering *adelantados*, and the government assumed a more settled form. In Tucumán the formal powers of the governors were much the same as elsewhere in the empire. They included a degree of jurisdiction in the distribution of *encomiendas*, responsibility to exercise military leadership and raise settler militias, authority to found new settlements, the provision of public works, the supervision of commerce, and the regulation of labor drafts (*repartimientos*). The governors also shared responsibility with the *cabildos* in organizing food supplies and setting food prices. The only major limit to their authority was in the sphere of revenues: to reduce opportunities for graft, tax collection was largely entrusted to other authorities.

But here the imperial bureaucracy never evolved into the aloof,

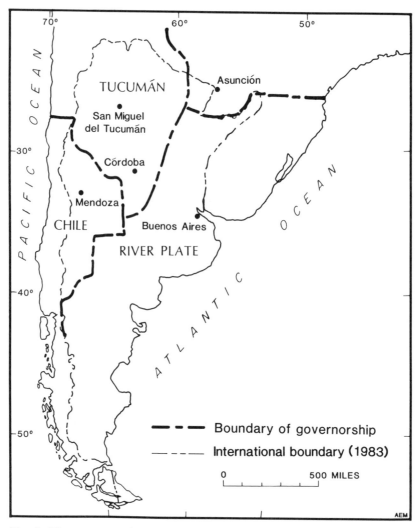

Map 3. The seventeenth-century governorships.

inflexible instrument of metropolitan interests it became in the wealthier, more populous areas of the empire. Except for Toledo, the viceroys in Lima remained remote and inaccessible, their presence felt only in moments of extreme crisis. The stabilization of the *gobernaciones* coincided with the dwindling of the Crown's control at large. The governors' salaries were usually paid in kind, or *monedas de la tierra*, in such produce as cotton bales, rather than in cash, and thus these officials were almost obliged to conduct themselves as much as entrepreneurs as agents of the Crown. Beyond sporadic attempts to ameliorate the lot of the Indians, and the more sustained endeavor to check contraband trading, the governors made little attempt to enforce the complex thicket of regulations emanating from Castile and frequently took refuge in the legal formula for noncompliance, "I render obedience but do not fulfill" (*Se acata pero no se cumple*).[23]

The last of the major colonial institutions was the Church. A bishopric established at Asunción in 1547 was not filled until 1556, and was again vacant between 1573 and 1585. The diocese of Tucumán was founded in 1570, and another in Buenos Aires in 1587. Regular orders of the Church, Dominicans, Franciscans, and from the late 1580s Jesuits, played an early prominent role in missionary activities. Franciscans were among the founders of the early settlements in Tucumán, and other churchmen created *doctrinas* and *curatos*, small Indian communities independent of the Spanish settlers. Soon Córdoba became the center of the Church's activities in this corner of the empire, finding favor owing to the fertility of the land and the easy availability of building materials from the nearby granite *sierras*. From this base, site of the country's first cathedral and from 1618 its first university, the Church soon assumed an important role in the economic life of the colonies. Churchmen, notably bishop Francisco de Victoria of Tucumán, a Portuguese Dominican of allegedly Jewish extraction, were instrumental in developing commerce between Tucumán and the coast of Brazil in the 1580s. By the early seventeenth century the Church had begun to organize *obraje* textile workshops, and soon, as elsewhere, it was drawn into rudimentary banking activities. The Church also patronized the germinal colonial culture and, by teaching craft skills to Indians and *mestizos*, enabled the construction of churches and the production of simple manufactures. Even so, with the exception of the Jesuits later on, the Church here never commanded the influence it had elsewhere in the empire. The poverty and isolation of the area attracted very few clergy, and into the seventeenth century bishoprics remained vacant for decades at a time.[24]

LABOR, PRODUCTION, AND TRADE, 1580–1630

The vain pursuit of precious metals and then a more fruitful scramble for Indians motivated Spanish expansion to the wider River Plate region. Under silver's influence and the growth of the market in Potosí, the fifty years after the refounding of Buenos Aires saw the formation of a typically Spanish colonial economy. At its base was Indian forced labor, and the creation of each city was closely followed by an assertion of control over surrounding Indian communities. Indians were seen as both a source of labor and a tradable commodity to be exchanged and hired out among the white settlers. From the 1570s into the seventeenth century Indians were sent into Upper Peru for service in the mines; such forced migration was especially common in Cuyo, where so many Huarpe Indians were sent to Chile that by 1620 only remnants of the native population remained. In Paraguay, where contact between the Spaniards and the Indians frequently took the form of polygamous unions with Indian women, native women were used for a time as units of exchange in commercial dealings.[25]

Encomienda was first applied on a large scale in Paraguay in the 1550s. Later it became equally prominent in Tucumán. At this relatively late stage in the institution's history, during the absolutist rule of Philip II, *encomienda* rights were invariably conferred by the Crown and its agents as a nonheritable usufruct rather than as a possession. Yet their juridical basis remained the same as formerly: the *encomendero* was charged with converting the Indians under his charge to Christianity; in return he had the right to labor services in the form of forced labor or tribute payments in cash or in kind, levied upon individuals or upon communities. In Paraguay the most common form of the institution, the *encomienda originaria*, consisted largely of services performed by women.[26]

A second form of forced labor was *mita*, more prevalent in Upper Peru, but also common in Tucumán. *Mita*, derived from the Incas and broadly resembling the feudal *corvée*, consisted of rotationary labor services by Indian communities. Whereas the Incas had used *mita* mainly for construction, the settlers used it for mining in Upper Peru and for agriculture and textile production in Tucumán. *Yanaconazgo*, a third labor system, also with Indian antecedents, developed during the 1570s. *Yanaconas* were those Indians uprooted from their original tribal ties, usually as a consequence of warfare, placed in new communities as the chattels of Spanish settlers, most often in newly settled areas whose native Indian population was small or difficult to subdue.

Yanaconas were used, for example, in the establishment of Salta in 1582, and in smaller numbers in Buenos Aires throughout most of the seventeenth century. Like *mita* workers they usually lived in family units on self-sufficient plots of land and performed rotationary services from within their own communities.[27]

Forced labor in Tucumán was immediately accompanied by abuses, hints of which can be deduced from regulatory ordinances drawn up by Governor Abreu in the late 1560s. These ordinances sought to enforce limits on the use of Indians as carriers; ordered the recongregation of displaced Indians in new villages; and attempted to regulate the *mita*, specifying that only one-tenth of the Indians between fifteen and fifty years old, and a maximum of thirty from each community, were to work for the Spaniards at any one time. The ordinances were also intended to check the buying and selling of Indians, that is, open enslavement, and to regulate the women textile workers. So far as the last, the ordinances specified that Indian women were to gather in the village plazas half an hour before sunrise and were to work until half an hour before sunset; the penalty for noncompliance was two hundred lashes.[28]

Here, as throughout the Americas, the coming of the Spaniards shattered the delicate balance of Indian society and swiftly effected a sharp demographic decline. Spanish confiscations, forced labor, and resettlement caused malnutrition and lowered resistance to European disease among the native population. Forced labor for Indian females and the occasional forced segregation of the sexes led to a sharp fall in the birthrate and an increase in the infant mortality rate. But as the population fell, the more onerous the tributary exactions became. Irrigated lands, once given to maize for subsistence, were confiscated for commercial crops like cotton. An attempt at gold mining in the San Juan region in 1600 led to a *mita* among the local Huarpes, obliging the men to spend 168 days in the mines each year.[29]

The apogee of Indian forced labor occurred between 1580 and 1610 (see Table 1). Questionable contemporary estimates for 1582 show that 12,000 Indians were held in *encomienda* in Santiago del Estero and 6,000 in Córdoba. Estimates in 1586 counted 18,000 in Santiago del Estero and 5,000 in Salta. By 1596 there were 12,000 *encomienda* Indians in Córdoba, 20,000 in the newly founded La Rioja, 8,000 in Santiago del Estero, and 5,000 in Mendoza. *Encomenderos*, in contrast, numbered no more than 300.

In the early seventeenth century, however, *encomienda* declined rapidly with the fall in population. Between 1596 and 1607 the number

TABLE 1. *Indians in Encomienda (Tucumán and Cuyo Regions),*
1582–1673

	1582		1586		1596		1607		1673	
	A	B	A	B	A	B	A	B	A	B
Santiago del Estero	48	12,000	–	18,000	–	8,000	100	6,729	34	3,358
Córdoba	40	6,000	–	3,000	–	12,000	60	6,103	16	430
Talavera*	40	6,000	–	13,000	–	5,000	33	1,636	9	10
San Miguel	25	3,000	–	3,000	–	2,000	32	1,100	33	2,303
Salta				5,000	–	5,000	30	1,800	20	1,984
La Rioja						20,000	62	6,000	51	1,390
Jujuy				3,000		3,000	8	690	9	1,515
Nueva Madrid*				1,500		1,500	10	188		
Mendoza				30		2,500		5,000		
Others										2,394
TOTALS		27,000		50,000		60,000		24,058		12,994

NOTE: A = number of Encomenderos; B = number of Indians in Encomienda (heads of families).
*Transitory Spanish settlements.
SOURCES: Data assembled from Jorge Comadrán Ruiz, *Evolución demográfica argentina durante el período hispano, 1535–1810* (Buenos Aires, 1969); Ricardo Zorraquín Becú, *La organización política argentina en el período hispánico* (Buenos Aires, 1959).

of subject Indians fell by at least half: to under 7,000 in Santiago del Estero, 6,000 in Córdoba, and only 6,000 in La Rioja. A similar picture emerges from contemporary estimates of the Spanish cities. Between 1586 and 1607 Santiago del Estero dwindled from 12,500 inhabitants to 7,700, and San Miguel del Tucumán from 3,300 to 1,800. Only Córdoba, due to the Church and its position on the trade routes, maintained itself, growing slightly over the same period from 6,400 to 6,600. *Encomienda* was not formally abolished till independence two hundred years later, but was already moribund by 1620. In 1673 there remained only 3,350 *encomienda* Indians in Santiago del Estero, 2,300 in San Miguel, and under 2,000 elsewhere; in Córdoba, only 430.[30]

Soon after 1600 the remaining Indians were "rationed" through wider use of the *repartimiento,* a labor draft organized by the governor or the *cabildos,* which normally avoided any direct or permanent entrustment of Indians to individuals. The rapidity with which the Indian population fell was also reflected in the frequent shifts in the location of the Spanish cities, as attempts were made to appropriate untapped reservoirs of native labor. As the Indian communities dwindled in number, *yanaconazgo* became more common compared with *mita*. Another result of the decline was the appearance of the *hacienda*, which typically emerged once the declining supply of Indians began to provoke food shortages and higher food prices in the Spanish cities. By the 1620s in Cuyo, for example, where the native population was dissipated most rapidly by forced migrations to Chile, erstwhile *encomenderos* became *hacendados*, developing a system of debt peonage among the surviving Indians to produce wheat and maize for sale in Mendoza and San Juan.[31]

Another example of this transition is the early history of the Catamarca region in the sub-Andean west. The first settlement, Londres— so called as an echo of the marriage between Philip II of Spain and Mary I of England—was created in 1558 by the Chileans. Although the Spaniards were soon evicted by an Indian revolt in 1562, they later returned with transported *yanaconas* to begin cotton growing. Thereafter the region, like Córdoba, maintained a fairly steady population by drawing people from contiguous areas. In a way typical of the rest of Tucumán, the Catamarca region developed on a blend of agricultural and pastoral products, its specialties being wine, tobacco, and textiles, the last of these under the direction of Franciscans. By 1607 flour mills had been established, and by the 1630s *haciendas* were rapidly forming, a land market having developed in various small pockets on the strength of land grants from the governors.[32]

In these regions the Crown's efforts to regulate Indian labor began very late, with the Alfaro Ordinances of 1613. The ordinances proclaimed the creation of new reservations, or *reducciones*, physically apart from the Spanish cities. They abolished labor services and established low fixed tribute payments in their place. The administration of the *mita* was delegated to the Indian communities themselves, and attempts were made to establish wage scales for work contracted by the settlers. The ordinances, however, proved a complete failure. At the first opportunity the Indians decamped in large numbers. Tribute returns shrank, to the detriment of the Crown, the Church, and the settlers alike. Within a short time even the regular clergy, though not the Jesuits, withdrew their support for the ordinances, which then became a dead letter.[33]

While the Indian population survived, commodity production in Tucumán centered on cotton and cotton textiles. After the introduction of cotton seeds from Chile in the 1550s, cotton was cultivated around nearly all the Spanish cities of the northwest. By 1600 Potosí was importing cotton goods from Tucumán to an annual value of 25,000 pesos. But production in Tucumán was small by comparison with elsewhere in the viceroyalty—Cuzco, Cochabamba, or Quito. Nor was the industry as highly advanced as elsewhere; there were many fewer *obrajes*, for example, although after 1580 some appeared in Córdoba, Santiago del Estero, and San Miguel del Tucumán. The *obrajes* of Santiago were the most prominent, producing a variety of coarse cotton and woolen goods (*paños, sayales, bayetas,* and *reposteros*). But most textiles in Tucumán were the product of native cottage industries. The low-quality and low-cost goods were intended for the lower end of the Potosí market; as such, they were not in competition with products from larger colonial centers or with Spanish imports.

The dominance of cotton in Tucumán was short-lived. The region suffered from shortages of dyestuffs, cochineal and indigo. More important, the attempt to promote a cotton monoculture hastened the demise of the Indian population. Cotton production swiftly reached a plateau and then declined steeply such that by the 1620s textile manufacture for outside markets was largely confined to pockets of the Catamarca region, La Rioja, and Santiago del Estero. Elsewhere, as part of the general transition to pastoralism in the wake of the population decline, cotton gave way to wool.[34]

Besides textiles the *encomienda* regime yielded tradable surpluses of wheat, maize, and flour, mostly from the Córdoba area. In 1603, for example, 90,000 *fanegas* of wheat and 50,000 of maize were exported to Potosí. As trade grew, silver flowed back in return. Soon silver had effected new interregional commercial ties that linked the governorships and fostered incipient specialization among them. Thus Tucumán became the chief source of textiles and cereals, Cuyo produced small surpluses of wine, and Paraguay yielded wine and sugar. Specialization, however, did not proceed very far, hindered by local mercantilism, and each community's desire for self-sufficiency. Communities sought to maximize their sales to Potosí and other neighbors while minimizing local imports, so as to leave the largest possible surpluses of silver for purchases of European goods. The same considerations led the *encomendero* classes and the Church to monopolize commodity dealings with Potosí; all other classes were legally obliged to conduct transactions through barter, using rates of exchange fixed by the *cabildos*.[35]

Of more interest to the Spanish communities than local commerce were intercolonial and intercontinental trade. Through Portuguese merchants in Buenos Aires commerce developed with Brazil. Besides silver, the grains, wine, and flour of Tucumán were exported to Brazil, sometimes in quantity. The main imports were Brazilian sugar, European manufactures, and slaves. Because European goods purchased through the Portuguese often cost only a third or half the price of Spanish goods from Lima, they immediately established themselves in the markets of the south.

Imports of slaves became more numerous as the native Indian population declined. The first to be sent to the River Plate arrived in the late 1580s, some directly from the Angola coasts, though a majority as reexports from Brazil. About one thousand slaves passed through Buenos Aires between 1587 and 1600, most en route to Chile or Upper Peru, though some remained in Tucumán, Cuyo, and Buenos Aires. In 1614, for example, forty-eight slaves were employed in the Santa Rosa region of Catamarca, and from an early date slavery became well established in Córdoba. Yet the economies of the region were too weak to promote a large-scale influx of slaves. Where slavery appeared, it did so invariably as an adjunct to the other labor systems without ever superseding them. Although slaves were widely employed in agriculture, their possession was largely limited to the small group of wealthy *encomenderos* trading with Potosí. Otherwise slaves dwelt in the towns as domestic servants and later as artisans' laborers.[36]

Besides Buenos Aires, Córdoba was the pivot of this nascent trading system that stretched from Potosí to Brazil and across the Atlantic. Between 1580 and 1620 a small group of commercial *encomenderos*, some of whom, like Bishop Victoria, churchmen, dealt regularly with factors in Brazil and as far afield as Lisbon and Seville. They largely controlled the silver flow to Buenos Aires, local agricultural, livestock and textile production, and the distribution of slaves and European imports to the markets in the west and the north. They also controlled the ox-drawn carts, which from an early date became the chief mode of transportation across the great plains of this corner of the Americas.[37]

BUENOS AIRES: THE EARLY YEARS

In Buenos Aires a somewhat different society took shape from that in the interior. Soon after the city's reestablishment in 1580, Juan de Garay managed to congregate a few score of the more docile local delta Indians for *encomienda* services. Small numbers of slaves were gleaned from Portuguese traders, and at various times during the late sixteenth and into the seventeenth century *yanaconas* were drafted from Tucumán and Paraguay to help with the construction of fortifications and develop local farming. The absence of a large local pool of Indians inhibited widespread use of *encomienda* or *mita*, and this lesser dependence on forced labor created distinctive population trends in Buenos Aires. While the population of the interior cities waxed and waned with equal speed, in Buenos Aires slow, uninterrupted growth proceeded from a minute base. The shortage of Indians also inhibited the growth of agriculture in Buenos Aires; during its first forty years on several occasions the city was obliged to import grain from Córdoba.

Although the conventional tribute system failed to evolve, Buenos Aires had other traits typical of early Spanish America. The white population quickly entrenched itself at the social apex, obtaining the best building lots in the city close to its central plaza, cornering the first permits to engage in trade, and monopolizing the herds of wild horses, legacies of Mendoza's expedition, and numerous wild cattle that appeared soon after 1580. The whites adopted the common Spanish-American practice of intermarriage between the daughters of leading creole citizens and Spanish immigrants, who came to staff the garrison or to hold Crown offices. Other racial groups were quickly excluded from positions of privilege or authority in the developing village caste system. The few Indians and blacks predominated in agriculture, while the *mestizos* became militiamen, cattle peons, or employees of artisans.[38]

Buenos Aires was also in part a community of Portuguese immigrants, whose presence became legal following the treaty of union between Spain and Portugal in 1580. From that time and through the seventeenth century, the city became the final link in a chain of Portuguese trading settlements along the Atlantic coast of South America from Curaçao southwards. Commerce with the Portuguese soon acquired substantial proportions, as up to 250 small boats a year embarked from Brazil with cargoes of silver, sugar, slaves, cereals, hides, and European consumer goods, along with commodities like bar-iron for the mines of Potosí. For much of the seventeenth century between a quarter and a third of the male population of Buenos Aires was Portuguese-born: in 1606, 33 of the 100 men in the city were Portuguese; in 1643, 370 of the male population of 1,500. Smaller Portuguese communities appeared in Santa Fe and Corrientes. Most of the Portuguese were merchants, but some were artisans indispensable to the communities they served. Many Portuguese were also reputed to be Jews, refugees from the Inquisition installed in Brazil in 1591 under Spanish instigation.[39]

In refounding Buenos Aires the Paraguayans had hoped to end the isolation of Asunción by strengthening their ties with Potosí and Spain. They sought also to organize ranching on the estuary and to export hides. Although pastoral activities, which required little labor, quickly outstripped agriculture, hopes of prosperity were frustrated, with hide exports few and returns from them small. Indeed, many inhabitants of Buenos Aires lived in the most straitened and impoverished circumstances, residing in rough straw or adobe huts and clothed in cattle hides. In 1599 a visitor described them as "poor devils without a shirt to their backs, and their toes sticking through their shoes."[40] From Buenos Aires came unending bitter complaints to Spain concerning the shortages of Indian service labor, the migration of clergy and skilled artisans to Upper Peru and Tucumán, and the deficiencies in manufactured goods—plowshares, weapons, bridles, locks, clothing, cooking oil, and soap. In Buenos Aires, it was said, a horseshoe cost several times more than a horse; as in Paraguay, those who owned European clothing took to the custom of wearing it only once a month or for special events.[41]

The weakness of the local economy thwarted cohesiveness within the community. Soon after 1580 a small hybrid rural population began to appear around the city. These escaped slaves, mestizo deserters from the militia, and other marginal elements of the city's population lived as the plains Indians had learned to, from the wild herds of cattle and horses. Soon the city authorities began campaigns to curb the growth of the semibarbarized race of "lost people" (*gente perdida*), who interfered with official cattle roundups from the city and further depleted an already scant reservoir of labor.[42]

Yet other indicators showed Buenos Aires to be thriving in its role as key intermediary in the trade between Potosí and Brazil. The wills and testaments of its merchants revealed that small fortunes were being made from trade. By 1600 some two hundred ox carts were arriving from Córdoba each year, and the influx of yerba mate from Paraguay and wines from Cuyo also demonstrated that the city had some significance as a market. Some public offices, especially those with jurisdiction over revenues such as the *alguacil mayor*, were eagerly sought by the traders and commanded a purchase price of several thousand pesos.

Buenos Aires was in fact a divided community. All commerce was in the hands of the Portuguese, who were not interested in exporting cattle goods—all the local economy could offer—but the silver that came by way of Córdoba from Potosí. Likewise, silver, not hides, bought imports. In this trade the Spanish-speaking inhabitants of the city, most of them descendants of Paraguayans, were largely bypassed; this was the source of their poverty.

Thus an uneasy relationship brewed between the two communities. The reluctance of the Portuguese to deal in hides led to recurrent efforts to be rid of them, and politics in Buenos Aires soon acquired a remarkable vitality for so small a community. Conflict was most virulent between 1610 and 1617, with the population split into two factions: the pro-Paraguayan *beneméritos* and the *confederados* who supported the Portuguese. The former were led by a white Paraguayan-born creole, Hernando Arias de Saavedra, or Hernandarias, who served as governor of Paraguay and the River Plate on six different occasions between the 1590s and 1620. In 1610 the Portuguese faction, led by Diego de Vega and Juan Vergara, usurped control over the *cabildo* of Buenos Aires and began open trading in Portuguese goods using counterfeit licenses. Hernandarias swiftly stepped in, establishing the Inquisition in the city to employ judicial torture and banishment in a campaign to quash all "Jewish" influence. Imports of slaves and sugar from Brazil were forbidden; the former to discourage the flow of silver into Buenos Aires, the latter to help rival Paraguayan sugar producers. Plans were also laid to create a shipping fleet, using timber from the upper Paraná, that would carry exports of hides to Spain.

The project failed. With the Portuguese gone, all trade ended. Hernandarias soon lost his local support, and the growing opposition to the Paraguayan interest he represented led to further isolation and still greater impoverishment. Soon after community leaders organized by Manuel de Frías began petitioning the Crown to separate Buenos Aires administratively from Paraguay. In 1617 the single governorship was divided with Buenos Aires achieving autonomy from Paraguay, and the Portuguese were then permitted to return.[43]

As the influence of the Paraguayans declined, there was less insistence on hide exports. Successive governors of Buenos Aires grew accustomed to accepting bribes from the Portuguese in return for tolerating their trading activities. When the Portuguese gained control of the *cabildo*, and at times even of the Inquisition, the trade proved impossible to extirpate. Portuguese ships would invoke the pretext of *arribada forzosa* (storm damage on the high seas) to land their cargoes. The issue was no longer whether the trade should be tolerated or stopped, but who was to benefit from it. The 1620s brought another long, acrimonious, and at times violent conflict between Vergara and the governor, Francisco de Céspedes, as each sought to monopolize the local slave trade. Here the Portuguese faction had the support of the city's bishop, one of Vergara's relatives, who excommunicated Céspedes. Later came other disputes between the two wings of the community. In 1628 intermarriage with Portuguese was forbidden; in 1640 came another effort to expel all the Portuguese.[44]

The conflicts were enacted against a background of shifting Crown policies. In 1580 the Crown supported the refounding of Buenos Aires not to create a new port on the Atlantic but as a military garrison. The Atlantic was rife with pirates and corsairs, and fears spread that the River Plate would be captured by foreigners, who would then launch an attack against Upper Peru. During the 1570s the Paraguayans were encouraged to believe that the Crown would subsidize a garrison at Buenos Aires, and this prospect had played a part in drawing them southward from Asunción. But the Crown failed to meet the commitment; rather than subsidizing Buenos Aires, it wanted the city to pay for itself. The city could do so only if allowed to trade, to breach the trade monopoly based in Lima. The Crown was apprehensive of such activity, worried that non-Spanish goods would invade the markets of Peru, that silver exported through Buenos Aires would go untaxed, and that through the Portuguese the silver would then fall into the hands of Spain's European enemies.

Trade through Buenos Aires with Brazil was first authorized by a royal order (*cédula*) in 1587. Four years later the Portuguese were permitted to import five hundred slaves a year from their colony in Angola. However, in 1593, after protests from the viceroy of Peru and merchants in Lima and Seville, the permits were revoked, and all trade through Buenos Aires was forbidden except for Spanish vessels licensed by the Crown. But very few such *navíos de registro* were forthcoming, mainly because they too were forbidden to trade in slaves or silver, and the Crown was soon inundated by petitions from Buenos Aires protesting shortages in essential supplies and threatening the city's abandonment.[45]

The Crown responded in 1602 by again permitting a measure of trade with the Portuguese for a trial period of six years. Small quantities of cattle and agricultural goods were to be exported from Buenos Aires in return for manufactures from Brazil. But the export of silver and the import of slaves remained under strict interdiction. This impractical measure again led traders to simply abandon Buenos Aires. During the next decade the continuance of trade depended on the inclinations of the governor. Hernandarias sought to stop it; others did not. Although in principle the Crown favored Hernandarias, it was not prepared to risk the collapse of Buenos Aires, which it still saw as essential to imperial defense. This concern was manifest when the Crown agreed to the subdivision of the governorship in 1617, a measure that also gave Buenos Aires administrative seniority over Paraguay.

At length in 1618 the Crown issued a new set of trade regulations. Two licensed Spanish ships of up to one hundred tons were allowed to voyage to Buenos Aires each year. They could bring Spanish goods but, to prevent the exchange of silver and slaves, could call at Brazil only on the return voyage with cargoes of hides. Once more all dealings in silver were emphatically banned. This scheme also failed. In 1622, as part of a broader effort to tighten the trade monopoly throughout the empire and thereby to increase revenues, a tariff line, the *Aduana Seca*, was established at Córdoba to halt the flow of silver southward. Buenos Aires was placed in a commercial *cordon sanitaire* intended to rupture its links with Córdoba and the cities beyond, and the city was allowed to export cattle goods from local herds alone: a little salted meat, tallow, hides, and flour. Finally in 1623, in an act that captured the essence of Crown policy but also its futility, an attempt was made to prohibit the use of money in Buenos Aires.[46]

The *Aduana Seca* persisted some hundred and fifty years with only one modification: the transfer of the tariff line from Córdoba to Jujuy in 1696, a change that helped bring Tucumán more closely within the commercial orbit of Buenos Aires. This final set of Crown measures again enjoyed only intermittent success, never completely eliminating the trade flow between Buenos Aires and Potosí. Buenos Aires could not survive exclusively on the meager exports of cattle goods allowed by the Crown's concessions. Few Spanish ships came to the River Plate after 1622, and the city was thus dependent on contraband and informal multilateralism. Otherwise its members served as a militia, sustained by subsidies from Potosí that the Crown grudgingly agreed to pay.

THE SEVENTEENTH-CENTURY DEPRESSION, 1630–1680

After 1630, during the prolonged Atlantic-wide recession that began in the 1620s, the River Plate territories too manifested symptoms of stagnation and decline. Their economies rested on the flow of silver southward from Potosí, the volume of shipping reaching Buenos

Aires, and the availability of Indian labor. But after 1630 less silver flowed southward, fewer ships came to the port of Buenos Aires, and the devastation wrought by forced labor substantially reduced the number of exploitable Indians. Consequently, the white population remained very small. In 1639 there were only 6,000 whites in the three governorships of Tucumán, Buenos Aires, and Paraguay; 2,800 in the cities of Tucumán; 1,400 in Buenos Aires, Santa Fe, and Corrientes; and 1,800 throughout Paraguay. Forty years later the largest cities, Buenos Aires and Córdoba, had populations of only 5,000.[47]

The long colonial dark age was characterized by recurrent political tensions reflecting the struggles for fixed and diminishing resources. Impoverishment bred dependency on outside subsidies. Among the elites military or administrative positions were prefered to mercantile careers. Weaker communities were absorbed by stronger, and capital squandered in vain searches for new resources. The main positive outcome of this period was the growth of the Jesuit mission settlements in the upper Paraná region east of Paraguay. By 1700 this area had become the most populous and vigorous of those subject to Spanish rule.

Silver output from Potosí reached a peak in 1595, when some 900,000 marks were produced. Decline began soon after 1605, continuing until 1735. By 1630, after a civil war in Potosí and recurrent flooding in the mines, production had fallen to around 600,000 marks; it fell further to about 500,000 marks in 1635, 300,000 marks by 1670, and below 200,000 marks between 1700 and 1735. By the last quarter of the seventeenth century, silver production was less than a third of that in the 1590s, roughly at the level of the 1560s before the adoption of the mercury amalgamation process.

This decline resulted from several conditions. The contraction of the Indian population in Upper Peru, again largely due to forced labor and the incidence of disease, eventually caused deficiencies in agriculture, food shortages, and rising food prices. As the population drifted back into agriculture, fewer Indians were available for *mita* services in the mines. Competition for labor between mining and agriculture led to the introduction of a wage system in the mines, which effected higher costs and falling profits at a time when the most accessible ores were becoming exhausted. Increases in taxation early in the seventeenth century had similar effects. As the relative profitability of agriculture increased, many Indian communities were granted the option of substituting payments either in cash or kind for *mita* services. This too depressed output from the mines.[48]

Simultaneously, demand for American silver in Europe fell. The declining market was due in part to the European depression and also to the appearance of competing mines in central Europe. Potosí was afflicted by growing shortages of mercury; output from Huancavélica was again affected by local labor shortages; and it became increasingly difficult to augment supplies from mercury mines in Spain itself. From the 1620s the Spanish trading system with the Americas began to deteriorate, as the exhausting wars in Europe left Spain with neither the goods nor the ships and the naval power to uphold the monopoly. By 1670 only 5 percent of American trade remained in Spanish hands. The sixty or seventy galleons crossing to the Americas each year in the 1580s dwindled to around fifteen in the 1670s.[49]

As a contraband port Buenos Aires had much to gain from the breakdown of formal Spanish trade. Despite falling production in Potosí and the *Aduana Seca*, silver continued to flow to the River Plate. Several seventeenth-century descriptions of Buenos Aires mention the silver ornaments and decorations possessed by the richer inhabitants. Throughout, silver was traded for slaves and European goods. In the mid 1650s the famous chronicle of a French visitor, Acarete du Biscay, reports cargoes of Rouen linen, silk, needles, swords, horseshoes, spices, and woolen goods being landed in Buenos Aires for dispatch to the markets of the interior and Chile.[50]

Nevertheless, several indications show that trade volumes declined markedly from about 1630, and further again after 1640. Between 1606 and 1615 the value of imported goods through Buenos Aires was estimated by Crown officials at 7.5 million *reales* (at 8 *reales* to the peso), with exports valued at only 1.1 million *reales*. The latter comprised legal trade, agricultural goods exported from Tucumán to Brazil, and the small volume of cattle goods from Buenos Aires itself. This unregistered discrepancy, 6.4 million *reales*, most of which reflected trade in contraband silver, is probably low given the considerable contraband in imports. A similar pattern appeared between 1616 and 1625, when registered imports rose to 7.9 million *reales*, while official exports fell to only 360,000 *reales*, a decline that probably resulted from the falling surpluses in Tucumán as the Indian population contracted. Between 1626 and 1635, following the introduction of the *Aduana Seca*, exports fell further to only 255,000 *reales*, but registered imports also fell, to only 1.8 million *reales*. By this point the visible balance of payments deficit, roughly the measure of silver exports, was now only 1.55 million *reales*, a trend that continued.[51]

A similar picture emerges from data on the imports of slaves. Although the slave trade was again largely contraband, the need to feed and clothe the slaves on their arrival made it more difficult to disguise their numbers than to conceal silver exports. Between 1606 and 1625 4,693 slaves were imported, an average of 234 a year. During the next thirty years the total fell to 2,488, or an annual average of only 83; and between 1636 and 1655 only 315 new slaves were recorded, for an annual average of 15.[52]

Yet another indicator of the economic decline after 1630 was a pronounced fall in the shipping reaching Buenos Aires. Contacts with Spain had always been meager. Until the 1660s, when the Crown began to grant private slave trade concessions and to increase the *navíos de registro*, only seven Spanish ships had called at Buenos Aires in forty years, most to deliver the governor. From the late 1620s Portuguese contraband trade also markedly declined. The Portuguese came under sustained attack throughout the Atlantic from the Dutch, who captured Pernambuco, and thereby control over the Brazilian sugar economy, in 1623. After taking Guinea in 1637 and Angola in 1641, the Dutch usurped dominance over the slave trade. Between 1640 and 1660 the metropolitan Portuguese were engaged in a war of separation against Spain. These conditions and a depression in the Brazilian colonies of São Paulo and Rio de Janeiro severely disrupted the earlier links between Buenos Aires and the Brazilian coast. By the 1630s Portuguese ships calling at Buenos Aires had fallen to only six or seven a year; between 1640 and 1655, during the War of Separation, only seventeen Portuguese ships reached Buenos Aires. To some extent Dutch traders replaced the Portuguese, but their activities were at most intermittent.[53]

In Buenos Aires complaints to Madrid over shortages of imports revived. After 1640 several wealthier members of the community emigrated to Upper Peru, taking with them their slaves and herds of cattle. Barter became increasingly common. The city simultaneously faced more-local difficulties as the Araucanian peoples of southern Chile began expanding across the Andes into Patagonia and then northward to the pampas. Quickly overcoming the scattered bands of Auca and Querandí, they began mustering the herds of wild cattle and horses, and driving them southward back to their homelands. By the 1660s the people of Buenos Aires were locked in perpetual conflict with the Indians for possession of the herds, and under their pressure the city's jurisdiction became confined to a narrow strip of territory along the estuary. At times, too, it proved difficult to maintain communications with Córdoba and the cities beyond.[54]

Even so Buenos Aires slowly advanced, its population rising from 1,100 in 1620 to a little over 5,000 in 1680, when the appearance of the first brick buildings gave the city an air of modest well-being, in contrast with its earlier look of a struggling infant community. By 1650 several members of the community had forty or fifty slaves, and to Acarete du Biscay the inhabitants seemed to live "very commodiously": "Except Wine, which is something dear, they have plenty of all sorts of Victuals."[55] With the Portuguese link in disarray, richer members of the community had turned to mule breeding, exporting the animals to Upper Peru. After 1640 the muleteers became a new oligarchy in the city, capturing control of the *cabildo* from the smugglers.[56]

Toward the end of this period Buenos Aires also grew by virtue of its garrison functions and the subsidies from Potosí. After 1625, amid recurrent fears of a Dutch attack, several governors with a military background were appointed to serve in the city. The first of these was Pedro Esteban Dávila, who arrived in 1629. During the next three decades intermittent attempts were made to improve the city's fortifications by drafting *yanaconas* and the rural "vagrants" from outside the city. In 1663, following rumors of an assault by English pirates from the Caribbean, the garrison was reinforced from Spain and an Indian militia brought from the Jesuit missions. One hundred and twenty-five troops arrived from Spain in 1670, and another 330 with governor Andrés de Robles in 1674. The influx of Spanish soldiers increased the city's white population and gave renewed impulse to the ethnic and caste divisions that had acquired elaborate forms. A dozen or so white families monopolized military and public offices, and profits from the mule, silver, and hide trades. The castes meanwhile were excluded from the priesthood and forbidden to bear arms, to purchase slaves, or to obtain licenses from the *cabildo* to profit from the musters of wild horses and cattle in the countryside.[57]

Like Buenos Aires, Córdoba escaped the worst effects of the seventeenth-century depression. It benefited from its sheltered location away from the nomadic Indians, its ecclesiastical functions, and the informal continuation of its commercial intermediary activities. In Córdoba Spanish *vecinos* increased from 60 in 1607 to around 1,000 in 1684, at a time when there were only 1,850 throughout Tucumán. In Salta, too, there was slow growth, mainly by virtue of the city's increasing role as the site of an annual market for the trade in cattle and mules with Upper Peru. Exports of live animals to Upper Peru increased slowly throughout the seventeenth century; in 1679 Crown officials estimated that some 40,000 cattle and 20,000 mules were passing northward through Salta each year.

Elsewhere in the interior, however, came either stagnation or decline, admixed with a shift from agriculture and cotton to pasturing. By 1679 exports of cotton cloth from Tucumán amounted to a negligible 2,000 *arrobas*. Silver shortages prompted the growth of barter and the renewal of expeditions in search of bullion-rich Indian kingdoms. By the late seventeenth century many of the interior communities required subsidies from Lima or Potosí. The crisis was most extreme in Paraguay and Cuyo, neither of which had sustained much beyond 1620 the exports created under *encomienda*. Sales of wine, tobacco, and sugar from Paraguay gradually ceased, leaving only yerba mate. Exports of wines and Indians from Cuyo also ended, and the settlements in Cuyo were little more than a small cluster of *haciendas*, subsisting on cattle sales to Chile.[58]

In the interior the midcentury brought growing conflict with the Indians and the militarization of the Spanish settlements. To overcome labor shortages, the whites repeatedly attempted to capture unsubdued pockets of Indians. In this era of unceasing Indian wars, the most gruelling was between the Spaniards and the Diaguitas in the Calchaquí valley. The first of two long struggles came in the 1630s, following rumors of gold discoveries in the valley and an unsuccessful attempt to impose a *mita* on the estimated 12,000 Indians still in the area. Toward the conclusion of the seven-year campaign, Spanish soldiers were billeted in the valley to prevent the Indians from sowing crops. Soon the natives' resistance collapsed in the wake of malnutrition and epidemics; those remaining were taken and distributed among the Spanish settlements as *yanaconas*.

A second war, briefer but greater in scale, occurred between 1657 and 1659. On this occasion the Indians were led by a messianic Spanish renegade, Pedro Bohórquez. Promising to organize *encomiendas* in the valley, Bohórquez persuaded the governor of Tucumán, Alonso Mercado y Villacorta, to grant him the title of lieutenant-governor of Calchaquí. Once installed there, he swiftly mobilized an army several thousand strong, which he then unleashed against the caravans en route to Potosí. But once more the Indians were forced into submission by dwindling food supplies. Bohórquez was captured in 1659 and sent to Peru; in 1667 he was executed there. Again retribution was exacted by expelling the Indians from the valley and distributing them as *yanaconas* among the Spanish communities, some as far away as Buenos Aires. The Calchaquí valley and its environs subsequently became a near-desert.[59]

Yet from these wars and numerous smaller ones, the Spaniards gained few rewards. If they augmented their labor supply, they reduced their store of capital. The wars provoked acute frictions among the communities over their respective military and financial obligations, and numerous other conflicts with the governors of Tucumán. By eliminating remnants of the settled Indian tribes, the wars left areas open for growing encroachments by the nomads, the Araucanians from the south and the Chaco tribes from the north. After 1660 the settlements in Tucumán were forced to the defensive. Esteco, a city northeast of Salta on the fringe of the Chaco, succumbed to the Indian onslaught and in 1692, after decades of slow decline, it was finally abandoned. In 1679 defense considerations forced the inhabitants of San Miguel to move to a new site. Conflicts with the Indians were equally acute among the Paraná settlements further east; throughout the seventeenth century Santa Fe, for example, was under constant siege from the surrounding tribes of Abipone, Chanás, and Timbúes.[60]

The slow, crumbling decline among most of the lay communities contrasted markedly with the early history of the Jesuit missions in the upper Paraná. The first of the Guaraní missions was founded in 1609, some thirty years after the coming of the Jesuits. During the next twenty years the missions grew steadily in number and population, supported by settler leaders like Hernandarias, who saw them as a means of expanding Spanish control from Paraguay to the coast of Brazil. But after a tranquil beginning, in 1628 the missions were suddenly invaded by bands of slave hunters from São Paulo, known as *bandeirantes* or *paulistas*. By 1631 eleven of the thirteen settlements had been destroyed, and most of their people carried off into captivity. However, the missions survived this early catastrophe, and soon after the *bandeirante* assault their remnants were removed to more-sheltered westerly areas. The Jesuits then established in the missions a standing army that defended against subsequent invasions. For the next hundred years or more this army remained the largest military machine throughout the wider River Plate area.

Before 1700 the missions rarely harbored more than a hundred Jesuits, and often fewer than forty, but their small numbers were amply compensated by their talents for organization. The missions were adapted to the Guaraní tradition of shifting cultivation, which helped preclude the disruption and depopulation of the Indian communities effected by the lay settlements. Until 1648 the missions also enjoyed the vital privilege of exemption from Crown tribute and from such other taxes as tithes and the *alcabala* on trade. The Jesuits were thus able to develop their missions on a firm subsistence-agricultural base without the need to extract large production surpluses. If mission society—dress, marriage, religious instruction, and daily living—was standardized and regimented to the last detail, labor was endowed with a festive and ritualistic quality, which stood in stark contrast with the grim, barefaced exploitation prevalent elsewhere. Here lay the secret of their success and progress: in the missions there was neither *encomienda* nor *mita*. Indeed, for several decades the Jesuits managed to isolate the missions from almost all contact with the outside world. The result was swift recovery from the *bandeirante* invasions and a steady growth in population. By 1650 there were twenty-two mission settlements in the upper Paraná, and thirty by 1700. By 1680 the missions harbored an Indian population of around 40,000, twice as many as in 1657.

After 1648, when the tribute exemption was abolished by a needy Crown anxious for whatever resources it could muster, the missions were gradually forced into closer contact with the colonial economy. To raise cash they became specialist producers of yerba mate, which until around 1670 was collected in a wild state from the surrounding jungles. As the trade grew, plantations appeared near each of the missions. There the crop was dried and shredded and sent southward along the Paraná to Jesuit merchants in Santa Fe and Buenos Aires, and then to markets as distant as Chile and Peru. By the late seventeenth century the missions had also begun marketing cattle, which were sent to the annual fair in Salta, and small quantities of hides, sugar, cotton, tobacco, textiles, ceramics, and timber products. Exports of these goods yielded silver, which in turn provoked Jesuit involvement in the import trade through Buenos Aires. The missions had now become the largest of the internal markets for imported agricultural tools and weapons. This market, more than any other, enabled Buenos Aires to survive as a commercial entrepôt.[61]

The sixteenth and seventeenth centuries thus witnessed Spanish occupation of several different areas within and immediately contiguous to the territory of modern Argentina. Among these by 1680 the Jesuit missions were the most populous and successful. Second was the governorship of Tucumán, which, despite its recent troubles, had the largest number of surviving Spanish settlements and the most diverse economy. After Tucumán came Paraguay and Cuyo, with the governorship of the River Plate still the least populous area.

The colonial system took shape during this first stage of conquest and settlement. Disappointed in their search for buillion, Spaniards sought to dominate the native agrarian cultures of the west, northwest, and northeast. Soon the Spaniards were extracting production surpluses from the Indians to enable trade with Potosí and the acquisition of imports in exchange for silver. The quest for silver encouraged the colonial elites to seek the same monopolistic controls over commerce that they possessed over labor and other resources. But all such monopolies sharpened the dichotomous patterns of income distribution and stratification. The resulting underconsumption then became another barrier to economic diversification, for an economy in which the mass lives at subsistence level is by definition largely confined to the production of subsistence goods.

The quest for silver also provoked rivalries among Spanish settlers in different communities. As each city strove to enhance its silver returns from trade, it tended to exclude or minimize commercial exchange with neighboring communities, since any such trade reduced the surplus income used to obtain silver and manufactures. Driven by their quest for imports, the Spanish cities thus became economic satellites of Potosí (and later of Buenos Aires), but at the same time largely separate from and independent of one another.

This local self-sufficiency hindered local specialization and became another barrier to economic development. By minimizing commercial contacts with their neighbors and largely replicating each others' economies, the Spanish communities were doomed to remain static and primitive, reliant on confiscating goods from the Indians and on breeding animals. Furthermore this type of economy, in which cities became largely self-contained mercantilist microcosms, fostered political regionalism and precluded integration.

At the same time suppliers of manufactures and agropastoral producers competed in their respective markets on unequal terms. The former enjoyed a captive market, monopoly power, and the ability to drive up prices. Agropastoral producers, however, competed against each other in the same markets, which caused prices to tend to drift downward. Such conditions of unequal exchange emerged during the early colonial period and exerted a major influence on the region in the eighteenth century. The same internal economic inequalities also contributed substantially to the prolonged political battles of the early nineteenth century, between a "federalist" movement, which represented regional interests, and "unitarist" advocates for import suppliers and mercantile purchasers of primary goods.

The early colonial economy had some capacity to produce manufactured goods; at its highpoint the *encomienda* system yielded textile manufactures as well as agricultural goods. But *encomienda* also meant forced labor, and manufacturing progressed only so long as the native labor reservoir remained. The subsequent swift decline of manufacturing illustrates the inherent self-destructiveness of *encomienda*. In contrast, the early history of the Jesuit missions shows that in the absence of tribute demands, the Indian population could flourish. The slackening of tribute demands during the seventeenth-century depression and the growing popularity of pastoral pursuits among the white elites eventually led to demographic recovery in lay regions beyond the missions.

The southward drive from Upper Peru to the River Plate, whose aim was *"abrir puertas a la tierra,"* illustrates the central role of foreign trade in the colonial system. Contact with Spain and access to European goods were of crucial cultural as well as economic significance. Without such European ties colonial society would have been absorbed or subsumed by the primitive American environment, or to use the contrast made famous by Domingo F. Sarmiento in the nineteenth century, without the external contact the society would have ceased to be "civilized" and have reverted to "barbarism." The early history of Paraguay, for example, reveals the importance of the external bond. For white Paraguayans a niche in the intercontinental trade flow seemed imperative for the salvation of colonial society. Besides bringing the artifacts of "civilization," trade also became a means to attract new white blood, protecting the ethnic and cultural identity of the ruling caste.

The same issue of transatlantic ties recurred in Buenos Aires: without trade and imports, as Crown petitioners from the city claimed, Buenos Aires lacked the necessities of *"la vida humana"* and would perish. In its early struggle for survival, Buenos Aires failed to develop a stable role in the imperial system and swiftly took to contraband. In the rise of contraband trade at the end of the sixteenth century lay the germ of the great Argentine tradition of commercial liberalism—a tradition that sparked the wars of independence and then played a central part in the political battles of the nineteenth and twentieth centuries. Contraband trading also gave Buenos Aires its beginning as an entrepôt, the foundation of its later political and economic primacy.

With its mercantile emphasis and the absence of a tribute pool, Buenos Aires developed distinctive features. Its ethnic diversity and large numbers of whites and mestizos gave a premature boost to social forms based on caste divisions, while the relative population scarcity, a high land-labor ratio, and abundant means of subsistence from the wild cattle herds tended to increase the wage share of total income. In Buenos Aires the dualism characterizing Spanish colonial society quickly assumed an additional dimension in the emergence of separate urban and rural societies: at the perimeter of the city's "civilized" population lived the "barbarian" society of the *gente perdida.*

By the end of the sixteenth century conditions had appeared that were to play a formative role in the city's and the country's history. From the *gente perdida* of Hernandarias's day evolved the nineteenth-century *gauchos.* Likewise, early efforts from Buenos Aires to suppress the vagrant population—to unify the local labor market, to check trends towards rising wage rates, and to enable the city elites to monopolize cattle resources—marked the inception of a centuries-long conflict between leveling pressures that arose from the pampas environment and a countervailing impulse toward elitism and monopoly.

Lastly, the middle and later seventeenth century illustrates the society's response to depression. As silver and imports grew scarcer, the whites first attempted to intensify their exploitation of the native peoples. When labor supplies continued to diminish, the whites shifted to pasturing activities. But as the economic crisis became more prolonged, they also tended to abandon entrepreneurship and to take refuge in externally subsidized administrative or military offices. As these career opportunities dwindled, political tensions and rivalries increased within the ruling caste, and the distinctions of rank, status, and hierarchy became more pronounced. The size of the ruling caste contracted, with those whites of lower social status and those who were losers in the political struggle forced out. Descendants of these groups lost the symbolic badge of elite status: *pureza de sangre,* undiluted European blood. Meanwhile, among the nonwhite social groups the depression intensified pressures toward environmental subsumption or "barbarization." As the cities became unable to support their population, and as the tribute nexus between Spaniards and Indians declined, larger numbers were drawn into the ranks of groups like the *gente perdida.*

II

THE RISE OF BUENOS AIRES, 1680-1810

I n the sixteenth and seventeenth centuries the development of
Spanish America was largely molded by the twin quests for
precious metals and Indians. Because the River Plate had neither in
any abundance, throughout this period it commanded little significance. Conditions altered in the wake of the eighteenth-century
commercial revolution. The population growth and economic recovery in Europe stimulated a slow but eventually massive increase in
transatlantic trade, with an expanding range of commodities. Contacts between suppliers and markets were also spurred by advances
in shipping technology that produced larger and more resilient vessels, able to handle cargoes of greater bulk and diversity. Commercial
profit became less governed by mercantilistic restrictions on supply
than by the volume and turnover of sales, and the ability to undersell
competitors and to reduce transportation costs.

Further change in the River Plate region came amid recurrent warfare between the leading powers of western Europe, conflicts whose
sources often lay in the contest for colonial markets and raw materials.
During the eighteenth century Britain and its ally Portugal went to
war with France six times, for a total of fifty-five years of conflict, and
Britain fought Spain on seven occasions for thirty-eight years, much
of the time once more in alliance with Portugal.[1]

All these events had repercussions for the River Plate region, especially for the city of Buenos Aires. Commerce enriched the city and
enhanced its standing in the Spanish empire; the wars eventually led

it into a struggle for independence. Until 1776 the Argentine territories remained at least nominally subject to Peru and Lima, but the Bourbon reforms—Spain's great effort to save and fortify the empire—belatedly freed them from this tie and gave them separate status as the viceroyalty of the River Plate. Buenos Aires flourished as capital of the viceroyalty and as a beneficiary of *comercio libre,* "free and protected" trade between Spain and its colonies, a system that disintegrated during the French revolutionary and Napoleonic wars.

COMMERCE AND RANCHING, 1680–1776

Buenos Aires emerged from the relative isolation of the seventeenth century several decades before the Bourbon reforms of the 1770s. In acquiring new connections with the Atlantic economy, it won growing dominance over the regions to its rear and also began expanding its jurisdiction over the pampas. These changes sprang indirectly from Portugal and Brazil during the last quarter of the seventeenth century. From 1660 the Portuguese, having regained independence from Spain, began to reconstruct their Atlantic commercial system, ejecting the Dutch from Brazil and from the slave bases on the African coast. The ensuing revival of Portuguese trade and sea power, assisted by commercial and naval alliances with Britain, spread to Brazil. By the 1670s the Portuguese were again expanding southward from Brazil toward the River Plate.

In 1676 a new bishopric was created in Rio de Janeiro, and papal authorization was secured to extend its jurisdiction to the east bank of the River Plate. To make good their claim, in 1680 the Portuguese established a new settlement, Nova Colônia do Sacramento, immediately across the estuary from Buenos Aires. Portuguese expansion to the east bank had four main objectives, the principal one being to regain access to Potosí and Spanish silver, now in heavy demand to finance Portuguese transcontinental trade. Second, the Portuguese intended to export cattle hides to serve the growing European market for leather, which expanded significantly during wartime; River Plate hides were considered to be of superior quality and size. Third, the east-bank settlement was seen as affording a means of communication along the Paraná and Paraguay rivers with the *bandeirantes,* who were moving into the Minas Gerais region of Brazil, where in the 1690s they discovered gold. Lastly, the settlement could be used to renew Portuguese pressure against the Jesuit missions in the upper Paraná.[2]

The founding of Colônia do Sacramento signaled a decisive break in conditions, although the transition took some time to complete. The presence of the Portuguese across the estuary was met by immediate hostility in Buenos Aires; in the Jesuit missions it brought panic. The two joined forces to expel the interlopers. An army, including some 3,000 Indians from the missions, was swiftly mobilized by the governor of Buenos Aires, José de Garro, and sent out against the Portuguese. In a sharp military encounter the army killed more than one hundred of the Portuguese colony's thousand-strong complement, captured the city's governor and many of its surviving inhabitants, and sent the rest fleeing back to Rio de Janeiro.[3]

When news of the capture reached Europe, the Portuguese threatened an invasion of Spain unless the Spaniards withdrew from the Plate's east bank and allowed the settlers to return. In its enfeebled state under Charles II, the last of the Hapsburgs, Spain quickly capitulated, and in 1682 the Portuguese returned to Colonia. The modest community thrived as the Portuguese settlers, many from the Azores, began to cultivate wheat and to export hides. By 1700 they were dispatching four or five thousand hides a year to Rio and Lisbon.[4]

But Colonia's major importance was as a source of contraband. As early as 1683 Portuguese merchants arrived there with cargoes of manufactured goods and slaves, which they exchanged for silver in Buenos Aires. Contraband trading from Colonia continued intermittently for the next ninety years. Portuguese skippers became adept at navigating their small launches through the labyrinthine rivulets of the Paraná delta to bring goods into Buenos Aires. As a result, for much of the eighteenth century Buenos Aires regained its position in the Portuguese Atlantic trading system. Once Portugal's alliance with Britain was firmly cemented by the Methuen treaty of 1703, Buenos Aires also became the entry point for a growing quantity of forbidden British goods on route to the markets of the interior.[5]

Despite the eventual longevity of the relationship, perennial frictions arose between the Spaniards and Portuguese, in part paralleling the European wars in which Spain and Portugal were usually on opposite sides. Closer at hand, disputes concerned the herds of wild cattle and horses on the east bank, which both sides claimed. In 1703 Portugal joined Britain in the War of the Spanish Succession; in 1705 Buenos Aires again attacked Colonia, which this time remained in Spanish hands until returned to Portugal under the Treaty of Utrecht in 1714.[6] Then, for much of the 1720s and 1730s Colonia lay under land siege from Buenos Aires, which sought to prevent the Portuguese from gathering cattle in the backlands. To help keep the Portuguese in check, several Spanish settlements were created on the Plate's east bank, chief among them Montevideo, founded in 1724.

More settled conditions emerged in the 1740s and 1750s, when Colonia's role as a contraband center reached its apogee. In 1762, however, during the Seven Years' War, the Spaniards again stormed and took the city; it was returned with the coming of peace a year later. The issue was concluded with the Treaty of San Ildefonso in 1777: after a fourth successful assault by the Spaniards, Portugal acknowledged Spanish suzerainty throughout the east bank, including Colonia.[7]

A second development affecting Buenos Aires was its growth as a slave port. In 1702, the new Bourbon king of Spain, Philip V, awarded a slave *asiento* concession to the French Guinea Company in acknowledgment of Louis XIV's assistance in supporting his succession. Buenos Aires was among the ports in Spanish America the company was authorized to use. During the next nine years some 3,500 slaves passed through the city in four French ships, only a third of the total authorized but a larger number than ever before. The concession was not intended to modify the *Aduana Seca* established eighty years before, which by this time had been moved back to Jujuy: prohibitions against the export of silver remained, and the import of European goods was to remain a Spanish monopoly. But these restraints were largely ignored by the French, who brought manufactured goods along with the slaves and also exported silver. In doing so, the French helped boost the commercial expansion of Buenos Aires.

The people of Buenos Aires were never entirely at ease with the slave trade in their midst. The city's own market for slaves was small; most were sent quickly to the interior. The slave compound in the city—on the site that a century and a half later became its chief railway terminal—was blamed as the source of periodic epidemics. But helping to allay the opposition was the willingness of the slavers to deal in hides, which during the war in Europe commanded higher prices than ever. The coming of the French thus brought unknown prosperity to local cattle interests. An estimated 175,000 hides were exported between 1708 and 1712, a quantity far surpassing previous levels. The French, moreover, made most of their hide purchases from the *cabildo* of Buenos Aires, which thus secured the power to set prices. With the arrival of the French the Portuguese had become both irksome competitors in the hide trade and superfluous as a source of contraband; the second attack on Colonia was launched in 1705.[8]

At the conclusion of the war of the Spanish Succession in 1714 the Treaty of Utrecht obliged Philip V to transfer the *asiento* from the French to the British South Sea Company. With brief interruptions it remained in British hands until 1739, when Europe again drifted into war, with Spain and Britain on opposite sides. In sixty-one voyages between 1714 and 1739 the South Sea Company brought some 18,000 slaves to Spanish America, about 8,600 of whom passed through Buenos Aires, which now became the largest slave port in Spanish America. In Buenos Aires the British slavers had rights denied their predecessors: unsold slaves could be transported to Chile and Peru, and slavers were permitted to bring in clothing for the slaves in ships that sailed directly from England. As the Spanish crown realized, but was powerless to prevent, this authorization was tantamount to an open warrant for smuggling. After 1714 British cargoes included arms and clothing, beer and spirits, powder, cotton and rice, tobacco, wax and medicines, cutlery and telescopes, combs and nails, buttons, stockings, and glassware. Though lured to Buenos Aires mostly by silver, the British also showed considerable interest in hides, buying some 45,000 in 1715, about 40,000 in 1718, and 60,000 in 1724. In this period tallow was exported from Buenos Aires for the first time, along with small quantities of wool from Tucumán.

Even so, like all previous foreign traders in Buenos Aires, the British were never fully secure. Another concession they gained in 1714 was an authorization to feed the slaves they held in Buenos Aires with meat acquired independently of local intermediaries. From here arose relations between the South Sea Company and the pampas Indians who provided them with cattle. The Indians thus became a source of cheap hides and a means to breach the monopoly claimed by the *cabildo* of Buenos Aires. The brief wars between Spain and Britain in 1718 and 1727–1730 were seized upon in Buenos Aires to eject or imprison the *asiento* merchants. When prolonged war returned once more in 1739, the British were expelled for good without hesitation or regret.[9]

The contraband and *asiento* trades of the early eighteenth century slowly transformed Buenos Aires. By 1740 the city had numerous brick houses, some of two stories. The hide exporters—beneficiaries of the growing market for leather goods in Europe—were now a wealthy elite parading the latest European fashions. The city's institutions, led by the *cabildo*, evinced strength and vitality. By 1744 population had reached 11,500, twice as large as any city in the interior. Scattered arrivals of immigrant Spanish soldiers and administrators enabled the white elites in the city to defend themselves against ethnic hybridization, although the city's population at large was becoming still more racially multiform. The recent decades of prosperity also enabled the purchase of growing numbers of slaves. By 1744 some 1,500 slaves and freedmen dwelt there, many performing the tasks previously allotted to the now-defunct communities of *yanaconas*.

Buenos Aires was also becoming a center of handicrafts. The city boasted a handful of silversmiths; cobblers plied their trade using local leather and imported tools; and tailors dealt in some of the finest European cloths. Skilled masons, builders, and carpenters had begun to form artisan guilds. Petty shopkeepers dealt in merchandise from silver to hardware and silks and spices. Beyond the city small farms, or *chacras*, and fruit orchards were growing in number.[10]

After 1739 Buenos Aires lost nothing from the expulsion of the British. They were immediately supplanted by the Portuguese in Colonia, who in any case dealt largely in British manufactures alongside slaves. Rather than marking any slowing in the city's growth, the period saw still faster advance. Before 1740 it had taken sixty years for the population to double from 5,000 to 11,000; after it doubled in little more than twenty years, reaching 20,000 by 1776. The midcentury growth of Buenos Aires was also due to increasingly closer connections with Spain, a tie that developed mostly through the much wider use of Crown-registered ships, the *navíos de registro*. From the 1720s onward Spanish ships brought still more slaves and manufactured goods, and they were used increasingly to transport mercury from Spain to Potosí. In the 1740s the *navíos de registro* were disrupted for a time by the naval wars against the British, but in the 1750s and 1760s they again prospered.[11]

Growing contact with Spain made it possible to wrest the slave *asiento* in Buenos Aires from foreigners and award it to Spaniards. The *navío de registro* trade also produced a new body of Spanish import-export merchants, or *comerciantes*, in the city. Some were factors for the great merchant houses of Cadiz, others fortune-hunting immigrants from various regions of Spain who worked their way up from the ranks of the artisans or petty shopkeepers. Though most newcomers settled in Buenos Aires, some went to the cities of the interior, establishing a new chain of mercantile relations in the River Plate. This chain began in Cadiz, passed through Buenos Aires, and from there to Paraguay, Chile, and Upper Peru. By 1760 this system had developed sufficiently to overshadow both the Portuguese connection through Colonia and the old routes down from Lima. The new Spanish merchants gradually assumed the role discharged earlier in some degree by the foreign slave merchants as suppliers of capital to local cattlemen and *hacendados* in the interior. In doing so, they gave Buenos Aires its beginnings as a financial center.

The Spanish merchants in Buenos Aires also assumed expanding political significance. By midcentury they had embarked on campaigns to end the city's administrative subordination to Lima and to abolish remaining restrictions on its trade, including the nominal *Aduana Seca*. These Spanish families were to play a lasting role in the country's history, dominating its commerce into the early nineteenth century, and later becoming the nation's wealthiest landed dynasties. Such were the Ramos Mexía, the Martínez de Hoz, the Sáenz Valiente, the Pereyras, the Canés, the Casares, and the Guerricos, and in the interior the Uriburus of Salta and the Iriondos of Santa Fe. The great Anchorena line began with the arrival in 1765 of Juan Esteban de Anchorena, who began building his family's fortune by selling slaves and dealing in contraband.[12]

Before 1776 Buenos Aires developed further as a military base. Its garrison grew from an ill-paid, neglected, and irregular force of around 500 in 1715 to about 5,500 by 1765, and to almost 7,000 by 1774. Initially an effort to keep the Portuguese in check in Colonia, this build up was later a response to fears that Buenos Aires might become a target for a British assault like the capture of Portobelo of 1739. The infusion of military personnel increased the city's population and its growth as a market, enriching the Spanish merchants who often made large profits from military contracts. Meanwhile military subsidies from Potosí, which during the early eighteenth century had been irregular and infrequent, increased during the wars of the 1740s. By 1750 the subsidy totaled 130,000 pesos, and it climbed to 200,000 pesos by 1760; altogether between 1750 and 1761 Buenos Aires received 1.5 million pesos from Potosí. The subsidy continued to rise even more steeply, reaching 600,000 pesos in 1774 and 650,000 pesos the year following.[13]

In the early eighteenth century Buenos Aires also developed a new cattle economy. Although exports of hides and other cattle goods were throughout secondary to silver and rarely exceeded 20 percent of total earnings, nevertheless cattle ranching and the hide trade helped increase the pace of the city's expansion.

During the seventeenth century Buenos Aires and the Paraná settlements of Santa Fe and Corrientes evolved the practice of provisioning themselves with cattle meat and hides for clothing and shelter—hides being a common roofing material—by periodic forays, *vaquerías*, into the surrounding countryside for wild cattle. Since cattle and horses were the region's sole resource of any value, the right to conduct *vaquerías* had always been a jealously guarded monopoly controlled by the *cabildo* through a licensing system. Licenses were granted only to a tightly knit inner circle of white notables, usually the *cabildo*'s officeholders. When hide exports began on a regular basis around 1700, the mode of exploiting the cattle herds changed. A concept of property based on the grant to conduct *vaquerías* gradually shifted to one based on control of land.

At the beginning, as the hide trade grew, *vaquerías* became far more frequent, better-organized and equipped ventures that penetrated much further than before into the surrounding plains. Capital, often culled from the foreign slave merchants, played a growing part in the operation, used to supply carts and horses and to hire peons to act as cattle drivers. The expansion of the *vaquerías*, however, intensified conflict with the Indians, especially the Araucanians. From time to time armed cavalry expeditions, *entradas*, were dispatched from Buenos Aires in an effort to drive the Indians back. But as demand for hides grew, the free-roaming herds were rapidly depleted; Indian resistance hardened, and returns from the *vaquerías* fell sharply. In 1715, in an effort to replenish the wild herds, the *cabildo* of Buenos Aires forbade *vaquerías* and the slaughter of cattle beyond the city's internal needs for a four-year period. *Vaquerías* thus ceased to be the regular annual events they had become.[14]

But this effort failed to match supply with demand, and a new initiative quickly followed. The more remote wild herds were abandoned to the Indians, and efforts were made to confine the remainder to specified territorial areas selected for the quality of their pastures and their access to water, with the rivers also serving as barriers to prevent the cattle from straying. Peons, who before had led the *vaquerías*, became permanent ranch hands, entrusted with the surveillance and protection of the herds. The *estancias*, as they were known, enabled more rational exploitation of the herds, matching the rate of slaughter with the needs of reproduction. In Buenos Aires this shift occurred between 1710 and 1730. By 1713 there were already some twenty-six *estancias* around Buenos Aires; *vaquerías* were then still common practice, although a decade later they had become a rarity. Between 1726 and 1738 some 185,000 hides were exported from Buenos Aires, mostly from *estancia* stock.

In the eighteenth century the term *estancia* did not usually denote private ownership of the land itself, which remained in the Crown's possession. Anyone seeking full title to land was obliged to submit to a lengthy and expensive procedure, the royal *confirmación*, before the claim was acknowledged. Instead possession of an *estancia* usually implied ownership of the cattle in a given locality, together with the usufruct of the land's other resources, its pastures and its water. Once more the *estancias* were closely regulated by the *cabildo*, and possession barred to social inferiors. From the start the *estancias* were vast in size: an income from hide sales worthy of the city's social elite required a large herd of cattle and control over a large grazing area. The basic land measure used throughout the grasslands of the River Plate was the *suerte de estancia*, a league and a half long and half a league broad, or about 2,000 hectares. But one such unit could support at most nine hundred cattle, or an annual yield of only ninety hides. As the *estancias* developed, they came to embrace tens of thousands of acres, the archetype for future landowning patterns in the pampas.[15]

The burgeoning pampas ranching economy spurred a demographic movement from the city into the countryside. The first rural settlers were few in number, partly because of the Indians and because the early *estancias* needed little labor. In the early years life on the cattle frontier was isolated, primitive, and risky. By 1740 the effort to control the Indians through the *entradas* was acknowledged to have failed. During the next decade or so the Jesuits attempted to establish reservations, or *doctrinas*, but they too failed. In 1752 a devastating spate of Indian attacks, massacres, and severe cattle losses led the *vecinos* of Buenos Aires to convoke the traditional general assembly, the *cabildo abierto*. The citizens agreed to organize a permanent rural militia, the *blandengues*, to be supported by taxing hide exports and the mule trains and ox carts destined for the interior. A line of forts was to be created, and a militia of self-sufficient small farmers, who would help supply the city with cereals. But not until the late 1760s was the militia fully operative and work seriously begun on the forts.[16]

In the early eighteenth century the same slow seepage of population from Buenos Aires and other Spanish cities of the littoral, which had earlier given rise to the "lost people" or "lost children" (*gente perdida, mozos perdidos*), continued. These migrants were usually of the lowest social class of the cities, escaped slaves or militia deserters, who exchanged the confines of urban life for a primeval existence as outlaws. In the eighteenth century members of the group were known as *vagos*, or vagrants, *changadores*, or *gauderíos*. Culturally, they were a hybrid mix of Indian, Spaniard, and African. To trap and kill the cattle from which they lived, they used the Indian *boleadoras* and Spanish hunting knives. They evolved a distinctive form of dress—bagged trousers, Spanish hats, and woven Indian shawls. Although this class was mainly male, some women, known as *chinas*, also dwelt in the countryside in rough huts made from canes and hides and scarcely distinguishable from the *tolderías* of the Indians.

Despite their isolated and peripatetic lifestyle, the *vagos* were involved in the hide trade from its beginnings, and thus played a growing part in the pastoral and mercantile society forming around Buenos Aires. Having obtained cattle from rustling on the *estancias*, the *vagos* sold the hides through rural trading posts known as *pulperías*. Hides were a means to procure essential goods: yerba mate (an essential nutritional supplement to diets consisting solely of meat), clothing, hunting implements, alcohol, and wine; and informal participation in the hide trade fostered the expansion of this free pastoral peasantry.

But as the numbers of *vagos* grew, they met increasing hostility from the colonial authorities and organized cattle interests. In Buenos Aires campaigns against "vagrancy" were pursued with growing energy, with the *cabildo* repeatedly seeking to enforce the *conchabo*, a mandatory licensing system intended to tie the rural population to the *estancias*, and to suppress the *pulperías*. In 1745 ordinances allowed the authorities to draft anyone convicted of vagrancy into military service. In 1753, to prevent illicit slaughter of cattle in the countryside, the carrying of knives was forbidden. In the 1760s the authorities were empowered to uproot and separate rural families judged as vagrants. But all these efforts proved fruitless as the roaming rural population continually defied all measures to suppress it.[17]

In contrast with the rapid growth of cattle ranching in the early eighteenth century, agriculture throughout languished, the output barely matching the growth of population. Such were the shortages of grains in Buenos Aires that the lower orders of the city, like those outside, often subsisted on meat and yerba mate alone. Farming was conducted on small holdings, or *chacras*, a maximum 500 hectares in extent, using slave or semiservile labor. The commercial farmers were mostly *mestizos*, who enjoyed none of the standing or political influence of the ranchers. They constituted an impoverished debtor class, financially dependent on the rural storekeepers (*pulperos*) or the lesser city merchants (*mercaderes*), through whom they also marketed their goods.

The weakness of farming originated in the general conditions of the region, the coexistence of an open frontier and a small population. Agriculture was in part a victim of the flight from the city that produced the rural *vagos*. Completely overshadowed by ranching because it required much more labor and produced no exports, farming always lost in the competition for land. High transportation costs confined it to the perimeter of the city. To an extent agriculture survived owing to support from the authorities. In Buenos Aires and other cities of the littoral, the *cabildo* was empowered to raise forced labor drafts for the harvest. Usually the militia or captured vagrants were assigned to this task, though on occasion urban craftsmen and artisans were mobilized. The *cabildo* intervened further to set aside land for agriculture, by creating lots known as *peonías*, and to fix land rents paid by the farmers. However, the *cabildo's* regulatory powers included control over food prices, and when it decreed lower prices during periods of shortage it undercut farmers' abilities to profit and accumulate capital.[18]

THE INTERIOR IN THE EIGHTEENTH CENTURY

Recovery in the interior, from Paraguay to Tucumán and Cuyo, also predated the Bourbon reforms of the 1770s, though it was less pronounced and more gradual than in Buenos Aires. But recovery manifested itself in a similar way, through a growth of production and population, and a resumption of commerce. Unlike Buenos Aires, none of the regions beyond became direct exporters; rather they remained satellites of other colonial economies—Upper Peru, Chile to a degree, and increasingly Buenos Aires itself. For the most part, development in the interior, unlike the littoral, followed the conventional Spanish-American pattern of agrarian *haciendas* and peasant agriculture, in which pasturing eventually became secondary.

The decades after 1680 marked the highpoint of Jesuit influence in the interior. From their position of supremacy in Córdoba, still the linchpin of the regions beyond Buenos Aires, the Jesuits created numerous *haciendas* in the seventeenth century. Jesuit colleges both in Córdoba and Buenos Aires educated the sons of the small colonial elites, and Jesuits controlled recruitment to the colonial administration. The stronghold of the Jesuits remained the twenty-two missions of the upper Paraná, to which eight new missions were added between 1682 and 1720 (see Map 4). By 1700 the missions harbored a

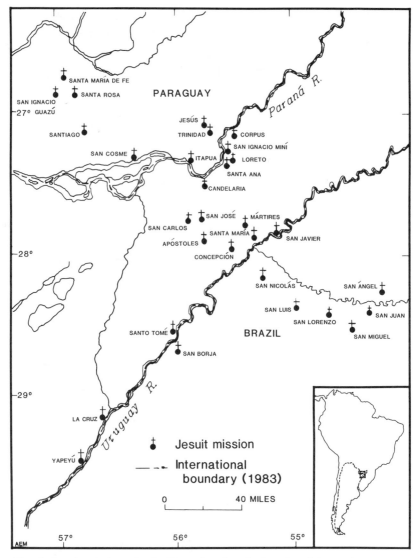

Map 4. Jesuit missions in the Paraná region during the eighteenth century.

population of perhaps 50,000 Indians, with the mean size of each mission settlement at about 1,000 during most of the seventeenth century. By the 1730s the larger missions had populations of between 4,000 and 6,000, equal to any of the lay communities except Buenos Aires (see Table 2). The missions continued to be administered by a cosmopolitan band of Jesuits, some now Spanish-American born, whose numbers rose to around 250 by the late seventeenth century and to almost 450 by the middle of the eighteenth.

The missions grew during the first decades of the century despite the incidence of disease and famine. The epidemic of 1717–1719, for example, only one of several, killed off almost one-sixth of their population. The Jesuits controlled almost all the Guaraní tribes of the Paraná-Paraguay region outside the adjacent lay settlements in Paraguay, Asunción, and Corrientes. Their attempts to expand among the hunting and gathering tribes of Mocoví southward toward Santa Fe, however, like the *doctrinas* around Buenos Aires, were much less successful. In the next forty years the Jesuits established another five

TABLE 2. *Population Estimates of Jesuit Missions, 1644–1768*

	1644	1702	1733	1750	1768
San Ignacio Miní	1,750	2,500	3,950	2,605	3,200
Loredo	1,700*	4,060	6,077	3,276	2,912
Corpus Christi	1,604	2,080	4,008	3,976	5,093
Candelaria	1,644	2,596	3,154	2,031	3,687
Santa Ana	1,000*	2,225	3,716	3,000*	4,000*
Concepción	2,000*	5,653	5,881	2,337	3,000*
Santa María la Mayor	1,000*	2,869	3,585	2,060	3,084
San Francisco Javier	1,560	4,117	3,663	1,946	3,000*
Santos Apóstoles	1,539	3,536	5,207	2,055	3,000*
Mártires	1,400	2,124	3,665	3,058	1,882
La Santa Cruz	1,000*	3,851	3,000*	2,410	3,523
San Carlos	2,300	5,355	3,369	1,628	2,500*
San José	1,441	2,594	3,605	1,866	2,341
Santo Tomé	3,000	3,416	3,494	2,793	2,400
Yapeyú	1,000*	2,300*	6,100*	6,578	7,000*
ROUNDED TOTALS	24,000*	49,000*	56,000*	42,000*	50,000*

NOTE: * = estimated.
SOURCE: Carlos Sempat Assadourián, Guillermo Beato, and José C. Chiaramonte, *Argentina: De la conquista a la independencia* (Buenos Aires, 1972), 200–201.

small settlements south of the Paraná missions, along with another half dozen westward on the southern flank of the Chaco.

In the early eighteenth century the Jesuit missions subsisted on pasturing and agriculture. Besides the numerous crops they produced, the Indians grew cotton and kept flocks of sheep for wool. Until around 1725 the missions provisioned themselves with cattle from *vaquerías*, which often penetrated as far south as the Plate's east bank. Afterwards, as in Buenos Aires, came a shift to *estancias* closer to the missions. San Ignacio Miní was typical of these larger settlements: according to inventories made in 1768 it possessed 3,000 sheep, 17,000 cattle, 800 oxen, seven yerba mate plantations, and an estimated 80,000 cotton plants.

The agricultural base of the missions throughout remained strong enough for the Jesuits to maintain a large standing army, ready for defense against the Brazilians or for offensive campaigns like the assaults on Colônia do Sacramento in 1680 and 1705. It also enabled them to develop thriving craft activities. Large numbers of women in the missions were employed in manufacturing textiles, while men were trained as masons, scribes, musicians, and decorative artists. Between 1715 and 1730 substantial improvements were made to the chapel buildings of the missions, many being completely rebuilt. The missions again expanded production and exports of yerba mate, using the trade to meet their tribute obligations to the Crown. The increasing output of yerba and the smaller quantities of hides, tobacco, and handcrafted furniture enabled the missions to be the first to exploit the growth of trade in Buenos Aires. Jesuit merchants there, known as *procuradores*, were large purchasers of weapons, agricultural implements, and construction tools. The missions also became one of the largest markets for slaves, who were placed mainly on the yerba mate plantations.[19]

Yet despite their numerous accomplishments, the missions were weaker and less firmly established than they seemed, ceasing to grow after 1730. The rising incidence of epidemics reflected a population that was outstripping resources. The missions were also confronted by growing political difficulties. Since their founding more than a century before, they had suffered recurrent harassment from the settler communities of Paraguay, who resented the Jesuits' success in gathering and maintaining a large Indian population, a valuable resource in extremely short supply. For the Guaraní the missions had long been a sanctuary from *repartimiento*, and they congregated there in large numbers.

In the early eighteenth century frictions revived and intensified. When supplies of manufactured goods and slaves from Buenos Aires began to increase, the lay settlers in Paraguay and Corrientes sought to follow the missions in expanding the production of yerba mate and tobacco, but they were halted by Jesuit competition and by labor shortages. Throughout the 1720s and until 1735 a long spate of disturbances, known as the *comunero* revolt, shook Paraguay and Corrientes. The *comuneros* first protested against the powers of the governors of Paraguay—officials nominated and largely controlled by the Jesuits—to impose taxes and administer labor drafts. Basing their claims on medieval Spanish law, the *comuneros* asserted such responsibilities rightfully belonged to the *cabildos*, and thus to themselves. The issue simmered in Asunción for more than a decade, but in 1732 it spread to Corrientes and provoked a military invasion of the missions. The assault was as devastating as the great *bandeirante* raid a century before. An ensuing famine and mass kidnappings ravaged the missions' population.[20]

Although the Jesuits survived the onslaught of the *comuneros*, the strange and exotic native civilization created by the missionaries began to wane. Enlightened despotism—the growth of royal power and bureaucratic centralism in all the Catholic states of mid eighteenth-century Europe—threatened the existence of the Jesuits as a wealthy, protected, and largely autonomous order, whose first loyalties were to the papacy. The new secular absolutism took hold in Spain on the accession of Ferdinand VI in 1746. As the tenets of enlightened despotism spread to South America, local enemies of the Jesuits in the River Plate renewed their challenge. They embarked on a war of propaganda, resurrecting old rumors that the missions harbored the fabled silver mines which the Spaniards had vainly sought for the past two centuries. They also complained repeatedly against the presence of foreign priests in the missions, insinuating they were agents of Spain's enemies.

These campaigns were soon rewarded: in 1750 an exchange treaty (*tratado de permuta*) concluded between Spain and Portugal stipulated that Spain would cede seven of the most easterly Paraná missions, and their 30,000 inhabitants, on territory claimed by the Portuguese, in return for Colônia do Sacramento. The Jesuits petitioned the Spanish crown to abandon the agreement, but once denied they turned to military resistance, instigating revolt among the missions. Braving renewed famine and the destruction of several settlements, the Indians warded off attempts by Spanish and Portuguese troops, aided by creole militias from Paraguay, to enforce the treaty. The exchange treaty was finally abandoned in 1759 on the accession of Charles III in Spain.[21]

But the Jesuits' victory was again short-lived. Their resistance to the treaty further undermined their position at court, where they were depicted as rebels against the Crown. Conflicts with enlightened despots had led to the expulsion of the Jesuits from Portugal and Brazil in 1758, and from France in 1764. In 1767 Charles III ordered their expulsion from Spain and the Spanish empire; early the following year the Jesuits in the missions and in the River Plate cities were rounded up on the authority of the governor of Buenos Aires and dispatched to Europe.[22]

For the past century and a half the Jesuits had been the most powerful of the clerical orders in the region, and their expulsion irreversibly weakened clerical influence there. Once the small band of autocratic leaders had departed, the missions began to disintegrate, with the merchants of Buenos Aires immediately assuming the Jesuit *procuradores's* franchise for marketing yerba mate. Upon discovering that the missions held neither gold nor silver in any quantity, the Crown abandoned all interest in them. Responsibility was vested in the governor of Buenos Aires, and immediate supervision entrusted to the Franciscans. This new regime was a disastrous failure, and the rituals of community discipline upheld by the Jesuits soon fell into abeyance. Paraguayans looted the cattle herds on the mission lands and captured and appropriated numerous Indians. Many of those who escaped gradually drifted into Brazil or onto the cattle *estancias* of Corrientes. By 1800 the population of the mission region dropped to under 30,000. Decline continued as the missions were once again devastated during the wars of independence. For the next hundred years, until its recolonization by Europeans, the mission region had no further significance.[23]

The growth of Buenos Aires, which in Paraguay and Corrientes provoked the *comunero* revolt and conflicts with the Jesuits, had less dramatic consequences in Tucumán and Cuyo. Although these settlements, led by Córdoba, participated somewhat in the slave and contraband trades, and in long-distance exchange with Chile and Upper Peru, for several decades after 1680 most continued to be the same enfeebled communities they had become in the seventeenth century. The cities' populations were counted in mere hundreds, frequently only in scores, and in many parts the economy consisted of little more than subsistence pasturing. Beyond the cities were scattered remnants of *encomienda* Indian communities living on *ranchos* and in crude shacks of thatch, sticks, and mud. Further beyond were the nomads.

During the early eighteenth century, Tucumán and Cuyo were perennially engaged in Indian wars, some intended to strengthen the settlements' defenses, others to augment their meager labor reserves or to keep open the routes into Peru and Chile. Warfare also fulfilled other functions, as the threat of an alien enemy encouraged cohesion among the Spanish communities. Most important, wartime needs were invoked to claim subsidies from Potosí. Throughout this period the Spanish towns were thus little more than lonely garrison points in the southern wildernesses of the viceroyalty. Writing to Philip V in 1708, Governor Urízar of Tucumán complained of the "miserable condition of this province, its frontier cities depopulated, their inhabitants largely destroyed or massacred (*casi destruídos o aniquilados sus habitadores*), the rest arms in hand in continual and necessary self-defense, lacking the time to attend to their own interests."[24]

Change came, apparently, less in the wake of the growth of Buenos Aires than of recovery in the mining economy of Upper Peru. In the 1730s a series of reforms implemented in the Potosí mines at last checked the century-long decline in silver output. Crown taxes were modified to create incentives to increase production, and a more flexible labor system was introduced to complement the *mita* and to develop more highly skilled workers. The practice evolved in Potosí of leasing the mines to Spanish immigrant entrepreneurs at fixed rents, which gave high returns to those able to increase production. Under the new system the mine shafts were deepened, and production gradually climbed, roughly doubling between 1740 and 1790 to reach the level of a century earlier. Potosí, however, became increasingly dependent on imported mercury as production at Huancavélica fell from approximately 4,000 *quintales* in 1700 to a mere 2,000 *quintales* by 1750.[25]

Recovery here, and more widely throughout Peru, gradually percolated southward. Its chief manifestation was the growth of the mule trade through Salta: from about 1740 through 1810 up to 70,000 mules a year passed through the annual market. As silver flowed back in increasing quantities, the Spanish cities embarked on new efforts to widen control in their hinterlands. New *estancias* and *haciendas* were formed; in drier regions like Santiago del Estero modest investments in irrigation were undertaken. Ox carts in teams of six, carrying up to a ton and a half of produce, once more traversed the trade routes.

Attempts were made to improve communications; for example, efforts abandoned since the 1620s to use the Rio Bermejo as a connection from Salta and Jujuy with the Paraná recommenced. As the new Spanish immigrant merchants appeared, developing and strengthening the new circuits of commerce, interest in military careers waned.[26]

Meanwhile, the population of the Spanish cities began to grow once more, and new Indian *curatos* appeared in their surrounding areas. Where demand for labor exceeded local supplies, as in Córdoba and Mendoza, black slaves were sent from Buenos Aires in growing numbers. By the middle of the eighteenth century all the cities along the main trade routes had substantial black populations. Still, slavery was relatively weak, in most parts the free black population being as large as the slave. Slavery was more common in the towns than in the country, and many slaves were women, the men often being allowed to earn their own subsistence among the *hacienda* peasants. Such conditions encouraged rapid racial admixture. Of an estimated population of 126,000 throughout Tucumán in 1778, 35,000 were white creoles or Spaniards, and a similar number were classified as Indians; there were 11,000 slaves and 44,000 free blacks, mestizos, mulattoes, and other ethnic permutations.[27]

Between the 1740s and the 1770s Tucumán and Cuyo suffered the same political tensions, arising from increasing market contacts that arose earlier in Paraguay and Corrientes. But here the focus of discontent was not the Jesuits nor in most cases the labor issue; rather, discontent sprang from disputes over taxes levied by outsiders and demands from the governors for funds and men to support distant and apparently unnecessary military adventures. In 1740, for example, the *vecinos* of Córdoba fought successfully against a Crown tax on the local mule trade, the revenues of which were destined to help Salta repel an invasion from the Chaco. Similar *comunero* movements in Catamarca in 1752, in La Rioja in 1758, and again in Corrientes in 1765 each reasserted the traditional liberties and prerogatives of the *cabildos*.[28]

By the 1770s Tucumán and Cuyo had changed substantially. In the towns populations now ranged between 2,000 and 7,500. Mendoza, for example, a town of 1,000 in 1724, grew to 4,000 by 1754 and to 7,000 by the 1770s. Beyond the towns was a substantial and growing rural population. Outside Córdoba in 1778 lived some 40,000 people, six or seven times the number that lived in the city; in San Miguel the rural population was roughly 20,000, in Santiago del Estero 15,000, and in La Rioja and Catamarca around 9,000 each. Between 1778 and 1809 Córdoba's rural population expanded to 60,000, Santiago del Estero's increased to 40,000, San Miguel's to 30,000, and Catamarca's to an estimated 24,000. By 1809 the total population of Tucumán and Cuyo reached about 250,000—roughly the same as at the time of the Spanish conquest.[29]

The towns of the interior had similar physical features. All were laid out in the classic Spanish colonial style of hectare blocks surrounding a central plaza bordered by a church and the *cabildo*. Homes were constructed of adobe, and the roofs from hides. In the patio gardens of the larger houses, and beyond into surrounding districts, were fruit orchards. Immediately outside the towns were small holdings producing cereals, often vines and a little cotton. Beyond were cattle and sheep *estancias*, peasant *ranchos*, and *curatos*, in which Indian or mestizo women labored on woolen or cotton textiles. Cooking pots or kettles were often the sole metal household implements, while heads of oxen served as seats. Many *estancias* and *haciendas* were self-contained entities: besides the animals they bred and the grains they cultivated, they frequently possessed soapworks, wine presses, warehouses for crop storage, and stills for the manufacture of *aguardiente* brandy. Among the ethnic strains in the countryside, the blacks were strongest in Córdoba and Mendoza, the Indians in the more upland areas. In Jujuy the pure Indian population remained throughout at about 80 percent, and in La Rioja half.[30]

Most communities of the interior were self-sufficient in wheat and corn, often in rice, olives, mules, wool, and cattle hides. Many contained tanneries, which produced numerous leather goods from lassos to wine casks and roofing materials. Local adobe brickworks flourished; in Córdoba a small glassworks grew up. The towns manufactured soap and flour, and carts for long-distance trading. Textile *obrajes* revived, most specializing in weaving. Some, like the old Franciscan *obrajes* in Catamarca, survivors from the late sixteenth century, now employed black slave labor; most spinning, however, was domestic. Cotton, wool, llama, and vicuña textiles were traded between communities and marketed widely among urban and rural communities alike, including the *vagos* of the littoral. Outside the main trade routes, cotton was still used as money and for tribute payments.

By 1750 a degree of local specialization had again arisen. Broadly, Tucumán was the source of textiles; Cuyo of wines and liquors; and the northeast, including the missions of subtropical farm goods, of sugar, cotton, yerba mate, and tobacco. Among the cities, San Miguel del Tucumán won note for its ox carts, Córdoba for its olives and its pastures for fattening mules, Mendoza for its wines, and San Juan for *aguardiente*. Santiago del Estero became a source of cochineal dye-stuffs, and wax and wild honey from the Chaco. In the northeast barrels and river barges were manufactured from local timber. Corrientes was noted for its coarse frieze and sackcloth. In Catamarca and La Rioja agriculture and textiles were supplemented by a small amount of mining for gold, silver, and copper.[31]

Nevertheless the communities' economies were still more competitive than complementary, with the settlements often duplicating each other's products. Except for mules, Mendoza wines, and the traffic in yerba mate or tobacco along the Paraná, little bulk trade was conducted between the communities in the goods each produced. As some of the *comunero* movements revealed, local mercantilism remained strong. Each community continued to strive to increase its exports, while importing a minimum from its neighbors and taxing goods from other communities; the chief object remained to amass silver to obtain manufactured consumer goods from abroad. Long-distance commerce seemed significantly greater than local. In 1805, for example, two-thirds of the incoming goods to San Miguel were of foreign provenance; of the other third about half were cottons from Catamarca, and most of the rest came from Chile. Goods from adjacent cities accounted for only around 15 percent of San Miguel's total consumption, and commercial contact with other settlements close by—Salta, Santiago del Estero, or Córdoba—was minimal. Of San Miguel's exports of cattle, hides, carts, and a little rice in 1805, almost all went to Buenos Aires or Potosí.[32]

Economic revival in the later eighteenth century occurred unaccompanied by changes in the system of production, local economic integration, or much alteration in the status of the subject races. Having survived the long depression of the seventeenth and early eighteenth centuries mostly on external subsidies, white elites still ruled the interior. Recovery in Potosí and Buenos Aires enabled them to revert to entrepreneurship and to replenish themselves ethnically through the stream of Spanish immigrants from the *navíos de registro*. Whites or near-whites were dominant in the cities and the countryside alike, retaining their privileges, rights to hold property, control over labor, and exemption from tribute. Meanwhile the population at large became subject to an increasingly elaborate caste system, which sought to institutionalize its inferior status. The caste system was an effort to stabilize and petrify the social order, to defuse pressures for social change, and to establish routinized forms of social control. In the eighteenth century repeated efforts were made to assign each racial subgroup to specific occupations and to a fixed rank. To protect the hierarchy, intermarriage among the castes was frequently forbidden. The castes were assigned distinctive modes of dress and, among other restraints, were prohibited from bearing arms and consuming alcohol. In some parts severe penalties were exacted against the castes if they ventured to acquire the blessings of literacy.[33]

THE BOURBON REFORMS

The expulsion of the Jesuits in 1768 was the prelude to a spate of reforms in the River Plate territories, which for a time gave renewed impulse to their development. The creation of the Viceroyalty of the River Plate in 1776 was accompanied by a wide program of change whose chief objects were faster local economic growth, more benefits for Spain from its imperial possessions, better defense against contraband trading and foreign invasion, and the embellishment of Crown authority.

The Bourbon reforms had their origins in the Enlightenment—its doctrines of secular absolutism, neomercantilism, and physiocracy—and in part, too, from simple imitation of other modernizing European powers. In the past the flow of resources from the empire to Spain had come from three main sources: tribute, taxes, and trade monopoly. With tribute now a much less important revenue source than under the Hapsburgs, the reforms made few changes beyond attempting to reduce evasion by conducting new population counts and by seeking to congregate those liable to tribute in new communities, or *reducciones*, accessible to imperial revenue officials. Taxes, now viewed as incentives to increase production, were generally reduced and simplified in the belief that any immediate decline in revenues would soon find compensation in the expansion of taxable goods and services. Taxation, too, became an instrument to modify the composition of production and exchange.

The reforms abandoned the earlier almost-exclusive concern with amassing bullion. Instead of directing investments so heavily into mining, an attempt was made to diversify the colonial economies and to export a wider range of colonial products, especially raw materials for Spanish industry. The final objective was to make the empire a self-sufficient entity; however, manufacturing would be centralized in

Spain, and competing colonial goods, such as wines and textiles, were to be discouraged and if possible eliminated.

The new concept of *comercio libre* brought major changes in the organization of colonial commerce. Instead of drawing profit through restrictions on the supply of European goods, the new aim was to maximize trade flows, basing returns on the increasing volume of transactions. Numerous new ports were opened up to trade, the old Crown commercial licensing system abolished, and the monopolies of Cadiz, Veracruz, and Lima abandoned. Even so, numerous limitations on trade remained such that *comercio libre* was an updated mercantilism rather than "free trade." Imperial trade remained a Spanish monopoly; the long struggle to combat contraband and European competition continued. Trade from each colony was to be conducted directly with Spain, and no attempt was made to integrate the colonies themselves. Spanish ships alone were to be employed in imperial trade. Any foreign goods imported by the colonies were to pay a duty double or more that of Spanish goods, and these goods were to enter only as reexports from Spain.[34]

The other major feature of the Bourbon reforms was a restructuring of imperial administration to promote efficiency, banish corruption, increase the tax yield, develop new raw materials for export, and widen the colonial markets for Spanish goods. The chief innovation was the establishment of intendancies, new territorial subdivisions in the viceroyalties. The intendants, the archetypal agents of the later Bourbon quest for active, positive authority, were granted wide responsibilities in their jurisdictions for taxation, investment and economic development, the organization of the militia, justice and the regulation of the *cabildos,* which in the wake of the *comunero* movements had fallen into some disrepute in Spain. The intendants were also to promote new public works, fresh mining ventures, credit institutions, and agricultural colonization. Theirs was the responsibility to discover and map out new resources and to develop commodities in demand in Spain, such as cotton. Further, the intendants inherited the powers of the governors, whom they replaced, to found new settlements, the rights of the old *corregidores* to create new Indian *reducciones,* and much of the former influence of the Jesuits in education. They supervised the collection of tribute and ecclesiastical tithes (*diezmos*). In the cities they assumed some of the earlier duties of the *cabildos,* such as the regulation of weights and measures, food prices, the guilds, and the castes. Finally, they became the chief authority through which royal *confirmaciones* to land claims were administered.[35]

Spain entered the Seven Years' War of 1756–1763 in 1761. Within two years it suffered major reverses at the hands of the British; the recapture of Côlonia do Sacramento from the Portuguese in 1762 was one of Spain's few successes. By 1763 the British, having vanquished the French in Canada and India, seemed to be readying themselves for another war, this to take key points in the Spanish empire. In response the Spaniards immediately embarked on military efforts to strengthen their possessions and to develop new trade routes safe from British attack. As the old route through the Caribbean was now largely in British hands, Buenos Aires began to be canvassed in Spain as a new official gateway to Potosí. Buenos Aires had progressively become stronger since the exchange treaty of 1750, and its governors, granted greater autonomy from Lima in the 1760s, now controlled the militias of Paraguay and Tucumán. During the assault on Colonia in 1762, the governor of Buenos Aires was authorized to call on subsidies from Peru and Potosí almost at will. In 1770 the destruction of a small British naval base on the Falkland Islands—territories claimed by Spain since the sixteenth century—viewed as a threat to Spanish shipping round Cape Horn, was also planned and executed from Buenos Aires.

However, plans to upgrade the status of Buenos Aires and fully to legalize trade there, were strongly opposed by the merchants of Lima, defenders of the old monopoly. As controversy mounted, Buenos Aires gathered support from two crucial constituencies: its new Spanish merchants and senior figures in the Crown bureaucracy. After 1763 the merchants intensified petitions and representations to the Spanish court, and they were strongly supported by three of the governors of Buenos Aires in this period: Pedro de Cevallos, military commander during the Jesuit war of the 1750s and the capture of Colonia in 1762; Francisco de Paula Bucareli, Madrid's agent in the expulsion of the Jesuits in 1768; and the Mexican-born Juan José de Vértiz y Salcedo. These governors joined the merchants in arguing that Buenos Aires had to be commercially developed in order to command sufficient military resources for defense against British or Portuguese attack.[36]

At length in 1776, as the British faced the outbreak of rebellion in their North American colonies, the opportunity came for decisive action. The war in the north left the Portuguese isolated in the south. Accordingly, early in 1777 under Pedro de Cevallos a military and naval expedition of 9,000 men was dispatched in secrecy from Spain to the River Plate. Cevallos's mission was to quash the Portuguese in Colonia, and then to confer on Buenos Aires the status of a viceregal capital. Both tasks were swiftly accomplished, as Cevallos over-whelmed Colonia and proceeded to Buenos Aires to proclaim the viceroyalty. The territories of the new jurisdiction embraced five regions: the governorships of Buenos Aires (including the Plate's east bank and the missions), Paraguay, Tucumán, the *corregimiento* of Cuyo, and Upper Peru. The last of these was indeed the vital acquisition, for Upper Peru possessed both half the population of the viceroyalty and the silver mines of Potosí (see Map 5).

Cevallos then abolished the *Aduana Seca*. In July 1777 he decreed that coined silver from the Potosí mint would henceforth be sent to Buenos Aires, and no longer to Lima. He also determined that Buenos Aires would serve as the official port of access for supplies of Spanish mercury. In 1778 *comercio libre* was proclaimed in Buenos Aires; the old trading licenses were abolished, along with many of the old taxes—*palmeo, tonelada, San Telmo, extranjería, visitas*. Only the *alcabala* and the *almojarifazgo* survived, the rates for both being reduced in most cases from 6 percent to 3 percent. Then a 7 percent duty was set for foreign goods arriving as reexports from Spain.[37]

Other expressions of Bourbon energy and innovativeness followed. To guard against British or Portuguese naval bases in the empty south, plans were laid for settlements along the Patagonian coast, to be supported by a new fishing industry. Cevallos also sought to establish a direct slave trade between Buenos Aires and Africa, dispensing with Portuguese intermediaries. He exhorted local ranchers to invest in salted-meat plants, and farmers to produce hemp and linseed.

In 1783 the intendants came to the viceroyalty as eight new jurisdictions were formed within it. Four of the intendancies were in Upper Peru (La Paz, Potosí, Cochabamba, and Charcas), and Paraguay also became an intendancy. Of the other three, the first embraced the vast territory of the former governorship of Buenos Aires from Tierra del Fuego through the city of Buenos Aires itself and the east bank to the former missions. The intendancy of Córdoba included Córdoba itself, the three cities of Cuyo (Mendoza, San Juan, and San Luis), and La Rioja further north. In the intendancy of Salta del Tucumán were Salta, Santiago del Estero, San Miguel, Catamarca, and Jujuy.

For the next twenty-five years, until 1810, the intendants discharged their responsibilities with characteristic Bourbon zeal. In Buenos Aires they were accorded the more senior rank of superintendant and given supplementary revenue duties. Here they also pursued,

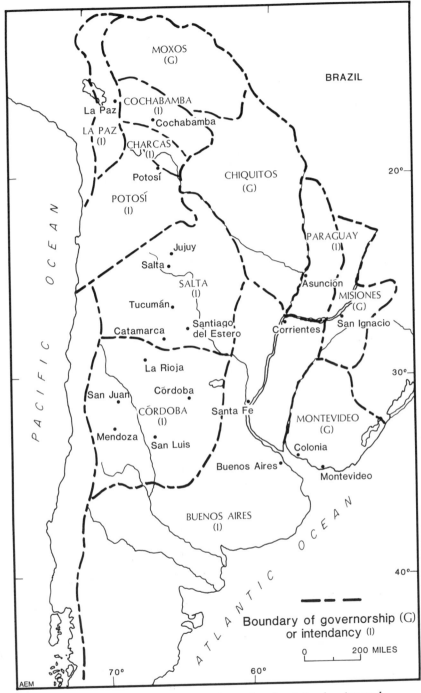

MOXOS
(G)

BRAZIL

La Paz
COCHABAMBA
(I)
· Cochabamba

LA PAZ
(I)
CHARCAS
(I)

Potosí

CHIQUITOS
(G)

POTOSÍ
(I)

20°

PARAGUAY
(I)

Jujuy

Salta ·

SALTA
(I)

Asunción

Tucumán ·

MISIONES
(G)

Catamarca

Santiago
del Estero

Corrientes

San Ignacio

La Rioja

30°

San Juan

Córdoba

CÓRDOBA
(I)

Santa Fe

MONTEVIDEO
(G)

Mendoza

San Luis

Colonia

Buenos Aires ·

Montevideo

BUENOS AIRES
(I)

PACIFIC OCEAN

ATLANTIC OCEAN

40°

Boundary of governorship (G)
or intendancy (I)

0   200 MILES

AEM

70°

60°

Map 5. The Viceroyalty of the River Plate, showing intendancies and
governorships.

though with little success, Cevallo's initiatives to develop meat-salting and fishing in Patagonia. Of the intendants the best known was Viscount Rafael Sobremonte of Córdoba, who organized numerous irrigation schemes, mining ventures, new Indian communities, and the construction of rural forts around Mendoza. Elsewhere, particularly in Paraguay and Salta, the intendants sought to promote production of cotton and cáñamo dyes. In Upper Peru they were active in silver mining and in regulating the *obrajes*.[38]

From the late 1770s the expansion of Buenos Aires accelerated. In the wake of Cevallos's expedition, real estate values in the city tripled, and for the next twenty years it enjoyed a sustained property boom. The population rose from 20,000 in 1766 to 27,000 in 1780, and to 42,000 by 1810. Although measures of maritime commercial activities in the city were still heavily distorted by contraband dealings, there were at least impressions of steady upward growth. Before the 1770s legal exports of hides averaged some 150,000 each year; between 1779 and 1795, some 330,000 a year. Revenues from imports displayed a similar pattern: before 1770, while the contraband link with Colonia still flourished, they were rarely greater than 20,000 pesos, but between 1779 and 1783 they climbed to an average of 150,000 pesos, and in the early 1790s to almost 400,000 pesos. Between the 1770s and the late 1790s the volume of shipping in the port of Buenos Aires doubled.[39]

Buenos Aires now changed substantially in other ways. Vértiz, who replaced Cevallos as viceroy in 1778, attained improvements in public works such as paving, lighting, and cleaning the city. The viceroy established an orphanage, a hospital, and a new school, the Colegio de San Carlos. Cultural resources also expanded, with the first theaters and the importation of printing presses from Spain, which enabled pamphlets and newsletters to circulate. There was also marked expansion among administrators, lawyers, and surgeons. At the conclusion of the American Revolution in 1783, in which Spain had eventually joined the victorious alliance against Britain, immigration from Spain gathered pace. In 1795 the city belatedly obtained its own chamber of commerce, or *consulado*, another typical late Bourbon institution. Alongside the intendants the *consulado* patronized new development projects, while encouraging experimentation and entrepreneurship. The *consulado* also led campaigns for the improvement in docking facilities in Buenos Aires, technical education, and new frontier explorations.[40]

With the final capture of Colônia do Sacramento Spaniards for a time enjoyed much greater control over commerce, and the two-centuries-old Portuguese community in Buenos Aires at last began to dwindle. There were now several thousand merchants of different kinds in the city. At the top rested some 150 *comerciantes*, the most powerful of whom, like their mercantile forebears, entrenched themselves in the *cabildo* and soon too in the *consulado*. The *comerciantes* controlled the lucrative trade from Spain, held the profitable royal contracts for transporting mercury and silver, oversaw local real estate dealings, and financed *hacendados* and other merchants in the interior.

Several thousand persons of African origin resided in Buenos Aires, about half of whom were slaves. Slaves and freedmen alike were widely employed in artisan activities. The artisan class also expanded during this period—among them, silversmiths, tailors, shoemakers, and a growing number of hatters, who used pelts of nutria from the nearby Paraná delta. By 1800 shoemakers in Buenos Aires were exporting goods to markets as distant as New York. Likewise, the 1780s saw rapid growth of the city guilds, though, perhaps due to their late beginning, they never attained quite the prominence of those in Lima or Mexico City, remaining dependent to some degree on the patronage of the *cabildo* or the intendants. In part the guilds attested to ethnic and social changes in the city. As immigration from Spain continued, the white population increased in size and diversity such that the number of career positions in administration or high commerce were inadequate. Many newly arrived whites had no choice but to enter the artisan trades, petty retailing, or transportation. Thus to some extent the growth of the guilds reflected the poorer whites' attempt to monopolize the crafts, expelling from them servile or caste groups.[41]

Of the other cities in the littoral beyond Buenos Aires, the largest was now Montevideo, on the east bank, which the reforms of the 1770s had also granted the right to trade under *comercio libre*. Though trade here never exceeded a quarter of that passing through Buenos Aires, Montevideo nonetheless had an important part in the hide and slave trades, and its population reached some 14,000 by 1805. In rural areas Vértiz improved and developed the frontier forts, which had been mere corrals. The forts were rebuilt with moats and stockades, and ten new forts appeared during the later Bourbon years, each quickly evolving into a small village. By 1800 the largest, Chascomús, had a population of about 1,000. Here, as in the interior, the rural population grew rapidly and spread into new zones. The first settlements now appeared in Entre Rios, between the Paraná and Uruguay rivers. Around Buenos Aires, the Plate's east bank, and Entre Rios alike, cattle *estancias* also grew in number; in the three regions combined, by 1795 an estimated million cattle a year were slaughtered for hides and meat. In Buenos Aires separate groups of ranchers and hide exporters now formed. In 1790 the latter created their own guild-type association, the *gremio de hacendados,* whose appearance typified the late–eighteenth-century trends toward increasing social diversification and stratification. Efforts to control the rural *vagos,* however, were still largely unavailing. A vigorous campaign by Cevallos in 1776 led to the capture and forced impressment of some 1,500 *vagos,* but nevertheless failed to check them. Other similar but less successful ventures followed.[42]

PROLOGUE TO INDEPENDENCE

In establishing the new Viceroyalty of the River Plate, Spain intended to create an efficient and enduring administration. The new colonial territory was given the financial resources and the military capability to resist invasion by Spain's enemies. But the outcome of the Bourbon reforms was not a revitalized imperialism, rather the decline and eventual extinction of the Spanish tie.

Deepening strains in the colonial system stemmed mainly from commerce and the increasing impracticability of *comercio libre.* Despite the intent of *comercio libre* to encourage direct trade with Spain and discourage trade with foreigners, throughout the period after 1776 most goods imported by Buenos Aires were foreign. Such goods included those that Spain was unable to supply—in particular, slaves—and manufactures that were preferable to Spanish products on account of higher quality or lower prices, discriminatory duties notwithstanding. Some foreign goods entered legally as reexports from Spain, others as contraband from other sources, often in foreign ships. Success in diversifying exports from Buenos Aires provoked further conflict after 1776. Whereas Bourbon administrators like the intendants encouraged export diversification to enhance ties with Spain, most new exports went not to Spain but to other colonial markets, another deviation from *comercio libre.*

Anomalies in the Spanish trading system became most acute in wartime. When the British navy seized control of the Atlantic, Spain could scarcely maintain commercial links with the empire, and the

Crown was forced to legalize trade with foreigners. But as a result colonial revenues, which in Buenos Aires came largely from trade duties, were increasingly dependent on foreign commerce. In 1779, for example, during the American War of Independence, revenues from imports of Spanish goods were a mere 20,000 pesos, compared with 114,000 pesos from foreign goods. By 1795, during the French Revolution, revenues from foreign goods climbed to 732,000 pesos, those from Spanish goods yielding only 118,000 pesos. Because revenues were crucial to the military effectiveness of Buenos Aires, during wartime the city found itself in the uncomfortable and anomalous position of having to increase trade with foreigners, and in doing so inviting a foreign attack, so as to be capable of defending itself. In sum, the final decades of the eighteenth century marked the increasing erosion of the bilateral relationship with Spain envisaged by the Bourbons. As the historic multilateral tradition in Buenos Aires reasserted itself, it eventually developed into a challenge against the whole colonial order.[43]

The first major difficulty with *comercio libre* concerned the slave trade. In 1778 Spain captured the west African slave bases of Fernando Pó and the Annabon Islands from the Portuguese. However, supplies of slaves from there were never sufficient to satisfy growing American demand in a period of economic expansion. The Spanish colonies remained heavily dependent on the Portuguese, and in Buenos Aires large numbers of slaves continued to be imported from Brazil. They came largely in Portuguese ships, which also brought forbidden Brazilian sugar and tobacco and British manufactured goods and which returned to Brazil with contraband exports, mostly silver.[44]

Second, in the 1780s both Buenos Aires and Montevideo began exporting jerked beef, a new trade initiated in part as a response to the economic diversification urged by Cevallos and later by the intendants and the *consulado*. Between 1785 and 1795 some 185,000 *quintales* of jerked beef were exported; by 1804 the annual export levels had doubled. But only a fraction of the meat exports went to Spain, with the great bulk marketed in Brazil and Cuba to feed slaves. From the 1780s growing commercial contact with Brazil and Cuba, fostered in part by the meat trade, led to the emergence of a body of new merchants in Buenos Aires outside the ranks of the official *comerciantes* dealing with Cadiz. Like the Portuguese, the shippers supplemented their cargo, jerked beef or hides, with exports of contraband silver and imports of slaves and foreign manufactured goods.[45]

In response to these peacetime issues in trade during the 1780s ranching and commercial vested interests emerged in Buenos Aires, both opposed to any strict application of *comercio libre* and in favor of increased multilateral links within the Americas. Subsequent events encouraged the growth of such groups. From the outbreak of the French revolutionary wars in 1793 until the Treaty of Amiens in 1802, Spain was at war first against the French, until 1795, and from the following year against the British. Throughout, the wars severely disrupted Spanish commerce with the Americas. In the war against France, Spain suffered the invasion of Catalonia, its chief manufacturing region; during the war with Britain, the Spanish mercantile marine was largely immobilized by naval blockades of Spanish ports. In Buenos Aires the 1790s brought recurrent commercial depression. Exports to Spain, for example, valued at 5.4 million pesos in 1796—for the most part a year of peace that brought unusually heavy trading to compensate for earlier losses—sank in the following year to a negligible 330,000 pesos and to a mere 100,000 pesos in 1798. Meanwhile, import shortages brought rapidly rising prices. Between 1797 and 1799 imported Spanish linen in Buenos Aires doubled in price, and Spanish wines and vegetable oil tripled.[46]

From Buenos Aires economic disruption spread into the interior, where already an undercurrent of unrest had become increasingly marked since 1776. The disagreements involved a variety of local conditions, but represented a shared opposition to the centralization of power in the viceregal capital. Montevideans, for example, were jealous of Buenos Aires's dominance in the import trade, while citizens on the east bank, in Santa Fe, and in Entre Rios resented the old claim of the *cabildo* of Buenos Aires to monopolize exports of hides. Potosí was embittered by obligations to provide Buenos Aires with subsidies for the upkeep of its administration and military forces, as Paraguay chafed at controls exercised from Buenos Aires over the trade in yerba mate and tobacco. Meanwhile, Mendoza and San Juan suffered from new preferences given Spanish wines in local markets under *comercio libre*. By the 1780s in Mendoza there were complaints that vintners were abandoning wine and reverting to cattle grazing for exports to Chile; in San Juan similar restrictions on access to outside markets gave rise to a recrudescence of *comunero* sentiments.[47]

Unrest in the interior worsened in the 1790s. The wars in Spain and the Atlantic blockades disrupted production and transportation of mercury used in the Potosí mines. Silver output thus began to stagnate, much of it flowing to Buenos Aires in search of scarce and expensive imports. The resulting shortage of money for internal trade compelled resort to debased *macucina* coin and provoked rising interest rates. Throughout the interior monetary contraction thus negated any advantages gained from falling competition from Spanish imports. Here, too, was commercial depression.[48]

Spain's response to the rising clamor of complaints throughout the American colonies in the 1790s was to relax *comercio libre*. Subject to the discretion of local colonial authorities it allowed more flexible use of colonial shipping, trade with allies or neutrals conducted by their ships, and direct trade within the Americas without the irksome and frequently impractical halt in Spanish ports. Thus in 1795, immediately before the outbreak of Spain's war with Britain, Buenos Aires briefly enjoyed the right to send its jerked-beef exports to British colonies in the Caribbean, and to import sugar and some manufactured goods in return; in 1797 the city was authorized to trade with neutral powers using its own or their ships. A flourishing trade with the United States developed as the Americans, mostly from Boston, joined the Portuguese as suppliers of slaves, manufactured goods, and spices and silks from the Orient. Contact between Buenos Aires and Brazil also grew markedly. Between 1796 and 1798 nineteen of the thirty slave ships that arrived in Buenos Aires were from Brazil.

Thus while trade as a whole fell sharply in the 1790s, much of what remained was outside the Spanish link and *comercio libre*, making these good years for the new merchants of Buenos Aires who dealt in the inter-American trade. Between 1797 and 1809 Tomás Romero, the most active and best known among them, chartered thirty-five ships from Buenos Aires and Montevideo, only two of which sailed to ports in Spain. According to their manifests, they transported more than 200,000 cattle hides, mostly to Brazil in exchange for slaves. But while merchants like Romero prospered, the "monopoly" *comerciantes* dealing with Cadiz fell victim to the shortages of Spanish goods and the blockades against Spanish ports.[49]

Commercial disruption quickly aggravated political tensions in Buenos Aires. In 1793, as the Crown began relaxing *comercio libre* and allowing exports to destinations other than Spain, local cattle interests petitioned the viceregal authorities to comply with these authorizations. In immediate outcry the "monopoly" merchants demanded continuing adherence to *comercio libre*, claiming that the inter-American trade was used for illegal imports of British textiles, which curtailed the market for Spanish goods. The dispute placed the viceregal authorities in a quandary, for although their sympathies lay with the monopoly merchants, the decline in trade with Spain prompted shrinking customs revenues. Because revenue concerns superseded others, they decided to allow the intercolonial trade, which then continued for the rest of the decade.[50]

At length the peace of Amiens returned normal conditions to Buenos Aires. Regular communications with Spain were restored and *comercio libre* reinstated. During 1802, the number of ships docked at the city tripled, to 188, bringing goods valued at 4 million pesos. Even so, trade issues continued to simmer, becoming the subject of growing public debate in the *cabildo* and the *consulado*, in pamphlets and in numerous local newsprints. At the forefront of the controversy was a group of local-born intellectuals, whose ideas were shaped by the impetus toward planning and experimentation initiated by the Enlightenment and the Bourbon reforms. Several held senior positions in the viceregal administration, positions they used in the 1790s to sponsor innovation—schemes to promote agricultural colonization, rural education programs to "civilize" the vagrant population, new techniques for the treatment of cattle hides, and efforts to develop exports of cattle meats, hemp, and linseed. By 1802 they had also become the leaders of a campaign to legalize permanently the inter-American trade and the multilateral connections beyond it.

The group's chief figure was Manuel Belgrano, son of an immigrant Italian merchant, who had received a Spanish education and in the mid 1790s became secretary of the *consulado*. Among Belgrano's followers were his deputy Juan José Castelli, Manuel José de Lavardén, and Juan Hipólito de Vieytes. Lavardén, an intermittent business associate of Tomás Romero, became well known in the 1790s as the author of *Nuevo aspecto del comercio del Rio de la Plata,* a radical tract that called for the termination of all restrictions on trade, the distribution of Crown land on the pampas in private property, and the creation of a local merchant marine. The group at large began promoting Lavardén's position, most of all the issue of free trade. Open commerce, they argued, would strengthen the local cattle economy, ensure a regular supply of cheap imports to enhance consumption and living standards, check inflation, and provide a dependable source of revenues. Free trade, however, remained anathema to the Spanish *comerciantes*, who continued to demand strict *comercio libre* to protect Spanish exporters and the Spanish merchant fleet. The monopoly faction sought to enlist support in the interior by contending that if trade were liberalized markets for domestic producers would become even narrower, that still larger quantities of silver would flow into

Buenos Aires, and that growing unemployment and vagrancy would befall the interior.[51]

Indeed, by this point tensions in the interior were increasing, not only on account of the trade crisis but also in the wake of conflicts arising from taxation. Between 1776 and the early 1790s the viceregal administration in Buenos Aires derived revenues from foreign trade, but often far more significant was the transfer of funds from Potosí. In 1791, for example, around 60 percent of the revenues of Buenos Aires came from Potosí, a proportion that rose further after the outbreak of war and the increasing disruption of foreign trade. Altogether in 1791–1796 Potosí supplied almost 79 percent of the total revenues of Buenos Aires. However, from the mid 1790s and especially after the peace of Amiens, which allowed uninterrupted sailings between Europe and the Americas, the Crown began to divert the bulk of the Potosí revenues to Spain in order to help defray her debts from the late wars. As a result, by 1801–1805 scarcely 6 percent of the revenues in Buenos Aires came from Potosí. The viceregal administration grew more reliant on revenues from trade, and the proportion of its income from this source reached 30 percent by 1801–1805, compared with only 17 percent a decade before. But to make up revenue shortages, the administration in Buenos Aires sharply increased the taxes levied on the interior. Here then, after 1800, rising tax demands, increasing commercial dislocation, and economic depression combined to place still greater cumulative strain on relations between Buenos Aires and the hinterland.[52]

In late 1804, after only a two-year respite, war between Spain and Britain recommenced. Within a year the Spanish navy was shattered by the British at Trafalgar. Regular contact between Spain and the River Plate was again obstructed by naval blockades, and another severe commercial recession battered Buenos Aires. In response, the Spanish crown again relaxed *comercio libre*, and the intercolonial trade revived once more.

At this point Buenos Aires suddenly received a much more direct shock from the war abroad. Without warning in late June 1806 the city was invaded by a British naval and military force some 1,600 strong that swept aside the Spanish militia and quickly won control over the city, sending the viceroy, the Marquis de Sobremonte, fleeing to Córdoba. The invasion of Buenos Aires was unplanned and unauthorized by the British government. Led by Sir Home Popham, it was rather a detour from a recent expedition against the Dutch in Capetown. But although Popham acted without orders, news of his adventure was welcomed in London, where other reports were bleak: British trade and industry were suffering as Napoleon controlled nearly all Europe and barred access to European markets. The prospect of trade in Spanish America through Buenos Aires presented itself as a much needed alternative, and plans were immediately laid to consolidate control by dispatching a second expedition. British merchants prepared some seventy ships laden with goods to accompany it.

But as the British made their preparations, the situation in Buenos Aires changed. During two months of appearing to submit to the invaders' presence, the city had secretly taken careful measure of the enemy's numbers and strength; now the city rebelled en masse. While Popham was stranded on board in the estuary, General George Beresford, commanding the land force, was captured with all his surviving officers and men. Both sides held to their positions until early the following year, when the second British expedition led by General George Whitelocke arrived. Whitelocke first took Montevideo, which became a base for the British merchants following him. He then landed on the Plate's west bank, some distance from Buenos Aires, where he was swiftly met by fierce resistance. Marching his troops in narrow file along the city's streets, Whitelocke watched as they were cut down in scores from the rooftops, by cannon and musketry captured from the first invading force. With no choice but unconditional surrender, Whitelocke returned to Montevideo with the remnants of his forces, leaving behind the merchants who had followed, and then quit the shores of the River Plate forever.[53]

The people of Buenos Aires drew great pride from these events, from having overcome the greatest challenge in the city's history. In the face of the British threat, years of wrangling on trade issues yielded to a tide of patriotic sentiment approaching the passion of a religious crusade. For a time supporters of the Spanish trade monopoly exploited this solidarity to gain ground from their rivals. One of the great heroes of the resistance was Martin De Álzaga, a Basque of humble origins, now president of the *cabildo* and the leading figure among the Spanish monopoly *comerciantes*. Belgrano, in contrast, as secretary of the *consulado* had left with Sobremonte, returning to the city only after the British had departed.

The British invasions of 1806–1807 shattered the Spanish administration. The regular army had been defeated by Popham and Beresford; the viceroy had fled and was soon afterward deposed. Victory had been achieved by Álzaga, the *cabildo*, and an irregular ad hoc militia of 8,000 that had been established between Beresford's defeat and Whitelocke's arrival. The militia had been formed by Santiago Liniers, a French-born soldier employed in the regular army, and consisted largely of common folk, divided into separate regiments of local-born creoles, blacks, and Spaniards. In 1807, pending the appointment and arrival of a permanent successor to the disgraced Sobremonte, Liniers became interim viceroy and with his army, Álzaga, and the *cabildo* ruled Buenos Aires.[54]

Before the new order in Buenos Aires had fully taken shape, events in the Iberian peninsula supervened. In September 1807, alleging defiance of his ban on trade with Britain, Napoleon invaded Portugal, provoking the Portuguese royal family to flee to Brazil on a British warship. Then the French turned on Spain. In March 1808 Napoleon forced the abdication of Charles IV; his heir, proclaimed King Ferdinand VII by legitimists, was taken and imprisoned, and Napoleon's brother, Joseph Bonaparte, imposed in his place. At this Spain revolted, forming a *junta central* to uphold Ferdinand VII. The same year a British army landed in Portugal to support the uprising. Napoleon and the French were now enemies common to all, and after having been at war with Spain for eight of the past twelve years, Britain suddenly became an ally.

In Buenos Aires, Liniers immediately became suspect on account of his French background. As tensions heightened between him and Álzaga, the viceregal administration in Buenos Aires was also becoming enmeshed in a financial crisis. The creation of the militia had multiplied administrative costs, but revenues had fallen consistently since the outbreak of the Anglo-Spanish war in 1804. To maintain its army in readiness against what was now an anticipated French invasion, Buenos Aires desperately needed new funds. A simple remedy lay at hand, as most of the British merchants who had followed Whitelocke were still sitting with their cargoes in Montevideo. Having failed to raise loans among the city's merchants, Liniers lifted restrictions on imports of British goods in November 1808. As these goods entered the city, financial pressures on the administration began to abate, and the freeing of trade established itself as a popular cause in the militia, whose members for the first time in several months began to receive salaries. Equally important, the freeing of trade by Liniers also boosted Belgrano's group, enabling it to overcome the political isolation it had suffered after the British invasions.[55]

In a desperate effort to rescind the measure, the monopoly faction led by Álzaga turned openly against Liniers, branding him an agent of the French. Álzaga argued that Buenos Aires should follow the procedure adopted in Spanish cities after the French invasion: convoke a *cabildo abierto* and appoint a junta to supersede the viceroy. When the proposal was ignored, Álzaga and his followers attempted a coup d'etat, but their rebellion against Liniers on 1 January 1809 failed. Among the militia the coup was supported only by the Spanish battalions, who were swiftly defeated and disarmed by the larger native segment, the Patricios regiment commanded by Cornelio de Saavedra. The coup thus discredited the monopoly faction and strengthened native voices against Spanish in the militia.

The failure of the Álzaga revolt thus marked another redistribution of power in Buenos Aires, this time toward the native-dominated militia. By this point Buenos Aires was only months away from the revolution that sparked the struggle for independence. While becoming the fulcrum of power, the militia also served as an instrument of social control that ultimately prevented the revolution from spilling over into a radical popular rebellion. The militarization of Buenos Aires after 1806 through the mobilization of around 30 percent of the adult male population amounted, by virtue of the wages and stipends paid to the militia, to a substantial income transfer to the general population. Such redistribution offset the unsettling influence of fluctuations in commerce and rising prices, arresting the formation of independent popular associations and protecting the supremacy of political elites at a time of increasing elite factionalization and division.[56]

In August 1809 a new viceroy, Viscount Balthasar de Cisneros, arrived from Spain to replace Liniers. Cisneros owed his appointment to the junta of Seville, now one of the few remaining outposts of Spanish resistance against the French. His arrival briefly calmed the atmosphere in Buenos Aires, for no one knew whether the viceroy was an absolutist, who would side with the monopoly traders, or a liberal who would grant the city the same trading conditions as Liniers. The viceroy's sympathies soon surfaced: he revoked Liniers's trade measures. But in late 1809, as revenues declined and the salaries of the militia once more fell in arrears, a group of British merchants requested authority to resume landing their goods.

Cisneros submitted the issue to the *cabildo*, which proved to be a major miscalculation. The two factions uncompromisingly restated their respective positions, and the long conflict escalated to a new threshold of intensity. The supporters of *comercio libre* again contended that trade with the British threatened Spanish manufacturing, exporting, and shipping; that such trade would undermine domestic manufacturing in the interior; and that, by channeling scarce supplies of money into Buenos Aires, it would disrupt regional commerce. In sum, if the British were to become resident consignees in Buenos Aires, Spanish trade would be disrupted and the Spanish merchants would face ruin.

Among the numerous rebuttals, the most influential was the *Representación de los Hacendados,* an unsigned tract written on behalf of local cattle ranchers by Mariano Moreno, a young creole intellectual. The *Representación* bluntly enunciated the concept of free trade asserted by Adam Smith, arguing that the foundation of economic progress lay in specialization. Specifically, since the country was weak in manufacturing, but strong in cattle goods, it should ignore the former and promote the latter. Further, Moreno rejected the view that to admit British goods would damage Spanish industry. Even before the recent wars, he argued, most goods from Spain were simply reexports of British or other European manufacturers; Britain had thus long ago proved superior in production techniques, and imports of British goods were thus inevitable. If the administration failed to legalize them, they would enter anyway as contraband. Meanwhile, restricting their legal import would only bankrupt the exchequer.[57]

Again having failed to raise revenue through voluntary loans from local merchants, Cisneros eventually tendered a compromise measure on trade. To improve revenues, he acquiesced in renewed imports of British goods; however, in a final reprise of Hapsburg policy, he banned all exports of silver by foreigners. But, as the controversy over trade still raged, Cisneros's policies began alienating the militia led by Saavedra. Pleading the need for economy, Cisneros first sought to reduce the militia's strength and numbers. Then he proposed to reform the Spanish contingent, while dispatching the Patricios regiment to Upper Peru to quell a revolt in Chuquisaca. Both actions prompted fears that the viceroy was plotting to repress the free-trade "patriots," as they now styled themselves. In January 1810 Belgrano began planning for revolution. He established a new newspaper, the *Correo de Comercio,* that continually paraded the trade issue before the public. His followers—Castelli, Vieytes, and others—formed patriot literary clubs, which furnished pretexts for a web of conspiracies and meetings with Saavedra.

The dénouement in Buenos Aires was once more provoked by events in Spain. In March 1810 came news of the French seizure of Gerona, and Seville seemed fated to fall next, leaving Cadiz as the final outpost of resistance. By March Saavedra decided that the fall of Seville would be his signal to undertake what Álzaga had urged late in 1808: convoke a *cabildo abierto* and establish a junta to replace the viceroy. In the second week of May came news of the fall of Seville. On 22 May Cisneros agreed to convoke a *cabildo abierto*, persuaded that he would become head of the new junta. Although some 450 notables were entitled to attend the assembly, only 200 did so, the rest kept away by mobs and the presence of the militia in the streets. Motions were quickly passed acknowledging the demise of the legitimate government in Spain and therefore the viceregal administration in Buenos Aires; power thus passed to those gathered in the *cabildo abierto*, which was now free to establish a new government. On 25 May, Cisneros was deposed and arrested by Saavedra. The new junta was sworn in, with Saavedra as its president and Belgrano, Castelli, and Moreno, the vanguard of the free-trade "patriots," among its other members.[58]

In sum, the eighteenth century witnessed a society in ascent, a society spurred continuously by an array of external forces. But the century closed with the long drift into crisis that began in the early 1790s, concluding in an explosion of revolutionary forces. After 1680 Buenos Aires at length emerged as an entrenched and successful entrepôt whose powers and functions were typical of Spanish colonial mercantile centers. The city and the interior had a relationship that was in part symbiotic, in part parasitic, with Buenos Aires as the chief supplier of imports, the largest of the local urban markets, the chief embarkation port for exports, the main recipient of subsidies and taxation revenues, and the chief source of finance capital. As the city expanded as a commercial, military, and administrative center, its society increased in diversity and, ultimately, in political self-awareness.

By 1800 Buenos Aires had also become the center of a growing local cattle economy. Both ranching and hide exporting were conducted in the monopolistic mode that typified the early colonial economy. Small elites entrenched in the *cabildo* struggled continuously to dominate access to land, to appropriate cattle herds in adjacent regions like the east bank, and to control the hide export trade. Early colonial operational practices also persisted in the small farming economy around Buenos Aires, among them the use of forced labor and the regulation of grain prices.

To the legacy of monopoly, forced labor, and state economic regulation the eighteenth century contributed several new conditions, ones that were to reappear in broadly analogous forms throughout Argentine history. The early hide trade, for example, developed in response to market demand engendered by the war of the Spanish Succession; throughout the nineteenth century foreign wars would again impel the expansion of the pampas economy—motivating wool production in the early 1860s and beef around 1900. As events from the early 1790s first highlighted, wars abroad, by disrupting external commerce, provoked local political instability. Import shortages brought inflation and declining state revenues, a combination that undermined the strength and effectiveness of government just as pressures on the political system were aggravated. Comparable situations were to appear in the late 1820s, the early 1840s, the mid 1870s, and during World War I.

In 1810 warfare abroad inflamed political conflict in Buenos Aires to the point of revolution. Conflicts between monopolists and free traders pitted against one another defenders of an obsolescent external partnership and supporters of new, but untested, alternatives. In scale this conflict had only one later parallel: the collapse of conservatism and the rise of Perón. Although these two great political transitions of 1793–1810 and 1930–1946 were vastly different in substance and outcome, they possessed certain broad similarities: incited by changes in the international balance of power, each of these crises generated economic breakdown and chronic political instability.

The growth of manufacturing in Buenos Aires during the eighteenth century mirrored the city's expansion as a market. In the manufacturing sector, too, some enduring patterns first became visible. Manufacturing in Buenos Aires constantly faced a threefold barrier: labor scarcity and relatively high production costs, lack of many raw materials, and competition from imports. The artisan industry thus developed narrowly, largely restricted to crafts for which raw materials were exceptionally cheap and abundant. Local manufacturers could produce competitively priced leather shoes or hats made from nutria pelts, but textile manufacture, as distinct from simple tailoring, was virtually unknown. Similarly, the silversmiths were by far the strongest of the early guilds, since silver was a readily available raw material.

By 1800 strains between Buenos Aires and Spain represented only one aspect of the late-colonial crisis, as other tensions evolved in relations between Buenos Aires and the interior. Toward the external Atlantic economy Buenos Aires had become increasingly liberal, but toward the interior increasingly exploitive. As a growing faction in Buenos Aires begrudged the tie with Spain, a similar faction in the interior grew restive at dominance from Buenos Aires.

In the interior economic recovery in the eighteenth century accompanied the revival of Potosí. The inflow of silver again prompted local elites into reconstituting a native or nonwhite labor force. By this time an elaborate caste system had replaced the simple two-class order of earlier rural society, which had become more closely linked with the colonial economy. Specialization was more highly developed among the interior cities, commerce embraced a larger volume of goods, and artisan manufacturing, too, was advancing. Yet even so, the economy of the interior was still based on an exchange of primary goods for imported manufactures, with each community continuing to strive for trade surpluses to augment the inflow of cash and imports. As the *comunero* movements showed, to achieve trade surpluses the cities had to compete constantly against one another for markets, labor, or livestock resources. Institutional rather than market mechanisms governed the labor force throughout the interior and a rigid, racially stratified system governed society.

While the eighteenth century brought some progress in the interior, it remained a mélange of backward and relatively static local economies subject to a series of crises. First, parts of the interior suffered from declining demand for their products when *comercio libre* gave preference to competing Spanish goods such as wines and textiles. Next came the commercial and financial disruptions of the 1790s, disruptions unique in their duration and intensity. Supplies of silver and money became increasingly volatile: when imports were scarce, silver was abundant; but as imports eventually arrived, large quantities of silver and coin vanished into Buenos Aires. Economic disruption in the interior became even more severe immediately before 1810. As the British increased their trade in and through Buenos Aires, cheap manufactures flooded the markets, and more silver passed to British merchants. After 1810, with the war, markets and silver contracted still further, occasioning economic collapse in the interior.

Indian pictography from the Córdoba region, probably of late sixteenth-century origin, showing the coming of the *conquistadores* on horseback. Reproduced from Dick Ibarra Grasso, *Argentina indígena y prehistoria americana* (Buenos Aires, 1967), 559.

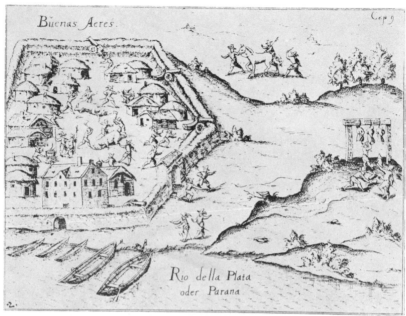

A late–sixteenth-century impression of Querandí Indian attacks on the newly created city of Santa María del Buen Aire following the expedition of Pedro de Mendoza in 1536. To the right Spaniards hack off pieces of flesh from the bodies of men hanged for killing horses. Based on the chronicle of the expedition by Ulrich Schmidel, published originally by Levinus Halsius (Nuremburg, 1595). Reproduced from Guillermo Furlong, *Historia social y cultural del Río de la Plata, 1536–1810: El trasplante social* (Buenos Aires, 1969), 1:509.

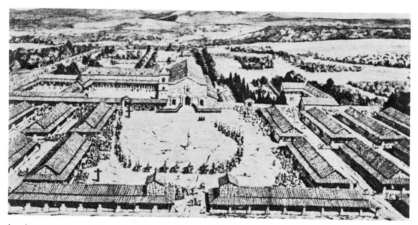

An impression of the Jesuit mission at San Ignacio Miní during the early eighteenth century, showing a parade of the Indian militia. Painting by Leonie Malthis, belonging to the Museo Histórico Provincial, Rosario. Reproduced from Diego Abad de Santillán, *Historia argentina* (Buenos Aires, 1965), 1:175.

Transporting bar iron to Potosí in the early nineteenth century. The mule train remained the most common mode of transportation throughout the colonial period, and the only means of access to the *altiplano* of Upper Peru. The original sketch appears in Peter Schmidtmeyer, *Travels in Chili, over the Andes, in the years 1820 and 1821, with some sketches of the productions and agriculture* . . . (London, 1824). Reproduced from Diego Abad de Santillán, *Historia argentina* (Buenos Aires, 1965), 1:348

"*El cordobés*" (the man of Córdoba) by Juan Mauricio Rugendas, depicting the traditional garb of men in the rural interior during the early nineteenth century. Reproduced from Guillermo Furlong, *Historia social y cultural del Rio de la Plata, 1536–1810: El trasplante social* (Buenos Aires, 1969), 1:219.

Mariano Moreno (1777–1811) by Juan de Dios. Author of the *Representación de los hacendados*, and secretary of the First Junta, 1810–1811. Reproduced from Diego Abad de Santillán, *Historia Argentina* (Buenos Aires, 1965), 1:427.

José Gervasio Artigas (1764–1850) by Juan Manuel Blanes. Leader of the movement for independence in the east bank of the River Plate, and the most prominent of the early Federalists. Reproduced from Diego Abad de Santillán, *Historia Argentina* (Buenos Aires 1965), 1:507.

Bernardino Rivadavia (1780–1857). Leading Unitarist reformer after 1810, and president of the United Provinces of the River Plate, 1826–1827. Portrait attributed to J. M. Turner, and belonging to the Museo Histórico Nacional, Buenos Aires. Reproduced from Diego Abad de Santillán, *Historia argentina* (Buenos Aires, 1966), 2:133.

Juan Manuel de Rosas (1793–1877), governor of Buenos Aires 1829–1832 and 1835–1852. Portrait by Juan Manuel de Blanes in 1840. Reproduced from Diego Abad de Santillán, *Historia argentina* (Buenos Aires, 1966), 2:306.

Juan "Facundo" Quiroga (1788–1836), *caudillo* governor of La Rioja from 1820, and Rosas's chief ally in the interior during the early 1830s. Lithograph by César Hipólito Bacle. Reproduced from Diego Abad de Santillán, *Historia argentina* (Buenos Aires, 1965), 2:179.

A depiction of Rosas's personal militia, the *Colorados del Monte*, during the late 1820s, featuring Rosas's most characteristic slogan, "Long Live the Argentine Federation."

Merchants and settlers come ashore in carts at Buenos Aires in the 1840s. The use of such carts continued until the modernization of the port in the 1880s. Lithograph by César Hipólito Bacle. Reproduced from Diego Abad de Santillán, *Historia argentina* (Buenos Aires, 1966), 2:164.

Daguerrotype portrait of Justo José de Urquiza (1801–1870), governor of Entre Rios during the 1840s, leader of the revolt that overthrew Rosas in 1852, and president of the Argentine Confederation, 1854–1860. Reproduced from Archivo General de la Nación, Buenos Aires.

Domingo F. Sarmiento (1811–1888), writer, educator, and politician. Pictured here in official dress as second elected president of the Argentine Republic in 1868. Reproduced from Archivo General de la Nación, Buenos Aires.

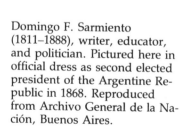

The Last Paraguayan by José M. Blanes. A sentimental portrayal of the destruction of Paraguay in the war of the triple alliance, 1865–1870. Original belongs to the Museo Nacional de Bellas Artes, Montevideo. Reproduced from Diego Abad de Santillán, *Historia argentina* (Buenos Aires, 1967), 3:177.

Caricature, origin and date unknown, of the rural cockfight, a sport that retained its popularity into modern times. Reproduced from Diego Abad de Santillán, *Historia argentina* (Buenos Aires, 1968), 4:342.

Wool and hide warehouses in Buenos Aires, 1876. The high-wheeled carts, drawn by oxen, are survivals from the early colonial period. Sketch reproduced from Desiré Charnay, *A travers la Pampa et la Cordillère* (Paris, 1876).

Emigrants depart from Marseilles to the River Plate in 1872. This engraving seems an idealized portrayal in that most emigrants were working-class men. Reproduced from Diego Abad de Santillán, *Historia argentina* (Buenos Aires, 1967), 3:184.

The riverfront in Buenos Aires 1885 with its daily population of servant washerwomen. Reproduced from Reginald Lloyd, ed. *Twentieth-Century Impressions of Argentina* (London, 1911), 363.

A country land auction in the province of Buenos Aires at the start of the Juárez Celman land boom, 1886. Sketch by Alfred Paris; reproduced from Diego Abad de Santillán, *Historia argentina* (Buenos Aires, 1967), 3:356.

General Bartolomé
Mitre (1821– 1906) in
old age. Early in his
sixty-year political ca-
reer, Mitre served as
first president of the
newly united republic
(1862– 1868). Repro-
duced from Archivo
General de la Nación,
Buenos Aires.

General Julio A. Roca
(1843–1914). "Con-
queror of the
Wilderness" in 1879,
Roca served two terms
as president,
1880–1886 and
1898–1904. Symbol of
the "oligarchy" dis-
placed by the Sáenz
Peña law of 1912. Re-
produced from Ar-
chivo General de la
Nación, Buenos Aires.

III

REVOLUTION AND DICTATORSHIP, 1810-1852

The May revolution brought the end of the colonial order and a bitter and lengthy struggle for independence. Although self-government was seized in an effort to deepen and quicken commercial prosperity, instead it brought prolonged economic disruption, decades of intermittent civil war, the shattering of central government, and a universal plunge into dictatorship. But amid these events came slow readaptation and recovery. The early nineteenth century saw the consolidation and expansion of the coastal cattle economy of Buenos Aires and the rise of a new land-based elite such that by midcentury Buenos Aires was preparing once more to reclaim its leadership over the lands beyond.

THE WARS OF INDEPENDENCE, 1810–1820

The decade following the overthrow of the last Spanish viceroy was marked by the emergence of a maelstrom of competing political forces, which made this period one of the most complex in Argentine history. Yet the decade's general features are clear enough: the region gradually made good its claim for self-rule, and eventually *de jure* emancipation, but at the price of territorial segmentation, the collapse of effective transregional authority, and an economic breakdown of unparalleled magnitude. The decade divides into three major phases. First, in 1810–1811 came territorial dismemberment, the loss of Upper Peru, Paraguay, and in a less direct way the Plate's east bank. Second, between 1812 and 1816, widening fissures developed between Buenos Aires and its northern and western hinterland, from Santa Fe to Tucumán and Cuyo. Frictions between a Unitarist, or centralist, faction in Buenos Aires and a Federalist, or provincial, faction beyond led eventually to spasmodic civil war alongside the struggle with Spain; the outcome was the rise of regional warlordism or *caudillismo*. The third phase, from 1816 to 1820, brought a temporary truce in the civil wars, which furthered the cause of emancipation from Spain, but in 1819–1820 reintensified civil war returned. The war's climax brought the conquest of Buenos Aires and of the Unitarists by Federalist *caudillos*, and the extinction of central government.

In May 1810 the new junta led by Saavedra had to confront the task of establishing its writ over the rest of the viceroyalty, a daunting prospect for a city of scarcely forty thousand facing a territory the size of India. To enhance and legitimize its authority, the junta quickly reiterated the invitation made earlier by Cisneros: to convoke a congress of delegates from the interior to consider responses to recent events in Spain. Declaring itself willing to broaden its membership and to include representatives from the cities beyond, the junta hoped to ally the regions with the metropolitan rebellion.

In much of the interior—Santa Fe, Corrientes, the Cuyo cities, and throughout the intendancy of Salta—the revolution received immediate and often enthusiastic support, for there, as in Buenos Aires, the Bourbon regime was unpopular. Many were vexed by the long crisis in trade, which in the past year or two had become increasingly severe and disruptive, and in many parts opposition to the autocratic rule of the intendants was considerable, accompanied by hopes for a redistribution of public offices that would favor the native elites. On news of events in Buenos Aires patriot militias were speedily formed and soon controlled the *cabildos* and the local administrations.[1]

Yet support for the revolution was far from universal. Montevideo and Asunción, which remained in the grip of Bourbon loyalists, rejected collaboration with Buenos Aires and proclaimed allegiance to the new Council of the Regency in Spain, a body established to replace the fallen junta of Seville, and now the focus of resistance to the French. Opposition also came from Upper Peru, where a year earlier a creole insurrection in the intendancies of Chuquisaca and La Paz was quickly stifled by a Spanish army led by General José Manuel de Goyeneche, in part with troops sent from Buenos Aires by Cisneros. Goyeneche's force now posed a major threat to Saavedra's power. Lastly, opposition in Córdoba was led by the intendant, Juan Gutiérrez de la Concha, and former viceroy Liniers, who was anxious to redeem his career by a show of loyalty to Spain. To resist the junta, the two organized a small army, which was first to link up with Goyeneche in Upper Peru and then march on Buenos Aires. To counter the resistance and to ensure that the interior selected for the proposed congress delegates who would support the revolution, the junta swiftly equipped two of its own military forces, one destined for Córdoba and Upper Peru, the other for Paraguay. Thus began the wars of independence.[2]

In July 1810 the force gathered by Gutiérrez and Liniers in Córdoba was routed by the army from Buenos Aires. The defeated leaders were summarily shot, as ordered by Mariano Moreno, now secretary to the junta and a proponent of ruthless measures intended to assert the revolution's authority, increase its momentum, and preclude any agreement with Spain that would halt the revolution. Since the coup in May, Moreno constantly decried the mere erection of a junta—a procedure that simply imitated events in Spain and sustained allegiance to Ferdinand VII. Moreno urged more momentous acts: a declaration of independence and the proclamation of a republic. Also, in what came to represent the first manifestation of the regional issue, Moreno insisted on full control of the revolutionary movement from Buenos Aires. In this demand, he sought to uphold, indeed enhance, political centralization, allowing Buenos Aires to enforce the free-trade measures demanded in the *Representación* of 1809.

But in all these spheres Saavedra was cautious and conservative. He supported self-rule under the "mask of Ferdinand"; he was also a leading advocate of shared government with the regions. In almost every respect Moreno's radical, if not jacobinical, program seemed to Saavedra too extremist. In the wake of the Córdoba executions, which Saavedra privately assailed, a power struggle erupted between the two—the first of the revolution's multitudinous internal crises.

In late 1810 Moreno's followers made a bid for control over the Buenos Aires militia. This effort, intended to spark a second coup in Buenos Aires, failed as the militia remained firmly united behind Saavedra. The collapse of the rebellion was swiftly followed by Moreno's resignation from the junta and his embarkation for Europe. Within weeks, Moreno died at sea. He had, however, correctly identified many of the issues that were to dominate politics in the years ahead: What kind of relations should prevail between Buenos Aires and the interior? Was the revolution's object independence or merely greater self-government and freedom of trade? Would the new order be a monarchy or would it adopt a republican form?

For the moment Saavedra clung to his moderate and conciliatory course. The junta was broadened to include representatives from the interior and renamed as the *junta grande*. Saavedra also authorized the formation of local *juntas provinciales* in the interior.[3]

Meanwhile, fateful events were taking shape in Upper Peru. Under Juan José Castelli, another of the radicals in the original junta, the army from Buenos Aires destroyed resistance in Córdoba, crossed Tucumán, and ascended the *altiplano*. As it went, the army augmented its forces with local volunteers. At first success seemed guaranteed, the expeditionary force likely to carry its triumphs to the gates of Lima. After a victory over the Spaniards north of Jujuy at Suipacha in November 1810, the army was warmly welcomed in Upper Peru, but this welcome proved short-lived. Castelli was lured into accepting a truce with the Spaniards, which enabled Goyeneche to gain reinforcements from Peru. Seven months later Goyeneche's larger force of regulars soundly defeated the motley, ill-disciplined patriot army at Huaquí, immediately south of Lake Titicaca. The remnants of Castelli's troops streamed back to Tucumán in complete disarray, leaving the road to Salta open to the Spaniards. Castelli's star, like Moreno's, waned as fast as it had risen.

The abortive campaign in Upper Peru in 1810–1811 had several crucial consequences. The expanding economic crisis in the interior was exacerbated to the point of near-collapse, as after the battle of Huaquí the exchange of mules and silver, the pillar of the eighteenth-century commercial system, was largely destroyed. Potosí was increasingly devastated by war, and Salta and Jujuy were for long periods occupied by the Spaniards. The flow of silver southward thus rapidly dwindled to a mere trickle, while silver coin continued to slip away to Buenos Aires in search of imports. In 1806–1810 the viceregal administration had managed to extract 1.1 million pesos in taxes from the interior. Revenues plummeted to a mere 180,000 pesos in 1811–1815, reflecting both political breakdown and the extent of economic dislocation in the interior.

The military campaign of 1810–1811 also further alienated Upper Peru from Buenos Aires. On his arrival Castelli initiated a series of reforms that included the abolition of Indian labor services and the *mita*, still the mainstays of the region's social system. Although Castelli's intention was to mobilize Indian support against the Spaniards, his chief accomplishment was to antagonize the local creole elites, whose will to expel the Spaniards was largely motivated by a desire to increase their own control over local resources, above all the Indians. Castelli's intervention thus brought to a climax some thirty years of growing resentment by the elites of Upper Peru at control from Buenos Aires. Earlier grievances had largely focused on taxation; to them now was added the issue of Indian labor. Future support for efforts to expel the Spaniards was offered by the elites of Upper Peru only to win local self-rule. Huaquí thus proved a first step in the sequence of events that led to the creation of the Republic of Bolivia in 1825.[4]

The expedition to Paraguay in 1810 fared no better than that to Upper Peru. Command over the second force from Buenos Aires was entrusted to Manuel Belgrano, whose military career continued without interruption until his death in 1820. In late 1810 Belgrano overcame heavy seasonal rains to reach Paraguay, but once there he erred by dispersing his forces. Early the next year he was twice defeated by the intendant of Paraguay, Bernardo de Velasco. A truce was eventually concluded, under whose terms Belgrano returned to Buenos Aires, his mission unaccomplished. Neither he nor any other military leader from Buenos Aires was to return to Paraguay for more than fifty years, and the area, which had little of the economic or strategic significance of Upper Peru, was left to its own devices. In 1811 Velasco was overthrown by a rebellion among the local creole elites, led by José Gáspar de Francia. Decades of complaints against Buenos Aires's control over Paraguayan trade left these elites as antagonistic toward Buenos Aires as toward Spain. Under Francia's dictatorship Paraguay became an independent republic, severing the bond between Buenos Aires and Asunción that had begun with the expedition to the River Plate led by Pedro de Mendoza.[5]

Within a year the revolutionaries in Buenos Aires thus suffered a succession of military setbacks that shattered control over two major segments of the viceroyalty, including Potosí. Meanwhile they were embroiled in a third conflict, with Montevideo, also over issues that lingered from the eighteenth century. Buenos Aires and Montevideo had long been commercial rivals, each aspiring to dominate trade with the interior, but tensions had become increasingly acute since the British invasions. In 1808 Montevideo repudiated the authority of Liniers; in 1810 it rejected the May junta. Later in 1810 Francisco Javier de Elío, the governor of Montevideo during Liniers's regime whom Cisneros had dismissed as a potential rival, returned from Spain as Cisneros's accredited successor as viceroy. Elío's orders were to destroy the Buenos Aires junta, and the naval forces at his command first seized control over the River Plate estuary and imposed a blockade against Buenos Aires. Elío had also been authorized in Spain to enlist military support from the Portuguese in Brazil, which he hastened to do, augmenting his forces and his funds among the towns, villages, and *estancias* of the east bank outside Montevideo.

But as Elío prepared to attack Buenos Aires, rural revolt suddenly engulfed the Plate's east bank. In the environs of Montevideo were ranches and villages of some 20,000 inhabitants, many of whom supported the May revolution in Buenos Aires. Despite the growth of Montevideo during the past forty years its rural environs were still administered from Buenos Aires, an arrangement that allowed considerable informal autonomy and the benefits of lax taxation. Elío's attempts to impress and tax the local population thus met prompt resistance, which flared into rebellion. Like the insurrection in Paraguay, that on the east bank was not merely an anti-Spanish revolt; it soon became a full-blown revolutionary movement for local independence and self-government. The east bank rebels took up arms under the leadership of José Gervasio Artigas, a former officer in the rural militia, and quickly overwhelmed loyalist forces outside Montevideo. Then Artigas bore down on the city itself, leaving Elío under siege within.

For Buenos Aires, Artigas's rebellion came at an opportune moment, saving it from invasion by Elío, and the grateful city dispatched reinforcements to the east bank. Elío faced the two armies outside the city until he was relieved for a time in September 1811 by the arrival of an army from Brazil. The Portuguese forced Buenos Aires into concluding a hasty truce, and Artigas to flee west into Entre Rios. But under British pressure in Rio de Janeiro—intended to avert a war in the River Plate that would disrupt commerce—in July 1812 the Portuguese withdrew, and the siege of Montevideo recommenced.[6]

Subsequently, the struggle for independence ebbed and flowed in other locales. In 1812-1813 troops from Buenos Aires, led by Belgrano, made a second effort to take Potosí and Upper Peru. Belgrano redeemed his reputation by early victories at Las Piedras, near San Miguel de Tucumán, and Salta, battles that ended the occupation of the Tucumán region by the Spaniards and quashed the threat of a loyalist thrust toward Córdoba. But in late 1813 Belgrano attempted a new incursion into Upper Peru and was soundly defeated at Vilcapugio and again at Ayohoma. As he retreated, the Spaniards advanced once more to take and occupy Salta.[7]

This second stage of the independence struggle thus began in the midst of stalemate, Upper Peru and Paraguay lost, neither side able to win superiority on the east bank. Now, too, the revolution became overtly overshadowed by regional tensions, the focus of which was Artigas. From the very start, following the successful rural revolt on the east bank against Elío, relations between Artigas and the leaders and generals of Buenos Aires were strained. To the generals, Artigas was a subordinate; in his own eyes, however, he was an independent ally and an equal who rightfully resisted acknowledging the generals' authority. Artigas's movement on the east bank, which had mobilized the lower orders of the towns and villages and the *vagos* of the countryside, thus possessed not only a strong republican thrust but also a popular and egalitarian character. As Artigas's ideas rapidly spread to the littoral, they provoked a growing crisis in relations between his followers and Buenos Aires.

In late 1810 Corrientes, Entre Rios, and Santa Fe had each been placed under military governors from Buenos Aires, who sought to raise troops and funds as Elío had on the east bank. Throughout the littoral arose complaints that military levies denuded the *estancias* of laborers and left the frontiers open to Indian invasions. There were other more deep-seated grievances. Santa Fe, which had been a major producer of mules, now suffered heavy losses from the disruption of commerce with Upper Peru. Corrientes, a center of native textiles, evidenced similar unrest at the growing quantity of competing British goods entering the country since the liberalization of trade under Liniers, Cisneros, and the May junta. Throughout the littoral sprang the same cry for autonomy—from Spain and also from Buenos Aires—that Artigas had kindled on the east bank.[8]

These were the first germs of the Federalist movement. Meanwhile, in Buenos Aires an opposing Unitarist movement was taking shape. The Saavedra faction in Buenos Aires, which espoused conciliation and moderation toward the interior, had managed for a time to surmount Moreno's challenge, but the group fell into total discredit in the aftermath of the first abortive expedition into Upper Peru. In September 1811, following the defeat at Huaquí, Saavedra and his cumbersome committee-style rule were replaced by an executive triumvirate. Saavedra made only feeble efforts to resist the change. On this occasion he was easily outmaneuvered by his opponents, lost his control over the Buenos Aires militia, and afterward passed into obscurity. The triumvirate that replaced him proved to be strongly anti-Artigas and largely insensitive to provincial concerns or interests. In December 1811, in a clumsy and provocative effort to stifle the radical ideas associated with Artigas, the triumvirate dissolved the *junta grande* and soon after the *juntas provinciales*. Then, it postponed convening the congress that had been planned at the inception of the revolution, arguing that the project was impractical because large parts of the country were under occupation by loyalists. Instead the triumvirate issued a provisional statute (*Estatuto Provisional*) creating a general assembly of limited powers. Although the assembly purported to represent the interior, most of its delegates were nominated in Buenos Aires. When provincial demands began to surface even in this regimented body, it too was dissolved by the triumvirate's police.[9]

The triumvirate, having abandoned Saavedra's effort to conciliate the interior, initiated aggressive efforts to defend and enhance the political primacy of Buenos Aires. As under the viceroyalty, all local officials of any rank were to be appointed from the capital and serve at its pleasure. Other measures to strengthen the system further originated with the triumvirate's energetic secretary, Bernardino Rivadavia, one of the reformer-intellectuals earlier associated with Belgrano. Among Rivadavia's projects were a maritime insurance scheme to promote trade from Buenos Aires, a discount bank to enhance the city's financial activities, the creation of new meat-salting plants (*saladeros*), and land colonization by European immigrants.

Most of these ideas had been first conceived in the 1790s, when the wars in Europe and the Atlantic had encouraged members of the creole intelligentsia in Buenos Aires to discussion of strengthening and developing the local economy. Most, too, had been as closely associated with Moreno's faction as they were with Belgrano's, or now with Rivadavia's. However, compared with Moreno, the new Unitarists, the followers of Belgrano and Rivadavia, were much more conservative and were inclined to a monarchical rather than a republican solution to the issue of self-government.

Immediately after the French invasion of Spain in 1808, when the prospect of *de facto* self-rule seemed likely, members of the free-trade group in Buenos Aires had occasionally hinted at instituting a new kind of relationship with Europe. From other European powers Buenos Aires could obtain benefits Spain had failed to provide: not only wider opportunities for trade, broader markets, and cheaper imports but also a new infusion of resources and investment funds as had occurred in the late 1770s. Such investment from abroad would enable the city to inaugurate the numerous schemes bruited and propagated before the revolution, among them harbor improvements, new *saladeros*, and the expansion of the cattle frontier. By 1809 Belgrano's group had seen such a partnership developing with Britain, the world's leading commercial, maritime, and industrial power. After the British invasions they were careful to avoid suggesting any formal tie with Britain, least of all that the River Plate became part of the British empire, but they envisaged indirect political links that would yield economic benefits without affronting patriotic sentiment. Their plan was to form a constitutional monarchy and enthrone Queen Carlota of Portugal, sister of the imprisoned Ferdinand VII, who resided in Rio de Janeiro under British protection. Her consecration, they hoped, would appease the local loyalists and legitimists, who were determined to uphold the connection with Spain, and satisfy the local merchants and ranchers who urged faster economic expansion. The idea failed: Carlota was unwilling to become a constitutional ruler, as opposed to an absolutist; in any event, her candidacy was opposed by both the monopoly faction in Buenos Aires and the British, who feared it would disrupt their alliance with Spain against the French.

In 1811, however, the triumvirate, urged on by Rivadavia, made a new bid for British support. Rivadavia hinted at the abolition of the slave trade, which Britain had abolished in 1807, and promised British merchants that they would at last be allowed to market their goods directly in Buenos Aires, without using local consignees. He further proposed full internal free trade through the abolition of provincial tariffs, excises, and transit taxes. At this point the triumvirate also revived the idea of a constitutional monarchy, which in part had become a scheme to fend off Spanish hostility and a bid for the support of Spanish liberals. But the idea was also consistent with the conservative social attitudes of the triumvirate's leaders and their dislike for the egalitarian impulses associated with Artigas, and as an imitation of British institutions, it suited the search for British patronage.[10]

Regional opponents of centralized government from Buenos Aires were angered, first by the triumvirate's attacks on representative organs like the *juntas provinciales*, then by Rivadavia's schemes that threatened to destroy whatever local autonomy remained. Throughout the interior Rivadavia's program was thus flatly dismissed as a plot to bolster the capital at everyone else's expense. Most of the littoral preferred Artigas's vision of republican self-rule and rejected talk of monarchy, constitutional or otherwise. Simultaneously, a rising sense of disquiet and an increasingly relentless opposition emerged in the interior concerning free trade. As spokesmen for the old Spanish monopoly traders repeatedly pointed out, for much of the interior free trade was a major potential threat to markets, employment, and native artisan production. For a brief period, however, renewed political instability in Buenos Aires checked the interregional conflict. Rivadavia and the triumvirate, like Saavedra before them, proved unable to sustain their regime, and after the truce in Montevideo they displayed less interest in the struggle with Spain, becoming immersed in plans for domestic reform. In early 1812 a new political movement gained popularity in Buenos Aires, led by José de San Martín, an American-born veteran of the peninsular wars, raised in the northeast mission region; Carlos de Alvear, a young member of a leading local family and, like San Martín, recently returned from Europe; and Bernardo de Monteagudo, a survivor from Moreno's group. Together they founded the Patriotic Society (*Sociedad Patriótica*) under the slogan "Independence, Constitution, and Democracy," demanding more vigorous pursuit of emancipation and, to conciliate Artigas and the interior, the convening of the postponed congress.

For some months these demands were unavailing, but then the *Sociedad Patriótica* seized the chance to act following another abortive rebellion by the weakened but not totally subdued Spanish loyalist faction in Buenos Aires, a group composed mostly of the old monopoly merchants. Since May 1810 a succession of forced loans had been levied on Spanish merchants in Buenos Aires. In July 1812, the loyalists, led once more by Martín de Álzaga, attempted a coup d'etat, but, like Álzaga's earlier rebellion against Liniers, it was immediately put down. Soon after Álzaga and two score of his followers were hanged in the Plaza de la Victoria, the main square of Buenos Aires. The leaders of the *Sociedad Patriótica* then exploited a wave of hispanophobia to redouble their attacks on the triumvirate, eventually provoking its fall in October.[11]

A second triumvirate survived for fifteen months, until January 1814, while the war with Spain took precedence over domestic matters. The struggle necessitated increased revenues, which the new government raised by extending concessions to British merchants. For the first time ever, the British were permitted to export silver on payment of duties, and during the next year silver was exported from Buenos Aires in large quantities. This measure benefited the exchequer in Buenos Aires, but exacerbated economic strains in the interior. In February 1813 the government purged all remaining Spaniards from the public administration, while inflicting new forced loans on the diminished Spanish mercantile community. San Martín then reorganized the army by dissolving the militia created in 1806 and the

Patricios regiment, and installing a new regular and highly disciplined force led by the elite Mounted Grenadiers. The army altered profoundly in both complexion and sociopolitical function. Army recruits now came from all parts of the country, and many were slaves. No longer did the militia serve, as it had before 1810, as a vehicle for progressive income distribution among the population of Buenos Aires. A near-dictatorship now controlled the city, regimenting the lives of its inhabitants, invoking trade and whatever other revenue device lay at hand to raise cash for the purpose of war.

Soon after the advent of the second triumvirate the Congress planned in 1810 finally met, with care taken to afford due representation to the interior. The Congress stopped short of a full declaration of independence, but it declared itself sovereign in what were now for the first time called the United Provinces of the River Plate. It also enacted a spate of reforms, which, unlike Rivadavia's measures a year or so before, were less an attempt to institute a new order than largely symbolic gestures to sweep away the past. Modeled after the actions of the Constituent Assembly in France in 1789, the new measures were primarily propaganda, intended to excite popular support for the revolution. The Congress abolished Indian labor services, Indian tribute, and long-defunct institutions such as *encomienda*. It similarly abrogated other nominally extant Spanish institutions, including the Inquisition and judicial torture. Titles of nobility and landed estates inherited through primogeniture (*mayorazgos*) were also annulled, although few of either existed in this part of the empire. The slave trade was abandoned and, while slavery persisted, the children of slaves were declared free; also, any slaves from abroad became free once they entered the territory of the United Provinces.

The second triumvirate also made substantial efforts to conciliate the interior. After petitions from Mendoza, San Juan, and San Miguel del Tucumán, the Congress dismantled the intendancies of Córdoba and Salta, and granted the three cities self-government and recognized jurisdiction over their hinterlands; Corrientes gained the same status. Indeed, by the end of 1814 most of the cities in the interior and their surrounding regions had been formally reconstituted as "provinces." Meanwhile the term *governor*, with its connotation of local autonomy, replaced the alien and authoritarian-sounding *intendant*. [12]

Thus the second triumvirate, as opposed to the first, focused on emancipation as the core of its policy. In an effort to forge unity and popular support, it instituted numerous reforms, though most were only cosmetic or symbolic. But the costly war against Spain compelled the regime to adopt an unprecedented free-trade policy, which, combined with the loss of Potosí, intensified the economic crisis throughout the interior. At the same time, the second triumvirate was obliged to use force to raise troops and supplementary revenues for the war. Thus despite all its concessions to the interior, it was unable to alleviate or override regional tensions. In the provinces the Federalists extended their grip; in Buenos Aires, despite the fall of Rivadavia's group, the Unitarists continued to gain strength.

Renewed conflict between the two groups first flared on the issue of a constitution. Proposals from the interior that strongly endorsed provincial rights met such uncompromising opposition from Buenos Aires that all discussion on a constitution soon ceased. It was Artigas who again kindled the greatest dissension. In April 1813 he dispatched delegates from the east bank to the Congress with a list of radical federalist demands: an immediate declaration of independence; a republican constitution that would create a loose confederation in which the provinces would elect their own governors, conclude commercial treaties with one another, and raise their own armies; a central government with jurisdiction over only the "common affairs" (*negocios generales*) of the provinces, such as foreign policy; and the establishment of the capital outside Buenos Aires.

In June 1813 the Congress, bowing to pressure from Buenos Aires, denied admission to Artigas's representatives. Subsequent negotiations failed, and the following January Artigas formally renounced the alliance with Buenos Aires, again withdrawing his troops from the siege of Montevideo. When the Congress declared him an enemy of the state, he toured Entre Ríos and Corrientes to gather support. Both provinces nominated him their "protector," while also breaking relations with Buenos Aires.[13]

As the rift widened, the war against the Spaniards proceeded with some success. Since the withdrawal of the Portuguese in 1812, Montevideo had been under constant land siege, first by the coalition of forces from Buenos Aires and Artigas's troops, and then by Buenos Aires alone. Throughout Montevideo held out by revictualing itself from the river, using the island of Martín García as a base. It seemed impossible to defeat the city except by sea power.

In early 1814 the Congress in Buenos Aires replaced the triumviral government by a single executive, naming its first incumbent, José Gervasio de Posadas, "supreme director." The change consolidated the anti-Spanish, military, or "patriotic" faction led by San Martín and

Carlos de Alvear. To vanquish Montevideo, the Posadas regime constituted a naval squadron under the command of William Brown, an Irish-born deserter from the British navy. Brown quickly defeated the small loyalist fleet that held Martín García and then blockaded Montevideo. Siege by land and sea forced the city to capitulate to the forces of Buenos Aires, led by Alvear, in June 1814. The fall of Montevideo was a significant victory, depriving the Spaniards of their only remaining base in the River Plate. Without Montevideo, the task of invasion and conquest from the peninsula became almost insuperable.[14]

But Artigas supervened once more. After the fall of Montevideo he returned to the east bank to demand possession of the city. He harassed Alvear's troops for several months, eventually coercing them to withdraw. In Montevideo Artigas declared an independent Eastern State (*Estado Oriental*). He abolished slavery and issued ambitious plans for land colonization and the redistribution of land to his rural followers. This revolutionary egalitarian program also addressed economic issues that had long divided Montevideo from Buenos Aires. Because the two remained competitors for international trade, Artigas set duties lower than those across the estuary. To his power throughout the east bank, Artigas soon added control over the littoral. In 1815 the governor of Santa Fe, appointed and also imposed from Buenos Aires, was overthrown by local Federalists. Santa Fe then joined Entre Rios, Corrientes, and Córdoba in a Federal League led by Artigas, who was designated "protector of the free peoples of the littoral." In early 1816 a force from Buenos Aires commissioned to capture Santa Fe was defeated by Artigas's lieutenant, Estanislao López, a victory that marked the summit of Artigas's power. He now had proven military superiority over Buenos Aires and was dissuaded from marching to seize the city only by lavish indemnities in cash, cattle, and arms.[15]

For Buenos Aires, with the capture of Montevideo, 1814 had been a year of triumph, but 1815 and much of 1816 brought recurrent setbacks. With Artigas and the Federalists now supreme on the east bank and in the provinces, the city was plunged into a period of internal turmoil. In January 1815 the loss of Montevideo to Artigas contributed to the fall of Posadas. Alvear, his successor as director, made a desperate bid for British support that proposed a secret plan for British annexation. But Alvear survived in office barely three months, overthrown in April, and a string of weak successors followed. In November 1815 a third expedition to Upper Peru was defeated by the Spaniards at Sipe-Sipe near Cochabamba. The front was finally abandoned, along with all prospect of taking Potosí; further resistance to the Spaniards in the northwest was purely local, taking the form of guerrilla warfare in the Salta region. The rural patriots here fell under the command of Martín Güemes, another former militia-man, who resembled Artigas in his equal hostility toward Buenos Aires and the Spaniards. [16]

Despite the internal political confusion, the commitment to emancipation persisted. At the end of 1815 a second congressional session was convened in the city of San Miguel, or Tucumán as it was now more commonly known. Like its predecessor, the Congress was dominated by Unitarists, and was therefore ignored by Artigas and his allies. Though most of the proceedings were spent in denouncing Artigas, in desultory efforts to enact a constitution, and in a hopeless quest to win acceptance for constitutional monarchy, the Congress effected one memorable achievement: on 9 July 1816 it declared the independence of the United Provinces of the River Plate. [17]

This formal declaration of independence exemplified the renewed vigor of the revolutionary movement, which now entered its third and final phase. Juan Martín de Pueyrredón, a triumvir in 1811-1812, was elected as director by the Congress in May 1816, and his tenure brought a period of greater internal political stability. For a time Pueyrredón eluded further conflict with the Federalists, which enabled him to give first priority to the war with Spain, in which the key site of contention was now Chile. Since 1814 San Martín had been planning an attack across the Andes from Mendoza, and in early 1817 the assault on Chile was finally launched. San Martín's crossing of the Andes with an army of 5,000 men, among the great epic feats of the Spanish American wars of independence, owed its success in good part to the firm logistical and financial backing supplied by Pueyrredón in Buenos Aires. [18]

More-settled conditions under Pueyrredón also followed from a sudden reversal in Artigas's fortunes. In June 1816 a second Portuguese invasion of the east bank was committed to destroy the government erected by Artigas, which was viewed in Brazil as a "barbarian democracy" that would instigate revolt among the slaves. The Portuguese invasion quickly destroyed Artigas and his ideas as a social and political force, accomplishing what Buenos Aires had failed to do during the past five years. With the coming of the Portuguese, Artigas was forced to abandon his feud with Buenos Aires, over which he no longer claimed to be master. His desperate defense of his domain was breached in January 1817, when Montevideo fell to the Portuguese. Buenos Aires now had its revenge on Artigas, as Pueyrredón repeatedly ignored his pleas for assistance. For the next three years Artigas fought unsuccessfully to repel the invaders. As he was pushed slowly westward to the River Uruguay, he found himself increasingly reliant on his allies in Santa Fe and Entre Rios, but both grew restive at his exactions, and the Federal League crumbled. The coup de grace came in 1820 as López and Francisco "Pancho" Ramírez, leaders of Santa Fe and Entre Rios, repudiated Artigas. Driven northward into Corrientes by Ramírez, Artigas eventually found refuge with Francia in Paraguay. There he remained until his death in 1850, playing no further part in events.[19]

The slow demise of Artigas temporarily weakened Federalism, but it soon revived in a more virulent form under López and Ramírez. Since 1816 the two provincial leaders had grown increasingly hostile to Pueyrredón's new methods of disciplining the littoral. Instead of direct political dominance, Pueyrredón sought to impose economic sanctions: he began bottling up the mouth of the Paraná so as to control the flow of goods along the river, thus threatening the littoral with even greater economic disruption. The policy only inflamed regional grievances against Buenos Aires. A renewed crisis erupted in 1819 when Pueyrredón endorsed a narrowly unitarist Constitution that empowered Buenos Aires to continue to nominate local officials, among them provincial governors. The document also pointedly and provocatively left open the possibility of establishing monarchy. To impose the Constitution Pueyrredón committed the cardinal error of sending an army into Santa Fe. López repelled the invasion, as he had in 1816, at which Pueyrredón resigned as director. Then López and Ramírez joined forces for an assault on Buenos Aires.

With Pueyrredón's downfall in June 1819, all vestiges of central authority perished. Throughout the provinces *cabildos abiertos* met to proclaim local self-rule. Provincial warlords, *caudillos* as they were known, like López and Ramírez formally took power: Bernabé Araoz in Tucumán, Juan Bautista Bustos in Córdoba, Felipe Ibarra in Santiago del Estero, and Güemes in Salta. Several provinces followed the lead of Entre Rios and declared themselves independent republics; others, like Salta and Tucumán, turned against each other in numerous petty civil wars. In early 1820 the joint cavalry forces of Santa Fe, Entre Rios, and Corrientes defeated José Rondeau, Pueyrredón's successor as director, at Cepeda, outside Buenos Aires. The victorious *caudillos* then entered the city to dictate their terms: the abrogation of the Constitution of 1819; acceptance by Buenos Aires of the kernel principle of Federalism through the election of its own governor and legislature; free navigation of the rivers and no further interference with the commerce of the littoral. López received 25,000 cattle as a gratuity, and with this prize returned to Santa Fe. Having defeated Buenos Aires, the two *caudillos* finally turned against Artigas. Factional struggle once more enveloped Buenos Aires, while a string of governors followed one another in rapid succession, each unable to maintain power. The conflict abated in September 1820, when Martín Rodríguez was acknowledged as provisional governor and concluded negotiations with López and Ramírez. Rodríguez also suppressed an internal rebellion against him, a victory that gave his authority a semblance of stability.[20]

The year 1820 marked the first hiatus following the outbreak of revolution against Spain and the consequent internal conflict and political disarray. Conditions broadly resembled those of the seventeenth and early eighteenth centuries in that interregional and inter-elite conflicts were set against increasing local militarization. Like his seventeenth-century predecessors, López, when not fighting Buenos Aires, spent much of his time in pursuit of Indians in the north. Those he captured were distributed as slaves among the *estancias* of Santa Fe, as the *yanaconas* once had been.

As the Unitarist movement took shape under leaders like Riva-davia in Buenos Aires, it attempted to maintain the continuities between the old Bourbon order and the new era of self-rule. But in following the ideas of Cevallos or Vértiz, and later Belgrano or Moreno, and seeking to strengthen the leadership of Buenos Aires, it provoked an explosion of grievances that had seethed during thirty-five years of forced centralization under the Bourbons. For its part, Federalism marked a recrudescence of the *comunero* and local mercantilist traditions rooted in the seventeenth century. For Federalism was not directed against Buenos Aires alone; its targets included several other beneficiaries of the late-colonial order—Montevideo, Córdoba, and Salta. It thus became a protest not only against centralization in the capital but also, at the local level, against the intendancies. Such local resistance to forced appropriations and military impressment crystalized the movement: on the east bank, the rise of Artigas and his followers; in Santa Fe, Estanislao López. Similarly, Ibarra's success in Santiago del Estero resulted from local dissatisfaction with wheat confiscations imposed by the local regime under orders from Buenos

Aires and with the dissolution of the provincial militia, which led to southward invasions by Abipone Indians from the Chaco. External conditions—the disruption of links with Potosí and growing commercial penetration by the British in Buenos Aires—impelled the movement's momentum.

The new *caudillos* were mostly men like Artigas, upwardly mobile former militiamen with strong roots in the countryside, from which they gathered their retinues of slaves, peons, and *vagos*, or *gauchos* as they were now known. Indeed the rise of the *caudillos* was in some measure a conquest of the towns by the countryside, the overthrow of the mercantile *cabildos* by rural forces whose social and political influence had become steadily more pronounced during the preceding half century. With the economic decline that began in 1810, city life in the interior entered a period of prompt deterioration. As in the seventeenth century, social militarization had its counterpart in ruralization.[21]

For most the era of independence brought acute hardship and increasing penury. Among its beneficiaries, however, were several species of war profiteers, including merchants who supplied the contending armies, and those artisans and wage earners who having escaped impressment profited from labor shortages. Slavery was not abolished by the revolution, but the need for troops frequently persuaded its leaders to offer emancipation in exchange for voluntary enlistment. Former slaves often bore a disproportionate burden of the fighting, with the result that by the mid 1820s slavery had markedly diminished in many parts of the country.[22]

As throughout Spanish America in this period, fortunes were sometimes made and dazzling feats of social ascent accomplished by a career under arms in the service of the revolution. The wars attracted numerous foreign adventurers. William Brown, who had arrived in Buenos Aires a penniless fugitive, immortalized himself during the siege of Montevideo. Peter Campbell, another Irish deserter from Beresford's army in 1806, became a leading henchman of Francisco Ramírez and commander of a small naval flotilla on the Paraná. In Santiago del Estero, Ibarra enlisted the services of Jean-Jacques D'Auxion Lavaysse, reputedly a former Bonapartist general.

From mid 1810 British merchants entered Buenos Aires in growing numbers. There they overmatched the competition from Spaniards and natives alike, continually sidestepped the forced loans, and for several years enjoyed virtually unlimited freedom to pursue their business. By 1813 the British shippers and wholesalers had branched out into retail and consignment ventures and captured the market by flooding it with goods—Lancashire muslins and calicos, hardware products from the Midlands—that they transported to the interior; likewise, they took over the carrying trade to Buenos Aires from the Portuguese and Americans. The British also assumed dominance in the hide trade. After 1810 heavy cattle slaughtering to feed the troops left a large supply of hides at low prices, and to keep prices low the British merchants created buying pools. Yet other British merchants profited from buying up the short-term negotiable bonds that the second triumvirate began issuing in 1813. British merchants bought great quantities of bonds at discount and then used them at par value to settle duties on imports. The use of such bonds provoked persistent inflation in Buenos Aires and also helped augment the flow of imports, while reducing real revenues from them. Lastly, British merchants flourished in the guise of arms suppliers, largely monopolizing government contracts for the provision of war *matériel.*[23]

As the British eclipsed the existing merchant communities in Buenos Aires, the native elites were forced to discover a new economic niche for themselves. After 1810 growing numbers of former mercantile families began cattle ranching on the Indian frontier and entered the meat-salting business. In 1812 *saladero* products were freed from export duties; by 1817 seventeen *saladeros* were operating in the city. Their products were marketed throughout the plantation zones of the Americas: Brazil, Cuba, and to a lesser degree in the American South. While the old mercantile society based on silver crumbled, the cattle economy expanded to supersede it.[24]

THE AGE OF RIVADAVIA, 1820–1829

The victory of the *caudillos* over Buenos Aires in 1820 proved short-lived, as the champions of centralization in Buenos Aires made another concerted bid for power under the leadership of Bernardino Rivadavia, the former secretary of the first triumvirate. After his overthrow in 1812 Rivadavia spent several years in Europe, from there playing a major role in the efforts of the Unitarists to find a candidate for the constitutional monarchy they hoped to establish. In 1821, however, Rivadavia became a member of the Rodríguez government. For a brief period in 1826–1827 he was president of the United Provinces, as a second attempt was made to impose a unitarist constitution.

The reversal of the *caudillos's* fortunes began in 1821, when the alliance between López and Ramírez suddenly shattered. After the victory at Cepeda, Ramírez began behaving like an Artigas, pronouncing himself the senior partner in the alliance and seeking to extend his authority over Corrientes and Córdoba. López resisted; Ramírez was defeated, pursued, captured, and killed. In a spectacle that had become common during the civil wars, his head was displayed in an iron cage in the main church of Santa Fe. Afterwards López proclaimed himself "patriarch of the federation." But without Ramírez he no longer had the military power to impose himself on Buenos Aires.

Buenos Aires soon resumed blockading the Paraná, which enabled it to monopolize foreign trade and the revenues from trade. Since the other provinces lacked the military capacity to retaliate, they could only capitulate to their growing isolation and poverty. On this occasion trade controls from Buenos Aires achieved the desired submissiveness in the provinces, which by 1822 were ready to call another national congress and resume discussions on a constitution. This cycle of events encapsulated the provinces' plight for the next forty years: the provinces wanted freedom from Buenos Aires, but once free their economic needs swiftly drew them back into relations. Complete local autonomy induced commercial isolation, which only condemned the provinces to continuing decline.

At peaceful stalemate with the *caudillos*, the Rodríguez government turned to a campaign against the pampas Indians. Its aims were to end widespread rustling and attacks on the frontier settlements and also to extend the frontier to develop cattle ranching. The first southward sally under Rodríguez, and another in 1828, enjoyed great success, opening up millions of acres of new land. In the 1820s the *estancias* spread across the Rio Salado, which bisected the province of Buenos Aires some seventy miles south of the city. Meanwhile, beginning with Tandil in 1823, a chain of new settlements emerged on the southern and western frontiers. The expansion of the frontier hastened Buenos Aires's transition from commerce to ranching. Specie exports declined from about 80 percent of total annual exports before 1810, to less than 15 percent in 1829, when hides and salted meat accounted for about 65 percent of total exports. Meanwhile, by 1822–1824 import duties had become the source of almost 84 percent of provincial revenues. The new economy was becoming firmly grounded. With the growth of ranching, men like Rodríguez himself and former Spanish commercial families like the Anchorenas, began amassing fortunes from *estancias* and investments in *saladeros*. Buenos Aires now embarked on a period of peace and expansion that its inhabitants later recalled, when times changed once more, as its "happy experience" (*la feliz experiencia*).[25]

In July 1821 Rivadavia reentered public affairs and, with Rodríguez's concentration fixed on the frontier wars, soon became the administration's leading figure. As partially evident in his earlier programs, Rivadavia represented an interstice between the late-eighteenth and early-nineteenth centuries: belonging fully to neither, he was both a precursor and an anachronism. His advocacy of free trade, foreign investment, and land colonization by Europeans injected ideas that would transform the country two generations later. In other respects, too, he subscribed to contemporary liberal doctrines. He continued the experiments with popular voting begun a decade earlier, helping to design and implement a new suffrage law in Buenos Aires. An enthusiastic disciple of Bentham, he introduced modern accounting techniques in government. He campaigned against the clergy, leading a successful bid to abolish clerical immunities, or *fueros*, and to lower the tithe. When the *cabildo* of Buenos Aires resisted such measures Rivadavia suppressed the venerable institution, which had played a central role in the city's affairs since its creation, and established a new municipal administration, once more along Benthamite lines.

Other administrative reforms patronized by Rivadavia emphasized centralization and the formation of specialized institutions. Here the influence appeared more French or Spanish than British, and illustrated the eclectic slant in Rivadavia's measures alongside the more apparently doctrinaire. In 1821 Rivadavia signed the decree establishing the University of Buenos Aires and awarding it a state subsidy. This measure had been first mooted under Pueyrredón; it was now carried to a successful conclusion. Later, Rivadavia stacked the university's library with the latest works on medicine, science, and political economy. Finally, his campaigns for European immigration bespoke an awareness of current events and issues in the United States; like Thomas Jefferson, he aspired to create a pioneer agrarian capitalism.

Yet alongside these liberal impulses was Rivadavia's conservative desire to recreate Buenos Aires in its late-eighteenth century guise as a commercial and financial entrepôt, with merchants and bankers controlling the economy and the state; his notion of strong, active, and centralized authority was in some respects more neo-Bourbon than liberal. Rivadavia also wanted to revive bullion as the chief export from Buenos Aires, and during his tenure encouraged a quest for new mines with the same dedication as the sixteenth-century *adelantados* or the Bourbon intendants. He revived colonial methods of dealing with rural vagrancy, enacting a measure in 1823 that divided the rural population into "owners" and "servants," and obliged the latter to furnish themselves with papers signed by an *estanciero*; failure to do so carried a penalty of five years' service in the militia.[26]

The most significant of Rivadavia's measures was the Law of Emphyteusis of 1826. After the campaign led by Rodríguez the government had the task of administering and adjudicating the frontier lands wrested from the Indians. In the 1820s the land law remained much the same as under colonial rule: land was open to exploitation by private parties, yet for the most part titles belonged to the state. To uphold state ownership of the frontier lands, Rivadavia applied the Roman law system of emphyteusis: he granted long-term rights of access and use on land that remained state property. By this policy he hoped to impose a quasi-tax on the land in the form of land rents that would enable him to reduce duties on trade; thus ranchers and farmers were to pay more, and merchants less. Under the legislation the government could lease land to individuals or companies for a rent equal to 8 percent of the assessed value of pasture land, and 4 percent of that of crop land.

The scheme's numerous flaws soon surfaced, and its results were largely the opposite of what Rivadavia intended. Instead of enhancing the mercantile interests, it hastened the transition to ranching. Furthermore, as a revenue instrument, the measure was a complete failure because the land assessments were made by the lessees themselves, who submitted undervaluations, and because the government lacked the administrative machinery to collect the rents. Subsequently, taxes on state land never exceeded 3 percent of the total revenues. Emphyteusis, in effect, enabled speculators to obtain land on a long-term basis without cost; they paid no purchase price and virtually no rent; they simply registered claims. The law, moreover, failed to limit the land area lessees could claim. An estimated 6.5 million acres were alienated under emphyteusis contracts to 122 persons and partnerships; ten grantees received more than 130,000 acres each. The main consequence of emphyteusis was thus the spread and consolidation of large landholdings, the acceleration of ranching and of the functional separation of ranchers and merchants.[27]

In the 1820s Rivadavia renewed his efforts to promote closer economic ties with Britain. Again interested in investment as much as trade, he hoped that foreign capital would spawn new brokerage, banking, or insurance opportunities for local mercantile and financial groups. Commerce with Britain had lagged for a time after 1815, as the internal market had become saturated with imports, and supplies of silver were largely exhausted. Then Pueyrredón had attempted to subject British merchants to forced loans. By 1822, however, Britain was again the source of almost half of Buenos Aires's total imports and almost all its imports of manufactured goods. By 1824 some 1,300 Britons lived in the city, most dealing in the import-export trade.

The British merchants now received lavish concessions from the government of Buenos Aires. Most originated less with Rivadavia himself than with the minister of finance, Manuel José García. But Rivadavia at least endorsed them and several times facilitated their enactment. To allay British merchants' fears of new forced loans or tax levies like the *contribución de comercio*, the government abolished its own authority to levy them. In 1822 it chartered a new discount bank, which it then allowed to become dominated by British merchants, who used it to finance their own operations. The concessions met a warm response in London. In 1824, as the last Spaniards were being driven from Peru, Britain conferred diplomatic recognition on the United Provinces. Under the Treaty of Friendship, Navigation, and Commerce, the two countries gave each other the status of most-favored nation in trade, along with security of property for each others' residents, freedom of religion, and exemption from military service.[28]

While visiting London in 1824 Rivadavia helped found the River Plate Mining Company, a venture intended to bring British capital into the search for new mines. The company received a concession to develop the new and promising, but as yet largely unexplored, Famatina silver mine in the western mountains of La Rioja. Also in 1824 Rivadavia supported and took a part in instigating a loan—ostensibly to underwrite the construction of new harbor facilities and waterworks in Buenos Aires, and fortifications on the cattle frontier—from Baring Brothers, the British merchant banking house. The loan became an issue of immediate controversy when the government of Buenos Aires received scarcely half of the £1 million borrowed, the remainder taken by brokers and other intermediaries as commission. In Buenos Aires speculators rushed to buy up depreciated government securities, which had been issued in recent years to finance recompensations for forced loans, severance compensation for demobilized soldiers, and other such projects. The speculators then pressed for the proceeds of the Baring loan to be allotted to convert the present internal debt to a foreign debt, with the conversion at the par value of the securities they had amassed. On his return from Europe, Rivadavia instead used much of the loan to finance a new national bank (*Banco Nacional*). Like its predecessor the bank was largely dominated by British merchants, who used its discounting facilities to finance a new wave of imports from Britain.[29]

A last major product of the Rivadavia years was the Constitution of 1826, the outcome of two years of deliberation by the Congress selected by the provinces in 1822. The Constitution differed from its ill-fated predecessor in precluding a monarchy by declaring a republic. It provided for the election of a president and a Congress, and a separation of powers on the model of the United States. It declared the rights of the provinces to self-government and proffered schemes for the sharing of revenues from Buenos Aires. Nevertheless, the Constitution contained several markedly unitarist features that immediately affronted the Federalists: it gave the executive power a nine-year term and numerous personal prerogatives, among them the power to appoint and dismiss provincial governors. It proposed placing the government in Buenos Aires: the city was to be detached from its surrounding province and be recast as a federal jurisdiction. The provinces would disband their militias; abolish local tariffs, transit taxes, and stamp duties; and cede land to the national government in return for the cancellation of provincial debts, with such land to be placed under the scope of the emphyteusis legislation.

In 1826, while debating the Constitution, the Congress elected Rivadavia president of the United Provinces of South America. The Constitution and the new regime alike were immediately repudiated by the *caudillos*, who distrusted the government's promises of revenue sharing and refused to dismantle provincial tariffs. They also refused to disband their forces, arguing that to do so would be to invite military encroachment from Buenos Aires. In the past few years the provinces had become troubled by Rivadavia's anticlerical measures, and the slogan *Religión o Muerte* ("Religion or Death") now echoed throughout the interior. Rivadavia faced similar unrest among local cattle interests in Buenos Aires. They complained that his two banks were monopolized by British merchants, and they strongly disapproved of his plan to separate the city and the province of Buenos Aires, perceiving the plan as a ploy to strengthen the political grip of mercantile interests, while depriving the cattlemen of funds and military support in the frontier wars.[30]

Thus early in Rivadavia's presidency, staunch support for his administration was restricted to a small coterie of mercantile and financial interests, most of them associated with the *Banco Nacional*. Soon even this support collapsed, in the wake of war between the United Provinces and Brazil. In 1822 Brazil had declared independence from Portugal. The Plate's east bank, wrested from Artigas two years earlier, was rechristened the Cisplatine Province and formally incorporated into the empire of Brazil. The annexation met strong opposition in Buenos Aires, in part because of the area's Spanish history and memories of the long conflicts the century before, and in part because the ranchers in Buenos Aires who held land on the east bank feared its loss or confiscation. Plans were soon laid for the east bank's redemption.

In 1825 a small guerrilla band of exiled "Easterners" (*orientales*) departed from Buenos Aires led by Juan Antonio Lavalleja, a former lieutenant of Artigas. He landed at Colonia, and from there rapidly mobilized local support. Like Elío fifteen years before, the Brazilians were quickly pinned down in Montevideo. Brazil then declared war on the United Provinces, which replied by sending military support to the east bank. Rivadavia strongly supported the war, which gave him the opportunity to raise an army. Once the campaign on the east bank was concluded, the army was to impose the constitution on the provinces. "We shall make unity with sticks" (*Haremos la unidad a palos*), declared Julián Segundo Agüero, one of his close followers.

The plan misfired. Lavalleja and the army from Buenos Aires were unable to take Montevideo. Though the Brazilians' land forces were weak, their strong navy retaliated by blockading Buenos Aires, subduing repeated defensive efforts by the still-active William Brown. The blockade of Buenos Aires was never fully enforced, but it created havoc with revenues, as trade in 1827 plummeted to one-third of that in 1824. In 1825–1828 duties provided scarcely 20 percent of revenues, against more than 80 percent early in the same decade. Yet revenues amounted to only 55 percent of actual expenditures. With 20,000 men under arms at the height of the war with Brazil, yearly land and naval war expenses made this war far more expensive than the struggle for independence. Soon the Brazilian blockade had forced the government in Buenos Aires to default on repayments on the Baring loan. The government also borrowed heavily from the *Banco Nacional* and flooded the city with paper money. The already marked inflation, a result of the expansion of credit after the Baring loan, accelerated its soaring pace.

The Brazilian blockade also exacerbated opposition to the government from the cattlemen, whose earnings from exports fell sharply, and from the British merchants, for whom inflation imposed a crippling indirect tax. British exports to Buenos Aires, valued at £1 million in 1824, plunged to £200,000 in 1827.

By early 1827 Rivadavia's presidency, barely six months old, was on the brink of dissolution. Four provinces—Córdoba, La Rioja and its client, Catamarca, and Santiago del Estero under their leaders Bustos, Juan "Facundo" Quiroga, and Ibarra—had formed a military alliance to resist the Constitution. In July 1827, as rumors spread of a cattleman's revolt in Buenos Aires and both the mercantile interests and the British abandoned the administration, Rivadavia resigned.[31]

Another bitter spate of civil war supervened. To placate the *caudillos,* Manuel Dorrego, Rivadavia's successor, nullified the Constitution, reacknowledged the autonomy of the provinces, and himself reassumed the title of governor of Buenos Aires. The former United Provinces were now the Confederation of the River Plate, or the Argentine Confederation. To end the Brazilian blockade, Dorrego declared support for peace on the east bank and eagerly accepted an offer of mediation that Rivadavia had ignored, from the British envoy, Lord Ponsonby. Hostilities ceased in 1828 when a British peace proposal was accepted by Brazil and Buenos Aires. Both agreed to abandon any claims to the east bank, agreeing to its independence as the Eastern Republic of Uruguay (*República Oriental del Uruguay*), which would serve as a buffer state between them. In this way, Uruguay joined Paraguay and Bolivia as the third independent state to arise from the ashes of the former Viceroyalty of the River Plate.[32]

In late 1828 the army that had fought on the east bank returned in two detachments; troops under General Juan Lavalle went to Buenos Aires, those led by José María Paz to Córdoba. Both immediately made a bid for power in the name of the deposed Unitarists: in Buenos Aires the hapless Dorrego was seized by Lavalle's men and shot; in Córdoba Paz overthrew Bustos and repelled an invasion by Quiroga from his stronghold in La Rioja. Lavalle, however, was unable to hold Buenos Aires in the face of a militia of *estancia* workers and *gauchos* led by General Juan Manuel de Rosas. Having unfurled the Federalist banner in Buenos Aires itself, Rosas formed an alliance with López in Santa Fe. In April 1829 Lavalle was defeated by Rosas and López at Puente de Márquez, and he fled to Montevideo. In late 1829 Rosas became governor of Buenos Aires, greeted as a savior after two years of anarchy. The legislature of Buenos Aires, the *junta de representantes*, bestowed upon him "extraordinary faculties" (*facultades extraordinarias*), unbridled dictatorial powers. For the moment Buenos Aires, hitherto the bastion of Unitarist centralism, was ruled by a Federalist, and the Federalist interior was dominated by the Unitarist Paz.[33]

THE RESTORER OF THE LAWS

Once he had gained power in Buenos Aires, Juan Manuel de Rosas proved extremely difficult to dislodge, remaining governor of Buenos Aires until 1852, except for a brief, voluntary retirement between late 1832 and early 1835. Contemporary opponents reviled Rosas as a bloody tyrant and a symbol of barbarism, while a later generation canonized him a nationalist hero, but he is more accurately depicted as the embodiment of the Federalist *caudillo*, a conservative autocrat dedicated to the aggrandizement of his own province and to its ranchers and *saladeristas*. For Rosas all other concerns were secondary, to be ignored, circumvented, or obliterated.[34]

Rosas, the "Caligula of the River Plate," was born into a ranching family whose ancestors included one of the eighteenth-century Spanish governors of Buenos Aires, but despite this pedigree he inherited no family fortune and made his way by personal endeavor. In 1815, at the age of twenty-two, he became a partner in a new *saladero* enterprise, a successful venture that led him into cattle raising. His political debut came in 1820, when at the head of a rural militia force, the *colorados del monte*, Rosas had a leading part in consolidating the Rodríguez government. He also helped negotiate the cattle indemnity that bought off Estanislao López after the battle of Cepeda. Next, Rosas participated in the southern frontier wars, leading the campaign of 1828. Initially well disposed toward Rivadavia, Rosas broke with him over the Constitution of 1826 and over attempts made in Buenos Aires to discharge him from his command of a regiment in the provincial militia. By the time of Rivadavia's fall, now complaining constantly that the government had failed to assist frontier ranchers in their efforts to repel the Indians, Rosas had become one of the most vocal opponents of the Unitarists.[35]

As his political influence grew during the 1820s, Rosas repeatedly revealed a strongly authoritarian temper. He viewed the body politic as a large-scale *estancia* or regiment whose hierarchy of interdependent parts required firm direction and control. Such inclinations were strengthened by the economic and political crises he inherited upon becoming governor in 1829: Buenos Aires was saturated in worthless paper money; the effects of the Brazilian blockade still lingered; and drought afflicted the cattle ranches. Drawing freely on his dictatorial powers, Rosas first formed an army, placing under his own command the remnants of the Unitarist force that had fought on the east bank. He then silenced his enemies and critics by censorship, intimidation, and banishment. Soon after he organized a personal retinue among the urban poor of Buenos Aires. Its members, many of them blacks and mullatoes, quickly became his most devoted and frequently fanatical supporters. Yet the rise of Rosas expressed first and foremost the accession to power of the new ranching interests, developing since 1810, and the displacement of the mercantile clique that had sustained Rivadavia. In the early 1830s, as commerce remained depressed and the administration attempted to meet debts it had inherited from the war with Brazil, government spending fell to only three-quarters of the early 1820s. Despite the contraction, Rosas engineered a major shift in spending from the city to the countryside for such purposes as frontier expeditions, fortifications, and Indian subsidies. In 1830–1834 real rural spending increased threefold by comparison with 1822–1824; nonmilitary urban spending halved.[36]

Once he had firm control in Buenos Aires, Rosas turned his attention to Paz in Córdoba. Paz, having defeated Quiroga in early 1830, now occupied the adjoining provinces. He had replaced their Federalist governors with Unitarists and had created the League of the Interior, styling himself after Artigas as its "protector." To defeat Paz, Rosas and López banded together once more, forming their own alliance in the littoral—the Federal Pact. While López gathered forces for an invasion of Córdoba, Quiroga regrouped in the west with funds and supplies from Rosas. Paz was unable to withstand the dual onslaught; he was gradually pushed east with his dwindling forces, and in 1831 he was captured by López. The Federalist regimes that Paz had destroyed were restored, as one by one the western and northern provinces succumbed to Quiroga.[37]

After the four years of civil war that followed the return of Lavalle and Paz from the east bank, three men dominated the Confederation—Rosas, López, and Quiroga. But Rosas, controlling Buenos Aires and the trade revenues, soon revealed himself the strongest among them. The campaign against Paz concluded, Rosas began once more isolating Buenos Aires from the other provinces, withdrawing or reducing his subsidies and taxing provincial trade. Events repeated those of the early 1820s, as the *caudillos* called for the convening of a new congress to draft a federalist constitution that would grant them both self-government and guaranteed shares in the trade revenues. The constitutional issue thus circumscribed a quest for subsidies. Rosas skillfully deferred action, neither openly refusing the demands of the *caudillos* nor making any effort to meet them. He had no intention of instituting formal revenue sharing—a measure that would siphon resources from Buenos Aires and deprive Rosas of his chief instrument for controlling provincial politics.[38]

In November 1832, his three-year term complete and the country at peace, Rosas left office. For some time he engaged in another frontier expedition in the south, penetrating as far as the Rio Negro, some 700 miles from Buenos Aires. At length, however, politics again intervened: the provinces were agitating once more for a new constitution, while rumors spread of new Unitarist conspiracies. In February 1835 Facundo Quiroga was assassinated, and a new civil war seemed imminent. Buenos Aires hastened to renominate Rosas as governor. He requested and received renewed dictatorial authority, investing him with the "plenitude of the public power" (*suma del poder público*).

Negotiation and new subsidies soon brought peace to the provinces. Rosas continued to serve one term after another as governor of Buenos Aires, legitimizing his rule through plebiscites, ritual displays of public support, and periodic endorsements from the other provinces. The principal agents of his personal will were the army, a ruthless vigilante police force (the *mazorca*), and the Church. By implicit agreement with Rome, he maintained control over ecclesiastical appointments, as each government had since 1810. Meanwhile, the courts, the *junta de representantes,* and the University of Buenos Aires—now moribund because underfunded—were reduced to passive tokens. By the late 1830s the government began requiring the citizens of Buenos Aires to parade wearing the crimson colors of the Federalists. The legend *Viva la Federación y Mueran los Salvages Unitarios* ("Long live the Federation and death to the unitarist savages") became an obligatory preamble to all public documents, newsprints, and personal correspondence. Throughout the Rosas years, whenever such bureaucratic or symbolic regimentation failed to enforce total political obedience, the government made liberal use of terror and assassination. Scores of its opponents perished by throat-cutting at the hands of the *mazorca.*[39]

The trade depression that began in 1826 continued throughout the early 1830s; not until 1837 did commerce recover to the level of 1825. But the economy now evinced greater stability and suffered less from the severe cycles of the past twenty years, as markets were swamped by imports. After Rivadavia's fall the British connection weakened perceptibly. The number of British ships disembarking cargoes at the port of Buenos Aires dropped from 128 in 1821, to 110 in 1824, and to 44 in 1831. Default on the Baring loan forestalled prospects of renewed British investment, which in any case Rosas saw no need for. Heavy losses during the civil wars had compelled many British merchants to leave the country, and in the 1830s Buenos Aires's import trade diversified. French, American, German, Spanish, and Italian shippers and merchants were each much less important than the British, but collectively now outstripped them. By the 1840s the total volume of commerce had again begun to grow substantially, but trade with Britain accounted for only a quarter of the total. Whereas in the 1830s an annual average of 288 foreign ships traded in Buenos Aires, in the 1840s the average climbed to 488. Exports—hides, salted beef, and growing quantities of tallow made in steam vats in the *saladeros*—doubled between 1837 and 1852.[40]

Despite commercial recovery in the 1840s, Rosas could not suppress the burdensome inflation that had mounted during the war with Brazil. His failure was partly due to recurrent military emergencies and subsidies to the provinces; in 1841, for example, military expenses absorbed three-quarters of the budget of Buenos Aires, and for most of the decade Rosas maintained a standing army 20,000 strong and a militia of around 15,000. Military demands on the budget, which rarely dropped below half total expenditures, helped prolong lax monetary policies. However by this time the landed classes of Buenos Aires had discovered the beneficial effects of inflation. As exporters they were paid at fixed external rates, but as the domestic currency depreciated, their local costs fell. Inflation thus shifted income to the landed interests, enabling them to increase profits and accumulate capital more rapidly, and it was used tacitly, but deliberately, to advance their interests.[41]

Rosas's benevolence toward the ranching interest was highlighted in his land program. In distributing land appropriated by the 1832 expedition, Rosas abandoned emphyteusis and state ownership. Land titles were granted to members of the expedition in lots proportionate to military rank, the same procedure in essence, as that used by the Spanish *conquistadores* in distributing *encomiendas*. Many soldiers sold their properties, these large tracts of land passing to the great cattle ranchers. A second aspect of Rosas's land program concerned the emphyteusis contracts established by Rivadavia, which expired in 1836. South of the Salado River the contracts were renewed, but lessees north of the river were given the option of purchase. The government justified this procedure by citing its revenue needs, but concurrently doubled emphyteusis rents, making rental in some cases more expensive than purchase. The measure prompted an immediate massive shift to private ownership north of the Salado, and in 1838 the practice was repeated for land south of the river. The landed classes found this program a satisfying way to contribute to the public exchequer. By the 1840s several ranchers held title to more than a million acres; by the 1850s the Anchorenas—the greatest exemplars of the elites' transition from commerce to land—owned almost two million acres, and Rosas's own estates totaled 800,000 acres, on which grazed some 500,000 cattle.[42]

Rosas's munificence did not extend to other social sectors of Buenos Aires. A tariff law enacted in 1836 prohibited imports of cattle goods, maize, timber, and butter, ostensibly to protect local suppliers. A broader scale of duties was established, and many goods were reclassified into higher-duty categories, among them certain textile and metallurgical goods. In submitting the measure to the *junta de representantes*, Rosas declared the object was to help "agriculture and the middle classes," farmers in the province of Buenos Aires and artisans in the city—groups in which he enjoyed substantial political support. But the government exaggerated the protectionist content of the measure, which in some cases increased duties on goods for which there were no domestic equivalents. Rather than protecting local producers, the law merely increased the burden of taxation. Since the government refused to increase substantially the revenues from land, it remained as dependent as before on income from tariffs.

The tariff measure was also allegedly to benefit producers in the provinces beyond Buenos Aires. But this claim proved unsubstantiated when the new law was accompanied by increased duties on many provincial goods entering Buenos Aires. Rosas's measure ignored pleas from Cuyo, Tucumán, and Corrientes to restrict imports of European wines, Brazilian sugar, and Paraguayan yerba mate, while widened access to the Buenos Aires market was made contingent on the provinces' lowering their own duties. But lower duties would have made them vulnerable once more to European imports, from which Buenos Aires alone would receive the revenue benefits. In sum, although the tariff law of 1836 has been frequently portrayed as an early essay into economic nationalism, the claim is scarcely warranted: for the most part the law exemplified Rosas's practice of firmly placing the parochial interests of Buenos Aires above all others.[43]

After 1835 Rosas's influence beyond Buenos Aires increased notably. Estanislao López's prominence was fading, and after his death in 1838 ten years elapsed before the provinces erected another *caudillo* of his or Quiroga's stature. Throughout, Rosas continued to resist demands for a new constitution and to maintain a firm grip on trade revenues. The first new major challenge to him was external rather than internal in origin. Commercial diversification and recovery in the 1830s prompted the appearance of new coteries of foreign merchants in Buenos Aires, among them a sizable French colony. France, however, failed to obtain from Rosas a trade treaty like that offered Britain by Rivadavia. French citizens living in Buenos Aires thus found themselves to have the same legal status as the natives, liable to military service and special taxes. Their frequent complaints of harassment and persecution fueled a series of diplomatic incidents between Rosas and the French government.

A similar French community developing in Montevideo obtained much better treatment from the local authorities. As relations there strengthened, a consortium of French and other merchants in Montevideo, which had arranged a loan for the Uruguayan government, was rewarded with control over the port revenues. Subsequently, most French goods, although eventually destined for Buenos Aires, passed first through Montevideo. Rosas was determined to stop this practice, which gave the Uruguayans and the French revenues that under direct trade would have gone to Buenos Aires, and he included among the provisions of the tariff law of 1836 discriminatory duties on reexports from Montevideo. The measure provoked angry complaints from the French, inflaming the prevalent bitterness evoked by the alleged mistreatment of French subjects. In 1838, as Rosas refused both commercial concessions and indemnities, a French fleet blockaded Buenos Aires.[44]

The blockade persisted with varying degrees of effectiveness for some two years, giving Buenos Aires a taste of protectionism far beyond the 1836 legislation and, like the Brazilian blockade a decade earlier, causing severe shortages of essential goods, diminished export earnings and revenues, and a wave of unrest and inflation—the last substantially due to a near tripling in the paper money supply. In the wake of the blockade came another civil war. In 1839, with support from the French, Juan Lavalle, the exiled Unitarist general, invaded Entre Rios from Montevideo. Uruguay also declared war on Rosas, and the Bolivians invaded the northwest. Simultaneously, a rebellion of cattle ranchers south of the Salado River around Chascomús was sparked by demands for new land grants from the government and difficulties caused by the blockade. The Chascomús rebellion seemed a strange affair: here were cattlemen revolting against Rosas, the very embodiment of cattlemen's rule. However, the blockade brought a fall in meat prices on a scale that induced many ranchers to cease marketing cattle and to concentrate instead on increasing the size of their herds. But in the Chascomús region ranchers had difficulty in acquiring more land to pursue this investment option, and they were forced to continue marketing cattle at a loss. Immediately before the rebellion, ranchers in Chascomús were complaining bitterly at the low prices they received for cattle from the *saladeros* in Buenos Aires. These were the chief factors in the revolt.[45]

One by one Rosas crippled his enemies. In the northwest his supporters quickly expelled the Bolivians. In November 1839 the insurrection at Chascomús was defeated by an army led by his brother; after a spate of land confiscations and executions, the district was laid waste. In the war with Uruguay, Rosas exploited local factionalism to raise a force of Uruguayans who pinned down his enemies in Montevideo. Meanwhile, police despotism kept the city of Buenos Aires under firm control. The British, concerned with their own trade losses, pressured the French into ending the blockade in 1840, with Rosas agreeing to pay a token indemnity. Lavalle was gradually thwarted, defeated first at Sauce Grande in Entre Rios, then in Santa Fe, and he was finally driven north into Salta. In 1841 he was killed in a skirmish in Jujuy, and his death ended this bout of civil war. Only Montevideo, which in early 1843 fell under siege by Rosas's Uruguayan allies led by Manuel Oribe, survived as a last outpost of resistance.[46]

Rosas's victories in 1839–1841 reconfirmed his position as the supreme political force throughout the Confederation and its surrounding region. Subsequently, the Rosas regime developed a substantially new identity, one geared to conditions of almost perpetual war. Rosas now maintained a large standing army, which he financed in part through the profits of state-run cattle ranches, many of them confiscated from his enemies. Inflation also financed the army: the government collected its revenues from trade at a gold rate but paid its dependents, military and nonmilitary, in depreciating paper.

By the 1840s Rosas became less an instrument of the cattle-exporting interests than an increasingly autonomous military dictator. But as the regime's permanent military expenses grew, Rosas was constantly forced into measures to amplify revenues. As a result, politics in the wider River Plate region began to assume a guise reminiscent of the early eighteenth century, when the *cabildo* of Buenos Aires had fought constantly to monopolize the hide trade against Colônia do Sacramento. Rosas now strove for a similar monopoly to help generate resources to support his military state. As part of this effort, he prolonged the siege of Montevideo, which dragged on for year after year and eventually won for Montevideo the sobriquet of "the Troy of the River Plate." The ostensible aim of the siege was to contain the Unitarists, and to bring Oribe to power in Uruguay. But in disrupting the flow of goods to Montevideo, the siege served Rosas's other purpose of forcing trade through Buenos Aires, and thereby increasing Buenos Aires's share of the trade revenues.[47]

Second, Rosas attempted to eliminate trade competition from the littoral provinces. In 1845 he set up controls over the river trade along the Paraná at Vuelta de Obligado, an action that immediately embroiled him in renewed conflict with France, which this time enlisted British support. Both European countries, in the throes of severe depression, were conducting an aggressive drive for new foreign markets and denounced Rosas's restrictions. In August 1845, as naval fleets again blockaded Buenos Aires, an Anglo-French naval squadron swept upriver to reopen commerce with the littoral. Once more Rosas surmounted the challenge, his forces repelling the French and British marines who tried to land on the banks of the Paraná. In Buenos Aires the *mazorca* again ruthlessly battened down on the slightest sign of unrest. By 1847, the British saw that they were losing more trade in Buenos Aires than they stood to gain in the littoral, and they abandoned the blockade, which promptly collapsed. In 1848 Rosas again closed the Paraná, triumphantly displaying acknowledgments from Britain and France of his right to do so.[48]

But by this time Rosas had encircled himself with enemies. In once more closing the Paraná, he estranged Brazil, which demanded access along the river to develop communications with the Mato Grosso. Rio de Janeiro also blamed Rosas for political unrest in the Rio Grande region immediately north of Uruguay, another of the areas competing with Buenos Aires in the hide and salted-beef trades. And Montevideo, which Rosas had failed to subdue, remained a refuge for his Unitarist enemies. Although most of the Unitarist leaders from Rivadavia's generation were dead, the movement continually gained new recruits among political exiles from Buenos Aires, and a torrent of anti-Rosas propaganda was smuggled across the estuary.

Nearer to home, Rosas had alienated the province of Entre Rios, whose river links had been cut by the prevailing blockades, which had also threatened the alternative routes through Montevideo. Entre Rios, moreover, was now rapidly gaining economic and political significance. Between 1830 and 1850 its population grew from 30,000 to 48,000, and by the midcentury it boasted seventeen *saladeros*, an estimated six million cattle, and two million sheep. The province was firmly united under its *caudillo*, Justo José de Urquiza, who had led local resistance to Lavalle in 1839. After becoming governor in 1841, Urquiza undertook a land distribution program in Entre Rios like that initiated in Buenos Aires during the 1820s and 1830s. Soon he was the province's largest and wealthiest landowner, and its leading *saladerista*, but his possessions were worthless if Entre Rios were denied the means to trade.

After 1848, when Rosas refused to reopen the Paraná, Urquiza grew increasingly restless. As he did, it became apparent that Rosas had committed a major strategic error in having designated Urquiza his leading provincial military commander and in having entrusted him with a large part of his military forces. At length, his demands unsatisfied, Urquiza turned to rebellion. Gathering allies from Brazil and Uruguay, in May 1851 he challenged Rosas by denying his reelection as governor of Buenos Aires with power over the Confederation's foreign affairs—the power invoked by Rosas when he had closed the rivers. At the same time Urquiza reiterated the long-standing demand of the provinces for a national assembly to commence deliberations on a new constitution. When Rosas ignored him, he moved first against Oribe and in September 1851 raised the siege of Montevideo. Then, with an army of 28,000, comprising *entrerrianos*, Unitarists, Brazilians and Uruguayans, Urquiza marched on Buenos Aires. The regime immediately disintegrated for Rosas not only had alienated Urquiza and the Brazilians but also had lost much of his following in Buenos Aires. During the past decade Rosas's army had become a major competitor for manpower in a labor-starved economy. Many ranchers and merchants perceived the army as a great barrier to exploiting rising external commercial opportunities. Rosas had also forfeited the backing of his own bureaucracy by having kept the nominal stipends of civil administrators stationary, despite inflation, and thereby reducing many to genteel poverty.

In early 1852, completely deserted by his local followers, Rosas was defeated outside the city at Caseros. Urquiza entered Buenos Aires, where his troops immediately massacred several hundred of Rosas's former supporters. Rosas himself, who in recent years had made his peace with the British, was taken on board a British naval vessel and transported to England, where he remained until his death in 1877.[49]

In many respects these forty years of war and dictatorship brought little more than superficial change to the region. At midcentury *caudillos* still reigned in the provinces; in Santiago del Estero, for example, Ibarra had been master for thirty-five years. Rosas's fall in 1852 seemed a reenactment of 1820 or 1828–1829: once more the provinces united against Buenos Aires to overthrow its government. Ox carts and mule trains continued to ply the old routes between Buenos Aires and the interior, and, despite the frontier campaigns led by Rodríguez and Rosas himself, immense regions in the far north and south remained unconquered and untrammeled. In the settled regions most people still lived as simple herdsmen, peons and peasants, artisans, muleteers or ox drivers. The only permanent social change effected in this period was the elimination of the Spanish bureaucracy and mercantile classes. After suffering some disruption during the wars of independence, the old caste system had an informal resurgence. Slavery declined but still persisted; until persuaded by the British to desist, Rosas had allowed the slave trade to revive. In the countryside bands of free *gauchos* still roamed.[50]

Beyond Córdoba was uniform decline: the towns' churches and public buildings were crumbling, silver and money had largely disappeared, and barter once more supervened. In the commercial boom year of 1824 revenues in Buenos Aires were 2.5 million pesos; in Córdoba they were only one quarter of this, in Tucumán a mere ninth. In 1839 revenues in Jujuy, the poorest of the provinces, were a mere 9,000 pesos. The governor of Jujuy received a salary of 1,500 pesos, and the militia swallowed up almost all the rest, with the result that public education, for example, was allocated only 480 pesos.[51]

Throughout the interior the mix of local products resembled that of a century before. Despite the influx of British goods after 1810, local protectionism enabled the survival of native textiles in Catamarca and Corrientes. Tucumán remained a specialist producer of ox carts, while in Santiago del Estero wax, cochineal, and honey were still gathered wild in the Chaco, and near the capital traditional flood-farming prevailed. In La Rioja, where the famed Famatina silver mine of the 1820s had proved a continual disappointment, cattle herding in the *llanos*, or flatlands, was combined with a bit of fruit farming close to the small provincial capital. In Corrientes, yerba mate, tobacco, and fruits were cultivated, to supplement the textile products. Throughout this period, the interior provinces, while striving to defend themselves against commercial penetration from Buenos Aires, had maintained their colonial commercial links with adjacent regions. In the 1850s Salta still exported mules to the *altiplano*. In the Cuyo provinces viticulture had again declined, and the area now subsisted largely from cattle sent live across the Andean passes into Chile.[52]

Even so, stagnation, decline, or reversion were not universal. In some quarters the foundation for deep-seated change was laid. From its base in Montevideo in recent years the Unitarist movement had revived and renewed itself. From the late 1830s it gathered together a new intelligentsia, known as the Generation of 1837. Like Belgrano's followers fifty years earlier, this group began popularizing liberal or now romanticist ideas current abroad. For the most part the Generation of 1837 pledged itself to an oligarchic or authoritarian form of government, but also a government committed to the intensification of material progress. The effect of such ideas and propaganda was to foster a new receptiveness to innovation and renewed support for national unity. By the mid 1840s three figures were most prominent: Esteban Echeverría, Domingo F. Sarmiento, and Juan Bautista Alberdi. Echeverría had in the 1830s organized a series of literary salons in Buenos Aires to disseminate progressive ideas. In 1838 he was accused by the government of pro-French sympathies. He fled to Montevideo, and there for more than a decade led the propaganda war against Rosas. Sarmiento, a native of San Juan, in 1845 published a classic indictment of Federalism and the *caudillos* in a work depicting the colorful and sanguinary career of Facundo Quiroga: *Facundo, or Life in the Argentine Republic in the Days of the Tyrants*. Influenced by a visit to the United States, Sarmiento was also a distinguished campaigner for popular education. Alberdi, from Tucumán, became known in the late 1840s as a devoté of Alexis de Tocqueville. He was also the leader of this generation's supporters of European immigration and colonization, celebrated for the aphorism *gobernar es poblar*, "to govern is to populate."[53]

The decades of war failed to arrest the steady growth of population that had begun in the seventeenth century. In 1816 population throughout the Confederation was estimated to be 0.5 million; by 1857 it reached 1.1 million. Growth was fastest in the city of Buenos Aires, the great beneficiary of revenues from commerce. Between 1810 and 1859 the city grew from a little over 40,000 inhabitants to about 95,000. Buenos Aires had become a cluster of former villages, linked by dirt roads, that still possessed many traditional features: its population remained ethnically mixed; the poor still subsisted on beef and yerba mate alone; and the beggars sought alms from horseback. But there were changes: by midcentury 4,000 immigrants arrived in the city each year from Europe, and in several neighborhoods foreigners were preponderant and dominated most commercial and artisan activities in the city.[54]

The province of Buenos Aires had also changed. After Rosas's frontier campaigns it had come to embrace three concentric zones of settlement. Closest to the city was an area of *chacras* (small farms) dotted with homes built from Paraná timber, or from cane and bulrushes from the nearby delta. During the past two or three generations farming had undergone little change, and it continued to be overshadowed by ranching. For a period after 1810 local farmers faced stiff competition from imported flour from the United States, but under Rosas, due in some measure to the 1836 tariff, conditions began to improve. From then onward the cereal zone and the agriculturally employed population roughly kept pace with the growth of the city itself, and the *chacras* expanded onto land used a century before by the early *estancias*. In this first settled belt outside the city, the principal pasturing activities were fattening cattle destined for the *saladeros* and providing dairy goods for the city.

In the second zone beyond the city, farming was secondary to pasturing; transport costs and labor shortages kept agriculture confined for the most part to the villages. Sheep farming was rapidly developing, and sheep were now expelling cattle to the outer perimeter. Closest to the frontier were the cattle *estancias*, where most conditions were as harsh and primitive as a century before, and Indians and *gaucho* bandits still plagued the ranchers. Although Rosas had recurrently banished convicted prostitutes to the region, *estancia* society remained overwhelmingly male.[55]

By 1850 Entre Rios had become a smaller replica of the province of Buenos Aires. Paraná, its capital, had a population of only 7,000, but like Buenos Aires was based on *saladeros*, tanneries, and river commerce; the capital also attracted small numbers of European immigants. The province, a region of massive cattle ranches surrounding small agricultural and sheep enclaves, was dominated by a clutch of great landowners led by Urquiza. Of the other provinces, Córdoba was still the most advanced, benefiting once more from the expansion of foreign trade in Buenos Aires in the 1840s. Between 1840 and 1860 the population of the city of Córdoba doubled, and the city remained the country's leading ecclesiastical center: from here sprang the cry *Religión o Muerte* and the revolt against Rivadavia in 1826. Among the traditions that persisted in Córdoba was mule breeding for Salta and Bolivia; the novelties included cattle ranches in eastern parts of the province, which were linked with the *saladeros* in Buenos Aires. Santa Fe, meanwhile, had undergone political eclipse after the death of López, and was now a weak client state of Buenos Aires. Santa Fe was also a cattle region, but there had been no sustained effort to extend the frontier. Beyond the provincial capital and its small hinterland, wild Indians still prevailed. Only the small river port of Rosario in the south betrayed a hint of impending change, emerging as an entrepôt for goods from Córdoba and the interior.[56]

On the whole Argentina appeared to be entering a new transition by 1850. Forty years earlier the war for independence and the civil wars had shattered the Bourbon economy and the late-colonial political system. The wars precipitated the growth of segmentary, largely isolated local economies and a profusion of microstates. At the inception of the revolution, cleavage between Buenos Aires and the interior became manifest and it persisted for two generations, till after the fall of Rosas. Latent tensions exploded following the loss and destruction of the mines of Potosí, whose silver had been for more than two centuries the chief buttress of the colonial economy, the main source of its stability and of whatever capacity it possessed to expand and develop. Decades elapsed before the pampas cattle economy had advanced enough to substitute for silver effectively and to become a sufficient force to overcome political sectionalism.

The duration of the crisis after 1810 also resulted from the failure to develop new external connections to replace the shattered link with Spain. Britain at times appeared willing to become a new partner, and Buenos Aires and the Unitarists were often eager to accept British patronage, but a British link was thus far impractical. If the British were willing to sell in the River Plate markets, they were unable to buy there in like measure, and until the 1830s British trade provoked chronic payments deficits. Such trade demonetized the local economy and provoked defensive protectionist impulses in the provinces, which accelerated the tendency toward provincial isolationism. Commerce with Britain thus became a major source of political strife and failure after 1810. In helping to revitalize colonial mercantilist and *comunero* traditions in the new guise of Federalism, British trade eased the way for the rise of the *caudillos*.

Conditions in the early nineteenth century evoked those of the seventeenth in several ways. Depression again gave military command disproportionate importance as an avenue of social mobility; weaker communities grew increasingly reliant on subsidies; and economic decline again brought "barbarism." Once more, too, economic crisis failed to spur any considerable economic diversification. Recurrent blockades against Buenos Aires and Buenos Aires's own blockades against the interior illustrated the continuing crucial importance of imports. Likewise, the failure of the political system in the early nineteenth century prompted neither social revolution nor successful egalitarian social movements. *Caudillismo* became a means to revive elitism and patriarchalism, allowing the elites to adapt rather than disappear, while society at large upheld its hierarchical form.

Once more, the elites used the device of monopoly to protect themselves. After 1810 monopoly became an increasingly prominent feature of landownership, as opposed to mere land use. Land monopoly enabled Bourbon merchant families to move into ranching, in much the same way the early colonial smugglers had turned to mule breeding. Among other echoes of the past were the renewed efforts to suppress rural "vagrancy" and Rosas's chauvinistic defense of the Buenos Aires meat and hide export interests, the policy that eventually led to his downfall.

IV

THE FORMATION OF THE NATION-STATE, 1852-1890

The fall of Rosas was followed by a wave of change. Politically, the country ceased to be a segmented imbroglio of *caudillo* chieftainships, and it gradually surmounted its interregional conflicts to form a national state that gained undisputed authority throughout the republic. Economic expansion occurred on unprecedented scale. The frontiers advanced rapidly as the Indians were driven away and the free *gauchos* at last suppressed. A massive network of railroads superseded the old system of transportation by ox carts and mules. In the River Plate steam packets eventually replaced sailing ships, and railways and steamships together revolutionized production and commerce. The concurrent social change was of comparable magnitude. The first national census in 1869 revealed a country in which four-fifths of the population was illiterate and housed in mud-and-straw shacks. Twenty years later, although conditions varied greatly among the regions, in some areas education, housing, and consumption standards bore comparison with the most-advanced parts of the world. By the late 1880s the nation's population was increasing by threefold every thirty years. Argentina was now becoming a society of white immigrants and large cities. Meanwhile, its landowners and merchants gathered hitherto unknown riches from the fertile pampas.

Economic growth and political unification were reciprocal and mutually reinforcing. As the prospects of growth and a share in its fruits increased, the conditions that had earlier fostered political fragmentation diminished. The provinces were persuaded to accept government from Buenos Aires, which in turn gave them a share in prosperity and power. Unification was accomplished amid a succession of export and foreign investment booms, which were largely the result of a new relationship between Argentina and Britain. In the years immediately after 1810 British commercial activities in the River Plate region had been heavily disruptive. By flooding the markets with cheap manufactures, they fostered social dislocation and severe commercial deficits. Toward 1870, however, Britain became an expanding market for Argentine exports, which improved the stability of the Argentine economy, and British investment financed the physical transformation of the pampas.

Complementarity and mutual interest lay at the heart of the new relationship between Argentina and Britain, and both countries unquestionably benefited from it. Yet in Argentina the relation effected a society bearing many of the classic traits of neocolonialism. Argentine landowners and merchants came to epitomize the "collaborating classes" of the "periphery" in partnership with an advanced industrial power. As a specialist primary producer, Argentina became increasingly vulnerable to demand and price fluctuations in export markets, and it incurred foreign debts that at times threatened to overwhelm it. The period also witnessed rapid development in the agrarian sector, but relatively little in manufacturing industry. Despite political unification, growth enhanced rather than erased regional disparities. By the early 1880s land prices in the province of Buenos Aires were as much as forty times higher than in the interior. By 1883 revenues of the province of Buenos Aires were 11.6 million paper pesos, in Córdoba they were 800,000, and 94,000 in the province of Catamarca.[1]

Despite rapid change, society continued to bear a crucial imprint from its Hispanic past. The great *estancias* survived and continued to spread across the frontiers, while most new immigrant farmers rented land rather than owned it. The result was a still rootless and unstable society in the pampas, and a situation in which a high proportion of the new immigrants were absorbed in the cities, despite the rural base of the economy. In the late nineteenth century Argentina became the most dynamic and opulent of the Latin American republics. It also acquired new structural imbalances and distortions that were to afflict its later development.

The forty-year period from 1850 to 1890 divides into three stages. In the 1850s the Federalists made a final bid for supremacy against

Buenos Aires, but in the early 1860s they were overcome. Buenos Aires then led the way in consolidating the new national state, which by 1880 had achieved complete supremacy. In the 1880s came a great economic boom, whose climax was a collapse into depression and revolution in 1890.

THE CONQUEST OF FEDERALISM, 1852–1880

Urquiza's victory over Rosas failed to resolve the issues that had bedeviled relations among the provinces since 1810, but proved a substantial step forward. Under the influence of liberal intellectuals like Sarmiento and Alberdi, the quest for a constitution and the concept of political unity were now inextricably intertwined with the aspiration for economic recovery and progress. The provinces were prepared to modify certain long-cherished attitudes and make concessions.

After Caseros the provinces each sent delegates to a convention in San Nicolás, a small city in the north of the province of Buenos Aires, close to the border with Santa Fe. Here they reissued the old Federalist demands for the sharing of trade revenues and an end to restrictions on river commerce, while Urquiza and other large landowners in the littoral pressed for subsidies and credits from Buenos Aires. But in several areas traditional Federalist ideas had weakened. There was now little insistence on provincial autonomy and local protectionism, which had failed to produce any benefits and which liberal propaganda associated with the backwardness or, to use Sarmiento's term, the "barbarism" of the *caudillos*. At the conclusion of the convention, the *Acuerdo de San Nicolás*, as the agreement was called, endorsed the preparation of a new constitution that would both erect a strong central government and eradicate internal restraints on trade. Some provinces now openly espoused ideas earlier identified with the Unitarists, among them the old plan to make the city of Buenos Aires a federal district. Like Rivadavia, the provinces saw in this a means to weaken the landed classes of Buenos Aires—the groups that had backed Rosas.[2]

Thirty or forty years earlier much of this program had been heartily endorsed by Buenos Aires, but in the early 1850s the majority opinion in Buenos Aires opposed it. In the city the overthrow of Rosas had evoked little regret, for during the last decade his rule had grown increasingly asphyxiating. However, acquiescence in the fall of the dictator did not imply a willingness to jettison the privileges he had given the province. Buenos Aires wanted neither to open up the rivers nor to surrender control over its revenues. Nor would Buenos Aires agree to demands from the other provinces that it have only the same number of representatives as each of them in the forthcoming constituent assembly. Finally Buenos Aires rejected another idea that had surfaced in San Nicolás, namely, granting Urquiza undefined supreme executive power. Resistance to the San Nicolás program in Buenos Aires quickly united in June 1852 in a new movement known as the *Partido Liberal.*

The Liberals of the 1850s were an urban clique of merchants and local functionaries, among them both former supporters and opponents of Rosas. Their conception of the future order resembled the city-state of antiquity: the port-city would enjoy complete political and economic primacy, using the provinces as markets, a source of exportables or local food supplies, essentially as tributaries to be exploited or ignored at will. In September 1852, scarcely six months after Caseros, the Liberals, or *setembristas* as they were first known, staged a revolt in Buenos Aires that succeeded in displacing Urquiza's puppet governor, Vicente López y Planes. Although the coup met resistance from rural Federalists in Buenos Aires, led by Hilario Lagos, under Valentín Alsina's leadership the *setembristas* persevered, defying another invasion by Urquiza. In early 1853 the Liberal regime in Buenos Aires rejected the San Nicolás accord and withdrew from a constitutional convention sponsored by Urquiza. Later that year a new constitution was promulgated, which was eventually ratified by all the provinces except Buenos Aires.[3]

The immediate aftermath of the fall of Rosas was thus another series of confrontations between Buenos Aires and the provinces. In 1854 Urquiza became president of a new Argentine Confederation with its capital at Concepción del Uruguay in Entre Rios. Buenos Aires severed all links with his regime and declared itself independent under its governor. For the next six years the two governments coexisted uneasily, sometimes engaging in token wars, more commonly resorting to blockades or discriminatory tariffs. If Buenos Aires lacked the military strength to impose itself on the provinces, it continued to receive the lion's share of foreign trade and most of the revenues. In contrast to the city's prosperity, the Argentine Confederation was continuously plagued by acute financial difficulties, its paper money almost worthless from the moment it was printed. After offering favorable terms for commerce, in 1853 Urquiza won diplomatic recognition from Britain. But Alberdi, his representative in Europe, failed to secure a British loan. Urquiza's aim throughout the 1850s was to foster new commercial growth in the littoral, using the Paraná to service Entre Rios and Rosario for goods from Córdoba and beyond. His efforts boosted commercial expansion in Rosario, whose population grew from a mere 3,000 in the early 1850s to 23,000 by 1869, and British observers calculated that customs revenues in Rosario soared from £116,000 in 1855 to £172,000 by 1860. But this success was insufficient to redress the Confederation's lack of access to Buenos Aires. Throughout the 1850s it proved difficult to attract shipping along the Paraná, as most merchants found carrying their goods upriver an irksome and otiose venture, when the main market and source of exportables lay immediately at hand in Buenos Aires. Urquiza tried time and again to circumvent this obstacle. Unable to persuade Buenos Aires to accept goods destined for the interior without levying duties on them, he then dropped the duties in the Paraná region below those in Buenos Aires. But whatever scheme he tried, he could not reclaim the Confederation from the brink of bankruptcy. As the years went by, his creation moved inexorably toward collapse.[4]

At length in desperation Urquiza returned to force. In October 1859 he again invaded Buenos Aires, defeating its army at Cepeda. Soon after, Buenos Aires pledged a large monthly subsidy to the Confederation. Nevertheless, another round of eventually inconclusive civil war seemed likely. Urquiza had shown repeatedly that he could defeat Buenos Aires, and if he wished take the city, but he had never been able to maintain his position for any length of time in the face of local resistance. However, unexpected events ensued: for several months Urquiza managed to keep Alsina's faction from recapturing control in Buenos Aires. In March 1860 Bartolomé Mitre, a veteran of the defense of Montevideo against Rosas and military chief of Buenos Aires under Alsina, assumed power as governor. Despite his position in the Alsina regime, Mitre had for some time ceased supporting the independence of Buenos Aires and instead pressed for unity, but on terms quite different from Urquiza's. Whereas Urquiza sought to reduce the power of Buenos Aires and impose an equitable sharing of the revenues, Mitre's concept of unity endorsed the paramountcy of Buenos Aires.

In the past few years, Mitre had exploited local grievances against the confederation's burdensome taxes to create pockets of personal support in Urquiza's provinces. Upon becoming governor of Buenos

Aires, Mitre encouraged his outlying followers to make their own bids for power. In 1860 and 1861 a series of *"mitrista"* provincial revolts were staged against Urquiza, to which he eventually replied by again invading Buenos Aires. But in the battle of Pavón in September 1861 Mitre's city militia, equipped with new imported rifles and cannon, at last managed to withstand Urquiza's *gaucho* cavalry. Pavón, however, was scarcely a military victory for Buenos Aires, for Urquiza elected to retreat; faced with stiffening resistance in Buenos Aires and the revolt in his rearguard, Urquiza finally lost faith in his own vision and capitulated.[5]

At the same time, new economic conditions suddenly favored Mitre's plan at the expense of Urquiza's. In 1861 the economy of the littoral witnessed an unprecedented boom led by wool exports. But to profit from the boom the littoral provinces needed an accord with Buenos Aires that would preclude Buenos Aires from blockading the Paraná or denying funds and credits to provincial landowners. The boom also helped undermine separatist sentiment in Buenos Aires. During the preceding decade of intermittent civil wars, which had redirected troops away from the frontier garrisons, the Indians had again moved northward such that by 1860 the frontier line in some parts lay closer to Buenos Aires than it had forty years before. As the wool boom developed, attempts from Buenos Aires to acquire new land for sheep breeding were thus pushed northward and westward into Santa Fe and Córdoba, on territory in the Confederation. Both the provinces and Buenos Aires, therefore—one wanting trade outlets and investment funds, the other seeking new land—had reason to support peace and cooperation. Immediately after Pavón, Urquiza buried himself in his personal business affairs in Entre Rios. Without his backing the Confederation, now under its second president, Santiago Derquí, swiftly crumbled. When Mitre finally marched unopposed into Santa Fe, the advance was greeted as a tacit acknowledgment of submission to Buenos Aires by Urquiza and the provinces. In 1861 Buenos Aires and the other provinces thus finally conceded their mutual needs, a complementarity of interest that bred both conciliation and consensus.[6]

In the confusing intermission between Cepeda and Pavón, the province of Buenos Aires, having secured a number of amendments, at last ratified the Constitution of 1853. The new articles of government established a federal regime, an elected bicameral legislature, and an independent judiciary. They contained a bill of rights and prohibitions against slavery and the slave trade, though both were already almost extinct practices. Drawing on late Bourbon and Unitarist ideas, in particular a recent tract by Alberdi, *Las Bases,* the Constitution enunciated commitments to increasing population through immigration, the development of communications, and the promotion of new industry. Congress was given wide scope to initiate educational programs, foster immigration, award railroad concessions, organize colonization grants, and seek loans from abroad. The Constitution banned all internal restraints on trade, and in this represented a great symbolic break with the colonial mercantilist and *comunero* traditions. Even so, there were still echoes of Federalism; for example, the Constitution provided for a national Senate, a body designed to safeguard the landed classes of the interior. Senatorial elections were placed in the hands of provincial legislatures, and eligibility for election was restricted to those of relatively high incomes. Senate members were privileged with lengthy terms, nine years with one-third of the body selected triennially.

As a document originating among the provinces, the Constitution of 1853 contained surprisingly strong reminiscences of its ill-fated Unitarist predecessors in 1819 and 1826. While establishing Catholicism as the state religion, it followed Rivadavia in establishing full liberty of conscience while exempting foreigners from forced loans and military service. It created a strong national executive: although the president was barred from immediate reelection, he was given a six-year term and wide powers to initiate legislation, to nominate and control the cabinet, and to suspend constitutional rights by declaring a state of siege. The national government, and when Congress was not in session, the president alone, also had the faculty of federal intervention (*intervención federal*), which under certain circumstances authorized the dissolution of the provincial administrations and direct rule over the provinces pending the election of new authorities. This provision represented a survival of the earlier claims of the Unitarists to appoint provincial governors, and the Bourbon Crown's powers of appointment over the intendants.

Yet ratification of the Constitution by Buenos Aires left several issues unresolved. In its original version the Constitution declared the city of Buenos Aires the federal capital. But the 1860 amendments, while suggesting some ultimate intent to federalize, erected cumbersome procedures that made the measure unlikely if not impossible. In this way the province of Buenos Aires upheld its earlier position as *primus inter pares.* At the same time the province's currency became acceptable as legal tender but only alongside other currencies such as Bolivian silver. The province of Buenos Aires, through its official bank, thus acquired control over national monetary and financial policies, but it was both ill-defined and incomplete. Meanwhile, each of the provinces, including Buenos Aires, was permitted to keep its own militia. Further, the relationship between the national government and the government of Buenos Aires was highly anomalous in that the former in effect rented land and facilities from the latter in the city.[7]

In 1862 an electoral college of delegates from the provinces voted Mitre the first president of a newly styled Argentine Republic (*República Argentina*). As he took formal command, he immediately invested the settlement with substance by establishing new organs of state. The Mitre years saw an institutional revolution, as the country's ablest jurists, led by Dalmacio Vélez Sársfield, were given the task of creating a national legal system, a bureaucracy, and a taxation system. The first fruit of their labors was the establishment of a national treasury and national customs office in 1862. A national judiciary followed the year after, when Congress passed a national voting law. In 1864 the embryo of a new national army was formed. Subsequently, attempts were made to create a national postal system, and a civil law code was promulgated in 1870. By the early 1870s Argentina had also acquired its two great establishment press organs, *La Prensa* and *La Nación*, the latter Mitre's personal vehicle and mouthpiece.[8]

At first the new order was largely sustained by the wool export boom. Prosperity alleviated political tensions and gave the government a store of resources to augment its popularity. Mitre became adept in the dispensation of subsidies to the provinces, using them with particular adroitness to keep Urquiza at bay in Entre Rios. His great concession to the provinces, however, was a government-sponsored railroad between Rosario and Córdoba. Construction of the line, which had been discussed in the 1850s under the Confederation, began in 1862 and was completed in 1870. It helped draw Córdoba and the interior closer to the Paraná and to the burgeoning market of Buenos Aires. It also provided another major spur to the growth of Rosario, where customs revenues increased from £172,000 in 1860 to £295,000 in 1870. After 1862 Argentina succeeded in attracting private British capital. In 1857 Buenos Aires had commenced repayment on the defaulted loan of 1824, a step that removed the major obstacle to new investment. Within weeks of Mitre's inaugural in 1862, preparations were afoot to establish several British banks and railway companies. During its delicate first years the main pillars of national unity were thus high export earnings and a matching land boom, foreign investment, and handouts from Buenos Aires to the provincial landed classes.[9]

Yet not everyone benefited from the new order. Throughout the 1860s old-style Federalists and *mitrista* cliques battled fiercely in the provinces on issues like local tariffs. During the six years of Mitre's tenure there were no fewer than 117 unscheduled local changes of government. Conflict was most bitter in the interior, where support for the national government was frequently narrow and tenuous. Mitre's two principal allies were Domingo Sarmiento, who had become governor of San Juan during the collapse of the Confederation, and the Taboada brothers, who ruled Santiago del Estero.

Mitre's first major antagonist in the interior was Vicente Peñaloza, known as *El Chacho*, the *caudillo* heir of Facundo Quiroga to the leadership of the pastoral *montonera* and *gaucho* clans of the province of La Rioja, a bastion of Federalism. With a population of only 34,000 in 1860 La Rioja was the most backward corner of the impoverished west. Subsidies from Urquiza had once kept the province relatively peaceful, but the subsidies ended abruptly on the demise of the Confederation. The immediate unrest was accompanied by suspicions toward the new national tariff, which was seen locally as a threat to the old cattle trade with Chile. In 1862 Peñaloza repudiated the unification settlement and launched his army on San Luis to the southeast. For some time he controlled large areas in the west, but in 1863 La Rioja was invaded by an army from Santiago del Estero, led by the Taboadas and equipped and financed from Buenos Aires. After his ragged followers were routed, Peñaloza himself was hunted down and shot.[10]

After *El Chacho* came Felipe Varela, his former lieutenant, who in 1866 led another desperate attempt to revive Federalism. In widely publicized manifestos Varela reasserted the rights of the provinces to impose local tariffs protecting cottage industries. Meanwhile, he sought to cultivate Urquiza in Entre Rios, attempting to fashion an alliance that would turn once more against Buenos Aires. But Urquiza was too enmeshed in business dealings with Buenos Aires to contemplate renewed war, and in 1867 Varela was destroyed by the Taboadas. By the early 1870s the national government imposed its writ on the interior through local garrisons and by liberal use of its powers of federal intervention. Though the intervenors were originally to arrange elections and quickly restore authority to local governors, instead they found themselves ruling for long transitional periods.[11]

Unlike Rivadavia, whose conflict with Brazil swiftly precipitated his downfall, Mitre was successful in using war to consolidate national unity. The war with Paraguay between 1865 and 1870 both revived the flagging new order in Argentina and also eliminated one of the major threats to its survival and aggrandizement.

Since 1811 Paraguay had been ruled by a line of autocrats, first José Gáspar de Francia, then Carlos Antonio López, and then the latter's son, Francisco Solano López. Fifty years of stiff political controls had produced an unusual society in which a primitive subsistence agrarian base coexisted alongside a highly developed state apparatus. In Paraguay there was no countervailing power against that of the ruler: the Church's wealth had been expropriated under Francia, and most landed and mercantile groups suffered the same fate. Much of the land and nearly all the country's small export trade—mainly yerba mate and tobacco—were vested in the state, which thus disposed of the bulk of surplus production. Toward midcentury some of this wealth was used to give Paraguay a superficial veneer of modernity. In the 1850s Carlos Antonio López pioneered the establishment of railways and telegraphs in Latin America, and he had European experts construct an iron foundry, a shipyard, and an arsenal. But he plowed the bulk of his resources into supporting and equipping what by South American standards was a massive military force. In 1864 Paraguay had a standing army of 28,000 peasant soldiers, with another 40,000 in the reserves—compared with an army of merely 6,000 in Argentina, and the 20,000 men Mitre eventually raised at much cost after the war had begun.

By the 1860s the resources supporting the military state in Paraguay had been developed to their maximum and could be increased only by expanding the territory and population under the state's domain. Such constraints impelled Solano López, who succeeded his father in 1862, to seek control of the upper reaches of the Paraná, from which he intended eventually to strike against the Brazilian states of Paraná and Mato Grosso. Brazil responded to the threat by drawing closer to Mitre's government in Buenos Aires. Mitre needed little inducement to join forces as he feared that an alliance between Solano López and Urquiza might emerge and subsequently support dissident *caudillos* like Varela in the interior.

The immediate cause of the war was political strife in Uruguay, where in recent years there had been unending conflict between the mainly mercantile or *colorado* ("red") faction based in Montevideo and the *blancos* ("whites")—Uruguayan federalists representing the cattle interests in the hinterland. Both Brazil and Argentina backed the *colorados*, Brazil because the *blancos* had long been suspected of fostering rebellion in the Rio Grande region, Argentina because the *blancos* were again potential allies of the domestic *caudillos*. Solano López, however, strongly supported the *blancos*. To help them and to assert control of the upper Paraná, he mobilized his army, declaring war on Brazil. To reach Brazil he marched his forces through the Argentine territory of Misiones, the site of the former Jesuit settlements, and then invaded Corrientes, where he set up a puppet regime. Mitre replied with war. In 1865 Paraguay thus faced an alliance embracing Brazil, Argentina, and their *colorado* clients in Uruguay; though Paraguay had by far the largest army, these were nevertheless daunting odds, which López worsened by a serious tactical error as the war began. He launched his fleet too early and it was quickly destroyed, leaving his enemies full control of the rivers.

Despite their early advantage, the allies took five years to defeat the Paraguayans, who fought with skill, indomitable courage, and an often savage ferocity, repeatedly proving their mettle against the ragged black slaves drafted by Brazil and the peasants and *gauchos* frog-marched into service by Mitre. Asunción held out until January 1869, and only fifteen months later were López and the last of his followers captured and executed in the outlying forests. The war had a devastating effect on Paraguay, whose population declined from about 400,000 in 1865 to 230,000 in 1871. In some parts of the country observers estimated that by the end of the war women outnumbered men by fourteen to one.[12]

The Argentine government entered this long and bloody war in a blaze of jingoistic enthusiasm, which evaporated as the war dragged on and resistance grew to its tax demands and the military draft. Mitre and his clients, the Taboadas, used the war to strike new blows against *caudillismo* in the interior, provoking trouble by rustling cattle and instituting press-gangs. In the ensuing melee they subdued the Varela rebellion, numerous other smaller outbreaks, and also a secessionist movement in Salta. Though the eventual cost of subduing the interior amounted to half that of the war itself, the result was a much stronger central authority in the north and the west.

The war with Paraguay also helped resolve economic difficulties and resurgent political divisions in the metropolitan and littoral regions. It came as the wool boom had passed its peak and was beginning to subside. The war did little for wool producers but enriched some members of the old cattle sector, enabling some ranchers to make enormous profits supplying meat, leather, and cavalry mounts to the troops. Hide prices, for example, rose from 12.7 pesos in 1865 to more than 17 pesos in 1870. The war also boosted production of wheat and maize in new agricultural colonies in Santa Fe and Entre Rios. Meanwhile, the merchants of Buenos Aires waxed fat on Brazilian gold, which flowed into the city in payment for supplies to the Brazilian army, and the government profited by taxing goods en route from Brazil to Paraguay. Among the greatest beneficiaries of the war with Paraguay was Urquiza: by 1869 he had amassed a personal fortune said to include 600,000 cattle, 500,000 sheep, 20,000 horses, and more than two million acres of land. However, Mitre's followers, too, gained substantially from the war, and Mitre's party now became known as the "Purveyors' Party" (*partido de los proveedores*). Thanks in part to the Paraguayan war, export earnings increased by 62 percent in 1867–1873, and government spending by 120 percent.[13]

By 1870 the struggle against Federalism was nearing completion. The last of the great *caudillos* was Ricardo López Jordán in Entre Rios, who took control of the province after his followers assassinated Urquiza in 1870. For several years López Jordán resisted attempts from Buenos Aires to eliminate him, but in 1874 he was defeated. Federalism had now become little more than an unsavory memory of a troubled past. Scattered bands of surviving *montonera* served for a time in different parts of the country as mercenaries of the central government; yet by 1880 they too had largely disappeared.

The preceding twenty years had effected radical changes in Argentine politics, which now functioned in the form of complex interlocking networks and alliances radiating from Buenos Aires. Formal politics, however, remained a narrow preserve of the mercantile and landed elites. The electoral law of 1863, which purported to allow popular participation in the political process, from the beginning proved itself a sham. Elections were invariably ritualistic parodies, stage-managed by lackeys of the powerful, with only a minute fraction of the electorate participating. By 1880 the term *caudillo* was losing its earlier connotation of regional or provincial leader and now referred to the local political bosses who controlled elections on behalf of their elite patrons.[14]

The transition came at a time when provincial interests were expanding their influence at the national level at the expense of the province of Buenos Aires. Hamstrung by the war in Paraguay, Mitre failed in the presidential election of 1868 to manipulate the victory of a handpicked successor. The presidency thus passed to Domingo Sarmiento, who became the first of four successive presidents from provinces other than Buenos Aires. Sarmiento had won fame as an eloquent and vitriolic critic of the *caudillos* and Federalism, and his was the administration that finished off Solano López and López Jordán. Sarmiento's other main achievement lay in his commitment to popular education: between 1868 and 1874 educational subsidies from the central government to the provinces quadrupled. Yet by and large his administration was a disappointment, with Sarmiento failing in an effort to develop mining in his native San Juan and his attempts to promote farm colonies in the province of Buenos Aires stymied by the opposition of local landowners.[15]

Some of the shortcomings of the Sarmiento government resulted from renewed rivalries between Buenos Aires and the other provinces. The advent of a *provinciano* to the presidency divided the politicians of Buenos Aires, with many, among them Mitre, viewing the event as a threat to the special position conferred on Buenos Aires in the settlement of 1862. Even so Sarmiento managed to attract support from a breakaway faction in Buenos Aires, which called itself the Autonomist Party and in coalition with provincial groups developed into the National Autonomist Party (*Partido Autonomista Nacional* [PAN]), a movement that was to have a vital role in politics during the next generation. In the election of 1874 the PAN candidate, Nicolás Avellaneda of Tucumán, resoundingly defeated Mitre, gathering 146 votes in the electoral college against 79. In some quarters the victory was interpreted as a mandate to consummate the federalization of Buenos Aires, for which some of the provinces had been noisily campaigning during the past few years. Mitre bitterly opposed the plan, and after the election his supporters issued allegations of fraud and then rebelled to prevent Avellaneda's succession. But with support from the Autonomists the revolt was defeated by Sarmiento and Avellaneda.

The 1874 rebellion was intended to restore the presidency to Buenos Aires; yet it seemed odd that Mitre, earlier the leader of national unity, in attempting a revolution was behaving like the Federalist *caudillos* he had repeatedly fought. However, despite his reputation as the architect of national unity, Mitre had always without exception placed Buenos Aires first, and his uprising illustrated the lingering power of provincial allegiances. It also demonstrated the extent to which national unity had been constructed on economic expansion, for the revolt came in the midst of a trade depression. A decade or so before, when the shepherds and ranchers of Buenos Aires were seeking new lands, and its merchants new markets, Mitre had led the movement for national unity. But once the provinces began scrambling among themselves for scarce resources, he swiftly backtracked to provincial chauvinism. The price of his defeat was that national government resources, which Mitre wanted for the landed and commercial interests of Buenos Aires, were diverted into provincial ventures, among them the construction of a state railroad from Córdoba to Tucumán, Avellaneda's native province.[16]

The festering issue of the special status the province of Buenos Aires had obtained in 1862 was finally resolved in 1880. The presidential elections of that year produced yet another victory for the candidate of the PAN and the provinces, Julio A. Roca, who defeated the nominee from Buenos Aires, Carlos Tejedor, the province's governor. Accusations of electoral improprieties again quickly flared into rebellion. But after several pitched battles, which left a reported three thousand dead, Tejedor's militia was routed by troops of the line commanded by Roca. Eighteen years earlier the province of Buenos Aires had supported a national government in the belief that the nation would be its captive; but in 1880 the province instead became the last and greatest prize of its own creation. Soon after the defeat of Tejedor the city of Buenos Aires was detached from the province and named the federal capital of the republic; standing armies in the provinces were abolished; and the province of Buenos Aires also lost its power to issue currency. Deprived of their center of government, civic leaders in the province soon turned to the construction of a new one, which gave birth to the city of La Plata some thirty miles from the capital.[17]

THE ECONOMIC REVOLUTION, 1852–1890

Political change in this period was closely shaped by economic growth, which in turn resulted from a simple trinity: foreign investment, foreign trade, and immigration. Before 1890 British investment came to Argentina in two waves bisected by the depression of the 1870s. While the first, until 1873, was small and tentative, the second gathered startling momentum in the 1880s such that by 1890 the British had inundated Argentina with an estimated £157 million of investment capital. The great symbol of the new British connection was a burgeoning railroad system, inaugurated with six miles of track open to traffic in 1857 and extended by 1890 to 5,800 miles—most of it in the hands of private British companies—over which were transported 10 million passengers and 5 million tons of cargo. Foreign trade similarly expanded: in 1861 total foreign trade, both imports and exports, was valued at 37 million gold pesos; by 1880 at 104 million, and at more than 250 million by 1889.

Meanwhile, the nation's population increased from an estimated 1.1 million in 1857 to approximately 3.3 million by 1890, with the rate of growth much faster in the littoral than in the interior. Between the provincial census of 1854 and the second national census in 1895 the population of the city and province of Buenos Aires almost sextupled; Santa Fe's population increased tenfold, and in Córdoba, Entre Ríos, and Corrientes fourfold. In Tucumán and Mendoza, the major growth centers of the interior, population doubled between 1869 and 1895 alone. In Catamarca, however, the increase was from 79,000 in 1869 to only 90,000 in 1895; in Salta, from 88,000 to 118,000. In 1869 half the nation's people dwelt in the five pampas or littoral provinces of Buenos Aires, Córdoba, Entre Ríos, Santa Fe, and Corrientes, but by 1895 the proportion was three-quarters. Throughout this period the pampas, as the heartland of the new export economy, drew migrants from the interior and immigrants from across the Atlantic. Net immigration increased rapidly: in the 1850s the annual balance of immigrant arrivals over departures was under 5,000; by the 1880s the annual average was 50,000, and at its nineteenth-century peak in 1889 net immigration exceeded 200,000.[18]

Growing opportunities for profit attracted foreign investment, while relatively high wages and prospects for social mobility drew immigrants. Both were the result and the source of Argentina's success in carving out new overseas markets for its primary goods. Among the most striking features of this period was the concurrent stagnation of trade in Latin America and the boom in transatlantic commerce. Among exports in the later nineteenth century most, but not all, were new products. The old salted-beef industry flourished for several decades after 1850, as it had done before, and in 1895 the thirty-nine *saladeros* in Argentina employed 5,500 men. The main markets for beef were still among the plantations of Brazil and Cuba, with the Brazilian market continuing to expand until 1886 when Brazil imposed a high tariff on meat goods from Argentina. The tariff was in part a response to demands from Brazilian ranchers in Rio Grande do Sul, in part a retaliation against similar restrictions in Buenos Aires on Brazilian sugar. The other main cattle exports, hides and tallow, had always been marketed in western Europe, especially Amsterdam and Le Havre. Hide exports continued to climb, especially in the mid 1850s when competing supplies from Russia were interrupted by the Crimean War. Tallow exports eventually declined, as oil-lanterns and later gas began to replace candles, but the cattle sector fared reasonably well until near the end of the nineteenth century. However, it increasingly seemed a relic from the past, and the abolition of slavery first in Cuba and later in Brazil at length undermined the *saladeros*. Soon after 1890 most disappeared from Buenos Aires and Entre Rios, and by 1900 they were to be found only in marginal cattle country like Corrientes.[19]

Throughout cattle remained secondary in the new export economy, and before 1900 played no part whatsoever in attracting to Argentina its eventually copious store of immigrants and British capital. After 1850 the first of the great export booms was wool, which overtook salted beef and hides in the early 1860s and soon after dwarfed them. In its early years, under Rosas, sheep grazing on the pampas was closely associated with the first immigrant communities—Basque refugees from the Carlist Wars in Spain (1837–1842), then the 15,000 or so Irish who came to the River Plate in the aftermath of the potato famine of 1846. The early shepherds used a poor-quality stock, mostly degenerate varieties of Spanish merinos, whose short, rough fleeces were of value only for carpet manufacture, and the animals themselves for tallow. Before 1860 much of Argentina's wool was exported to the United States, where machines picked the fleeces clean of burrs from the pampas.

In the early 1860s the merino flocks were gradually displaced by imported long-wool Rambouillet breeds, which made possible wool exports for garment manufacture, and in the 1880s came imports of Lincoln pedigrees, enabling exports of frozen mutton. In 1852 sheep outnumbered people in Argentina by about seven to one; by the late 1880s, although the human population was also growing rapidly, the ratio was around thirty to one. The number of sheep increased from 7 million in 1852 to 23 million in 1864, to 57 million in 1875, and to a prodigious 87 million by 1888 (see Table 3). Sheep also outnumbered cattle; for example, in the province of Buenos Aires in 1875 were an estimated 5 million cattle and 45 million sheep. In the 1880s it was

TABLE 3. *Sheep Population and Wool Exports,*
1830–1880

	Sheep Population (millions)	Wool Exports (metric tons)
1830	2.5	1,812
1840	5.0	1,610
1850	7.0	7,681
1860	14.0	17,317
1865	—	54,908
1870	41.0	65,704
1880	61.0	92,112

SOURCES: Herbert Gibson, *The History and Present State of the Sheep-Breeding Industry of the Argentine Republic* (Buenos Aires, 1893), 50; José C. Chiaramonte, *Nacionalismo y liberalismo económico, 1860–1880* (Buenos Aires, 1971), 36.

claimed that Argentina had more sheep than any other country in the world.

Wool exports rose accordingly, from 300 tons in 1829 to 7,600 tons in 1850, then more than doubled to 17,000 tons in 1860, and increased threefold in the next five years to 55,000 tons. Subsequently, the pace of expansion slackened, but continued its upward course, with wool remaining the largest export earner until after 1900. Exports were 65,000 tons in 1870, 91,000 in 1875, and 111,000 tons by 1882.[20]

The expansion of the wool economy led to substantial changes in pampas rural society. Such tasks as shearing, carting the fleeces, and constructing fences and sheds attracted a larger population onto the land. Sheep farming was also more suitable to family labor than cattle ranching and thus helped augment the rural female population. In some measure the rise of sheep farming helped break up the largest of the *estancias,* as the luckier shepherds—the Irish being the best example—gathered the capital to set themselves up as landowners, usually on small plots under 1,750 hectares in size. However, such independent shepherds were exceptions, and most sheep farming was conducted under sharecropping contracts. Before 1860 terms of such contracts frequently favored tenants, but in time the original half-shares of the wool crop (*mediería*) usually became thirds (*terciaría*).[21]

The sudden spurt in wool exports during the early 1860s, which had a central role in consummating the political settlement of 1862, was largely an outcome of the American Civil War, as cotton short- ages provoked a surge both in wool prices and in demand from several new markets overseas—France, Germany, the northern United States, the Netherlands, and Britain. The end of the Civil War, however, brought a sharp fall in prices: by 1867 wool prices were 13 percent less than in 1865, and by 1869 28 percent less. Argentine exporters suffered severely from a protective tariff adopted by the United States in 1867, which at a stroke eliminated a fifth of Argen- tina's foreign market. After 1867 western Europe was almost the only market for Argentine wool.

The slump following the American Civil War was exacerbated by domestic financial conditions. In the early 1860s the province of Bue- nos Aires issued large quantities of paper money, ostensibly to defray debts from the recent wars with the Confederation. But, as had hap- pened with the cattle ranchers under Rosas, the resulting inflation greatly benefited shepherds and wool exporters, whose incomes were high, based on gold, and whose debts—for labor, land, and credit— were paid in depreciating paper. The great disadvantage of inflation was its deterrent effect on foreign investors, who earned paper money only to watch its value depreciate. As part of Mitre's campaign to attract foreign investment, in 1863 the Bank of the Province of Buenos Aires announced a program of monetary stabilization and currency convertibility. As a first step it began withdrawing paper money from circulation, but as the economy continued to expand throughout 1864, the resulting pronounced money shortage provoked the paper peso to appreciate rapidly. As it did so, the earlier bounty to exporters van- ished and interest rates surged. The ensuing contraction in foreign demand and the fall in wool prices were such that by 1866 most profits on the wool crop were swallowed up by loan repayments to the banks. The shepherds and wool merchants were not alone in their suffering. The recent expansion of wool had fanned an enormous land boom, but between 1864 and 1866 land prices fell by 20 to 25 percent, bringing bankruptcy and ruin to many speculators. By this time, how- ever, Argentina had embarked on the war against Paraguay, which helped contain the fall in land prices and head off the rumblings of political discontent that accompanied it.[22]

Following the wool boom came a revolution in Argentine agricul- ture. As late as 1869 only 3 percent of the population of Buenos Aires was employed in farming, and the country was still heavily de- pendent on wheat and flour imports from the United States and Chile.

By the late 1880s, however, Argentina was rapidly becoming a major world producer of temperate cereals—wheat, corn, oats, and barley—and a major industrial crop, linseed. For example, wheat exports increased by a factor of twenty-three between 1880–1884 and 1890–1894 (see Table 4).

Agriculture first expanded in areas of the littoral linked with Buenos Aires by the Paraná River, its emergence resulting from the widening of the internal market and the freeing of the river trade in 1862. Although agricultural exports began only in the late 1870s, by the early 1890s a vast semicircular farming belt had appeared around the city of Buenos Aires. From Entre Rios in the north it ran across central and southern Santa Fe and eastern Córdoba, then traversed the province of Buenos Aires to the port of Bahía Blanca in the south. Almost nonexistent in the early 1850s, the cultivated area grew to almost 600,000 hectares by 1872, reaching 2.5 million hectares by 1888. Half this area was devoted to wheat and about one-third to corn, with linseed, barley, and oats following. As the land was settled by farmers, fences built, trees planted, windmills and homesteads constructed, and wells dug, agriculture prompted a rapid leap in rural investment and imports of agricultural capital goods. By the early 1890s annual imports of barbed wire, for example, stood at 20,000 tons.[23]

The new agricultural system preceded the national unification in the 1850s with the establishment of the first successful colonies of European farmers. In 1853 the government of Corrientes contracted to locate one thousand French families on land in the province. From this beginning several hundred farm colonies and roughly the same number of new towns and villages were founded in Corrientes, Entre Rios, Córdoba, Santa Fe, and Buenos Aires. Many of these farms were

TABLE 4. *The Wheat Trade, 1870–1895*
(*In metric tons, five-year averages*)

	Exports	Imports
1870–1874	77	2,110
1875–1879	5,700	1,200
1880–1884	34,400	6,100
1885–1889	115,200	600
1890–1894	782,000	300

SOURCE: James R. Scobie, *Revolution on the Pampas: A Social History of Argentine Wheat*, 1860–1910 (Austin, 1964), 170.

sponsored by the provincial governments, which drew up contracts with European entrepreneurs. The former selected and prepared land for colonization, subdividing it into lots of usually between thirty and forty hectares, and provided the farmers with animals and seed, while the contractors assumed responsibility for recruiting and transporting colonists from Europe. Once settled on the land, the colonists received additional subsidies until they were able to discharge their debts. There were many highly successful ventures of this kind. By 1870 the colonies were the source of around 20,000 tons of wheat, about half total domestic output. By 1880 there were 365 colonies and some 20,000 small farms in Santa Fe, 146 colonies and 18,000 farms in Córdoba, and 184 colonies and 15,000 farms in Entre Rios. Private railroad and land companies also actively promoted colonization schemes and eventually took the leading role.[24]

The largest region of farm colonies was central Santa Fe, formerly the domain of *caudillos* like Estanislao López and then subject to rival clutches of cattle ranchers. An overwhelming proportion of the province's nominal territory lay still in the hands of wild Indians. As colonization projects began to be discussed in Santa Fe around 1850, the prevailing backwardness of the province proved to have certain advantages. Supporters of colonization could argue that farmers posed no threat to the ranchers, as the farms would be located on new land and thus serve as a buffer against the Indians, and that farmer immigrants would broaden the tax base, allowing ranchers' taxes to be reduced. Colonization projects began in Santa Fe with the foundation of Esperanza in 1856. Soon after Swiss, German, French, and above all Italian farmers rapidly transformed the province. Between 1860 and 1895 the cultivated area in Santa Fe increased from almost no acreage to 1.5 million hectares, and the number of rural villages in the province grew from four in 1869 to sixty-two by 1895 (see Map 6). By 1895 three thousand miles of railroads in Santa Fe enabled agriculture to expand far beyond the Paraná. Between 1858 and 1869 the population of Santa Fe doubled, rising from 41,000 to 89,000; by 1895 it had again quadrupled, to almost 400,000. Agriculture gave yet another fillip to Rosario, which by 1895, with a population of 91,000, had become the second city of the republic.[25]

Agricultural colonization in Santa Fe was based on smallholdings that enabled farmers to gain full title to their lands. The result, especially in central regions of the province, was a stable, well-rooted rural middle-class society similar in many ways to the Midwest of the United States. Similar middle-class pockets also emerged in Entre Rios

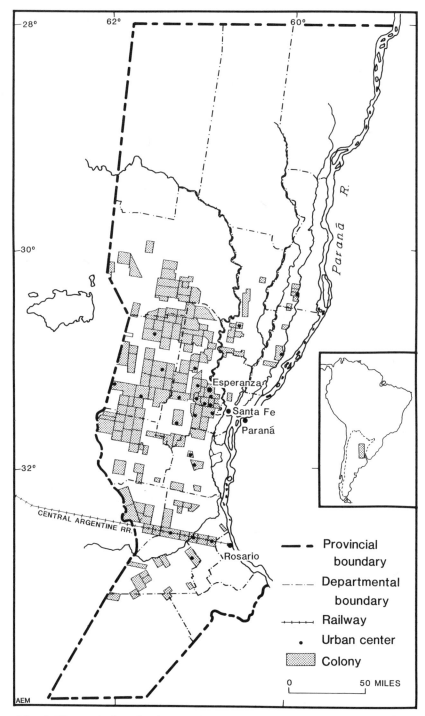

Map 6. The agricultural colonies of Santa Fe (circa 1890).

and Córdoba. They were much rarer, however, in the province of Buenos Aires, which by and large remained an area of sizable, undivided *estancias*. The failure of the colonization movement here reflected in part the traditional salience of extensive cattle ranching in the rural economy of Buenos Aires, the abundance of land, and shortages in labor and capital. Such conditions long promoted large-scale landholding and detained pressures toward subdivision. However, the spread and survival of *latifundismo* (large landholdings) also resulted from the continuation of the methods used by Rosas to alienate state land, and throughout the nineteenth century *tierra fiscal* in Buenos Aires was viewed not as an instrument of social pioneering but as a source of ready cash. In 1859, for example, the province sold off enormous lots to pay for the war against the Confederation and resume payments on the defaulted loan of 1824. It did the same in 1864 to back the currency conversion scheme and to support rail construction projects. In 1867 state lands in Buenos Aires were being sold at prices reportedly lower than those under Rosas thirty years before. In the early 1870s came another spate of land grants, like those in years past, to veterans from the war with Paraguay.[26]

The shortcomings of such practices were fully obvious to contemporaries. They flagrantly contradicted Alberdi's dictum, *gobernar es poblar*, which implied that planned American-style immigrant colonies were the key to economic progress and good governance. When Sarmiento assumed the presidency in 1868, he declared his intent of founding "a hundred Chivilcoys," referring to one of the few farming zones in the province of Buenos Aires. In the event, he produced none. Others made diligent, yet ineffective, efforts to halt the growth of the great estates through legislation. A land law enacted in 1871, for example, alienated four million hectares on condition that purchasers settle it with farmers, but the requirement was almost completely ignored and the government rarely reclaimed title. In late–nineteenth-century Buenos Aires land was first and foremost a commodity for speculation. Buyers would acquire land from the government in the largest lots possible and then await the coming of the railroad. The land appreciated rapidly once linked with the ports, and speculators reaped enormous profits.[27]

In the competition to buy land on the open market, the native speculator interests enjoyed a decisive advantage over immigrants: easy and abundant credit. The land credit system in effect from about 1870 onward gave the best terms to those offering land they already possessed as collateral for new purchases. A land mortgage bank

(*Banco Hipotecario*), founded in the province of Buenos Aires in 1872, provided interest-yielding bonds, or *cédulas*, rather than cash, to prospective land purchasers. Borrowers were allowed to draw up to half the value of their current real estate assets in *cédulas*, which they would then sell to raise cash. The market for *cédulas* in the 1880s was good, especially in Europe, mostly in Britain. The ease with which landowners could obtain *cédula* credit helped yield a profile of land prices that bore only a limited relationship to the actual revenues the land produced. As a result, land purchase was far beyond the means of most immigrant farmers, who had no land to offer as collateral and were therefore unable to acquire *cédula* credit. Although they could borrow cash from ordinary banks, these usually offered only short-term loans, of a type quite unsuitable for farmers, at considerably higher interest rates. Further, those farmers managing to obtain such credit usually incurred a heavy insurance premium against the high weather risks associated with agriculture.[28]

European immigrants to Argentina were thus welcomed as farmers, but found themselves increasingly enjoined from landownership. Except for railroad companies and consortia of foreign land developers, proprietorship was a privilege largely reserved to the speculators and the magnates whose ancestors had benefited from emphyteusis. In 1895 only about 8 percent of the immigrant population, which was approaching one million, were landowners. But those with access to mortgage credit were irresistibly tempted to acquire as much land as possible in the largest segments. Ideally, the land would be located close to a projected railway line, where values appreciated fastest, and the owner could embark on cattle ranching or sheep farming, or settle immigrant farmers as tenants or sharecroppers. As he did so, he became the beneficiary of the sometimes staggering rates of appreciation that followed the coming of the railroad. In the 1880s, for example, land values increased by as much as 1,000 percent in the province of Buenos Aires, 750 percent in Córdoba, and 370 percent in parts of Entre Rios. Landowners also received an income from livestock or tenants' rents, and they could immediately use their land as collateral to obtain more credit and more land. The most-prized land was that nearest the coast, where transportation costs to the ports were less and profits to the landowners greater.

Thus, outside relatively small pockets like central Santa Fe, the late nineteenth century witnessed the further consolidation of *latifundismo*. Although the country was undergoing profound change and development, and a new population was forming, no concomitant change occurred in the distribution of wealth nor in the power structure. In different parts of the country landowning and mercantile groups had slowly patched up their earlier differences, but the outcome of this accommodation was a society heavily biased toward oligarchy.[29]

Despite this bias, immigrants arrived in enormous droves: between 1871 and 1914 some 5.9 million newcomers, of whom 3.1 million stayed and settled. Altogether between 1830 and 1950 Argentina absorbed some 10 percent of the total number of emigrants from Europe to the Americas. About 80 percent of the immigrants to Argentina came from Mediterranean countries; half were Italians, a quarter Spaniards, the others Ottomans, Russians, French, and Portuguese. Immigration increased in tempo during the American Civil War as the United States became a less attractive destination, and as shipping rates to the River Plate fell in conjunction with the wool boom. Between 1880 and 1885 there were 200,000 arrivals; more than triple that number—670,000—arrived between 1885 and 1890 (see Table 5). Between the two national censuses of 1869 and 1895 the foreign-born population of the province of Buenos Aires increased from 19.8 percent to 30.8 percent, in Santa Fe from 15.6 to 41.9 percent, and in Córdoba from 0.8 to 10.1 percent.[30]

Immigrants were drawn to Argentina in part by deliberate government programs. In 1862 Congress authorized the contracting of immigrants for colonization ventures in the national territories, regions beyond the constituted provinces ruled from Buenos Aires. One fruit of this legislation was a small Welsh colony in Patagonia, in the territory of Chubut, founded in 1865. In 1869 an immigration bureau was established in Buenos Aires, the *Comisión Central de Inmigración,* and in 1876 the bureau inaugurated the practice of appointing agents in Europe to recruit settlers. Under other schemes new arrivals were given several days' free lodging in the port of Buenos Aires and exempted from duties on their tools and personal possessions. Later, as agriculture expanded, harvest workers from Europe received free rail transportation to different zones of the country.

But above all immigration was a response to economic incentives. The influx would slow or reverse itself in periods of depression; amid prosperity it would rapidly gather momentum. If eventually only a small proportion of the immigrants realized the dream of becoming landowners, opportunities on the land as shepherds, sharecroppers, tenants, or simple seasonal laborers, or in the cities as artisans and

TABLE 5. *Immigration, 1871–1890*

	Immigrants	Emigrants	Balances
1871	20,933	10,686	+ 10,247
1872	37,037	9,153	+ 27,884
1873	76,332	18,236	+ 58,096
1874	68,277	21,340	+ 46,937
1875	42,036	25,578	+ 16,458
1876	30,965	13,487	+ 17,478
1877	36,325	18,350	+ 17,975
1878	42,958	14,860	+ 28,098
1879	55,155	23,696	+ 31,459
1880	41,651	20,377	+ 21,274
1881	47,484	22,374	+ 25,110
1882	51,503	8,720	+ 42,783
1883	63,243	9,510	+ 53,733
1884	77,805	14,444	+ 63,361
1885	108,722	14,585	+ 94,137
1886	93,116	13,907	+ 79,209
1887	120,842	13,630	+107,212
1888	155,632	16,842	+138,790
1889	260,909	40,649	+220,260
1890	110,594	80,219	+ 30,375

SOURCE: Ernesto Tornquist and Co., *The Economic Development of Argentina in the last Fifty Years* (Buenos Aires, 1919), 15.

wage earners, were sufficient to sustain the inflow. Many early immigrants, the farmers of Santa Fe and the shepherds of Buenos Aires, achieved swift social mobility. But after 1870 immigration to Argentina was essentially a movement of proletarians and mostly a movement of men.[31]

Sheep, agriculture, and *gringos* transformed society in the pampas. Here, as in early modern England, where "the sheep ate the men," the spread of sheep farming drove the free *gauchos* to the far periphery where they rapidly disappeared as an identifiable social group. The growth of farming had much the same effect. Economic and social pressures of this kind underlay the revolt of "Tata Dios" in the Tandil area of Buenos Aires in 1870–1871, a movement that began as a religious revival among the native rural population and turned into a bloody assault against local immigrant settlers. Nativist reactions to immigration were not confined to the poorer segments of the creole population, nor always to the victims of social change. After 1870 members of the ruling classes became increasingly fearful of an immigrant revolution that might displace them from power. Toward the end of his life even Sarmiento turned against the immigrants, denouncing campaigns to simplify naturalization procedures. Yet throughout, the direct political influence of the immigrants was surprisingly small. They wanted cash rather than power, and in their fluid, mobile state they were notoriously slow to organize. Between 1850 and 1930 fewer than 5 percent of immigrants took Argentine citizenship, partly because as noncitizens they remained legally exempt from military service. Also, the native Argentines showed little interest in bringing the newcomers into the political system.[32]

With the coming of the immigrants, Bahía Blanca, Rosario, and eventually the new city of La Plata grew from villages into large towns. Meanwhile Buenos Aires and Córdoba grew faster than ever before, the former now developing such that soon after 1900 it became the largest city in Latin America. In 1854 the population of Buenos Aires was only 90,000; by 1869, with 41,000 Italians and 20,000 Spaniards in its midst, the population had increased to 177,000; and by 1895 it approached 670,000. Similarly, the proportion of the nation's total population that dwelt in Buenos Aires grew: from 12.5 percent in 1869, to almost 20 percent by 1895, and more than 25 percent by 1914. Throughout this period Buenos Aires upheld its historic role as the emporium of foreign trade. After 1860 it also emerged as the nodal point of the new railroad system, and by 1876 it possessed telegraph links with Europe. The city was the center of banking, insurance, and land transactions; the principal domicile of the great pampas landowners, who financed a succession of urban construction booms; and both the seat of government and the major beneficiary of central government spending.

As the city grew, its physiognomy rapidly changed. Formerly, the bulk of its population, rich and poor alike, was concentrated close to the site of the old colonial fort and the Plaza de Victoria, but by the 1860s conditions there were becoming congested and unhealthy. The city had a mortality rate of 42 per 1,000, double that of contemporary London, and in 1871 an epidemic of yellow fever claimed more than 7,000 victims. After the epidemic the rich began moving northward into the new neighborhoods of Barrio Norte, Palermo, and Belgrano. Meanwhile, the coming of the first tramways in the early 1870s spurred many of the poor southward into Barracas and the Boca, the latter the port for the coastal shipping trade. At the same time came a gradual westward movement of population toward the village of Flores, which by 1900 had become a residential zone of a burgeoning urban middle class employed in government, commerce, and banking. In the center of the city immigrant tenements were constructed, along with imposing public buildings and banks. The pace of change was fastest during the 1880s, when, in imitation of Haussmann's Paris, sections of the city were leveled and repaved to create four parallel avenues: Santa Fe, Córdoba, Corrientes, and the Avenida de Mayo, the last linking Government House and the new Hall of Congress a mile and a half westward.[33]

Labor for the construction of this new economy came mainly from the Mediterranean, but much of the capital was British. In the early 1860s Argentine bonds began being quoted on the London Stock Market, and between 1862 and 1873 total investment in British-owned companies in Argentina, including government loans, was estimated at £23 million. Following the depression of the mid 1870s, in 1880 the total rebounded to about £20 million. It then increased eightfold in the 1880s, to reach £157 million by 1890. In 1880 only a ninth of Britain's total investment throughout Latin America was vested in Argentina. A decade later the proportion was roughly one-third.[34]

Initially most British investment comprised direct government loans or flowed into ventures for which the government guaranteed a minimum-profit return, particularly the railroads. Before 1880 the Argentine government employed its loans primarily to serve the cause of unification, in ventures like the war in Paraguay and the campaigns against the *caudillos*. Foreign funds were also deployed in the construction of state-owned rail links with the interior, the chief of which ran to Tucumán and Mendoza from Córdoba; the state lines there fed into the private system of the littoral. The government undertook this construction when private capital revealed itself reluctant to venture beyond the pampas, and the state railroads often ran at a deficit. Emanating from the political settlement of 1862, they became another form of subsidy to the interior designed to foster commercial and political links with Buenos Aires.[35]

Private foreign investment flowed into banks and railways, and after 1880 into *cédula* land bonds. In 1863 the Bank of London and the River Plate was established with £1 million in capital. Specializing mainly in commercial and exchange dealings, the bank doubled its original capital in its first seven years of operation. Other British banking and insurance ventures followed, among them the River Plate Trust Company, which dealt mainly with ranchers and sheep farmers.[36]

The coming of British railroads to the pampas swiftly subverted traditional modes of transportation: ox carts had a maximum capacity of some two tons, freight trains hundreds and soon thousands; and the journey from Rosario to Córdoba that once took a month, was accomplished by railway in less than forty-eight hours. But the price of this revolution was the disappearance of a whole stratum of employment, which had thrived during the recent wool boom. Until this displaced mass was absorbed by ranching, agriculture, or urban occupations, the railroads—like sheep, wire-fencing, and immigrant farmers—were a subject of embittered controversy.

The first railroad in Argentina was the Western Railway (*Ferrocarril del Oeste*). Construction began in 1854, and eight years later the line extended some twenty-five miles from the city of Buenos Aires into the surrounding countryside, carrying fruit and grains into the city, and some wool for export. Initially a local private venture, the Western was acquired by the province of Buenos Aires in 1863 and remained under the province's control until 1890. Before 1890 local investment had an important role in the railways, with 45 percent of rail investments coming from domestic sources as late as 1885.

However, the second rail line, the Central Argentine Railway, was owned and in large part financed by the British. This was the venture sponsored by Mitre to link Rosario with Córdoba, the centerpiece of his efforts to attract support for the political settlement of 1862. The company began construction from Rosario in 1863, having received generous terms from the government in Buenos Aires: exemption from duties for its imported coal fuel, rolling stock, and other materials; a government-backed 7 percent minimum-profit guarantee; and a land grant one league in width on either side of the track, which it was encouraged to colonize with immigrant farmers. Later, in an effort to speed up construction, the government bought a substantial share in the company's stock. Having completed the Rosario-Córdoba link in 1870, the company embarked on a new line from Buenos Aires to Rosario. Although the Central was conceived to enhance communication with the interior, its major contribution lay in opening up the prairies of southern Santa Fe and eastern Córdoba to agriculture. Here it traversed almost virgin territory and had to populate the land before it could garner profits. As a result, during its first twenty years the company's earnings were relatively low, and for some time it was heavily dependent on its profit guarantee.[37]

In contrast, a second British railroad, the Buenos Aires Great Southern, which began service in 1864, owed relatively little to government sponsorship. It developed as a spontaneous venture among British merchants in Buenos Aires and Argentine landowners, the former serving as a nexus with private investors in Britain. Because the company serviced a region already settled, mainly by sheep farmers, profit was speedily forthcoming. By the late 1860s the Great Southern was already generating sufficient revenues to release it from reliance on its government profit guarantee, with subsequent returns on its ordinary shares climbing as high as 10 percent.[38]

Other British railroad companies followed these, for a total of seven by 1880. On the flat pampas, railways were easy and cheap to construct: track length tripled during the 1870s, and by 1880 some 1,600 miles were in operation, about half of which belonged to either the national or provincial authorities. In 1880 the railways carried 3.25 million passengers annually and an estimated 1 million tons of cargo. By now too the Argentine railroad system had acquired its characteristic fanlike shape, radiating out from the city of Buenos Aires.

After 1860 Argentina was enveloped by the dramas and conflicts that typified the rail era elsewhere in the world. The nation swarmed with entrepreneurs, contractors, and engineers, while in Buenos Aires pools of generously remunerated lawyers and legislators lobbied for concessions. Railroads underpinned the sometimes fabulous fortunes made from land, but resentments stirred as the railroads drove out the old ox carts and inflicted high monopoly rates on consumers. Only in the 1880s, when the major trunk lines had been completed and the companies brought to compete, did rates fall appreciably. Conflicts also arose between the railroad companies and landowners on issues like monetary policy. To avoid exchange losses on remittances, the companies wanted a gold-standard currency or at least a gold-based schedule of rates; the landed interests pressed continuously for gold-free paper money. Other clashes concerned the siting of new track. The companies preferred to construct in settled regions, where returns were swifter and surest, but the government and Congress, encouraged by speculators, favored a forward policy of expansion across the frontiers, leaving the settlers to follow. Throughout this period domestic groups charged repeatedly that the railways abused their franchises and privileges, that they bribed members of Congress to obtain concessions, and that they understated their profit margins to draw illicitly on government guarantees.[39]

During the late 1860s and early 1870s foreign investment also became a means for the government to disguise trade deficits (see Table 6), to import more than was being exported while covering the disparity with foreign borrowings. To justify the practice it was argued that much of the import excess comprised railroad materials, producer goods that would quickly yield larger exports and the resources to cancel out the indebtedness. Another habit adopted by governments from Mitre's onward was to pay interest and amortization charges on past debts by contracting new ones. In periods of prosperity, when export earnings grew rapidly, this refinancing worked, but it led to serious problems in times of depression.

The first of Argentina's great foreign investment crises erupted in the aftermath of the Franco-Prussian War (1870–1871). France's defeat and heavy reparations debt left the French market in disarray. From there came a decline in British exports and a payments deficit in Britain that the Bank of England sought to correct by increasing its discount rate. Simultaneously, a railroad boom in the United States collapsed. The outcome was financial panic, a universal flight of British funds back to London. In Argentina the cessation of new investment, and the swift outflow of old, immediately terminated the practice of settling past debts by arranging new ones; now the foreign debt had to be serviced from internal resources alone. The financial crisis in Europe was followed soon by an industrial depression, which provoked a collapse in demand for Argentine wool and hides. The sharp decline in Argentina's export earnings widened the payments gap and forced a parallel fall in imports (see Table 6).

The Argentine government soon found itself enmeshed in a severe debt crisis. While British investments were still fairly small, in recent years debt services had grown substantially as a portion of government revenues. Revenues, moreover, were closely tied to import duties, so that as imports fell revenues too slumped. At the same time the contraction in trade brought a decline in railroad earnings, which further increased the government's debt responsibilities under the profit-guarantee scheme. Between 1872 and 1874 revenues shrank from 20 million gold pesos to 13 million (see Table 7), and by 1875 the government was responsible for approximately 80 percent of the foreign debt; of this total 56 percent comprised state loans and 25 percent railroad profit guarantees.[40]

In its efforts to grapple with the situation the government severely curtailed its expenditures, withdrew its deposits from the Bank of the Province of Buenos Aires, and borrowed heavily from domestic banks. Both the depression and the government's attempts to cope

TABLE 6. *Foreign Trade and Balance-of-Trade Deficits, 1865–1875 (In millions of gold pesos)*

	Imports	Exports	Deficit
1865	30.2	26.1	4.1
1866	37.4	26.7	10.6
1867	38.7	33.1	5.5
1868	42.4	29.7	12.7
1869	41.9	32.4	8.7
1870	49.1	30.2	18.9
1871	45.6	26.9	18.6
1872	61.5	47.2	14.3
1873	73.4	47.3	26.0
1874	57.8	44.5	13.2
1875	57.6	52.0	5.6

SOURCE: José C. Chiaramonte, *Nacionalismo y liberalismo económico, 1860–1880* (Buenos Aires, 1971), 195.

with it immediately sent severe shock waves through the economy and the political system. Unemployment rose, incomes and consumption fell, and land prices collapsed. The withdrawal of government funds from the provincial bank reduced the bank's reserves, leaving insufficient capital for loans to private borrowers. A spate of bankruptcies and foreclosures among landowners followed. This severe economic disruption formed the background for the political struggle of 1874; Mitre, the candidate of the landed and commercial debtor classes in Buenos Aires, was for many the only hope of financial salvation. When he failed to win the election, pressure from his commercial constituency helped impel him to rebellion.

Some of the political backlash from the depression was also directed against the British. In Santa Fe the depression had forced several local mortgage banks into liquidation, and in 1876 provincial government supported the local landowners' campaign to force the local branch of the London and River Plate Bank into easing its restrictions on discounts. When it refused, its manager was imprisoned and the bank forcibly closed. The British government retaliated by sending a gunboat to Rosario. But this armed pressure proved ineffective, and the British then turned to the authorities in Buenos Aires. A recent arrangement between the Argentine government and British railroad interests had enabled the former to win postponement on the

TABLE 7. *National Revenues and Expenditures, 1873–1880 (In millions of gold pesos)*

	Revenues	Expenditures
1873	20.2	31.0
1874	15.9	29.7
1875	17.2	28.5
1876	13.5	22.1
1877	14.8	19.9
1878	18.4	20.8
1879	20.9	22.5
1880	19.5	26.9

SOURCE: Ernesto Tornquist and Co. *The Economic Development of Argentina in the Last Fifty Years* (Buenos Aires, 1919), 276.

payment of a profit guarantee to the Central Argentine Railway. The British now threatened to abrogate this agreement unless the government of Santa Fe abandoned its campaign on the bank. The Argentine government was forced to concede, for the loss of the guarantee deferment would so exacerbate its difficulties in servicing the foreign debt as to perhaps necessitate open default, a step likely to impair permanently Argentina's reputation in London and preclude any future loans. Thus the government intervened with a promise to Santa Fe of future financial assistance if it let the bank reopen. After further negotiation the offer was accepted, and the dispute ended, but not without illustrating the influence the British had come to command in Argentina. Although they could do little by force, they had secured great power in their guise as the government's creditor.[41]

The depression also provoked a lengthy debate on the issues of protectionism and economic diversification. Protectionists of earlier generations had been concerned largely with the defense of archaic economic forms like native textiles. By the 1870s the focus centered on the new economy and means of strengthening it. Discussions were prolonged, often sophisticated and in some quarters acquired an unusually modern ring, anticipating twentieth-century nationalist and anti-imperialist ideas. During a congressional debate on the tariff in 1877 three separate schools of opinion emerged. Supporters of protection, led by Vicente F. López, criticized the country's heavy reliance on funds and investment from Britain, contending that it would inevitably produce repeated foreign-debt crises. They also attacked Argentina's dependence on a small range of pastoral exports, which left it vulnerable to the vagaries of the world market. In arguing for plans to diversify the economy, López invoked protectionist and nationalist doctrines current in Germany and the United States. He wanted protection to foster "infant industries"; free trade, he declared, was a conspiracy of the strong nations to dominate the weak. López held out Potosí, now only a husk of its former self, as a portent of the country's eventual fate if it remained a purely primary producer.

A second group, whose most prominent member was Carlos Pellegrini, also favored protection, but more moderately and less ambitiously. In Pellegrini's view protection was justified only to promote goods that would quickly become competitive with imports. Because Argentina's natural resources, particularly coal and iron ore, were limited, Pellegrini urged protection only for such goods for which raw materials were potentially cheap and abundant, mostly agricultural or pastoral products. Efficiency and the protection of consumers against exploitative domestic monopolies, he maintained, made it desirable to continue importing most manufactured goods; diversification should proceed only within the prevailing agrarian framework. Lastly, a strong orthodox free-trade lobby also surfaced during the debate. It opposed any kind of deliberate protection and wanted tariffs limited to their traditional role as a source of state revenues. It argued against protection on the grounds that such measures would encourage contraband and increase the cost of living.[42]

The argument continued for several years in Congress and the press. López's program was soon forgotten, as the country plunged into another export boom, and the outcome of the debate rested in a policy that fell between that advocated by Pellegrini and orthodox free trade. Although most changes in tariffs were enacted solely to raise revenue, the tariff law of 1877 did grant protection to two important new products, and soon after a third. The first was flour, for the country was now fully self-sufficient in wheat, and second was sugar, with protection conferred as the state railroads reached Tucumán. Two years later, as the rail link reached the city of Mercedes in San Luis, the same concession was made to the vintners of Mendoza and San Juan.

Flour, sugar, and wine were thus the only "infant industries" the legislators of the late 1870s saw fit to support through protection; they completely ignored manufacturing. Nevertheless their measures served to benefit Tucumán and Mendoza, whose relatively late development made them the last of the major beneficiaries of the political and economic order established after 1860.

Sugar had been cultivated in the northwest during the days of *encomienda* but, like almost every other agricultural activity at that time, was soon abandoned. Cultivation revived in the late seventeenth century under the Jesuits, but then again disappeared after their expulsion. A second revival began in Tucumán soon after independence, developing into an appreciable commerce in sugar between Tucumán and Buenos Aires during the French blockade of the late 1830s. The industry began fully establishing itself in the 1860s, when a diverse group of local entrepreneurs—descendants of colonial mercantile families, political refugees from Salta and Catamarca, and a sprinkling of French and British immigrants—began to import milling machinery from Europe and set up sugar refineries known as *ingenios*. At first the *ingenios* were little different from traditional *haciendas*, from which in fact most evolved. They were largely self-sufficient entities dealing primarily in local markets, and besides sugar, they produced hides, cereals, and flour.[43]

The number of *ingenios* grew rapidly until the depression of the mid 1870s, when shortages of capital and credit induced sudden contraction and concentration, resulting in a smaller number of larger and stronger units. The depreciation of the peso during the depression, however, also increased the competitiveness of domestic sugar against imports. The coming of the railroad in 1876, which brought a massive fall in freight rates between Tucumán and Buenos Aires, and tariff protection granted the *ingenios* the following year, effected a rapid spurt in sugar production. In 1870 sugar production was around 1,000 tons; it had tripled by 1876, tripled again by 1880, and increased from 9,000 tons in 1880 to 41,000 tons in 1889, at which time local producers were supplying about 60 percent of domestic needs. Meanwhile, the land area employed for sugar, which also included small pockets in Jujuy, multiplied from 1,700 hectares in 1872 to 40,000 in 1895.[44]

Sugar production came to take over land once occupied by subsistence peasants: in 1874 maize and wheat accounted for 73 percent of the cultivated area of Tucumán; by 1895 the proportion had fallen to 36 percent. As sugar monoculture spread, part of the shortfall in staple foods was remedied by mobilizing supplies from surrounding provinces, flour from Catamarca, corn from Salta and Santiago del Estero. In this way the surrounding provinces were gradually transformed into satellites of the sugar economy. Furthermore, Tucumán's relatively dense peasant population could not supply sufficient labor for cane cutting, and the low wages and poor housing conditions made it impossible to attract and retain Europeans in the region. Thus in the 1880s a contract labor system was devised to recruit seasonal workers from surrounding regions and eventually, as the rail links penetrated northward, to bring in harvesters from Bolivia and the Chaco. The outcome was a society very different from that taking shape in the pampas, where the wage system was becoming universal. Tucumán instead developed a neoseigneurial system based on modified forms of traditional debt peonage.[45]

The growth of Mendoza wines paralleled sugar's course. In the early 1860s French and Italian immigrants began to arrive and to create new small holdings around the city of Mendoza, taking over land previously devoted to alfalfa and fattening cattle for export to Chile. Tariff protection and the coming of the railroad, which reached Mendoza from Mercedes in 1885, greatly benefited the new wine economy, as did an interventionist provincial government, which created local banks, instituted tax exemptions for farmers, organized irrigation schemes, and laid down roads between the vineyards and the railheads. As in Tucumán, seasonal contract labor was used, for grape picking, but Mendoza managed to attract and retain European immigrants and thus largely avoided the acute social disparities of Tucumán. The distinctive feature of society in Mendoza was the emergence of a rural and urban middle class, smaller but essentially similar in character to that in central Santa Fe.[46]

BOOM AND COLLAPSE, 1880–1890

Argentina lifted itself from the depression of the 1870s by simply increasing the production of exportables. Throughout the depression the railroad system had continued to grow on the strength of concessions made before 1873. As it did so, it opened up new land for shepherds and farmers. In the late 1870s exports of cereals began, and thereafter increased rapidly. With the advent of steam-powered shipping, ocean freight rates in 1886 were half those of 1877. Also, the depreciation of the paper peso during the depression cheapened Argentine goods against competitors in North America and Australia, and lowered costs of production relative to export prices. As a result, although markets for a time remained weak, exporters could still profit, and the more they produced, the higher their returns. Occupation and colonization of virgin land in the pampas thus proceeded rapidly. As exports grew, imports followed suit; revenues then recovered, the foreign-debt crisis receded, and the government's demands on the banks dwindled; interest rates fell, and credit flowed more freely. As current government spending advanced, the domestic economy revived and employment rose.

Conditions in Europe were also improving such that by 1880 Argentina faced a new era of opportunity. Having avoided default on the foreign debt, the nation enjoyed an untarnished reputation in the eyes of the British merchant banking houses. As foreign markets expanded once more, Argentina expected another generous slice of Britain's capital surplus, which would finance more railroads and the construction of a deep-water port in Buenos Aires. The stage was set for another period of expansion, a renewed influx of immigrants, and the attenuation of recent political conflict.

Indeed, the achievements of the 1880s dwarfed those of any preceding decade. In these ten years the nation's population increased from 2.4 million to 3.4 million; the population of the city of Buenos Aires almost doubled, from 286,000 in 1880 to 526,000 in 1890. As the city grew, British companies built tramways and created gas and electricity services. Buenos Aires now acquired its avenues, many of its great mansions, and a modern sewage system that dispelled the threat of new epidemics of yellow fever. During the 1870s the net addition to the population through immigration was 250,000; in the 1880s it was 850,000, with immigrants outnumbering emigrants by 220,000 in 1889 alone. Shipping using Argentine ports climbed from 2.1 million tons in 1880 to 7.7 million tons in 1889. Between 1881 and 1889 export earnings increased from 58 million gold pesos to 123 million, and imports climbed from 56 million gold pesos to 165 million, an increase from 18 pesos per capita to 50. In 1881 Argentina received foreign loans totaling 56 million gold pesos; in 1889 the total was 154 million. Throughout the 1880s foreign investment grew by almost 800 million gold pesos; investments in railroads alone climbed from 63 million gold pesos to almost 380 million, and the railroad track length increased from 1,570 miles in 1880, to 2,790 miles in 1885, and to 5,850 miles by 1890.[47]

In the 1880s the inflow of British investment was accompanied by marked expansion of trade with Britain (see Table 8). In 1880 Britain provided 28 percent of Argentina's imports; by 1889 the proportion was 41 percent. Throughout the decade imports from Britain, the

TABLE 8. *Argentine Trade with Britain,*
1870–1889 (Quinquennial averages in millions
£ sterling)

	Imports	Exports
1870–1874	1.85	3.11
1875–1879	1.33	2.08
1880–1884	0.96	2.06
1885–1889	2.03	6.88

SOURCE: H. S. Ferns, *Britain and Argentina in the Nineteenth Century* (Oxford, 1960), 492–93.

largest of them now coal and railroad materials, doubled. In 1880 Argentina's main export market was Belgium, which took much of its wool, with the British share only 9.2 percent; by 1887 it had grown to 20.3 percent.[48]

At the end of the nineteenth century Argentina's greatest asset was its vast reserve of prime land. But much of the land was still the domain of wild Indians, who from time to time launched invasions on the *estancias* and pampas villages. One such Indian attack in 1876 penetrated to within 60 leagues of Buenos Aires, departing afterward with a reported 300,000 cattle and 500 white captives. Throughout the 1870s conditions on the frontier became the subject of almost incessant debate in Buenos Aires. A second but growing concern was that Chile had begun to lay claim to parts of Patagonia, still almost completely unoccupied by Argentina. Finally in 1879, after several trial runs during the previous seven years, General Julio A. Roca led a military expedition across the southern frontiers and in one sweep accomplished the "conquest of the wilderness" (*la conquista del desierto*). Under his command five columns departed from Buenos Aires, Córdoba, San Luis, and Mendoza to converge on the Rio Negro. Along the way they subdued, drove out, or exterminated the scattered Tehuelche and Araucanian tribes in the region, stopping at last their depredations against the southern *estancias* and opening land access to Patagonia. After Roca's campaign the southern passes into Chile were garrisoned and closed, and the surviving Indians driven onto reservations. Like many of its forerunners, this military venture was financed by prior land sales, with as much as 8.5 million hectares passing into the hands of 381 persons.[49]

To reward Roca for his exploit the PAN nominated him to succeed Avellaneda as president. The candidate was a formidable figure: like

Avellaneda, his family background was in Tucumán. In his youth Roca had fought with Urquiza at Cepeda and Pavón. Later he was prominent in the struggles against Peñaloza and Varela, and in the war against Paraguay. In 1874 he helped suppress uprisings in the provinces supporting Mitre's rebellion in Buenos Aires. He then began creating a personal power base in the western provinces such that by the late 1870s he had become a master of contemporary politics, astute in the arts of compromise and coalition making. In 1877 he was appointed minister of war, a position that put him in command of the wilderness campaign. With the support of Avellaneda and the PAN he emerged an easy victor in the presidential election of 1880, a triumph that was completed by his defeating the Tejedor rebellion.[50]

This military victory and a favorable economic outlook afforded Roca a much stronger position than any of his predecessors. On assuming the presidency he pledged himself to "peace and administration"—firm government that would grant priority to economic expansion. Like other Latin American positivists of his generation, Roca stressed material progress and offered grandiose visions of the country's future in the wake of material accomplishments. During his tenure as president Roca ruled from Buenos Aires through the PAN, which now functioned as a network of alliances between the president and a "league of governors." Roca sustained the *situaciones* (ruling provincial cliques) by subsidies and patronage, while controlling dissidents through managed elections and federal interventions. For their part the provincial governors were required to endorse the president and send representatives to Congress who would be obedient to his will.

The federalization of Buenos Aires in 1880 was followed by the establishment of state elementary education in the capital. This measure and one permitting civil marriage led to conflicts with the Church, the expulsion of the papal nuncio, and ultimately the rupture of diplomatic relations with the Vatican. In the city of Buenos Aires Roca also established a new municipal government and federal law courts. Other laws formalized administration in the national territories of the far south and the far north, creating the jurisdictions of La Pampa, Neuquén, Rio Negro, Chubut, Santa Cruz, and Tierra del Fuego in the south and southwest, and in the north Misiones, Formosa, Chaco, and Los Andes (see Map 7). These laws also fixed the boundaries between the provinces of Buenos Aires, Córdoba, San Luis, and Mendoza, and thereby prevented Buenos Aires from fulfilling a long-cherished ambition to absorb Patagonia.[51]

After a relatively trouble-free term, in 1886 Roca was succeeded by

Map 7. Provinces and national territories, early twentieth century.

his kinsman, Miguel Juárez Celman, a native of Córdoba and in recent years governor of the province. Most observers expected Juárez Celman's administration to be a continuation of Roca's, with the retired president commanding power behind the scenes. However, in a display of independence the new president usurped control of the PAN and then erected a system more authoritarian than Roca's, which his enemies dubbed the *unicato* (one-man rule). He then initiated a new, energetic, and highly successful bid for foreign investment: between 1886 and 1890 foreign investment totaled 668 million gold pesos, compared to 150 million gold pesos between 1880 and 1885. But the result of this program was the crisis of 1890, when the country again tottered at the brink of bankruptcy and revolution.[52]

Juárez Celman's regime was dominated even more so than its predecessors by land speculators who sought to open new land at the fastest possible rate. Many were from Córdoba, the president's native province, a region as yet relatively unaffected by the coming of the railroad and the appreciation of land values. In 1881 Roca's government had returned to the gold standard, which after being introduced in the 1860s had been abandoned in 1876 during the depression. The chief purpose of the measure was to satisfy foreign investors, who demanded gold earnings to preclude losses on exchange. In 1885 a brief recession reduced gold reserves, and the government again suspended convertibility. Although Juárez Celman took office when recovery was underway and the reserves climbing, he did not restore the gold standard. Instead, his government made large issues of paper money, a deliberately inflationary policy adopted largely under pressure from speculators, who profited from being paid in gold and settling debts in depreciating paper. Speculators' interests were further served by the government's new railroad program, under which more rail concessions were granted between 1886 and 1890 than throughout the past thirty years. To protect investors from domestic inflation, almost all the new ventures received gold-backed government minimum-profit guarantees. Meanwhile, as economic expansion bid up land prices and landowners' collateral, vast quantities of *cédula* land bonds were issued by an array of new mortgage banks.[53]

These banks, most of them in the provinces, were also the chief source of new paper-money issues after 1886, issues which trebled the amount of paper money in circulation and accelerated its depreciation against gold—the gold premium—to a rate of 94 percent by 1889. In 1887 Congress passed legislation, a "law of guaranteed banks," whose declared objective was to reduce the foreign debt. It gave local banks the right to issue paper currency in exchange for an equal sum of gold deposited with the National Bank in Buenos Aires, which would then be employed to settle accounts with foreign creditors. But instead of depositing local gold, many provincial banks borrowed gold from abroad, with the result that by 1890 the provincial banks and provincial governments, which were also heavy borrowers, held some 35 percent of Argentina's foreign debt. The banking law thus expanded, rather than reduced, the nation's external indebtedness.

Furthermore, the provincial banks' issues of paper money often exceeded their gold deposits. The worst culprit was the Bank of Córdoba, which issued 33 million paper pesos against deposits of 8 million gold pesos, disbursing the paper at discount to some two hundred local politicians and landowners. In sum, in a five-year period, new borrowings by the government in Buenos Aires, new railway profit guarantees, and foreign loans to the provincial banks and provincial administrations almost tripled the annual cost of servicing the foreign debt. The annual debt service rose from 23 million gold pesos in 1885 to 60 million in 1890—this latter figure equal to 60 percent of the year's total export earnings. Except for *cédulas*, most such debts were fixed-interest securities payable in gold. Until the new railroads were fully operative and the lands they opened up settled, the government could not expect to keep pace with the mushrooming foreign debt; it simply gambled that foreign investment would continue, enabling the repayment of older loans by new ones. Moreover, since the abandonment of the gold standard in 1885, government revenues from imports were collected in paper pesos. Thus while gold debts increased and the gold premium rose, revenues fell.[54]

The inevitable crisis erupted in late 1889, when Baring Brothers of London, which in recent years had again been prominent in funneling British funds to Argentina, failed to attract subscribers for a loan it had underwritten to reorganize the water supply in Buenos Aires. The failure of the loan triggered panic; new British investment ceased abruptly; and although Argentina's exports increased appreciably in 1890, their prices declined and export earnings fell by some 25 percent. The government found itself trapped, as the growing payments deficit, resulting from the cessation of new investment and lower export earnings, produced a larger outflow of gold and an upward leap in the gold premium. Simultaneously, revenues from imports, collected in paper, shrank and revenues slipped still further. In a desperate effort to cope with the foreign debt, the government tried to buy gold on the open market. But this strategy only drove up the gold premium still further: the more paper pesos the government sought to sell, the less gold it obtained. Next, it introduced gold-based tariff duties, but these duties merely depressed already-declining imports, yielding no gain in net revenues. Then the government resorted to disposing of its assets, selling a state railroad, the *Central Norte*, to a British business group; the province of Buenos Aires did the same, and in 1890 the Western Railway also passed into British hands. However, both sales stipulated government gold-backed minimum-profit guarantees, so that the transactions did little more than convert one liability into another. When even these measures proved insufficient, in mid 1890 the government lurched toward default on the foreign debt.[55]

Meanwhile, the provincial banks continued to issue still more paper money, sometimes secretly at the behest of speculator interests. The faster the gold premium rose, the better speculators could shield themselves from falling export earnings. The rising gold premium, however, was accompanied by a commercial depression stemming from financial crisis in Britain: as a result, unemployment grew and real wages in Buenos Aires fell by around 50 percent. The net gain of 220,000 immigrants in 1889 was replaced by a gain of only 30,000 in 1890, and a net loss of 30,000 in 1891. Throughout 1890 thousands of new immigrants were stranded in Buenos Aires unemployed, often homeless, and financially unable to seek refuge in Europe. There was severe distress among importers and artisans, and public employees were dismissed in droves as the government began curtailing expenditures. Between 1889 and 1893 wool prices halved, while many unwitting landowners were caught by the 50 percent slide in land prices between April 1889 and April 1890.[56]

The first organized opposition to Juárez Celman began in mid 1889 among university students who christened their movement the Youth Civic Union (*Unión Cívica de la Juventud*). Early the following year this group developed into a broad coalition of the government's opponents, including Bartolomé Mitre and his following of mercantile and landed groups in Buenos Aires. The coalition also attracted Catholic groups, hostile toward both Roca and Juárez Celman since the introduction of civil marriage and educational reforms in the early 1880s, and an incipient popular and democratic group in Buenos Aires led by Leandro N. Alem and Aristóbalo del Valle, both veterans of metropolitan politics. In April 1890 a protest staged by the coalition, which now called itself simply the Civic Union, was attended by some 30,000 demonstrators. Mitre soon began enlisting military support for the coalition, which in July 1890 launched a full-blooded revolt against the government.

The *Revolución del Noventa* was the outcome of several years of breakneck economic expansion whose climax was financial and commercial collapse. If the movement expressed the depth of antagonism toward Juárez Celman in Buenos Aires, rekindling the earlier tradition of interregional conflict, it also revealed a deeply divided opposition, whose factions aspired to contradictory objectives—a foretaste of the political issues that were to dominate Argentina's future. Although the Civic Union had rallied support by demanding political reform and crusading for popular democracy, only Alem's group was serious in this quest. The Catholics were essentially concerned with the annulment of anticlerical legislation, while Mitre wanted a second term as president, and the groups backing him demanded the preferential economic relief measures they had sought in 1874. To achieve power the latter were prepared to pay lip service to popular democracy, but they had little intention of implementing it.

Before the July rebellion Mitre engaged in a secret negotiation with Roca, from with the following deal emerged: Roca agreed to support the overthrow of Juárez Celman, and Mitre conceded that his immediate successor would be the incumbent vice-president, Carlos Pellegrini, one of Roca's men; Roca would then endorse Mitre in the forthcoming presidential election of 1892. To realize this plan, they needed to stall the rebellion, above all to keep Alem in check. Thus when Alem led a hastily assembled popular militia against the government's forces, Mitre's army, led by General Manuel Campos, made a suspiciously inept effort to press home the challenge. While Campos dallied, the rebels were defeated. But the insurrection proved the end for Juárez Celman, who resigned a few days later. And Pellegrini stepped into his place.[57]

The debacle under Juárez Celman showed the extent to which Argentina had been drawn into the international economy, and the price an indiscriminate drive for prosperity could exact. Unitarism, or Liberalism as it was now known, had finally predominated, with the Liberals having used war to establish a national state and then leading the country into breakneck economic expansion. Change in the late nineteenth century was revolutionary in scope but had several important limitations: landownership remained highly concentrated, political power remained undemocratic, and economic change was largely confined to the farm sector.

In Buenos Aires especially, attempts to change land tenure failed to surmount opposition from native landed interests, whose power enabled them to nullify or vitiate most homestead and colonization schemes. Their power also enabled them to bias in their own favor the new market or credit mechanisms through which land was bought and sold. The metropolitan landed interests also protected themselves through their powers of political veto, as events in 1874 and to an extent those in 1890 illustrated. If the government refused to accommodate the landed interests of Buenos Aires, it risked rebellion and the destabilizing of the new national order. Liberalism had proclaimed a commitment to expunge monopoly; yet monopoly survived, sometimes in new guises, alongside agrarian capitalism.

An important consequence of the unevenness of socioeconomic change was a weak rural middle class and a disproportionately large urban middle class. Immigrants were attracted to the pampas by opportunities for wealth and social mobility, and many achieved such objectives. Yet, by comparison with their counterparts in North America and other English-speaking colonial regions—regions in which state power more forcefully equalized access to land—immigrant farmers in Argentina were an unstable and politically passive group; for example, the renewed pressure for political change in 1890 emanated not from rural society but from the city of Buenos Aires and other large cities. The urban reform movement lacked both an agrarian and an industrial program, emphasizing issues of distribution rather than structural reform. The movement thus instigated change and a measure of redistribution, but within a lingering colonial structure.

V

FOUR SEASONS OF DEMOCRACY, 1890-1930

The late nineteenth and early twentieth centuries again witnessed advance unparalleled in Argentina's history. The long cycle of expansion and national consolidation that began with the political settlement of 1862 reached its apogee around 1914. Once one of the world's emptiest backwaters, Argentina was now among its most prosperous countries. Yet amid prosperity was striking ambiguity. Throughout this period Argentina remained a producer of food and raw materials; it lived from the pampas, still failing to diversify substantially into manufacturing. By 1914 and again in 1930 disparities between the littoral and the interior became more pronounced. The east was the center of investment and consumption, and its heart, the city of Buenos Aires, an embodiment of advanced civilization. Much of the area beyond still exemplified the most backward parts of Latin America: rambling *haciendas,* an impoverished Indian or mestizo peasantry, feeble towns, inertia, and stagnation.

Among the chief features of the period between the two great depressions of 1890 and 1930 was the nation's failure to achieve political development that matched its social and economic change. Argentina was among the leaders in Latin America in adopting representative democracy, at a time when politics was also increasingly overshadowed by new class-based conflicts. After 1890 a new ruling party emerged, the *Unión Cívica Radical,* whose leader, Hipólito Yrigoyen, dominated his period much as Rosas, Mitre, or Roca had earlier done. In 1916 Yrigoyen won the presidency after the first national elections under universal male suffrage; two years into his second term he was ejected by the military coup d'etat of September 1930. With Yrigoyen's demise, prospects of a stable democratic order perished.

After the Baring crash of 1890, the investment links between Argentina and Great Britain were successfully rekindled, and immediately before World War I Argentina and Britain were closer than ever. But after the war the tie failed to further develop and showed signs of obsolescence. The waning of the British link was a harbinger of crisis; by the late 1920s, despite its outward air of prosperity, Argentina faced an uncertain future.

THE GREAT STEP FORWARD, 1890–1913

The 1890s began in the depths of depression. Several grueling and lean years followed the fall of Juárez Celman in August 1890, as the struggle continued to avoid default on the foreign debt. In January 1891 Pellegrini negotiated a debt moratorium with Baring Brothers. But the depression continued to intensify, the gold premium climbing from an average of 151 percent in 1890 to 287 percent the following year. After a brief improvement in 1892, the next year's wheat harvest failed and export earnings, still affected by low world prices, plummeted sharply. The Argentine government was forced to renegotiate the foreign debt once again in 1893. With the Romero Deal (*Arreglo Romero*), named after its author, the Argentine minister of finance, many interest charges were deferred until 1898, and amortization repayments delayed until 1901. At this time the national government assumed many of the debts the provinces had contracted during the past decade. In return, the provinces were obliged to surrender control over certain local revenues and taxes. The depression thus enhanced the concentration of power in Buenos Aires.[1]

Severe as it was, the depression eventually abated. In the 1890s Argentina still possessed an enormous land reserve in the pampas; once more progress lay in opening up the frontier and increasing production. Again a high gold premium proved to have advantages: domestic costs fell faster than world prices, fostering opportunities for profit and incentives to produce. Recovery was also assisted by railway construction undertaken at the height of the depression, contracted and financed before it. Between 1890 and 1892 railroad track was extended by more than 25 percent, and the cultivated area increased with it, from 2.4 million hectares in 1888 to almost 4.9 million hectares in 1895. The decade was thus a partial vindication of Juárez Celman, whose error had been simply to attempt too much too quickly.

Economic recovery was led by agriculture, particularly wheat. In the 1880s annual wheat exports were less than 250,000 tons, but by 1894 they climbed to 1.6 million tons (see Table 9). With the construction of new railroads and grain elevators in Rosario, wheat farming now spread so rapidly in southern Santa Fe that between 1887 and 1897 the province's wheat acreage tripled. Wheat farming was also

TABLE 9. *Wheat Production and Exports, 1892–1914*

	Area Sown to Wheat (1,000 hectares)	Production (1,000 metric tons)	Exports (1,000 metric tons)
1892	1,320	980.0	470.1
1893	1,600	1,593.0	1,008.2
1894	1,840	2,238.0	1,608.3
1895	2,000	1,670.0	1,010.3
1896	2,260	1,263.0	532.0
1897	2,500	860.0	101.8
1898	2,600	1,453.0	645.2
1899	3,200	2,857.1	1,713.4
1900	3,250	2,766.6	1,929.7
1901	3,380	2,034.4	904.3
1902	3,296	1,534.4	644.9
1903	3,695	2,823.8	1,681.3
1904	4,320	3,529.1	2,304.7
1905	4,903	4,102.6	2,868.3
1906	5,675	3,672.2	2,248.0
1907	5,692	4,245.4	2,680.8
1908	5,760	5,238.7	3,636.3
1909	6,063	4,250.1	2,514.1
1910	5,837	3,565.6	1,883.6
1911	6,253	3,973.0	2,286.0
1912	6,897	4,523.0	2,629.1
1913	6,918	5,100.0	2,812.1
1914	6,573	2,850.1	980.5

SOURCE: Ernesto Tornquist and Co., *The Economic Development of Argentina in the last Fifty Years* (Buenos Aires, 1919), 28.

extended into the western and southern parts of the province of Buenos Aires, into eastern Córdoba, and into the territory of La Pampa. With expansion in the south, growth in the port of Bahía Blanca rivaled Rosario's. By 1904, less than thirty years since Argentina had imported wheat, wheat had surpassed wool to become the country's largest export.[2]

By 1896 the last traces of the depression were gone. Between 1895 and 1900 export prices were around 25 percent higher than the average for 1890–1895. The country now resumed its forward march at an accelerating pace. As prosperity returned, the government was able to make payments on the foreign debt before the date specified by the 1893 agreement. The peso began to appreciate, with the gold premium declining from an average of 257 percent in 1894 to 125 percent in 1899. As the gold premium fell, however, exporters were confronted with rising internal production costs, and they pressured the government to return to the gold standard in 1899. In addition to containing production costs, this return signaled a new commitment to financial stability and the extrication of finances from government interference. Currency issues were henceforth automatically to follow fluctuations in gold reserves and the balance of payments. A conversion board was established to release or withdraw paper money at the fixed ratio of 0.44 gold pesos per paper peso, an arrangement that persisted essentially unchanged until 1914.[3]

Except for two brief recessions in 1899 and 1907, after 1895 each of the major sectors of the economy experienced swift, uniform expansion. The gross national product increased by roughly 6 percent a year, as it had in the 1880s. Farmland in use increased from under 5 million hectares in 1895 to 24 million hectares in 1914. The wheat acreage tripled during this period, a sixfold increase by comparison with 1888. Corn acreage quadrupled and linseed quintupled.[4]

Between the second national census of 1895 and the third of 1914 population rose from 3.9 million to 7.8 million. Specifically, the city of Buenos Aires grew from 660,000 to more than 1.5 million inhabitants, the province of Buenos Aires from 900,000 to a little over 2 million, Santa Fe from 400,000 to almost 900,000, and Córdoba from 350,000 to 735,000. Again growth was much less rapid in the interior, and negligible in some parts. Between 1895 and 1914 La Rioja's population, for example, increased from only 79,000 to 83,000, and Jujuy's from 76,000 to 80,000.[5]

Population growth was due in part to a rising birthrate and a falling death rate, and as such indicates improved living standards.

Argentina also witnessed a renewed and still more massive wave of immigration from southern Europe. During the 1890s net annual immigration was about 50,000, less than half the immediate predepression rate in 1887. But immigration soon regained its momentum, which peaked in 1904. For the next ten years the annual balance of immigrants over emigrants exceeded 100,000 (see Table 10). By 1914 around one-third of the country's population was foreign-born, and around 80 percent of the population comprised immigrants and those descended from immigrants since 1850. Almost 1 million Italians and more than 800,000 Spaniards lived in Argentina. There were also

TABLE 10. *Immigration, 1891–1914*

	Immigrants	Emigrants	Balance
1891	52,097	81,932	− 20,835
1892	73,294	43,853	+ 29,441
1893	84,420	48,794	+ 35,626
1894	80,671	41,399	+ 39,272
1895	80,989	36,820	+ 44,169
1896	135,205	45,921	+ 89,284
1897	105,143	57,457	+ 47,686
1898	95,190	53,536	+ 41,654
1899	111,083	62,241	+ 48,842
1900	105,901	55,417	+ 50,485
1901	125,951	80,251	+ 45,700
1902	96,080	79,427	+ 16,653
1903	112,671	74,776	+ 37,895
1904	161,078	66,597	+ 94,481
1905	221,622	82,772	+138,850
1906	302,249	103,852	+198,397
1907	257,924	138,063	+119,861
1908	303,112	127,032	+176,080
1909	278,148	137,508	+140,640
1910	345,275	136,405	+208,870
1911	281,622	172,041	+109,581
1912	379,117	172,996	+206,121
1913	364,878	219,519	+145,359
1914	182,672	243,701	− 61,029

SOURCE: Ernesto Tornquist and Co., *The Economic Development of Argentina in the last Fifty Years* (Buenos Aires, 1919), 15.

some 94,000 Russians and Poles, 86,000 French, and almost 80,000 Ottoman Turks, including Lebanese and Syrians.

During the wheat boom of the early 1890s many immigrants settled in the pampas; but soon after, the trend of the late 1880s resumed as the majority settled in the cities. Between 1895 and 1914 the rural population increased from 2.3 million to 3.3 million, but the urban from 1.6 million to 4.6 million. In 1914 in Buenos Aires, Rosario, and Bahía Blanca alike foreign-born men substantially outnumbered native men. In the province of Buenos Aires foreigners, males and females together, constituted roughly a third of the population; in Santa Fe, three-fifths; and about a quarter in Córdoba. Outside the littoral, in contrast, in 1914 foreigners comprised only 10 percent of the population of San Luis and Tucumán; elsewhere, except for Mendoza and the national territories, only 5 percent or less.[6]

This period witnessed spectacular growth in foreign trade. In 1893, a year of low prices and harvest failure, the value of exports was less than 100 million gold pesos. But exports reached 203 million gold pesos in 1903 and 519 million in 1913, a fivefold increase in twenty years. After 1901 export earnings grew by 7.5 percent annually. Following wheat in the early 1890s came the rapid expansion of corn production, with exports of corn climbing to almost 5 million tons in 1912 and 1913. Linseed exports also increased, from a little over 100,000 tons in the early 1890s to more than 1 million tons in 1913. By 1913 foreign sales of wheat and corn each yielded around 100 million gold pesos, and linseed around 50 million. Imports meanwhile grew at a parallel rate from a depressed 96 million gold pesos in 1893 to 496 million in 1913 (see Table 11). Foreign trade as a whole, 190 million gold pesos in 1893, exceeded 1 billion gold pesos in 1913. Shipping in

TABLE 11. *Values of Exports and Imports in Argentina, 1890–1914*
(Annual averages in million gold pesos)

	Exports	Imports
1890–1894	103	98
1895–1899	131	106
1900–1904	197	130
1905–1909	335	267
1910–1914	402	359

SOURCE: Ernesto Tornquist and Co., *The Economic Development of Argentina in the Last Fifty Years* (Buenos Aires, 1919), 140.

Argentine ports multiplied from 10 million tons in 1895 to almost 30 million tons in 1913. Trade thus expanded at more than double the rate of population, from a per capita average of around 50 gold pesos in the early 1890s to 132 gold pesos in 1913.

By 1914 Argentina had become a primary exporter *par excellence* serving the industrial economies. Ninety percent of its exports were farm goods from the pampas region; more than 85 percent of these went to western Europe. Land use followed the growth in foreign trade: both expanded fivefold between the early 1890s and 1913. Throughout this period Britain was still Argentina's leading trade partner, buying at least 20 percent of her exports and in some years, such as 1907, as much as 40 percent, mostly meat and cereals. From Britain came around one-third of Argentina's imports: coal (accounting for 10 percent of total imports), other railroad materials, and finished metal and textile goods. By 1913 a sizable trade had also developed with Germany, although it remained only half that with Britain. In 1913 Argentina exported to Germany goods—led by unwashed wool—valued at 84 million gold pesos; among imports from Germany the leaders were machinery and electrical goods. Other substantial trade partners included France, which imported a large quantity of wool and sheepskins, Belgium, the Netherlands, and Italy, the last supplying in return large quantities of dyed cotton cloth. On the American continent substantial exports of wheat and flour to Brazil were balanced by large imports of coffee and yerba mate; however, trade with Brazil was less than one-sixth of that with Britain. The United States, now the main outlet for Argentina's cattle hides and ranking seventh among its trading partners, exported few manufactured goods to Argentina but was the main supplier of oil.[7]

Foreign investment once more played a major part in priming Argentina's economic growth. In the 1890s, as successive governments struggled to cope with the legacy of Juárez Celman, new investment was negligible. The mid 1890s thus saw a pronounced lull in railroad construction; rising export earnings at this time were largely the result of rising prices. British investment recommenced on a large scale soon after the readoption of the gold standard in 1899 and climaxed between 1904 and 1913, when Argentina received more funds from Britain than it had throughout the entire nineteenth century. The pattern of foreign investment changed: public investment became much less salient and the private British railroad companies accounted for the lion's share. Railroad investment rose from 346 million gold pesos in 1890 to 1,358 million in 1913. Between 1894 and

1914 the railroad track length more than doubled. From 8,820 miles in 1895, track length had increased to 10,350 miles by 1900. There were 17,495 miles in 1910, and 20,940 miles in 1914. Between 1890 and 1913 railroad cargoes increased from 5 million tons to 42 million tons, and railroad revenues from 8 million to 52 million gold pesos. In 1907 Congress adopted a new railroad code, the *Ley Mitre*, named after its sponsor, Emilio Mitre. This legislation abolished the profit-guarantee system adopted in the 1860s but upheld the companies' exemption from all duties on imported equipment and materials, and gave them considerable autonomy over rates. The new law prompted the fastest-ever wave of railroad expansion: between 1907 and 1914 the system grew at an average annual rate of 1,100 miles (see Map 8).[8]

After 1900 Argentina also received substantial investment capital from France and Germany. The French had a secondary role in railroad construction; Germans largely controlled the new electricity industry. Nevertheless, in 1913 more than 60 percent of foreign investment in Argentina was British; and British investment there was roughly 10 percent of Britain's total investment abroad. In 1898 British engineers finally completed construction of a deep-draught port in Buenos Aires. There and in several other cities they developed lengthy tramway networks along with a multitude of gas and sewage facilities. In 1914 foreign investments, both public and private, represented about half of Argentina's total capital stock, and their value was two and a half times that of the gross domestic product.[9]

Between 1895 and 1914 manufacturing establishments doubled in number, and capital investment in manufacturing quintupled. The dairy industry, insignificant in 1890, appeared by 1914 to have a great future. Between 1895 and 1914 flour milling expanded fourfold, sugar refining threefold, and beer eightfold. From the introduction of the conversion law in 1899 money in circulation climbed from 295 million paper pesos to 823 million in 1913.[10]

The last major feature of this period was a third revolution on the land. After 1900 both sheep and agriculture were subordinated to a renascent cattle economy. Sheep were largely driven out of the pampas into Patagonia; between 1895 and 1916 the sheep population of the province of Buenos Aires declined from 56 million to only 18 million. Meanwhile, the spread of mixed farming in which cereals, fodder crops, and cattle pasturing were combined in rotation provoked substantial changes in agriculture. After a tenfold increase in production in the preceding twenty years, by 1914 alfalfa acreage exceeded that of wheat. Major changes also occurred among the cattle

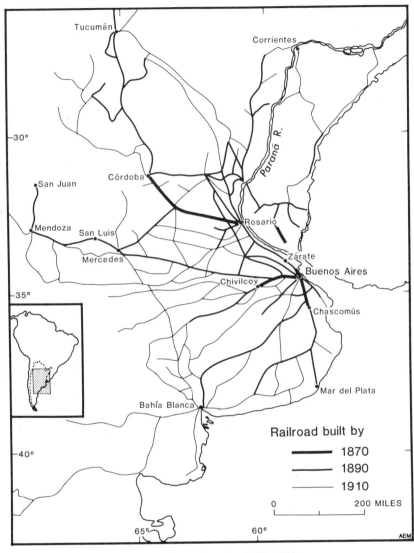

Map 8. Growth of the Argentine railroads, 1870–1910.

herds, as over much of the pampas the old creole stock was replaced by high-quality breeds imported from Britain, mainly Shorthorns and Herefords.[11]

These changes reflected the growth of high-grade beef exports and the creation of new meat-packing plants. Till 1900 the international beef trade was composed mainly of exports from the United States to Britain. However, as the internal American market expanded, the exportable surplus from this source steadily declined. At this point, Argentina replaced the United States as the major supplier to the British market. In Argentina primitive refrigeration techniques had been in use some twenty years before 1900, but solely for exports of lamb and mutton. The only cattle meats exported were dwindling quantities of salted beef and cattle on the hoof, a trade with Britain that grew during the 1890s as meat exports from the United States fell. But in 1900 Britain banned imports of live cattle from Argentina as a protection against hoof-and-mouth disease. However, Britain's demand for canned and frozen beef increased with the need to provision its troops during the Boer War in South Africa, and several British meat-packing firms were established in Argentina to export frozen beef. Within a decade beef exports from Argentina to Britain exceeded those from the United States.

The main phase in the industry's early development began in 1907 with the advent of American meat-packing companies from Chicago. The Americans could chill as well as freeze beef, which enabled them to produce a much higher-quality product. Chilled beef soon dominated the trade, and in early 1914 constituted three-quarters of beef exports. The marketing of chilled beef also boosted ranchers' investments in higher-quality stock, promoted the growth of mixed farming, and prompted specialization among ranchers, who began separating into an outer ring of breeders (*criadores*) and an inner core of fatteners (*invernadores*). The former sold to the latter, who in turn dealt with the packers. During the early years Argentina's cattle ranchers welcomed the Americans, who in competition for control with the British paid high prices for stock. Breeders and fatteners alike thus made handsome profits during a succession of "meat wars" between rival segments of the industry.

These meat-packing plants (*frigoríficos*) were the first major investment link between Argentina and the United States. By 1914 American interests, led by Armour and Swift, controlled between a half and two-thirds of production, yet more than four-fifths of Argentina's cattle meat exports went to the United Kingdom and virtually none to the United States. Recurrent efforts by the meat packers to win access to the American market from Argentina foundered consistently against opposition from American ranchers and the American public's hostility toward the "meat trust."[12]

ARGENTINA IN 1914

By the outbreak of World War I Argentina had experienced almost twenty years of prodigal expansion. Per capita income equalled that in Germany and the Low Countries, and was higher than in Spain, Italy, Sweden, and Switzerland. Having grown at an average annual rate of 6.5 percent since 1869, Buenos Aires had become the second city of the Atlantic seaboard, after New York, and by far the largest city in Latin America. In a great compendium on the republic's affairs issued in 1911, Lloyd's Bank of London observed that until around 1903 the value of foreign trade in Argentina and Brazil was roughly equal. But six years later Argentina's aggregate was half again larger than its leading rival in Latin America. Except entrepôts like Holland and Belgium, no country in the world imported more goods per capita than Argentina. By 1911, Argentina's foreign trade was larger than Canada's and a quarter of that of the United States. Argentina was the world's largest producer of corn and linseed, second in wool, and third in live cattle and horses. Though it ranked only sixth as a wheat producer, it was the third, and in some years the second, largest exporter. Despite the competition for land from cattle and forage crops, the expansion of wheat farming after 1900 outpaced Canada's.[13]

In 1914 Argentina was overshadowed to an even greater degree by the city of Buenos Aires. In many respects the city was still, as Sarmiento had depicted it, an outpost of civilization at the margin of the vast territories to its rear. As the pivot of the railroad system, the city continued to exploit its position at the interstices of foreign trade. If it had lost some export trade to Rosario and Bahía Blanca, and dealt more in meat than in grains, it was still the port of entry for almost all Argentina's imports. It remained the emporium of banking and finance, the hub of government, state spending, and state employment, drawing resources from the pampas through landed rentiers and commercial intermediaries.

With the completion of new port facilities in the late 1890s, incoming immigrants or visitors were no longer obliged to disembark into skiffs on the outer port roads to reach the shore. The city's great railroad stations in Plaza Constitución and Retiro—the latter the site of the slave compound two hundred years earlier—were replicas of those in London or Liverpool. With its solid and imposing central office blocks, its capacious avenues lined with jacarandas, its sidewalks made of Swedish granite, Buenos Aires seemed as well endowed a city as any in the world. Three-quarters of the city's children attended primary school, and although around 20 percent of the population died from tuberculosis, the epidemics of yellow fever and cholera that had afflicted earlier generations had long since ceased.

By 1914 some of the territory that had been designated part of the federal capital in 1880 remained undeveloped. Agriculture and grazing survived, mostly toward the west and southwest. But new construction, mostly single-story flat-roofed dwellings laid out in the rectangular grid created by the Spaniards, had advanced rapidly during the recent boom. Tramways affected land values in the city as the railroads did outside: between 1904 and 1912 real estate in the city appreciated up to tenfold. Buenos Aires was now divided into clearly demarcated zones (see Map 9). To the north were the well-to-do, the *gente bien*, in an area that stretched from the mansions of Barrio Norte and Palermo toward the city center through Belgrano across to the suburban *quintas* of Vicente López, Olivos, and San Isidro in the province of Buenos Aires. In the center and west of the city were its middle-class neighborhoods. The south, the *barrios* of Nueva Pompeya, Barracas, Avellaneda, and the Boca, were the working-class and manufacturing zones.[14]

At the apex of this highly diversified urban society was an elite of rural and city landowners, bankers, merchants, and investors. The elites had changed substantially in the past fifty years. Although their ranks included many long-established lineages, some descended from the Bourbon mercantile families of the late eighteenth century, others had more-recent immigrant antecedents. Among those of Italian ancestry was Antonio Devoto, the founder and patron of Villa Devoto, an expanding middle-class neighborhood in the western part of the city. In a way typical of the elites as a whole, Devoto had multiple interests in land, banking, trade, public works, and manufacturing. Among his landholdings in 1910 were 80,000 hectares and seven *estancias* in the province of Buenos Aires, 26,000 hectares in Santa Fe on two *estancias*, another 75,000 hectares in Córdoba among four, and 30,000 on one *estancia* in the more remote La Pampa territory. Devoto also possessed extensive urban properties in central Buenos Aires and was founder and president of the Banco de Italia y Rio de la Plata. Luis

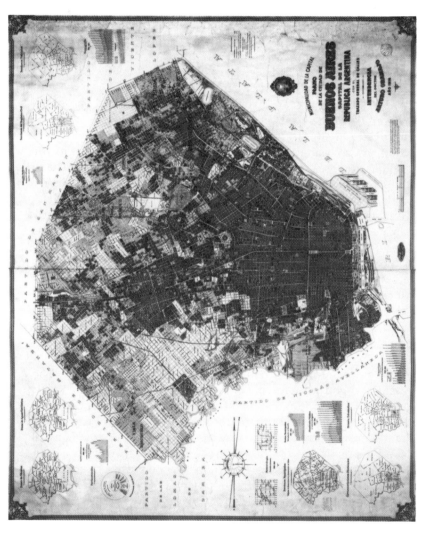

Map 9. Buenos Aires in 1916.

Zuberbühler, a second generation Swiss-Argentine, had a comparable fortune distributed among *estancias*, land-colonization companies, forestry, and manufacturing. Nicolás Mihanovich, who had arrived a penniless immigrant from Dalmatia some fifty years before, had a near-monopoly on the coastal steamships plying between Buenos Aires and Asunción along the Paraná or southward to the Atlantic settlements of Patagonia.[15]

The middle class of Buenos Aires, the largest group of its kind in Latin America, had an overwhelmingly immigrant background. The lower stratum of this class embraced numerous petty manufacturers and shopkeepers, some 40,000 in 1914, about four-fifths of them foreign-born. Scattered throughout the city were multitudes of bakers, tailors, shoe and sandal makers, brewers, chocolate and cigarette manufacturers, printers, carpenters, blacksmiths, and match and soap makers, along with a roughly equal number of street-corner shopkeepers (*almaceneros*). The upper stratum of the middle class was employed in the professions, public administration (the fastest-growing segment), and white-collar positions in such fields as transportation. Unlike the manufacturers and shopkeepers, most members of this upper stratum were first-generation Argentines, sons of immigrants, typically upwardly mobile children of the manufacturing and commercial classes. Among them an increasing concern with issues of higher education was apparent; secondary school diplomas and university degrees were passports into the professions and public administration.[16]

Of the working class in Buenos Aires in 1914 some three-quarters were immigrants. Around 400,000 strong, the working class made up some two-thirds of the city's employed male population. Workers were concentrated in large numbers in the port, the railroads, the tramways, and in a variety of public services. Others worked in manufacturing, either in large concerns like the meat-packing plants or in the numerous small workshops that served the local market, and in domestic service. A fifth of the employed working class were women and children. Among unskilled workers before 1914, many drifted to and fro across the Atlantic, or alternated between work in the city and harvest labor outside. Stabler, skilled groups were employed among the crafts, in construction, metallurgy, and transportation.[17]

Despite the stratification within the working class, its members shared common conditions and difficulties, chief of which was housing, a perennial problem in Buenos Aires. In 1914 it was estimated that four-fifths of working-class families lived in one-room households.

Many, perhaps 150,000 in all, dwelt in *conventillo* tenements close to the city center. The older *conventillos*, two-story rectangular constructions with Spanish-style patios in their interiors, had a half-century earlier been residences of the rich. But as they moved out after the epidemic of the early 1870s, the buildings were acquired by speculators, some of whom later constructed similar new buildings. The *conventillos* had been designed to accommodate a single extended family in some style. In the early years of the twentieth century they had become slums, with one dwelling occupied by as many as a score of families.[18]

In regard to other types of working-class consumption, imported goods, which the government taxed on entry, were often expensive but were offset by the abundance and variety of most common foodstuffs. By and large, working-class conditions in Buenos Aires were much the same as in western European cities. A preponderance of Italians and Spaniards among the immigrants, and their close cultural and linguistic affinities, enabled different sectors of the working class to mix easily. By comparison with American cities in this period, Buenos Aires was relatively free of ethnic ghettoes, and its highly mobile labor force made it also a city with little permanent unemployment. Among its bleaker features, however, was prostitution, which reflected the marked lack of women immigrants. Early in the twentieth century Buenos Aires had ill-fame as the center of a white-slave traffic from Europe, with some three hundred registered brothels in the city in 1913. Many other expressions of misery and wretchedness prevailed. Among the large foreign employers, the meat-packing plants were notorious for low wages and oppressive working conditions. Some of the worst abuses against workers were perpetrated by the immigrant middle-class store owners, who paid paltry wages and made eighteen-hour shifts commonplace.[19]

Outside Buenos Aires, the pampas region—except for its drier fringes in parts of San Luis, Córdoba, the territory of La Pampa, and Entre Rios—was markedly the most advanced. The area was covered by a dense network of railroads, its farms and estates delineated by barbed wire, and its landscape dotted with small towns, windmills, scattered homesteads, and water troughs. Immediately after World War I, the Argentine economist Alejandro E. Bunge claimed that this part of the country, including the city of Buenos Aires, had more than 90 percent of the nation's automobiles and telephones; that the region boasted no less than 42 percent of all the railroads in the whole of

Latin America; and that from the pampas came half of Latin America's total exports.[20]

Such exaggerated claims nonetheless had at least figurative validity: the pampas was by far the richest and fastest-expanding region in Latin America. During the past two generations townships had sprouted in great abundance throughout the pampas. Some had developed upon the hamlets or the *pulperías* from the days of Rosas or earlier, while others, beyond the old frontier, were the outcome of colonization ventures. The chief function of the pampas towns were as railheads, but they were also centers of local banking and petty crafts. Many had grown at roughly the same rate as the national population as a whole, at least doubling in size since 1890. Most had large congregations of immigrants, who established newspapers, schools, hospitals, and libraries. Yet most of the pampas towns were still small. Azul, with a population of 40,000 in 1914, was the fourth largest township in the province of Buenos Aires after Avellaneda, a working-class suburb of the capital; La Plata, the provincial capital; and Bahía Blanca, the leading port in the south. In a province the size of France only ten townships had populations greater than 12,000.

Much of the pampas appeared a society of rural capitalist pioneers. With the demise of older cattle activities linked with the *saladeros*, little remained of the earlier pastoral patriarchalism. Labor was free and highly mobile, and the wage form almost universal. Nevertheless, outside rural middle-class enclaves like central Santa Fe, aspects of the past endured—in the large estates, the uneven distribution of wealth, and the large transient population. In 1914 only a quarter of the region's land area was occupied by smaller farms between 500 and 1,000 hectares, while farms over 1,000 hectares accounted for 61 percent, with the largest 584 holdings in the pampas constituting almost one-fifth of the total area. Neither the boom of the 1880s nor its successor after 1895 had placed a large propertied population in the countryside. For the most part the rural population was composed of a thin sprinkling of farm tenants, cattle peons or shepherds, and seasonal laborers. Population density in areas devoted to beef herding was no more than one or two persons per square kilometer, in areas dominated by wheat farming generally three or four persons. The highest population densities were associated with corn, with up to fifteen persons per square kilometer.[21]

In part these low population densities identified the region as an area of new settlement in which development had occurred through continual expansion across the frontiers onto new land. However,

they were also due to the institutions employed in the land's settlement, for over most of the pampas farming was still conducted
under tenancy or sharecropping; as an example, in 1916 only 31 percent of cereal farms were worked by their owners. Agricultural tenancy, particularly in the province of Buenos Aires, had thirty or forty
years of history behind it, and during the previous twenty years
general trends in the pampas economy had again strengthened the
institution rather than weakened it. After 1895 the revival of cattle
ranching—at first through the expansion of cattle exports on the hoof,
and soon after through exports from the *frigoríficos*—encouraged landowners to adopt mixed rotational farming techniques, combining cattle with grains and using tenants to grow alfalfa as cattle fodder. Cattle
also provoked a general and frequently rapid upward movement in
land prices. As a result farmers usually found it more attractive to rent
relatively large land parcels than to buy small farms, especially since
the larger units of production would yield a higher output and higher
incomes. By leasing a larger tract, rather than trying to buy a smaller
one, farmers could also avoid high initial purchase and start-up costs.

The revival of cattle ranching, and the subsequent appreciation of
land values, thus combined to make tenancy neither unpopular nor
irrational. Farmers prospered more quickly as tenants than as independent smallholders, and their prosperity over time may also have
been greater. Even so, both tenancy and the new *estancia* system had
a long-term regressive effect on the pampas economy and the pampas
society. Rent payments eventually reduced the proportion of the revenues generated on the land that were spent or reinvested there.
Instead, substantial revenues drained out of the rural sector and went
to feed the expansion of the city of Buenos Aires. By 1914 in many
parts of the pampas there was abundant evidence of social and economic distress among tenants, many of whom dwelt in mere shacks.
Tenant farmers still lacked adequate credit facilities, and many were
chronically indebted to landowners, rural shopkeepers, or the great
cereal export houses in Buenos Aires that had emerged in the
1880s—among them Bunge y Born, Weil Brothers, and Dreyfus and
Co. Oligopsony in the commercialization of farm products left most
tenant farmers in the ever-vulnerable position of price-takers.

After 1900 farm machines were widely adopted in the pampas, but
farming remained heavily dependent on seasonal labor. During harvest periods the rural population would swell by as much as 300,000.
In areas farther away from Buenos Aires, like Santa Fe or Córdoba, the
harvesters were often migrants from the interior. However, the major-

ity of those who entered the province of Buenos Aires before 1914, when the war brought an end to the system, were immigrants from Europe who returned there after the harvest. Such "swallows" (*golondrinas*), as they were known, resurrected the tradition of social rootlessness that had prevailed in the pampas in the days of the now-extinct *gauchos*.[22]

South of the pampas colonists had been settled for some time in the well-irrigated Rio Negro valley, which had become a prosperous fruit-growing area, marketing its products in the city of Buenos Aires. Also in the south there seemed a promising future for the territory of Chubut. In 1907, during an attempt to tap supplies of artesian water, rich oil deposits were discovered in the area christened Comodoro Rivadavia. Additional oil discoveries were made in Neuquén, west of Rio Negro, at Plaza Huincúl. But beyond these enclaves and the still-struggling Welsh colonies in Chubut, Patagonia had evolved little beyond the naturalists' paradise encountered by Charles Darwin during the voyage of the *Beagle* some eighty years earlier. The great arid and windswept plateau contained nothing but vast sheep ranches. The mammoth land concentration prevailing in Patagonia was due in part to the land having only one-tenth of the sheep-carrying capacity of that in the province of Buenos Aires, but it also resulted from the methods adopted in distributing the land after the 1879 campaign. In 1885, for example, some 11 million acres were divided among 541 officers and soldiers from the conquering expedition. When the wool economy began to stagnate at the turn of the century, the arrival of sheep in Patagonia did little to develop the region.

In 1914 the population of Patagonia, about one-third of the country's territory, was a mere 80,000 people, or slightly above 1 percent of the total, most of whom settled in the Rio Negro region. Throughout Patagonia Argentine-born settlers were relatively few, mainly shepherds, token military and naval personnel, and a sprinkling of national government administrators. Many of the landowners of Patagonia, on sheep ranches and fruit farms alike, were British. The area also had a marked Chilean influence, as land hunger across the *cordillera* had recently incited substantial numbers of peasants to migrate. Thirty years earlier a similar emigration of Chileans to Bolivia and Peru had led to war and the annexation of land by Chile. Chileans were therefore treated with some suspicion by the Argentine authorities.[23]

At the other end of the country, the northeast, the old site of the

Jesuit missions, and south into Corrientes and Entre Rios constituted an area of greater physical variety than Patagonia, but one scarcely more developed. The great days of Entre Rios ended with the death of Urquiza and the suppression of López Jordán's rebellion in the 1870s. The province had railroad connections with the Paraná ports, but beyond clusters of small, often Jewish, farm colonies, it remained a traditional cattle region, using creole herds to produce hides and salted beef. Most of Corrientes further north was similar, though there some Guaraní peasant agriculture persisted. In 1914 some 10,000 hectares of Corrientes, on peasant smallholdings, were devoted to tobacco cultivation. Misiones, almost empty since the expulsion of the Jesuits a hundred and fifty years before, showed greater progress. Like the Rio Negro valley, this area had begun to attract immigrants, often Poles and Germans, who cultivated forest clearings and established new yerba mate plantations. Like Tucumán, the yerba mate region was gaining an ill reputation for its use of contract and forced labor. Meanwhile, the eastern Chaco, around the city of Resistencia, had begun to develop cotton crops. The northern reaches of Santiago del Estero, Santa Fe, and parts of Corrientes and the Chaco were devoted to the extraction of quebracho hardwood. Throughout this period the virgin quebracho forests were decimated with reckless energy, mainly by British consortia. Only token efforts were made to replace the forest cover, and vast tracts became desolate, dust- or brush-covered wastelands. The timber of the northwestern forests was largely used for railroad ties, and that of the east for its tannin, which was exported to Europe for the treatment of leather. During the war quebracho also became a substitute for imported coal on the railroads.[24]

To the west in Cuyo viticulture continued to flourish. Between 1895 and 1910 the area devoted to vines quintupled to 120,000 hectares. By 1914 annual wine production was approaching 4 million liters, an output that exceeded Chile's and was double California's. Vines had spread beyond Mendoza into San Juan and small pockets of Catamarca and La Rioja. Still largely an area of small holdings the vine region helped speed the growth of the city of Mendoza, which by 1914 had a population of 59,000, four times that of the medium-sized provincial capitals of the interior, such as Santiago del Estero or Salta, and ten times that of the poorest, La Rioja and Catamarca.[25]

In Tucumán sugar also prospered. Between 1900 and 1914 production again increased by threefold, and sugar had come to occupy roughly the same land area as vines. The sugar economy of Tucumán continued as a diverse mix of modern, highly capitalistic features and other characteristics that evoked the precapitalist past. Beyond the pampas, this region was one of the few to attract foreign investment. Many *ingenios* had now evolved into joint-stock ventures with foreign shareholders, and these mills used imported machinery, often British. In contrast, 80 percent of the sugar farmers of Tucumán eked out a living on small plots of seven or eight hectares, and some on even smaller plots. Sugar remained heavily reliant on contract labor, which caused acute social polarization throughout Tucumán. Lloyd's Bank, for example, called sugar a "big, bad blot" on the country and commented, "While the wealthy landowners and the big employers, the latter mostly of overseas nationality, are reaping increasingly rich rewards, those who perform toilsomely the actual labor that gives that reward are allowed to pass their lives in conditions that do not conform to the lowest standards of existence."[26]

The rest of the interior remained largely unchanged. The state railroads, which now linked all the provincial capitals with Buenos Aires, failed to induce the development or expansion that occurred elsewhere. Beyond the immediate radius served by the railways, goods were still transported by ox cart and mule. The age-old dream that the *cordillera* region would develop mining remained unfulfilled, while some small silver mines in La Rioja and elsewhere had collapsed in the wake of the late–nineteenth-century fall in silver prices. Traditional *haciendas* still held sway, with peasant communities subject to seigneurial levies. Peasant cottage industries languished against the incessant competition of imports and their own technological backwardness. With the exception of sprinklings of petty merchants, many of them Levantines, the area had few new residents. Its small cities, crumbling and downtrodden in aspect, mirrored the indigence of their surroundings.

The population of the interior was wracked by bronchial pneumonia, tuberculosis, and a variety of gastric ailments. The infant mortality rate was double and often treble that of Buenos Aires. Illiteracy approached 50 percent. Yet the interior was also empty, less so than Patagonia, but more so than the pampas. In 1910 it was estimated that only 1 percent of its land area was under cultivation, the rest remaining in a pristine state as *sierra* or desert. In the most backward parts, La Rioja and Catamarca, the distribution of a precious water supply from the mountain streams was conducted according to the same time-worn rites as in colonial days. At the end of the nineteenth century came a temporary revival in the old cattle and mule trades into

Chile and Bolivia. The Chilean trade followed the growth of mining and the development of the nitrate fields, while the Bolivian resulted from the resurgence of the Salta route to the River Plate following the loss of Bolivia's coastal panhandle in the War of the Pacific in the early 1880s. For a time this trade helped the *llaneros* of La Rioja, and revived Salta as an entrepôt. Yet by 1914 the trade had again declined or shifted in direction toward the local growth poles in Mendoza and Tucumán.

The lesser provinces lingered on in a state of unspecialized semi-autarky, many of them reliant on subsidies from Buenos Aires for the upkeep of their administrations. In 1914 Santiago del Estero had the same mixed agricultural and pastoral economy as a hundred and fifty years before. Flood farming along the Rio Dulce enabled the production of sugar, wine, cotton, and tobacco; mules were still being bred for export to Bolivia. But all these activities were small in scale, faster development being constrained as in centuries past by the high saline content of the soil. Until the growth of sugar in the 1920s, Jujuy in the far northwest had only minimal contact with the markets to the south. Local indigenous communities exchanged alpaca and llama wool for Bolivian salt and the narcotic *coca* across a scarcely acknowledged frontier. Tradition remained strong even in the city of Córdoba, which had attracted numerous immigrants, and its province remained governed by a conservative oligarchy of local families. The University of Córdoba continued to be hidebound by scholasticism and clericalism.[27]

By 1914 Argentina had thus evolved into an extremely mixed and diverse society. Across its regions extreme modernity and immutable backwardness coexisted. Expectations remained high that the imbalances would steadily recede as the present wave of growth continued, for there was still much to accomplish. Despite two generations of immigration the country had a population of a mere 8 million in a land mass the size of continental Europe. But in which direction would it now turn? And how much progress could it achieve? By 1914 reserves of good land were dwindling, the remainder offering only meager returns to investors and pioneers. Argentina appeared perhaps to be reaching a saturation point in its capacity to absorb foreign capital and immigrant labor.

Despite the recent growth of manufacturing, the country was far from being a fully fledged industrial society. Manufacturing was heavily dependent on a market that grew in proportion to exports and the inflow of foreign investment. Despite the wide adoption of steam-power, most industries remained simple handicrafts. Locally manu-factured foodstuffs, for which raw materials were cheap and abun-dant, were of high quality but were essentially an outgrowth from the export economy. Metal and textile industries were still weak; local metallurgical plants used imported raw materials, and their survival depended on the maintenance of low ocean freights. A new textile industry in Buenos Aires, which functioned largely on a "putting-out" basis among seamstresses, was notably less developed than Brazil's. In 1911 Argentina had 9,000 spindles and 1,200 looms, compared with Brazil's estimated 1 million spindles and 35,000 looms.

Prospects seemed limited for a deepening and broadening of the manufacturing sector, as Argentina lacked even an embrionic heavy or capital goods industry. Its scant reserves of coal and iron ore lay in distant and still inaccessible regions, mostly in the far southwest. Experiments with tariff protection had failed to foster domestic goods other than sugar, wines, and flour that were able to compete effec-tively with imports. Limited markets narrowed the scope for ad-vanced technology and economies of scale. The home market was rich but still relatively small; foreign markets were dominated by the world's industrial giants. Moreover, Argentine society seemed poorly prepared for industrialization. The elites were closely linked with the export of farm goods, and the high living standards of the new urban population rested on the inflow of cheap imports and continuing commercial reciprocity with western Europe. A strong preference for free trade was accompanied by a marked disinclination to support efforts to industrialize. Overall in 1914 Argentina's economy was a high-wage, high-consumption complex that largely disclaimed the need or attractiveness of diversification.[28]

THE COMING OF REFORM, 1890–1916

Political change at the turn of the century had its genesis in the 1890 depression. In 1891, after the failure of the rebellion against Juárez Celman and the secret deal between Roca and Mitre, Leandro N. Alem and his followers renounced the Civic Union and set up a rival organization, the Radical Civic Union (*Unión Cívica Radical* [UCR]). The new movement pledged itself to renewed insurrection to implant popular democracy. For a time the government held the Rad-icals at bay, but in 1893 they led a new spate of uprisings in the provinces. For a brief period led by Alem's nephew, Hipólito Yrigoyen, they took La Plata. In Santa Fe, the Radicals exploited the hardships caused by the depression and resentments against provincial taxes imposed by the dominant ranching interests to muster a large following among the agricultural colonists. But here, as in Buenos Aires and elsewhere, they were defeated. In 1896, disillusioned by failure, Alem committed suicide. Yrigoyen inherited his movement, but the UCR had ceased to command much influence. As the economy revived, political unrest abated.[29]

Throughout the 1890s the dominant political figure was Roca. In 1892 Roca reneged on his promise to Mitre two years earlier to support the latter's candidacy for president. Instead Roca manuevered the election of the colorless Luis Sáenz Peña, and when he resigned in 1895, his replacement by the equally pliant vice-president, José Evaristo Uriburu. Neither administration achieved much of moment beyond sorting through the aftermath of the depression. At length in 1898 Roca himself returned to the presidency. With economic recovery fully underway, his second term promised to be as successful as his first. During this second term the Argentine political system grew to resemble that of Mexico under Porfirio Díaz. Both regimes viewed foreign investment and immigration as the keys to progress, and both controlled the provinces by mixing patronage and subsidies with the threat of force. In both countries only a small fraction of the nominally enfranchised population voted in elections, which local bosses regulated by manipulating the electoral rolls or by simple bribery and intimidation. Aspirants to elected positions usually purchased the services of the bosses, who reliably delivered the vote. The provinces resembled inflated versions of the pocket boroughs of unreformed England, with the difference that possession over them rotated with the ebb and flow of local factional conflict.

Yet Roca's system, like Díaz's, was less stable than it appeared, and the forces that would promote political change were in gestation. After 1900 the ruling classes became increasingly divided between those supporting Roca and others of a more progressive bent who favored reform and democratization. The latter were in part influenced by events in Europe: from Spain to Russia, nations were moving from absolutism or oligarchy toward popular democracy. The Argentine elites were becoming aware of the unfolding similarities between western European societies and their own, with the growing cities and the emergence of new social classes. Democracy's attractiveness lay in its promise of protecting political stability, for if political exclusion were maintained, they argued, the nation risked a repetition of the upheavals of the early 1890s. To contain and control the effects of social change and to buttress their own position, the elites contended, the country needed new institutions, genuinely popular political parties to replace the present oligarchic factions, and an active participating public opinion. While the dominant ideological influence on the reformers was the democratic liberalism of John Stuart Mill, the reform campaign also had a subsidiary corporatist quality deriving mostly from the papal encyclical of 1881, *Rerum Novarum*. Advocates of political change sometimes invoked an organic conception of society and the normative functions of institutions that belong within the corporatist tradition: they emphasized the need for new inclusive party associations, and the role of such associations in promoting social solidarity and the common good. This new outlook gained strength and adherents in the wake of symptoms of unrest among the urban middle classes and the working class. After 1900 the former were mobilized by the Radicals, while the later became divided between a militant anarchist movement and a new reformist Socialist Party.[30]

For almost ten years after Alem's death in 1896 the Radicals were little more than one among a string of minor factions. Once firmly under Yrigoyen's leadership in 1898, they ceased contesting elections in protest against electoral misconduct. At this time Radicalism was more a secret society than a political party, its adherents pledged to two simple rules: "abstention" from fraudulent elections and "intransigence" against compromise on the commitment to renewed revolution and against efforts at cooptation by the government. To minimize internal factionalism, which had recurrently weakened the party during the 1890s, Yrigoyen made few pronouncements on specific political issues but attacked Roca's system rather by impugning its morality. The present ruling classes, "the Regime" (*El Régimen*), as he called it, upheld itself by fraud and violence in defiance of the Constitution; the historic mission of Radicalism, "the Cause" (*La Causa*), was to overthrow the Regime and implant democracy. Year after year Yrigoyen sought to publicize this message in long, rambling manifestoes, yet he adopted an air of conspiratorial secrecy, making no public appearances nor ever speaking in public. He also made a cult of personal austerity and lived with deliberate frugality, constantly affecting poverty although he was a landowner of some substance.

Under Yrigoyen's leadership Radicalism upheld an uncompromising commitment to popular democracy and to the principles of government accountability and honest administration. However, the group lacked a constructive or detailed plan for reform and tended to present democracy as a panacea. Behind their rebellious exterior most Radicals were largely conservative in orientation, their attitudes for the most part falling within a continuum between conservative paternalism and liberal laissez-faire. The doctrines of Radicalism also betrayed more corporatist influences. Radicals proclaimed their ethical superiority to their political rivals. They were less concerned with the instrumental significance of popular democracy than with its normative functions to promote the common good. Radicalism was not a "party" linked to a certain set of interests but a "movement," an inclusive aggregation of citizens committed to achieving social solidarity. Also, solidarity was their goal, rather than a specific list of reform priorities on behalf of sectional interests.

In 1905, suddenly and unexpectedly, Yrigoyen led another revolt against the government, but this rebellion, a pale shadow of its forerunners in 1890 and 1893, was put down immediately. Yet in that it was executed less in expectation of victory than for publicity and propaganda, it proved a spectacular success, both reviving public interest in electoral reform and frightening the government, since it attracted some support from the Army, mainly among junior officers of immigrant background. When the former rebels were granted amnesty in 1906, they immediately launched a vigorous campaign for popular support. A profusion of local political clubs was gradually molded into a hierarchical chain of party committees. Through their committees the Radicals diversified their regional following and began capturing the support of the urban middle classes. Soon the latter were at the vanguard of a new movement for political reform.[31]

Anarchism in Argentina first appeared in the 1880s among immigrants from Italy and Spain. Its heyday came after 1899, when resumption of the gold standard ended the recent upward trend in real wages that accompanied the appreciation of the paper peso. As the influx of immigrants increased in tempo, wages were again under pressure and rents surged upward. When labor unrest surfaced, the anarchists renounced their earlier individualism and plunged into organizing trade unions. Of the several anarchist federations, the most durable and influential was the FORA (*Federación Obrera Regional Argentina*), founded in 1904. Although FORA's 20,000 members represented only around 5 percent of the Buenos Aires working class, for several years the group had a major role in the city's political life.

The popularity of anarchism in Buenos Aires and other larger cities of the littoral lay in its expression of a simple confict ideology and a philosophy of action that workers could invoke in the day-to-day struggle to improve their lot. Its utopian and millenarian qualities were readily accepted by a population seeking a bridge from its peasant agrarian background to its present urban condition under petty capitalism. On half a dozen occasions between 1899 and 1910 disputes between workers and employers were transmuted under anarchist influence into militant political struggles against the state through the weapon of the general strike. These movements, all of them stirring and dramatic interludes in the politics of Buenos Aires, invariably commanded great enthusiasm, which led to massive popular demonstrations and street battles with the police. In response, different governments repeatedly imposed a state of siege and restrictive legislation: the Law of Residence of 1902 and the Law of Social Defense in 1910 allowed the police to deport or imprison those suspected of anarchist affiliations. The conflict reached its climax in 1910, when anarchists threatened to sabotage the forthcoming national centennial celebrations. To thwart the threatened strike, bands of civilian vigilantes attacked anarchist meeting places, burning books and destroying printing presses. A spate of imprisonments and banishments followed, and the repression achieved its intended result. Although anarchism lingered on in the working-class movement, it never fully recovered from this blow.[32]

Argentine socialists were men of different stamp from the anarchists, and soon their bitter rivals for control over the working class. The socialists were moderates, influenced more by bourgeois liberalism and positivism than Marxism. Like the Radicals, they were strong supporters of popular democracy, but they also endorsed numerous other complementary measures. Overall their program addressed the redistribution of income rather than wealth: better credit facilities for agricultural tenants, government housing schemes, and measures to reduce the cost of living. The last of these issues was the most prominent, and to lower consumer prices an extreme free-trade policy was advanced. Socialists also supported the separation of Church and state, and the replacement of a standing army by a civilian militia. They became the first champions of women's suffrage in Argentina and led campaigns against the white-slave traffic. Other positions included the legalization of divorce, an eight-hour workday, a progressive income tax, and higher spending in primary education.

The Socialist party (*Partido Socialista*) was founded in 1894 by Juan B. Justo, a medical practitioner who remained the party's leader until his death in 1928. In building a party leadership Justo attracted other professionals and a sprinkling of skilled workers with trade-union experience. The party was thus less a pure workers' movement than an alliance between some of the professional sectors, upper echelons of the working class, and small segments of the petty manufacturers. It differed from all other political movements in Argentina, including the Radicals, in its tightly knit organization and its small, carefully sifted membership. The emphasis on internal organization and the adoption of a detailed party program became the foundation of the Socialists' claim that theirs was the only "modern, organic" party in the country. Radicalism they regarded as an atavism of "creole politics" (*política criolla*), dismissing its members as a collection of pseudodemocrats and descendants of earlier oligarchic factions. The Socialists had perhaps even less in common with the anarchists, for, as rigid constitutionalists, the Socialists opposed violence and direct action, including the anarchists' general strikes. This stance cost them a base among the trade unions, most of which ignored the Socialists, who turned instead to the immigrant communities, sponsoring naturalization drives to qualify the immigrants to vote. But these efforts were largely unsuccessful, the overwhelming majority of the immigrants preferring to uphold their citizenship of origin. Before 1912 the Socialists' only electoral success came in 1904 when one of their leaders, Alfredo Palacios, was returned to Congress from the Boca district of Buenos Aires.[33]

Radicals, Socialists, and indirectly the anarchists helped fuel the movement for reform during the early years of the twentieth century. Progressives among the elite feared the growing popular support for the Radicals, wondering when their next revolt would come, and were equally apprehensive of the anarchists. These progressives advocated reform as a means to domesticate the workers, enhance the moderate Socialists, and undermine the extremists. However, Roca's presidency precluded possibilities of change.

The decline of Roca, the country's foremost political figure since the desert campaign of 1879, began in 1901, three years into his second term as president. Carlos Pellegrini, Roca's long-time ally and present minister of finance, proposed mortgaging the customs revenues to a consortium of foreign bankers in exchange for funds to consolidate the public debt. The scheme was badly received by Congress and the press, which attacked it as a surrender of national sovereignty to foreigners. As the opposition became manifest, Roca disavowed the idea and jettisoned his friend. Pellegrini resigned. The rift between the two men was irreparable, and Pellegrini became one of the most ardent patrons of electoral reform. Institutional links between government and public opinion, he argued, were necessary to enable the citizens to influence policy and to bypass politically unacceptable schemes like that which had provoked his own downfall.

Roca appeared to ride out these difficulties. To neutralize the opposition, he sponsored electoral legislation, which when implemented in 1904 increased voting turnouts and to a degree broadened representation in the Chamber of Deputies; it was at this point that the Socialist Palacios won election. But the measure failed to check bribery and was soon permitted to lapse. It also failed to quiet Pellegrini such that in 1904, for the first time in twenty years, Roca found himself unable to dictate the presidential succession. The new president, Manuel Quintana, was a compromise between Roca's candidate and Pellegrini's. However, Pellegrini's faction prevailed in the selection of the vice-president, José Figueroa Alcorta. When Quintana died in 1906, Figueroa Alcorta succeeded him.

The year 1906, which also saw the death of the still-active Bartolomé Mitre as well as that of Pellegrini, was the turning point in the battle for reform and the decisive moment in the fall of Roca. Figueroa Alcorta swiftly curbed Roca's influence by using federal interventions to root out his followers in the provinces. When Congress launched a protest, the president closed the session and had its members turned away by the police. Succeeding elections gradually gave the supporters of reform a majority, and in 1910 Figueroa Alcorta arranged to be succeeded by Roque Sáenz Peña, no less a member of the old ruling class than his predecessors, but for the past twenty years its leading advocate of electoral reform.

The Sáenz Peña Law, as the reform legislation became known, was debated by Congress in 1911 and implemented the following year. Two separate enactments established universal male suffrage for natives over eighteen years of age and an electoral roll based on the military conscription lists. The legislation had several peculiarities: to foster habits of civic involvement and participation, voting was made compulsory; and to minimize malfeasance, the Army was given custodial duties during elections. A device known as the "incomplete list" made it possible to award a third of the seats in each jurisdiction to the leading runner-up in each election. This mechanism was intended to give representation to minority parties and thus to draw controversial issues into Congress while reducing the scope for less easily controlled political action outside. However, the new law did not extend voting rights to noncitizens, nor did the government make any attempt to simplify the cumbersome naturalization procedures. For the foreseeable future the landed interests, the upper middle class, and to a lesser extent the conservative interior were to dominate the electorate. There was no discussion whatsoever of the enfranchisement of women.[34]

Whatever its limitations, the Sáenz Peña Law brought sweeping changes to Argentine politics. Where it was once highly exceptional for a third of the nominal electorate to vote, turnouts now reached 70 and 80 percent. Methods of electioneering altered dramatically, and the worst kinds of political skulduggery were banished. But the reform also brought surprises. Sáenz Peña and his supporters had espoused electoral reform in the belief that the old oligarchic factions would adapt to the new conditions and unite into a strong conservative party that would enjoy large popular support. The progressives expected Sáenz Peña to be able to hand over the presidency to a kindred progressive conservative, whose administration would be strengthened and legitimized by its victory in open and fair elections.

Instead, the conservatives repeatedly failed in their efforts at unity and self-democratization. After 1912 they were split along regional lines among supporters of Marcelino Ugarte, the governor of the province of Buenos Aires, and those of Lisandro De la Torre, leader of the Progressive Democratic Party (*Partido Demócrata Progresista*), a democratic conservative group based in Santa Fe. At the same time Yrigoyen decided to end "abstention," and his followers embarked at once on the quest for electoral supremacy. In this last phase of coalition building, Yrigoyen's technique of promising change but hedging on its precise content began to pay dividends. Radicalism now emerged as a movement transcending regional and class divisions; from its base in Buenos Aires it rapidly spread throughout the rest of the country. If it made little headway among the working class, it successfully united substantial fractions of the landed and commercial elites with the enfranchised native-born urban and rural middle classes. After 1912 the Radicals began capturing control of the provinces, and increasing their representation in Congress. Finally in 1916, by the slender margin of one vote in the electoral college, Yrigoyen was selected to succeed to the presidency. The outcome of the conservatives' reform was thus to catapult the former rebels, and Yrigoyen himself, into power.[35]

Carting the wool clip to the railhead, province of Buenos Aires, circa 1900. Reproduced from Archivo General de la Nación, Buenos Aires.

Spanish immigrants awaiting medical inspection at the port of Buenos Aires around 1905. Reproduced from Reginald Lloyd, ed., *Twentieth-Century Impressions of Argentina* (London, 1911), 99.

Railroad goods yard in Buenos Aires, 1910. Carting exportables from the railroad to the port was a major source of employment in the city during this period. Reproduced from Reginald Lloyd, ed., *Twentieth-Century Impressions of Argentina* (London, 1911), 79.

The grape harvest in Mendoza, circa 1905. The source of this predominantly female and child labor force remains unexplored by historians. The workers were most likely immigrants brought in seasonally by rail through Córdoba. Reproduced from Reginald Lloyd, *Twentieth-Century Impressions of Argentina* (London, 1911), 251.

Indian sugar workers, probably from the Chaco region, in Tucumán around 1905. The illustration is a graphic example of the uniqueness of agrarian capitalism in the sugar region. Reproduced from Reginald Lloyd, ed. *Twentieth-Century Impressions of Argentina* (London, 1911), 261.

An example of the survival of traditional Argentina beyond the pampas: the upper Paraná, probably Corrientes, around 1905. Reproduced from Reginald Lloyd, *Twentieth-Century Impressions of Argentina* (London, 1911), 775.

A downtown restaurant in Buenos Aires decorated in typical Italian style. Sketch by Alejandro Sirio, originally published in *Caras y Caretas*, a popular current affairs weekly in the early twentieth century. Reproduced from Diego Abad de Santillán, *Historia argentina* (Buenos Aires, 1968), 4:54.

Looking for Lodgings. A sketch, also from *Caras y Caretas*, conveying the atmosphere of the urban slum, or *conventillo*. Reproduced from Diego Abad de Santillán, *Historia argentina* (Buenos Aires, 1968), 4:61.

Supporters of the *Unión Cívica* defending the barricades during the rebellion against Juárez Celman, 26 July 1890. Sketch by M. Lenz; reproduced from Diego Abad de Santillán, *Historia argentina* (Buenos Aires, 1967), 3:373.

Hipólito Yrigoyen, bearing floral bouquet, leads a demonstration of Radicals in support of electoral reform, 1912. Reproduced from Archivo General de la Nación, Buenos Aires.

The arrest of a demonstrator in Buenos Aires, May Day 1905. An incident typical of the highpoint of anarchist influence in Argentina. Reproduced from Archivo General de la Nación, Buenos Aires.

Labor demonstration in Buenos Aires, New Year's Day, 1909. Reproduced from Archivo General de la Nación, Buenos Aires.

Caricature from *Caras y Caretas* of federal interventions in the provinces under Yrigoyen, 1916–1922. Reproduced from Diego Abad de Santillán, *Historia argentina* (Buenos Aires, 1968), 4:81.

The workers' procession of 9 January 1919, burying the victims of conflicts between police and strikers, and the prelude to the *Semana Trágica*. Reproduced from Archivo General de la Nación, Buenos Aires.

Strikers burning automobiles in Rivadavia Avenue, Buenos Aires, 10 January 1919. Reproduced from *Revista Popular* 13 January 1919.

Demonstration of the middle classes against the general strike, 11 January 1919. Reproduced from *Revista Popular* 13 January 1919.

REVISTA POPULAR

Año II. — Núm. 42. Buenos Aires, Lunes 20 de Enero de 1919. Defensa 179.

CUÍDATE DE LOS PERROS QUE NO LADRAN

El sueño de los maximalistas y de "algunos otros" también...

Yrigoyen, prisoner of the "Bolsheviks," January 1919. The placard, written in misspelled Spanish to satirize working-class immigrants of dubious political loyalties, reads "Long live Maximalism (Bolshevism): Peace, Labor, and Dynamite." Reproduced from *Revista Popular* 20 January 1919.

Hipólito Yrigoyen (1852–1933) in later life, around 1928, at the commencement of his second term as president. Reproduced from Archivo General de la Nación, Buenos Aires.

A student march in Buenos Aires, late August 1930. One of the immediate preludes to the overthrow of the Radical government. Reproduced from Archivo General de la Nación, Buenos Aires.

General José F. Uriburu proclaims the *de facto* military government from the balcony of the Casa Rosada, 6 September 1930. Reproduced from the Archivo General de la Nación, Buenos Aires.

Cartoon satirizing the monopolistic pretensions of the British-led Transit Corporation in 1936. Original from *Caras y Caretas*; reproduced from Diego Abad de Santillán, *Historia argentina* (Buenos Aires, 1969), 5:84.

Revolution of 4 June 1943. Infantry being conveyed toward the Casa Rosada. Reproduced from Archivo General de la Nación , Buenos Aires.

Cavalry enter Buenos Aires during the June Revolution, 1943. Reproduced from Archivo General de la Nación, Buenos Aires.

President Ramírez flanked by General Edelmiro Farrell (left), and Colonel Juan D. Perón in September 1943. Reproduced from Archivo General de la Nación, Buenos Aires.

THE WAR AND POSTWAR ECONOMY, 1913–1929

On the surface the Argentine economy behaved much the same in the 1920s as before World War I. By 1929 growth had kept pace with Canada and Australia. Argentina was presently the world's largest exporter of chilled beef, corn, linseed, and oats, and was third in wheat and flour. Average annual exports for 1910–1914 and 1925–1929 increased as follows: wheat from 2.1 million tons to 4.2 million tons, corn from 3.1 million to 3.5 million, and linseed from 680,000 to 1.6 million tons. Annual exports of chilled beef, which averaged only 25,000 tons between 1910 and 1914, increased to more than 400,000 tons between 1925 and 1929. Annual export values as a whole, which in 1910–1914 averaged 4,480 million paper pesos (at 1950 prices), increased to 7,914 million paper pesos between 1925 and 1929. Per capita incomes in Argentina continued to compare favorably with most of western Europe, and the standard of living again rose while illiteracy fell. Large segments of the population enjoyed prosperity and well-being. By 1930 there were 435,000 automobiles throughout Argentina, a substantially larger number than in many western European countries, and a sevenfold increase from eight years earlier. Assisted once more by immigration, population rose by almost 4 million between 1914 and 1930, from 7.9 million to 11.6 million. Domestic oil production underwent spectacular growth: from less than 21,000 cubic meters of oil fuel in 1913 to 1.4 million cubic meters by 1929.

Even so, expansion was notably less rapid and less smooth than immediately before the war. Export volumes grew by more than 5 percent a year before 1914 but by only 3.9 percent after, and the annual rate of growth of the land area sown for crops fell from 8.3 percent to 1.3 percent. Expansion in land use in the pampas was negligible, with no increases in Santa Fe, and minimal ones in Córdoba, Entre Rios, and Buenos Aires. Similarly, population in the pampas continued to grow, but at a slower rate: between 1895 and 1913 the rural population increased by 1 million, but by only 270,000 between 1914 and 1930, with the average annual rate of increase declining from 50,000 to 22,500.

In the 1920s increasing farm output was achieved mainly by mechanization. Argentina was now a large market for imported farm machinery. Machines, estimated to represent 24 percent of the capital stock in the rural sector in 1914, accounted for around 40 percent in

1929. By the latter year an estimated 32,000 harvesters, 16,000 tractors, and 10,000 threshing machines were in Argentina. To some extent, too, increases in agricultural output during the 1920s were illusory, the result of substitutions in land use. A near doubling in production of cereals and linseed between 1922 and 1929, for example, followed in part from a decline in the cattle population by 5 million and a shrinkage in the acreage devoted to alfalfa fodder. The cattle stock contracted from an estimated 37 million in 1922 to only 32.2 million in 1930, while land devoted to alfalfa dropped from 7 million hectares to 5 million. Meanwhile, mechanization prompted a decline in the land used for pasturing horses. Such conditions enabled land devoted to cereals to rise from 11 million hectares to 19 million. In 1921–1922 cereals and linseed represented 56.5 percent of the cultivated area in the pampas; by 1929–1930 the proportion was 73.5 percent.

After 1913 Argentina absorbed substantially less private foreign investment (see Table 12). Between 1913 and 1927 only 750 miles of new railroad track were added, most of which was on branch-lines or was government-built track in the interior. Between the quin-quenniums 1865–1869 and 1910–1914 the railroads were expanded at an annual average rate of 15.4 percent; between 1910–1914 and 1925–1929 the rate was 1.4 percent. British investment to Argentina ceased completely during the war and immediately after, recovering to only a comparative trickle during the later 1920s. Overall foreign investment was only a fifth of the prewar flow. Likewise, immigration virtually ceased for a decade after 1913; net annual immigration was 1.1 million between 1901 and 1910, but only 856,000 between 1921 and 1930.[36]

TABLE 12. *Stock of Foreign Capital in Argentina, 1900–1927*
(Millions of dollars at 1970 prices)

	1900	1913	1927
Britain	912	1,860	2,002
United States	—	39	487
Other countries	—	1,237	984
TOTAL	1,120	3,136*	3,474†

*Stock includes $1,037 million invested in railroads.
†Stock includes $1,187 million invested in railroads.

SOURCE: Carlos Diaz Alejandro, *Essays in the Economic History of the Argentine Republic* (New Haven, 1970), 30.

While the period between 1895 and 1913 witnessed steady upward growth, that between 1913 and 1929 divides into two cycles of depression followed by recovery. The first depression, between 1913 and 1917, was succeeded by recovery and renewed boom between 1918 and 1921; the second, between 1921 and 1924, by an expansion that continued till 1929. These recessions, which resembled those in the last quarter of the nineteenth century, sprang from contractions in international demand for Argentine goods. The resultant balance-of-payments deficits were corrected eventually by falling imports, but at the cost of falling government revenues. The depression of 1913, as in 1873 and 1890, was exacerbated by a cessation in foreign investment. In 1914 the gold standard and peso-convertibility schemes established in 1899 were abandoned, to be restored for only a brief two-year period between 1927 and 1929. Both depressions brought unemployment, falling urban and rural land values, a spate of bankruptcies, and severe credit squeezes. However, in 1913 Argentina managed to avoid a repetition of the overseas debt crises of 1890 in that around three-quarters of the foreign investment was private, and the government was largely exempt from its earlier obligation to afford gold-based guaranteed minimum profits.

The depression of 1913 began when the Bank of England raised interest rates to correct a payments deficit in Britain and to check financial uncertainty caused by wars in the Balkans. The measure immediately prompted an outflow of capital from Argentina. Conditions worsened with a downward plunge in world cereal and meat prices, and with the failure of the 1913–1914 harvest. Some months later, as matters appeared to be improving, the outbreak of World War I brought transatlantic trade to an almost complete standstill, forcing the Argentine government to decree a financial moratorium in August 1914. Foreign trade resumed in 1915, but Britain and France had shifted to munitions production, and an Allied blockade was imposed against Germany. Argentina's growing shortages of imports were only partly remedied by supplies from the United States.

Depression persisted until the end of 1917. Export prices then rapidly advanced under the stimulus of wartime demand, especially for frozen and canned meat, enormous quantities of which were consumed by the Allied troops on the Western front. Export earnings, around 400 million gold pesos in 1913–1914, had almost tripled by 1919–1920 to 1,100 million. But imports increased much more rapidly, as an acute shortage of manufactured goods during the war weighted the terms of trade heavily against primary producers. Although the *volume* of Argentina's imports fell from an estimated 10 million tons in 1913, most of which was coal, to only 2.6 million tons in 1918, their *cost*, inflated further by the fourfold rise in shipping rates during the war, more than doubled, from around 400 million gold pesos in 1913–1914 to almost 850 million in 1919–1920 (see Table 13). As a neutral throughout the war, Argentina suffered no physical harm but it could not escape the war's highly disruptive economic consequences.

Until 1918 the workers of Buenos Aires endured an uncharacteristically high rate of unemployment: approximately 16 to 20 percent of the city's labor force in 1914. In the past it had been possible to "export" unemployment by encouraging immigrants to return to Europe. But although after 1913 emigrants consistently exceeded new arrivals, shipping shortages and the steep rise in shipping rates impeded this escape mechanism, bottling up some of the unemployment in Argentina. The first three years of the war thus brought falling wages, a longer working day, and highly unfavorable conditions for trade unions. Between the last year of prewar prosperity in 1912 and the end of 1916, there were no strikes of any significance.

In the public sector the fall in imports after 1913 brought a steep decline in government revenues, which compelled the government to use a larger proportion of its revenues to service the foreign debt. As during the mid 1870s and the early 1890s, depression forced stringent spending cuts by the national government, the provinces, and the municipalities alike. As day-to-day administrative spending

TABLE 13. *Indices of Foreign Trade, 1915–1922 (1914 = 100)*

	Volume of Exports	Volume of Imports	Value of Exports	Value of Imports
1915	127	84	116	114
1916	112	81	129	142
1917	79	70	171	176
1918	113	62	174	256
1919	135	86	190	244
1920	133	111	200	276
1921	116	103	138	228
1922	153	112	109	188

SOURCE: Guido Di Tella and Manuel Zymelman, *Las etapas del desarrollo económico argentino* (Buenos Aires, 1967), 320, 352.

decreased, unemployment and bankruptcies mounted. Pending changes in the taxation system to exact revenues independent of import duties, the government could reduce its cutbacks only by contracting new debts. Short-term loans were financed by banks in New York, and internal bonds were issued. Between 1914 and 1918 the public floating debt almost tripled, from 256 million paper pesos to 711 million. However, total expenditures in 1918, at 421 million paper pesos, were roughly the same as in 1914 and not far above the 375 million expended in 1916, the year of lowest spending throughout the period. All this changed dramatically after the Armistice, when imports began to flow once more. From late 1918 onward public spending rapidly increased, and in 1922 reached 614 million paper pesos, almost 50 percent higher than in 1918.

During the upward phase of the cycle between 1918 and 1921, a period of steep increases in export prices, the landed and commercial classes recovered rapidly and for a time enjoyed unprecedented profits. In 1918 some of the meat-packing plants had returns of 50 percent on capital invested. However, the export boom brought little immediate relief for other sectors of the population, since unemployment was now succeeded by inflation (see Table 14). Between 1914 and 1918 food prices increased 50 percent and prices of simple clothing goods, most usually imported, by 300 percent. The growth of domestic textile manufactures, which mainly used wool, afforded

TABLE 14. *Employment, Incomes, and Trade Union Membership, 1914–1922*

	Unemployed as % of Labor Force (winter levels)	General Cost of Living (1910 = 100)	Real Wages (1929 = 100)	Dues-Paying Members of Trade Unions
1914	13.4	108	—	—
1915	14.5	117	61	2,666
1916	17.7	125	57	3,427
1917	19.4	146	49	13,233
1918	12.0	173	42	35,726
1919	7.9	186	57	39,683
1920	7.2	171	59	68,138
1921	—	153	73	26,678
1922	—	150	84	

SOURCE: David Rock, *Politics in Argentina, 1890–1930: The Rise and Fall of Radicalism* (Cambridge, 1975), 159–60.

scant relief. It helped reduce unemployment—possibly more among women than men—but failed to check rising prices. For many working-class families in Buenos Aires, real wages fell by as much as half between the plunge into depression in 1913 and the Armistice in November 1918. Falling standards of living alongside a tightening labor market proved a politically explosive combination. Labor's earlier quiescence ceased abruptly. Between 1917 and 1921 trade unions in Argentina flourished on a scale previously unknown and not matched again until the mid 1940s; strikes, before so conspicuously absent, mounted in number, intensity, and eventually in violence.[37]

The instability of the war years continued in some measure until 1924. The postwar depression that began in 1921 led once more to unemployment, the collapse of the trade union movement, a decline in imports and another decline in state revenues. In 1920 imports were valued at 2,120 million paper pesos, but at only 1,570 million in 1922; because tariffs were increased in 1920, revenues fell during the same period by only 20 million. Yet public expenditures continued to climb, and the floating debt increased once more from 682 million paper pesos to 893 million. The postwar depression's severe effect on the cattle sector precipitated a shift back to agriculture, which by 1929 brought a large increase in land devoted to linseed and cereals.[38]

During the later 1920s much of the real growth in the rural sector, as opposed to mere substitutions in land use, occurred beyond the pampas region. In the northwest Salta and Jujuy now joined Tucumán as large sugar producers. In 1920 the two provinces contributed less than 16 percent of the national sugar output; by 1930 their share had risen to almost 26 percent. The more northerly sugar region differed from Tucumán in that production was mainly on large estates. From the 1920s and into the following decade, it became common for the *ingenio* owners of Tucumán to buy up *haciendas* northward. Some they used for cane production, but others they acquired apparently to gain control over their peasant occupants, whom they then pushed onto the plantations.[39]

There was also growth in fruit production in the Rio Negro valley; in cotton, rice, peanuts, and cassava in the Chaco; and in fruits and yerba mate in Misiones. Domestic cotton output increased from an annual average of 6,000 tons in 1920–1924 to 35,000 tons in 1930–1934, and yerba mate from 12,000 to 46,000 tons. The national government's energetic and highly successful colonization program in the national territories helped Rio Negro, Chaco, and Misiones to attract substantial numbers of new European immigrants. As a result, by 1930 small farming was more widely established than before the war, although most new farms lay in the periphery. In the pampas there was little change, and the large estates still prevailed. However, the new small-farming belt outside the pampas also contained precapitalist features, especially a dependence on contract labor. Large numbers of Chileans worked the farms of Rio Negro and Neuquén; and Paraguayans, *chaqueños*, and *correntinos* those in the northeast.[40]

After 1913 the growth of domestic manufacturing at least matched expansion in the economy at large, but it became notably faster after the war. During the war market opportunities for manufacturers were curtailed by the contraction of demand and shortages of raw materials. A degree of import substitution occurred in manufacturing, but amid near stagnation in manufacturing output at large. In 1914 the index of industrial production was 20.3 (index base, 1950 = 100). In 1918 it was only 22.1, but by 1929 it reached 45.6. During the war the index grew at an annual rate of 0.36 percent, after the war by 2.1 percent. The 1920s also witnessed a faster rate of diversification in the manufacturing of consumer durables, chemicals, electricity, and particularly metals. Between 1926 and 1929 the output index for the metallurgical industry increased from 29 to 43 (index base, 1950 = 100). Even so, much of the growth in manufacturing was in light and traditional industries, continuing the prewar pattern, and textiles were for the most part stagnant. The growth of manufacturing also failed to affect Argentina's high import coefficient, which in the late 1920s remained roughly the same as in 1914, at around 25 percent. On balance the period thus brought the country little nearer to integrated industrialization.[41]

Of the much smaller volume of postwar foreign investment, the major source was the United States. In the 1920s American investment was much higher than British, which all but came to a halt, with the result that by 1930 American investment had climbed to roughly one-third of the British total, having risen from 39 million gold pesos in 1913 to 611 million in 1929. American interests, once almost wholly confined to meat packing, became active lenders to the government and investors in local industry. Twenty-three subsidiaries of American manufacturing corporations were established in Argentina between 1924 and 1933. But these had little effect on the basic economic structure and, except for oil, failed to foster backward linkages in the economy at large. The machinery and much of the fuel and the raw materials used by the American companies were imported. Like the

railroads before 1914, private foreign investment thus tended to impose binding additions to the import bill, leaving manufacturing and
urban employment ultimately as dependent as before on foreign earnings from exports.

In the 1920s growing imports from the United States began to
strain Argentina's commercial links with Great Britain. In 1914 imports from the United States were valued at 43 million gold pesos;
they rose to 169 million by 1918, to 310 million in 1920, and to 516
million by 1929. During the war the Americans gained mostly at the
expense of Germany, but afterward they began capturing markets
from the British. The British share of the Argentine market fell from
30 percent in 1911–1913 to only 19 percent by 1929–1930, while the
American increased from 15 to 24 percent (see Table 15). After the war
the British increased exports of coal and railroad materials to Argentina, but they were unable to compete in the goods for which demand
was rising most rapidly: automobiles and capital goods for agriculture
and industry.

Changes in Argentina's import trade were not accompanied by a
parallel reorientation in exports. The striking feature of the 1920s was
Argentina's failure to balance its growing import reliance on the
United States by an expansion of exports to the American market.
Despite a temporary increase during the war years, exports to the
United States, which were 6.3 percent of Argentine exports in
1911–1913, remained at only 9.3 percent in 1928–1930. In the late 1920s
some 85 percent of Argentina's exports went to western Europe; indeed the trend for exports was almost the direct inverse of that for
imports. Although Argentina was now buying relatively less from
Britain, the proportion of exports that was sent to Britain increased

TABLE 15. *Argentine Trade with Britain and the United States,*
1913–1930 (Select years, as percentage of total)

| | Imports | | Exports | |
	Britain	U.S.	Britain	U.S.
1913	31.0	14.7	24.9	4.7
1921	23.3	26.9	30.6	8.9
1924	23.4	22.0	23.1	7.1
1927	19.4	25.4	28.2	8.3
1930	19.8	22.1	36.5	9.7

SOURCE: Colin Lewis, "Anglo-Argentine Trade, 1945–1965," in *Argentina in the Twentieth Century*, David Rock, ed. (London, 1975), 115.

from 26.1 percent in 1911–1913 to 32.5 percent in 1928–1930. While Argentina was developing a close association with the United States for imports, it remained heavily dependent on Britain for its export earnings—commercial trends that were to prove of major importance.[42]

WAR AND POSTWAR POLITICS, 1916–1930

Hipólito Yrigoyen's first term as president, which ended in October 1922, was far from being the smooth transition into representative government that supporters of electoral reform had desired. After 1916 the battle between conservatives and Radicals that originated in 1890 continued unabated. Conflicts were exacerbated by the wartime inflation, which heavily distorted income shares among the major social classes, and by the cycles of depression and expansion that affected state revenues and Yrigoyen's abilities to hold or consolidate his popular support.

In 1916 the new government's legislative proposals largely confirmed the views of those who had seen the Radicals as timid reformers, basically dedicated to the established order. The program was mild in character and included recommendations that had been under public discussion for some time. Yrigoyen requested from Congress funds for new colonization schemes on state lands, for subsidies to farmers caught by a recent drought, for a new state bank to improve farmer's credit, and for the purchase of shipping to counter high wartime freights. The program was a bid for popularity among the pampas' rural middle classes, especially in the province of Buenos Aires where the Radicals were still a minority. The conservatives, however, were determined to maintain control there. Pleading the need for economy during the wartime recession, Congress therefore rejected the plan.

To carry through his program Yrigoyen needed control over Congress. Like Roca, Pellegrini, and Figueroa Alcorta before him, he turned to the device of federal intervention, using it to supplant the conservatives and their party machines in the provinces. During his six-year term there were an unprecedented twenty interventions, fifteen of them by executive decree. Denounced by numerous conservatives as illegal and unconstitutional, these decrees constantly inflamed partisan controversies. A major uproar in April 1917, which sparked rumors of revolutionary plots among the conservatives, was provoked by Yrigoyen's decreed intervention against Marcelino Ugarte in the province of Buenos Aires. But largely because of the interventions, by 1918 the Radicals had a majority in the Chamber of Deputies. They failed, however, to gain control over the Senate, whose members were protected by nine-year terms. Continually stymied by the impasse in Congress, Yrigoyen's administration produced little legislation. With the conservatives also unwilling to cooperate on budgetary issues, Yrigoyen's term was disfigured by claims and counterclaims of illegal and improper government spending.[43]

Before 1919 the Radical government sought to strengthen its links with the middle classes by supporting *La Reforma*, the university reform movement that began in Córdoba in 1918 as the climax to growing agitation to expand higher education. Argentina had three universities: Córdoba, founded by the Jesuits in 1617; Buenos Aires, founded by Rivadavia in 1821; and La Plata, founded in 1890. Mirroring the expansion of the new middle class, attendance at these institutions had increased from around 3,000 in 1900 to 14,000 in 1918. By 1918 tensions had been rising in Córdoba for a decade or more. The university administration was controlled by conservatives, but the student body was increasingly dominated by middle-class groups of immigrant background. During the war long-standing demands for improvements in the university's teaching and for the streamlining of its curricula were radicalized by events in Europe and Russia and by the Mexican Revolution. The reform movement began in 1918 with a succession of militant strikes and an outpouring of manifestos organized by a new students' union, the *Federación Universitaria Argentina*. Demands were made for student representation in university government, the reform of examination practices, and an end to nepotism in the appointment of the professorial staff. As one of the students' manifestoes declared, "We rebelled against an administrative system, against a method of teaching, against a concept of authority."[44] For much of the year Córdoba was in turmoil. The following year the student strikes spread to Buenos Aires and La Plata.

Throughout the Radical government gave the students in Córdoba sustained support, implementing many of their demands and seeking to link the vague democratic ideals of Radicalism and the diffuse body of doctrine emanating from the reform movement. The government enacted similar changes at the University of Buenos Aires, and later all three universities were given new charters that supposedly enhanced their autonomy, but which actually brought them more directly under the budgetary control of the central government. In 1919 and 1921 new universities were created in Santa Fe and Tucumán under the same system. The Radical government's support for university reform represented one of its more positive and lasting achievements, for in this area Yrigoyen managed to challenge privileged interests and associate himself with democratization, without being checked by conservative opposition.[45]

His much less fruitful contact with the Buenos Aires working class and the trade unions stemmed from rivalries between Radicals and Socialists for a popular majority in the federal capital. Conflict for the working-class vote, already a leading issue in the presidential election in 1916, continued unabated. The Radical offensive began at the end of 1916 on the outbreak of a strike in the port of Buenos Aires, the first of many such movements in the wake of the wartime inflation. The authorities responded with a show of sympathy for the strikers and refused to summon the police—hitherto the most common practice. Instead members of the government and the government press announced they would pursue "distributive justice" and a policy of "social harmony," familiar notions in the corporatist concept of the organic state, but experienced so far in Argentina as little more than esoteric theories. Subsequently, several union leaders were brought before members of the government and urged to accept their arbitration. The strikers thereby obtained a settlement that met most of their grievances.[46]

Government intervention in this strike and others won the Radicals a measure of popularity among the voting working class, which helped the Radicals defeat the Socialists in the congressional election of 1918. But victory was accomplished at the cost of inflamed conservative opposition, which moved quickly beyond Congress and the press to embrace special interest associations led by the Argentine Rural Society (*Sociedad Rural Argentina*), the main organ of the cattle owners. In 1917 and 1918 the strikes spread to the British railroad companies. Largely due to the high cost of imported coal, working conditions had deteriorated and wages had fallen steeply. When the administration again appeared to take the strikers' side, opposition spread to British business groups. Primed by leading British companies, employers established a strike-breaking body, the National Labor Association (*Asociación Nacional del Trabajo*), which pledged itself to an all-out war against union "agitators."[47]

In early January 1919 working-class discontent suddenly further intensified, and the subsequent events, known as *"La Semana Trágica,"* are remembered as one of the great benchmarks in the history of Argentine labor. Metallurgical workers in Buenos Aires had called a strike the month before. During the war the metallurgical industry had suffered perhaps more than any other because of its dependency on imported raw materials. High shipping rates and acute shortages due to arms manufacture caused the cost of raw materials to reach astronomical levels, and as costs climbed, wages fell. By the end of the war the metallurgical workers' situation was desperate, their strike a battle for survival. Violence immediately ensued, and the city police force intervened. When the strikers killed a policeman, the force organized a retaliatory ambush. Two days later five bystanders were killed in an affray between the two sides.

At this Buenos Aires erupted. On 9 January 1919 workers struck *en masse*, and more outbreaks of violence followed. As the Army intervened to quell the movement, the Radical government fell captive to a conservative-led reaction bent on exacting revenge for the disorders. In the strike's aftermath civilian vigilante gangs appeared in the streets. Their manhunt for "agitators" claimed scores of victims, among them numerous Russian Jews who were falsely accused of masterminding a Communist conspiracy. When the violence finally subsided, the vigilante groups organized themselves into the Argentine Patriotic League (*Liga Patriótica Argentina*). With backing from the Army and Navy, the League remained active during the next two or three years, constantly vigilant against "Bolshevik" conspiracies, repeatedly threatening the government with force whenever it made renewed moves to conciliate organized labor, and conducting education campaigns among the immigrant communities to inculcate the values of "patriotism." The outcome of Yrigoyen's dabblings with the unions was thus the crystallization of a new Right with authoritarian and protofascist tendencies. Behind it stood the Army, both of them ready to attack the government and thereby to bring to a swift conclusion the experiment with representative government. After 1919 Yrigoyen was compelled to give the new Right virtually free rein; for example, strikes of shepherds and rural workers in Patagonia in 1921–1922 were met by army intervention and a series of massacres.[48]

Labor unrest in this period illustrated the difficulties of attempting reform or broadening democratization without the backing of the conservative elites. It now seemed that the true intent of the Sáenz Peña Law was less to foster change but to restrain it by coopting native groups, including the new middle classes, into formal politics as a buffer against the immigrants and the workers. Labor conflicts also precipitated the armed forces into politics. Armies and militias had performed a central role in Argentine politics throughout the nineteenth century, and this role survived the Army's reform and modernization under Roca soon after 1900. Yet the events of 1917–1919 showed the Army in a more prominent political role than ever before, as the arbiter in the fate of representative government. The Army's lingering politicization was due partly to Yrigoyen and the Radicals. Before 1912 they had made numerous efforts to capture its support in their campaign against the conservatives, and they continued to do so afterwards. But it was now apparent the Army's (and still more so the Navy's) sympathies lay with the conservatives; the Army too was another great obstacle to Yrigoyen's efforts to promote reform and deepen political change.[49]

The political crisis of 1919 helped provoke major changes in Yrigoyen's style of political leadership and the subsequent development of Radicalism. To counter the threat from the Right, Yrigoyen took the path of populism. After mid 1919, as imports and revenues recovered, state spending began a steep ascent. Alongside it grew the bureaucracy, as Yrigoyen began using his powers of patronage to reconstruct his popular support. The technique soon brought returns as the Radicals again defeated their electoral challengers, leaving the conservatives once more isolated. However, as Yrigoyen's popularity grew in the electorate at large, conservative opposition to him continued to harden. After the debacle with organized labor and now the steep expansion in public spending, he was vilified as a demagogue. In 1916 the conservatives had acquiesced in Yrigoyen's succession in the belief he would protect continuity and stability. In most areas the hoped-for continuity was achieved, since the Radicals accomplished negligible reform, but by 1922 genuine stability remained as distant a goal as ever. [50]

Yrigoyen's successor in 1922 was Marcelo T. de Alvear, a descendant of Carlos de Alvear and a member of one of the country's wealthiest landowning families. Alvear gained a convincing victory over a divided opposition and took office at the height of the postwar depression. Three chief issues, each with complex implications, faced him: crisis in the beef industry, tariff reform, and the public debt. The first issue illustrated the power wielded by the foreign meat-packing plants in Argentine politics, while the second revealed the prevalence of nineteenth-century attitudes toward the tariff and industrial development. Alvear's handling of the debt issue had a central bearing on politics throughout the decade, becoming a major divisive factor in the Radical party in 1924 that enabled Yrigoyen's resurgence as a popular leader in readiness for the presidential election of 1928. The prewar chilled-beef trade, which had arisen mainly under American direction since 1907, was oriented toward the more affluent sectors of the British consuming public. When war came in 1914 chilled-beef exports declined steeply, as controls, quotas, and rationing were imposed in Britain. At the same time the British, and in some measure the French, began to purchase much larger quantities of cheaper and less-sophisticated meat products for their troops on the Western front. Thus while exports of chilled beef fell, shipments of frozen and canned beef rapidly increased. The shift toward inferior-quality meats made it unnecessary for Argentine ranchers to use high-grade stock fattened on special pasture before slaughter. As a result the prewar trend toward specialization between breeders and fatteners largely ceased, and all ranchers serviced the frozen- and canned-meat business. During the war, while profits for meat packers skyrocketed, several new plants were created in Zárate in northern Buenos Aires, in Concordia in Entre Rios, and in La Plata. Prosperity also reached into the more peripheral cattle regions of Entre Rios and Corrientes, where the herds were mostly traditional creole breeds. Equally urban interests from Buenos Aires and Rosario were drawn into ranching on a large scale, borrowing heavily from the banks to do so. Between 1914 and 1921 the cattle stock in Argentina increased by almost 50 percent, from 26 million to 37 million.

The boom ended abruptly in 1921 when the British government ceased stockpiling supplies from Argentina, abolished meat control, and began to liquidate its accumulated holdings. In Argentina the number of cattle slaughtered for export in 1921 was less than half that in 1918, and prices also dropped by half. Production of frozen and canned beef declined precipitously, and all but disappeared. What little beef trade remained was again, after a seven-year lapse, dominated by chilled beef. For a time all sectors of the cattle economy, from the humble alfalfa farmers to the great meat-packing plants, suffered from the depression. But because of the vertical organization of the industry, the losses were unevenly distributed. Some businesses protected their profit margins by lowering the prices they paid to the subordinate sectors that serviced them. The greatest power and freedom to maneuver resided with the meat-packing plants. Cattle ranchers with Shorthorn stock were also able to avoid the full impact of the depression by reverting to the chilled-beef trade, and specialist fatteners cut prices to breeders. Besides the breeders, the main victims of the depression were the cattle owners of Entre Rios and Corrientes, who only had creole stock, and the gamut of wartime speculators, who faced a crippling burden of debt.

At the height of the depression a group representing the cattle breeders won control over the Rural Society. This prestigious institution was employed to bring pressure on the government to intervene against the meat-packing plants, which were accused of operating a buying pool to protect their own profits. To counter the meat-packers' pool the Rural Society proposed creating a locally owned plant that would pay higher prices than the American and British buyers. Other recommended measures were intended to assist ranchers overstocked with creole cattle: the introduction of a uniform minimum price, determined by weight rather than pedigree, and the exclusion of foreign meat packers from the domestic market, which would thus be reserved for those with lower-grade stock. In 1923, with support from Alvear, Congress passed legislation that incorporated most of these proposals, but this regulatory effort proved a spectacular failure. The packers replied by imposing an embargo on all cattle purchases, an action that quickly reduced the ranchers to confusion and division. The government soon shelved the entire scheme and did not attempt renewed intervention. The episode was a dramatic and unprecedented demonstration of the power of foreign-dominated monopsonies.[51]

Alvear's proposals to Congress in 1923 for changes in the tariff have sometimes been interpreted as a strong shift toward protectionism in support of domestic manufacturing. This claim was first made by Alejandro E. Bunge, Argentina's leading economist in this period, an early apostle of industrialization and a proponent of protectionist programs emulating Japanese practice. However, Bunge's claims and those made by later economic nationalists are scarcely borne out by the evidence. One part of Alvear's proposed measure stipulated reducing duties on imported raw materials used by the metallurgical industry; rather than a protectionist effort, this was a freeing of trade to assist an import-dependent industry. Another part suggested extending protection to cotton, yerba mate, and temperate fruits—a proposal that simply returned to the policy advocated by Pellegrini in the mid 1870s, which had led to tariff protection for flour, sugar, and wine. Once more the aim was to diversify the agricultural sector, in this case to assist government colonization schemes in the

Chaco, Misiones, and Rio Negro. Lastly, the measure of 1923 recommended a substantial increase in tariff valuations (*aforos*), the notional values applied to each category of imports upon which variable schedules of duties were imposed. This proposal was also squarely in the nineteenth-century tradition, which used tariffs not as an instrument of protection but as a source of revenues. By the early 1920s the real incidence of the *aforos* had declined substantially, due to the wartime inflation, and government revenues along with them. The 1923 readjustment, together with one made by Yrigoyen in 1920, had no greater effect than to restore duties to the level of 1914. Rather than any essay into protectionism, this was clearly a pitch for "normalcy" with revenue considerations foremost.

In the early 1920s Argentina remained unwilling to launch an effort to industrialize. Policy makers were deeply aware of the likely costs of such a venture and markedly reluctant to incur them, attitudes strongly colored by experience during the past decade. Since 1913 local manufacturing had enjoyed unprecedented, if also involuntary, protection as a result of the steep decline in worldwide industrial production. But to contemporary observers this protection seemed to have achieved only a wave of severe inflation, profiteering by local monopolies, and a spate of strikes that appeared in early 1919 to be at the point of provoking a workers' revolution. Thus the attitude toward national industry continued to echo a nineteenth-century theme, that protection was justifiable only to support local products that would quickly become price competitive with imports, for the most part only agricultural goods. To support "artificial" industries, it was argued, would induce chronic inefficiencies and social tensions.[52]

The Alvear government began its tenure with a large floating debt, inherited from the high-spending Yrigoyen. Fiscal conservatives in its ranks were uneasy with the rampant populism of recent years and were determined to dilute it. The effort at economy was pursued with some determination, but when large-scale dismissals affected appointees from the previous administration, Alvear quickly lost the support of his party. In mid 1924 the Radicals split. The majority, overwhelmingly middle class in composition and mainly the beneficiaries of government patronage and jobbery, renounced Alvear, readopted Yrigoyen, and from henceforth styled themselves *yrigoyenistas*. The rump, mainly the party's conservative and patrician wing, organized itself into the Antipersonalist Radical party (*Unión Cívica Radical Antipersonalista*). An embittered struggle for supremacy erupted between the two sides. At first Alvear aligned himself with the Antipersonalists, but in 1925 he broke with them, refusing their demand for federal intervention against the *yrigoyenistas* in the province of Buenos Aires. With Alvear neutral and politically impotent, the way was open once more for Yrigoyen. After the party split his followers rapidly reconstructed their organization, again using the local committee system that the Radicals first developed after 1906. Then they embarked on a bid for popular support. The *yrigoyenista* campaign of 1925–1928 was pursued with an energy, dash, and commitment hitherto unknown in local politics. By 1926 it had proved remarkably successful, with the *yrigoyenistas* defeating all challengers. As Alvear's term drew to its close in 1928, Yrigoyen was poised for a triumphant return to power.

Yet as these events unfolded, it was evident that Yrigoyen still had powerful enemies. Undeviating hostility toward him prevailed in the Army and among leading conservative institutions, whose forces were now augmented by the Antipersonalists and other smaller parties. The provinces of Mendoza and San Juan, under the grip of the Lencinas and Cantoni families respectively, had become centers of a virulent local populist *anti-yrigoyenismo*. Their dislike of Yrigoyen dated to the federal interventions he had ordered a decade earlier to unseat local Radical governors and impose others from Buenos Aires. In effect, Yrigoyen's interventions had provoked a local neo-Federalist backlash.

Among all these various groups Yrigoyen's return prompted not only distaste but also some fear. He had spared no effort to reconstruct his popularity, frequently engaging in blatant rabble-rousing and fanning expectations of a return to the spoils bonanza of 1919–1922. Many of his opponents suspected him of plotting a popular dictatorship. With the prospect of his return to the presidency, support among conservative groups for the Sáenz Peña electoral reform was rapidly dwindling, and some contemplated recourse to a military coup. Among the most extreme anti-*yrigoyenistas* were several new right-wing groups styling themselves nationalists, committed to the overthrow of representative government, to the erection of a military dictatorship that would destroy "demagogy" while restoring social order and "hierarchy," and to the extirpation of all "imported" or "foreign ideologies." By 1927 nationalists had begun to draw together in a movement styled the *Nueva República*. But as yet all Yrigoyen's opponents together amounted to only a scattering of disunited minorities. In 1928, with Yrigoyen at the zenith of his popu-larity, any attempt to forestall his return risked provoking a civil war. For the moment Yrigoyen's opponents had to wait.[53]

During the election campaign of 1928 the *yrigoyenistas* found one issue that, more than any other, helped carry their leader back into power: a state monopoly over oil. This nationalist crusade was also focused against American oil interests, particularly Standard Oil of New Jersey, and thereby became a central element in a growing crisis in relations between Argentina and the United States.

This oil campaign was inaugurated some twenty years after the discovery in 1907 of the rich Patagonian oil fields at Comodoro Riva-davia and other smaller fields in Neuquén, Mendoza, and Salta. From the start, the Argentine state had a leading part in the oil industry, reflecting a strong determination to prevent oil resources from falling into foreign hands. In 1910 legislation established a state reserve of 5,000 hectares in Comodoro Rivadavia, from which all private claims were for a time excluded. The government soon commenced drilling operations there, while private interests were initially confined to the smaller fields elsewhere.

In its early years the industry's progress, with the state sector acting as a leader, was disappointing. Hopes of reducing oil imports, which came mainly from Texas and Mexico, were unfulfilled, and local production before 1914 was barely 7 percent of total con-sumption. Various factors caused such shortcomings: Congress was unwilling to increase taxes to provide funding; difficulties were en-countered in obtaining skilled personnel and equipment; and during the war the United States embargoed exports of drilling and refining equipment. Although attempts to increase production were sup-ported by the Army and Navy, to satisfy defense needs, progress did little to alleviate the crisis caused by shortages of imported British coal. Furthermore, only a fraction of the small output of crude could be refined.[54]

The wartime fuel crisis eroded some Argentines' arguments against foreign involvement in the industry. Such foreign in-volvement came to be seen as a necessary evil to increase the pace of development, an opinion largely shared by the first Radical govern-ment. Indeed, between 1916 and 1922 Yrigoyen was perhaps less nationalistic on oil than his conservative predecessors, registering no opposition to the presence of a private sector dominated by foreign interests. Under his administration private companies increased their share of production from a diminutive 3 percent to 20 percent. Yrigoyen used Comodoro Rivadavia, like the rest of the government, as a source of political patronage. His efforts at oil reform, like so many other proposals, fell foul of a hostile Senate. His most significant step came in 1922 with the establishment of a new supervisory and managerial board for state oil, the *Dirección Nacional de los Yacimientos Petrolíferos Fiscales*, known as the YPF.[55]

Under Alvear came more favorable conditions for the import of oil equipment, and he placed the YPF under a vigorous and independent military administrator, General Enrique Mosconi. Many of the state sector's early difficulties were now resolved. In 1925 a large refinery was opened at La Plata. The YPF established its own retailing network for gasoline and kerosene. But despite the expansion of the YPF—the first vertically integrated state petroleum industry outside the Soviet Union—the 1920s saw even faster growth among the private companies, which by 1928 had increased their share to almost 38 percent of nationwide production. Private companies were the source of almost a third of the output from Comodoro Rivadavia, two-thirds of that from Plaza Huincúl in Neuquén, and all the output from the smaller fields in the provinces. Among the private companies Standard Oil was the most prominent. The leading importer of oil, it also controlled the main channels of internal distribution, had substantial interests in refining, and had the largest share in kerosene and car fuel sales. Standard Oil also controlled the oil industry in Salta, where it had amassed a vast area, overlapping northward into Bolivia, to which it held exclusive exploration and drilling rights.[56]

Beginning around 1925, amid a highly publicized battle for supremacy between the private oil companies and the YPF, public opinion at large returned to its prewar hostility toward foreigners in the industry, and the *yrigoyenistas* plunged into a campaign to exploit the popular mood. In July 1927 they pledged to bring all the nation's oil fields under state control and to extend the state monopoly to refining, subproducts, and distribution. They began depicting this measure as the sovereign remedy for the nation's ills: the oil revenues would enable the repatriation of the foreign debt; manufacturers would be endowed with a limitless source of cheap power; a state oil monopoly would enable the elimination of all other forms of taxation. The nationalization program was accompanied by a strident campaign against Standard Oil.[57]

By the late 1920s a sharp note of anti-Americanism had appeared in Argentina. Its origins were several, including cultural biases, but among its chief causes were longstanding disputes over trade. The principals in these disputes were not so much the middle classes nor the Radicals as the pampas' landed interests and the conservatives. Since the turn of the century, first with Texas oil and then with cars and other consumer and capital goods, the Americans had obtained a large share in the Argentine market, but Argentina had been unable to develop reciprocal exports to the United States. After the American Civil War Argentina suffered the closure of the American market to its wool. Later it failed to win access for its major grain and meat products. Although exports to the United States had increased tenfold in value during World War I, in 1922 the Fordney-McCumber tariff restored and in some measure extended the earlier policy of exclusion.

As a result, Argentina remained heavily dependent on its exports to western Europe, especially to Britain. But this long connection was now threatened by the shift in Argentina's imports from Britain to the United States. By the late 1920s Argentina's trade surplus with Britain roughly matched its deficit with the United States. Argentina feared that Britain would soon respond with discriminatory action, cutting its purchases from Argentina to relieve its trade deficit. If, for example, the campaign in progress for Imperial Preference in Britain were successful, British Dominion producers—Canada, Australia, New Zealand, and South Africa—would usurp Argentina's share in the British market.

Trade questions also bore closely on the issue of Standard Oil. In 1926, the Coolidge administration, pleading the need for protection against hoof-and-mouth disease, banned imports of dressed beef from the River Plate. Buenos Aires viewed the measure as another act of deliberate discrimination and immediately sought to retaliate by moving against Standard Oil. For Yrigoyen's part, the campaign against Standard Oil enabled him to ride with the popular tide while presenting himself as a champion of wider national interests and the pampas' landowning elites. While attacking Standard Oil, the *yrigoyenistas* carefully refrained from giving offense to the British, who were also active in the oil industry, mostly through Royal Dutch Shell. Yrigoyen apparently intended to give the British the role of chief oil importers and suppliers of equipment required by the YPF, a concession that would both reduce the trade surplus with Britain and improve Argentina's bargaining position in the face of Imperial Preference.[58]

In the 1928 election the *yrigoyenistas* swept aside all opponents. Yrigoyen regained the presidency with around 60 percent of the popular vote, a victory that marked the acme of a public career which had spanned more than half a century. But it was the last of his personal triumphs. Less than two years later, in September 1930, he was over-thrown by a military coup d'etat.

Despite his advancing age, which led to rumors that he was senile, Yrigoyen returned to the presidency with what seemed a much clearer sense of purpose than he had had twelve years before. Despite his popularity, he knew his political survival rested on his ability to keep at bay the conservative and military opposition. The oil question re-mained unresolved, as the nationalization measure submitted by the *yrigoyenistas* in 1927 had passed through the popularly elected Cham-ber of Deputies, but was ignored in the Senate. Again Yrigoyen did not have enough allies in the Senate to enact his program: the oil measure required a Senate majority. Because senatorial elections were pending in Mendoza and San Juan, the bastions of the Lencinas and Cantoni families, Yrigoyen gave much of his immediate attention to politics in Cuyo. The *yrigoyenistas* became embroiled in an embittered conflict for supremacy. In late 1929 they assassinated Carlos Wáshing-ton Lencinas, the leader of the Mendoza opposition, and the year after successfully impugned the election of Federico Cantoni and one of his supporters as senators for San Juan. By mid 1930 the *yrigoyenistas* had quashed much of the opposition in the interior and were at the brink of a Senate majority. The administration planned to resubmit the oil legislation when Congress reconvened in 1931.[59]

While enhancing his position in Congress, Yrigoyen was for a time also successful in dealing with the conservatives in Buenos Aires. With them he continued to exploit the issue of trade relations with Britain and the United States. In 1927, soon after the United States had widened the ban on imported Argentine meat, the Rural Society led a campaign for preferences for British goods against American in the import trade. Its slogan "Buy from those who buy from us" (*Comprar a quien nos compra*) won strong support from the new administration. When Herbert Hoover, as president-elect, visited Buenos Aires in late 1928 on a tour to promote trade with the Latin American republics, he met with a hostile reception and was slighted by Yrigoyen. In con-trast, a year later a British trade mission received a quite cordial wel-come. To its leader, Lord D'Abernon, Yrigoyen offered a "moral gesture" to Britain in acknowledgment of the "close historical ties" between the two countries. He promised numerous concessions to British firms and British goods in the Argentine market, including an exception to the practice of open international bidding that would allow Argentina to acquire all future supplies for the state railroads from Britain.[60]

For some time Yrigoyen thus successfully balanced his followers' aspirations and the elites' concerns about trade and international relations. But in late 1929, on the heels of the Wall Street crash and after two years of falling export earnings and diminishing gold reserves, the Great Depression struck Argentina. *Yrigoyenismo* began to collapse as the depression forced the government to cut state spending. Yrigoyen finally had to pay the price for the methods he had used since 1919 to attract popularity and free himself from the grip of the conservatives.

On Yrigoyen's return to power in 1928, his supporters had immediately snatched control of the bureaucracy. The administration soon became a vast employment agency serving the government's political ends. Although 1928 saw a 10 percent fall in revenues against the previous year, state spending increased by 22 percent. In 1929 revenues rose against 1928 by 9 percent, but spending did so too by 12 percent. Thus by 1929 revenues were one percent lower than in 1927, but spending around 34 percent greater. Finally in 1930, as revenues again declined to around the low 1928 figure, an 11 percent decline in spending left spending still 23 percent higher than in 1928. In 1930 the deficit on current spending amounted to 350 million paper pesos, while the past several years of accumulating deficits had produced a floating debt of 1,200 million paper pesos. Nevertheless, in 1930 the government had begun to cut spending, and in doing so it enhanced the deflationary pressures that resulted from the decline in export prices. As had happened in the mid 1870s, the early 1890s, and to a lesser extent in 1922–1923, government retrenchment accelerated the fall in incomes and the growth of unemployment, thereby shattering the government's political base and leaving open the road to revolution.[61]

In 1930 Yrigoyen fell into a trap similar to that which snared Alvear in 1922–1924 but with far more devastating consequences. The revenue crisis and the depression at large swiftly unhinged his party and his popular backing. In the congressional elections of March 1930, the *yrigoyenista* vote was 25 percent lower than two years before, and in the city of Buenos Aires the *yrigoyenistas* lost an election for the first time since 1924, defeated by the Independent Socialist party, a newly formed offshoot from the old Socialist party now aligned with the conservatives. Disillusionment with the government escalated into inflamed opposition. Events in the Cuyo provinces now attracted intense debate. The press issued long, detailed exposés of administrative corruption. University students, since *La Reforma* among Yrigoyen's most vocal supporters, demonstrated against him, with rival factions of *yrigoyenistas* and their opponents fighting for control of the streets. As reports of the president's senility circulated with growing frequency, the cabinet disintegrated into warring factions. At last Yrigoyen's opponents had their opportunity to destroy him. In early September 1930 Yrigoyen was overthrown by military rebellion.[62]

Democracy's long spring season began with Alem and ended with the Sáenz Peña Law; its brief and tempestuous summer coincided with the war years and lasted through 1919; autumn lingered throughout the 1920s, until its winter finally arrived in September 1930. Despite a long burst of economic expansion after 1890, this political cycle mirrored the shortcomings of Argentina's late–nineteenth-century transition. Representative government might have fared better had its social and economic base been different: had the mid–nineteenth-century liberals succeeded in destroying the monopoly in landownership; had manufacturing developed sufficiently to create a larger and more powerful class of industrial producers; had politics been less susceptible to the manipulation of foreign business interests; had renascent regional conflicts not prevented the elites from uniting in a popular conservative party, as Sáenz Peña had urged in 1912. But actual conditions were the outcome of historical factors that had proved impossible to correct; democracy fell victim to Argentina's colonial heritage.

The political reform of 1912 was far from a capitulation by the old ruling classes; least of all was the reform an invitation to structural change. Indeed, none of the competing power groups demanded such change. At most, reform was a strategic retreat by the elites to buttress the existing social order. The boundaries of concession quickly revealed themselves: reform was intended neither to change the status of worker-immigrants nor to ameliorate their lot. Seeking to limit state spending, conservatives also sought to limit concessions to the urban middle class. When Yrigoyen regained power, he discovered that as long as he could spend, he would survive. Once government spending contracted, he forfeited the support of the middle class and was overthrown. But by 1930 renewed political instability was only one of Argentina's critical problems. Expansion in the rural sector was slowing; difficulties loomed with export markets. For the past seventy years Argentina had prospered largely on account of its close European connection. After 1930 the country was increasingly compelled to search for substitutes.

VI

FROM OLIGARCHY TO POPULISM, 1930-1946

The change of government in 1930 was a conservative, and to some an "oligarchic" restoration. Led by the Army, the revolutionaries seized power as popular support for the Radicals collapsed in the wake of the depression. Throughout the 1930s, dubbed "the Infamous Decade" (*La década infame*), the conservatives repeatedly rigged elections to keep themselves in power. Yet they also initiated substantial reform, which assisted them in successfully steering their way through the depression. The real gross domestic product, which had fallen by some 14 percent between 1929 and 1932, recovered rapidly: by 1939 it was almost 15 percent higher than in 1929, and 33 percent above its 1932 level.

Despite its successes, the conservative restoration was briefer in span than the preceding period of Radical dominancy. After 1939 new political forces took shape, forces the conservatives were unable to control and which finally overwhelmed them. In June 1943 they too were overthrown by a military coup d'etat. During the *de facto* regimes of Generals Ramírez and Farrell, the next two and a half years brought political change arguably greater in scope than any since the early 1860s. Its outcome was the election of Juan Perón to the presidency in February 1946. Backed by a new movement whose base was the trade unions and the urban working class, the *peronistas* swept into power brandishing a program of radical social reform and industrialization.

This period was shaped first by the Great Depression and then by World War II. The former sparked a much greater level of government

214

involvement in the economy. Among its other by-products were the rapid growth and diversification of industry and major social change. The war, however, brought a prolonged crisis in Argentina's relations with the United States. From these conditions—an increasingly active state, the expansion of manufacturing, and wartime international issues—emerged Perón's "national-populist" movement.

THE CONSERVATIVE RESTORATION

Between the Sáenz Peña Law of 1912 and the military coup of 1930, Argentine politics is best pictured as an exercise in informal power sharing between the traditional elites and the urban middle classes. Although this relationship was subjected to a multitude of strains and had the appearance of perennial conflict rather than compromise, it functioned due to the expansion of the economy and the unwillingness or inability of government to attempt major reform. After 1916 the status of the elites changed little, and for most of the period the Radicals had the material largesse to satisfy the interests of the middle classes. But the onset of the Great Depression in 1930 immediately pitted the elites and the middle classes against each other in a contest for rapidly shrinking resources. Each began to demand incompatible policies toward government spending. The elites wanted to curtail the state sector, mainly to free funds to help protect themselves against the Depression. The middle classes, however, demanded its still-greater expansion to defend employment and contain the fall in personal income. Caught in the middle, the government failed to satisfy either side and became a target for both. In 1930 its popular support and party base collapsed; this was the prelude to its overthrow.[1]

The deposition of the Radical government on 6 September 1930—the first of the Army-led coups in Argentina in the twentieth century—was accomplished with remarkably little planning and with only small forces. Most of those who marched from the Army garrison at Campo de Mayo to take possession of Government House, the *Casa Rosada*, were junior officer cadets. They completed their task swiftly, with little bloodshed, and against only token resistance.[2]

The leaders of the coup, if united by long hostility toward Yrigoyen, were otherwise divided into two groups that differed fundamentally on the broader objectives of the revolution. On the extreme right was a "nationalist" faction led by General José F. Uriburu, who became president of the provisional government. Uriburu and his associates had been prominent opponents of Yrigoyen's wartime labor policies. Former leaders of the Patriotic League of 1919, they exemplified a nationalism that perpetuated the league's virulent anticommunism and its cult of chauvinistic myths and values. During the 1920s the nationalists had become increasingly antidemocratic and antiliberal. They subscribed to the clericalist doctrine of *hispanidad*, which had developed in Primo de Rivera's Spain, and to some extent they were also influenced by Italian fascism.

In September 1930 to enforce a complete break with the immediate past, the nationalists were prepared to suspend or make radical revisions to the Constitution of 1853, to suppress elections and the political parties, and to create an authoritarian system based on corporate representation. Nationalists elevated state power to an extent quite unknown in the past except perhaps under Rosas, while espousing a more extreme and complete corporatism than any of their predecessors within the recent conservative tradition: the state would no longer simply mediate among subsidiary interest groups, while assisting them in the pursuit of "organic" development; interest groups would now subsist at the state's behest and dictation.[3]

Yet although they held titular leadership, the nationalists were a minority in the revolutionary coalition that overthrew Yrigoyen. The dominant voice, as soon became clear, lay with liberal conservatives led by General Agustín P. Justo, who had served as minister of war under Alvear. The liberals opposed any extreme measures; they saw their task as restoring rather than destroying the Constitution, by purging society of the "corruption" and "demagogy" of the *yrigoyenistas*. Unlike Uriburu's group, the liberals did not want government set above society at large in the corporatist or fascist style, but one directly responsive to the commercial and landed elites.[4]

Soon after taking power, Uriburu sought to strengthen himself by patronizing a paramilitary organization, the *Legión Cívica Argentina*. Justo meanwhile intrigued persistently to undermine him. The twelve months after the revolution were overshadowed by this secret power struggle and by relations with the deposed Radicals. The September revolution had been accompanied by enthusiastic popular demonstrations in Buenos Aires and other cities—street mobs had burnt and ransacked Yrigoyen's home. But the euphoria was short-lived: the depression deepened, and the provisional government's emergency measures began to take their toll. Public opinion took another violent swing, this time in favor of the ousted regime.

Uriburu, however, did not apprehend this change in the popular mood. In April 1931, intending to stage a quasi plebiscite on his own behalf, he allowed a trial election in the province of Buenos Aires to select a new governor. To his consternation, the Radicals were victorious. Three months later an attempted pro-Radical rebellion among military personnel in Corrientes caused the president to annul the April election, severely punish the military dissidents, and conduct a mass roundup of Radical sympathizers. In a desperate bid to regain his standing with the military, Uriburu concocted a deal to allow military officers to cancel their personal debts. Nevertheless, his reputation in the Army plummeted, and within months the nationalist regime had collapsed in disarray. Uriburu had no choice but to set the date for the presidential election he had earlier promised. The election was held in November 1931, but the Radicals were excluded by proscription and by the arrest or exile of their leaders. Justo, who had carefully upheld his military constituency while collecting endorsements from the leading power groups, swept the elections. In early 1932 Justo assumed the presidency; within weeks of leaving the office Uriburu was dead of cancer.[5]

The election of 1931 restored power to the same broad complexion of groups that had controlled it before 1916—the pampas' exporting interests and the lesser landowners in the provinces. The restoration was accomplished thanks to the Army's backing, the proscription of the Radicals, and some crude electoral manipulation. In various parts of the country the police confiscated the ballot tickets of known opposition supporters. Justo's followers falsified voting registers, and in some jurisdictions the dead were resurrected in multitudes to cast their votes. Ballot rigging became a pandemic practice in the 1930s. A common trick of the time was to bribe voters into accepting sealed voting envelopes with premarked ballots. The complicit voter then smuggled the marked ballot into the voting booth and surrendered the legitimate blank ballot card as proof of having accomplished his mission. One of the most notorious areas for election fraud was the city of Avellaneda, just outside the federal capital, where the political bosses were heavily involved in gambling and prostitution. To retain electoral control, they switched ballot boxes, placed a police guard on voting booths, and had members of the opposition arrested on polling day on trumped-up charges. In the 1938 election in Avellaneda, votes cast outnumbered registered voters. Until 1935 the Radicals simply gave up contesting elections, resuming the posture of "abstention" they had endorsed before 1912.[6]

Justo's civilian support embraced an unwieldy coalition of parties known from its inception as the *Concordancia*. Its principal components were three. First were the old-style conservatives of pre-1916 vintage, who shortly before the 1931 election named themselves the National Democratic party. But few of its members were genuine democrats, and given their continual poor showings in many parts of the country, they were never fully national. Second was the Independent Socialist party, a right-wing offshoot from Juan B. Justo's original Socialist party formed in 1927. From this group, which represented the *Concordancia* in the city of Buenos Aires, the Justo regime obtained two of its most talented figures, Federico Pinedo and Antonio de Tomaso. Last were the Antipersonalist Radicals, the most important of the three groups throughout the 1930s. From their ranks came the *Concordancia's* two elected presidents, Justo and his successor, Roberto M. Ortiz.[7]

Compared with Uriburu, whose brief tenure had been disfigured by bouts of persecution and repression, Justo was a far more tolerant and benign ruler. He remained hostile to the nationalist factions, repeatedly outmaneuvering them for control of the Army, while avoiding resort to open dictatorship. On taking office Justo lifted the state of siege that had prevailed since the coup. He released and amnestied political prisoners, among them Hipólito Yrigoyen, who was permitted to spend the last few months of his life in the seclusion of his home in Buenos Aires, where he died in July 1933. Justo also reinstated university professors who had been dismissed for their pro-Radical sympathies. He sharply curbed the activities of paramilitary groups like the *Legión Cívica*. In dealing with the few labor disputes during the early years of the depression, he avoided Uriburu's practice of immediate resort to the police, and at least attempted conciliation. Yet his more enlightened style failed to dispel a growing air of public disillusionment with the regime that followed the coup of 1930 and the election of 1931. Justo's fiction that both had been carried out in the interests of institutional defense, conservation, and continuity was never widely accepted.[8]

Yet throughout Justo's regime there was neither effective nor organized opposition offering genuine alternatives. The old Socialist party, weakened by the schism with the Independent Socialists and the death of Juan B. Justo in 1928, dwindled in membership and influence during the 1930s. Members of the party were elected to Congress from the city of Buenos Aires, thus defeating the government's fraudulent tactics, but most of its leading figures were relics who paraded much the same ideas they had propounded before 1916. As the new order consolidated itself under Justo, the initially spirited reaction of the Radicals soon flagged. Radicalism functioned best in times of prosperity, when it had something to offer the electorate, but during the depression it floundered constantly, strong on moral imperatives but usually weak on content, and divided perennially on tactics and strategy.[9]

In the 1930s the oil question became less significant. Uriburu and Justo buried the idea of a state oil monopoly but avoided inflaming the issue by holding fast to the status quo, treating the state oil directorate—the YPF—and its foreign competitors for the most part equally. This arrangement enabled a tripling in oil output between 1930 and 1946, and a high 9.8 percent growth rate between 1927–1929 and 1941–1943. In the early 1930s, the YPF's share of the market fell to a little over one-third of the total, but when oil imports rapidly declined during World War II, the YPF's share expanded again to reach two-thirds by 1943. A law enacted in 1932 exempted from customs duties equipment imported by the YPF, but, in return, the YPF was required to contribute 10 percent of its profits to the national exchequer. In 1935 a comparable tax was imposed on the foreign companies. In 1936 Justo resolved a price war between the YPF and its competitors by establishing market quotas.[10]

Oil issues gave the Radicals few opportunities to launch a campaign against the government. As time passed, the Radicals became more influential in local and regional affairs, under leaders like Amadeo Sabbatini in Córdoba, than in the national sphere, and in Buenos Aires they largely drifted. Between Yrigoyen's death in 1933 and 1942 they were led, for the most part colorlessly and uninspiringly, by former president Alvear. Having made his peace with the *yrigoyenistas,* or the "intransigents" (*intransigentes*) as they now styled themselves, Alvear devoted most of his nine-year party leadership to a vain attempt to cleanse his party of its rabble-rousing reputation, to reconstruct it in its pristine form as a coalition between the elites and the middle classes. In the 1930s and into the 1940s there seemed even less difference in substance between Radicals and conservatives than a generation before. As Felix Weil declared in 1944, "The conservatives stand for 'moderate progress and honest government,' and the Radicals a 'tempered program and clean government.' Neither of them means it."[11] Even so, the Radicals continued to enjoy a much stronger popular base than their opponents. They maintained their support from both the urban and rural middle classes such that they were able to carry elections whenever the government relented in its use of fraud.

On assuming power in 1930, the conservative regime was immediately confronted by the depression: a 34 percent fall in export earnings against the previous year, a 14 percent decline in aggregate output between 1929 and 1932, and the cessation of immigration. Among the longer-term results of the depression was a substantial fall in population growth. The birthrate dropped (see Table 16); the proportion of foreign-born in the population declined from around 40 percent in 1930 to 26 percent by 1947; the net population increase fell from a rate of more than 30 per 1,000 before 1920 to under 25 per 1,000 after 1935.[12]

The conservatives' first responses to the depression were highly orthodox. Before the coup they had bruited rumors that the Radicals planned to default on the foreign debt; they now gave this matter urgent priority. But, in fact, the much lower rate of foreign investment in the 1920s alongside substantial postwar economic growth had made the burden of external indebtedness light by comparison with 1873 or 1890. During the past thirty years public foreign investment had declined substantially against private. Public foreign investment, which had constituted as much as three-quarters of the total in the late nineteenth century, was now less than a quarter. Of a total estimated foreign investment of 4,300 million gold pesos in 1934, only 900 million comprised loans to the national government and other public authorities. The public foreign debt had also largely ceased to carry gold guarantees and was mostly redeemable in paper currency. But

TABLE 16. *Birthrates and Death Rates, 1915–1945*
(Rates per 1,000 inhabitants)

	Birthrate	Death Rate
1915	35.1	15.5
1920	31.5	14.7
1925	n.a.	n.a.
1930	28.7	12.2
1935	24.7	12.5
1940	24.0	10.7
1945	25.2	10.3

SOURCE: Carlos F. Diaz Alejandro, *Essays in the Economic History of the Argentine Republic* (New Haven, 1970), 426.

the peso had depreciated by as much as 25 percent against gold with the abandonment of convertibility under Yrigoyen in late 1929. This, too, helped mitigate the foreign-debt crisis because many large foreign concerns, among them the railroad companies, abstained from effecting remittances pending an improvement in exchange rates. Finally, since 1914 a large segment of Argentina's public debt had shifted from London to New York. When the dollar was devalued in 1933, Argentina began to repatriate its debt in the United States on favorable terms. After 1930 American loans of this type fell substantially, from $294 million in 1931 to $190 million in 1945; overall foreign investment during the period declined from an estimated 30 percent of total investment in 1930 to only 20 percent by 1946.[13]

Besides the foreign debt the conservative government had to cope with an internal debt that had risen rapidly after Yrigoyen's return in 1928. Uriburu responded with heavy public spending cuts, discharging an estimated 20,000 government employees in Buenos Aires alone between 1930 and 1931. The national government's expenditures fell from 934 million paper pesos in 1929 to 702 million in 1934. Under Justo the peso was devalued in 1933, and the gold profits from this transaction were used to finance the debt's conversion. In 1931 the public floating debt amounted to 1,341.9 million paper pesos; by 1934 it had fallen to 872 million; and by 1935, after the conversion measure, it had dwindled to a mere 110 million.[14]

The same determined approach governed measures adopted to confront the large balance-of-payments deficit provoked by the depression. Cuts in public spending helped depress the demand for imports, as did Uriburu's increased tariffs (see Table 17). In October 1931, following the example of a score or more other countries, Argentina introduced exchange controls. By mid 1932, if at the expense of a large overall contraction in foreign trade, the payments deficit had been eliminated. It recurred in 1933, however, as world cereal prices plummeted to their lowest point in forty years. Wheat, which had sold at 9.68 paper pesos per 100 kilos in 1929, fell to 5.28 paper pesos in 1933, and maize from 8.11 to 4.00 paper pesos. Yet by 1934, after another induced contraction in imports, the trade balance was again restored. The unequal and disproportionate fall in prices between industrial and farm goods during the early years of the depression is illustrated by the comparative declines of exports and imports between 1925–1929 and 1930–1934: the export quantum fell by 6 percent, imports by 40 percent.[15]

By 1933, the government's orthodox policies—balancing the bud-

TABLE 17. Terms of Trade, 1926–1932 (1937 = 100)

	Export Volumes	Import Volumes	Export Prices	Import Prices	Terms of Trade
1926	84	101.2	92.7	118.6	78.2
1927	112	108.3	88.7	115.4	76.9
1928	104	119.6	99.7	102.1	97.6
1929	104	125.0	90.2	100.6	89.7
1930	72	109.6	83.9	98.4	85.3
1931	100	75.6	63.0	99.7	63.2
1932	92	57.6	60.5	93.2	64.9

SOURCE: Guido Di Tella and Manuel Zymelman, Las etapas del desarrollo económico argentino (Buenos Aires, 1967), 410.

get, meeting payments on the foreign debt, eliminating trade deficits—started to ramify toward reform and innovation. Once the conservatives began to employ tariffs to block imports, they could no longer continue the traditional reliance on tariffs as the chief source of revenues. In 1933 Justo replaced his first minister of finance, Alberto Hueyo, an exponent of orthodoxy, by Federico Pinedo. In November Pinedo imposed a series of emergency measures to address the revenue decline caused by the renewed slump in trade. Among them was the introduction of an income tax, an idea first discussed under Yrigoyen in 1918 but one long resisted by conservatives. With the advent of direct taxation, tariffs and duties contributed a smaller proportion of total revenues. Having accounted for 80 percent of total revenues during the 1920s, revenues from trade represented about 50 percent by 1940; by 1946, after the wartime disruption of trade, they were a mere 10 percent. This amounted to a fiscal revolution, which swept away a system that dated to colonial days.[16]

In 1933 Pinedo also reformed the system of exchange control adopted two years earlier. The original regulations directed the government to purchase foreign exchange from exporters and to then sell it in open auction. The reform limited the range of purchasers through a system of permits, and those who lacked permits were obliged to purchase foreign exchange on a parallel market at prices frequently 20 percent above the government's rate. This new system enabled the government to regulate not only the volume of imports but also their content and their source, and the system became a central component in bilateral trading during the 1930s.

The reform enabled the government to collect substantial profits on its exchange dealings. Between 1934 and 1940 these profits amounted to one billion paper pesos, a sum larger than the 1936 budget. Some of these revenues were employed to fund the foreign debt, but most were used to develop a new system of price supports for rural producers. Supports were administered by regulatory boards (*juntas*), which were created for grains, meat, cotton, wines, milk, and other goods. Throughout the 1930s these boards performed like their counterparts in such countries as Brazil and the United States: financing production, purchasing surpluses, and seeking to promote price stability.[17]

The centerpiece of Pinedo's reforms was the Central Bank, created in 1934. The previous banking system made it impossible to control the money supply and manage the economy at large by such methods as buying or selling securities, rediscounting, or changing bank reserve requirements. When the gold standard was in force, as between 1927 and 1929, the domestic money supply was determined by gold holdings, a mechanism that produced a rigid, inelastic monetary system, one which invariably tended to enhance rather than attenuate business cycles. In the early 1930s the traditional alternative of inconvertibility was deemed unsatisfactory because depreciation heavily penalized foreign investors wishing to repatriate their earnings; Pinedo believed that economic recovery ultimately depended on renewed foreign investment.

The Central Bank was thus intended primarily as an alternative to the gold standard, one that would uphold the peso at a fixed parity and enhance the country's attractiveness to new foreign investors, while avoiding the pains of automatic deflation as gold reserves fell. The bank was also empowered to regulate the money supply. By 1935, under Raúl Prebisch, its youthful and resourceful director-general, the bank, however, had developed quasi-Keynesian functions through its capacity to control credit and stimulate demand. The Central Bank was empowered to serve as the financial agent of the government, thereby precluding the recurrence of situations in which the government and the private banks both competed for funds from the Banco de la Nación.[18]

Another hallmark of economic policy in the 1930s was the effort to protect the historic connection with Britain through bilateral commerce. Yet bilateralism emerged more out of necessity than choice. After years of debate, in 1932 Britain adopted Imperial Preference, a scheme reminiscent of Spanish *comercio libre* in the late eighteenth century: Britain would import as much as it could from its empire and, in return, enjoy highly preferential access to the empire's markets. It seemed doubtful, however, whether Britain intended to apply the idea rigidly and cease trading with Argentina, for commercial ties between the two countries were quite extensive and mutually beneficial. But for some time the British had been restive at American competition in the Argentine market, and they were willing to use trade issues to help British companies in Argentina, companies whose earnings had fallen steeply since 1929. During the negotiations on Imperial Preference in Ottawa, Britain therefore agreed to proposals from Australia and South Africa to curtail severely imports of Argentine beef. The plan was to enact monthly cuts of 5 percent during the first year of the agreement. Reports of the plan provoked an immediate outcry in Buenos Aires, and the Justo government hastily dispatched to London a team of negotiators, led by Vice-President Julio Roca, Jr. In 1933 the nations concluded a bilateral treaty known as the Roca-Runciman agreement.[19]

From this treaty Britain undoubtedly received the far greater benefits. Britain agreed to continue admitting the same quantity of Argentine beef as in 1932, at least pending any further severe fall in beef prices in Britain. It also agreed that Argentine-owned *frigoríficos* would provide 15 percent of the nation's meat exports to Britain—a stipulation intended to counter protests in Argentina that the foreign meat packers, as in the early 1920s, had formed a buying pool to hold down prices paid to ranchers. These two were the only substantive concessions made by the British. They applied to beef alone, and they merely kept trade at the same level as early 1932.

In return, Argentina agreed to reduce tariffs on almost 350 British goods to the rates of 1930 and to refrain from imposing duties on goods, such as coal, that were still on the free list. Argentina also committed itself to the "benevolent treatment" of British companies, which were to be given priority in the distribution of permits under the newly reformed exchange control system. Remittances of British companies deferred by the depreciation of the peso—which Britain insisted on treating as a form of forced foreign loan—were to be effected by automatic subtractions from Argentina's sterling earnings on its exports; any blocked funds not released in this way were to be regarded as an interest-earning foreign loan. The treaty also included two concessions to the British railroads: an exemption from certain labor legislation, such as the funding of pension programs, and the

promise of favorable remittance terms in the event of future devaluations in Argentina. Finally, the treaty left almost all trade between
the two countries in the hands of British shippers. In sum, by this
treaty Argentina contrived to hold its meat exports at the levels of
1932, but Britain won what amounted to a return to the conditions of
1929 and in some respects to those of the prewar era.[20]

Following the Roca-Runciman agreement, Argentina concluded
several bilateral treaties with other countries such that by the late
1930s some 60 percent of its imports were procured through bilateral
trade. But throughout, the United States refused any bilateral *quid pro
quo*, continuously unwilling to open its markets to Argentine meats
and cereals. In Buenos Aires importers of American goods thus encountered the twin obstacles of the new high tariffs imposed since
1930 and the requirement to purchase expensive foreign exchange on
the parallel market. Discrimination in the use of exchange control had
been another major concession to the British. After 1933 Britain's
share in the import trade increased substantially; with even greater
speed the American share dwindled (see Table 18).[21]

The term of the Roca-Runciman agreement was three years, and in
1936 it was renewed by the Eden-Malbrán treaty. On this occasion the
British won the option of imposing excise taxes on its meat imports
from Argentina. Second, in return for reducing freight rates for
wheat, the British railroads received even more-favorable terms for
effecting remittances.[22]

Another major issue in British-Argentine relations concerned the
tramway companies of Buenos Aires. Along with the railroads, which
suffered a 40 percent fall in revenues during the early 1930s, receipts

TABLE 18. *Argentine Trade with Britain and the United States,
1927–1939 (Select years, as percentage of total)*

	Argentine Imports		Argentine Exports	
	Britain	*U.S.*	*Britain*	*U.S.*
1927	19.4	25.4	28.2	8.3
1930	19.8	22.1	36.5	9.7
1933	23.4	11.9	36.6	7.8
1936	23.6	14.4	35.0	12.2
1939	22.2	16.4	35.9	12.0

SOURCE: Colin Lewis, "Anglo-Argentine Trade, 1945–1965," in *Argentina in the Twentieth Century*, David Rock, ed. (London, 1975), 115.

on the tramways fell from 43 million paper pesos in 1929 to only 27 million in 1934. But the tramways' declining revenues resulted not only from decreasing traffic during the depression but also from growing competition between the tramways and a newly developing microbus system. In 1935, as the expiration of the Roca-Runciman treaty approached, the largest of the British tramways, the Anglo-Argentine, proposed a citywide transport monopoly under a private corporation, the *Corporación de Trasportes*. This plan, a thinly disguised plot to subject the buses (*colectivos*) to the hegemony of the tramways, called for all parties providing transport services in the city to receive shares and voting power in the transit corporation proportional to their capital assets. In such a corporation the tramways would immediately control the buses, since the latter were mostly one-man businesses operating heavily on credit.

In 1935 the Anglo-Argentine Tramway Company also sought to exhume the guaranteed-profits system of the late nineteenth century, proposing that the city guarantee the transit corporation a minimum 7 percent return on capital. Fearing British retaliation against meat exports, the Justo government acquiesced in the creation of the transit corporation but resisted the demand for guaranteed profits. It subsequently made every effort to ignore and subvert the agreement, doing little to compel the *colectivos* to participate in the plan and repeatedly refusing requests from the tramways to charge higher fares. After 1935 the *colectivos* continued to flourish, and the tramways to lurch at the brink of insolvency.[23]

While the Justo government eventually managed to outmaneuver the British and to concede relatively little on the transit issue, the administration emerged much less unscathed from another episode involving foreign capital. In the early 1930s the meat packers formed a pool, as they had in the early 1920s, intended to force ranchers to bear the brunt of falling prices. Between 1929 and 1933 the price paid to ranchers for live steers declined from 34 *centavos* a kilo to only 17 *centavos*, but between 1930 and 1934 meat packers' profits ranged between 11.5 percent and 14 percent on capital invested. The Roca-Runciman treaty attempted to combat the pool by allowing exports from locally owned *frigoríficos*. But since there were no nationally owned plants in the metropolitan area able to deal in chilled beef, the concession proved meaningless.

The ranchers' complaints intensified, and a congressional investigation in 1935 substantiated most of their charges that a pool was in operation. In a minority report to the committee, a leading member of the Senate opposition, Lisandro De la Torre, went further: he denounced a variety of fraudulent accounting practices among the *frigoríficos* and their evasion of income tax and exchange control regulations. De la Torre also alleged that members of the government had personally profited from the pool. These accusations were debated in the Senate amid hot-tempered denials from senior administration figures. The atmosphere of growing recrimination reached a bizarre climax when Enzo Bordabehere, De la Torre's fellow senator from Santa Fe, was shot dead on the floor of the Senate.[24]

The Justo government justified its conduct toward foreign business interests by claiming that the depression limited its freedom to maneuver; without economic concessions, the country would lose its foreign markets. The administration also pointed to its efforts to reduce dependence on foreigners in constructive ways that helped fight unemployment, citing the example of the road-building program begun in March 1931 and financed by a tax on automobile fuels. Indeed, this program continued throughout the 1930s, often in the teeth of extreme opposition from vested interests like the British railroad companies. Between 1930 and 1940 the road system doubled, and expenditures for highway improvements in 1940 were twice the 3 million pesos spent in 1920.[25]

But by the mid 1930s those pacified by the government's excuses were rapidly dwindling in number. Old provincial conservatives like De la Torre attacked the government's relations with the meat packers. The Radicals denounced the favors given the railroad companies under Pinedo's reformed exchange control system. Socialists, the traditional defenders of consumer interests in the city of Buenos Aires, leapt to the forefront in the controversy over the transit corporation. From all sides came accusations that senior administration officials had made corrupt deals with foreign interests.

Overshadowing all these issues was the intense controversy provoked by the Roca-Runciman treaty, whose opponents flatly denounced it as a betrayal of national interests. They rejected the government's view that the protection of the meat market was a matter of vital necessity; in 1933 chilled beef was a mere 16 percent of total exports. Concessions to the British, they alleged, were out of all proportion to the country's gains. The real object of the treaty, they contended, was to safeguard the elite cattle fatteners, the *invernadores*, whom they saw as the government's main prop. Such attacks on the government were increasingly followed by bitter propaganda campaigns against the British, campaigns that soon evolved toward economic nationalism.

Nationalism emerged as a major force in Argentine politics in the mid 1930s and soon after became a central one. The nationalist movement had diverse historical strands and antecedents. Chauvinistic impulses had surfaced among conservatives since before the turn of the century, a legacy of the conscious effort at nation building made by Mitre and his successors. Protonationalist sentiments were also evident, at least in Buenos Aires, as early as the war with Paraguay. As nineteenth-century economic expansion reached a climax and confidence in the future soared, the elites adopted a form of Manifest Destiny, which at times threatened, like its northern prototype, to permutate into aggressive territorial expansionism. Around 1900, for example, Argentina entered serious disputes with Chile concerning boundaries in Patagonia, and Tierra del Fuego and its adjacent islets. In the event, however, such impulses were curbed by the realization that war might well jeopardize prosperity, a view the British in particular were at pains to encourage, and they eagerly accepted invitations to arbitrate the territorial disputes. Second, Argentina came to recognize that beyond the pampas lay little of real value, little worth seizing or attempting to annex, and that for the present, at least, local resources were well sufficient to satisfy any incipient appetite for land. Nevertheless, the idea that Argentina was a nation graced by Nature and by God, predestined for power and greatness—an idea whose origins lay in Roca's generation and the positivist tradition—lingered on into the 1930s, becoming the foundation for the eventually intimate association between nationalism and the armed forces.

There had also long been a latent, half-articulate filament of economic nationalism in Argentina. Its nineteenth-century thread consisted of the suspicion that foreigners—particularly the British—were making undue profits compared with the benefits they offered Argentina through investment or trade. Such perceptions did not precisely constitute economic nationalism, however, and from the early 1860s till the 1930s very few specific, overt efforts were made to restrict the accumulation of property by foreigners. Land distribution, for example, began to favor native interests not because of any express policy of exclusion but through the subtle operation of market and credit mechanisms; if few immigrant homesteaders gained land titles, a large number of foreign consortia led by the British certainly did.

Before 1930 deliberate exclusion for consciously nationalist motives occurred in one sector alone—the oil industry. Other arguments and sentiments that passed as economic nationalism usually amounted to little more than rhetoric, intended as a bargaining strategy to secure better deals from foreign investors. Landowners, for example, repeatedly campaigned against high freight rates on the railroads; urban consumers attacked the rates set by public utility companies. These protests, often expressed as vague xenophobic grumblings, reached a highpoint during the war, as rates climbed alongside the increasing scarcity of imported coal. Campaigns against foreign capital in the 1930s were in part a legacy of the wartime protests, but the earlier grumbling gave way to outright rejection and repudiation.

Yet another precursor of the new nationalism lay in *yrigoyenismo.* The university reform movement of 1918 had grafted a branch of radical, anti-imperialist doctrine, imported mainly from Mexico and indirectly from Russia, onto the concerns of the new middle class to widen avenues of social mobility. This hybrid bore new fruit during the oil battle of the late 1920s. The *yrigoyenistas* perceived the oil battle as the climax to the struggle for democracy and the downfall of "oligarchy." It is perhaps more accurate to depict it as an incipient symptom of economic stagnation and a narrowing of the channels of social mobility in that it reflected an unconscious yearning for industrialization or a quest for new middle-class jobs. The same general impulses became apparent in a Radical youth nationalist movement founded in 1935, known as the FORJA (*Fuerza de Orientación Radical de la Juventud Argentina*). The FORJA combined the old Radical commitment to "complete democracy" (*democracia integral*) with the kind of blunt, uncompromising nationalism enshrined in the slogan: "We are a colony; we want a free Argentina" (*Somos una Argentina colonial; queremos ser una Argentina libre*).[26]

As yet, however, nationalism with the apparent leftist thrust epitomized by the FORJA was a rarity. Impediments to the growth of working-class nationalism sprang from the structure of the working class and also from the programs of working-class leaders. Until the 1930s much of the working class was foreign-born, and as the low rate of naturalization suggested, transatlantic loyalties overshadowed local. The early anarchist leadership of the working class was similarly cosmopolitan and internationalist in outlook. Leaders with firmer local ties, like the Socialists, directed their energies to defending real wages and consumption. The Socialists were extreme advocates of free trade; they viewed foreign investment as a necessary instrument of economic development and modernization. Among its natural working-class constituency nationalism of the left thus lacked a social and political base, foundations it did not develop until urban manufacturing began its rapid ascent during the late 1930s.

Yet despite such varied and complex origins, until the mid 1930s "nationalism" was best exemplified by right-wing figures like Uriburu. The mainstream nationalist movement flowed from the Patriotic League of 1919, which imbued its nationalist vision with xenophobia, nativism, and clericalism, with anti-Semitism, antianarchism, and above all anticommunism. By the late 1920s this strain of nationalism was also *anti-yrigoyenista* and authoritarian, becoming increasingly penetrated by corporatist and sometimes by fascist doctrine. It was on the extreme political right that radical anti-imperialism made its greatest mark during the 1930s, and it was from this base that the nationalist movement metamorphosized into a comprehensive political program.

After the Roca-Runciman treaty a profusion of new nationalist writers and factions began to appear. For a time the nationalist movement was largely dominated by historians who sought to fuel the campaign against the British. These historical "revisionists" began to reexamine the nineteenth century and to catalogue Britain's imperialist encroachments: the British invasions of 1806–1807, Britain's role in the foundation of Uruguay in the late 1820s, its seizure of the Falkland Islands in 1833, the blockades under Rosas, the later collaboration between the ruling oligarchy and British business interests—the same "antinational" alliance that had concluded the Roca-Runciman treaty. A cult now enveloped the figure of Juan Manuel de Rosas, who was depicted as a symbol of national resistance to foreign domination. Raúl Scalabrini Ortiz resurrected the seamy side of the growth of the British railroad interest after 1862. Propaganda of this kind made a deepening imprint on public opinion and helped sustain nationalist sentiments in the Army. Justo, though throughout the master of the situation, was obliged to be constantly on guard, alert to a multitude of minor plots and intrigues against him.[27]

The Justo presidency came to an end in early 1938 amid some division and confusion in the aftermath of the nationalist campaigns. A split had arisen within the *Concordancia* over whether it should continue to regulate the political process by controlling elections or should seek to enhance its legitimacy by liberalization. The division was mirrored in the new administration, with the presidency going to Roberto M. Ortiz, leader of the factions favoring conciliation. The new president, the self-made son of a Basque grocer in Buenos Aires, was a former Antipersonalist who had served Alvear as a minister of public works and Justo as minister of finance. Ortiz belonged squarely among the liberal-conservatives of the Sáenz Peña tradition. He was unpopular among the more authoritarian-leaning nationalists on account of this background and because he had long served as an attorney for several British railroad companies.

Frictions among the ruling parties prevented Ortiz from nominating his own running mate, and the vice-presidency went to Ramón S. Castillo, a former dean of the law faculty of the University of Buenos Aires. Notorious as an archconservative of pre-1912 vintage, Castillo had served in the Justo government since 1936 as minister of justice and public instruction. Castillo was a native of Catamarca, one of the most backward western provinces and still dominated by a small landowning clique; there the most extreme forms of election fraud flourished unabated.

Ortiz and Castillo were victors in an election diligently stage-managed by the outgoing Justo. But once installed as president, Ortiz declared his intent to cease rigging elections and pursue conciliation with the Radicals. In interim congressional elections in early 1940, the Radicals largely swept the board and, after a ten-year lapse, they again had a majority in the Chamber of Deputies. In March 1940 Ortiz intervened in the province of Buenos Aires to displace its governor, Manuel Fresco, a corporatist who was flirting with fascism and was a leading opponent of political liberalization. To the chagrin of his vice-president, soon after Ortiz carried out a similar intervention in Catamarca. Toward mid 1940 the conservatives, as during the past thirty years, were thus still struggling with the issue of representation, groping for the elusive formula to unite the traditional ruling classes with the population at large.[28]

THE RISE OF IMPORT SUBSTITUTION

Compared with most of the world's industrial nations or some of its Latin American neighbors like Chile, Argentina suffered relatively little from the Great Depression. Its urban unemployment rate, never much above 5 percent, remained far below that in western Europe and the United States. Despite commercial difficulties with the British, substantial economic recovery was underway by 1934, although another recession followed in 1937–1938, mainly caused by adverse weather conditions. Immigration resumed; government spending rose by 27 percent between 1932 and 1937; exports increased, led by grains (see Table 19). Indeed, for several years in the mid 1930s Argentina was the world's largest exporter of corn, partly in the wake of droughts in the United States and Canada, and partly because the tribulations of the cattle sector effected a new decline in the acreage devoted to livestock. In 1936–1937 grain exports reached a record volume; between 1934 and 1939 average prices paid to grain producers rose by 22 percent.[29]

In the early 1930s the depression had also enveloped domestic manufacturing. But once the export recovery primed demand, while imports continued to be restrained by exchange control and bilateralism, Argentina embarked on industrial import substitution. Between the triennial averages of 1927–1929 and 1941–1943, manufacturing grew at an annual rate of 3.4 percent, as against only 1.5 percent in the rural sector and 1.8 percent in gross domestic product. Imports of manufactured consumer goods, around 40 percent of total imports before 1930, had fallen to less than 25 percent by the late 1940s. The 1914 census had catalogued some 383,000 industrial workers; by 1935 the number had risen to 544,000, by 1941 to around 830,000, and by 1946 to over 1 million. Similarly, the number of industrial firms grew from less than 41,000 in 1935 to more than 57,000 in 1940, and to around 86,000 by 1946. In 1935 the value of industrial production was still 40 percent below that of the agrarian sector; in 1943 industry surpassed agriculture for the first time.

Rapid growth in manufacturing began in the mid 1930s and gained

TABLE 19. *Production and Exports of Wheat and Corn, 1933–1939*
(Thousands of metric tons)

| | Wheat | | Corn | |
	Production	Exports	Production	Exports
1933	6,556	3,929	6,802	5,018
1934	7,787	4,793	6,526	5,471
1935	6,550	3,859	11,480	7,047
1936	3,850	1,594	10,057	8,367
1937	6,782	3,887	9,135	9,085
1938	5,009	1,940	4,500	2,641
1939	10,319	4,746	4,424	3,196

SOURCES: Guido Di Tella and Manuel Zymelman, *Las etapas del desarrollo económico argentino* (Buenos Aires, 1967), 427; Carlos F. Diaz Alejandro, *Essays in the Economic History of the Argentine Republic* (New Haven, 1970), 437, 478.

further momentum during the war. But the new manufacturing sector embraced only consumer goods, as import substitution failed to extend into heavy industry. Much of local industry also remained extremely small in scale. In 1939 more than 60 percent of firms catalogued as industrial by census-takers had ten or fewer employees; of the remainder, three-quarters had fewer than fifty employees. In contrast, reflecting the continuing salience of large traditional, export-oriented industries, like the meat-packing plants, firms with more than three hundred workers employed some 40 percent of the total industrial workforce. As the manufacturing sector grew during the 1930s and 1940s, it thus maintained its earlier composition; a few large companies, numerous small firms, and relatively little in between. Also manufacturing, whether large or small, was still a mainly foreign occupation: in 1939 half the owners of small manufacturing plants were foreigners, many of the newcomers Jewish refugees from central Europe. Another conspicuous feature of manufacturing was its overwhelming concentration in the city of Buenos Aires and its immediate environs. In 1939 some 60 percent of the nation's industrial firms, 70 percent of its industrial workers, and around three-quarters of its industrial wages were in Greater Buenos Aires.[30]

Some of the main growth fields of the 1930s and 1940s, such as textiles and processed foods (chocolate, edible oils, dried fruits and vegetables), developed on a base established before 1914. Some of the novelties, particularly such electrical and rubber goods as lightbulbs and tires, were created by subsidiaries of foreign firms. The growth of the latter was one of the unforeseen results of high tariffs, bilateralism, and exchange control. Several American companies that once exported to Argentina from the United States, after 1933 sought to circumvent the discriminatory use of exchange controls by creating local branches in Buenos Aires. Although American investment as a whole fell during the depression and war years, investment in manufacturing subsidiaries increased by an estimated $30 million between 1933 and 1940. Between 1935 and 1939 fourteen new American companies were created in Argentina, employing a workforce of 6,500.[31]

But it was textiles that led import substitution during this period. The textile sector grew even in the depths of the depression: between 1929 and 1934 textile factories in the federal capital increased from twenty-five to thirty, and the workforce in these larger factories from 8,000 to 12,000. In 1930 domestic manufacturers provided less than 9 percent of Argentina's total consumption of textiles, but by 1940 their share rose to 46.9 percent, and to 82 percent by 1943; conversely, imported textiles fell from around 25 percent of total imports in the late 1930s to only 14 percent by the late 1940s. Overall in the 1930s and 1940s textiles achieved an annual growth rate of 11 percent. Between 1935 and 1946 the textile labor force additionally rose from 83,000 to 194,000, a rate matched only by the "food and drink" sector, in which employment increased from 111,000 to 235,000 (see Table 20).

The textile industry benefited from a unique set of conditions. During the early 1930s the price of raw cotton halved, while land devoted to cotton cultivation doubled, from an average of 101,000 hectares between 1927 and 1931 to 225,000 hectares between 1932 and 1936. The expansion of cotton cultivation was assisted by one of the new government regulatory boards established after 1933, the *junta de algodón*. Second, textiles had the advantages of inelastic market demand and relatively low investment capital needs; the former pushed up prices and profits for entrepreneurs when foreign supplies were short, while the latter enabled the intensive use of labor. These factors made the industry highly appropriate to local conditions. By contrast with textiles, manufacturing sectors that remained dependent on imported raw materials, like metallurgy, grew at a slower rate after 1935 than before 1929. Third—as the nationalist critique failed to perceive—domestic textiles were an indirect beneficiary of bilateralism and exchange control, which tended to drive out cheaper foreign suppliers like the Italians or Japanese in favor of relatively expensive British goods. In this oblique way the Roca-Runciman treaty may have helped trigger the expansion of Argentine textile manufacturing.[32]

Closely linked with the growth of manufacturing from the late 1930s onward was internal migration from rural areas into Buenos

TABLE 20. *Indices of Industrial Output 1935–1945 (1960 = 100)*

	All Manufacturing	Textiles	Food and Drink
1935	38	—	—
1937	42	32	85
1939	47	47	90
1941	48	43	90
1943	55	74	101
1945	58	83	94

SOURCE: Carlos F. Diaz Alejandro, *Essays in the Economic History of the Argentine Republic* (New Haven, 1970), 443.

Aires; these migrants came to constitute a large proportion of the new urban industrial working class. Between 1914 and 1935 perhaps 5 percent of the growth of Greater Buenos Aires was due to an influx of population from the hinterland; between 1937 and 1947 the rate leapt to 37 percent. As industrial growth quickened, annual migration increased from an average of 70,000 between 1937 and 1943 to 117,000 between 1943 and 1947. The population of the city of Buenos Aires grew from some 1.5 million in 1914, to 3.4 million in 1935, to 4.7 million by 1947. Numerous migrants also settled in working-class suburbs of the Capital like Avellaneda, which by 1947 had a population of more than 500,000. Altogether between 1937 and 1947 some 750,000 migrants arrived in Greater Buenos Aires. Migration consisted mainly of an outflow from the pampas until 1946, when the movement of population spread more widely into the interior and also beyond the frontier into surrounding states. Before 1946 an estimated two-thirds of the migrants came from the pampas, perhaps as much as 40 percent of them from the province of Buenos Aires alone (see Table 21). Initially, migration thus involved movements over relatively short distances.[33]

While the growth of manufacturing attracted migrants to the city, the contraction in pampas agriculture pushed them out of the countryside. Severe rural unemployment resulted from wartime dis-

TABLE 21. *Migration to Greater Buenos Aires by 1947*

	Migrants *(in thousands)*	*Percentage* *of Total*
Littoral	1,016	59.6
Northwest	117	6.8
Center-west	61	3.5
Northeast	17	0.9
South	53	3.1

NOTE: Littoral includes provinces of Buenos Aires, Sante Fe, Entre Rios, Corrientes, Córdoba; northwest, those of Catamarca, Tucumán, Santiago del Estero, La Rioja, Salta, Jujuy; center-west, provinces of San Luis, San Juan, Mendoza; northeast, those of Chaco, Formosa, Misiones; and south includes La Pampa, Neuquén, Rio Negro, Chubut, Santa Cruz, Tierra del Fuego.

SOURCE: Walter Little, "The Popular Origins of Peronism," in *Argentina in the Twentieth Century*, David Rock, ed. (London, 1975), 165.

ruptions in foreign trade. Cereal exports fell from 17 million tons in 1937 to only 6.5 million in 1942. Corn was the war's chief casualty, as exports that had averaged 6.1 million tons a year between 1935 and 1939 dropped to only 0.4 million between 1941 and 1944. During the war some 8 million tons of grains were simply burnt, between 1940 and 1944 agricultural prices fell to less than two-thirds of those during the previous quinquennium. The average acreage devoted to cereals declined by some 3 million hectares between the periods 1932–1939 and 1940–1945.

To some degree the decline of the staples was offset by the expansion of forage crops, like barley and oats, and new industrial crops like sunflower. Between the periods 1935–1940 and 1944–1946, sunflower production increased by 300 percent, barley by 164 percent, and oats by 123 percent. Yet, as during World War I, the major trend was the substitution of livestock for cereals. While grain prices collapsed during the war, meat prices climbed: chilled beef, for example, fetched 26 cents a kilo in August 1939 but 38 cents in July 1943. In the six-year period after 1939 agricultural prices declined against livestock prices by almost 30 percent; cattle stock increased by almost 25 percent between 1937 and 1947; the 44.2 million hectares devoted to livestock in 1940–1944 represented a record acreage; hog farming, spurred by an abundance of cheap corn, doubled between 1935–1940 and 1944–1945. Argentina's export data show the same trends: between 1939 and 1943 meat increased from 44 percent to 57 percent of total exports, while agriculture's share fell from 49 percent to less than 23 percent; by 1943 more than 20 percent of exports were manufactured goods.[34]

Somewhat fragmentary evidence suggests significant wage and income disparities between rural and urban workers during the war. In 1941 the typical working man with a family of three children living in Buenos Aires earned 127 pesos a month. Officials in the National Labor Department, who monitored urban wages, regarded this sum as about 20 percent below their assessment of the required minimum living wage. Low wages compelled many working-class families in Buenos Aires to reside in the infamously congested *conventillo* tenements, some of which were a century old. Yet this standard of living, which roughly reattained the level of 1929, seemed significantly higher than that in the countryside. In 1937, for example, most head foremen of *estancias* earned less than 100 pesos a month; half of the ranch hands earned less than 40 pesos (though some enjoyed rent subsidies), and half of the agricultural day laborers allegedly earned less than 75 pesos a month. Moreover, during World War II inflation affected urban wages much less than during World War I, and cereal products remained cheap. Also the growth of urban employment helped protect and increase real wages, which by 1947 were 14 percent higher than in 1940 or 1929.[35]

On balance, whatever its shortcomings, life in the city appeared markedly preferable to that in the country. In the early 1940s pampas rural society retained all the unstable features bequeathed by the preceding generations. In 1932 legislation required that agricultural tenants receive five-year contracts and be reimbursed for investments in the lands they farmed. Yet estimates in 1937 showed that more than half the tenants worked without written contracts. Itinerant seasonal laborers composed a large proportion of pampas society, as reflected in a low rural marriage rate and a low rural birthrate. Meanwhile the proportion of absentee landowners climbed from 50 percent in 1914 to around 62 percent in 1937. Landholding remained as highly concentrated as twenty or thirty years earlier. In 1937 some 20,000 landowners held title to as much as 70 percent of the pampas' land area; 3,500 persons or companies owned half the land in the province of Buenos Aires.[36]

Before 1940 the rise of manufacturing and its concomitant social change were frequently noted by observers, but as yet neither had substantially affected Argentine politics. Conservatives had foreseen that some industrial growth would result from the changing conditions in importing, but they were still far from offering any deliberate support for industrialization. They perceived the value of industrial growth and diversification in essentially traditional terms, and their attitudes were scarcely any different from those prevailing sixty or seventy years earlier: some new industry would strengthen the balance of payments and provide employment, thereby staving off political unrest. Both the Justo and Ortiz governments thought economic progress lay not in industrialization but in an expeditious return to the predepression past. They wanted to uphold primary exporting and to strengthen the economy through new foreign investment. Still, their discourse drew heavily on the theory of comparative advantage, and they repeatedly emphasized the constraints on industrialization: meager native reserves of coal and iron ore, an absence of adequate power and transportation facilities for industrial ventures, limited supplies of capital, and the small size of the domestic market. Except for a small band of economic nationalists, such views also prevailed among the other political parties.

An organized lobby of industrial interests was slow to develop. Established organs like the Industrial Union (*Unión Industrial Argentina [UIA]*), founded in 1886, claimed to represent manufacturers but did so inadequately. The UIA was dominated by export-linked groups; in the early 1940s half its membership, expressed by the sum of their assets, was engaged in food processing for export, and another substantial component embraced the subsidiaries of foreign firms that had appeared during the past fifteen years. The new manufacturers engaged in import substitution had little voice or influence. Indeed the UIA occasionally opposed demands among importers for a return to free trade and issued demands for legislation against dumping. The UIA also sought tax credits for manufacturers who exported, but the body had no overarching, coherent, or sustained program. Other smaller business associations, such as the *Federación Argentina de Entidades Defensoras del Comercio y la Industria,* had similarly confined horizons. Their chief concerns were taxation and what they viewed as constraints on market competition exercised by trade unions.[37]

THE WARTIME CRISIS

By mid 1940 international conditions were soon to sweep away Argentina's lingering caution toward industry, and in scarcely three years industrialization became a high-priority national goal. Although Argentina had only the most token role as a belligerent in World War II, upholding neutrality until March 1945, the very eve of Germany's capitulation, the war brought changes whose magnitude exceeded any earlier in the century. In spring 1940 the Germans occupied most of Scandinavia, France, and the Low Countries. A British naval blockade then closed access from the Atlantic to all the markets of western Europe except Spain and Portugal. Because Argentina's major grain markets were in continental Europe, earnings from grain fell steeply, and commerce was also severely disrupted by the threat of German submarines. By late 1940 shipping to and from Argentine ports was less than half that of a year earlier: exports had fallen below the lowest point of the depression and imports followed suit (see Table 22). Supplies from western Europe were almost completely cut off, and imports from Britain fell steeply as resources there were shifted into arms production. During the twelve months after June 1940, import values plummeted to less than half their level in the prewar period,

TABLE 22. *Foreign Trade 1938–1945 (1937 = 100)*

	Export Volumes	Import Volumes	Export Prices	Import Prices
1938	66	92.4	91.8	101.5
1939	83	81.4	82.0	105.5
1940	69	69.9	89.6	137.6
1941	63	55.9	100.6	146.5
1942	61	44.8	126.9	183.4
1943	63	30.7	150.6	197.1
1944	69	30.2	148.0	214.2
1945	69	32.7	156.0	226.6

SOURCE: Guido Di Tella and Manuel Zymelman, *Las etapas del desarrollo ecónomico argentino*, (Buenos Aires, 1967), 485.

with Argentina's import coefficient, 36.7 percent in 1935–1939, falling to only 19.5 percent in 1940–1944. Coal imports declined by two-thirds between 1939 and 1941, and by half again between 1941 and 1943, and oil imports between 1939 and 1942 declined by half, and by half again in the next year.[38]

These conditions required resourcefulness and versatility, and throughout Argentina an army of ingenious repair specialists quickly learned to improvise with existing materials. When the railroads could no longer obtain coal, they turned once more to burning quebracho and soon too to corn—at the height of the war grains were the source of one-third of total energy consumption. Although the YPF made strenuous efforts to increase production, eventually doubling output from the wells at Comodoro Rivadavia, linseed in part replaced oil as a fuel and a lubricant. Meanwhile, manufacturers pressed forward with import substitution. So far as increasingly severe electricity shortages permitted, twenty-four–hour shifts became commonplace in the factories of Buenos Aires.[39]

In late 1940 the government responded to the trade crisis with the *Plan de Reactivación Económica*, known more commonly as the Pinedo Plan, after the minister of finance, its chief author. It was intended as a countercyclical measure to revive demand, minimize inflation, safeguard employment, and prevent "social repercussions of unforeseeable results"—a veiled reference to labor agitation during World War I. Pinedo proposed to help agriculture by extending the crop-financing scheme he had established seven years earlier. Second, he hoped to encourage import substitution and initiate the export of manufactured goods, and he therefore advocated a new state-backed credit fund for industry and "drawbacks" (*reintegros*)—reimbursements to exporters for the tariff costs incurred in acquiring imported machines and raw materials. The Pinedo Plan also contained ideas for a southern-cone *Zollverein*, a free-trade agreement among the Latin American neighbors that would open up adjacent markets to Argentine manufacturers. A final component of the plan was government support for the construction industry and a program of cheap housing, actions that Pinedo hoped would create around 200,000 new jobs. However, the segment of the plan devoted to relief for agriculture was by far the most prominent, as the sum allotted for industrial credits was only one-sixth of that destined for farmers. For Pinedo's attitude toward industry was still hesitant, and his plan, he declared, was to support only "natural industries"—a phrase evoking the debates on protectionism in the 1870s. He saw industry as having a secondary or supplementary role in the economy at large; when arguing the measure with Congress, he talked of farm exports as the "master wheel" of the economy, and his intent to promote industries as "lesser wheels" at its side. [40]

Although the Pinedo Plan was an imaginative formula for gradual, controlled change that would minimize social unrest, it failed to win acceptance. As Pinedo introduced his proposal, the country fell victim to political crisis. Ortiz, a chronic diabetic, suffered bouts of blindness that forced him to vacate his office to Castillo, the archconservative vice-president. For almost a year, until Ortiz finally resigned, Castillo was only the acting president, but nevertheless he quickly undertook to reverse his predecessor's liberal policies. In the ensuing bitter partisan conflict, one of the first casualties was the Pinedo Plan. The legislation passed through the Senate, but the newly elected Radical majority in the Chamber of Deputies refused even to discuss it, dismissing the government's appeal for a "patriotic accord" on the plan and demanding redress for recent cases of ballot rigging allegedly connived at by Castillo. [41]

The Pinedo Plan thus fell victim to the fifty-year–old feud between the conservatives and Radicals. Yet aside from this, the plan had certain inherent weaknesses that would have made its success problematical even had Congress accepted it. To develop manufacturing Argentina needed imports of capital goods and many raw materials; to get those it had to export or, failing that, to obtain credits. Exports were also essential to the success of the new, extended crop-financing system. But with the current closure of the continental markets for its grain, Argentina's only large market was Britain, which took much of its meat but relatively little of its grain. Britain, however, could no longer export to Argentina, neither coal, machinery, nor consumer goods. Throughout the war Argentina's export earnings from Britain thus accumulated as credits, called "blocked sterling balances." This sum reached 295 million pesos by the end of 1942 and 714 million pesos a year later; by December 1944 it stood at more than 1 billion pesos, or £80 million. The British were prepared to guarantee the blocked balances against a future devaluation of sterling but, intending to resume exports to Argentina after the war, would not release them for any purpose other than importing British goods. Thus the British repeatedly refused Argentina's efforts to apply the blocked balances to the foreign debt or to stock purchases in British-owned firms like the railroads; the latter had been powerful bargaining assets at the time of the Roca-Runciman treaty and the British were unwilling to lose them. Likewise, the British rejected Argentina's attempts to convert the blocked funds into dollars, for such a conversion would have reinstated the trading pattern of the 1920s, when the proceeds of sales to Britain from Argentina were used for purchases in the United States. After 1940 Argentina thus found itself locked into its prewar bilateral relationship with Britain but in a way that rendered trade virtually useless to the effort to promote economic recovery.[42]

Pinedo and his adviser Raúl Prebisch foresaw the United States developing as an alternative import supplier and as a new market for Argentina; this seemed the germ of a long-term master plan. After the vicissitudes of the 1930s and the wartime disruption of transatlantic commerce, the conservative classes at large sensed they were approaching a crossroads in their own and the country's history. In 1940 and for some time afterward, they feared that the demise of the long connection with Britain was imminent. Among them was a half-formed notion of creating a new but essentially similar partnership with the Americans. As the creole elites had jettisoned Spain in 1810, their descendants now contemplated discarding Britain. If a new external partnership could be secured the existing social order would be fortified while the traditional ruling classes would perpetuate their historic role as a collaborating elite with an outside industrial power. Among hypothetical partners, the United States at this juncture had numerous advantages over an alternative like Germany. For although trade with Germany had increased rapidly immediately before the war and German supremacy in Europe now seemed imminent, Germany was now inaccessible and any overture to Germany would prompt retaliation from Britain. In contrast, communications between Buenos Aires and the American eastern seaboard remained completely open, and only the Americans had the surplus goods and capital Argentina needed. In 1940 Panamericanism suddenly acquired quite unwonted popularity in Argentina. Relations between leading Argentine politicians and the British noticeably cooled, as enthusiasm for the United States grew. Argentine manufacturers and some labor leaders, interested in American imports or the prospect of new jobs, also began to espouse closer ties with the Americans. For a time not only members of the government but broader sectors of society moved toward what Pinedo called "close and complete cooperation" (*estrecha y completa cooperación*) with the United States.[43]

Deciding to approach the United States was one thing, but making the approach successful was quite another, and therein was the Pinedo Plan's great objective flaw. Throughout the 1930s relations with the United States had continued to be poor. In 1930 the Hawley-Smoot Act strengthened the barriers to imports from Argentina by raising tariffs on meat, linseed, corn, and wool, and for the first time duties were levied on hides. Furthermore, the Agricultural Adjustment Act of 1933 raised prices of American farm goods above international levels; soon after a ban was imposed on all foreign farm goods that undersold domestic; and in 1936 a new tariff was imposed on Argentine tallow. In the 1930s the Americans again cited sanitary regulations, intended ostensibly to prevent hoof-and-mouth disease, to impose another form of commercial restraint. Both Uriburu and Justo persistently strove to surmount such restrictions, the latter issuing several proposals for a bilateral trade treaty with the United States. But the United States refused any concession to a farm producer like Argentina whose goods duplicated those of its own heavily depressed rural sector. Thus for most of the 1930s Argentine exports to the United States were less than half those in the previous decade. Argentina retaliated by playing politics with oil. Behind the scenes the conservatives, like the Radicals, harassed corporations like Standard Oil, which in 1936 made an effort to cut its losses and sell out. Argentina's discriminatory use of exchange controls simultaneously induced a steep fall in imports from the United States, especially American trucks, tractors, and automobiles (see Table 23).[44]

Dissonance between the two countries over trade issues increasingly extended into the spheres of diplomacy and Pan-American

TABLE 23. *Imports from United States, 1928–1939*
(In thousands of current dollars)

1928	178,899	1934	42,688
1929	210,288	1935	49,374
1930	129,862	1936	56,910
1931	52,652	1937	94,183
1932	31,133	1938	86,793
1933	36,927	1939	70,945

SOURCE: Harold F. Peterson, *Argentina and the United States, 1810–1960* (Albany, 1964), 342–58.

affairs. The Roosevelt administration's Good Neighbor policy toward Latin America was received in Argentina by repeated denunciations couched in colored nationalist terms; even some conservatives dismissed it as an imperialist plot. Before and immediately after the outbreak of World War II, Argentina continually rebuffed American invitations to join the Pan-American defense alliance. By 1939 some observers in the United States understood that Argentina's uncooperative diplomatic posture had its explanation in commerce. Despite Roosevelt's support for a plan to purchase Argentine canned meat for the U.S. Navy, the proposal was rejected by the U.S. Senate. In 1940 and 1941 the Americans offered loans and credits to facilitate Argentine purchases in the United States, but they obdurately resisted pressures to diversify the range of purchases from Argentina.[45]

Another area of conflict now emerged. Under the Lend-Lease Act of January 1941, the United States began furnishing arms to several Latin American nations. Because of its refusal to join the defense alliance, Argentina was accorded low priority and virtually denied supplies. The bulk of the lend-lease arms went to Brazil, which provoked immediate speculation in Buenos Aires that this tactic was intended to pressure Argentina. Tension between the two countries mounted as the Americans grew more insistent in urging Argentina join the Pan-American alliance, and Argentina became increasingly stubborn and recalcitrant.[46]

In mid 1941, after several approaches to the United States from Pinedo and Prebisch had failed, the Castillo government made a last effort to break the impasse by opening formal discussion with the United States on trade. The subsequent commercial treaty between Argentina and the United States, signed in October 1941, was the first between the two countries in almost a century; but in terms of

Argentina's immediate and long-term interests, it was a complete failure, for each side offered only token concessions. Argentina renounced bilateralism and exchange control, both dead issues now that the United States had become almost the sole supplier of manufactured goods. For their part the Americans offered little more than to lower tariffs on those goods from Argentina they already imported, such as linseed and hides. The only new goods to be admitted were certain rare minerals like tungsten and beryllium, both in high demand among arms manufacturers, and dairy products and wines, which before the war the United States had imported from France and Italy. But the door remained almost shut to Argentina's major staples, its meats and cereals. Argentine observers concluded that the Americans regarded the treaty as no more than an emergency wartime expedient. Although Argentine exports to the United States began to increase rapidly, eventually to exceed imports, as before the relationship had no stability and no promise of permanence. Merely a variation of a traditional wartime pattern, the treaty fell far short of the dynamic association to which liberal-conservatives aspired.[47]

The failure to reach agreement with the United States was accompanied by the abrupt decline of the pro-Panamerican movement of 1940, the weakening of the liberal faction in the government, and strengthening of isolationists and nationalists. In March 1941 the liberal foreign minister, José Luis Cantilo, was replaced by a proclerical hispanophile, Enrique Ruíz Guiñazú. In January 1941 Pinedo had also left the government, partly it seemed out of frustration and disillusionment at his difficulties with the Radicals, partly following probes instigated by nationalists into his activities as a lawyer for the British railroad companies. A proliferation of new nationalist groups appeared and, like their forerunners in the past decade, they were proclerical, anticommunist, and sometimes anti-Semitic, and they supported a corporate state. Many, as well as being strongly anglophobic, were still more stridently anti-American. Among them a variety of new proposals surfaced. The *Federación Patriótica Argentina*, founded in 1942, for example, wanted state-controlled unions, as a barrier against communism, and the expropriation of foreign-owned public services. As the dispute over lend-lease arms mounted, others bruited the idea of a military strike against Brazil to gain control over its iron and steel foundries, the prelude to a crash program of arms manufacture. From the same groups came heady talk of a war of conquest to refashion the old viceroyalty of the River Plate, and give Argentina control over adjacent Latin American markets.[48]

Throughout 1941 Germany attempted to exploit Argentina's confused situation. Nazi propaganda intensified, with hints of trade concessions to Argentina at the end of the war. In some quarters these overtures helped stimulate interest in a possible German alliance, but their influence was limited since Germany could do little to give its promises any substance. When the Germans invaded Soviet Russia in May 1941, no realist could fail to recognize that the Ukraine would be the granary for the new German empire and that a German tie for Argentina was scarcely more viable than one with the United States.[49]

As Argentina's options narrowed, the country found itself isolated, increasingly captive to nationalist propaganda. Nationalists were now arguing openly and publicly that Argentina should produce whatever manufactured goods it could not import and the arms it needed to meet the threat from Brazil. In 1941 the General Directorate of Military Manufacturers (*Dirección General de Fabricaciones Militares*) was formed under Army command to produce arms. The directorate was not an entirely novel concept, for the Army had been running a small experimental airplane factory in Córdoba since 1927, and a munitions plant since 1935; and the armed services had been involved with the oil industry since World War I. Even so, the appearance of the directorate marked a major advance into manufacturing by the Army and also betrayed the growing influence of nationalist ideas in its ranks.[50]

Toward the end of 1941 the Castillo government was weakening. Among the Radicals, still in uproar about electoral fraud, were intrigues to gain military support for a coup. With the defection of Pinedo's liberal wing of the *Concordancia* the government was no longer a coalition of conservatives but rather a tool of the reactionaries from the far interior, like Castillo, and ultramontane figures like Ruíz Guiñazú. Unable to overcome congressional opposition, Castillo began ruling by decree, using the Japanese attack on Pearl Harbor as the pretext for a state of siege and for police measures against dissidents. Yet Castillo's authority was declining. Unable to curb the opposition and broaden his base of support, he was forced back on the goodwill of the military, to courting the generals by lavish banquets.[51]

Simultaneously, the diplomatic rift with the United States was becoming more pronounced, as under Ruíz Guiñazú neutrality developed into anti-American isolationism. In the Pan-American conference held in Rio de Janeiro in January 1942, soon after Pearl Harbor, Argentina blatantly obstructed efforts by the United States to persuade the Latin American nations to break relations with the Axis.

Instead it intrigued to create an alliance of neutrals. The Americans retaliated: Secretary of State Cordell Hull imposed a complete arms embargo; some months later the Export-Import Bank halted credits, and supplies of oil tankers and machinery were curtailed. Campaigns launched in the United States labeled the Argentine government fascist and pro-Axis. To support this view the Americans pointed to subsidies from the German embassy to sections of the Argentine press, like the nationalist *El Pampero*, the tolerance among successive governments for Axis propaganda, the granting of visas to known German spies, government dealings with German firms, and the fact that Buenos Aires was sometimes used by the Germans to market looted securities. In 1942 rumors in Buenos Aires of an impending invasion from Brazil grew more frequent, as did reports of a planned takeover of Comodoro Rivadavia by American marines.[52]

Amid all this Castillo received some support from the British, who intervened in an effort to restrain American pressure. Unlike the Americans, the British appeared quite content with Argentina's neutrality, which offered better protection for the meat shipments against German submarines. Neutrality also served British interests in Argentina, since Argentine membership in the Pan-American alliance might well lead to its becoming an American client state. Moreover, the British Foreign Office was reluctant to share the American view of Argentina as an Axis supporter. It appeared readier to acknowledge the practical difficulties of administering neutrality in a country where several of the leading belligerents had multiple business interests and substantial communities of citizens. If there was some German influence in the press, there was also Allied, and the allies monopolized the telegraph and telephone systems, issued an abundance of propaganda in Argentina, and no doubt had an abundance of spies stationed there. The British also recognized the absence of an overwhelming public desire in Argentina to forgo neutrality. Although opinion at large favored democracy and feared totalitarianism, the popularity of the Allies was offset by past conflicts with British business interests, and by almost universal fear and distrust of the United States.[53]

On balance it seemed that rather than secretly supporting the Axis, Castillo had no real policy and was bent on a stubborn holding operation. His aim was to sit out the war, hoping the Americans would eventually cease pressurizing him and normal trade with western Europe resume. If he inclined toward any one of the belligerents, he was pro-British. He made no real efforts to use the meat shipments to force concessions from Britain on the blocked sterling balances, and he also sought to enforce the Transport Corporation, driving the free *colectivos* from the streets of Buenos Aires in 1942. But his personal authority continued to dwindle, and presidential elections were scheduled for late 1943. Toward June it became known that the president's choice for a successor was Robustiano Patrón Costas, like Castillo a politician from the interior, and the most powerful of the Tucumán sugar barons. Although Patrón Costas was reputed to favor the Allies, and especially the British, more strongly than Castillo, to most of his compatriots he was another aging oligarch whose election would prolong the fraud and corruption of the 1930s, and the present line of drift and repression.

News of the candidacy of Patrón Costas triggered an Army intervention on 4 June 1943, a revolt that unseated Castillo as easily as the Army had deposed Yrigoyen in 1930. The coup's leaders made little attempt to alert the public, and in some quarters the rebellion came as a surprise, though it had been in the wind for months. By the time of Castillo's fall, the *Concordancia* was a husk of its original self, as leading liberal conservatives of the Pinedo school had by this time joined the opposition. The government's overthrow was endorsed by the Radicals and also by the United States. For its part the Army was tired of election fraud and the air of scandal and racketeering that pervaded this government, like its immediate predecessors. Furthermore, the Army remained obsessed with the threat from the United States and Brazil, rejecting Castillo's implied position that the country's only future lay as a weak dependency of the moribund British empire.[54]

In 1943, as in 1930, the Army seemed unanimous on the need for revolution; once more, however, it was divided on how to proceed afterward. One faction, at the time of the coup the more substantial in number and seniority, inclined to moderation: a liberal-leaning coalition government like Ortiz's that would command the support of the major parties and interest groups, and an international policy of accommodating the Americans, eventually accepting their chief demand—a diplomatic break with the Axis. The second faction, however, was composed of nationalists who had been hardened by recent events in their determination to resist American pressure, preserve neutrality, arm the nation, and promote military independence by encouraging industry. Some months before the coup about twenty nationalists had formed a pressure group, or *logia*, known only as the GOU, an acronym usually thought to denote *Grupo de Oficiales Unidos*, the United Officers' Group. Some of the GOU members were relatively junior officers, about half at the rank of lieutenant-colonel or below. Although the body conducted its proceedings in secrecy, before and after the coup it had an influential role in developing the nationalist position and gaining adherents for it in the Army at large. Two ideas dominated the GOU: anticommunism and "economic sovereignty."[55]

Division in the Army was apparent from the inception of the revolution. The titular leader of the coup was General Arturo Rawson, whose popularity in the Army and Navy enabled him to unite them against Castillo. On assuming power, Rawson produced a list of cabinet nominations, somewhat heterogeneous in complexion but overwhelmingly civilian. Other leaders of the coup felt the new government bore too great a resemblance to the old, and within three days Rawson was deposed. The office then passed to General Pedro Ramírez, Castillo's minister of war, who appointed a cabinet dominated by the military.

The choice of Ramírez seemed to imply that the Army had elected for domestic and international conciliation. As Castillo's minister of war, Ramírez had been the target of Radical intrigues to promote a military rebellion. Rumors had circulated that Ramírez had agreed to be the Radicals' candidate in the forthcoming elections, which as president he now pledged to carry through. Ramírez's installation was also warmly welcomed in Washington, which hastened to recognize the new government and to lift some of its restrictions on commerce. Meanwhile the German embassy had burnt its secret files, for in the third quarter of 1943 Argentina appeared to be readying itself for a break with the Axis.[56]

Such appearances, however, masked the political infighting in the government and the Army, as the nationalists led by the GOU began maneuvering to consolidate their position. In the weeks after the coup Ramírez made no move to fulfill his pledge on elections, and tensions with the Radicals soon surfaced. In early September 1943, in a letter to Cordell Hull from Admiral Saturnino Storni, the minister of foreign affairs, Argentina intimated its willingness to break relations with the Axis on the condition that the United States first lift the arms embargo and thus cease using Brazil as a threat, a proviso intended to absolve the government of charges that in breaking with the Axis it was yielding to foreign pressure. Storni's letter was thus an appeal from moderates in the government for American assistance in the internal struggle against the nationalists, but the U.S. State Department failed to apprehend the message. Three weeks later Storni's proposal was curtly and imperiously rejected by Hull, who demanded Argentina take the first step and break relations with the Axis. To have complied with Storni's request would have weakened the nationalists. But Hull's refusal instead undermined the moderates, and the nationalists gained the upper hand in the Ramírez government. Only weeks later, in October, the cabinet was again reshuffled; Storni and the rest of the moderates resigned. General Edelmiro Farrell, a military hardliner, was promoted from minister of war to vice-president, and Enrique Martínez Zuviría, a former novelist with a reputation for anti-Semitism, became minister of justice and public instruction.[57]

THE RISE OF PERÓN

By October 1943 the nationalists had the whip hand in the Ramírez government, which now abandoned negotiation with the United States, reiterated neutrality, and began searching for allies in Latin America. Efforts begun under Castillo to expand trade with surrounding states were intensified. Commercial treaties were signed with Chile, Paraguay, and Bolivia; Bolivia was afforded technical assistance in the exploitation of its oil. Exports of manufactured goods had climbed to almost a quarter of Argentina's total exports, and for a time Buenos Aires renewed its late–eighteenth-century guise as the commercial and political nerve center of this region of South America. Toward the end of 1943 a military coup in Bolivia effected the assumption of power by a neutralist pro-Argentine, but anti-Brazilian and anti-American faction. The United States, having recently frozen the assets of Argentine banks and urged other Latin American countries to refuse to trade with Argentina, now accused Argentina of plotting and supporting the uprising, and of intriguing a similar rebellion in neighboring Uruguay.[58]

On the domestic front the nationalists made vigorous efforts to consolidate their position. The Army was firmly united behind them, but the rift between Ramírez and the Radicals left the nationalists isolated in the midst of growing civilian opposition. The government was soon inundated with petitions demanding the restoration of civil liberties, an end to the state of siege, which had prevailed almost continuously since December 1941, and the announcement of a date for elections. Opposition to the government's economic program arose among a wide range of sectors historically linked with the free-trade economy: Radicals, Socialists, urban consumers, and the so-called *Fuerzas Vivas*—the leading interests, which included the Rural Society, exporters, importers, and the largest of the foreign companies.

The government responded with a blend of strident propaganda, nationalist enactments, repression, and populism. From the generals came proclamations concerning the "nation in arms" and resonant slogans like *Honestidad, Justicia, Deber* ("Honesty, Justice, Duty"), which evoked Pétain's *Travail, Famille, Patrie* ("Work, Family, Nation"). The government launched a drive against corruption by purging the public administration. In October 1943 Martínez Zuviría ordered the police to suppress a strike of university students. He then instituted curricula that emphasized "patriotic" education and restored religious instruction, which had been absent from the schools since Roca's measures in the early 1880s. The curricular changes were just one example of the extravagant efforts he and other members of the government made to cultivate the Church.

Repression under the nationalists consisted mostly of an intense dose of long-established, familiar measures: the provinces succumbed to a wave of federal interventions; political parties were banned by decree; restrictions on the press increased; and opponents of the regime were threatened and harassed. For a time the trade unions bore the brunt of such measures. A strike among meat-packing workers in Buenos Aires and La Plata in October and November 1943 was answered by mass arrests. All other strikes were banned, and management of the largest railroad unions, *La Fraternidad* and the *Unión Ferroviaria*, was placed under government nominees. Panic gripped the Jewish community as rumors, which proved false, spread that the government was setting up concentration camps in Patagonia.

The government also made several efforts to trigger popular support. Ignoring the protests of landowners, it decreed a 20 percent reduction in rural rents. In Buenos Aires it compelled the tramways to cut fares, abolished the hated Transport Corporation, and took over the British-owned Primitiva Gas Company which, having been starved for coal since 1939, had long intimated its willingness to be nationalized. Meanwhile, determined efforts were made to unlock the sterling balances held in London and to repatriate the public debt. In another gesture to small farmers, the government took over the grain trade, grain elevators, and warehouses in April 1944. It also imposed a rent freeze in Buenos Aires, and attempted to control food prices.[59]

Many of these enactments, however, were less a mark of strength than of desperation; the government cast its net in various directions in a scramble for support. Self-preservation similarly guided its international dealings. In late 1943 the United States resumed its campaign against Argentina, again cutting supplies and once more, with even greater vehemence, denouncing the Argentine government as fascist. The United States also increased arms shipments to Brazil, which caused anxieties in Buenos Aires over a Brazilian invasion to approach hysteria. While pushing forward plans to manufacture arms, the government attempted to secure weaponry from Germany. The effort proved a major miscalculation, as Ramírez's secret agent was arrested by the British in the West Indies en route to Spain.

In the six months since the June coup, the British had watched and waited, reluctant to intrude in Argentine affairs as long as the meat shipments continued. But this incident, in concert with recent hostile behavior against British companies, seemed a vindication of the American thesis on Argentina. When Ramírez's agent was arrested, the Foreign Office immediately informed the United States government. Armed with this evidence of collusion with the Axis, the Americans abruptly ordered Ramírez to break relations with Germany or face a total embargo on supplies from the United States. Ramírez capitulated and formally announced the diplomatic break in late January 1944. But soon after, the Army dismissed Ramírez, installed Farrell, and then attempted to continue as if nothing had happened. Farrell thereby failed to win full diplomatic recognition from the Allies. The U.S. Board of Economic Warfare further tightened the restrictions on commerce with Argentina; only British pleas prevented a complete trade ban.[60]

By the time of Farrell's takeover, the nationalist government had embarked on a large-scale mobilization of men and resources. Its plan now seemed to transcend the quest for "sovereignty" to almost a search for autarky. Army personnel were drafted into the construction of new roads, and experimental heavy industrial plants were created under Army control and supervision. Military spending, which had almost tripled between 1941 and the end of 1943, continued to rise steeply, accounting for 43 percent of total government expenditures in 1945, compared with 17 percent two years earlier. The officer corps increased by 40 percent, and the Army forces grew from 30,000 in June 1943 to 60,000 by mid 1944, and to 100,000 by late 1945. Whereas before 1944 the military draft had absorbed less than one-third of those eligible for conscription, by 1945 almost all eligible men were drafted.[61]

Meanwhile the Army conducted intense searches for industrial raw materials throughout the Andean region. In April 1944 the government established an industrial credit bank to promote manufacturing of "national interest." Arms had first priority, followed by consumer goods made from local raw materials. In June tariffs were substantially increased, quotas were imposed on imports competing with domestic goods, and the system of drawbacks for exports of manufactures was extended. The government continued to restrict the press, imposing a five-day closure on the great conservative daily, *La Prensa*, in April 1944. It deluged the country with propaganda, and Farrell officiated over great fascist-style torchlight processions through central Buenos Aires. Still seeking rural support, the government promulgated a "peon's statute" (*Estatuto del Peón*) that established a minimum wage for rural workers.[62]

An often impenetrable air of secrecy surrounded the inner machinations of the military government. As the first half of 1944 passed, it became clear that Farrell himself was little more than a figurehead, that the government's most powerful figure was Farrell's aide, Colonel Juan Perón. Though Perón remained a somewhat shadowy figure, he was quietly emerging as the most energetic, imaginative, and politically adroit of the revolutionary leaders.

Like most military nationalists of the early 1940s, Perón came from an immigrant middle-class family. His experience in the complex, devious, and secretive recess of military politics dated to 1930, when as a young captain he had acted as courier and intermediary between the Uriburu and Justo factions. During the 1930s he performed several missions abroad; while stationed in Italy between early 1939 and early 1941, he witnessed the outbreak of war and the Axis conquest of Europe. If his political ideas bore the imprint of the earlier phase of the nationalist movement—its anticommunism, its corporatist and quasi-fascist bent—they also exemplified its more recent emphasis on economic sovereignty, anti-imperialism, and neutrality. As a leader of the GOU in 1943, Perón had a major role in the overthrow of Castillo. After the coup he opposed and helped outmaneuver the generals ready to capitulate to the Americans. He was also prominent in the nationalist victory in October 1943, which eliminated the moderates from the Ramírez government. Although Perón was only a colonel, he had close attachment to Farrell, whom he championed to become Ramírez's minister of war in June 1943, as vice-president in October, and president the following February. When Farrell became president, Perón succeeded him as minister of war, and in June 1944 as vice-president.[63]

As minister of war Perón hastened his ascendancy in the government, using the position to enhance his popularity among the officer corps at large. The war ministry served as the nexus in communications between the government and the armed services, and controlled the distribution of supplies and promotions, an increasingly influential charge as the military budget continued to grow with unprecedented rapidity. From his ministry Perón projected himself as a leading figure in the struggle to create an independent military capability. In a highly publicized speech in La Plata in June 1944, Perón appealed to the lingering fears of a Brazilian invasion and placed himself at the epicenter of the campaign to arm the country; and in October 1944 it was Perón who spearheaded the formation of an air force separate from the other two services.[64]

From the beginning Perón was closely involved in the military regime's efforts to shield itself from popular opposition by enlisting its own body of civilian support. He endorsed the various measures by which the government hoped to court the tenant farmers, agricultural workers, and urban consumers. He joined the effort to suppress communism, assisting in the purge of communist union leaders during a meat-packers' strike in La Plata in September 1943. For a time, he also took a lead in efforts to recover the backing of the Radicals. But as this effort failed, he began casting about in new directions. In the government reshuffle of October 1943 Perón took control of the National Labor Department in Buenos Aires, a body that collected information and statistics on labor affairs and arbitrated strikes. Under Perón the department was swiftly upgraded in rank and responsibilities, and restyled the Secretariat for Labor and Social Welfare (*Secretaría de Trabajo y Bienestar Social*). Perón sought to use the secretariat to win support among the political parties, but once more had scant success.

Popular opposition to the government markedly intensified, sparked in part by the liberation of Paris in August 1944. Once more attention focused on the suppression of political liberties, the ultramontane drift in education, and the high government expenditures for manufacturing and the military. The Farrell government trembled for several weeks during the third quarter of 1944, when a sudden wave of strikes were undertaken by meat packers, sugar refiners, bakers, metal plants, textiles, and some of the railway and tramway companies.

Perón now turned to labor, the unions, the strikes, and his role as defender and protector of the working class. During recent months Perón had already established preliminary contacts with labor leaders, especially leaders of the railroad unions. In an agreement with the largest of the rail unions, the *Unión Ferroviaria*, in December 1943, Perón's new Secretariat granted railwaymen generous pay and fringe benefits, such that Perón was greeted by rail workers' leaders as "Argentina's Number One Worker" (*Primer trabajador argentino*). In March 1944 rail workers also led a demonstration on Perón's behalf, and repeated such demonstrations on several later occasions. However, Perón's main bid for working class support began in mid 1944, as he began to search for the mass constituency that he had failed to generate among the political parties, and at the same time to head off the opposition thrust. In December 1943 labor and trades union subjects were still minor items among Perón's speeches. Six months later Perón talked of little else. From the Secretariat now poured a stream of enactments improving workers' conditions—pay, vacations, pensions, housing, accident compensation—and establishing new labor courts. As secretary for labor, Perón had powers that exceeded those of his predecessors in the old National Labor Department. While they could only offer arbitration in strikes, he could impose it and make its results binding. Amid a fanfare of radio and press publicity, Perón began intervening in the strikes and issuing settlements highly favorable to the workers. He cultivated labor leaders with offers of generous social security schemes devised by the secretariat. Perón then developed the practice of dealing only with those unions recognized by his secretariat as possessing full legal standing (*personería gremial*). By this means he isolated those union leaders opposed to dealing with him, and he prompted union affiliates into electing leaders who favored cooperation.[65]

For the preceding quarter century, since the early 1920s, organized labor's political influence had been slight. During the period of slack demand for labor before 1936, strikes were few, most unions small and unrepresentative. Despite the creation of the General Confederation of Labor (*Confederación General del Trabajo* [CGT]) in 1930, allegiances were split among several rival groups: Socialists, Syndicalists, Communists, and a small sprinkling of anarchists. Among the factions the Communists were stronger in manufacturing, the Socialists in transportation. Some change began around 1936. Communist influence in the unions now increased, especially in construction, as Communists began adopting Moscow's line of supporting a Popular Front strategy to combat international fascism. At this point, too, many labor leaders followed the swing toward economic nationalism, and began to espouse the nationalization of foreign-owned public services. Labor nationalism was thus far from Perón's creation. Nationalism began during the late 1930s, though only attained hege-

mony during the mid 1940s. Also from around 1936, as import substitution gradually tightened the labor market, union membership and
the number of unions steadily increased. Individual affiliations rose
from 369,000 in 1936 to 447,000 in 1941 (see Table 24), and the number
of unions affiliated with the CGT doubled, largely due to the spread
of unionism in construction and new manufacturing. This pattern
continued during the war, as union memberships climbed from
447,000 in 1941 to 522,000 in 1945, and unions affiliated with the CGT
almost tripled, rising from 356 to 969 (see Table 25).

The growth of the union movement in the early 1940s differed
substantially from trends during World War I, when, although many
new unions were formed, the overriding feature had been a sharp rise
in affiliations. The differences are easily explained: during World War
II the crippling inflation of World War I was absent. By 1940 real
wages had reattained the level of 1929. Subsequently, new urban jobs
and cheap grains enabled wages to keep pace with the rising cost of
living, even to show some increase by 1945. Between 1914 and 1918
the cost of living in Buenos Aires increased by around 70 percent. The
increase was 10 percent between 1939 and 1944, while it was estimated that workers' family incomes grew by almost 18 percent between 1939 and the first half of 1945. Under such conditions strikes
were less frequent during the early 1940s than twenty-five years earlier: between 1940 and 1944 the strike rate, measured in worker hours
lost, was only one-third of that between 1915 and 1919, despite
roughly a doubling in the labor force between the two periods (see
Table 26). Until late 1944 most strikes were confined to sectors with
special wartime problems, like metallurgy, for which raw materials
were scarce and expensive; this sector alone accounted for two-thirds
of the stoppages in 1942. Labor was not only less militant than it had

TABLE 24. *Trade Union Affiliations 1936, 1941, and 1945*

	1936	1941	1945
Industry	72,282	144,922	212,518
Services	131,317	154,907	149,570
Transport	151,834	117,709	130,326
Other	13,296	29,674	29,674
TOTAL	369,726	447,212	522,088

SOURCE: Louise M. Doyon, "Organised Labour and Perón, 1943–55: A Study in the
Conflictual Dynamics of the Peronist Movement" (Ph.D. diss., Univ. Toronto, 1978),
119, 254.

TABLE 25. *Number of Unions by Sector, 1941 and 1945*

	1941	1945
Agriculture	10	44
Chemicals	2	29
Clothing	10	37
Commerce and finance	69	77
Communications	2	32
Construction	34	79
Electricity	4	8
Entertainment	14	32
Food	39	205
Hotel	25	46
Land transportation	30	91
Maritime transportation	14	31
Metallurgy	4	21
Paper and printing	2	29
Professionals	5	14
Sanitary works	8	30
State	15	42
Textiles	2	8
Wood	10	17
Other	57	91
TOTAL	356	969

SOURCE: Louise M. Doyon, "Organised Labour and Perón, 1943–55: A Study in the Conflictual Dynamics of the Peronist Movement" (Ph.D. diss., Univ. Toronto, 1978), 251.

been in World War I; now many unions also pressed for different goals. Wages had dominated the period after 1915; after 1940 the primary issue was fringe benefits—vacations, sick pay, insurance, accident compensation, and the like.[66]

In this climate, Perón began his overtures to labor, having a somewhat easier task before him than Yrigoyen had faced a generation before. Fringe benefits were more easily delivered than wage increases, and they were the kind of support Perón could offer through the secretariat. It was also simpler to appease labor now that the issues at hand concerned the amelioration of acceptable conditions rather than bare survival. Equally, labor's more modest exactions and the

TABLE 26. *Working Days Lost in Strikes, 1916–1920 and 1941–1945*

1916	233,878	1941	247,598
1917	2,100,269	1942	634,339
1918	2,191,773	1943	68,290
1919	3,262,705	1944	41,384
1920	3,693,782	1945	509,024

SOURCE: Louise M. Doyon, "Organised Labour and Perón, 1943–55: A Study in the Conflictual Dynamics of the Peronist Movement" (Ph.D. diss., Univ. Toronto, 1978), 33, 439.

rapidly rising demand for labor discouraged employers from uniting in opposition. Lastly, Perón was able to take advantage of division and weakness among the unions and the CGT. Following a Communist takeover attempt, in March 1943 the CGT had split into two factions. Then came repression under Ramírez, which led to the dissolution of the Communist group in July. This action eliminated many of the most powerful and independent Communist union bosses, the ones most capable of resisting Perón.[67]

From mid 1944 Perón pursued his quarry with a brazen persistence that contrasted sharply with Yrigoyen's caution and tentativeness a generation earlier. Even so, Perón's approach somewhat recalled Yrigoyen's as he echoed the Radicals in talking of the "harmony of classes," "distributive justice," and "humanizing capital." Among the clearest statements of his objectives toward labor were his remarks before the *Bolsa de Comercio* (stock exchange) in August 1944:

> Businessmen [*señores capitalistas*]: Don't be afraid of my unionism [*sindicalismo*]. Never has Capitalism been firmer than now. . . . What I want to do is to organize the workers through the state [*estatalmente*], so that the state shows them the way forward. In this way revolutionary currents endangering capitalist society in the postwar can be neutralized.[68]

Perón's emphasis on the need for defense against a leftist workers' revolution kept him in the mainstream of the nationalist movement. For a time it helped him deflect criticism of his activities among his fellow members of government, who were persuaded that concession to the working class represented a much more effective form of control than coercion. Perón agreed that repression would lead to a "rebellion of the masses," and urged instead that the state lead a "peaceful revolution":

If we fail to carry out the Peaceful Revolution, the People will accomplish the Violent Revolution. . . . And the way to do this is to carry forward Social Justice for the masses. . . . Naturally this is not a popular idea among rich men. . . . Undoubtedly this path will meet with their resistance. But they are their own worst enemies. Better to offer 30 percent now than in several years or perhaps even months to lose all they have, including their ears.[69]

In this way an incongruous spectacle evolved: a government of anticommunist zealots propitiated labor while attacking capital. Perón's tactics exploited the deep-seated phobias within the nationalist movement against Communism and working-class revolution. Perón also drew heavily upon corporatist doctrines, ideas peripheral to traditional conservatism and usually secondary in Radicalism, but central to the nationalist movement since the late 1920s. Social justice and state-controlled labor unions were typical of corporatist political thought. They sprang from corporatism's stress on the normative basis of the state, and the state's responsibilities in promoting social integration and in the regulation of the community to the common good, and from the idea that associations like unions existed in some measure on the basis of state concession.[70]

However, both nationalism and corporatism were still minority doctrines in a society that remained largely liberal in character and inclination. Perón played the game of mobilizing the unions with consummate skill, taking full advantage of all opportunities. But the game was becoming dangerous, as opposition to the Farrell government began focusing on Perón himself in late 1944. At the end of the year tensions rose when the *Unión Industrial Argentina* (UIA) publicly broke with Perón over the year-end bonuses (*aguinaldos*) for workers that he had decreed. Numerous employers now joined the *Fuerzas Vivas* and the parties in assailing Perón as a fascist demagogue.

In early 1945 both Perón and Farrell gained some measure of relief from the opposition following an unexpected shift in American policy toward Argentina. Over the past six months the Americans had been tightening the pressure on the military regime. In June 1944 they withdrew their ambassador, persuading the reluctant British to follow suit. In August Argentine gold assets in the United States were frozen, and in September the export embargo was extended to all oil machinery, automotive spare parts, paper machinery, and railroad supplies. Throughout this period Hull was issuing accusations that Argentina had become a refuge for escaped Nazis, and was plotting an imperialist war against its Latin American neighbors. In November 1944, however, Hull resigned as Secretary of State.[71]

Responsibilities for Latin American affairs in Washington then passed to a new under secretary, Nelson Rockefeller. With Rockefeller came a quite new approach. For a time the United States tried conciliation. The Americans now lightened the trade embargo and hinted at an end to the restrictions on lend-lease arms. The change of policy—warmly endorsed by many American manufacturers and exporters interested in widening access to the Argentine market—swiftly brought results. In February 1945 Argentina became a signatory to the Act of Chapultepec, which pledged the American nations to cooperation on mutual defense and trade. Finally, toward the end of March, Argentina at last declared war on Germany and Japan. When it did so, the United States accorded full diplomatic recognition to the Farrell government.[72]

The *rapprochement* was short-lived, however. Upon Roosevelt's death in mid April, Truman became president; in the reshuffle at the State Department, first conciliation and soon Rockefeller himself were dropped. With Germany's unconditional surrender on 7 May, the Americans were at last free of Britain's restraining influence in Latin American foreign policy. They quickly reimposed trade sanctions on Argentina and demanded immediate elections as a prerequisite for their removal. Among the leaders of this hard-line approach was the new American ambassador in Argentina, Spruille Braden. Braden made several inflammatory speeches in Buenos Aires, deliberate attempts to prime the military government's opponents into an all-out rebellion. After several months of relative quiescence, a political explosion seemed imminent, as class fissures between labor and capital, which focused on Perón's activities as secretary for labor, widened. In mid June 1945 a manifesto of the *Fuerzas Vivas* attacked the government's social reform program. The trade unions issued a countermanifesto "in defense of the benefits obtained through the Secretariat for Labor and Welfare."

Events moved to a climax in the third week of September. On 19 September a great demonstration, dubbed the "Constitution and Liberty March," was held in Buenos Aires. Thousands upon thousands of the regime's opponents tramped through the streets hurling protests and abuse. Throughout the country people talked of civil war. On 24 September General Arturo Rawson, the three-day president of June 1943, staged an abortive coup. Farrell began to slide toward surrender, first promising elections and then appearing ready to cede power to a caretaker administration headed by the Supreme Court. In early October, amid myriad controversies among the Army commanders and members of the cabinet, Farrell was prevailed upon to dismiss Perón from his multiple posts and to imprison him. The *Fuerzas Vivas*, and behind them Braden, seemed victorious.

But the unity of the opposition to Perón immediately revealed itself to be spurious, for once he was gone the opposition collapsed into inner wrangling, as the ancestral feuds that had divided the old parties reappeared. The opposition failed to agree on the composition of a caretaker government. The proposal that the administration be vested in the Supreme Court met with increasing resistance in the Army. If the Army was now willing to divest itself of Perón, it refused to abrogate the 1943 revolution, which it believed handing over power to the Court implied. As a result Perón's departure left a political stalemate and a growing power vacuum. But then as the opposition hesitated, Perón's partisans acted. In the days following his imprisonment several of his closest followers canvased the working-class neighborhoods of greater Buenos Aires, launching a campaign to free Perón. Among them were Cipriano Reyes, a meat-packing workers' leader; Colonel Domingo Mercante, Perón's closest associate in the Secretariat for Labor; and Eva Duarte, Perón's youthful and glamorous mistress. On 17 October 1945 thousands of workers suddenly took to the streets and began marching toward the presidential palace. From the Plaza de Mayo they demanded Perón's release and reinstatement. At this show of strength Farrell's opposition collapsed in disarray, and the president resumed control with Perón at his side. Perón's opponents in the government, led by General Eduardo Ábalos, resigned. Within days Farrell announced presidential elections for February 1946.[73]

Later that October Perón's working-class and union supporters gathered together in the new Labor Party (*Partido Laborista*). Perón also gained the endorsement of a minority faction in the Radical Party, which called itself the *Unión Cívica Radical—Junta Renovadora*. Its leader, Hortensio Quijano, became Perón's running-mate in the February 1946 presidential election. Perón also won the support of several nationalist factions, chief of which was the *Alianza Libertadora Nacionalista*, along with the endorsement of several clerical groups. In the provinces he succeeded in enlisting the services of a number of the old conservative party bosses. Thus, though the backbone of Perón's constituency remained the organized urban working class, by early

1946, *peronismo* had become highly heterogeneous. In the meantime the opposition groups resolved some of their earlier differences and formed themselves into the Democratic Union (*Unión Democrática*), a coalition that enjoyed support from such divergent groups as conservatives and Communists, though at its core were the Radicals.

On the eve of the 1946 election the United States government, largely at Braden's instigation, made a final bid to turn public opinion against Perón and toward the Democratic Union. A blue book issued by the State Department in February detailed charges that leading members of the Argentine military, as well as members of successive Argentine governments, had collaborated with the Axis during the war; several accusations were directed against Perón. But once more American intervention backfired, as Perón invoked the blue book to proclaim a stark choice before the country: *"Braden o Perón"*— surrender to the Americans or its alternative, a bold thrust for Sovereignty and Social Justice. Perón carried the election with 54 percent of the vote.[74]

The dramatic shifts in Argentine politics during World War II resulted from a complex interplay between external and internal conditions: the decline of Argentina's European connections and its failure to obtain a substitute alignment with the United States. For these issues underlay the collapse of the conservatives in 1940–1943, which left the way open for the nationalists, from among whose ranks Perón rose.

VII

THE APOGEE OF PERÓN, 1946-1955

A t the end of World War II Argentina found itself on an entirely new course, with Perón promising a "New Argentina" founded on "social justice, political sovereignty, and economic independence." His particular amalgam of social reform and national emancipation marked an abrupt break with the past, but his was a revolution never to be consummated. In September 1955, a little less than a decade after his election as president, Perón was unseated by a military coup, his country consumed by political divisions as profound as any throughout its history. Peronists and Anti-Peronists confronted each other with diametrically contrasting visions of what Perón had achieved.

To Perón's numerous adherents, he was the architect of striking progress, especially in the area of social reform. The innovations instituted on behalf of Argentina's urban working class included: pension schemes and protection against layoffs, a working day of statutorily defined length, paid vacations and a new rigorously enforced Sunday rest law, improved working conditions for factory workers, accident compensation, regulated apprenticeships, controls on female and child labor, compulsory and binding conciliation and arbitration procedures, subsidized housing and legal services, vacation resorts, full legal status for trade unions, employment agencies, and annual bonuses (*aguinaldos*). Workers' basic rights were guaranteed by the Constitution, whose provisions included the "right to work," which implied a state commitment to full employment, and the rights to "just pay," retirement, education, and access to "culture."

Perón's concept of "social justice" had also meant a substantial increase in wage earners' incomes against those of other sectors. In 1935–1936 the wage share in national income was estimated at 38.3 percent; by 1953–1955 it was 46.4 percent. During Perón's administration around 500,000 new homes, most of them low-cost workers' apartments, were built, some 100,000 homes in 1954 alone. The per capita rate of new construction in the early 1950s (8.4 units per 1,000 inhabitants) was among the highest in the world. Construction also included large numbers of new schools, hospitals, clinics, and recreational facilities.[1]

To the poor and underprivileged, those Perón called the "shirtless masses" (*masas descamisadas*), Peronism also gave a sense of dignity (*dignidad*)—an elevation in status and at least vicarious role in the system of power. Before his rise, except briefly and fitfully before 1920, the political significance of organized labor was negligible. By 1955, the *Confederación General del Trabajo* (CGT) had become one of the most powerful organizations in the country, its membership having grown from around 520,000 in 1945 to almost 2.3 million in 1954. Many trade unions had become wealthy associations administered by complex bureaucracies that controlled large funds and networks of social services. Several working men ascended to positions of power in Perón's administration: Ángel Borlenghi, minister of the interior for nine years, had previously led a small commercial workers' union in Buenos Aires; José María Freire, a former glass worker, was minister of labor during the late 1940s; Juan Bramuglia, foreign minister during the same period, had been a lawyer for the railroad union, the *Unión Ferroviaria*; and José Espejo, once an apartment *concierge*, served as secretary-general of the CGT between 1947 and 1952.[2]

Peronists claimed similar accomplishments in pursuit of sovereignty and economic independence. Perón had almost eliminated the foreign debt, they asserted, and the substantial fall in private foreign investment they interpreted as a halt to foreign control over the economy. Indeed, by 1955 private foreign investment was only three-fifths of that nine years earlier, and sectors of the economy once in foreign hands—railroads, power plants, and telephones—became wholly "Argentine." Between 1946 and 1955 the government created thirty-seven hydroelectricity plants and a pipeline from Comodoro Rivadavia to feed the oil refineries of La Plata and Buenos Aires. Perón also created a national airline and a merchant shipping fleet, which by 1950 transported 16 percent of Argentina's overseas trade.[3]

Perón's supporters and apologists pointed further to the 75,000 new manufacturing firms that appeared between 1946 and 1953. Manufacturing's share in the economy increased from 27.5 percent in 1940–1944 to an average of more than 30 percent between 1946 and 1955. Industrial advance once more reduced dependence on imported manufactures; for example, finished consumer goods accounted for around 40 percent of total imports in 1930 but under 10 percent by the early 1950s.[4]

Peronism, its constituents claimed, also made a major contribution to the nation's "spiritual" development. In a world divided by the Iron Curtain, the doctrines of *justicialismo* offered an alternative to both capitalism and communism. To its adherents *justicialismo* was a social-Christian philosophy rooted in Catholic and Aristotelian precepts of justice and harmony. Like the Socialist ideal, *justicialismo* paid or protected each according to his needs and opposed unearned privilege or power, and wealth based on inheritance. In the quest for harmony *justicialismo* sought to transfuse particularist class or corporate loyalties into a broader national allegiance, to balance the economic sphere of the state against private enterprise. While establishing the "compromise state" (*Estado de Compromiso*), it sought to fashion the "organized community" (*La Comunidad Organizada*), giving a stable rank and network of associations to each of its constituent groups. *Justicialismo* also entailed a new posture and morality in international affairs. What Perón called *la tercera posición*—"the third position"—was among the first of the doctrines of nonalignment, an attempt to achieve effective national sovereignty on a foundation of independence and equidistance from the two rival world power blocs.[5]

Justice, sovereignty, welfare, emancipation, harmony, progress—such were the myths of Peronism and the keywords in its discourse. But for Perón's opponents the legacy of the "New Argentina" was a shattered and divided society, a bankrupt economy, and a nation vitiated by dictatorship. For many "social justice" had meant imprisonment or exile, and some claimed torture. Peronism was denounced as a "pornocracy" that governed by fraud, indoctrination, false propaganda, and persecution.

The anti-Peronists charged that the rewards to Perón's followers, the "zoological flood" (*aluvión zoológico*) as they were dubbed by one of the regime's critics, were accomplished by confiscations from the rest of the community and by the disruption of key sectors of the economy. They pointed first to agriculture, in which output had stagnated and export volumes and earnings had fallen steeply; products that had once been exported, they argued, were now being consumed at home by a bloated urban population. Industry, they alleged, had fared little better, with negligible growth in recent years. In 1955 industrial self-sufficiency remained as distant a goal as in 1946, for industry had experienced neither structural change nor development, and its largest components were still processed foods and textiles. The country remained a workshop rather than a factory producer of most manufactured goods. Of the new industrial enterprises the Peronists claimed to have created, a vast majority were little more than one-man businesses: producers with fewer than ten employees, although employing only 20 percent of the workforce, comprised more than 80 percent of the nation's "industrial firms." Medium-sized firms, those employing fifty to three hundred workers, the most typical segment of an emergent industrial capitalist economy, showed little or no growth. The rest of industry still exhibited marked monopolistic features; in the metallurgical sector, for example, one firm, ACINDAR, controlled 40 percent of production.[6]

Besides Perón himself anti-Peronists blamed the trade unions and the workers for this poor performance. The price of high wages and new fringe benefits was low investment; union power on the shop floor had led to featherbedding and sometimes grotesque inefficiency. Industry's shortcomings were also intimately related to the decline of agricultural exports. If Argentina now imported fewer manufactured consumer goods than before, it had grown desperate for intermediate goods and raw materials, but agriculture could no longer provide the foreign exchange to enable adequate supplies of these goods. The resulting chronic balance-of-payments deficits and the "balance-of-payments bottleneck" continually throttled industrial expansion and development.[7]

Decline and stagnation were pervasive throughout the economy. Per capita gross national product was only 3 percent higher in 1952, and 16 percent higher in 1955, than in 1943. In the early 1950s Venezuela overtook Argentina as the Latin American nation with the highest per capita income, and Brazil surpassed Argentina in the value of foreign trade. Under Perón had come the worst inflation in generations; during 1952 the cost of living rose by almost 40 percent. Between 1946 and 1955, production only crawled upward, but money in circulation increased eightfold. To disguise growing unemployment, Perón had swollen the state sector, with the number of national government employees soaring from 243,000 in 1943, to 398,000 in 1949, and 541,000 in 1955. By 1955 some 10 percent of the total working population was employed by state bodies. Service activities, including construction, absorbed an estimated 51.7 percent of new investment between 1940 and 1944; by 1955 this share had increased to 57.3 percent. Perón's high spending, including the vaunted housing program, it was argued, was a major factor in the stagnation of agriculture and industry, and had also stoked the furnace of inflation.[8]

Perón's claims to have enhanced national sovereignty were similarly impugned by his enemies. His administration had inherited massive foreign reserves, which were then depleted to near-exhaustion, standing in 1955 at less than a quarter of their levels in 1946. Vast sums were squandered on vainglorious schemes like the nationalization of the railroads. Having at first posed as the scourge of foreign capital, Perón later began to court it, even making a deal with the infamous Standard Oil.[9]

Deeply divided opinions of Perón predated his election as president in 1946, but cleavages intensified as he shifted resources among different social sectors, often resorting to force to quell resistance. The ways in which Perón used and abused power were also symptomatic of the much deeper conflict between ends and means. His effort to amalgamate nationalist and egalitarian aspirations contained elements of both naiveté and risk, but at the time of its formulation his program was largely consistent with reputable and impartial forecasts of the country's opportunities in the postwar world. Perón's great error, which sprang from his need to increase his legitimacy and his means of political self-defense, was to commit all his resources too early on the assumption that these forecasts and expectations were correct. When they proved largely wrong, he was left with an impractical program and severe, worsening economic problems. But he was too committed to his path to retrench and embark on another, and his efforts to salvage what he could became increasingly desperate. From such efforts arose many of the political divisions that constituted his chief legacy in 1955.

THE POSTWAR REVOLUTION, 1946–1949

By 1946 the military-popular alliance erected by Perón had proved itself the master of its opponents in two great trials of strength, that of October 1945 and then in the February election. Despite these

victories the coalition remained a fragile *mélange* of largely uncoordinated groups. Among Perón's most pressing tasks were to organize his support, develop his party, and deepen his association
with the unions and the workers, the "vertebral column" of his movement. He knew that only such accomplishments could keep his enemies from seizing the earliest opportunity to oust him.

In measuring the prospects for the future, Perón and his advisers
reexamined the aftermath of World War I. Both the labor and manufacturing sectors feared a repetition of the events of 1919 to 1921,
when the end of hostilities was followed by a spate of commercial
dumping from abroad; many held this postwar dumping responsible
for bankrupting the local manufacturers who had appeared during the
wartime disruption. If this pattern were to repeat itself the results
would be far more severe, for industry now employed thousands of
new workers, many of whom were rural migrants. The wartime
changes in farming, led by the shift from agriculture to cattle raising,
severely reduced the prospect of migrants' returning to the rural sector. A new industrial collapse would cause massive unemployment
and threaten Perón's alliance with labor. Many also believed it would
leave the door open to communism.

In 1946 Perón's overriding concern was thus to protect—and if
possible augment—employment in the urban manufacturing sector.
Second, to consolidate his grip on labor, he intended to enhance the
flow of benefits to the unions and extend the social reforms begun by
the Secretariat for Labor and Welfare. Of necessity, Perón's early
concern with the "organization of the masses," and his emphases on
"social justice" and "economic sovereignty" remained closely intertwined: the defense of native industry was essential for the protection
of his political base.

Equally, Perón was now the prisoner of the nationalist sentiments
he had repeatedly manipulated throughout his rise to power. Nationalism was inherent to his definition of sovereignty, and appeasing
nationalist aspirations was also in some measure central to his success
in holding together his coalition and keeping at bay the opposition. In
1946 Perón was thus pledged to root out the symbols of the "colonial
past." He had to nationalize public services owned by foreigners,
reduce foreign indebtedness, and uphold an independent line in foreign affairs.

Perón's ministerial team reflected his varied concerns. Although
most of his appointees were typical of those who had served in past
governments, men with university or military college educations, and
in some cases upper–middle-class backgrounds, among them were

several unusual choices. Two members of the cabinet, Minister of the Interior Borlenghi and Foreign Minister Bramuglia had trade-union antecedents or connections. Two other senior officials were self-made manufacturers representative of a subclass that had risen to prominence since the mid 1930s. Rodolfo Lagomarsino, once a hat maker, was appointed secretary for industry and commerce, and Miguel Miranda, millionaire owner of a canned-foods business, served from late 1945 until mid 1947 as president of the Central Bank, then as president of the newly established National Economic Council, a body created to formulate and execute economic policy.

In contrast, the administration contained surprisingly few members of the nationalist groups prominent since the mid 1930s. They now paid the price for their shifting loyalties in 1944 and 1945, and from their ranks Perón took "many ideas but few men." The main nationalist figure among his inner retinue was José Figuerola, a Spaniard who in the late 1920s had advised Primo de Rivera, the Spanish dictator. Although Figuerola was a leading ideologue of state economic planning and state-controlled unions, Miranda quickly emerged among the team as the most powerful after the president. Later dubbed the "Czar of Argentine Finance," Miranda was also the high priest of domestic manufacturing interests and industrial development. From the Central Bank and the National Economic Council he exercised a firm grip on economic policy and planning during the crucial first two and a half years of the Perón regime.[10]

Perón's program was thus initially a continuation of the previous administration's and a natural emanation from the movement he had constructed. Dictated in part by political interest and necessities, the program could also be depicted as having a higher, more objective rationale. During the war an important supplementary stimulus to the growth of manufacturing in Argentina had come from adjacent Latin American nations, which also suffered acute shortages of imports. Between 1941 and 1945 manufactured goods, mainly textiles and shoes, marketed in Latin America represented 13.6 percent of Argentina's exports. This trade reached a peak in 1945–1946, when manufactured exports were valued at $114 million.[11]

The coming of peace made it impractical to base industrial development on this regional export scheme. The other Latin American states had little to sell in return; Argentina could accept only so much Brazilian coffee, Chilean copper, Bolivian tin, or Peruvian sugar. Second, several of the larger Latin American nations—Brazil, Mexico, and Chile—had also effected import substitution and were likewise anxious to defend and expand their accomplishments. Each, with its large peasantry acting as a brake on increases in wages and production costs, enjoyed an inherent competitive edge over Argentina. If this alone proved insufficient protection, the other Latin American nations could invoke tariffs as a second line of defense. Third, in the smaller Latin American markets Argentina's exports of manufactured goods now began to suffer ill-effects from high postwar exchange rates, which Perón's government adopted to direct food goods into the domestic market and drive up prices of farm exports to western Europe.

Finally, most of the goods the larger Latin American countries could not produce for themselves could now be obtained from the United States. With the coming of peace the Americans immediately resumed their prewar commercial offensive in Latin America, making goods available at prices or on lavish credit terms that Argentina had no hope of matching. In some cases the Americans reentered the Latin American markets with the deliberate aim, it seemed, of destroying Argentina's commerce. Until as late as 1948 the Americans were still concerned with Argentina's wartime attempts to establish a southern block in opposition to the Pan American Union. Recognizing the crucial role of commerce to this design, they made vigorous efforts to check Argentina's commercial expansion in a campaign that extended beyond issues of direct trade. In 1947, for example, Argentina and Chile agreed that all maritime trade between them should be reserved for their own vessels to the exclusion of outsiders. The agreement brought immediate American protests, and when the Latin Americans tried to buy ships in the United States, sales restrictions were imposed to defeat the project.[12]

After becoming president, Perón made some effort to protect Argentina's manufactured exports, mostly through offers of bilateral agreements and loans. In late 1946 he proposed an economic "union of the southern lands" (*unión de los países del sur*) with Chile and Bolivia. The United States immediately intervened with generous counteroffers that frustrated the plan. In the wake of these various unfavorable conditions, Argentina's exports of manufactured goods declined steeply: between 1947 and 1949 their value was less than a third of that in 1945–1946; by this time they also comprised less than 5 percent of Argentina's total export trade. Recovery never came: between 1940 and 1947 Argentina exported some 600,000 pairs of shoes, but between 1950 and 1954 a mere 15,000.[13]

Argentina's effort to pursue industrial development thus by necessity focused on the domestic market. But such "inward-led" growth (*desarrollo hacia adentro*) required that the domestic market be widened by expanded demand. The leading Latin American economists were aware that income in the hands of the rich or the middle classes tended to enhance demand for luxury or consumer durable goods, most of which were obtainable only through imports, while income in the hands of the poor or the working classes increased demand for wage goods. Because the latter products—manufactured foods, textiles and shoes—were the ones the national industry could provide most competitively, continuing industrial growth thus became incumbent on progressive income redistribution. This relationship further enhanced the close association in Peronism between manufacturing growth and "social justice."

Another issue in 1946 was the relative priority of heavy and light industry. Amid wartime fears of American or Brazilian intervention, the military nationalists, who had largely dictated economic policies since the failure of the Pinedo Plan in 1940, had given high priority to heavy industry to develop arms manufactures. But as the war drew to a close and the need for arms grew less pressing, there came a slow shift in favor of light manufacturing, which seemed a better use of resources when capital was relatively scarce and labor abundant. Planners were also beginning to acknowledge that heavy manufacturing required an impossible level of domestic savings and investment, and that the smallness of the domestic market conspired against the necessary economies of scale. Meanwhile, despite continuing American export embargoes on militarily strategic goods—oil machinery, tires, galvanized wire, and steel bars—many other American capital goods were becoming plentifully and cheaply available. The sensible course, it seemed, was to concentrate on light industry, while importing capital and intermediate goods and technology. This view was adopted after 1945 not only among Perón's advisers but also throughout Latin America, and its wisdom was upheld as late as 1949 by the newly founded United Nations Economic Commission for Latin America (ECLA). Argentine analysts noted that the country had endured a seven-year dearth of imports, and some attributed the industrial recession in 1945 to the heavily depleted stocks of imported machinery. A resumption of growth, and again interests of political stability, thus made it imperative to pursue replenishments with the utmost speed.

Thus far Perón's approach to the economy reflected at least some logic as well as political expediency. It was essential to protect and develop industry to avoid unemployment and social unrest; industrial development necessitated the redistribution of income to ensure the expansion of the market. It was also rational to prefer light manufacturing to heavy, while importing capital goods and raw materials as fast as possible to escape recession. But Perón's policies also contained features of dogma, risk, and naiveté. For Peronism was also the legatee of the nationalist campaigns of the 1930s to curb foreign business.

The nationalists claimed that a reduction of foreign economic influence would enhance the country's bargaining power, ending humiliations like the Roca-Runciman treaty, and stem the loss of resources through profit remittances and interest payments abroad. Yet although the expropriation of public services owned by foreign corporations seemed to promise freedom, the cost would be high. After fifteen years of depression and war, many of the foreign-owned public services were neglected and obsolete, near-bankrupt relics; among the keenest, however silent, supporters of their expropriation were often those who owned them. These assets were thus of questionable value, and their acquisition would reduce the resources available for new investment.

The foreign debt posed a similar problem. Through his election campaign Perón followed the nationalist line and promised to cancel the foreign debt. But the facts of the matter dictated pragmatic caution rather than sweeping pledges, for since the 1920s few new debts had been contracted, and interest rates on the debt were fixed and usually low. The incidence of debt services against export earnings was therefore now much lower than twenty years before and was steadily dwindling of its own accord.

The forming of long-term economic plans obliged Perón and Miranda to forecast the probable course of the postwar world. In 1946 the outlook seemed bleak: much of Europe was devastated, and the two superpowers appeared to be moving toward renewed warfare. In essence Miranda expected a repetition of the 1920s and 1930s, but encapsulated into a five-year span. As in 1919–1921, a short-lived trade boom would be followed by depression, on whose heels would come renewed bilateralism and the return of autarkic blocs like the British Imperial Preference system—all as prelude to another war between East and West. From these assumptions Miranda concluded that Argentina needed to act swiftly to stockpile imports, guarding against the time they would again cease to be available. But at this point Miranda's hypothesis drifted away into speculation and mere hopes that if enough machinery or raw materials were in stock Argentina could develop in isolation for an indefinite period. Miranda appeared to believe self-sustaining industrialization could be accomplished in a single quinquennium.

The same assumptions and forecasts colored the attitudes among Perón's policymakers toward the agricultural sector. In the short term they were determined to avoid a repetition of 1918–1921, when high export prices had brought enormous windfall gains for the *estancieros* and exporters, but at the cost of heavy inflation and severe popular unrest. This they intended to forestall by taxing farmers and subsidizing foodstuffs, the latter also essential to the program of income redistribution as it would assist efforts to broaden the market for manufacturers and hold down wage costs. Beyond this Perón's advisers thought it pointless to pay much attention to agriculture, for once the anticipated world depression came export earnings would fall, as in the 1930s. If war were renewed, Argentina could again expect increased exports but, as World Wars I and II had shown, it would no longer be able to import.

As a radical populist preaching the destruction of "oligarchy," Perón had the outward credentials of a land reformer. But he knew that changes in land tenure were likely to provoke a short-term fall in agricultural production. Export earnings would thus decline just as the effort was being made to reequip industry with replacement capital goods and raw materials. If agricultural output fell, domestic food prices would rise and thereby restrict the expansion of manufacturing. Because any land reform project would pose a conundrum of economic and political problems, Perón thought it ill-advised to precipitate such problems needlessly. Also, conditions suggested that in time progressive change on the land might occur spontaneously. Perón proposed to tax the farmers and, partly to reduce the rural exodus, to continue the policies in force since 1943 that protected agricultural tenants and raised rural wages. In doing so, the government would squeeze the incomes of the large landowners, who would then face a simple choice: drastic self-reorganization to increase productivity or bankruptcy. Again such reasoning was not illogical but was predicated on two risky assumptions: that the best approach to agriculture was to apply penalties rather than rewards, and that longer-term export earnings from agriculture were unimportant.[14]

When Perón succeeded Farrell as president in early June 1946, the third anniversary of the 1943 coup d'etat, he had all the necessary political implements at hand. The February elections gave him not only the presidency but also substantial majorities in both chambers of Congress, and he also controlled most of the provinces. His position was thus quite unlike Yrigoyen's, most of whose time as president had been spent in vain pursuit of parliamentary majorities. Perón also had an advantage over his more immediate predecessors in that his power was derived from a popular vote in a cleanly won election. Though he faced opposition from former supporters of the Democratic Union, he had the backing of the Army, the unions, and the goodwill of the Church. Perón further strengthened the executive branch by the creation of a parallel cabinet of advisers, entitled secretaries, who were accountable to the president alone. The state ministers, in contrast, were constitutionally subject to congressional scrutiny through the procedure of interpellation.[15]

The state apparatus Perón inherited had grown extremely powerful in recent years. During the 1930s the government had begun to control the farm sector through the *juntas reguladoras*. It supervised exchange rates, import licenses, and the money supply through the Central Bank and could direct commerce through its powers to negotiate bilateral treaties. After the 1943 revolution the government had taken over public services and industries. It now controlled the largest gas company in Buenos Aires, the former Primitiva Gas Company, and thirty-eight formerly German-owned firms that had been expropriated on the declaration of war in late March 1945. It had indirect control over what existed of heavy industry through the *fabricaciones militares*, and a major role in investment and financing through new institutions like the Industrial Bank. It could set food prices, freeze rents, and oversee collective bargaining through the Secretariat for Labor and Welfare.

Between February and June 1946 the outgoing Farrell administration had augmented the power of the state still further. In March, in a measure instigated by Miranda and supported by Perón, Farrell nationalized the Central Bank and the deposits of private banks. This action eliminated the Central Bank's formal autonomy, which it had enjoyed since its creation twelve years earlier, and its system of administration by a board of nominees from private banks. The measure also extended the rediscount nexus between the Central and private banks, and established uniform reserve requirements for issuing loans. Nationalization of the Central Bank thus enhanced the centralization of economic management.[16]

Second, at the end of May 1946, again following Miranda, the

Farrell government created a new agency to direct the buying and selling of exportables, the Institute for the Promotion of Trade (*Instituto Argentino para la Promoción del Intercambio* [IAPI]). The IAPI was given a monopoly over foreign sales of cereals and meat, indeed over all major exports except wool. This monopoly was justified as essential for dealings with a new monopsony abroad, the International Food Council, set up by the Allies to procure food for Europe. The IAPI's task was to ensure the highest-possible earnings from exports and favorable terms for the acquisition of imports. At the same time it became the sole buyer of farm goods from domestic producers. The IAPI was thus to be the chief instrument in the plan to redistribute income from the rural to the urban working-class sectors, as well as the primary source of new investment funds for national industry. The IAPI would buy cheaply from the farmers and sell dearly abroad, with the profits going to finance Perón's urban programs. It would also be a vehicle to prevent profiteering among farmers and oligopolistic intermediaries: the meat-packing plants and the four big grain-exporting houses led by Bunge y Born, which before the war had controlled around 80 percent of grain exports. Among other supplementary functions of the IAPI were purchases of fuel and supplies for public companies and the armed forces.[17]

In mid 1946 Perón also appeared to enjoy a much more favorable international situation than any of his predecessors since at least the 1920s. Europe, still struggling with the aftermath of the war, was producing foodstuffs at a rate 25 percent below 1939 levels. With the end of the wartime blockades and the freeing of shipping, agricultural prices immediately leapt upward: the predicted postwar boom had arrived. Argentina's other great asset in 1946 was its massive foreign reserves, the result of wartime trade surpluses, which at $1,687 million amounted to one-third of the total foreign reserves throughout Latin America. From its wartime commerce with Britain alone Argentina had a sterling balance whose value approached £150 million. All these funds Perón now hoped to employ in the plan to reequip the country with machinery and raw materials.[18]

Mid 1946 also marked a noticeable attenuation of the wartime feud with the United States. In late 1945 the United States had refused to supply coal and fuel to Argentina, apparently so as to disrupt its exports. However, with the coming of the Cold War, the Americans were less interested in harassing alleged relics of fascism like Perón. Although they still sought to curb his influence elsewhere in Latin America, they were now prepared to accept him at home as a bulwark against the Communists. America's attitudes toward Perón also changed as it became more aware of the commercial opportunities afforded by Argentina. Last, in the aftermath of the blue-book debacle, Spruille Braden's influence had waned in the State Department. In May 1946 the Truman government sent a new ambassador to Buenos Aires, the conciliatory George Messersmith, whose task was to smoothe away earlier disagreements and open the Argentine market for American goods. To assist his efforts, the United States unblocked Argentine gold assets held in American banks.

Perón's first act on taking office, a resumption of diplomatic relations with the Soviet Union, seemed intended to antagonize the United States, but this proved little more than a gesture of independence for home consumption. Soon after came friendlier behavior: in September the Argentine Congress ratified the Pan American defense treaties negotiated eighteen months earlier at Chapultepec and Argentina's 1945 pledge to join the United Nations. In August 1947 at the Rio de Janeiro conference, Argentina also became a signatory to the Pan American alliance, although this was not immediately ratified by Congress. Throughout this period Perón publicly appeared vehemently anti-American, repeatedly proclaiming nonalignment and refusing to foreswear exchange control and bilateralism, the main conditions for joining the newly created International Monetary Fund and later the General Agreement on Tariffs and Trade (GATT). Yet in private contacts with American diplomats Perón was often cordial and accommodating, continually emphasizing his determination to fight Communism. In this way he persuaded the Americans to relax restrictions on exports of tires, some shipping machinery, and technical assistance.[19]

In late 1946 Perón's regime issued its economic program in the form of a five-year plan (*Plan de Gobierno*) drawn up under the auspices of Miranda and Figuerola. The plan, a crude first effort, as much propaganda as a statement of policy, was eventually submitted to Congress as twenty-seven separate items of legislation. It began with a ringing declaration: "In 1810 we were liberated politically; today we long for economic independence," but it neither detailed costs nor itemized priorities. Its chief goals, however, were clear enough and highly ambitious: Argentina was to achieve a self-sufficient mixed agro-industrial economy by 1951; the target for five-year industrial growth was 43.2 percent. The government would repatriate the foreign debt, drastically reduce foreign ownership of public services, increase consumption through income redistribution, and maintain full employment. The plan also mentioned generous and comprehensive public health and housing provisions, and a variety of new benefits to labor—paid vacations, the year-end *aguinaldo* bonus, up to three months' sick benefits, and maternity leave for female workers. The plan's significant and striking omission was agriculture, which was ignored except for promises of credits to small farmers and the protection of rural tenants.[20]

As the five year plan was implemented the new state purchasing and marketing board, the IAPI, came to the fore. Throughout the late 1940s the IAPI customarily conducted its operations by announcing at planting time the prices it would pay farmers. Between 1947 and 1949 wheat farmers, for example, were paid less than half the prevailing world prices for their products. After the harvest, with goods in hand, the IAPI embarked on an aggressive sales campaign abroad. The IAPI also took over meat purchases and sales, for a time making enormous profits by pushing down the incomes of the cattle ranchers while squeezing the meat-packing plants. These profits were then siphoned off to the banks to be spent on import purchases, loans to manufacturers, and the government's welfare programs.

The plan yielded immediate and striking results. Between 1945 and 1948 the gross national product grew by around 29 percent, and manufacturing increased at a similar rate, led once more by textiles, some chemicals, foods, oil, and metals (see Table 27). To push growth to its maximum the Central Bank adopted a mildly inflationary strategy, increasing the money supply at an average annual rate of 12.7 percent, roughly double the growth of output. Another prime agent in the fast growth of manufacturing was the Industrial Bank, founded in 1944, which from mid 1946 provided up to 80 percent of total credits

TABLE 27. *Indices of Manufacturing Production, 1945–1948 (1950 = 100)*

	Production
1945	76.5
1946	86.3
1947	99.5
1948	100.7

SOURCE: Guido Di Tella and Manuel Zymelman, *Las etapas del desarrollo económico argentino* (Buenos Aires, 1967), 507.

to manufacturers. Interest rates were highly favorable, and for certain earmarked priorities negative interest rates were offered. Between 1945 and 1949 credits for industry increased fourfold. Manufacturing was also supported by tariffs and stiff exchange controls. Many finished consumer goods enjoyed absolute protection; others were safeguarded by stringent quotas. In contrast, many capital goods and raw materials were subject to minimal tariff rates or no tariffs at all. The exchange-control system, established fifteen years earlier, acquired a sophisticated, multivariate form with no fewer than five different rate levels.[21]

Perón's government had a vital role in shaping the economic environment, generating the resources, and mapping out the conditions for the postwar surge in industry-led growth. However, industrial expansion occurred mostly in the private rather than the public sector, an expression of the postwar shift from heavy to light industry. Most of the nation's heavy industry, roughly 10 percent of the total industrial capacity, was state-owned. After 1945 investment in the state industries declined markedly; simultaneously, an effort was made to streamline and reorganize them. In 1947 the former German-owned firms were grouped together in a National Directorate of State Industries (*Dirección Nacional de Industrias del Estado* [DINIE]). The military-administered factories, which had expanded rapidly during the war, were similarly placed under an umbrella body, the *Dirección Nacional de Fabricaciones e Investigaciones Aeronaúticas y Metalúrgicas del Estado* [DINFIA]. Despite reorganization and falling investment in the state sector, several new entities appeared during the late 1940s, including a state shipbuilding concern (*Astilleros y Fabricaciones Navales del Estado* [AFNE]) and a steel plant (*Sociedad Mixta Siderurgia Argentina* [SOMISA]). The latter was created as a mixed public and private venture under the DINFIA, with the government having an 80 percent share.[22]

Outside banking and trade activities, the renewed expansion of the state in the economy was most visible in the sphere of public services, as Perón carried through his pledge to nationalize foreign interests. By the end of 1946 he had negotiated the takeover of the small network of French-owned railroads. He did the same with the *Unión Telefónica*, a company formed by the British that had been acquired by the International Telephone Company of New York (ITT) during the late 1920s. Perón also began fulfilling his promise to repatriate the foreign debt, and his actions effected a substantial fall in foreign investment, from $2,651 million in 1945 to $1,487 million in

1953. Yet the centerpiece of this aspect of Perón's policy was the nationalization of the British-owned railroads in February 1947. The expropriation of the railroads accounted for more than 2,000 million pesos, or 59 percent of the total decline in foreign-owned assets—3,400 million pesos—between 1945 and 1953. Other major expenditures in this area included 1,000 million pesos for debt repatriation and 370 million pesos for the purchase of the *Unión Telefónica*.[23]

The nationalization of the British railroads was by no means a new idea; it had been under desultory discussion for ten years, was eagerly desired by the nationalist factions led by the writer Raúl Scalabrini Ortiz, and since the late 1930s the British had acknowledged that nationalization was almost inevitable. Perón, however, despite his nationalist rhetoric, was circumspect, reluctant to offer too much for what he called "old iron." But he was forced into the issue because the Mitre Law of 1907, which had served as the general railroad code for the past half century, was due to expire in 1947.

Meanwhile, Perón faced a second pressing matter in relations with Britain, the blocked sterling balances, the earnings from wartime trade with Britain that for the past six years had piled up in the Bank of England. At first he and Miranda made new efforts to unfreeze the funds and mobilize them for import purchases. But the British refused, for they had many similar debts with other countries, some much larger than Argentina's, and if they bowed to Perón would have to do so elsewhere. In the Eady-Miranda treaty of September 1946 Argentina agreed to postpone its claims and in return received new safeguards against the devaluation of the blocked balances and the payment of a nominal interest on the debt. For its part, Britain promised to cease blocking Argentina's future sterling earnings, which were to be freely convertible, and received a four-year contract for meat imports at favorable prices. Britain also gained from Argentina a promise of "favorable treatment" for its British-owned railroads, an echo of the Roca-Runciman treaty of 1933.

This last provision resulted in the formation of a new joint state and private holding company to administer the railroads. Under this "condominium" agreement the British retained some of the benefits extended under the Mitre Law, such as the importing of supplies free from duties. The Argentine government also agreed to return to the nineteenth-century practice of guaranteed minimum profits for the railroads, with the rate set at 4 percent, and pledged further to provide subsidies for replacement rolling stock. In return it received a financial share in the railroads and a schedule under which it would gradually obtain a controlling interest.

But within weeks Perón discarded the agreement and committed himself to full-scale nationalization through outright purchase. This abrupt change was effected in part by the interplay of domestic forces. The condominium agreement was received unfavorably in Buenos Aires, amid protests from the nationalist groups and the railroad unions. Perón, who was waging a battle for greater control over the unions and the CGT, clutched at nationalization as a means of strengthening his political position.

British interests, however, and indirectly American, played an equally crucial role in what transpired. In 1945 Britain had obtained massive recovery loans from the United States in return for pledges to restore the convertibility of sterling and to release the wartime blocked balances. In imposing such conditions the Americans sought to open up the sterling area to their trade, enabling sellers to Britain to make return purchases from the United States. To the Americans the Eady-Miranda treaty, by failing to release the blocked balances, was a violation of the conditions Britain had accepted for the recovery loans. In the face of growing American pressure, the British decided that the solution to this difficulty was to liquidate the sterling balance through the sale of the railroads. They reopened negotiations with Perón who, despite his domestic preoccupations, still sought to drive a hard bargain. For some time the two sides placed markedly disparate values on the railroads' assets. The talks were about to collapse, but Ambassador Messersmith intervened, and an agreement was soon reached.

Opinion was divided as to whether Argentina or Britain had the better of the final deal. The purchase price was £150 million, or 2,028 million pesos, far below Britain's initial valuation of £250 million, yet higher than the London Stock Market valuation of £130 million, which had recently increased as news of the negotiations reached holders of railroad stock. Argentina had acquired control over a railroad system some 30,000 kilometers in length, but around half its rolling stock predated 1914, and large sections of the system had fallen into serious disrepair, casualties of the preceding fifteen years of depression and war. Lastly, the price Argentina paid for the railroads slightly exceeded the blocked sterling balances; the remainder would be settled from future sales of meat.

The nationalization of the railroads seemed in some respects as much an American as either a British or Argentine design. Messersmith's anxiety to consummate the deal reflected more than American concern with the blocked sterling balances, for the Americans also here perceived an opportunity to further their generation-long endeavor to loosen Britain's grip on the Argentine market. Without the railroads, they believed, the British would find it much harder to strike trading bargains with Argentina like those they had won during the 1930s, to the detriment of American exporters.[24]

The negotiations on the railroads also revealed something about Perón, casting him in the guise of a somewhat reluctant nationalist, ready to make new deals with foreign capital but constrained from extreme measures by the need to protect himself politically. He played this same role in his dealings with American oil interests later in 1947. Publicly Perón was pledged to a basically *yrigoyenista* policy on oil— favoring the YPF, the state oil directorate, while shunning the foreign- ers. Privately, however, he appeared to acknowledge criticisms of this position: Argentina's oil needs were rising with the growth of manu- facturing, and a narrow nationalistic line would provoke a growing oil deficit, compelling additional oil purchases from abroad, and thereby reducing the amount of foreign exchange available to import capital goods for industry. As part of his early efforts to repair relations with the United States, Perón thus made known his willingness to strike an agreement with Standard Oil, using the same mixed-company prin- ciple he first adopted with the railroads. But Standard Oil demurred. It criticized recent enactments freezing its prices while granting its workers a 20 percent pay increase, and it also attacked government favoritism toward the YPF, which was allowed to import oil duty-free, a privilege denied the foreign companies. Resolving these grievances became Standard Oil's precondition for any future negotiation. Perón was unwilling to meet these demands. In discussions with American diplomats, he described the oil issue as "political dynamite," implying that although he favored greater concessions he was constrained po- litically from offering them. The idea soon lapsed.

Throughout this period Perón used the decline of foreign in- vestment and his nationalization schemes to score propaganda victo- ries, while covertly courting the Americans. But the American re- sponse was invariably the same: no new investment would be forthcoming until American companies, notably the meat-packing plants, ceased to be persecuted by bodies like the IAPI, and until the companies were permitted to increase their earnings and repatriate their profits without restraint.[25]

Once in office Perón swiftly began to punish those who had led the efforts to unseat him the previous year. He purged the universities, dismissing some 1,500 members of the professorial body. In July his followers in Congress tabled an impeachment motion that charged members of the Supreme Court with partisan behavior in the events of October 1945, and the following May the measure carried. With the ejection of all but one of the judges, Perón enjoyed complete control over all three branches of government. By this time he had also taken over the *Unión Industrial Argentina*, thereby stilling its criticisms of labor legislation and other aspects of his program.

Freedom of the press was somewhat restrained by rationing newsprint and favoring *peronista* tabloids. In 1947 the long-established Socialist daily, *La Vanguardia*, was briefly closed down by the police after a virulent campaign against the government. Afterward *La Vanguardia* ceased to appear, although its demise seemed due as much to the plummeting popularity of the Socialists as to continuing persecution. The same year a Radical deputy, Ernesto Sanmartino, was expelled from Congress as punishment for his spate of personal insults at Perón and his wife. Amid such cases of undue heavy-handedness, Perón made some effort to fulfill the promise issued on his inaugural that he would seek political reconciliation. He curbed the anti-Semitism that had been simmering since 1943. Accusations that he deliberately harbored escaped Axis war criminals seemed largely fictitious. Like the Americans and the Russians, Perón was interested in attracting persons with scientific expertise to the country. His dealings with alleged Nazis went little further than this, though throughout his presidency he showed keen interest in developing atomic power in Argentina, and he longed to give teeth to his "Third Position" through the atomic bomb.[26]

Perón's relations with the armed services were conducted with care and circumspection, but with few immediate difficulties. Efforts to depoliticize the military included awarding the officer corps several pay increases, reportedly raising the salaries of some senior ranks above those of their counterparts in the United States, and military pension benefits were increased. Meanwhile, senior officers continued in high government posts and as managers of state firms in the energy and transportation sectors. Whenever he could overcome or ignore continuing American reluctance, Perón also provided the military with new weaponry; in 1947, for example, he made a large purchase of British jets. However, he rapidly scaled down overall spending on the armed forces, chiefly by ceasing to apply universal conscription. The share of the national budget devoted to the combined services fell from about half in 1945, to about a quarter by 1949, and thereafter remained at around one-fifth. But while the number of enlisted men fell, the officer classes steadily grew such that, for example, in 1951 there were twice as many generals as six years earlier. The basic strategy was thus to encourage military careerism.[27]

The major political issue in 1946 and 1947 was Perón's relations with the coalition of the unions and the CGT that had backed his bid for the presidency, and he hastened to strengthen his control. Perón had begun his quest for power by seeking to create a kind of state syndicalism: a trading of benefits and support with the working class, a plan that entailed mass unionization and the subordination of the workers to the state through the nexus of the unions. During the crisis of September-October 1945 he had been compelled to retreat from this concept and to accept a relationship with labor that was more akin to power sharing. The *Partido Laborista* formed in late October 1945 had adopted Perón only as its "candidate" in the February elections, while pointedly avoiding the term *leader*. He was the party's "first affiliate," a title that implied *primus inter pares* among an assembly of largely autonomous union leaders, who intended to uphold their power through the *laboristas* in Congress and to maintain their control over the union rank and file. From the start Perón was dissatisfied with this arrangement, which left him without direct control over his political base. Once he became president-elect, he made ready to return to his original plan.

In May 1946 the outgoing Farrell promulgated the Organic Statute of Political Parties—rules for the legal recognition of political parties and the terms on which they could contest elections. Among the stipulations of the statute was a ban on the kind of *ad hoc* party coalitions that had been formed during the February elections. The measure was regarded in most quarters as a ploy to stifle attempts to recreate the Democratic Union, or leftist Popular Front movements dominated by the Communist party. However, Perón immediately seized on the enactment to justify purging the *laboristas*. Soon after he announced the dissolution of both the Labor party and Radical *Junta Renovadora*, and the formation of the *Partido Único de la Revolución Nacional* (Single Party of the National Revolution). The *laboristas* were denied positions in the cabinet.

In the ensuing conflict Perón's chief opponent was Cipriano Reyes, the leader of the meat-packing workers' union who had been among the chief instigators of the workers' march of 17 October 1945. To counteract Perón's measures against the *laboristas*, Reyes led some of the meat workers in a protest strike. Perón stifled the demonstration by calling in the police. In mid 1947 Reyes attempted a comeback but was arrested. In September 1948 he was again detained, on a trumped-up charge of plotting to assassinate Perón, and spent the next several years in prison.[28]

During his first confrontation with Reyes in late 1946, Perón was also turning against the *laboristas* in the CGT. Another prominent *laborista*, Luis Gay, defeated Perón's nominee, Ángel Borlenghi, in the November elections for the position of secretary-general of the CGT. For the moment the president appeared to accept the verdict. But three months later, Gay suddenly resigned after charges of disloyal collusion with an American labor team that had come to enlist the CGT in a newly established Pan-American labor association. The Peronist press claimed that agents of Spruille Braden were among the American delegation sent by the American Federation of Labor and Congress of Industrial Organizations (AFL-CIO). The campaign against Gay coincided with the announcement of the plan to nationalize the railroads, and the wave of popularity engulfing Perón undercut all opposition. The fall of Gay demonstrated that Perón would brook no power in the unions except his own. By late 1947, when José Espejo took over the position of secretary-general, any residue of independence in the CGT had evaporated, marking the end of the *laboristas* and their aspiration for autonomy and shared governance.[29]

As Perón fashioned undisputed leadership at the apex of the working-class movement, he did so at its base by fostering the renewed growth of the unions and their affiliation under Peronist leaders with the CGT. The urban labor force continued to grow rapidly, as the annual rate of migration from the country to Greater Buenos Aires increased, from an average of 3.4 percent in 1935–1945 to 4.4 percent in 1945-1960. The population of Greater Buenos Aires, 3.4 million in 1936, had reached 4.7 million by 1947, and continued to climb at the same or even higher rates, reaching almost 7 million by 1960. Migrants arrived from the pampas, from the interior, and from neighboring Latin American states, and a half million new European immigrants were admitted between 1947 and 1951. The new population was inescapably visible throughout the metropolitan area in a mass of new suburban settlements. Migrants swelled the numbers of new urban workers in industry, transportation, and services, becoming the backbone of the swift upward surge in union membership during Perón's first years as president. Between 1945 and 1949 union affiliations almost quadrupled, rising from 530,000 to 1.9 million.

Here lay Perón's popular base, greater and soon more solid than any earlier coalition. Trade unions grew during the late 1940s in the aftermath of a great crop of strikes that far exceeded previous protests. In 1946 an estimated 334,000 workers took part in strikes, and 2 million working days were lost. In 1947 strikes involved 541,000 workers and 3.4 million days lost, and the next year 278,000 workers and 3.1 million days lost. Wages, which were around 40 percent of national income in 1946, rose in the aftermath of the strikes to 49 percent by 1949, and between 1945 and 1948 real wages of industrial workers increased by 20 percent. During the strikes of the late 1940s Perón almost invariably sided with the unions, thereby gaining the political credit for the swift amelioration in workers' living standards.[30]

Perón further consolidated his grip on the organized working class by using the law of Professional Associations (*Ley de Asociaciones Profesionales*) enacted in December 1945. The measure gave the government, through the Labor Secretariat, the power to confer on individual unions *personería gremial*, the full legal standing necessary to engage in collective bargaining before the government and employers. Unions lacking this status were reduced to mere mutual aid societies; their strikes unrecognized by the government, they were unable to share in the rewards bestowed on the union movement at large. *Personería gremial* thus became a major tool to impose government tutelage on the unions.

Almost all the unions cheerfully sacrificed autonomy for material self-advancement, but Perón encountered occasional pockets of resistance. He had some difficulties with middle-class associations, such as bank clerks, and with unions in the food sector, where pay scales were affected by his discriminatory policies against agriculture. Other opposition surfaced in some older unions, anxious to preserve their independence, despite the destruction of the *laboristas*. In most cases if a denial of *personería gremial* proved insufficient, the CGT would enter into conspiracies with opponents of the dominant union factions. On the pretext of resolving internal conflict, the CGT would then forcibly intervene, reorganizing the union under a *peronista* leadership. This technique was applied to the metal workers' union in 1946, to the telephone workers in 1947, to the printers' union (the *Federación Gráfica Bonaerense*) in 1949, and to the sugar workers' union in Tucumán. In 1951 the last of the great traditional unions, the railway footplatemen's union, *La Fraternidad*, fell under *peronista* control.

As his authority over the unions expanded, Perón reorganized them into industrywide blocs under a hierarchical bureaucracy, supported by compulsory dues from rank-and-file members, a structure that better lent itself to control from above than did skill- or plant-based organizations. Under the new system unions became increasingly omnipresent agents of power. By 1950 union leaders were commonly selected as senior public officials, and on the shop floor many unions acquired control over promotions, layoffs, seniority bonuses, and retirements. Beneficiaries of union social security schemes multiplied, from 500,000 in 1943, to 1.5 million by 1946, and 5 million by 1951.

In dealing with the workers, Perón grew increasingly adept at using propaganda, theatricality, display, and charismatic authority. In 1946 he declared October 17, the anniversary of his return from imprisonment the year before, a national holiday, *Día de la Lealtad* (Loyalty Day). In February 1947, immediately after the nationalization of the British railroads, Perón issued the Rights of the Workers (*Derechos de los Trabajadores*), ten principles summarizing his commitment to ameliorate the lot of the humble. On 9 July 1947, Independence Day, he went to Tucumán, site of the declaration of independence in 1816, to issue his Declaration of Economic Independence. Throughout this period he dwelt unceasingly on his achievements in nationalizing public services and repatriating the foreign debt; among his claims was that Argentina now belonged to a privileged triad of creditor nations. To uphold, propagate, and externalize allegiances he conducted numerous mass rallies of his *descamisado* followers, usually in the Plaza de Mayo outside Government House. On these occasions scores of thousands would gather to applaud *El Líder* and the benefits he bestowed upon them.[31]

Yet as this nexus grew tighter and firmer, Perón also seemed to distance himself from the workers, steadily abstracting himself from their day-to-day affairs and behaving as if the state and himself were separate from and suspended above society at large. His opponents interpreted this as further confirmation that Peronism was simply a form of fascism, but Perón's mix of several authoritarian-populist styles defied easy labels or characterizations. The rallies in the Plaza de Mayo evoked the triumphs of the ancient Caesars; the notion of Social Justice executed from above had Bismarckian connotations; and in his self-proclaimed guise as mediator between competing social forces, Perón sometimes evoked Marx's rendering of Louis Bonaparte. If the emphasis on mass organization recalled Mussolini or Primo de Rivera, its application to the unions echoed Cárdenas in Mexico or Vargas in Brazil.

In the late 1940s Peronism remained much closer to corporatism than to totalitarianism. Despite the regimentation of the unions, in other spheres society continued to uphold numerous pluralist features, and a considerable degree of decentralized autonomy: Argentina was still a long way from the complete absorption of civil society by the state that characterizes totalitarian systems. To a large extent, as was true in 1944–1945, the unions were primarily a defense barrier against a variety of potentially hostile forces from outside. As a political *parvenu*, aware of his fragile legitimacy, Perón was obliged to play by most of the established political rules: to hold elections, tolerate the presence of an opposition in Congress, and grant much greater freedom of expression than was customary under fully authoritarian or fascist regimes.

In some measure Peronism also evoked *yrigoyenismo*, as Perón depicted himself the leader of a "movement," rather than a "party," an association open to all sharing his enmity toward imperialism and oligarchy, and his vision of social justice and national sovereignty. Thirty years earlier the Radicals had constructed a strong grass-roots movement based on precinct committees and individualized services to the population. The Peronists now did the same through what were known, following Perón's penchant for military vocabulary, as "basic units" (*unidades básicas*). Again following Yrigoyen, Perón continually preached the goal of "class harmony."

By 1948 Perón had begun referring to his political ideas as *justicialismo*, which he defined as "Christian and humanist" with the "best attributes [of] collectivism and individualism, idealism and materialism." Only by semantic legerdemain could such a remarkable eclecticism as *justicialismo* be called a "philosophy"; rather, and again following Yrigoyen's example, Perón intermixed alluring propagandistic clichés to give his movement an inclusive, universal appeal.[32]

After *El Líder* himself, the regime's most intriguing and colorful figure was Eva Perón, the former actress who at the age of twenty-four became Perón's mistress in 1944; they married soon after the victory of October 1945. Enjoying a wide network of associations in the Army and the trade unions, "Evita" already possessed substantial political influence in her own right by the time Perón became president. It was she, for example, who reputedly procured the appointment of Ángel Borlenghi as minister of the interior. As first lady she sought with energy and ruthlessness to enhance her power, assuming a prominent role in the campaign against Cipriano Reyes and in the conspiracy that overthrew Luis Gay. In early 1947 she purchased the newspaper *Democracia* and converted it into a personal propaganda organ. During a spectacular tour of Spain, Italy, and France in mid

1947, she boldly propagated the cause of the New Argentina. By the end of the year she was again embroiled in the internal politics of the CGT, exerting decisive influence in the selection of José Espejo, known widely as her political puppet, as secretary-general. Subsequently, despite having no official position or standing, she remained the most powerful figure in the CGT leadership.

Evita Perón's second field of operations was charitable work, which in her hands became another powerful propaganda tool. In June 1946 Perón's enemies among the *Fuerzas Vivas* denied her the position customarily filled by the wife of the president as head of the *Sociedad de Beneficencia*, a long-established patrician charity association. She replied by instigating a government takeover of the society, which she then purged of her adversaries. Soon after she founded the Social Assistance Foundation (*Fundación de Ayuda Social*), which in June 1948 was renamed the Eva Perón Foundation. Both organizations received generous state subsidies, tax exemptions, and contributions from the CGT; both funded clinics and hospitals, subsidized pharmacies, organized periodic food and clothes handouts, and provided disaster relief in Argentina and abroad. Through her foundation Evita claimed personal credit for an expansion in hospital beds, from 15,400 in 1943 to 23,300 in 1949, and for increasing the nation's schools by a fourth during the same period.

Lastly, Eva Perón led a campaign for women's political rights. Her efforts were directly responsible for the enfranchisement of women in 1947 and for the creation of the Women's Branch (*Rama Feminina*) of the Peronist party in 1949. On these foundations Perón launched a bid to capture the loyalties of the *descamisadas* as he had earlier gained the support of their men.

This dynamic, captivating, magnetic, but also mercurial and vindictive woman wielded power that was never defined nor formalized, and which was therefore often unchecked and unlimited. During a crisis she was indispensable to Perón; at other times her most easily identified functions were those of broker, liaison, and propagandist between Perón, the CGT, and the working-class masses. Having taken a leading part in the subjugation of the unions, Eva Perón afterward directed the creation of the lines of communication between the upper hierarchy and the base. Her charity activities were directed to the same goal. As she dispensed succor to scores of daily supplicants at her foundation, she revived on a grand scale the activities of the traditional political boss, exchanging favors and benefits for support and allegiance.

Evita also served as a symbol and a myth in the Peronist movement. Her charity work cast her in the role of a providential Madonna, the *Dama de la Esperanza*, "Lady of Hope," or *Abanderada de los Humildes*, "Standard-Bearer of the Humble." Her marriage to Perón exemplified the greater marriage between the leader and his followers, for she was an iconic image of the elevation of the *descamisados* to power and status, and a romantic vision of the pilgrimage of the internal migrant from the wretchedness and squalor of the pampas village to the glamor of the metropolis. She was at once the glittering ceremonial showpiece who acted the part of a monarch and yet the coarse, venemous demagogue or feminist crusader who instigated the destruction of oligarchy and privilege. As one Peronist slogan put it, *Perón cumple, Eva dignifica:* through him achievement and accomplishment; through her its ennoblement and beatification.[33]

In December 1947 Perón's party, known for the preceding eighteen months as the *Partido Unico*, was rechristened the *Partido Peronista*, a change that attested to his standing and personal control. In the interim congressional elections early the following year, the Peronists completely crushed the opposition, carrying the election by two to one, and leaving the Radicals with fewer than a fourth of the seats of the Chamber of Deputies.

In early 1948 Perón's position seemed impregnable, and his strong and self-confident air was soon mirrored by the successful execution of constitutional reform. The issue was first taken up in Congress in May 1948. In the December elections to convoke a constitutional convention, the Peronists once more won two-thirds of the vote. The convention opened in January 1949, pledged to create a "Justicialist" successor to the Constitution of 1853. Within less than a year it had completed the task, as heated protests from the Radicals and others were ignored or overridden.

Although the Constitution of 1949 was a revision of its predecessor, rather than an entirely new set of articles of government, the changes and additions were profound. Its most controversial provision was to permit an incumbent president to seek reelection to an unlimited number of six-year terms. Also, the electoral college was abolished, allowing the direct election of the president. Likewise, national senators were no longer to be selected by the provincial legislatures but by direct popular vote, and the terms of congressional deputies were extended from four to six years. The Constitution of 1949 thus established election by plebiscite, eliminating the sectional and regional weightings that were legacies of nineteenth-century federalism. Furthermore, it widened presidential authority to intervene in the provinces and gave the president discretion to impose a "state of internal war" to protect against rebellion or insurrection. Thus the long process by which power had become increasingly centralized and also personalized here reached its acme.

The Constitution of 1949 contained several other characteristically *peronista* elements. Its preamble reiterated the familiar covenant to a "Nation socially just, economically free, and politically sovereign." Article 33 comprised the "decalogue," the ten rights of the workers proclaimed by Perón two years earlier. The former constitution's classically liberal emphasis on freedoms and rights of the individual was replaced by corporate rights emanating from the state. The document's other pronounced *etatiste* and nationalistic features included the assertion of inalienable national ownership over nonrenewable natural resources such as oil, the authorization of the state to nationalize public services and regulate foreign trade through bodies like the IAPI, and the extension of the government's control over coinage and money. In defining private property as a "natural right" limited by its "social function," the Constitution of 1949 implied that the state had the power to expropriate property, either business or land, to ensure its "full productive use" for the benefit of the community at large—a power whereby the executive branch could, if it wished, initiate land reform.[34]

THE ADVENT OF CRISIS, 1949–1952

The Constitution of 1949 was hailed as another of Perón's great victories, but it was also one of his last. Though his veneer of monolithic, unassailable strength remained uncracked, economic conditions put him on the defensive. The surge in manufacturing after 1945 came in the wake of large increases in imports: between 1935 and 1945–1949 annual average imports of raw materials increased by 38 percent, capital goods by 49 percent, fuels by 27 percent, and goods employed in transportation, construction, and commerce—tires, excavators, locomotives, trucks—by 143 percent. From a low wartime base in 1945, by 1948 imports were estimated to have quadrupled. Supplies were contracted at frantic speed, sometimes piling up in the ports for weeks before they could be moved. More than half the nation's total imports came from a single source, the United States. In 1937 imports from the United States had totaled $55 million and were a mere $37 million in 1939. After the war, however, they soared, reaching $328 million in 1947, and $192 million in 1948.[35]

Argentina made these purchases on the strength of reserves accumulated during the war and by virtue of new earnings from exports, the value of which doubled between 1946 and 1948. Its resources appeared more than sufficient to reequip the country with the goods that were unobtainable during the war. In 1946, for example, the reserves alone were enough to maintain imports at the current rate for two and a half years. However, there was no simple correlation between the capacity to import and either the foreign reserves or new earnings from exports. Argentina was again enmeshed in difficulties that stemmed from its old triangular trading relationship with the United States and western Europe, particularly Britain: buying from the United States far more than it could sell, while in Europe obliged to sell more than it wished to buy. In the 1920s currency convertibility among Argentina's major trading partners had eased this problem: Argentina could sell to Britain, for example, while buying from the United States. But during much of the late 1940s sterling and most other European currencies were inconvertible. Bilateralism, the road taken during the 1930s, was also of limited value, since the nations to which Argentina exported were unable to reciprocate with the goods required by domestic manufacturers.

During the immediate postwar period the United States imported from Argentina significant quantities of raw wool, canned meats, and quebracho extract. But it still kept the door firmly shut against most Argentine meats and grains. For several years after 1945 Argentina thus sold to the United States only a quarter of what it bought, covering the deficit by drawing on its wartime dollar reserve. At $569 million in early 1946 the dollar reserves were substantial, but already by the end of the following year they were nearing exhaustion. In contrast, the western European countries, each struggling to surmount severe food shortages, for a time took whatever Argentina had to offer. But Europe had virtually nothing to sell: the British would offer whiskey, the French perfumes, and the Spaniards or Italians light manufactures of the type Argentina was now producing. In 1946 about three-quarters of Argentina's foreign reserves were held in western European or Latin American currencies almost all of which were inconvertible. That year Argentina added some $425 million to its foreign reserves, but two-thirds of these funds were inconvertible and piled up as useless credits vulnerable to devaluation. Meanwhile, in the same year two-thirds of imports came from the United States.

By late 1948 Argentina had thus amassed a commercial deficit with countries upholding convertibility—in particular, the United States— of $880 million (see Table 28). [36]

With memories of numerous previous failures, Perón's economic advisers, led by Miranda, seemed to abandon any hope of prizing open the American market. The centerpiece of their commercial strategy was Britain, still the largest and apparently most secure of Argentina's foreign markets; foremost in Miranda's mind was Britain's pledge to the United States to restore sterling convertibility. In the Eady-Miranda treaty of September 1946, although Britain refused to release the wartime blocked balances, it pledged to cease blocking Argentina's future sterling earnings, which were to be convertible. In the next eleven months Argentina was able to convert some $200 million in sterling to dollars. However, in August 1947 Britain faced a widening trade deficit and a run on sterling, and suspended convertibility.[37]

Britain's suspension of convertibility was a major blow to Argentina. Yet, another highly promising alternative immediately presented itself. In mid 1947 the United States launched the reconstruction of the western European economies through the Marshall Plan. As part of this project, under the European Cooperation Administration (ECA) the Europeans were permitted to use Marshall Plan dollars for overseas food purchases. Perón later claimed to have received verbal assurances from American diplomats in Buenos Aires that the Europeans would be allowed to make some of these purchases from Argentina, which would have enabled Argentina to export to Europe and be paid in American dollars. With this expectation, Argentina continued to make heavy purchases from the United States in late 1947 and into the following year. In doing so it drew upon its severely

TABLE 28. *Trade Balances with Major Trading Areas, 1945–1948*
(*In million current pesos*)

	Sterling Area	Western Europe	U.S.
1945	+ 562	+309	+ 417
1946	+ 790	+967	+ 39
1947	+1,477	+949	−1,466
1948	+1,094	+779	−1,493

SOURCE: Jorge Fodor, "Perón's Policies for Agricultural Exports, 1946–1948: Dogmatism or Common Sense," in *Argentina in the Twentieth Century*, David Rock, ed. (London, 1975), 146.

depleted dollar reserves but assumed that they would be speedily replenished from trade with Europe. The IAPI sought to increase the wheat surplus for export by announcing purchase prices for wheat that were relatively high compared with competing farm products. At 6.5 million tons, the 1947–1948 wheat harvest was the largest since before the war.[38]

In early 1948 the Americans made what for Perón was a crucial and fateful decision: Marshall Plan dollars could not be used to purchase Argentine goods. Instead the Americans planned to provision Europe from their own, Canadian, and other British Commonwealth grains. The Agricultural Act of 1948 laid out the project: the American federal government would increase grain production by subsidizing American farmers and would finance grain sales in Europe.

Perón frantically attempted to persuade the Americans to change their plan. In April he met at length with the American ambassador, James Bruce, who had replaced Messersmith the year before. Throughout the exchanges Perón indulged in craven appeals for American goodwill. He told Bruce, for example, that any of his apparently anti-American remarks were merely domestic rhetoric. He abdicated on nonalignment, declaring himself a faithful supporter of the Pan American and western alliances. The "Third Position" Bruce reported him as saying "is a political device for use in peacetime . . . it has no application and would not even exist in the event of war between the United States and Russia."[39] In a revealing statement concerning his dealings with the trade unions, Perón reiterated to Bruce his commitment to the struggle against communism; Bruce's report of Perón's comments continue:

> There are two distinct ways of combating communism: one a process of extermination, and two, buying off (the workers) . . . the latter [is] more effective and in the long run much less expensive. [Perón] explained that by buying them off he meant raising wages and improving living conditions to such an extent that there would no longer exist a fertile field for Communist activities.[40]

Despite Perón's pleas the American policies remained unchanged; in cutting Perón adrift the Americans had the final and decisive word in their five-year feud with him. By August 1948, as an international crisis loomed over the status of Berlin, Bruce was reporting that Perón and Miranda now saw war as their only salvation: wartime food shortages would compel the Americans to finance sales of Argentine goods to Europe. In September Bruce mentioned Argentina's "acute shortage of exchange" and noted that "many of the projects included in the five-year plan have been abandoned at least temporarily because of a lack of dollars to pay for machinery and equipment."[41]

Argentina's situation was indeed critical. Two years of substantial trade deficits had depleted foreign reserves by two-thirds, to $524 million, most of which was inconvertible. By January 1949 the dollar fund was completely exhausted, and Argentina owed the Americans around $150 million. Although Perón seemed at the pinnacle of his power, with the revised constitution nearing completion, and his control over the unions undisputed, confusion and uncertainty plagued the regime's upper levels.

In private discussions with Bruce, Perón broached the possibility of the United States' extending a loan to Argentina, but it could not be called a "loan," only a "credit," since Perón did not want his countrymen to see him as having borrowed from the United States; he far preferred to pretend the Americans owed him these credits. Miranda, meanwhile, was at the limit of his strength and resources. Bruce criticized his reluctance to give higher priority to exports to the United States, despite what he called "many constructive suggestions." Moreover, Bruce reported, Perón and Miranda were still hoping the Berlin crisis would spill over into war: "[They] have based their entire policy on the assumption that war between the U.S. and Russia is inevitable." [42] As the sparks of war still failed to ignite, in January 1949 Perón suddenly reshuffled his cabinet and dropped Miranda.

Perón had fallen into a trap. Under the Marshall Plan Argentina's export sales totaled a mere $21 million, only 3 percent of the total food goods bought by the Europeans, while American grain exports in the early 1950s were eight times greater than prewar sales. Between the mid 1930s and 1948–1952 Argentina's share of the world wheat market fell from 23 percent to only 9 percent, the share for corn from 64 percent to only 23.5 percent; in the same period the United States' share of world trade in wheat increased from under 7 percent to 46.1 percent, for corn from 9 percent to 63.9 percent. Denied access to the markets that were recipients of Marshall aid, Argentina could only aim at hitherto secondary markets, such as Spain and Brazil. Grain sales to the latter, for example, tripled between 1943 and 1950, and grew sevenfold during the next three years—but this was little recompense for what had been lost. Furthermore, neither Spain nor Brazil could reciprocate with the exports Argentina needed; nor for some time could they pay in dollars.[43]

The debacle over markets proved only a beginning, as large flaws in Argentina's five-year plan were becoming apparent. In 1946 Miranda had assumed that as the country replenished its stock of capital goods and raw materials, its need for foreign exchange would diminish. Instead, manufacturers' insatiable appetite for new machines, intermediate goods, and fuels caused imports to grow at a near-exponential rate. Instead of the anticipated five-year transition to autarky, markets shrank, export prices began to fall, and the supply of exportables diminished. The resulting steep fall in economic growth incited new political tensions.

In 1949 Perón concluded a trade agreement with Britain that in essence assured the exchange of meat for British-controlled Middle East oil. To the Americans, ostensibly inveterate champions of multilateralism, the renewed resort to bilateral barter was a revival of unacceptable habits and potentially the "most serious blow to American business interests since the Roca-Runciman treaty."[44] The new agreement recalled that of 1933 in other ways as well. Argentina entered the negotiations in a weaker bargaining position than at any time throughout the past fifteen years, and in one important respect a position even weaker than that during the early 1930s: having nationalized the railroads and repatriated much of the foreign debt held in London, Argentina no longer had the means to pressure Britain into an agreement. "Economic sovereignty," contrary to Perón's claims and the Americans' expectations in 1947, had weakened rather than strengthened the country. In 1949 the British drove a very hard bargain, Perón reportedly emerging from the agreement bitterly disappointed with the prices obtained for his meat. Ironically, Perón as a nationalist dealt perhaps less successfully with the British in 1949 than the "oligarchs" of 1933. Within months of the agreement, Argentina's desperate shortage of dollars was compounded by its almost-exhausted sterling reserves.[45]

This new meat deal also illustrated the radically changing conditions of world commerce. By 1949, only two years after the inception of the Marshall Plan, a new and hostile era was dawning for those primary food exporters, like Argentina, who were outside the privileged handful of the plan's beneficiaries. Immediately after the war farm goods had been in extreme short supply, and prices were high. Now, as American farmers rapidly increased production and agriculture in Europe began to recover, prices were sliding. For two or three years after the war Europe had often met Perón's imperatives; by 1949 the roles were reversed. Several European countries that had earlier evinced sympathy for Argentina's campaign to be included in the Marshall Plan were by 1949 often averse to buying from Argentina at any cost, in retaliation for the hard bargains the IAPI had driven. Between 1945 and 1948 Argentina enjoyed highly favorable terms of trade; in 1947 and 1948, for example, the index of the terms of trade (1935–1940 = 100) was 133 and 132. By 1949 the index slipped back to 110, and in 1950 to 93—in other words, between 1948 and 1950 for each unit of imports, exports had to increase by more than 30 percent, yet Argentina could not possibly increase exports on this scale.[46]

In 1946 and 1947 grain production had shown signs of recovery from the wartime blight, and the future was expected to bring a repetition of the mid 1920s and the mid 1930s, both periods of agricultural revival. But in 1949, partly due to drought, output in the farm sector declined by more than 8 percent against the year before, and by a further 6.7 percent in 1950. Between 1946 and 1948 wheat harvests averaged around 6 million tons; the two following years, under 5 million tons. Similarly, maize and other farm products declined after 1950. Between the late 1930s and the mid 1950s, some 4.5 million hectares were removed from production; land devoted to wheat decreased by 30 percent, maize by 50 percent, and linseed by 75 percent (see Table 29). Some land had been converted from these three crops to others—alfalfa, sorghum, or sunflower—and the decline in acreage exceeded the fall in yields because marginal areas were the first to be abandoned. But despite some offsetting improvement in productivity, the grain sector was in a severe crisis.[47]

Certain causes of this decline could not have been averted by any set of policies, for with the exception of the years 1946 to 1948 farming faced highly unfavorable conditions throughout the decade: the wartime blockades and shipping shortages, the effects of the Marshall Plan, and postwar American competition. Farming also encountered domestic competition for land and labor from cattle and industry. But discriminatory government policies in the late 1940s aggravated agriculture's weakness and exacerbated its decline.

Specifically, during the boom of 1946–1948 farmers suffered from the IAPI's pricing practices and the forced channeling of investment into manufacturing. When the government repeatedly froze agricultural rentals the landowners did not sell out or subdivide their holdings but rather withdrew from new tenancy contracts and allowed people to drift away from the land; between 1943 and 1952 tenant farms shrank from 44 percent to 33 percent of the total. The government also increased farmers' costs, by extending minimum-wage leg-

TABLE 29. *Areas Planted to Select Crops, 1935–1955 (In thousand hectares)*

	Wheat	Corn	Linseed	Oats	Barley	Rye	Rice	Sunflower
1935	7,613	7,029	3,279	1,428	815	864	15	84
1936	5,750	7,630	2,660	1,195	785	708	15	124
1937	7,793	6,091	3,499	1,619	679	1,269	17	207
1938	8,384	6,066	2,864	1,608	693	1,199	22	319
1939	8,621	5,300	2,707	1,401	835	975	33	333
1940	7,217	7,200	3,075	1,395	859	929	33	506
1941	7,085	6,098	2,875	1,596	868	1,346	31	574
1942	7,300	5,000	2,730	1,424	798	1,077	34	750
1943	6,873	4,139	2,474	1,935	589	1,767	42	674
1944	6,811	4,412	2,284	2,147	718	1,825	56	1,573
1945	6,233	4,017	1,956	2,011	761	1,615	52	1,492
1946	5,762	3,951	1,865	1,708	1,043	1,504	49	1,639
1947	6,674	3,612	1,905	1,570	1,371	1,944	46	1,609
1948	5,450	3,319	1,573	1,323	1,049	1,766	51	1,533
1949	5,806	2,691	1,305	1,394	942	1,835	50	1,806
1950	5,692	2,156	1,078	1,230	803	1,863	48	1,491
1951	6,554	2,439	1,087	1,311	896	2,191	54	1,628
1952	4,791	2,532	641	1,189	872	1,997	62	1,604
1953	6,066	3,354	1,020	1,702	1,108	2,483	71	820
1954	6,354	3,268	732	1,500	1,085	2,445	71	571
1955	5,937	3,002	739	1,376	1,090	2,493	65	559

SOURCE: Carlos F. Diaz Alejandro, *Essays on the Economic History of the Argentine Republic* (New Haven, 1970), 440–41.

islation to rural laborers in 1947. By 1949 all this seemed a gross error. If the country was to master its looming economic crisis, it had to increase the volume and competitiveness of farm exports, which meant shifting resources back into agriculture with all possible speed—but all the resources had been spent.[48]

Other difficulties stemmed from the recent government-maneuvered redistribution of income toward the urban sectors. This effort had helped expand the market for domestic manufacturers, but it also increased domestic consumption of farm goods, leaving fewer goods for export. Between the late 1930s and the early 1950s the total output of farm goods, both grains and meats, remained roughly constant, yet domestic consumption of foodstuffs increased by around one-third, and export volumes declined by two-thirds. Whereas 47 percent of grain production was exported in 1935–1939, in 1945–1949 the proportion was 23 percent, and 22 percent during 1950–1954.

Domestic meat consumption showed the same pattern, rising steadily by around 100,000 tons a year between 1946 and 1950, reaching 1.8 million tons in 1950, compared with meat production, including lamb and pork, of about 2.2 million tons. In 1946 domestic consumption accounted for 75.2 percent of meat production, by 1951 well beyond 80 percent (see Table 30). Rising internal consumption coupled with falling world prices could not but yield plummeting export earnings. Between 1940 and 1944 meat prices were high and foreign earnings from meat totaled $1,295 million; ten years later prices were lower and earnings were only $566 million. Per capita exports of meat fell from over 70 kilos in the late 1920s to less than 17 kilos in the early 1950s.

Although Argentina could with some justice blame its falling cereals trade on American intrusion in the world grain markets, such arguments had little validity concerning meat. Throughout, meat prices were falling but Britain represented a ready market. However, the steep increase in domestic consumption coupled with stagnant production impeded Argentina from meeting the quotas for 1949 specified in the recent bilateral agreement. One startling and unprecedented result of the continued inability to meet quotas was that in 1950 Argentina's exports to the United States were greater than those to Britain. Before the war Argentina provided more than 40 percent of Britain's meat imports, in 1950 only 28 percent. As meat exports fell,

TABLE 30. *Percentage Shares of Meat Consumed Domestically and Exported, Select Years, 1914–1951*

	Home Consumption	Exports
1914	59	41
1928	60	40
1938	68	32
1949	77	23
1950	79	21
1951	86	14

SOURCE: Colin Lewis, "Anglo-Argentine Trade, 1945–1965," in *Argentina in the Twentieth Century*, David Rock, ed. (London, 1975), 121.

so did total trade with Britain, stabilizing in the mid 1950s at around half the level of the immediate postwar. In 1947 Britain was Argentina's second largest trading partner. But Britain slipped to third in 1949, to twelfth in 1951, and to eighteenth by 1952. Lacking the meat to sell, Argentina thus lost the means to exploit Britain's economic recovery in the early 1950s. A century before the British had come to Argentina cherishing the belief that "trade follows investment." Under Perón the reverse also proved true, as the fall in British investment in Argentina during the late 1940s was followed by a decline in trade in the early 1950s. In this way the ninety-year Anglo-Argentine connection dissipated, and Argentina, having throughout the 1940s failed to obtain a substitute, faced the world alone.[49]

Simultaneously, Argentina was contending with a worsening fuel and energy crisis. Despite continuing postwar restrictions on exports of oil machinery from the United States, between 1947 and 1952 the YPF increased production by 22 percent, an increase far short of the demand spurred by the growth in manufacturing. Between the late 1930s and the early 1950s dependence on imported oil grew, from around a third to a half of total consumption, and now represented around 23 percent of total imports. Nor did coal production keep pace with demand, though mines opened in Patagonia had produced some 16,000 tons of coal by 1949. Two years later a new railroad was completed connecting the mines with the Atlantic port of Rio Gallegos, but this resource contributed little to satisfy the demand for coal, almost all of which continued to be imported. Recurrent coal and oil shortages hindered the growth of the electricity supply, which also failed to keep pace with demand. Overall between 1945 and 1955 capacity increased from 1.29 million kilowatts to 1.62 million, an annual rate of only 2 percent.[50]

By the late 1940s the balance-of-payments bottleneck had become the major ruling force in the Argentine economy. Already in 1948 exports were 25 percent less than those in 1935–1939, and imports 38 percent higher. By early 1949 Argentina had exhausted its dollar reserves, could no longer import from the United States, and had export earnings 30 percent less than a year earlier. The crisis in commerce and agriculture soon provoked the contraction of industry, employment, and incomes; inflation compounded the crisis. Per capita gross national product (1943 = 100) fell from 130 in 1948 to 116 in 1949. Gross domestic product grew by 13.8 percent in 1947, by only 1.2 percent in 1948, and declined by 4.6 percent in 1949. Likewise manufacturing output, which increased by 13.2 percent in 1947, rose by only 0.7 percent in 1949, while employment in industry also fell in comparison with the previous year. A final measure of the crisis was inflation: in 1947 the cost-of-living index rose by 12.2 percent, in 1948 by 13.0 percent, and in 1949 by 32.7 percent.

In 1950 agricultural output again declined, for a fall of 12.8 percent since 1948. Even so, export earnings rose by 25 percent, largely due to the outbreak of the Korean War in June 1950, which prompted a sudden leap in export prices. This recovery swiftly rebounded on the rest of the economy, bringing a 0.3 percent increase in gross domestic product in 1950 and a 3.9 percent increase in 1951. The outbreak of the Korean War was thus greeted by Perón with thinly disguised jubilation, but the economic boost it afforded proved both partial and short-lived. The United States released large quantities of stockpiled grains, and Argentina's wartime gains were from wool more than from cereals or beef. These events put the final seal of bankruptcy on the 1946 five-year program. War had come, yet had helped Argentina only very little.

In 1950 Argentina ruthlessly pruned imports, especially from the United States, and managed to achieve its first payments surplus since 1946. When some of these extreme controls were relinquished the following year, the deficit immediately recurred; by 1952 the deficit doubled, to a little less than $400 million. If 1949 was a critical year, then 1952 was a disastrous one: agricultural output plunged once more to 14.9 percent less than 1951; the gross domestic product followed, declining by 5.9 percent; and manufacturing output fell by 2.6 percent. Per capita gross national product was estimated to be a mere 3 percent higher than nine years earlier, while the cost-of-living index increased by nearly 40 percent, and the export quantum was only half that in 1950. The terms of trade also suffered another severe setback; the index declined by 25 percent against 1950; each unit of exports now bought only three-quarters the imports of two years before, and only half those of 1947 (see Table 31).

Drought, which had caused harvest failure and major cattle losses, was largely responsible for the economic plunge of 1952. However, the acreage sown to wheat, 4.7 million hectares, was the lowest since 1904, and the wheat harvest of 2.1 million tons was the lowest in decades. In 1950 Argentina had exported 2.7 million tons of wheat; in 1952 a mere 480,000 tons. Yet nature, it seemed, merely quickened the forces that had prompted agriculture's decline during the previous decade. The fall in production in 1952 was partly a result of falling

TABLE 31. *Terms of Trade, Export and Import Volumes, 1945–1952*
(1950 = 100)

	Terms of Trade	Export	Import
1945	86.5	106.1	44.4
1946	96.0	123.0	81.5
1947	101.3	115.5	162.5
1948	117.6	97.3	165.4
1949	101.0	72.5	116.8
1950	100.0	100.0	100.0
1951	97.2	78.6	114.0
1952	73.3	51.0	82.3

SOURCE: Guido Di Tella and Manuel Zymelman, *Las etapas del desarrollo económico argentino* (Buenos Aires, 1967), 524.

land yields, which could be traced to overcropping on natural pasture and thereby linked to the decline in tenancy that had disrupted long-established rotational practices. The wider use of fertilizers could restore the soil's organic and mineral content, but Argentina had neither the means to produce fertilizers nor to import them in the required quantities.[51]

The economic crisis that began in 1949 quickly elicited substantial changes in government policy intended to revive agriculture and exports, while minimizing the ill-effects of this shift on industry, the urban sectors, and the working class. Miranda's successor, Alfredo Gómez Morales, reformed the system of exchange control to favor priority imports such as oil and spare parts for machinery. The import of nonpriority items, which had to be purchased at the most unfavorable exchange rates, was further restricted by the devaluation of the "free market" peso by 90 percent in October 1949. Credits to industry were pruned, and more funds made available for agriculture such that 1949 marked at least the beginning of a new deal for farmers. Foreign exchange became more easily available for imported agricultural machinery; in 1950–1954 imports of tractors were double those in the preceding five-year span. Farmers received seed for planting at prices below cost, and the IAPI paid them a much higher percentage of world prices, although prices had fallen so steeply that the concession meant little in practice. These various adjustments enabled Gómez Morales to achieve the trade surplus of 1950, but imports that year were 40 percent lower than two years earlier.[52]

Throughout this period Perón oscillated between strident anti-Americanism and forlorn secret appeals for American support. In 1950 he was again currying sympathy. The Congress at last ratified the Pan-American defense treaty of 1947, and in June 1950 Argentina endorsed the United Nations' intervention in Korea, but gains from these gestures were minuscule. A trade agreement with the United States in 1950 recalled its ill-starred predecessor in 1941. The Americans, already substantial importers of Argentine wool, agreed to take more wool—needed by troops in Korea—but still resisted admitting the major agricultural and pastoral goods of the pampas. By May 1950 Argentina's outstanding debts to the United States totaled $245 million, forcing Perón at last to seek an American loan. An agreement was soon reached for a $125 million loan from the Export-Import Bank of New York, but the transaction brought Perón little satisfaction. While he had hoped to obtain a much larger sum to enable a fuller resumption of imports to aid manufacturing, he received only enough to settle arrears on the present debt.[53]

In 1949 the government announced a plan to reduce the public-spending deficit, which in 1948 was 14 percent of the gross national product. This plan also proved a failure, as the coefficient of public spending against GNP remained at 28.5 percent between 1950 and 1954, compared with 19.5 percent between 1940 and 1944, and 29.4 percent between 1945 and 1949. Rather than making any serious attempt at economy, the government for a time deliberately chose the path of inflation. In 1949 the Central Bank's gold-reserve obligation for new currency (25 percent gold backing) was abolished, and the bank was authorized to hold a larger quantity of government bonds, a step that facilitated the inflationary financing of public deficits.

Industry stagnated, prices rose, and real wages fell by some 20 percent between 1948 and the end of 1952. The government exacerbated the decline by curtailing the food subsidies adopted in 1946, a measure also intended to increase export surpluses. At the same time, Perón struggled to hold down unemployment. Although an estimated 80,000 jobs in manufacturing were lost between 1949 and 1953, many displaced workers found alternative employment in the government's housing program. Housing was given immediate emphasis under Gómez Morales, with the argument it was labor intensive and added little to the import bill. The newly nationalized railroads were used for the same purposes. The steep postwar increase in the number of railroad employees continued, rising from 184,000 in 1949 to 210,000 in 1957. Altogether between 1943 and 1957 the railroad workforce grew by 60 percent, although traffic volumes were roughly static. With freight and passenger fare rates falling by an estimated 32 percent between 1947 and 1953, the railroads quickly became a major source of the heavy deficit in the public sector.[54]

As the regime juggled with the economy, pursuing a set of largely incompatible objectives, its character shifted toward authoritarianism and overt demagoguery. Before 1949 on several occasions the government had arbitrarily abused its power, yet its most distinctive quality during its first phase was an open, expansive populism. Perón had employed the largesse from an expanding economy to retain and enhance the allegiance of his supporters, while rarely needing to attack his enemies. But as the economic crisis limited his freedom to maneuver, insecurity replaced brash self-confidence, and the regime retreated into an increasingly threatening and repressive shell. In September 1948 Bruce, the American ambassador, perceived a close relationship between the dollar shortage and Perón's stance on domestic and international issues. He commented:

> If Perón should reach the conclusion that there is no hope of increasing exports to the United States or of obtaining ECA dollars, his position would become more desperate, he would be filled with resentment towards the United States, and his course of action would probably become more totalitarian.[55]

Events soon bore out Bruce's assessment. In October 1948 the regime issued allegations of an assassination plot, a pretext for arresting Cipriano Reyes and for conducting a brief anti-American campaign, as the Americans, behind whom it was said stood Spruille Braden, were declared the plot's instigators.

Bruce also perceived links between the economic crisis and Perón's adoption of constitutional reform in late 1948, which Bruce explained as a "diversionary tactic" in the midst of threatened strikes and inflation.[56] In relations with the unions Perón now adopted a form of control he called *verticalidad*, a pyramidal bureaucratic chain of command reaching out from the CGT through the unions to the rank and file; to consolidate the structure he led campaigns to form middle-level cadres. His earlier tolerance for strikes ended abruptly, reflected in the sudden decline in working days lost in strikes. In 1949, despite growing pressure on wages from inflation, the days lost were some 500,000, one-sixth of those a year earlier. Further, in 1950 Perón again purged the CGT; its earlier chief functions of promoting and advertising the regime's social programs was dropped, and the CGT now did little but issue interminable exhortations to "loyalty," while battening down the slightest signs of unrest. Now, too, Eva Perón's influence in the CGT reached its acme, and the last of the independent unions suffered intervention and "peronization." Despite some indications of worker alienation, such as a steep fall-off in attendance at union meetings, Perón's firm control over the labor movement was challenged only once, by wildcat railroad strikes in late 1950 and early 1951. Perón responded by declaring the strikers liable to military conscription, and therefore subject to military courts and punishments; after the strikes collapsed, he gave the workers the increases they were seeking.[57]

Perón was markedly less successful in stemming opposition from the middle and upper classes, the source of increasingly bitter campaigns that focused on charges of government corruption. A favorite target was the Eva Perón Foundation, many of whose millions, it was alleged, were being pocketed by its patroness. Another issue was the corrupt sale of import licenses, the possessors of which were able to become wealthy from bribes. In 1950 the opposition predictably pounced on Perón's accepting the loan from the Export-Import Bank, gleefully reminding him he had earlier promised "to cut off [his] hands" before putting his name to such a venture.

Unable to stanch such attacks, the regime resorted to repression. In late 1949 new restrictions were applied to the press, and in November the police raided the leading metropolitan dailies, *La Prensa, La Nación,* and *Clarín,* and also the offices of the United Press and Associated Press. To enforce the government's policies, the powers of the police were broadened and several new police bodies created, among them special sections to invigilate the trade unions and the political parties. Reports soon circulated that beatings and sometimes systematic torture were becoming routine police procedures.

In 1950 Congress resurrected decrees from the *de facto* regimes of the early 1940s in passing a new treason and espionage law that broadened the definitions of crimes against the state and increased the powers of the police to investigate them. A new contempt law (*Ley de Desacato*) likewise expanded the definitions and increased the penalties for libel, slander, or defamation against public authorities. *Desacato* quickly became a catch-all to silence Perón's critics and was also employed to subvert the traditional immunities of members of Congress. Among those falling victim to the measure was the rising Radical leader Ricardo Balbín, who in November 1950 received a five-year prison term. Many prominent members of the opposition sought refuge in Montevideo, as the gag on the press became still more stifling. In early 1951, soon after the railroad strikes, Perón resolved a long and acrimonious conflict with *La Prensa*, the oldest and most prestigious newspaper in the country, by closing it, expropriating its properties, and converting it into an organ of the CGT.[58]

The regime issued ever-swelling torrents of propaganda. The Peronist press, augmented by new acquisitions, filled its pages with endless sycophantic eulogies to Perón and Evita. To enable Perón to pose as the heir of José de San Martín, Argentina's greatest national hero, 1950 was declared the "Year of the Liberator." To educate citizens and thereby give substance to *verticalidad*, Perón taught classes in the arts of "political leadership" and inundated the country with copies of his lectures. In 1951 Eva Perón produced a ghost-written pseudoautobiography, *La razón de mi vida*, "a book," she declared "from the most intimate corner of my heart," concerning "the figure, the soul, and the life of General Perón and my undying love for his person and his life." [59] Portraits of both now smiled out from every corner of the republic, and endless batteries of slogans were promulgated.

Justicialismo was reemphasized and elevated to a "national doctrine," its teachings compulsory in the schools. In 1951 the government created a Peronist college (*Escuela Superior Peronista*) and, in a bid for the support of intellectuals and apologists, several Peronist Athenaeums (*ateneos peronistas*). But as its standing ascended, *justicialismo* became still more vapid. Among the "twenty truths" of *justicialismo* issued by Perón in late 1950 were such verities as "For a Peronist there is nothing better than another Peronist," and "True Democracy is when the Government does what the people wants and defends one interest alone: the People." The regime also expanded its charity activities, in a scramble to produce surrogates for the improvements in living standards it could no longer deliver. Between 1949 and 1952 the real budget of the Eva Perón Foundation increased tenfold, and the beneficiaries of its bounties numbered in the thousands. Lastly, echoing the classic style of Latin American dictators, Perón gave himself a string of new titles. Having been "First Worker of the Republic" soon after the 1943 revolution, and *El Líder* in 1946, in 1952 he became "Liberator of the Republic." To Evita went the title "Spiritual Chief of the Nation" (*Jefa Espiritual de la Nación*).[60]

Despite his difficulties, Perón clung on and at least gave the appearance of increasing his popular support. In the November 1951 elections, the first under the new constitution, he swept into a second term as president. Following the introduction of female suffrage, the Peronist vote grew from 1.4 million, or 54 percent, in 1946 to 4.6 million, or 64 percent five years later. In 1946 Perón's margin of victory had been 260,000 votes; in 1951, 2.3 million. His party won majorities in each of the provinces and the capital, and carried every seat in the Senate. In the Chamber of Deputies the Radical bloc fell from forty-three to fourteen; nine out of ten deputies were now Peronists.

But the election was yet another pretense of strength rather than its proof. The victory was heavily tainted by numerous forms of fraud, and gerrymandering made the Peronist vote far more impressive than it really was. Throughout the campaign the Peronists had monopolized the media, broken up meetings held by the opposition, and silenced dissenters with arrests for *desacato*. Yet in the city of Buenos Aires, the Radicals still carried 45 percent of the popular vote, although that translated into fewer than a fifth of the seats in the Chamber of Deputies.[61]

By 1951 Perón's relations with the Army were also showing signs of growing strain, although he still sought to maintain control by the dispensation of special favors. If he could no longer provide much in the way of new weapons or equipment, he gave the armed forces frequent cost-of-living allowances, and officers received privileged access to the dwindling quantities of new imported cars. Perón also continued to ease promotions in the services, inflating the senior ranks. Nonetheless, restlessness fermented among the military. Three months before the election Eva Perón's followers in the CGT wanted to nominate her as candidate for vice-president, but the Army immediately interposed with a veto. A month later General Benjamín Menéndez, a retired cavalry officer, attempted an ill-planned coup, supported by only three tanks, a handful of junior officers, and two hundred men. Although the coup was immediately silenced by the government, Perón saw that the alliance he had proclaimed between the Army and the people was beginning to crumble.[62]

Perón again responded with harsh measures. More than two hundred officers were purged, and Menéndez received a fifteen-year prison term. Loyalty tests were imposed in army promotions; *doctrina peronista* was added to the required courses of the military academy, the *Escuela Superior de Guerra*. Two top-ranking military adherents of the regime, the Army minister General Franklin Lucero and Rear Admiral Alberto Teissaire for the Navy, were assigned to monitor the troops for any indications of disaffection. Eva Perón formed her own response to the Menéndez uprising: a secret transaction to stockpile a cache of imported weapons and the laying of plans for a worker's militia.

Finally, Perón used his powers under the new Constitution to declare a "state of internal war," and he launched the police on renewed roundups of his opponents. This was the climate in Argentina at the time of the presidential election in 1951. That same year an American observer, George Blanksten, perceived "an unstable and uneasy regime . . . beset by tensions and uncertainties" and forecasted that "the Army will probably fall on Perón's head one day. . . . or perhaps it be the Church."[63]

DECLINE AND FALL, 1952–1955

Perón began his second six-year term in June 1952, but he endured scarcely three more years, until the coup of September 1955. His decline and fall were enacted against the background of a stagnant economy and a cauldron of social unrest. Projects to restore economic growth failed, at the same time provoking a gradual shrinkage in the regime's power base. As opposition to the regime intensified, groups that had been neutral or benevolently disposed to Perón gradually joined the opposition. Creeping demoralization overtook Perón's followers in the unions.

Throughout 1952, the year of extreme economic decline, the general repressive atmosphere prevailed, with relentless censorship and new bans on travel to Uruguay. In February the uncovering of another assassination plot triggered a renewed spate of police arrests. But 1952 was overshadowed by the death of Eva Perón at age thirty-three, of cancer. For eight years Evita had played a major role in the Peronist movement, the source of much of the mystique surrounding Perón in the eyes of the *descamisados*. In death Perón made use of her once more.

Eva Perón's illness had determined her relatively passive response to the Army's veto on her candidacy for the vice-presidency. Almost permanently bedridden by the time of the Menéndez coup, she was unable to establish the workers' militia she envisioned. After this she could manage only occasional personal appearances and addresses by radio, in which "in her voice so sweet and so harsh at the same time," she continued her cult of Perón and her diatribes against his enemies, real and mythical. For months the country observed her slow decline; she died in late July 1952.

For two weeks Eva Perón's body lay in state and thousands filed past to pay homage. The country was at a standstill: a year of disastrous harvests, decaying industry, spiraling inflation, and sliding living standards were for a time forgotten amid the mawkish ritual. Perón exploited his wife's death to stage an artificial show of unity and backing for his government. He had her body embalmed imperishably and announced plans to enshrine it in a great national mausoleum. Eva Perón, the "Lady of Hope" and the "Spiritual Chief," in death became "Martyr of the *Descamisados.*"[64]

Throughout 1952, however, the president and his advisers pondered a new economic strategy and issued their second five-year plan. Compared with its predecessor, this plan struck a much more sober and modest note. Gone were the lavish promises of 1946, when Perón and Miranda had pledged self-sufficiency in five years. The new goal was to achieve the maximum growth in industry compatible with "economic and social equilibrium." The plan's primary objective was the suppression of inflation, now perceived as the source of myriad ills, from recent political unrest to low investment in agriculture and industry. To this end the plan sought to propagate the idea of a "social compact," through which rewards and sacrifices would be shared among major segments of the community, farmers, manufacturers, and unions.

Most aspects of the new plan marked a complete reversal of Perón's earlier policies: it favored agricultural development over urban, capital and profits over labor and wages, heavy over light industry, and exports over domestic consumption. Perón tacitly acknowledged that in neglecting the farm sector, while stimulating internal consumption, his programs had exacerbated the economic crisis since 1948. By shifting more resources back to agriculture, he hoped to increase export earnings and overcome the balance-of-payments trap. The plan's provisions included a 50 percent increase in the land area sown to crops during the following five years; yet-higher priority for imports of tractors, harvesters, and fertilizers; and the construction of new silos and grain elevators. To overcome the acute shortage of agricultural labor—the result of the preceding decade's rural exodus—army conscripts were to be drafted for harvest work. After 1951 the IAPI began to purchase farm goods at prices higher than those on the world market, to lead campaigns to diversify the rural economy and to create agricultural cooperatives to eliminate commercial middlemen.

To promote industrial recovery the new five-year plan emphasized wage and price controls and increased productivity. In February 1952 collective bargaining contracts were required to have a two-year duration, during which period prices would be frozen and excess profits taxed. Perón planned a negotiated agreement between unions and management to increase productivity. Light manufacturing was to be of lesser priority than heavy industry and capital goods—steel, chemicals, metals, and eventually motor vehicles—which were to be financed by redeploying credits from the Industrial Bank and by favoring large businesses over small ones. The government also laid plans to develop the state-run sectors of industry, particularly SOMISA, the steel complex, which had thus far received negligible funding or attention. Likewise, energy was to receive new emphasis through projects to increase the output of oil, coal, and electricity.[65]

Perón also began to ponder the means to recommence exports of manufactured goods. In May 1952 he created a new international labor association, known as the ATLAS (*Agrupación de Trabajadores Latinoamericanos Sindicalistas*), whose official task was to disseminate the doctrines of *justicialismo* in Latin America; but Perón hoped to use the ATLAS to build contacts that would ultimately serve as a vehicle for commerce. Toward this goal Perón similarly sought closer relations with his counterparts in Brazil and Chile, Getulio Vargas and Carlos Ibañez. In 1953 he concluded a bilateral trade agreement with Ibañez, the Act of Santiago, and made similar agreements with Ecuador and Peru.[66]

In 1952 Perón's regime also began seeking new foreign investment, now sharing the view that underinvestment and decapitalization were among the chief causes of the economic crisis. Domestic capital, Perón's advisers reasoned, was insufficient to satisfy the competing claims of agriculture and manufacturing, nor could it ensure a continuity of investment throughout the economic cycle. By attracting foreign investment, Argentina could gain access to new technology and new products, which would improve efficiency in the economy and relieve once more the burden on the balance of payments.

Argentina's association with the multinationals began in 1952, with an agreement between FIAT of Italy and the Army-controlled manufacturing plants (*fabricaciones militares*) to assemble tractors, and later cars and trucks, in newly constructed factories in Córdoba. In 1953 Perón took advantage of the advent of a new Republican administration to reopen contact with the United States, with which relations had been icy since the expropriation of *La Prensa* two years earlier. After a visit to Buenos Aires by President Eisenhower's brother Milton, an agreement was concluded with the Export-Import Bank for the construction of a steel mill in the city of San Nicolás. In August 1953 Congress passed Law 14226, intended to establish a favorable climate for foreign investment by allowing profit remittances and promising support from the Industrial Bank. The same year Perón began negotiations with a second automobile manufacturer, Kayser of Detroit, to establish new factories in Argentina; an agreement was reached in March 1955. Throughout this period Perón and his advisers agonized over national oil, eventually reversing themselves: in March 1955 Standard Oil of California was granted permission to develop the Patagonian oil fields.[67]

A last aspect of the five-year plan concerned successive cuts in domestic consumption. The two-year wage freeze left workers' incomes at the low point to which they had sunk since 1949. Faced with the recent losses from drought, the government issued directives for the adulteration of wheat bread with other cereals. To increase meat exports, it imposed periodic bans, *vedas*, on domestic retail sales. A final measure, which aimed to correct the acute shortage of rented housing, was to lift the freeze, imposed in 1943, on rents in the capital.[68]

Though the new plan was a retreat into conservative orthodoxy, nevertheless it was beset by contradictions, by traces of the efforts that had prevailed since 1949 to achieve compromise and to match incompatibles. Regarding public spending, for example, Perón was pledged to a war on inflation—the plan bluntly stated that state spending would increase only at the rate of prices—yet the plan also proposed increased public investment, not specifying where cuts in public consumption would occur. Here lurked the prospect of continuing deficits and recurrent inflation.

Second, in 1952 Perón rejected the option of a new devaluation, although in principle it represented a quick way to eliminate balance-of-payments deficits and lay the foundation for faster economic growth led by exports. In theory, devaluation would shift income to the farmers, because they would be able to obtain the prevailing international price for their products while borrowing or settling their debts in devalued pesos. Higher profits would then encourage farmers to save and invest more, and to increase production and therefore exports. Devaluation was also predicted to help the balance of payments by reducing aggregate demand for both exportables and imports: food prices would rise for domestic consumers, forcing them to consume less; import prices would also rise for manufacturers, forcing imports to fall.[69]

But neither public spending cuts nor devaluation could be reconciled with the foremost Peronist goal of "equilibrium." To cut state spending was to invite reactions like the wildcat railroad strikes and the price of devaluation was an urban recession, which threatened simultaneously to alienate labor, manufacturers, and the middle classes. Even as it stood, the plan opened Perón to severe political risks: losing union support due to declining living standards, and alienating manufacturers by the shift of resources to agriculture and heavy industry; for most of the population the plan offered at best a continuation of the present climate of austerity. In inviting renewed foreign investment, Perón also risked accusations of *"entreguismo"*—selling out to foreigners.

To succeed the plan had to improve the capacity to import, increase farm output and exports, restore industrial growth, and curb inflation. Three economic indicators in 1953 provided evidence for some optimism: the gross domestic product rose by 6.1 percent, after a 5.9 percent drop in 1952; the balance of payments showed the largest surplus since 1946; and the cost of living increased by only 4.3 percent, compared with nearly 40 percent the year before. However, there was no growth in manufacturing, and in agriculture a recovery of only 3 percent after the almost 15 percent drop in 1952. Indicators in 1954 showed more balanced improvement: the gross domestic product grew by 5 percent, industry by 9.1 percent, prices by only 3.5 percent; once more the balance of payments was favorable, though the surplus was smaller than the year before. Yet growth in agriculture was only negligible. In 1955 the gross domestic product grew by 7.2 percent, industry by 12 percent, and agriculture by 3.7 percent. But the balance-of-payments deficit, at almost $240 million, was the largest since 1952, and prices had begun to rise more rapidly, climbing by 12.1 percent.[70]

The five-year plan of 1952, in sum, enjoyed only partial and short-lived success. For a brief period it quelled inflation, restored the balance of payments, and encouraged a moderate rate of growth. But it failed to resuscitate agriculture: farm production in 1955 was no higher than in 1950. The payments deficit in 1955 indicated the completion of a triennial cycle that was becoming a central feature of the Argentine economy. In the first phase higher export earnings, accomplished mostly by curbs on domestic consumption and the financing of sales abroad by the IAPI, produced a balance-of-payments surplus.

This surplus, in the second phase, enabled a loosening of the restrictions on manufacturers' ability to import. Finally, as manufacturing employment and aggregate demand grew, while agriculture stagnated and the export surplus fell, a new payments deficit quickly supervened, forcing renewed curbs on imports; meanwhile rising wages and ongoing public-sector deficits refueled inflation. The early 1950s also demonstrated that the economy could grow only from a starting point of recession, which meant that overall throughout the cycle it largely stagnated.

By 1955 the main features of the Argentine economy were inertia and acute imbalance. Per capita GNP was only 16 percent higher than in 1943. Agriculture had shrunk from 24.7 percent of the economy in 1940–1944 to only 16.6 percent in 1950–1954; agricultural output in the pampas region was only 84 percent of that in 1935–1939. In recent years, too, industry had been largely stationary; only the service sector showed growth. Perón's foreign investment program enjoyed but limited success: although fourteen foreign companies created subsidiaries in Argentina between 1953 and 1955, net foreign investment was only $50 million. Energy independence was still a distant goal; in 1955 Argentina imported more than 90 percent of its coal and 60 percent of its oil. Increases in pig-iron production were negligible between 1944 and 1955. During the same period steel production increased from 133,000 tons to only 217,000 tons. Recent efforts to develop exports of manufacturers were also a failure, and the increased salience of capital goods and raw materials among imports left the country short of numerous consumer goods that it was unable to produce domestically. By 1954, for example, the average automobile in Argentina was reportedly seventeen-years old.[71]

Among the apparent economic bright spots was a substantial increase in agricultural production in the interior, 39 percent between 1935–1939 and 1950–1954. Growth in the interior followed the expansion of demand in the cities, which triggered increasing production of such goods as sugar, wines, yerba mate, cotton, and fruits. Yet this advance had its negative effects, in many parts promoting the expansion of large landholdings at the expense of small farmers. Peasant and small farming plots were subdivided into increasingly smaller segments (*minifundios*); the bulk of the population in the interior became still more impoverished; and out-migration swiftly increased. Beginning about 1948, urban manufacturing could no longer absorb the swelling urban labor force, and most new migrants were condemned to the rapidly proliferating shantytowns that adumbrated

Greater Buenos Aires. Perón made some effort to address the issue through his housing programs but, beyond some rural labor minimum-wage legislation and encouragement for agricultural cooperatives, he did little to attack the problem at its rural source. By 1955 Perón's colonization and land redistribution measures had aided only 3,200 farming families.[72]

The plan of 1952 proved a severe test of Perón's political control. Unable to buttress his support with real improvements in living standards, he was obliged to rely still more heavily on ersatz benefits, exhortation, and manipulation. The activities of the Eva Perón Foundation were accelerated and publicized, and government propagandists milked public events, popular festivals, and sport contests in search of political gains. Perón blamed the ailing economy on "sabotage" by the "landed oligarchy" or the opposition parties, and he uttered threats of agrarian reform. Such incitements to class hatred sometimes instigated ugly incidents: in April 1953 Eva Perón's brother either committed suicide or was murdered by the police while under investigation for corruption. The incident severely embarrassed the government and gave renewed encouragement to its opponents. A week later as Perón addressed his party and the unions at a mass rally, a bomb exploded in the crowd and he urged retribution against his enemies. Mobs of citizens complied, ransacking and torching the Jockey Club, the greatest of the traditional *estanciero* associations in Buenos Aires. They then did the same to the headquarters of the Radical and Socialist parties, the *Casa Radical* and the *Casa del Pueblo*. But neither Perón's barrages of self-publicity nor political scapegoating could check the growing demoralization among his supporters. Attendances at union meetings continued to fall, absenteeism increased in the factories, and notably smaller crowds gathered to applaud him at party rallies.[73]

For a year or more Perón managed to suppress open expressions of labor unrest. In April 1954, however, the metallurgical workers went on strike, suddenly and apparently spontaneously. Other groups of workers quickly joined them; there were more strikes throughout 1954 than in the past three years combined (see Table 32). At this juncture, as the economic cycle peaked, imports and the manufacturing sector were expanding, the urban labor market was tightening, and pressure on wages increasing. In April 1954 Perón hurriedly lifted the wage freeze imposed two years before, but the ensuing swift upsurge of wages caused prices to climb and threaten the anti-inflation program.[74]

TABLE 32. *Working Days Lost*
in Strikes, 1949–1954

1949	510,352
1950	2,031,827
1951	152,243
1952	313,343
1953	59,294
1954	1,401,797

SOURCE: Louise M. Doyon, "Organised Labour and Perón, 1943–55: A Study in the Conflictual Dynamics of the Peronist Movement" (Ph.D. diss., Univ. Toronto, 1978), 439.

In relinquishing the wage freeze, Perón alienated the urban manufacturers, previously a divided or neutral group. Perón had given them subsidized credit, tariff protection, and an expanding internal market, at least during the 1940s. However, manufacturers had been increasingly hamstrung by unions and a variety of new taxes. In recent years their share in national income had undergone a steep decline such that by 1954 many concluded that Perón was a liability. Manufacturers were also becoming increasingly obsessed with "productivity," a euphemism for complaints against falling profits and the unions' powers. Like other disaffected groups, including the farmers, manufacturers began attributing their difficulties to over-regulation of the economy. To curb the power of organized labor, they now looked to the downfall of its political backers. [75]

During this period Perón also tried, but once more failed, to break the opposition among the political parties and the middle classes. After the assault on the Jockey Club in April 1953, he again resorted to severe repression. But in December, apparently motivated by a desire to present himself more favorably to foreign investors, he announced a program of reconciliation. Large numbers of political prisoners were released, as the regime attempted to coopt leading members of the opposition. In this new plan to strengthen his political grip, Perón also abandoned his recent threats to institute agrarian reform.

Perón's political pronouncements a decade earlier had proposed fashioning social harmony, balance, justice, and solidarity through the establishment of concentrated corporate blocs under state authority. These blocs were depicted as the key to both economic progress and political stability. Whereas in the 1940s the application of such ideas had stopped short at the unions, in December 1951 the government established a *Confederación General Económica* (CGE) to group small and medium employers for collective bargaining with the CGT. In late 1953 Perón resurrected this concept on a much larger scale in a project he called "the organized community" (*La Comunidad Organizada*): he would now extend corporatism even beyond the unions and manufacturing employers. By establishing a range of new institutions embracing other major social groups, he hoped to reify and bureaucratize his authority, acquire new organs for indoctrination and propaganda, and thus reduce his reliance on brute repression as a means of enforcing political control. As the project unfolded, the *Confederación General de los Profesionales* (CGP) was created for the middle-class professions, the *Unión del Personal Civil de la Nación* for government employees, the *Confederación General de los Universitarios* (CGU) for university students, and the *Unión de Estudiantes Secundarios* (UES) for high school students. Meanwhile Peronist propaganda was again accelerated; for example, school textbooks were radically revised, and stringent political tests were applied in the selection of teachers.

As had once happened among the unions, the new entities immediately began to compete and overlap with traditional associations, to swallow them and "peronize" their memberships. The CGE became the single representative for employers, as the old *Unión Industrial* was abolished, and the CGU replaced the student's federation (the FUA) founded during the university reform movement in 1918. The government expedited the transition by using all the police and propaganda powers it had amassed since 1943. Resistance in the universities, for example, was quashed by the imprisonment of some 250 students.[76]

But in mid 1954 Perón crashed headlong into the Roman Catholic Church. The Church had been another of his semiallies and had supported him in the 1946 election, for which it was rewarded in March 1947 by legislation establishing religious instruction in the schools. Once the regime began invading spheres and activities traditionally dominated by the Church, however, relations cooled. The Church was affronted by the government's political exploitation of organized charity and by Perón's designation of *justicialismo* as a "doctrine," its adherents as "believers," and himself on occasion as its "apostle." In 1952 the Church refused to support a campaign for the canonization of Eva Perón, and during the next two years it was scandalized by reports of Perón's amorous liaisons with teenaged girls. Lastly, the Church strongly opposed the Peronist invasion of the schools.

As the rift widened, the Church's political influence was expanding. By mid 1954, among all major civil associations and institutions, the Church stood alone in having eluded purges and "peronization." Standing aloof from the "organized community" in jealously guarded autonomy, it had become almost a last refuge for Perón's opponents. Soon it also became the focus of conspiracies to overthrow him.

After the metalworkers' strike in April 1954 Perón became increasingly suspicious of efforts at political penetration of organized labor by outsiders. In July he suddenly accused Church leaders of supporting a newly formed Christian Democrat Party, which he alleged was seeking adherents among the unions. In September the traditional celebration of the coming of the southern spring was the source of intensified friction. In Córdoba two rallies and marches for high school students were planned, one by the Peronist UES, the other by the Church sponsored *Acción Católica*. Reports estimated the Peronist marchers at 10,000 and the Catholics at 80,000, an indication of the depth of anti-government sentiments and of the Church's role as an instrument of unity for the opposition.

Perón responded with a tactic he had often used against the independent unions in the late 1940s: he withdrew legal standing (*personería gremial*) from Catholic associations like *Acción Católica*. But he acted too late, for the Church had already emerged as the great symbol of resistance. In December 1954 the conflict was again renewed when, following another series of Perón's verbal attacks on the Church, the annual Church procession in Buenos Aires to celebrate the Immaculate Conception gathered an enormous following, again far exceeding attendance at a rival government-sponsored event. Perón replied by annulling the legislation concerning compulsory religious instruction in the schools. He also ended state subsidies to private church schools and announced pending measures to legalize divorce and prostitution.

The prolonged conflict was an acid test of the limits of Perón's authority. Although the government controlled the press, it was unable to halt a tide of street pamphlets and manifestos accusing it of corruption, tyrannical abuses of power and, after the deal with Standard Oil in March 1955, the betrayal of national sovereignty. In May the government announced a plan to introduce a constitutional amendment to establish a formal separation of Church and state; soon after Perón began imprisoning priests. On 11 June the annual Church procession in Buenos Aires to celebrate Corpus Christi attracted an estimated 100,000 participants, a multitude that marched through the streets silently bearing the papal flag.

At length the confrontation erupted into violence. Five days after the Corpus Christi march Perón replied with a counter-demonstration, convoked by the CGT, in the Plaza de Mayo. As thousands of workers and trade unionists gathered, naval planes began traversing the square. Seeking to destroy the presidential palace, they showered bombs on the multitudes below, killing several hundred people. That evening bands of Peronists roamed the streets of the capital, burning its churches.[77]

The air attack had been intended to kindle a general rebellion of the armed forces, but it failed. A few scattered mutinies were immediately quashed by the Army commander, Lucero. Perón still remained president but was ceasing to be master; he survived in office thanks only to the Army, which now dictated to him. The Army wanted conciliation and had Perón reshuffle the cabinet, eliminating Borlenghi, who became the scapegoat for recent provocations against the Church, along with Minister of Education Armando Méndez de San Martín, who in recent years had led the efforts to impose Peronist doctrine in the schools. Changes were also made in the leadership of CGT. In early July Perón issued a call for national unity, declaring a political truce and the end of censorship and a recently imposed state of siege; he also resigned as head of the Peronist party. Finally, in an address on 15 July he proclaimed the end of the "Peronist Revolution" —henceforth he would be president of "all Argentines."

In succeeding weeks, first this effort at moderation and then a renewed resort to force both failed Perón. Liberalization was seized upon by his opponents to intensify the campaign sparked by the Church. In late July Arturo Frondizi, a leading Radical and candidate for the vice-presidency in 1951, made an impassioned attack on the government in a radio address. He detailed the regime's numerous infringements of personal freedoms and attacked its corruption and its policies, notably the contract with Standard Oil. The streets of Buenos Aires filled with students and middle-class demonstrators demanding that their traditional associations be freed from *peronista* subjection.

At this new wave of protest and on the pretext of another assassination plot, Perón launched the police on a roundup of his opponents. Those who had spoken publicly, like Frondizi, were arrested on charges of *desacato*. Then, seeking to rekindle the spirit of 17 October 1945, Perón made a final dramatic plea to the CGT, the unions, and the *descamisados*. In a mass rally on 31 August, he offered to resign before the CGT. When the crowd rejected this, he issued a strident call to arms and a chilling threat. *"Cinco por uno,"* he proclaimed: for each dead Peronist he would kill five of his enemies. The state of siege was restored, and rumors spread that Perón was arming workers to prepare for civil war.

These actions at last pushed the Army into the opposition camp. On 16 September simultaneous military revolts erupted in Córdoba and Bahía Blanca. The larger, in Córdoba, was led by General Eduardo Lonardi, a veteran nationalist who had been implicated in the abortive 1951 rebellion and had spent the past several years in forced retirement. Within two days loyalist forces from Buenos Aires appeared to have Lonardi encircled and trapped, but the revolt then spread to the garrisons in Cuyo. Meanwhile, Buenos Aires was under blockade from the Navy under the command of Admiral Isaac Rojas. On 19 September, following Rojas's threats to shell oil installations in Buenos Aires and La Plata, Perón resigned, ceded his power to a junta led by Lucero, and took refuge on a Paraguayan gunboat in the River Plate. After two days of negotiations between the rebels and Lucero, Lonardi flew to Buenos Aires to be sworn in as president of the new junta. Lonardi's first act was to proclaim nonreprisal against the defeated Peronists. This "revolution of liberty" (*revolución libertadora*), he affirmed, would produce "neither victors nor vanquished" (*ni vencedores, ni vencidos*). This phrase was not new; with the same words Urquiza had entered Buenos Aires a hundred and three years earlier, after defeating Rosas.[78]

On Perón's departure his enemies gave themselves to days of unbridled celebration. His critical mistake, it seemed, was to have attacked the Church, for that action had initiated the chain of events that culminated in Lonardi's investiture as president by awakening the dormant resistance of segments of the old pluralist order to Perón's grand corporatist design. Yet it seemed, too, that Perón was propelled into this conflict as much by irresistible external forces as by the dictatorial caprices imputed to him by his enemies. His efforts to revive the economy failed in their goals and instead provoked friction by continually shifting resources among different sectors of the community. When repressive measures then failed to subdue social unrest, he resorted to the totalitarian formulas that inflamed the conflict with the Church.

In late 1955 the prospect that Perón's successors could triumph where he had failed seemed unpromising. The economy was slipping into another triennial depression. Furthermore, like its predecessors, the coup had been accomplished by a coalition of divergent forces:

among the anti-Peronists were liberal democrats, Catholic nationalists large and small farmers and manufacturers, and factions from the right, the center, and the left—all had rallied behind the Church. For the moment they were behind Lonardi.

Argentina's economic stagnation and Perón's failure to revive prosperity so exacerbated social and political conflicts that his task of political management and control eventually became insuperable. Were stagnation and the ensuing political strife inevitable? The orthodox anti-Peronist critique suggests that Perón could have avoided both had he not blundered between 1946 and 1948. His chief mistakes were to let the farm sector languish and decline, while manufacturing grew too fast, and to grant labor far too many concessions before a firm base had been established for sustained growth. Higher agricultural production and exports during the late 1940s, critics argue, would have created a larger fund of reserves to cushion the economy against the later fall in export prices; in the longer term agriculture would then have provided resources allowing the still-faster expansion of manufacturing and urban employment. Implicit in the anti-Peronist analysis is the insinuation that someone like the resourceful but pragmatic Pinedo, rather than the flamboyant and demagogic Perón, could have surmounted the postwar challenge. Had the liberal conservatives remained in power, Ortiz until 1944 and Pinedo succeeding him, the country's course might have been quite different.

This critique, however, contains several questionable assumptions. It ignores, for example, Argentina's experience during the fifteen-year period of depression and war, which by 1946 made the farm sector appear an unpromising vehicle for economic recovery in comparison with manufacturing. The critique also assumes an impossible farsightedness among Argentina's political leaders in 1945–1946 concerning the international postwar economy, which recovered more rapidly than anyone could have predicted.

Similarly, the critique ignores the complex international and domestic pressures that destroyed conservatism in 1943, leaving the country in the hands of the nationalists. Specifically, the critique underplays the effects of mass migration and import substitution. Liberal-conservative policies during and immediately after the war would have had to contend with numerous market forces that, regardless of Perón, would have increased the wage share of national income and domestic food consumption, and therefore reduced the export surplus. The critique makes the quite unreasonable assumption that in 1946 Argentina could have won wider access to the United States market or, alternatively, that under a different government Argentina could have gained inclusion in the Marshall Plan. These issues are crucial because only a large, sustained inflow of dollars could have maintained the pace of expansion in manufacturing; only dollars could have enabled the large-scale investment in agriculture necessary, although perhaps not sufficient, for renewed agrarian expansion.

Other Latin American nations—Chile, Brazil, and Uruguay among them—had no wartime Perón or developed his analogue only later. Unlike Argentina, some of these countries quickly joined the Allies, accepting their new role as American client states but receiving few benefits from it. Some Latin American countries adopted substantially different policies and husbanded their wartime gains from trade more successfully than did Argentina. Yet by the mid 1950s these countries also faced crises of growth and distribution that sapped the authority and effectiveness of the state.

In sum, Argentina was destined for crisis with or without Perón, although he deepened and intensified the crisis, making its resolution more difficult. Perón's legacy was a nation that continued to be ensnared by the same problems he had failed to surmount.

VIII

A NATION IN DEADLOCK, 1955-1982

After Perón's fall Argentina began a long, unavailing struggle to surmount the economic impasse that had arisen during the 1940s. But the country failed to regain prosperity and growth; chronic inflation and recurrent cycles of recession and recovery arrested its progress toward industrialization. At the same time, social and political divisions grew increasingly tense and violent; successive administrations proved unable to prevent progressive institutional decay. Now a second-rank nation in Latin America, Argentina seemed unable to find a stable international position and was largely isolated in the world community.

Argentina's social problems became more extreme and appeared ineradicable. Unemployment and underemployment afflicted all the major social sectors, while the high living standards that had once distinguished Argentina from the rest of Latin America slowly eroded. During the 1960s and 1970s only 50 percent of the school-age population completed primary school, a proportion no higher than fifty years before, and only 22 percent completed secondary school. By 1970 a fifth or more of the population dwelt in makeshift housing: the shanty town population in the capital was reckoned at 750,000, perhaps double this number in Greater Buenos Aires.[1]

Once more Argentina failed to achieve a consensual political order and stumbled along in volatile stalemate. Frequently, a roughly synchronized regularity linked the behavior of the economy and the cyclical flow of politics; as the economy waxed and waned, regimes came and went.

Economic progress repeatedly revealed itself incompatible with representative government. Military rule supervened with increasing frequency, and by the late 1970s Argentina had become notorious for its political violence and repression. In the early 1980s internal conflicts drove the country into a disastrous war with Britain over possession of the Falkland Islands.

CONTEMPORARY ISSUES: A SKETCH

A measure of long-term economic growth occurred after 1955 peaking at around 3.5 percent annually during the late 1960s. Though per capita living standards and incomes no longer compared with western Europe, they remained higher than those in most of Latin America. With its small peasantry, its large and stratified middle and working classes, a manufacturing sector whose size and weight in the economy at large compared with several advanced industrial nations, Argentina was an oddity in the underdeveloped world. However, it shared those nations' structural inertia and inability to harness resources fully.[2]

Stagnation became the most striking feature of the economy: both agriculture and manufacturing suffered glaring shortcomings. Annual growth in agriculture was a mere 1.5 percent between 1958–1962 and 1974–1978; by 1970 agriculture represented only 13 percent of the gross domestic product and employed only 12 percent of the total work force. Between the late 1930s and the mid 1960s farm export volumes increased by only 3.2 percent.[3] After 1955 farm exports continued to suffer from adverse terms of trade and, at least with cereals, unequal access to markets. Export prices remained fairly stable until the 1970s but at roughly the same low level of the early 1950s. Argentina's share of world trade in agricultural goods declined, from 1.92 percent in 1950 to only 0.57 percent in 1968, as North America, Australia, and, from the mid 1950s, Europe dominated the market. Between 1950 and 1968 world trade grew at an annual rate of 7.8 percent, Argentina's trade, by less than 1 percent.

The outlook for markets brightened briefly in 1960 with the formation of the European Economic Community, but it soon became clear that the community's intent was agricultural self-sufficiency. Unable to secure a preferential trade agreement with the Common

Market, Argentina was obliged to circumvent its elaborate agricultural protectionism, which included sliding-scale tariffs, like the *prélèvement*, responsive to changing farm prices in the Market's member nations. Again Argentina found itself in the subordinate status of a reserve supplier whose goods were intermittently sought to overcome short-term scarcities; only with Italy did Argentina establish a degree of sustained commercial reciprocity.

The creation of the Latin American Free Trade Association (LAFTA), also in 1960, raised similar expectations. During the 1960s trade among members increased at twice the rate of that with nonmembers, but growth lagged during the 1970s. Despite LAFTA Argentina was unable either to break the dominance of the United States in the Latin American grain trade or to win a secure position for exports of manufactured goods. By the mid 1970s disenchantment superseded the earlier optimism. Meanwhile, freight rates that were uncompetitive with those from North America or Australia precluded Argentina from making much headway in the Japanese market. Meat exports oscillated with outbreaks of hoof-and-mouth disease; twice in the 1960s and again in the mid 1970s Britain banned the imports of Argentine meats. International cartels—the dominance of the United States in the grain trade, the linseed cartel based in Rotterdam—posed yet other obstacles to trade.

The main export successes came in the mid 1960s with the opening of trade with China and the Soviet Union. Yet although Argentina's foreign markets were extremely diversified—its markets for meat, for example, included a score of countries (see Table 33)—for the most part it pursued its customers year to year. For much of the period after 1955 Brazil was Argentina's best market for wheat, and Italy for its corn and sorghum. Trade with the Soviet Union suddenly spurted in the early 1980s, following an American embargo on grain sales. Trade with the United States showed an almost-permanent deficit.[4]

In a period of rapidly expanding world trade, however, the major issue in agriculture was no longer markets but production. Nor was it plausible to blame stagnating exports on domestic consumption of exportables, though some antiurban conservatives did: the main reason for increasing farm exports was to obtain foreign exchange for manufacturers; price increases in domestic food costs helped exports, but disrupted the market for manufactures, making it pointless to increase manufacturing investment. Rather, production was the central, inescapable issue. The expansion of agricultural acreage in the interior, which began in the 1930s, continued until around 1960 but leveled off as expansion spread to more-marginal areas (see Table 34).[5]

TABLE 33. *Meat Export Markets, 1966–1968*

	Average Annual Volume (thousand metric tons)	Percentage Share of Market
Britain	122	25.4
Italy	56	11.7
Spain	48	9.2
United States	46	9.6
Holland	40	8.3
Latin America	25	5.2
Israel	21	4.4
West Germany	19	4.0
Belgium	13	2.7
Japan	4	0.8
Rest of the world	86	17.9
TOTAL	480	100.0

SOURCE: República Argentina, Presidencia de la Nación, Secretaría del Consejo Nacional de Desarrollo, *Plan nacional de desarrollo, 1970–1974* (Buenos Aires, 1970), 5:96.

TABLE 34. *Index of Cultivated Areas, Pampas and Nonpampas Regions, 1935–1939 to 1965–1967* (1935–1939 = 100)

	Pampas	Nonpampas
1935–1939	100	100
1940–1944	103	111
1945–1949	100	137
1950–1954	89	167
1955–1959	98	194
1960–1964	94	194
1966–1967	95	191

SOURCE: Darrell F. Fienup, Russell H. Brannon, and Frank A. Fender, *El desarrollo agropecuario argentino y sus perspectivas* (Buenos Aires, 1972), 67.

In the pampas cattle raising maintained the dominance it had gained in World War II and until the mid 1960s continued to take land from farming. The cattle sector also benefited substantially from the introduction of artificial pastures. Between the late 1930s and the mid 1970s the total livestock population, led by cattle, increased by around 80 percent.

Farming underwent considerable diversification, as sorghum, soya, and sunflower appeared alongside the old staples. Sorghum cultivation increased from 32,000 hectares in 1954 to 3.8 million hectares in 1970. Yet diversification failed to trigger growth. Earlier patterns repeated themselves, as the gains of one farm product came mostly at the expense of another. In 1970, for example, the corn crop was massive, but wheat acreage shrank to its lowest level since 1903.

Nor did substantial mechanization stimulate growth in production. Although the number of tractors, for example, increased from around 30,000 in 1953 to 128,000 in 1969 and released land once used for pasturing horses, they also displaced human labor, thereby prolonging and intensifying the flight from the rural sector. More-genuine improvements followed the adoption of hybrid seed; during the late 1960s yield increases as high as 42 percent for wheat and 60 percent for corn were reported in some localities. With corn and sorghum, substantial increases in productivity followed the combined application of mechanization and hybrid seed. Yet despite evidence of many specific improvements or innovations between 1945 and 1973 average grain yields in Argentina increased by only 25 percent; in Australia the increase was 89 percent, and in the United States 140 percent.[6]

Agriculture's weaknesses elicited a host of explanations, both technical and political. Observers noted that in 1960 Argentina had only one agronomist for each 7,000 farms. Critics denounced anomalies in the tax system, which provided no incentives for farmers or ranchers to increase output and efficiency.[7] Until the late 1970s a continual debate raged on land reform. Reformers argued that many estate owners viewed their land more as a badge of status or protection against inflation than as a source of income from production. Opponents pointed to the absence of conclusive evidence that smaller farms outperformed larger ones. In the late 1950s, for example, government-sponsored loan schemes had induced substantial land redistribution, but no discernible effect on output.[8]

Argentina's agricultural stagnation contrasted with the rapid postwar expansion of agriculture in North America, Australia, and western Europe. The most striking differences between Argentina and these other countries lay less in land tenure (since trends elsewhere sometimes favored land concentration) but in differential access to state subsidies, price supports, and new technology. Subsidies and price stability were constantly undermined by inflation and the counterpull of the urban sectors. Between 1945–1959 wheat prices, for example, in Argentina varied by 54 percent, against only 5 percent in Canada and 9 percent in the United States. While agricultural prices and profits remained highly variable and unpredictable, low investment and output characterized most farms, largely regardless of size. Such conditions helped maintain Argentina's farms as underspecialized, undercapitalized concerns, geared to swift substitutions from one basket of goods to another as profit-making opportunities altered. Conditions stymied innovative, progressive farmers and hindered adaptations in land tenure necessary to promoting efficiency.

Despite improvements in agricultural productivity and yields after 1960, agricultural technology in Argentina was rarely available in a balanced, sustained package; rather, it came in sporadic doses and was relatively far more expensive than elsewhere. In 1969 for example, a tractor in Argentina cost as much as 143,000 kilos of wheat; in Australia the price was 64,000 kilos, and in the United States 75,000 kilos. On a similar measure, phosphate fertilizers were seven times more expensive in Argentina than in Australia, and an extreme example of the undercapitalization in Argentine agriculture concerns the use of fertilizer. In 1969 in Argentina, an average of two kilos of fertilizer were applied to each hectare of cultivated land; in Holland, the average was 456 kilos. Argentine farmers were similarly constrained in their use of insecticides, fungicides, and herbicides: farmers in the United States in 1963 used almost threefold the fungicides, more than fourfold the herbicides, and ninefold the insecticides of their Argentine counterparts.[9] Conditions in the farm sector symptomized the vicious cycles that ruled the Argentine economy. Agriculture's access to subsidies and technology depended fundamentally on a more successful and mature industrial base and on a more prosperous and stable urban economy. However, industry's growth largely depended on agriculture's capacity to provide higher export earnings. Underdevelopment in one sector thus constantly barred the progress of the other.

While production units in agriculture were criticized for being too large, in much of domestic manufacturing they were undoubtedly too small. The manufacturing sector was still largely composed of artisan workshops and penny capitalists. With few exceptions, large domestic corporations were state-owned entities that straddled industry and public services: gas, steel, electricity, water, railroads, and oil. Among the country's thirty largest companies in the mid 1960s state firms had 49 percent of total sales, foreign companies 41 percent, and private domestic manufacturers only 10 percent. One salient feature of the postwar period was the expansion of the state sector at the expense of the private: by the early 1980s some 700 state firms accounted for 42 percent of the gross domestic product.[10]

Differences in scale aside, domestic manufacturing and agriculture shared the problems of poor growth, low investment, and technological backwardness. Like the farms, many manufacturing firms were geared to swift product substitutions to facilitate a response to volatile price changes, and efficiency was hindered by limited specialization. Outside the wage-good sector, much of domestic manufacturing could also be described as mercantilistic. Profit was based not on mass production and falling prices, but on high prices, near-monopoly, or state contracts in a limited market.[11]

Among the renewed efforts to resume manufacturing exports, a 1962 program combined old methods like drawbacks and tax incentives with new ones, including subsidies. But in 1963 scarcely 1 percent of finished manufactured goods were exported. The obstacles were numerous: wages were relatively high compared with those of competitors elsewhere in the underdeveloped world; manufacturers were often unable to import competitively priced raw materials and were obliged to use expensive domestic substitutes; when costs rose manufacturers could not increase prices of exports with the latitude they enjoyed in the domestic market. Such difficulties were eventually overcome in part by a lavish program of subsidies adopted in the late 1960s. By 1970 manufactured goods had increased to 15.6 percent of total exports, and to 21.5 percent by 1975. However, when the subsidies were withdrawn in 1976 a decline in exports immediately ensued.[12]

The regimes that followed Perón's witnessed another series of severe short-range cycles and recurrent, eventually chronic, inflation. Brief interludes of growth, of up to 8 or 9 percent annually, were followed almost invariably by declines of similar magnitude. By the early 1960s inflation averaged around 30 percent a year; since the mid 1970s it has stuck fast at a constant three-figure rate. Efforts to restore and maintain growth while curbing hyperinflation were of four types:

stabilization plans, devaluations, foreign investment by multinationals, and foreign loans. Perón's stabilization program in 1952 was followed by five similar ventures in 1959, 1962–1963, 1967–1969, 1973–1974 and 1976–1980. Each program managed to slow inflation only temporarily, and none successfully restored growth.[13]

Devaluation became a major instrument in economic management; in the mid 1960s and the late 1970s the "crawling peg," method was used, but more frequent was the single sharp stroke. In principle, devaluation was to correct balance-of-payments deficits by promoting exports and restraining imports; in practice it did this only after inflicting numerous and complex countervailing side effects. For example, expectations of devaluation promoted the stockpiling of imports, which added to the payments deficits, and devaluation redistributed income to wealthier groups, like the farmers, with a high marginal propensity to consume imports, often luxury goods.[14] The shortcomings of devaluation as a means to help exports were illustrated by the beef sector, the largest source of export earnings, and the "beef cycle." Cattle ranchers repeatedly responded to devaluation not by increasing slaughter for immediate profit, but by reducing slaughter to augment their stock. After the devaluation export earnings thus increased less than anticipated, and the stock-building would last for several years. Eventually, as calves matured and pressure on pasture land grew, the slaughter rate suddenly increased, and meat flooded the market, causing a steep fall in prices. With lower prices, domestic meat consumption rose. Exports also rose but, because of cheaper prices and increased domestic consumption, export earnings failed to reflect fully the increase in supply.[15]

At best devaluation was a short-term expedient, one that invariably prompted urban recession and increased political friction. After each devaluation food and import prices rose and consumption fell, which caused manufacturing output to fall and urban unemployment to increase. Recession, in turn, provoked a decline in government revenues, as the tax base narrowed and tax evasion spread. Government spending then declined, helping to hasten and deepen contraction throughout the economy. When spending did not drop quickly enough, the economic depression was accompanied by inflation. As events in 1954 first showed, political responses to devaluation were usually most potent in the aftermath of recession, once the balance of payments was improving, manufacturing again reviving, and unemployment falling. At this point, as the labor market tightened, the trade unions led strike campaigns to restore the predevaluation wage share in national income. But then as wages rose, so too did production costs and soon prices. The mounting inflation again channeled exportables into the home market. While manufacturers increased production, imports were also rising, which renewed the balance-of-payments crisis and required another devaluation. Through this chain of intersectoral income shifts, changes in relative prices, and inflation, each devaluation thus carried the seedling of its successor.[16]

After a weak beginning during Perón's regime, the multinationals descended on Argentina in growing numbers. They came mostly in three waves—1959–1961, 1967–1969, 1977–1979—in response to lavish inducements from governments seeking to diversify the industrial base, increase efficiency in manufacturing, and gain access to new technology. Between 1959 and 1973 foreign investment of this kind was an estimated $750 million. Among the multinationals the pioneers were automobile firms, such as Ford, Renault, FIAT, Peugeot, and Citroën. They were followed by other international giants such as Firestone, IBM, Duperial, Olivetti, and Coca-Cola. Before 1975 about half the multinationals were American in origin, and the rest western European. Yet between 1967 and 1975 Argentina received only 5 percent of total American investment throughout Latin America, and a mere seventh of that channeled into Brazil.[17]

The prominence achieved by the multinationals in the economy was arguably due as much to the competitive weaknesses of national firms as to their own predatory appetites. But local critics usually perceived only the latter and repeatedly accused the multinationals of disrupting native manufacturing while doing nothing to promote economic recovery or expansion. First among numerous complaints against the multinationals were charges of "monopoly" and "concentration." Instead of adding new resources to manufacturing and supplementing existing capacity, their detractors alleged, the multinationals grew at the expense of domestic industry, usurping domestic markets and bank credit, and transforming manufacturing into large foreign-held blocs. Critics claimed that the multinationals expanded at an annual rate of 8.8 percent in the 1960s (or 15 percent disregarding the older and moribund foreign firms like the meatpacking plants), double the rate of national firms. In 1955 foreign companies were the source of 20 percent of total manufacturing output; by the early 1970s their share reached one-third. Among the one hundred largest manufacturing firms fourteen were foreign-owned in 1957, but by 1966 fully half were; and by as early as 1963 multinational subsidiaries, about half of which had been established within the preceding five years, controlled as much as 50 percent of output in sectors like tobacco, rubber, chemicals, oil derivatives, machinery, electrical goods, and transportation materials. Of the eighty-eight manufacturing firms that employed more than 1,000 workers in 1963, thirty-five were foreign-owned.[18]

In the 1960s, critics further alleged, only a quarter of the total investments by the multinationals came from abroad; the rest was from domestic savings, often secured from the banks at highly favorable and discriminatory interest rates. As high-technology, capital-intensive concerns, the multinationals undermined the growth of manufacturing employment, thereby provoking downward pressures on wages. Because most goods they produced were luxury items in limited demand, rather than promoting egalitarian patterns of consumption, they exacerbated social dualism.

The multinationals were also decried as imperialists who invested or reinvested much less than they eventually repatriated as profit and who exacted monopoly royalty fees for the technology and expertise they provided. One account estimated investment during the 1960s at $600 million, but repatriated profits at $1,358 million; total payments for royalties and patents were estimated to have risen from $50 million in 1965 to $300 million by 1973. This outflow of capital magnified the balance-of-payments deficit, which then necessitated a larger devaluation; the greater the devaluation, the more the contraction in urban wages and consumption. In sum, critics concluded, the closer the ties with the multinationals, the steeper the price paid by the domestic economy.[19]

A source of equal contention was the issue of foreign borrowings. Loans from agencies like the International Monetary Fund (IMF) were granted on stringent conditions: government spending cuts to help curb inflation and the cessation of subsidies, price supports, and multiple exchange rates—all measures expected to deregulate and liberalize the economy and correct distortions in relative prices. However, like devaluations, such measures inexorably led to recession: spending cuts provoked unemployment; the curtailment of subsidies undermined wages and salaries; the enactment of a uniform exchange rate altered the composition of imports and intensified foreign competitive pressures on national producers. The foreign loans afforded Argentina temporary relief from balance-of-payments difficulties, but at the price of renewed political instability and sometimes crippling increases in indebtedness.[20]

The outcome of Argentina's economic failure was a heavily un-balanced society that made ill-use of its potential resources. In 1959 experts from the United Nations Economic Commission for Latin America concluded that 70 percent of the nation's land area—some 193 million hectares of a total 280 million—was usable for stockraising, agriculture, or forestry. But only a quarter of the usable land was actually in use, scarcely one-sixth of the total area. Aridity afflicted 45 percent of the land, yet less than 1 percent was under irrigation, scarcely an advance on 1930. The 1960s and 1970s brought little change: the pampas remained the source of 60 percent of cereals, 55 percent of forage crops, and, discounting Patagonia, an even larger proportion of livestock.[21]

Meanwhile, Argentina became still more heavily urbanized, such that by 1970 79 percent of the population lived in urban areas, a proportion matched by few other countries in the world. The rural population had peaked in 1949 at 5.9 million; by 1970 it had fallen to 4.9 million. This growing urbanization and centralization aggravated historic interregional disparities. In the 1960s and 1970s four-fifths of internal commerce was conducted within the littoral triangle between the cities of Buenos Aires, Santa Fe, and Córdoba. Although the growth of the oil industry and the development of temperate-fruit production effected migration toward the south, especially to Rio Negro and Neuquén, Patagonia at large remained a near-empty wil-derness. Demographic decline was marked in the northern regions: in the 1960s an estimated 164,000 people left Tucumán, some 140,000 left Chaco province, 100,000 left Santiago del Estero, and from Corrientes another 100,000 migrated. Some three-quarters of a million migrants settled in Greater Buenos Aires in the 1960s.[22]

Argentina had always subsisted in the shadow of Buenos Aires, and in the twentieth century its structural lopsidedness remained as acute and extreme as ever. In 1930 24.7 percent of the nation's 9 million people dwelt within or close by the capital; by 1980 the propor-tion was 34.3 percent—9.2 million of a total 27.2 million. Greater Buenos Aires was now the third largest conurbation in Latin America, stretching far into the western plains; its northern limits extended to Tigre, at the mouth of the Paraná delta, and its southern boundary was close to La Plata, thirty miles from the city center. The city's population density also increased, as its earlier single-floor dwellings were replaced by high-rise apartments. Here was half the country's manufacturing industry, employing one million persons in 1980; here too, among the shantytowns, in what were euphemistically termed *villas de emergencia*, was its growing army of indigent poor, estimated at around 1.5 million in 1970. A survey of one shantytown settlement in 1971 reported that 70 percent of the population had not completed primary school; though the country had almost as many cattle as people, 16 percent had never drunk milk. The only appreciable countervailing force against Buenos Aires was Córdoba, which from the late 1950s grew swiftly as an automobile manufacturing center. Between 1947 and 1970, Córdoba's population rose from 383,000 to almost 800,000.[23]

Other symptoms of social strain were a low birthrate, slow population growth, and structural unemployment. The birthrate began to decline around 1930; by 1960 it had fallen to 2.2 percent, two-thirds of the average elsewhere in Latin America. The decline was still more extreme in the cities: in Buenos Aires and Rosario in 1960 the birthrate was only 1.7 percent, a reflection of the falling marriage rate, the housing shortage, and insufficient incomes among the population of immigrant descent, the middle and skilled working classes. New European immigration was negligible after 1950. The foreign-born population, which had been 30 percent in 1914, first dwindled in the 1930s and 1940s, and fell steeply soon after, to less than 10 percent by 1970. Among resident foreigners perhaps three-quarters were displaced migrant peasants from surrounding Latin American states (see Table 35). In the 1960s immigration from Paraguay, for example, was estimated at 400,000. Although Argentina was the world's ninth largest nation in land area, in the early 1980s its population still languished below 30 million.[24]

Measurable unemployment rarely fell below 5.6 percent, or half a million persons; unemployment and disguised unemployment afflicted workers, the migrant poor, and the middle classes. In the 1960s and 1970s employment in manufacturing increased at an annual rate of scarcely 1 percent; as a sector of total employment, manufacturing fell slightly between 1950 and 1960 from 27.9 percent to 25.9 percent.

TABLE 35. *Percentages of Immigrants to Argentina by Area of Origin, 1895–1914 and 1960–1970*

	Europe	Latin America	Unknown
1895–1914	88.4	7.5	4.1
1960–1970	18.7	76.1	5.2

SOURCE: Alfredo E. Lattes and Ruth Sautu, "Inmigración, cambio demográfico y desarrollo industrial en la Argentina," *Cuadernos del CENEP*, no. 5 (1978), 10.

In the early 1960s Argentina each year lost some 10,000 members of the professions to emigration; this number then rose sharply during the 1970s.[25]

Socially and politically, Argentina represented a case of arrested transition. The legacy of the 1940s endured in the new migrant urban population, in the labor movement, which was the largest and strongest in Latin America, and in the survival of *peronista* populism. But the elites still largely dominated the land, and in the 1960s and 1970s they also recovered many of their traditional leadership roles in commerce and finance, reviving their political influence through power groups like the Army. The elites now entered manufacturing, less as entrepreneurs than as brokers and agents for the multinationals, thereby resuming their historical roles as collaborators and agents of foreign investors.[26]

Argentina's middle class survived in number and strength, although *embourgeoisement* became increasingly difficult. Throughout the period the number of professionals, white-collar workers, and state administrators—the type of middle class that appeared before 1930—continued to proliferate, and they were joined by the new petty capitalists spawned by import substitution. The middle class also grew as more women entered the labor market. Until 1960 women composed a roughly constant 20 percent of the workforce, with most employed as domestics or in manufacturing. By 1970 women represented 25 percent of the workforce, the increase due almost entirely to women's penetration of middle-class service occupations—banking, insurance, commerce, public administration, and the vocational professions.[27]

In this period the major social groups, classes, parties, corporate institutions—each highly organized in a multitude of special interest associations—were locked in almost perpetual conflict, often within and among themselves. No one sector was able to establish stable, durable alliances or an institutionalized system of dominance. Politics increasingly focused on competing sectoral claims to national income, state subsidies, and support; an acute polarization developed between civil society and the armed forces.

The period between Perón's fall and the Falklands war divides into three phases, which span sixteen changes of government (see Table 36). From 1955 until 1966 came a series of failed efforts to destroy Peronism and to erect a civilian alternative that could command majority support. Both military and non-Peronist civilian governments seized power but could not retain it; the Peronists were able to topple

TABLE 36. *Governments in Argentina, 1955–1982*

September 1955–November 1955	General Eduardo Lonardi
November 1955–May 1958	General Pedro E. Aramburu
May 1958–March 1962	Arturo Frondizi
March 1962–July 1963	José María Guido
July 1963–June 1966	Arturo Illia
June 1966–June 1970	General Juan Carlos Onganía
June 1970–February 1971	General Roberto M. Levingston
February 1971–May 1973	General Alejandro Lanusse
May 1973–July 1973	Hector Cámpora
July 1973–November 1973	Raul Lastiri
November 1973–July 1974	Juan Perón
July 1974–March 1976	María Estela Martínez de Perón
March 1976–March 1981	General Jorge Videla
March 1981–December 1981	General Roberto Viola
December 1981–June 1982	General Leopoldo Galtieri
June 1982	General Reynaldo Bignone

governments but unable to take power. Between 1966 and 1976 the struggle between the military and the Peronists intensified. In 1966 the Army established authoritarian rule and initiated a stabilization program to expunge inflation and restore economic growth. Violence and revolt forced the program to collapse in 1969, and serious political unrest persisted over the next seven years, despite the return of the Peronists in 1973. The third phase began in 1976, under a second group of military authoritarians whose regime was harsher and more resistant to compromise than any of its predecessors. The regime survived first an armed rebellion, then a steep and prolonged recession, throughout resisting pressures for a return to civilian rule. But having failed to resolve the chronic problems of stagnation and maldistribution, it too underwent spectacular and ignominious decline.[28]

FROM LONARDI TO ILLIA, 1955–1966

Like its predecessors in 1930 and 1943, the *revolución libertadora* of September 1955 was executed by a coalition of military leaders composed of nationalists and liberals. Like Uriburu and the ephemeral Rawson in 1943, Lonardi as the titular leader of the revolution belonged to the weaker faction, which was swiftly supplanted. The situation more closely resembled 1930 than 1943 in that Lonardi, like Uriburu, was a nationalist, but the liberals were once more the stronger faction.

Division in the new government swiftly crystalized on attitudes toward the deposed Peronists. Liberals clamored for root-and-branch suppression of the Peronist party, Peronist unions, and the Peronist state. Lonardi shared their antipathies to Perón and his inner clique but had a much less iconoclastic view of the *peronista* system. In years past he had supported insurrection mostly in reaction to what were perceived as Perón's excesses or deviations: the regime's increasing corruption, its takeover of the schools, its assaults on the Church, and the recent deal with Standard Oil. Although Lonardi was willing to purge the upper ranks of the Army, he was disinclined to dismantle Perón's bureaucratic controls over the economy, to undo his social reforms, or to alter the relationship that had evolved between government and organized labor. His plan, it seemed, was to assume Perón's position as a popular leader and to erect—to use a phrase that became common in the 1960s—"Peronism without Perón" (*peronismo sin Perón*). In October 1955 the Lonardi government appeared to show scant concern for workers' interests when it devalued the peso. However, Lonardi made at least cosmetic efforts to conciliate the unions by appointing a union lawyer and suspected Peronist as minister of labor and by leaving *La Prensa* in the hands of the CGT.

Lonardi's conciliatory approach had some backing from nationalists in the Army, but the liberals outnumbered the nationalists there and commanded overwhelming allegiance in the Navy and Air Force. They also enjoyed the support of a broad bloc of civilian groups: farmers, manufacturers, and large segments of the middle class. Soon after Lonardi's investiture the friction became manifest in a spate of internal military wrangles, disputes within the junta, and conflicts over policies and spheres of influence in the cabinet. Within sixty days, by mid November, Lonardi was gone—betrayed, disillusioned, and fatally ill.[29]

Under General Pedro E. Aramburu, Lonardi's liberal successor, the assault on Peronism began forthwith. The Peronist party was dissolved, the CGT placed under an interventor, and *La Prensa* re-expropriated. In late 1955 a wage freeze was decreed, though soon abandoned to facilitate a takeover of the unions by anti-Peronists. The Law of Professional Associations, which Perón had enacted in 1945, was annulled, and an effort was made to destroy the authoritarian hierarchical structure of the unions by granting legal recognition to several organizations, not just one, in each industry. Hundreds of union leaders were arrested, and the 60,000 who had held union offices during the preceding three years, when Perón's control was tightest, were expelled and banned. Similar exclusions were inflicted on the CGE, Peronist congressmen, and on all who had held public office since 1946. In May 1956 the Constitution of 1949 was abolished, and new penalties great and small were heaped on the Peronists. Their insignia and slogans were forbidden, as was even the mention of Perón's name. The former president was now referred to by a variety of insulting sobriquets, of which the best known was the "the fugitive tyrant" (*el tirano prófugo*), the tag given him by *La Prensa*. Meanwhile, the remains of Eva Perón disappeared without trace from their resting place in the CGT.[30]

The continuity between Lonardi and Aramburu was greater in economic policy. Immediately after the September revolution the new government commissioned Raúl Prebisch, until 1943 director of the Central Bank and now secretary-general of ECLA, to suggest economic reforms. Prebisch's plan was strongly liberal in that its major thrust was economic deregulation. Among his proposals were freer use of devaluation, the dismantling of the IAPI, some denationalization in the state sector, reduced government spending, the restoration of autonomy to the banks, and the cessation of price controls, subsidies, multiple exchange rates, and export taxes; lastly, he urged a more active effort to seek foreign investment and loans. Much of this program was accomplished, at least in part, in 1956. The next year Argentina, having also agreed to halt bilateral trading, had achieved the credentials for admission to international financial agencies, among them the IMF.[31]

Aramburu adhered to Lonardi's pledge of September 1955: the military government was provisional and transitional; it would remain only so long as necessary to destroy Peronism and to create conditions appropriate to the election of a non-Peronist civilian government. But it soon became apparent that these were impossible targets. During the September revolution and for some time after, the bastions of Peronism in the CGT and the unions had evinced confusion and disorientation. The Peronist leaders made no concerted effort to rally to Perón's defense, in part because they had lost the habit of taking the initiative; during Perón's last years their role had been simply to follow and execute his orders. Their attitude of blind obedience persisted after the revolution, encouraged by Lonardi's hints of magnanimity and by expectation that in practice affairs would be conducted much as before. Thus the advent of Aramburu and blunt persecution came as a stunning blow that was met by only feeble resistance.

Yet events soon seemed to vindicate Lonardi's conciliatory approach. Instead of destroying Peronism, Aramburu's persecution swiftly reinvigorated it and also restored workers' perceptions of Perón as their great benefactor. Such sentiments strengthened as the series of devaluations that began in October 1955 and the curtailment of food subsidies began to undercut workers' living standards. The provisional government further contributed to this response by more errors of judgment. In June 1956 General Juan José Valle led a small pro-Perón military rising in Corrientes. The rebellion posed little danger and was immediately stifled, but twenty-seven of its ringleaders were summarily shot. Not since the *caudillos* had military rebellion been punishable by death. The Peronists now had martyrs and an indelible grievance against the government; the incident was unforgettable and unforgivable.

The Peronists now initiated a movement that they called *La Resistencia*. Unions closed ranks against anti-peronists, and in August 1957 the Sixty-Two Organizations, a Peronist bloc, was formed in the CGT. With the ban on former union leaders, many unions now fell under a new generation of Peronist militants who were often young, less directly involved at senior levels in the fallen regime, and more susceptible to idealizing its accomplishments. Under their promptings came a campaign of industrial action that climaxed with two general strikes in September and October 1957. The Peronists also relied on passive resistance; for example, in July 1956, soon after the abolition of Perón's constitution, the provisional government held an election to select delegates for a constitutional convention but formally banned the Peronists from participating. The number of blank ballots cast in the election exceeded those of all other parties; in this way the Peronists reasserted themselves as the popular majority. When the anti-Peronist assault on the unions then evaporated, a large majority among the Sixty-Two Organizations were still under Peronist control.[32]

As the Aramburu government failed on the political front, it had no more success with the economy. Initially, it managed to achieve a balance-of-payments surplus, due largely to renewed devaluation, and an inflow of short-term capital from abroad. The surplus was sustained in 1957 owing mainly to the vagaries of the beef cycle, as a drought ended a phase of herd rebuilding and caused the herds to dwindle by an estimated 14 percent. Increased slaughter brought higher meat shipments and higher export earnings. But the following year, as rebuilding the herds began, meat exports plummeted, and another balance-of-payments crisis loomed. Such events exemplified a classic dilemma in economic policy making, one that recurred repeatedly in the 1960s and 1970s: the government had simultaneously to improve export earnings and avoid urban recession. The resulting erratic potpourri of measures, which recalled Perón's efforts between 1949 and 1952, produced another bout of inflation that destabilized the coalition established to overthrow Perón. Aramburu could point to only two achievements: the 16 percent increase in oil production between 1955 and 1958, and the creation of the Agricultural Technology Institute (*Instituto Nacional para la Tecnologia Agraria* [INTA]), which enjoyed some prestige in the 1960s as the initiator of recent improvements in the agricultural sector.[33]

The evaporation of its political base helped hasten the Aramburu regime's willingness to withdraw from power. Elections were scheduled for February 1958, but the ban against the Peronists continued. A lengthy rift among the Radicals came to a head in 1957 with the formation of two rival factions, the People's Radical Party (*Unión Cívica Radical del Pueblo*, UCRP), led by Ricardo Balbín, and the Intransigent Radical Party (*Unión Cívica Radical Intransigente*, UCRI), led by Balbín's running mate in the 1951 election, Arturo Frondizi. The two leaders had long been rivals for supremacy in the party, but now they also disagreed on the issue of relations with the Peronists. Balbín's faction wanted a complete dissociation, while Frondizi urged a kind of accommodation that he hoped would evoke support from the unions and the working class.

As the 1958 election approached, Frondizi courted the Peronist vote by taking a pro-union stance during strikes, promising new nationalization measures, issuing several vitriolic condemnations of the United States, and opposing the bans on the Peronists. These activities won him a secret endorsement from the exiled Perón, which carried him to electoral victory with some 4 million votes against Balbín's 2.6 million; another 1.5 million votes were shared among twenty minor parties, mostly remnants of the old conservative and Socialist parties, and 800,000 blank votes were cast. In surreptitiously aligning himself with the Peronists, Frondizi had adopted a risky course. He won the election, yet his behavior had placed him under suspicion in the Army, which remained dominated by extreme anti-peronists, or "gorillas." Meanwhile, Frondizi had also incurred a costly political debt with Perón, but had few resources to discharge it.[34]

As Frondizi assumed the presidency in May 1958, another balance-of-payments crisis was approaching. Ignoring this, he began practicing the populism he had preached during the election campaign. He immediately gave the unions a 60 percent wage boost and imposed a price freeze; pensions were increased, public transit fares reduced. The laws instituted by Aramburu that allowed several unions in each industry were replaced by a system like Perón's in which for purposes of collective bargaining the government recognized only the union with the largest membership—usually the Peronist segment. In other respects, too, Frondizi seemed to pattern his administration on Perón's. The Law of Industrial Advancement (*Ley de Promoción Industrial*) enacted in 1958 reversed Aramburu's tendency toward economic liberalism and restored in full the government's regulatory power over tariffs and exchange rates. In July 1958 Frondizi announced an agreement with several foreign oil concerns to commence new drilling operations in Patagonia. Although the measure treated the foreigners as contracted agents of the YPF and gave none of them concessions in the form of real property, it seemed a *volte face* of bizarre proportions, for Frondizi had long had the reputation of an ultranationalist on oil. Again, his policy seemed a return to Perón's line in 1955.

Frondizi's objectives in late 1958 were to consolidate his popular support, establish a firm bridgehead among the unions, and neutralize Perón's influence by imitating his policies. Frondizi hoped to use the Peronists, but soon they were exploiting him; each demand he met from them instantly prompted others, with the implied threat that they would turn against him unless he complied. Whatever the economic logic of his oil policy, it proved a major political liability. Early in 1959 a strike by oil workers prompted a state of siege. Meanwhile, caught between rapidly rising wages and the price freeze, many farmers and manufacturers complained bitterly against the government. Most of Frondizi's initial measures merely worsened the parlous situation he had inherited. By the end of 1958, as the reserves neared exhaustion and the balance-of-payments deficit ensnared him, Frondizi was obliged to change course; but in doing so, he shattered his alliance with Perón and the unions.[35]

At the end of 1958 Frondizi announced a new program with two main objectives: price stabilization and the conquest of the balance-of-payments bottleneck. Stabilization was to be accomplished with the assistance of foreign borrowings, the chief of which was a loan of $328 million from the IMF. The terms of the loan required the Argentine government to impose higher interest rates and tighter monetary controls, to end price controls and subsidies, to reduce the public deficit through higher transit rates and higher oil and electricity prices, and to attack featherbedding in the state sector; critics charged that the railroads alone harbored between 45,000 and 70,000 superfluous personnel. The adoption of a single exchange rate in January 1959 evolved into a large *de facto* devaluation when the Central Bank ceased to defend the parity of the peso and allowed it to depreciate.

The immediate outcome of the stabilization program was unprecedented recession admixed with hyperinflation. Whereas the plan sought to attack inflation by curbing excess demand, the substantial devaluation increased import prices, thereby in effect substituting for demand inflation an even greater wave of cost inflation. In 1959 the cost of living rose by 118 percent, and wholesale prices by 133 percent. Industrial output fell by 8 percent, the GDP by 5 percent, and per capita GNP by 7.5 percent. The fall in real wages was estimated at 26 percent. The wage share in national income had fallen from 56.1 percent between 1949 and 1955 to 53 percent between 1955 and 1958, and to only 45.8 percent in 1959; other calculations showed that the wage share had declined by one-fourth since 1954. Devaluation effected a net transfer of around $500 million to the farming sector; ranchers' incomes reportedly increased by 97 percent. Frondizi's alliance with Perón, which neither had hitherto acknowledged publicly, collapsed in June 1959, when Perón, from his refuge in Venezuela, revealed the secret deal he had made with Frondizi, the exchange of votes in the 1958 election for Peronist control over the unions and eventual legalization of the Peronist movement. As he made all this public, Perón also liquidated the alliance.[36]

Yet throughout 1959 Frondizi clung fast to the stabilization program and abandoned his earlier populist stance. In January he responded to a general strike, which the Sixty-Two Organizations proclaimed "revolutionary," with a bout of police measures. As his political isolation grew, Frondizi fell under the grip of the Army, which in June 1959 forced him to dismiss his economics minister, Rogelio Frigerio, because he had served as Frondizi's emissary to Perón before the 1958 election. In Frigerio's place came Álvaro Alsogaray, an orthodox conservative popular in the Army. Next the Army urged Frondizi to a series of repressive measures. In the aftermath of the strikes and the recent revolution in Cuba, the Army became obsessed with radical or leftist conspiracies, and it betrayed a growing inclination to conflate working-class or trade-union–based Peronist opposition with the new enemy: international or Cuban-based communism. To counter the threat the Army organized a new security network known as the Plan CONINTES (*Conmoción Interno del Estado*). Among the powers of this body were the arrest, detention, and interrogation of suspected but ill-defined "subversive elements." The year 1959 exemplified several common and persistent features of Argentine politics following the overthrow of Perón. The Army reappeared as a powerful and often irresistible pressure group constantly shaping, limiting, or vetoing government policies. At the same time, in order to win power and create a majority alliance, Frondizi had made many populist promises; but to control the economy he had to jettison these pledges. As austerity supervened, the government's political base shattered, and the president became little more than the Army's puppet.[37]

In 1959 Frondizi repeatedly avowed that the hardships would be brief, that economic recovery lay at hand. To complement the stabilization plan his administration sponsored a highly ambitious program of industrial development (*desarrollismo*). Frondizi and Frigerio, who after his ouster remained the president's close personal advisor, now argued the fruitlessness of pursuing economic recovery through agricultural exports because as agricultural production and protectionism continued to increase in the industrialized countries, agricultural prices and the terms of trade would continue to fall. The wiser course lay in intensified industrial development, which would reduce import needs and conquer balance-of-payments constraints on growth. Through industry, argued the *desarrollistas*, Argentine agriculture could overcome its chief handicap, the lack of access to new technology. Similarly, they contended that industry's chief shortcoming, the insufficiency of domestic savings and capital, could be allayed by a massive injection of foreign investment. Oil was their first target: the elimination of oil imports would in itself almost conquer the present payments deficit. Beyond this Frondizi and Frigerio aspired for national steel, petrochemical, and automobile industries.[38]

Frondizi's determined bid for foreign capital was highly successful: an estimated $244 million was invested in 1959, and a total of $344 million between 1959 and 1961. Around two-thirds of these investments flowed into petrochemicals and into newly constructed automobile plants, mostly in Córdoba. As the government had hoped, foreign investment brought the recession to a swift and sharp conclusion; the balance of payments showed a surplus and reserves grew rapidly. By the end of 1959 the extreme inflation had begun to decline, and oil production posted a 25 percent increase. Recovery continued throughout 1960 and into 1961, as the economy grew by 8 percent and 7.1 percent respectively. In 1960 real wages recovered by 17 percent; worker hours lost to absenteeism declined to 1.8 million compared with 11.1 million hours a year earlier.[39]

In the early 1960s the *desarrollistas* could point to several major accomplishments: oil production surged forward, increasing by 43.2 percent in 1960, 32.3 percent in 1961, and another 16.3 percent in 1962. Self-sufficiency was near, as oil imports fell from 40 percent of total oil consumption in 1961 to only 10 percent in 1963. Steel production was boosted when the first integrated steel plant was established in 1960. From the 200,000 tons of steel produced in 1955, output grew in ten years to 1.37 million tons, half of which came from the state steel complex, SOMISA. Argentine production of motor vehicles climbed from a mere 6,000 in 1955 to 200,000 in 1965. Lastly, Frondizi did much to overcome earlier electricity shortages, with output increasing by 150 percent in the decade after 1955.

Even so, these achievements were more an illusion of transformation than its realization. Like Perón, Frondizi was able to restrain inflation for only short periods. Prosperity in 1960 and 1961 depended on the influx of foreign investment; when the flow slowed in 1961, a classic new balance-of-payments crisis loomed. The expansion of manufacturing had provoked a steep increase in imports, while exports earnings were falling in response to increased internal consumption of foodstuffs, a tightening labor market, and rising wages; throughout agriculture still slumbered. However, adding to the payments deficit were onerous new foreign debts and profit remittances by new foreign investors. The crisis also revealed that the effort to promote national industry not only failed to reduce demand for imports but also in some respects increased it, shifting import needs to new schedules of goods. Instead of importing cars or oil, for example, the country now imported the machines or technology to produce them.[40]

As the economy worsened in 1961, Frondizi faced renewed political difficulties. In July, October, and November 1961 the CGT organized more strikes, whose climax was a six-week stoppage on the railroads in protest against government efforts to prune the labor force. Meanwhile, Frondizi's relations with the Army had again deteriorated. Throughout 1961, seeking a foreign-policy success to help him at home, Frondizi sought to mediate in the confrontation between the United States and Cuba. First, he cultivated the new Kennedy administration in Washington, and later in the year, briefly and secretly in Buenos Aires, he hosted Ernesto "Che" Guevara, the Argentine-born hero of the Cuban revolution. News of the encounter provoked a furor in the Army, which forced a diplomatic break with Cuba in February 1962.

Frondizi's diplomatic dabblings showed him again posturing on the side of progressive causes, as he had done before his election, and for similar motives. To survive the incipient recession without falling completely in the Army's hands, the government needed to muster popular support; crucial gubernatorial and congressional elections were pending in March 1962. With an eye to the elections and to postpone the adoption of a new austerity program, Frondizi had finally shed himself of Alsogaray in April 1961. All prospects of an electoral deal with the Peronists had disappeared, and the issue now was whether Frondizi would uphold their proscription, as the Army demanded. To do so, however, threatened to undermine Frondizi's status in Washington, where he was engaged in energetic efforts to secure funds under the new Alliance for Progress sponsored by Kennedy; the American funds were expected to be vital in attenuating the effects of the threatened recession. Frondizi's dilemma was finally resolved by three preliminary gubernatorial elections in late 1961, each of which was won by the UCRI. These victories persuaded him to abandon thoughts of proscribing the Peronists; instead he proposed to admit them and defeat them.

The gamble proved fatal. The Peronists, who had made only token efforts in 1961, massed all their forces for the March elections and carried ten of the fourteen provinces in which elections were held, including the province of Buenos Aires. The Army insisted that Frondizi annul the elections. When he refused, he was deposed, arrested, and held captive on the island of Martín García. In 1958 Frondizi had artfully manipulated the conflict between the Army and the Peronists to his own advantage, but four years later he became their victim.[41]

After Frondizi's departure recession struck swiftly. Between early 1962 and mid 1963 per capita GNP fell by 8.6 percent; in 1963 per capita income was estimated at a mere 1 percent above 1949. The new industries were paralyzed, with unused capacity climbing as high as 60 percent in some areas. Industrial output in 1962 fell to only 74 percent of 1961. Real wages also fell, to 80 percent of 1958, and unemployment grew to an estimated 15.1 percent by December 1962. Meanwhile, the older wage-goods industrial sector fell victim to a recession provoked by underconsumption. In 1962 there were twice as many bankruptcies as in 1958. Another "beef cycle" crisis compounded the depression, which reduced export earnings, and exacerbated the incidence of the large foreign debt contracted by Frondizi. A credit squeeze led many firms and individuals to defer or evade tax payments. Reductions in government spending provoked still higher unemployment and a second wave of bankruptcies. Industry's chief difficulties, it seemed, stemmed from the profit squeeze that resulted from rising import costs, high interest rates, and shrinking markets. Yet the native manufacturing associations led by the CGE now orchestrated campaigns against the multinationals, denouncing growing concentration and the monopolization of bank credits. Rising import prices, successive devaluations, which totaled 65 percent between March and December 1962, and heavy domestic borrowings by the government forced a swift leap in prices. In 1962–1963 wholesale prices rose by 67.8 percent, bringing the total increase between 1958 and 1962 to 323 percent. Lastly, the post-devaluation redistribution of income brought a substantial increase in imported luxury goods, although overall imports were falling.[42]

Nevertheless, within a year the recession was surmounted, the balance of payments restored, and conditions once more encouraged expansion. Recovery was due in part to forced cuts in consumption, administered once more by the dour Alsogaray, who resumed office under the military puppet regime led by José María Guido, former president of the Chamber of Deputies. Yet recovery resulted as much from chance as design, as in the mid 1960s world prices for Argentina's chief exports briefly climbed higher than at any point since the late 1940s. Between the late 1930s and 1953–1955 prices had fallen by as much as 32 percent; ten years later they had recovered to 93 percent of their value in the late 1930s. For three consecutive years favorable weather produced bumper wheat harvests. Only once before, in 1938–1939, had the wheat harvest climbed beyond 10 million tons; at its lowest point, in 1952, it was scarcely 2 million. But the 1963 harvest yielded 8.1 million tons, that of 1964 produced 9.1 million tons, and 1965, for the first time in a generation, the harvest surpassed 10 million tons. Argentina also gained access to new markets, selling large quantities of grains to the Soviet Union and China. Rising export earnings swiftly rekindled the domestic economy, which at the peak of the boom in 1965 grew at the unprecedented rate of 9 percent.[43]

The avoidance of open junta rule in 1962 was not motivated by a sudden fondness for constitutional proprieties in the Army. In some measure, a concern to protect Argentina's reputation in Washington, thereby maintaining its eligibility for support under the Alliance for Progress, motivated the pretense at legalities. But more important was serious internal division in the Army, which had become more pronounced during recent years as the Army's custodial and deliberative role had grown. This division embraced two major contenders. One faction, dubbed the "Blues" (*azules*), favored another attempt at constitutional government, but by exhuming Lonardi's plan of aligning the Peronists behind a new military leader. Such a movement, contended the *azules*, would be the country's best protection against communism. The other Army faction, the "Reds" (*colorados*) or "gorillas," was composed of militant anti-Peronists who rejected any kind of neopopulism and favored an indefinite military dictatorship. In 1962 and into the following year, the two factions clashed repeatedly and at times were close to open war. But at length, as the *colorados* finally backed out of the confrontation, the *azules* gained the upperhand and scheduled elections for July 1963. Recession, falling wages, and unemployment, however, undercut any chance of a "Peronism without Perón"; here the Blues failed, as the unions and the CGT firmly resisted cooptation.[44]

If economic recovery favored the return of an elected civilian government in 1963, in most other respects the outlook was bleak. Democracy was reborn from deadlock in the Army, yet unless it could master the Peronists and surmount economic stagnation, the Army seemed likely to intervene once more. The election of 1963 again exemplified democracy of a very imperfect kind. The Army banned a Peronist-front organization led by Vicente Solano Lima, nor would it permit Frondizi to resume power, although his prospects had become remote when the UCRI split. The only remaining choice was the UCRP candidate, Arturo Illia, a little-known country doctor from Córdoba. In July 1963 Illia received the largest number of votes, but these represented a mere 25 percent of the total. Some 20 percent of the voters followed orders from Perón and cast blank ballots; the UCRI came in third with 16 percent; and the remaining 40 percent was distributed among no fewer than forty-seven minor parties, mostly remnants of the old conservative and Socialist parties, several provincial offshoots from Radicalism, and a string of fringe rightist and left groups.

Illia's was thus a daunting task. He was to rebuild constitutional rule on the legacy of Perón and repeated political intrusions from the

Army, and he was to do so after a decade in which prices had risen at an average annual rate of more than 30 percent. The instrument he possessed was a highly unrepresentative government; in Congress the new administration controlled only a third of the seats, the rest shared among nine other parties. Unlike Frondizi five years earlier, Illia made no effort before the election to enlist Peronist support and therefore enjoyed no organized working-class backing. Upon his inauguration, the Army resumed its customary invigilatory role in the backrooms of power.[45]

As the direct heirs of *yrigoyenismo*, Illia and his followers had campaigned on the antiquated Radical slogans of honest, democratic government and a commitment to expunging foreign influence in the oil industry. Illia immediately annulled Frondizi's oil contracts. Helped by the upturn in the economy, he then quietly and unobtrusively began to rally popular support by promoting a large increase in consumption. In 1964 prices were frozen, but a 30 percent ceiling was set for wage increases. As a result, real wages grew by an estimated 6.4 percent, and automobile sales rose by 65 percent. But the state deficit that year increased by 140 percent and was largely financed by bank borrowings. Despite the price freeze, the program was patently inflationary. Although inflation usually subsided during the upward phase of the economic cycle, throughout 1963 and for two years following it held fast at around 25 percent. The price freeze swiftly collapsed, forcing the government into a 58 percent devaluation in April 1964. Subsequently, Illia resorted to creeping devaluation in an effort to help farmers and exports by keeping a consistent margin between costs and revenues in the farming sector. Manufacturers then began stockpiling imports, which again strained the balance of payments.

Despite the growth of consumption, Illia's program satisfied few outside the Radicals' traditional middle-class constituency, who gained substantially from the growth of state spending and state jobs. On the right, Illia fell foul of such organizations as the Rural Society and the Industrial Union, which had banded together in an antistatist, free enterprise association known as ACIEL, *Asociación para la defensa de la libre empresa* (Association for the Defense of Free Enterprise). They attacked the state deficit, the government's devotion to price and exchange controls, its favors to state companies like the YPF, and its continuation of the freeze on agricultural rents first introduced under Ramírez in 1943.

But the major opposition to Illia came from the unions and the CGT, and it followed upon a new effort by the government to divide

Peronism and coopt working-class support. In early 1964 the latter adopted a battle plan (*Plan de Lucha*), a campaign of selective strikes and factory sit-ins designed to win wage increases and harass the government. The first of these challenges came in May 1964, soon after the devaluation, and others followed later in the year and into 1965. As the onslaught mounted, Illia's position began to crumble; like Frondizi, he was obliged to gamble on an electoral success to shore up his authority. But in mid 1965 the Peronists were again victorious in the congressional elections, as the Blue faction, which still dominated the Army, failed to enforce the bans against them. In Congress the Peronists immediately began sabotaging the government's legislative program; political chaos soon prevailed once more.[46]

Early in 1966, the economy completed another three-year cycle and headed for recession. The government attempted austerity but had to abandon the new wage freeze in response to a wave of strikes. Illia now lost the backing of the Army. In late 1965 General Juan Carlos Onganía, leader of the Blues in 1963, had resigned as Army Chief of Staff. Everyone recognized in this the portent of a new coup. In preparation Onganía sought to repair the recent divisions in the Army and renewed the hints he had made in 1962 that a new military government would pursue a more popular line; once more "Peronism without Perón" was in the air. On 28 June 1966 the coup was executed cleanly and clinically: tanks and troops converged on Government House; when Illia refused to resign, they simply swept him out into the street. There was no other resistance, nor even much protest at the departure of constitutional government. Indeed, in many quarters, from the major business associations to the Peronist unions, the coup was welcomed as a new beginning, which it proved to be, although in unexpected ways.[47]

THE PEOPLE'S CHALLENGE, 1966–1976

The coup was expected to result in a neo-Peronist mediatory regime that would enjoy broad popular and corporate backing, a regime pledged to political balance and compromise. However, as quickly became clear, Onganía had discarded such ideas; they had provided a simple means to manipulate the unions and to quell immediate organized resistance among them. His government's implicit model was the military regime that had been established in Brazil in 1964. Following the Brazilians, Onganía sought to create a modernizing autocracy that would change society from above, with or without popular backing.

To intimidate potential opponents, Onganía's government made an ostentatious parade of its power. It banned the political parties and all political activities. In late July 1966 Onganía decreed an intervention in the national universities, ordering the police to use their clubs to expel students and faculty who allegedly constituted hotbeds of communism. In August the government also intervened in the sugar industry of Tucumán; to resolve the chronic problems of peasant *minifundios*, grinding poverty, and heavy unemployment, the government forcibly closed many small *ingenios* and amalgamated the larger ones. Later in 1966 it also became apparent that Onganía had no real intent of accommodation with the unions. A strike in the port of Buenos Aires elicited a military response, and the strike's leader, Eustaquio Tolosa, was sent to prison for an indefinite term. In early March 1967 the CGT replied by a general strike, but it was smothered by the government.

As the nation now realized, Onganía's was a hard-line regime prepared to make immediate resort to force to quell all competing institutions and any real or imaginary adversaries. Although the country had witnessed such behavior from earlier military governments, this one differed from its precursors in rejecting the label "provisional." Onganía declared his intent to remain in power indefinitely (*sin plazos*) and proclaimed *"La Revolución Argentina,"* a comprehensive program of national regeneration. He would first restore the economy, revive growth, and conquer inflation. He would then distribute the fruits of growth, thereby achieving "social peace," which would yield a "true democracy" (*la democracia verdadera*). The Onganía regime thus represented still another variant of corporatist thinking. Again the state would be employed in the pursuit of normative objectives like "social peace" or "true democracy." However, this one differed from past corporative schemes in rejecting the integration of interest groups with the state, and in postulating a largely isolated state power from which interest groups were explicitly excluded. Early in 1967, having completed his initial phase of consolidation, Onganía embarked on the first stage of his enterprise. In March he appointed Adalbert Krieger Vasena as minister of the economy, charging him with the conception and execution of a new stabilization plan.[48]

The Krieger Vasena Plan of 1967 shared some features with its forerunners in 1952, 1959, and 1962. Preceded by a steep devaluation of 40 percent, it sought to check the state deficit by increasing rates charged by public corporations. Following Frondizi's plan, it renewed the commitment to foreign investment and, like Perón's effort in 1952, set strict guidelines on wages. But it differed from other schemes in its elaborate and sophisticated safeguards against both the substantial redistribution of income and the steep urban recessions that had dogged most past stabilization ventures. This time the windfall profits of farmers and exporters induced by devaluation were to be taxed through "retentions" (*retenciones*), a system reminiscent in principle of the IAPI. These revenues would be plowed back into the urban economy to increase public investment and food subsidies, and promote exports of manufactured goods. To foster efficiency in domestic industry, Krieger Vasena lowered tariffs; to strengthen the war on inflation, he rewarded with public contracts those firms that kept their prices stable. In sum, the plan was intended to increase exports while protecting domestic consumption, to generate growth while avoiding an accumulating undercurrent of inflation.

For some time the plan effected an apparently magical transformation. By the first half of 1969 inflation had fallen to an annual rate of a mere 7.6 percent. This was accomplished, at least according to the government, while the aggregate wage share in national income remained roughly constant at 43 to 44 percent. Industrial growth surged, as the manufacturing sector recovered from the 1966 recession, expanding from 1.6 percent growth in 1967, to 6.9 percent in 1968, and 11.1 percent in 1969. Between 1966 and 1969 public investment increased at an annual rate of 22 percent, with new investment in energy doubling, and in roads, tripling. The government hastened construction of the huge Chocón Dam in Neuquén, a scheme intended permanently to alleviate power shortages in the metropolitan area. The Paraná and Uruguay rivers were spanned by new bridges. Many observers thought that the long and eagerly awaited Argentine economic miracle had at last arrived. From Washington in February 1969, the Krieger Vasena Plan was hailed as "one of the great economic success stories of the postwar."[49]

Meanwhile, after an initial flurry of repression, Onganía seemed to have imposed political peace. The failure of the general strike in March 1967 dissipated the energy of the CGT, which for some time had been torn by internal conflict. A "participationist" faction was headed by Augusto Vandor, leader of the metallurgical workers' union, the UOM; members of another faction called themselves *ortodoxos* or *Los 62 junto a Perón* (The Sixty-Two at Perón's Side). The *vandoristas* remained ready to strike a deal with the government; its opponents bitterly resisted it. As this rift widened, a third union faction appeared in April 1968, *La CGT de los Argentinos*, led by a young printer, Raimundo Ongaro. Exploiting such divisions, Onganía began ruling through executive councils with an aloofness and steadfastness reminiscent of a Bourbon viceroy. He eluded questions over the longer-term political future with Olympian references to a "community of solidarity" (*Comunidad Solidaria*), which would be the climactic stage in his grand revolutionary design. In the population at large an unusual quiescence prevailed. The banned political parties' occasional manifestos against the government passed unheeded.[50]

But suddenly and quite unexpectedly Onganía's construction lay in ruins, and the president was left scrambling desperately to salvage his shattered authority. In late May 1969 the city of Córdoba erupted in a massive riot, primarily instigated by university students and automobile workers. Declaring an active strike (*paro activo*), the protesters swept into the city center, burning cars and buses along the way. As the tumult unfolded, a broad cross-section of the city's population joined the strikers. For some forty-eight hours the city became a theater for pitched battles between rioters and police.

In scale the *cordobazo*, as the event became known, surpassed all popular demonstrations during the past generation, rivalling the great general strike during the *Semana Trágica* in early 1919 or the march of Peronist workers in October 1945. The strike immediately exposed the fragility of Onganía's "social peace"; recent quiescence now appeared not to have marked the extinction of dissent but a state of temporary dormancy; in cutting the normal institutional channels through which dissent expressed itself, the government had been merely winding a spring from whose recoil dissent reappeared in devastating force. The eruption in Córdoba divided the Army: Onganía and his followers blamed Cuban influence and wanted a determined show of force; the other contingent, led by the Army commander, General Alejandro Lanusse, preferred concession. The latter view prevailed, and within days Onganía replaced his entire cabinet, including Krieger Vasena.

Although the *cordobazo* shocked the population at large, which had failed to perceive the underlying unrest, it was far from a random, spontaneous outburst. If its style was reminiscent of recent popular outbreaks abroad, notably the Paris *événements* of May 1968, no evidence supported the government's contention that it had been provoked by "outside agents." Rather, the *cordobazo* was foremost the expression of a purely homegrown restlessness and aggression nurtured by a generation of inflation and mistrust for government, a latent discontent stirred to action by Onganía's methods and the effects of the stabilization plan.

In the universities, for example, the intervention of 1966 had been followed by the suppression of most established student union bodies. For three years students could but silently nurse their grievances in isolation; with the dissolution of their organizations, students' political activities could not but assume wildcat, apparently spontaneous forms. The longer their grievances accumulated, the more likely it became that a relatively trivial issue could trigger a violent response. The powderkeg was also lit by the Krieger Vasena Plan, which emphasized "efficiency" in the state sector and effected reductions in government subsidies to the universities. When the University of Corrientes sought to economize by leasing university refectories to private firms and proposing stiff increases in food prices, its students went on strike, in March 1969. In the ensuing melee, a student died at the hands of the police. From here the student strikes spread, first to Rosario and in May to Córdoba.

The automobile workers' participation in the *cordobazo* resulted in part from the fact that many day students worked nightshifts at the factories, and many young car workers were night students; these two groups served as a conduit between affairs in the university and those in the factories. Beyond this, the Córdoba car workers had an unusual position in the nation's labor movement. Nearly all the automobile factories postdated Perón, and their new unions had no tradition of Peronist regimentation from the CGT. In this new working-class city, which had doubled in size during the past twenty years, the unions were smaller, plant-based, more democratic and independent. Thus these union members were able to act even as the labor movement at large was paralyzed.

But the Córdoba auto workers were "the best paid in the country," a stupefied Krieger Vasena complained after his overthrow. Yet this simple measure of wage differentials had little relevance to the depth of their long-standing grievances and their militancy. During the recession in 1966 the largest of the automobile firms, FIAT and IKA-Renault, had laid off large numbers of men. The subsequent unrest persisted despite the later recovery, as militant shop stewards sustained the atmosphere of confrontation. Immediately before the May strike a management campaigned to deprive the workers of their traditionally free Saturdays, known as the "English Saturday" (*sábado inglés*), and to increase by four hours the forty-four–hour work week. The workers viewed the proposal as a conspiracy to impose new redundancies and called for a strike.

Finally, insomuch as the *cordobazo* involved wide segments of the city's population, it was sparked by malaise in the local economy and the unpopularity of the administration installed by Onganía in 1966. The press had observed trouble brewing shortly before the protest; in March 1969 a reporter commented: "The increase in taxes, the closing of some factories, and the dismissals in other industries of the province, added to the failure of the harvest, are capable of bringing a difficult situation in Córdoba toward the middle of the year." He predicted a "popular insurrection" in protest against the province's "oligarchic" government.[51]

In the months following the *cordobazo* the political calm of the past three years was repeatedly shattered by violence. At the end of June the "participationist" wing of the CGT suffered a major blow when an unknown gang assassinated Augusto Vandor. The next day, during a visit by Nelson Rockefeller, who had come as the Nixon administration's special envoy from the United States, bombs largely destroyed a chain of supermarkets in Buenos Aires in which the Rockefeller family had a controlling interest. In September Rosario witnessed a smaller reenactment of the *cordobazo*. Dissenters also issued a torrent of antigovernment propaganda that focused on Onganía's "dictatorship" and the "sell-out" to foreigners since 1966.

After replacing Krieger Vasena, Onganía attempted to prolong the stabilization plan, but as opposition mounted at year-end he was forced to solicit support by relaxing wage controls, a move that nullified the anti-inflation effort. The economy now began to reassume a familiar aspect. The *cordobazo* had abruptly reversed the steady influx of foreign funds and provoked a headlong flight of capital; the peso trembled against an onslaught of speculative pressures; the balance of payments turned sharply into a deficit, which was exacerbated by another crisis in beef exports. In 1969 some 13.5 million head of cattle were unloaded on the market for slaughter, and earnings from beef were high. But in 1970 the contraction in the meat trade was the most serious to date, prompting the collapse of Swift International, one of the oldest and largest of the American meat-packing companies. Like the handover of the British railroads in 1947, the nationalization of Swift in 1971 concluded another major chapter in the history of the Argentine economy.

In early 1970, only three years after Krieger Vasena had proclaimed the "last" such measure, the government was again forced to devalue. The renewed economic difficulties elicited reappraisals of the Krieger Vasena Plan, as it now seemed too simple to attribute its failure to political disorder alone. The fall in meat earnings, which many ranchers blamed on recent government tax measures, and signs even before the *cordobazo* that foreign investment had begun to slacken were in themselves sufficient causes for the current balance-of-payments difficulties. In this light the successes of the late 1960s could be interpreted as not so much the result of deliberate policy but in large part the outcome of the normal economic cycle, which in itself would have produced short-term growth and falling inflation. Like Frondizi, Krieger Vasena seemed merely to have increased the pace of short-term expansion through foreign investment; his failure to overcome the structural constraints on sustained growth imposed by agriculture's stagnation and industry's need for imports again led eventually to renewed recession. Further, although the stabilization plan had undoubtedly attenuated shifts in income distribution after the 1967 devaluation, as conditions in Córdoba had shown, it did squeeze certain sectors, provoking a fall in consumption. During the subsequent upward phase of the economic cycle, as the labor market tightened, came the familiar round of labor protest, rendered this time more virulent by the government's repression of the regular channels of communication.[52]

As the challenges mounted, the government's grip weakened. By early 1970 Córdoba was becoming ungovernable: student power now ruled the university, and radical left-wing unions, the largest and most militant of which was SITRAC–SITRAM (*Sindicato de Trabajadores Concord–Sindicato de Trabajadores Materfer*), organized in the two FIAT plants of Concord and Materfer. SITRAC–SITRAM, which called itself an exemplar of "class syndicalism" (*sindicalismo clasista*) and was directed by mostly Communist leaders, demanded a break with the IMF, the expropriation of "monopolies," default on the foreign debt, the suppression of "oligarchy," an end to "bureaucratic centralism" in the trade unions, and workers' control on the factory shopfloor.[53]

Finally, armed struggle came to Argentina. In March 1970 a guerrilla unit, the *Frente Argentino de Liberación*, kidnapped but later released the Paraguayan consul in the northeastern city of Posadas. In June a Peronist group, calling itself the *Montoneros–Comando Juan José Valle*, stunned the country by kidnapping former president Aramburu. The *Montoneros* proclaimed the abduction a reprisal for the execution of General Valle and his associates in 1956, and they demanded to be told the whereabouts of the body of Eva Perón, a mystery since the *Revolución Libertadora*. Aramburu was interrogated for six days and then executed.[54]

While guerrilla groups were not unknown in Argentina before 1970, earlier groups had exerted little impact. Several small organizations had sought to imitate Fidel Castro by leading a revolution from the northwestern *sierras*, in Salta or Tucumán: the *Uturuncos*, or "Tigermen," in 1959, the People's Guerrilla Army in 1963, and the *17 de Octubre* cadre in 1968; a right-wing group organized in 1964, the *Movimiento Nacional Revolucionario Tacuara*, was the only one to base itself in the cities. The rural guerrillas set up training camps on isolated farms or in the hills. From these bases they sought to link up with local peasant communities and also made small forays against the rural gendarmerie or village police posts. Nearly all members of these groups were middle-class students with ties to the numerous fringe parties that had arisen since 1955. Ill-equipped for the extreme privations of the rugged environment, some perished of undernourishment; the rest, except for the Tacuara leaders who fled to Uruguay, were captured or killed by the police. None of the cadres survived for more than a few months.

By the end of 1970, however, eighteen months after the *cordobazo* and six months after Aramburu's execution, three new Peronist groups—the *Montoneros*, the *Fuerzas Armadas Peronistas* (FAP), and the *Fuerzas Armadas Revolucionarias* (FAR)—as well as the non-Peronist People's Revolutionary Army, or *Ejército Revolucionario del Pueblo* (ERP), were active. The ERP represented the armed wing of a small Trotskyite party, the *Partido Revolucionario de los Trabajadores* (PRT), which formed in July 1970. For the next two years the guerrilla bands, none of them having more than a few score activists, conducted separate operations, the Peronists largely in and around Buenos Aires, the ERP primarily in Córdoba. They staged kidnaps, bank robberies, occasional assassinations of senior Army or police personnel, and Robin Hood escapades in which multinationals were forced to make charity handouts in the shantytowns in return for abducted executives. In 1973 the Peronist groups united under the *Montoneros*, a unification that conferred leadership on the original group of ten, under Mario Firmenich, that had kidnapped Aramburu.

Despite their individual ideological coloring, the guerrilla bands were composed overwhelmingly of lapsed students or newly qualified members of the professions, many from affluent middle-class families and nearly all in their early twenties. All, too, were disgruntled with the traditional left, its impotence in elections or among the unions, and they now proclaimed popular revolution as an immediate goal. This revolution was to be accomplished by attracting mass support and by gradually intensifying guerrilla activities in a succession of stages or "leaps" (*saltos*). All the guerrilla bands also had a high proportion of female combatants. Mirroring the sexual revolution of the 1960s, their cells often also made the guerrilla groups poignant symbols of the crisis afflicting the Argentine middle-class family.

These similarities aside, a considerable gulf separated the *Montoneros* and the ERP. The former emanated mainly from the eastern cities and closely identified with the urban-based, populist, and nationalist ideals of Peronism. They were committed to destroy "oligarchy," expel "foreign monopolies," uphold international nonalignment, return to the redistributive policies of the late 1940s, and expand the economic functions of the state. The *Montoneros* also inherited a radical leftist outlook within Peronism, one that had first appeared in the early 1960s. In 1962 one of the factions in the CGT had issued the "Program of Huerta Grande," which proposed land expropriation without compensation, higher protective tariffs for native industry, and renewed nationalization measures. A second major influence on the *Montoneros* was the late Peronist intellectual known by his nom de plume of John William Cooke, who in the early 1960s began propagating a view of Peronism as the Argentine counterpart of Castro's movement in Cuba. Cooke also popularized the doctrines of armed struggle. Within Peronism both the Huerta Grande faction and Cooke had strongly opposed "union bureaucrats" like Vandor, men ready to bend with the wind and collaborate with dictators. As Cooke's heirs, the *Montoneros* committed themselves to a struggle on two fronts—against the Army and against the less radical, conciliatory Peronists. Their advent marked the radicalization of a segment of the middle class, which sought to forge a popular, working-class base through control over organized labor.

The ERP, by contrast, exemplified the Argentine left's long-standing mistrust of Peronism, an unease that dated back to Perón's anticommunist measures in the mid 1940s. If Peronism could no longer be dismissed as "fascist," it was "bonapartist" or "bourgeois reformist" and, as such, lacked genuine revolutionary potential. The ERP thus rejected Cooke's view of Peronism as a "national liberation" movement. Many members of the ERP, among them its Tucumán-born leader Mario Santucho, were from cities and universities in the interior. Their aim was not the penetration and takeover of Peronism, but the mobilization of a new political constituency—non-Peronist workers in Córdoba through unions like SITRAC–SITRAM, the peasants of Tucumán still suffering the aftereffects of the intervention of 1966, the mestizo "black faces" (*cabecitas negras*) of the shantytowns. In 1973 the ERP disavowed the label *Trotskyite* and proclaimed itself "Guevarist," but either way its vision of revolution was much broader than that of the *Montoneros*. For the ERP the revolution was not a limited national and nationalist movement, but rather part of a pan-American struggle against imperialism. In this vein they aspired less to refurbish the nation-state than to transcend it.[55]

The coming of the guerrillas in mid 1970 immediately injected a new vicious dialectic into the country's conflict-ridden politics. In April 1970 an extreme right-wing group, reputedly composed of off-duty police, known as *Mano* ("Hand"), attacked the Soviet ambassador in retaliation for the kidnapping in Posadas. Counterterrorism escalated rapidly, and by the end of 1970 *Mano* and other clandestine right-wing groups conducted their own series of kidnaps, abducting students or union militants of Peronist or leftist affiliation. Most of these victims simply vanished without trace, and the few to reappear spoke of torture. By the early months of 1971 one such "disappearance" occurred on average each eighteen days.[56]

Meanwhile, the death of Aramburu had toppled Onganía's regime. Before his abduction Aramburu had been rumored to be intriguing Onganía's overthrow and his own return to power. When the former president disappeared the government made such suspiciously dilatory efforts to find him that some believed the government itself had contrived the whole conspiracy. The incident brought to a crisis the rift between Onganía and the Army that had arisen during the *cordobazo*. Since then Lanusse had pressed repeatedly for formal power sharing between the Army and the administration. When this demand was presented once more after Aramburu's kidnap, Onganía again demurred and was overthrown with the same lack of ceremony he had accorded Illia four years before.[57]

Lanusse chose to remain in the background and allowed the presidency to pass to General Roberto M. Levingston, a little-known figure who had recently served as military attaché in Washington. The keynote of late 1970 was further retreat by the government. Levingston attempted to restore the stabilization program, but when this effort failed, he abruptly altered course. By October he struggled to head off recession and to enact expansionist measures intended to deflect the flood tide of propaganda against multinationals and foreign investors. Thus he took a weak stance on wages and adopted a "Buy Argentine" law, which sought to give native manufacturers a larger share of the domestic market. To forestall any recurrence of the *cordobazo*, the government began a campaign to erase income disparities between Buenos Aires and the provinces.

Levingston's concessions had little effect. In December 1970 the still nominally banned political parties, including the Peronists, took the unprecedented step of issuing a joint manifesto. Entitled *"Hora del Pueblo"* ("Hour of the People"), it demanded the immediate restoration of civilian rule. In February 1971 Córdoba erupted in a second violent, explosive demonstration provoked by the local governor's verbal attacks on radical agitators in the province, whom he called "vipers" (*víboras*). The new movement, thus dubbed the *viborazo*, seemed even more dangerous than its predecessor and had an air of deliberate orchestration, with evidence that the ERP had a hand in mobilizing demonstrators and in committing acts of sabotage. The *viborazo* intimated that the guerrillas, unless checked, would soon be capable of engineering popular insurrection. The resulting internal furor in the Army produced yet another change of government, on 22 March 1971. After less than nine months in office, Levingston was replaced by Lanusse. The last remnants of the *Revolución Argentina* proclaimed by Onganía in 1966 were abandoned.[58]

Lanusse promised elections to restore civilian government, but military rule persisted for two more years. As the guerrillas expanded their operations, the three armed services were drawn steadily into a war on "subversion." Each blow struck by the guerrillas was matched in kind by clandestine groups on the right, and torture became a standard technique in the police interrogation of suspects. In August 1972 a group of imprisoned guerrillas, mostly members of the ERP held in the Patagonian naval garrison near Trelew, attempted to escape. Sixteen guerrillas, among them the wife of Mario Santucho, were immediately recaptured and summarily shot. In Mendoza, in the resort town of Mar del Plata, and in the cities of Cipolletti and General Roca, in Rio Negro, came a new spate of riots that resembled the *cordobazo* in that the participants came from both working-class and middle-class groups. The protests developed with apparent spontaneity in response to arbitrary municipal impositions related to inflation; the *mendozazo* of April 1972, for example, was provoked by stiff increases in local electricity rates.

Though Lanusse failed to prevent these outbreaks or to curb the guerrillas, he managed at least to contain them. His response to the riots in Córdoba mixed populist and repressive measures. The provincial government was directed to make at least a show of meeting local grievances, but to control the radicals the Army filled the city with troops and arrested student and union leaders. By the end of 1972 the Army had accomplished one major objective, the decline of *sindicalismo clasista* and SITRAC–SITRAM, and had forced the ERP to scale down its activities in the city. Although for some time Córdoba remained in latent ferment, the *viborazo* was the last major movement of its kind.

In Buenos Aires, where the government's fear of popular insurrection was most acute, Lanusse used concession, seeking to shore up or resurrect more-moderate institutions or associations, while again isolating the extremists. Seeing the unions as the key to control, the government minimized its own role in collective bargaining and allowed the unions and their leaders to gain popularity as agents of wage increases. The tactic proved a successful counter to Onganía's emasculation of the unions, which had provoked some, like Ongaro's *CGT de los Argentinos*, toward the radical position embraced by SITRAC–SITRAM in Córdoba. By the end of 1972 this trend had been largely overcome, and the CGT was reunited under conservative Peronists. This was a crucial accomplishment, since it preserved the unions and the workers from the influence of the *Montoneros*. Although the guerrillas continued to gain new recruits, they now faced the Army and the government on one side and the union "bureaucrats" on the other. Renewed inflation, however, proved to be the price of concessions to the CGT. When Levingston abandoned stabilization in late 1970, inflation leapt swiftly to 30 percent; between March 1971 and March 1972 it climbed to 58 percent, and it rose higher still over the next year.

Through the political parties Lanusse sought additional protection against radical dissidents. In July 1972 he proclaimed a "great national convenant" (*Gran Acuerdo Nacional*), inviting all "democratic forces" to unite with him in the struggle against "subversion" and in the drafting of procedures for a return to constitutional rule. Lanusse's idea, which recalled the program of the Blues in 1962, was to rally the parties to name him as the candidate of a national coalition. To this end the government frequently struck a populist pose: Minister of Agriculture Antonio Di Rocco encouraged debates on land reform, and another minister, Francisco Manrique, organized Evita-like handouts among the poor in the provinces. Yet the parties sensed that they needed to yield nothing to Lanusse and refused to cooperate. Lanusse then offered more concessions, and in a final effort to stem the unrest Lanusse did the unthinkable: he lifted the eighteen-year ban on Peronism. Although his intention was to undercut the passion for revolt and to restore nostalgia as the pivotal force in the nation's politics, Lanusse in effect resurrected Juan Perón as the cardinal figure in the country's affairs.[59]

After his hasty and largely unlamented departure in September 1955, Perón passed his exile in several Latin American countries whose governments were reminiscent of his own: Stroessner's Paraguay, Pérez Jiménez's Venezuela, Batista's Cuba, and Trujillo's Dominican Republic. Forced from most of his refuges either by pressure from Argentina or by revolution, in the early 1960s he took up residence in Madrid, where he remained for a decade under the protection of General Franco. Throughout his long exile Perón maintained close contact with his native land, keeping alive the expectation he would eventually return to power. Aramburu's vendettas had helped him retain a grip on the unions, and Perón also employed what became known as his "pendular" technique of bestowing favor first on one faction of his movement and then on another, while repeatedly playing them off against each other. He sent personal delegates to Buenos Aires to deliver and execute his orders; these emissaries were kept on short rein by constant replacements.

Throughout his exile Perón revealed remarkable political durability, but, by the mid 1960s his influence showed signs of waning. As he was now nearing seventy, the likelihood of the promised restoration (known among devout Peronists as *El Retorno*) seemed to diminish, while several of the most powerful union officials, led by Vandor, were gravitating toward *"Peronismo sin Perón."* To counter the threat Perón at times supported left-wing elements in his movement, the Huerta Grande faction and the followers of John William Cooke, and made occasional dramatic gestures to reassert personal control. In December 1964, despite threats that his plane would be destroyed in midflight, he declared his intent to return to Buenos Aires, but flew only as far as Brazil before returning to Madrid. Though this adventure helped rally his supporters, it did not unseat Vandor. Nor did Perón appear to gain much during the aftermath of the *cordobazo*, as events suggested less a revival of Peronism than the gestation of a new radicalism destined to supersede it.[60]

Perón's rehabilitation was due substantially to Lanusse, who invoked his name and fanned expectations of his return in order to curb the growth of the independent left and relieve the pressures on himself. In 1972 the government added a residence requirement to its new electoral law, which effectively barred Perón's candidacy in the forthcoming elections. But in every other respect Lanusse made Perón the center of attention, concessions that reached a climax in November 1972, when—to the acclaim of thousands of his supporters—Perón was allowed to return to Buenos Aires, for a brief visit.

Perón moved deftly and surely. He had already restored full control over the unions and, by joining in the rhetoric against the multinationals, soon enlisted domestic business associations like the CGE. In 1972 the Peronist Youth (*Juventud Peronista*), previously a minor component of the movement, was revamped into a major association for dissident youth groups. Peronism, in its new polymorphous guise, was suddenly all things to all men, an almost perfect prototype of Latin American populism. Perón's name now evoked multifarious associations and expectations. Workers and unions envisioned the restoration of the late 1940s, while the propertied classes saw him as Argentina's de Gaulle, the symbol of conservative stability and defense against revolutionary anarchy. Simultaneously, Perón basked in the image invented by Cooke: he was a leader of national liberation. In dealings with Lanusse he refused to disavow the *Montoneros*, whom he called the "special formations" of his movement; they were to be his leverage in extracting concessions from the government. Meanwhile, he cultivated the radical youth through hints of *"trasvasamiento generacional"*—his willingness to make them his political heirs.[61]

The unforeseen dénouement to Onganía's *Revolución Argentina* was thus the rebirth of Peronism on a breadth and scale even greater than thirty years before. In the election of March 1973 the Peronist alliance, the FREJULI (*Frente Justicialista de Liberación*), was victorious with almost 49 percent of the vote. Far behind trailed the Radicals with a little over 21 percent, with the rest of the vote taken by minority parties. Since Perón's candidacy had been vetoed by the Army, the president-elect was Hector Cámpora, Perón's most recent "personal delegate" in Argentina. Cámpora, typical of those who had served in this office, had no personal base in the movement, serving only as Perón's stalking-horse. Cámpora took office toward the end of May, to remain there a mere forty-nine days.[62]

Soon after Cámpora's inaugural latent tensions surfaced in the Peronist movement—products of its recent headlong growth, its extreme heterogeneity, and the power struggle between the *Montoneros* and the union leaders. Among Cámpora's first acts was to declare a political amnesty and the release of all imprisoned guerrillas. The *Montoneros* now abandoned clandestine recruiting and made an open bid to broaden their base and capture strategic positions of power. They took control of the Peronist Youth, established front organizations in the universities and among the shantytowns, and were similarly active among the unions, where the union "bureaucrats" promptly began to organize resistance. In June 1973 Perón made ready for his second return to Buenos Aires. An estimated half million people trekked out from the city to the airport at Ezeiza to meet him. As they waited, pitched battles erupted between armed hirelings of the unions and the *Montoneros*. Scores of persons, if not hundreds, died in the affray.

Ezeiza highlighted Cámpora's inability to control the movement and to hold at bay its contending forces. By June 1973 many observers, among them the Army leaders, were concluding that only Perón could abate the conflict and achieve stability. In July Cámpora was unseated after Perón theatrically withdrew his personal support from the government. The presidency passed to Raúl Lastiri, formerly president of the Chamber of Deputies, pending the September presidential elections. Perón received 60 percent of the vote, and on 17 October 1973, the twenty-eighth anniversary of his great triumph in 1945, he began his third elected term as president.[63]

Perón's restoration was an admission of political bankruptcy by a military now prepared to clutch at any straw to contain the radical left. Even so, his reinstatement constituted a quite remarkable change of fortune for Perón, still more so because the country now exuded a sense of deliverance and a sudden optimism rarely seen in recent decades. Yet Cámpora's fall had brought little abatement in political violence. The *Montoneros* undertook a campaign to annihilate union leaders; in September 1973 they assassinated José Rucci, secretary-general of the CGT. As the Peronists grew increasingly hostile, the ERP began preparing for renewed guerrilla warfare, amassing funds from kidnaps and robberies in late 1973. In January 1974 the ERP mounted a full-scale assault against an Army garrison in the city of Azul. Meanwhile, right-wing violence also increased. By early 1974 most kidnaps and murders of leftist militants were the work of a new secret organization, the Argentine Anticommunist Alliance (*Alianza Argentina Anticomunista*), known familiarly as the "Triple A"; evidence pointed toward the federal police as its guiding hand.

Perón's ability to succeed now also depended on his age and health, for he had resumed the presidency at age seventy-eight. To mask the divisions in his movement he had chosen his third wife, María Estela Martínez de Perón, "Isabel," as his running mate. Like Cámpora, she had been among his couriers to Buenos Aires and was politically inexperienced. In late 1973 the outcome of the recent political settlement seemed to depend first and foremost on Perón's own ability to survive.

As he had in 1946, Perón took the presidency at a fortuitous moment. In 1973 a world commodity boom brought an unexpected 65 percent increase in export earnings and a swift expansion of the reserves. Wheat prices, for example, which averaged $67 a ton in 1972, climbed to $116 a ton by early 1974; thus between 1972 and 1973 foreign reserves jumped from $465 million to $1.3 billion. Since the *cordobazo* extreme recession had been staved off by expansionist economic policies. Yet between 1970 and 1972 growth was under 3 percent; in 1973 it climbed to 6 percent. Throughout 1973 inflation steadily declined, from an annual rate of 80 percent in May to only 30 percent by October. As throughout the postwar period, improving economic conditions invariably favored greater political calm, which Perón immediately encouraged. As he took the presidency, he indulged in effusive shows of reconciliation with former political enemies, some of whom he had imprisoned or driven into exile twenty years earlier.

Despite any gestures to the contrary, eighteen years of exile, and the circumstances surrounding his recent return, had done little to develop Perón's ideas. As in 1946, the kernels of his programs were income redistribution in favor of labor, the expansion of employment, and renewed social reform. The new Peronism was to resurrect the IAPI, increase food subsidies, and tax farming; the state would once more control the banks, support native industry, and regulate trade through highly protective tariffs and multiple exchange rates; numerous plans were drafted to trim the influence of foreign corporations and to extend nationalization. Perón remained adept in the exploitation of symbols. During his negotiations with Lanusse in 1972 the embalmed body of Eva Perón was rediscovered in a secret resting place in Italy. Perón brought it back to Argentina and laid new plans for the construction of a national mausoleum.

Another facet of Perón's program in 1973 had its antecedents in the stabilization plan of 1952. To quell inflation the Peronists proposed that the CGT and the CGE, representing employers, negotiate an agreement on prices and incomes. Under this social compact (*Pacto Social*) the wage share in national income would rise over a four-year period to roughly the level of the early 1950s; the unions, after receiving an initial large wage boost, would agree to defer new collective bargaining agreements for a two-year period; and price controls would prevail, leaving profits to increase along with the expansion of demand. When the compact was first concluded under Cámpora in June 1973 inflation fell rapidly. In the first year of the agreement prices rose by only 17 percent.[64]

As recovery continued and inflation fell, public backing for Perón soared. Soon he felt himself strong enough to reinstate the political agenda of his first government—purge the movement, strengthen his personal grip, and eliminate independent factions. In 1946 his targets were the *laboristas*; in early 1974, the *Montoneros* and the Peronist Youth. Perón's demeanor toward them had begun to change after the Ezeiza incident in June 1973, and hardened into thinly veiled hostility after Rucci's assassination in September. It now became apparent that Perón had used the left as an instrument for his return to power and that the left, in a mix of blind ingenuousness and opportunism, had allowed him to do so. But his new plan, for which he had enthusiastic backing in both the Army and the CGT, was to destroy it. Soon after taking the presidency, Perón endorsed changes in the penal code providing stiffer sentences for acts of terrorism; however, he ignored the activities of the Triple A. He was also courting the leaders of the CGT, buttressing their authority by reinstating union verticality, another of his once-favored techniques. A new union law in early 1974 proposed the reconstruction of the unions as industrywide federations under the CGT, which would again enjoy full faculties of intervention in individual unions. To protect and stabilize the present union leadership, the law established a four-year interval between labor congresses.

As Perón closed ranks with the CGT, he began denouncing "infiltrators" in the movement, attacks that were interpreted as the signal for open purges of leftists in the provinces. The internecine conflict became manifest in May 1974, when Perón addressed the crowds in the Plaza de Mayo on Labor Day. Greeted by a barrage of remonstrances from the Peronist Youth and the *Montoneros*, he retorted angrily and unyieldingly, calling them "callow and stupid" (*imberbes y estúpidos*). The split in the movement was now public, and each side hastened to marshal its forces. But on 1 July 1974 Perón succumbed to heart failure and died.[65]

With Perón's death the political settlement of 1973 shattered. His widow assumed the presidency as political and economic crisis, a storm of violence and inflation, reconverged. The *Montoneros* tried once more to gain a voice in the regime, but when again repulsed they repudiated Isabel and proclaimed a return to clandestine operations in September 1974. Like the ERP the year before, they sought to finance their campaign by robbery and kidnap, extorting millions of dollars from such escapades. In September the *Montoneros* abducted Juan Born and Jorge Born, owners of the largest of the grain-exporting houses in Buenos Aires, exacting a ransom estimated somewhere between $20 million and $60 million. Another $14 million was paid for the release of an American oil executive.

Late in 1974 guerrilla warfare resumed with a wave of bombings and assassinations. The chief victims were army and police personnel, and to a lesser degree union leaders and politicians who had had a leading role in preparing the elections of 1973. In the next twelve months the guerrillas' tactics came to include open rebellion. In Tucumán the ERP began a drive for control of the province; the *Montoneros*, increasingly active in the east, in October 1975 orchestrated the storming of an Army garrison in the northeastern province of Formosa; five hundred guerrillas took part.

As the guerrilla war grew in scale, resistance stiffened. In the latter half of 1974 the Triple A murdered some seventy of its opponents, mostly prominent leftist intellectuals or lawyers; by early 1975 they dispensed with leftists at the rate of fifty a week. Throughout 1974 the Army sought to stay clear of the conflict, but in early 1975 it intervened in full force. In Tucumán it ruthlessly hunted the guerrillas and initiated reprisals against those suspected of harboring them. The three armed services were now on full war footing; supported by the state security police (*Coordinación Federal*), each formed espionage networks and clandestine operational units. These forces, which soon dwarfed their adversaries, imposed repression by the use of unchecked, random, indiscriminate violence that struck without warning or warrant. The definition of *subversion* was broadened and became increasingly capricious, encompassing the mildest protest, whether made by the parties, the press, the universities, the legal profession, or the unions. The number of persons who simply disappeared (*los desaparecidos*) mounted rapidly, with some held hostage to deter the guerrillas; guerrilla actions were answered by the execution of hostages. Corpses were found floating in barrels in the River Plate, or left charred and unrecognizable on refuse dumps; other captives were rumored to have been hurled to their deaths from aircraft. From the prisons came detailed accounts of systematic torture.[66]

Above this sordid contest stood a government whose authority was rapidly deteriorating. Isabel Perón at first made faint gestures toward repairing the rift with the left, but once its grievances focused against her she left the issue to the armed forces and the police. In November 1974, following the assassination of the Chief of Police Alberto Vilar, the government decreed a state of siege, which gave the Army *carte blanche* authority to deal with the guerrillas. Isabel Perón meanwhile succumbed to the influence and direction of José López Rega, a member of Perón's personal entourage from Madrid and since May 1973 the minister of social welfare. Under his guidance she became another Peronist parody, an image of Evita, who sought popular esteem by mimicking the former first lady's public style, oratory, and exploitation of organized charity. López Rega's influence was reflected in the national budget: in 1975 the Ministry of Social Welfare collected 30 percent of all federal appropriations.

The new government's prospects were quickly compromised by renewed economic crisis. In July 1974 outbreaks of hoof-and-mouth disease in Europe incited bans on imported Argentine meat. More important, while the domestic economy expanded, oil prices soared after the Arab-Israeli War in 1973. Argentina's oil bill rose from $58 million in 1972, 3.1 percent of total imports, to $586 million, or 15.1 percent of imports, in 1974. To pay for the oil, and for numerous other imports undergoing similarly sharp price increases, the government resorted to the reserves, which dwindled as fast in 1974 as they had risen during the short-lived export boom the year before. Once the reserves were exhausted, a huge payments deficit mounted. By the end of 1975 export earnings had fallen by 25 percent and the deficit had risen to $1 billion.

The new crisis was not solely exogenous in origin; internal conditions and recent policies also had a major bearing on its germination and intensity. Since Cámpora's administration wages and public spending had sharply increased, but when commercial conditions altered the government made no attempt to check the expansion of the economy. For a time inflation was held at bay by the liquidation of the reserves and by the price freeze imposed by Perón in 1973; by late 1974, however, the sudden rampant growth of the black market illustrated the rising undercurrent of inflation.

Had Perón lived, such conditions would have tested him to the limit; to some extent they were also his doing. Instead, it was Isabel

Perón who became ensnared in the classic trap of the Latin American populists. To fight inflation she had to attack wages and consumption; to safeguard her political base she had to hold fast to expansion. Her government lurched first down one road and then down the other, forfeiting control over the economy and suffering a fatal procession of political defections. "Zero inflation" Perón had boasted in early 1974; a year later prices were rising at three-figure rates. In 1974 consumer prices rose by 24.2 percent, in 1975 by 183 percent.[67]

The defection of the Peronist left wing was immediately followed by another bitter contest between the movement's right wing, led by López Rega, and the unions. While the former pressed for holding the line on wages, despite rising prices, the latter demanded renegotiation of the *Pacto Social*. In May 1975 the debate exploded. Unable to contain pressures from the unions, Economy Minister Alfredo Gómez Morales resigned. The unions then won wage increases of up to 100 percent and also managed to unseat López Rega, who retired abroad after naming Celestino Rodrigo to replace Gómez Morales. Rodrigo decreed a draconian austerity package: a devaluation of 160 percent, a doubling in rates charged by public corporations, and a limit of 50 percent on wage increases. The unions replied with a general strike, dubbed the *rodrigazo*, the first ever under a Peronist government.[68] Isabel Perón yielded to the pressure by disavowing Rodrigo, who then resigned. Suffering from nervous collapse, she absented herself from the presidency and spent the next few months in intermittent seclusion.

After mid 1975, with the CGT now its dominant force, the government struggled to prevent any fall in real wages. The new economy minister, Antonio Cafiero, introduced wage indexing along with price controls, a combination that produced some grotesque distortions in relative prices: in late 1975 farmers complained that one pair of shoes cost the same as two cows. Inflation continued to mount, by the end of the year at a monthly rate of 30 percent. Meanwhile, the newly created system of union rule was nearing breakup. Toward the end of the year even leaders of the CGT began hinting at the need for wage restraint, hints that incited a string of wildcat strikes that the guerrillas sought to exploit by kidnapping executives and demanding wage increases for workers as ransom. Soon the unions were divided between *verticalistas* supporting the CGT and *antiverticalistas* wanting to prolong free wage bargaining.

By the end of 1975 the government was sustained by little more than a small coterie in the CGT, which the recent struggles had left largely bereft of rank-and-file support. To crown the many ironies of Isabel Perón's rule, the CGT now pushed for a stabilization plan. A new series of devaluations in early February 1976 were followed by overtures to the IMF in March. But no amount of tacking or backtracking could save the regime. Some months earlier Isabel Perón was alleged to have diverted large sums from a public charity into her personal account. Congress seized on the issue to open impeachment proceedings against her, a move supported by much of the Peronist bloc.

For more than a year surging inflation had been accompanied by growing violence—the classic scenario for a coup d'etat. The Air Force attempted one in late December 1975 but failed to win support from the Army. While intensifying the war on the guerrillas, the Army waited until the last vestiges of the government's popular support had crumbled and Peronism lay shattered. At length, on 24 March 1976 the Army abducted the president as a prelude to dissolving the government.[69] Once in power, the Army embarked on the conquest of any lingering resistance to a revolution in government whose aim was the total dismantlement of the Peronist state.

POSTSCRIPT: THE NEW AUTOCRACY AND ITS DECLINE, 1976–1982

The junta of 1976, led by General Jorge Rafael Videla, came to power with greater strength and freedom of maneuver than any of its military predecessors. With the collapse of Peronism, the disruption of the unions, and the population at large prostrated by strikes, lockouts, inflation, and terror, only the guerrillas offered organized resistance, but by March 1976 their numbers, too, were declining. In the past two years their sympathizers had been weeded out of the public administration, the universities, the mass media, and the unions. Their press organs were suppressed; and possession of their literature was declared an act of criminal subversion. Throughout the past six years both guerrilla bands had failed to obtain a broader popular base, for the *Montoneros* had little success in penetrating the unions even at the height of the conflict between *verticalistas* and *antiverticalistas*. In 1975 one of their front organizations, the *Partido Auténtico*, joined with another Peronist group to contest an election in Misiones but gathered only 9 percent of the vote. The ERP fared no better. In 1975 its forces in Tucumán were eradicated by the Army; that December eighty combatants, all but one secondary or university students, were killed in an attack on an Army garrison at Monte Chingolo, in the province of Buenos Aires. Even so, at the time of the coup the rebels were still capable of audacious bombings and assassinations.

The last phase of the guerrilla war was its bloodiest and most terrifying: all due process of law was overturned; military patrols infested the country; thousands vanished into the prisons and police torture chambers. During the previous six years the guerrillas' victims had numbered at most two or three hundred; the price now exacted in retaliation, mostly through "disappearances," was at least 10,000. The repression quite deliberately it seemed, was arbitrary, uncoordinated, and indiscriminate, which intensified its powers of intimidation. After the coup the combination of terror and collapsing living standards induced thousands to seek refuge abroad. But by 1978 the Army had crushed the guerrillas. Almost all of those who had failed to escape were tracked down and liquidated. Santucho was killed in 1976; the following year Firmenich fled to Italy.[70]

On taking power in March 1976, Videla declared that the coming of the new junta signaled "the final closing of one historical cycle and the beginning of another." In this spirit the regime conducted its war on subversion, demolished many of the new institutions created by the Peronists, and quashed all political opposition. A similar iconoclastic élan characterized its approach to the economy. For some five years after the coup economic management was entrusted to José A. Martínez de Hoz, a member of one of the great landed families and a prominent figure in banking. He immediately attacked hyperinflation and the steep balance-of-payments deficit by an onslaught on consumption and wages. After the coup the CGT was abolished, strikes were banned, and the war on subversion was broadened to encompass union leaders and workers suspected of plotting resistance. An authoritative report, issued January 1978, on the "disappearances" estimated that fewer than 20 percent of the victims were guerrillas and some 37 percent were factory workers, mostly second-level or shop-floor union leaders.[71]

In 1977 the wage share shrank to only 31 percent of national income, its lowest level since 1935; the near 50 percent plunge in real wages in 1976 was the fastest and steepest ever. The fall began after the *rodrigazo* in mid 1975. But it accelerated after March 1976 following new increases in public service rates, much higher food prices, and the curtailment of welfare subsidies. Further cuts were enforced through the transfer of state services to the provinces unaccompanied by increased central subsidies. The government, however, was reluctant to provoke open unemployment, lest the guerrillas gain new recruits. At 2.2 percent in February 1978 unemployment was lower than any period since the late 1940s. The income wrested from wage earners in 1976 and 1977 was propelled into farming, which rewarded Martínez de Hoz with a bumper harvest in 1976–1977. In 1976 foreign loans helped reestablish the reserves; export earnings increased by 33 percent, imports fell by 20 percent, and the previous year's $1 billion payments deficit became a surplus of $650 million. Meanwhile the government managed to reduce a heavy public-sector deficit by indexing taxes and freezing salaries among government workers.[72]

With Martínez de Hoz came a commitment not only to restore order in the economy but also to change and reconstruct it. The minister and the leading members of his team, all extreme market economists, attacked the heavy concentration of economic power in the state and pushed for its dismantlement. They wanted a prolonged attack on inflation by monetary controls. Inefficiencies would be conquered by open competition, and price distortions overcome by ending subsidies, tariff controls, and regulated exchange rates, and by the creation of new financial markets. Through an aggressive pursuit of foreign investment, Martínez de Hoz aimed to broaden the infrastructure for industry and create a rejuvenated, diversified export sector.[73]

Along with wages, manufacturing bore the main brunt of his program. The collapse in demand in 1976 prostrated the wage-good sector of industry; the textile industry, for example, suffered a 50 percent contraction. Industry also had to endure a graduated reduction in tariffs, an end to subsidized exports, new internal terms of trade that favored agriculture, and competition from agriculture for funds in an open capital market. In July 1977 representations against such measures by the CGE were met by the closure of the institution. By the first half of 1979 manufacturing, which had accounted for 38.1 percent of the gross domestic product in the boom year 1974, shrank to 35 percent. Steel output dropped from 4.4 million tons in 1974 to only 3.3 million tons in 1978. Between 1976 and 1978 manufacturing employment declined by 10 percent.[74]

The Army's war on subversion and Martínez de Hoz's program elicited opposite responses from outside observers, who detested the extreme brutalities of the former but generally praised the latter. In many respects, however, the two policies were complementary and inseparable. The butt for both was the urban sectors: the unions, industry, and much of the middle class. The Army's task, with the

war against subversion in part as a pretext, was to shatter their collective bargaining power and their means of resistance; Martínez de
Hoz's role was to weaken and ultimately destroy the economy on
which they subsisted, for example, by eliminating the state as a major
source of employment and the chief agent distributing resources in
urban society. If manufacturing survived his onslaught, it was likely
to do so in still more concentrated blocs. Even on optimistic assumptions—successful export diversification, conquest of balance-of-
payments constraints on growth, and the emergence of an efficient,
competitive manufacturing sector—the outlook for the bulk of urban
society seemed bleak. If the export sectors and high-technology industry, both of which had a poor record for generating employment,
became dominant and the state sector and small-scale manufacturing
were shorn of resources, urban society would be forced to undergo
profound internal change. Although some members of the middle
and working classes would find niches in the new order, most likely
would not, and they would suffer progressive pauperization. Urban
society's relatively open and egalitarian character would thus become
more dualistic, more like the rest of Latin America and the rest of the
underdeveloped world.

In the event Martínez de Hoz's program was applied only in part,
mainly to accomplish short-term recovery, for by 1978 it was losing
momentum. If united in the war on subversion, the Videla junta was
divided into three broad factions on issues of the longer-term political
future. The faction led by Admiral Emilio Massera, which evoked the
army Blues of 1962 and the line initially taken by Lanusse in 1971,
urged military populism, a new "Peronism without Perón," that
would supersede Peronism, protect against renewed popular outbreaks like the *cordobazo*, and pose a barrier to the revival of the Left.
Because the economy precluded rallying popular support by wage
and other concessions, the method Perón once used, Massera at first
sought to forge popularity by inflating the threat from the guerrillas
or "international Marxist conspiracies" and by constructing a reputation as the leading architect of "national defense" against them. But as
the internal war subsided, he was obliged to seek alternative instru-
ments in an extreme nationalism. In mid 1977 the decision was announced of a British arbitration on a long-standing dispute between
Argentina and Chile for sovereignty over the Beagle Channel in Tierra
del Fuego. By and large the award favored Chile. Massera seized
upon Argentine dissatisfaction to foster a climate of military confrontation and used the Beagle Channel as a pretext to prolong the

atmosphere of national emergency, a prelude to attempts to penetrate, mobilize, and coopt popular institutions. Using Chile as the new enemy, he hoped to don the mantle of Perón and establish a popular dictatorship—Bonapartism in a raw form. In October 1978, when the dispute with Chile seemed likely to evaporate peacefully, Massera began calling for an invasion of the British-held Falkland Islands.

A second faction in the junta, led by Generals Carlos Suárez Masón and Mario Menéndez, appeared as heirs to the extreme anti-Peronist "gorillas" of the late 1950s and early 1960s. Like the *colorados* of 1962, its members supported indefinite military dictatorship backed by an unrelenting war on the Peronist party, the unions, and all leftist organizations. Theirs was Martínez de Hoz's program pressed to its fullest extreme—a succession of unremitting blows against the defense bulwarks of urban society.

Third was a group led by Videla and General Roberto Viola, who in May 1978 succeeded Videla as Army commander in chief. The Videla-Viola faction, which recalled Onganía's regime after 1966, envisaged a series of phases by which economic recovery would again serve as the foundation for eventual political liberalization. It thus regarded Martínez de Hoz's program mainly as a short-term plan to achieve recovery and control inflation, and it soon grew uneasy with the minister's more radical proposals—tightening the pressure on manufacturers, the permanent collapse of wages, and the dismantlement of the state sector.

As time passed, the Videla-Viola faction emerged supreme in the junta, and the government's inner power struggles enabled the faction to exploit growing military opposition against the plan to alienate state corporations. Since the coup most state corporations had fallen into the hands of military administrators, who now from their well-remunerated positions of power firmly opposed *privatización*. With backing from this group, by late 1978 Videla had repelled Massera and captured control over foreign policy from the Navy. The dispute with Chile, which in months past had threatened to bring war, was submitted to papal mediation, and the furor began to cool. In late 1979 Videla and Viola also managed to defeat the extreme anti-Peronists. The junta's new trade-union legislation, which upheld the dissolution of the CGT and abolished the closed shop, had been denounced as insufficient by the hard-liners. In October 1979 they revolted under Menéndez, but the rebellion failed to attract broad support and was swiftly put down by the government.[75]

As its standing increased, the Videla-Viola faction became more moderate and further diluted its endorsement of Martínez de Hoz; by late 1979 Viola publicly criticized low wages. Martínez de Hoz consequently found himself under growing pressure from the junta to accomplish a series of contradictory, if not incompatible, goals: to continue the war on inflation, but at the same time contain the fall in living standards and revive manufacturing. His inability to touch the public sector, however, deprived him of his main weapon against inflation, and in 1976 the price index rose by around 500 percent. Even after steep drops, inflation remained for much of the late 1970s at more than 150 percent. In 1977 and 1978 the high inflation was due in part to military mobilization and rearmament during the dispute with Chile, but also in part to continuing government deficits provoked by subsidies to public corporations.

In groping for methods to curb inflation, Martínez de Hoz continued the plan of graduated tariff reductions he had adopted in 1976, with the aim of encouraging imports to compete with domestic producers and thus force down prices. Although the policy showed little discernible influence in containing prices, it did impede recovery in the manufacturing sector, which remained in deep depression throughout the late 1970s. Meanwhile, to enhance the long-term competitiveness of manufacturing, Martínez de Hoz sought new foreign investment that would deepen the productive infrastructure and thereby reduce manufacturers' costs.

Recourse to foreign investment under the military regime followed legislation in March 1977 that established new tax benefits and favorable terms for profit remittances, including the removal of all restraints on convertibility. Foreign investment was also facilitated by new liberal banking regulations and high domestic interest rates. Changes in the banking laws, also in early 1977, led to the swift proliferation of new financial institutions known as *casas financieras*. High domestic interest rates strongly motivated the new *financieras* and the traditional banks to an energetic pursuit of funds abroad, and they soon became one of the government's chief means for attracting foreign investment. By 1978, following a marked decline in international interest rates, foreign investment also became available on relatively easy terms. The large and rapidly growing influx of funds financed oil and gas exploration projects, hydroelectricity and nuclear schemes—exactly the kind of projects that Martínez de Hoz hoped would eventually boost domestic manufacturing. But to accelerate the process still more, in January 1979 he eliminated the stipulation that required the banks and *financieras* to keep in reserve a margin of 20 percent of their funds from abroad. Arguing that major changes in parity would induce still higher rates of domestic inflation, he also instituted "crawling peg" devaluations, which caused the rate of peso depreciation to fall substantially behind the rise in domestic prices. The new measures of early 1979 complemented those instituted in 1977 to boost foreign investment. Investors could now purchase pesos and invest in local banks and *financieras*; when they withdrew from the market, reconverting their pesos, their returns reflected the high prevailing domestic rate minus the substantially lower peso depreciation rate. In 1979 returns on such investments climbed as high as 60 percent, and the scheme also gained a self-sustaining momentum: the faster the inflow of foreign investment, the higher the returns on it climbed, since new investment helped slow the depreciation of the peso, while sustaining inflationary pressure in the economy. Such opportunities for profit attracted large funds not only from foreigners but also from domestic private investors who customarily held their savings abroad, often in dollars in Miami banks. An increasingly overvalued peso accompanied by falling tariff duties also meant cheaper imports, which occasioned a growing influx of luxury consumer goods and buying sprees by state corporations. By late 1979 imports were growing three times faster than exports.[76]

In early 1980 the country appeared to have undergone a dramatic change. With the guerrillas vanquished, discernible repression had waned: the troops had returned to the barracks and the covert police squads, agents of the "disappearances," were no longer active. Although wages and manufacturers' profits remained bitingly low, the press gagged, and the unions cowed, much of the population found solace in speculation and the purchase of cheap imports.

But the storm only appeared to be passing; in truth the country stood in the eye of another, contrived by Martínez de Hoz. An overvalued peso pumped in foreign investment but swiftly disrupted foreign trade, and in the first half of 1980 the trade deficit reached $500 million. To control the deficit required a steep devaluation, one that would immediately eliminate the high returns earned by foreign investors. Martínez de Hoz knew that in all probability devaluation, even a rumor of devaluation, would provoke foreign investors into massive withdrawals that would cause the reserves and the peso to collapse, leading the economy into another deep depression.

By 1980 conditions had an inescapable air of 1889–1890, with Martínez de Hoz becoming a latter-day Juárez Celman. The first signs of financial strain came in early 1980 with the sudden collapse of the Banco de Intercambio Regional, one of the newer *financieras*, provincial in origin, that had undergone rapid growth. To compete with its numerous rivals, it had offered investors extremely high interest rates, but like most of the other *financieras*, it was lending at still higher rates, mostly to domestic manufacturers. The manufacturers' position had been enfeebled first by the aftermath of the 1976 recession and then by growing competition from imports as tariff levels fell; manufacturers' defaults on loans, it seemed, were the major cause of the bank's failure. But financial panic ensued: between April and June 1980, an estimated $1.9 billion in short-term speculative money fled the country. In July several other large banks and *financieras* declared bankruptcy. The grain export conglomerate SASETRU also failed, a reflection of the growing pressures on farm exporters from an overvalued peso.

Martínez de Hoz attempted to restore confidence and rebuild the reserves by a new injection of short-term foreign finance. In July 1980 foreign investors were permitted to open month-to-month accounts, and $700 million was thus deposited in July alone. But the new influx brought another large flood of imports and still greater pressure on the balance of trade. By October 1980 the financial system was reported "close to collapse," as a multitude of firms struggled to survive by renegotiating their debts through new short-term loans. In early February 1981, after another spate of bankruptcies, a sudden unprogrammed devaluation was followed by capital flight estimated at $2 billion. Between December 1979 and March 1981 Argentina's foreign debt had risen from $8.5 billion to $25.3 billion, from 14 percent to 42 percent of the gross domestic product. Interest charges on the foreign debt were 10 percent of exports in 1979, but more than 30 percent by the end of 1980. In 1980 export values fell in constant dollars by 3.9 percent, while imports grew 43 percent.[77]

On the expiration of Videla's term in March 1981, Viola became president, while Martínez de Hoz resigned. The new president began his tenure still cherishing hopes of political liberalization, but his position was at once imperiled by a financial crisis that soon exploded into a thunderous economic collapse. Further, numerous conflicts still divided the military, and within weeks Viola found himself embroiled with his Army commander, General Leopoldo Galtieri, over concessions to the Peronists, including the liberation of Isabel Perón, held captive for the past five years. In June 1981, when rumors of an impending coup led by Galtieri coincided with a new devaluation, the reserves fell by a reported $300 million in a single day; the financial crisis was now "without historical precedent."[78] In July, amid fears of popular demonstrations triggered by the Peronists, Viola proclaimed a pending "dialogue" with the political parties as a prelude to a political "opening" (*apertura*), an announcement that provoked new friction with Galtieri. By August steel production had fallen by 20 percent against a year earlier. In November a new run on the peso proved the end for Viola, whom Galtieri forced to resign in late December. Throughout 1981 the peso depreciated by over 600 percent of its value, the gross domestic product fell by 11.4 percent, manufacturing output by 22.9 percent, and real wages by 19.2 percent.[79]

The Galtieri coup marked the victory of those military factions committed to "firmness and action," qualities they regarded Viola's regime as lacking. Galtieri's outlook appeared to bring together the positions of the Massera and Suárez Masón–Menéndez factions four or five years earlier. He opposed even the slightest new concession to the Peronists and appeared to be preparing an attack against them as the prelude to forming a new mass movement dominated by the generals. But Galtieri's economic policy reinvoked the initial extremes of Martínez de Hoz's program, with pledges to renew the plan to alienate state industries and services into private hands. The regime also renewed the quest for still more foreign investment, aiming for a new partnership with the United States based on the ideological affinities between Galtieri and the Reagan administration. In November 1981, a few weeks before the overthrow of Viola, Galtieri had visited Washington and had reportedly offered the Americans military bases in Patagonia in return for investments in a new gas pipeline and in the oil industry, which were to produce Argentina's first exports of gas and oil. Galtieri also offered technical advisers and military support for the American-backed war against leftist rebellion in Central America.[80]

To his compatriots Galtieri appeared to be "[a] man of austerity while simultaneously presenting himself as a man of the people"—in essence the reputation Massera had sought in 1977. To test and enhance its popular standing, the government organized public barbecues (*asados*) in the provinces, events that critics dubbed the *Gran Asado Nacional*, a pun on Lanusse's *Gran Acuerdo*. But Galtieri's weakness, it was apparent, was a lack of political momentum. He neither sparked popular support nor overcame the persisting divisions in the armed services. In an effort to resolve these problems, Galtieri once more exhumed Massera's ideas and turned to foreign affairs. In late January 1982 Argentina mounted a new campaign against Chile over the Beagle Channel; in February came hints of pending military involvement in Central America; next, a diplomatic offensive against Britain concerning the Falkland Islands and a demand for an acknowledgment of Argentina's sovereignty. This last issue seemed most promising and gained increasing primacy. For if the regime escalated the tension with Chile, it risked a protracted war that could spread elsewhere in Latin America, perhaps ultimately sparking an invasion from Brazil. And if Argentina became too involved in Central America, domestic dissidents would charge that the government was acting as a mercenary to imperialism, a position that might unite the Peronists, prompt the revival of the Left, and incite renewed popular unrest. By comparison, action in the Falklands was "the easiest war of all." As the options were canvased in early 1982, Galtieri swiftly acquired the reputation of a "trigger-happy warmonger."[81]

In early April 1982 the junta invaded and took the Falkland Islands and their dependencies. It was the first time since 1870 that Argentine forces had engaged in a foreign conflict. In executing the invasion, the junta expected maximum gains and minimum losses, for the "reoccupation" of "*nuestras Malvinas*" was universally popular. Incipient protests against the government were replaced by massive demonstrations of solidarity that gave the junta the instrument of vicarious unity it required. The junta now posed as an agent of national redemption, dismissing its opponents, whatever their grievances, as "traitors" or "antipatriots." The takeover of the islands also deflected attention from the deepening economic depression, renewed political repression, and the crucial issue of the *privatización* of state corporations. Likely costs from the adventure seemed slight. Within Latin America the junta hoped that the invasion would be interpreted as a blow struck against "colonialism." It believed Britain's commitment to the islands too slight, and British power too weak, for the occupation to provoke much more than token protest. After Galtieri's recent concessions and promises of assistance in Central America, the junta believed the British would gain little backing from the United States.[82]

The junta, however, had misjudged. The invasion bought ephemeral domestic peace at the price of a swift and shattering military defeat. The British responded to the invasion by mobilizing their navy and dispatching a task-force flotilla to the South Atlantic. For some time the United States pursued efforts at mediation, but when Argentina resisted pressure to withdraw from the islands pending negotiations, the Americans sided with Britain. The British fleet reached its destination in May, and immediate naval and air encounters bottled the Argentine navy in its ports; the Argentine air force was almost completely destroyed. British troops and marines then landed on the Falklands, securing all their objectives in scarcely a month. Within three months of their arrival, 10,000 Argentine troops had surrendered their weapons and were transported back to the mainland. Galtieri resigned, plunging the services into renewed conflict. The streets of Argentina filled with protesters.

Argentina's claim to the Falkland Islands did not lack juridical persuasiveness. Throughout, since their forcible occupation in 1833, recurrent and unceasing demands had been made for a British withdrawal, but Britain repeatedly refused, citing the right of self-determination among the islanders—a reason that had a somewhat hollow ring when applied to the islands' community of fewer than two thousand landless shepherds. But for Argentina the Falklands were less important in themselves than as a nationalist myth. To the Galtieri junta, perhaps with memories of 1806 or of Mitre's conflict with Paraguay, war had become merely another technique in the struggle to build a new political order after Perón.

Though the Falklands War soon ended, the underlying issues remained: the failures of a debilitating forty-year–long struggle to industrialize. In late 1982 every sign seemed to indicate that Argentina's economic and social crisis would continue to be as politically destructive as they had been in the past. In the immediate future, if the military sought to cling to power, it risked a new outburst of popular revolt and a repetition of the events of the 1970s. If it ceded and restored civilian rule, it ran the risk of reprisals for its conduct in the "dirty war" against subversion. In the early 1980s, with the failure of the new autocracy of 1976, Argentina remained in deadlock and impasse. As long as the urban sectors and the populist impulse kindled by Yrigoyen and Perón remained strong, the future seemed likely to bring an endless repetition of the old economic and political cycles. If the urban and populist sectors weakened, or strategies like Martínez de Hoz's succeeded, the likelihood was increasingly severe social dislocation. Either way these were unhappy prospects.

Convivial relations between War Minister Perón and senior military colleagues, 1944. Reproduced from Archivo General de la Nación, Buenos Aires.

Perón chairs a meeting, probably of the National Council for the Postwar (*Consejo Nacional de la Posguerra*), late 1944. Reproduced from Archivo General de la Nación, Buenos Aires.

Peron's triumphant procession through the avenues of Buenos Aires after his inaugural as president, 4 June 1946. Reproduced from Archivo General de la Nación, Buenos Aires.

Members of the trade unions gather in the Plaza de Mayo to greet Perón on May Day, probably in 1947 or 1948. Reproduced from Archivo General de la Nación, Buenos Aires.

The Plaza de Mayo during the celebration of Loyalty Day (*Día de la lealtad*). The organized and orchestrated character of the demonstration suggests the year is 1950 or 1951. Reproduced from Archivo General de la Nación, Buenos Aires.

Poster commemorating Loyalty Day. The style is typical of Peronist propaganda art and seems modeled eclectically on both European socialist and fascist forerunners. Reproduced from Archivo General de la Nación, Buenos Aires.

Watched by Eva Perón, who died scarcely a month later, Perón takes the oath for his second presidential term, 4 June 1952. Reproduced from Archivo de la Nación, Buenos Aires.

Perón gratefully embraces his army commander, General Franklin Lucero, following the latter's successful intervention against military rebellion, June 1955. Reproduced from Archivo General de la Nación, Buenos Aires.

The Liberating Revolution (*La revolución libertadora*), late September 1955. Mobs burn Peronist propaganda in the streets of Buenos Aires. Reproduced from J. Halcro Ferguson, *The River Plate Republics: Argentina, Paraguay, Uruguay* (New York, 1965), 103.

President Arturo Frondizi, seated second from right, with John F. Kennedy, 1961. Reproduced from Archivo General de la Nación, Buenos Aires.

General Juan Carlos Onganía (no. 2), leader of the Blues military faction in 1962–1963, in attendance with interim president José M. Guido (no. 4) in 1962. Reproduced from Archivo General de la Nación, Buenos Aires.

The march of auto workers, May 1969 in Córdoba, that triggered the *cordobazo*—the great prelude to the violent political struggles in Argentina during the 1970s. Reproduced from Daniel Villar, *El cordobazo* (Buenos Aires, 1971).

Riot police attempting to clear street barricades during the *cordobazo*. Reproduced from Daniel Villar, *El cordobazo* (Buenos Aires, 1971).

An aged President Perón in early 1974 with his third wife, Vice-President María Estela ("Isabelita") Martínez de Perón. Reproduced from Archivo General de la Nación, Buenos Aires.

Perón's last moments of popular acclaim from the Casa Rosada, 12 June 1974, only nineteen days before his death. Reproduced from Gente y la actualidad, *25 de mayo de 1973–24 de marzo de 1976: Fotos. Hechos. Testimonios de 1035 dramáticos días* (Buenos Aires 1976).

A typical shantytown scene in Buenos Aires during the mid 1960s. Reproduced from J. Halcro Ferguson, Life World Library/*The River Plate Republics: Argentina, Paraguay, Uruguay* (New York, 1965). Photograph by Leonard McCombe Time-Life Books Inc., Publisher © 1965 Time Inc.

Epilogue

History has frequently repeated itself in Argentina. The sixteenth and early seventeenth centuries, much of the eighteenth century, and finally the years 1860 through 1930 were periods of expansion. The main features common to these upswings were growing foreign trade, complementary commercial and investment links, and relative social and political stability. On the other side—during the mid seventeenth century, the early nineteenth century, and the middle and late twentieth centuries—came three long downswings, the last of them still in progress. These downswings occurred as foreign markets were disrupted and external partnerships dissolved; internal social and political tensions then intensified the dislocation. Downswings in the seventeenth and early nineteenth centuries produced "barbarization," a phenomenon that has a rough modern counterpart in the severe social dislocation that has been Argentina's lot during the last twenty or thirty years. In the past social groups penalized by economic decline could escape into a peasant or pastoral economy, but today no equivalent refuge exists. Instead, Argentina's contemporary middle class is pauperized or expelled abroad; workers, too, suffer collapsing living standards; rural migrants are pushed into shantytowns. In the past long-term economic crisis also produced dictatorship or oligarchy. At present neither dictatorship nor oligarchy has acquired stable form, although since the 1960s dictatorship has become increasingly prevalent, while popular, egalitarian movements have grown increasingly ineffectual.

Analysts in the liberal tradition have long argued that Argentina's economic vulnerability stemmed from limited natural resources. Though rich in agrarian resources, Argentina was poor in basic industrial raw materials like coal, iron ore, or timber. The liberal argument, however, is oversimplified and misleading, for in principle the River Plate region could have developed in ways other than as it did, perhaps even along similar lines as the United States. Argentina's path was not determined by resources alone, but by the interaction of its resources and its early colonial institutions. Had those institutions been different, the resources would have been sufficient for the emergence of a small farmers' commonwealth. As in the United States, agrarian capitalism could have helped foster manufacturing, and, again like the United States, Argentina might have eventually conquered or annexed the resources for industrialization: Paraguayan timber, Chilean coal, or Brazilian iron ore.

Argentina's lack of labor and markets made agricultural capitalism impossible until the late nineteenth century. At that time, foreign investment and European immigration might have more thoroughly changed the country had the Argentine state been differently organized and constituted. But the structure of the state, then controlled by native landed interests, was itself an historical product impossible to discard. Subsequently, as Argentina entered the twentieth century, the nation had no politically effective middle class of producers. "Statist" or "clientistic" groups, less interested in structural reform or economic development than in increasing their share of national income, led an abortive effort to establish representative government. A belated attempt at industrialization came in the 1940s, led by another polymath movement, again largely governed by consumer groups. But unfavorable external conditions, compounded by Perón's errors, produced a stalled effort at industrialization and, into the early 1980s, a society still trapped by internal conflict.

Notes

PREFACE

1. J. P. Robertson and W. P. Robertson, *Letters on South America*; Charles Darwin, *Journal of Researches into the Geology, Natural History of the Various Countries Visited During the Voyage of HMS Beagle Around the World*; Jean Antoine Victor Martin de Moussy, *Description géographique et statistique de la Confédération Argentine*; William Henry Hudson, *Far Away and Long Ago*; M. G. Mulhall and E. T. Mulhall, *Handbook of the River Plate*; W. H. Koebel, *Argentina*; Ernesto Tornquist and Co., *The Economic Development of the Argentine Republic in the Last Fifty Years*; Alberto B. Martinez and Maurice Lewandowski, *The Argentine in the Twentieth Century*; Reginald Lloyd, ed., *Twentieth-Century Impressions of Argentina*; Colin Clark, *The Economics of 1960*.

2. Quoted in Lloyd, *Twentieth-Century Impressions*, 337.

3. Quoted in Mark Falcoff and Ronald H. Dolkart, eds., *Prologue to Perón*, 111.

4. United Nations, Comisión Económica para América Latina (CEPAL), *El desarrollo económico de la Argentina*, Carlos F. Diaz Alejandro, *Essays in the Economic History of the Argentine Republic*.

5. Quoted in Guillermo Gasío and María C. San Román, *La conquista del progreso, 1874–1880*, 73.

6. Tulio Halperín Donghi, *Politics, Economics, and Society in Argentina in the Revolutionary Period*; John Lynch, *Argentine Dictator*.

7. An example of such tendencies is Roberto Cortés Conde and Ezequiel Gallo, Jr., *La formación de la Argentina moderna*.

CHAPTER I

1. For population estimates see Jorge Comadrán Ruiz, *Evolución demográfica argentina durante el período hispano, 1535–1810*; Jean Pyle, "A Reexamination of Aboriginal Population Estimates for Argentina."

2. This brief geographical outline has been assembled from Jean Antoine Victor Martin de Moussy, *Description géographique et statistique de la Confédération Argentine*; Carlos M. Urien, *Geografía argentina*; Felix de Azara, *Descripción e historia del Paraguay y del Rio de la Plata*.

3. On these issues see the classic studies of the Spanish colonial system: J. H. Parry, *The Spanish Sea-borne Empire*; H. Chaunu and P. Chaunu, *Seville et l'Atlantique*; Lewis Hanke, *The Spanish Struggle for Justice in the Conquest of America*; Immanuel Wallerstein, *The Modern World System*.

4. On the prehistory of Argentina's indigenous peoples, see Dick Ibarra Grasso, *Argentina indígena y prehistoria americana*; Alberto González and José A. Pérez, *Argentina indígena*; Salvador Canals Frau, *Las poblaciones indígenas de la Argentina*.

5. The Diaguita have been studied by Ibarra Grasso, *Argentina indígena*, 348ff.; Canals Frau, *Poblaciones indígenas*, 473–503. See also Manuel Lizondo Borda, "El Tucumán indígena del siglo XVI"; Ramón Rosa Olmos, *Historia de Catamarca*, 9–24.

6. Cf. Ibarra Grasso, *Argentina indígena*, 264–80; Canals Frau, *Poblaciones indígenas*, 411–72; Lizondo Borda, "El Tucumán indígena"; Emilio Coni, *Síntesis de la economía argentina*.

7. For the Guaraní, see Branislava Susnik, *El indio colonial del Paraguay*; Elman R. Service, "The Encomienda in Paraguay."

8. For the plains Indians, see Antonio Serrano, *Los pueblos y culturas indígenas del litoral*; Coni, *Síntesis*, chap. 1; also Ibarra Grasso, *Argentina indígena*; Canals Frau, *Poblaciones indígenas*.

9. For the first expeditions see Julián M. Rubio, *Exploración y conquista del Rio de la Plata*, 13–96; Vicente D. Sierra, *Historia de la Argentina*, vol. 1; *1492–1600*; Ángel S. Caballero Martín, *Las corrientes conquistadoras en el Rio de la Plata*.

10. Luis L. Dominguez, *The Conquest of the River Plate*, 9–10. For other details of Mendoza's expedition, see Rubio, *Exploración*, 102–50; Caballero Martín, *Corrientes conquistadoras*, 50–75; Ernesto J. Fitte, *Hambre y desnudeces en la conquista del Rio de la Plata*, Enrique de Gandía "La primera fundación de Buenos Aires."

11. These events are recounted in Sierra, *Historia* 1:217–50; Efraín de Cardozo, "Asunción del Paraguay"; José L. Busaniche, *Estampas del pasado argentino*, 17–36.

12. For Almagro and Rojas, see Rubio, *Exploración*, 420–49; Roberto Levillier, *Nueva crónica de la conquista de Tucumán*; Manuel Lizondo Borda, *El descubrimiento del Tucumán*.

13. Quoted in Amílcar Razori, *Historia de la ciudad argentina* 1:136–37.

14. Cf. Rubio, *Exploración*, 471–76; Roberto Levillier, "Conquista y organización del Tucumán"; Olmos, *Historia*; Jorge Comadrán Ruiz, "Nacimiento y desarrollo de los núcleos urbanos y del poblamiento de la

campaña del país de Cuyo durante la época hispana, 1551–1810"; Juan Pablo Echagüe, "Los orígenes de San Juan: los Huarpes, la conquista y la colonización."

15. For silver mining in Upper Peru, see Pierre Vilar, *A History of Gold and Money, 1450–1620*, 119–42; Gwendolin B. Cobb, "Supply and Transportation for the Potosí Mines, 1545–1640"; Peter Bakewell, "Registered Silver Production in the Potosí District, 1550–1735"; D. A. Brading, "Las minas de plata en el Perú y México colonial: Un estudio comparativo."

16. Cf. Rubio, *Exploración*, 422–524; Levillier, "Conquista y organización"; Razori, *Historia*, vol. 1; Fermín V. Arenas Luque, *El fundador de Córdoba*; Atilio Cornejo, "El virrey Toledo y las fundaciones de Gonzalo de Abreu en el valle de Salta"; Madeline W. Nicholls, "Colonial Tucumán"; Lizondo Borda, *Descubrimiento*.

17. Roberto Leviller, "Enfrentamiento de las corrientes pobladoras del Tucumán y del Rio de la Plata"; Enrique de Gandía, "La segunda fundación de Buenos Aires"; Manuel M. Cervera, *Historia de la ciudad y provincia de Santa Fe, 1573–1853*, vol. 1.

18. For figures on the Spanish population, see Comadrán Ruiz, *Evolución demográfica*.

19. These procedures are described at length in Levillier, "Conquista y organización" and *Nueva crónica*; Rubio, *Exploración*; Sierra, *Historia*, vol. 1.

20. Ricardo Zorraquín Becú, *La organización política argentina en el período hispánico*; Alexey Shtrajov, "Trasplante de las instituciones españolas al Rio de la Plata en los siglos XVI y XVII."

21. Changes in territorial jurisdiction are described at length in Zorraquín Becú, *Organización política argentina*.

22. These conflicts are recounted in Levillier, *Nueva crónica*; Arenas Luque, *Fundador de Córdoba*; Rubio, *Exploración*, 492–504.

23. Cf. Zorraquín Becú, *Organización política argentina*, 105 et passim; José Torre Revello, "Los gobernadores de Buenos Aires (1617–1777)."

24. On the Church see Cayetano Bruno, *Historia de la iglesia en la Argentina*, vols. 1–3.

25. Cf. Álvaro Jara, *Importación de trabajadores indígenas en siglo XVII*; Ricardo Zorraquín Becú, "Migraciones indígenas en la época colonial"; José Luis Mérida, "La sociedad paraguaya hacia 1625"; Service, "The Encomienda in Paraguay"; Sierra, *Historia* 1:436ff.

26. The *encomienda* in early colonial Argentina has not received the detailed analysis accorded elsewhere in Latin America. The best study for the general region is Service's "The Encomienda in Paraguay." See also Comadrán Ruiz, *Evolución demográfica*, 197–217; Zorraquín Becú, "Migraciones indígenas."

27. For useful introductions to these differing labor systems, see Juan A. Villamarin and Judith E. Villamarin, *Indian Labor in Mainland Spanish America*;

James Lockhart, *Spanish Peru: A Colonial Society*, 149–207. For local details see Comadrán Ruiz, *Evolución demográfica*; Zorraquín Becú, "Migraciones indígenas."

28. For the Abreu Ordinances, see Sierra, *Historia* 1:359; Olmos, *Historia*, 48.

29. Cf. José A. Craviotto, "La minería durante la conquista"; Comadrán Ruiz, *Evolución demográfica*, 33–36.

30. Figures from Comadrán Ruiz, *Evolución demográfica*, 33–36.

31. Cf. Comadrán Ruiz, "Nacimiento y desarrollo."

32. The early development of Catamarca is recounted by Olmos, *Historia*.

33. See Enrique de Gandía, *Francisco de Alfaro y la condición social de los indios*.

34. See Carlos Sempat Assadourián, "Sobre un elemento de la economía colonial"; Emilio A. Coni, "La agricultura, ganadería e industrias hasta el virreinato"; Ceferino Garzón Maceda, *Economía del Tucumán: economía natural, economía monetaria, siglos XVI, XVII, XVIII*.

35. Garzón Maceda, *Economía del Tucumán*; Sempat Assadourián, "Elemento de la economía colonial."

36. Carlos Sempat Assadourian, *El tráfico de esclavos en Córdoba, 1588–1610*.

37. Sempat Assadourián, *Tráfico de esclavos*.

38. There are numerous commentaries on these conditions in Comadrán Ruiz, *Evolución demográfica*; Zorraquín Becú, *Organización política argentina*. See also José Torre Revello, *La sociedad colonial*.

39. The Portuguese are discussed in Raúl A. Molina, *Las primeras experiencias comerciales del Plata*; Alicia Piffer de Canabrava, *Comércio português no Rio da Prata, 1580–1640*.

40. Attributed to a Henry Ottsen. See José Torre Revello, "Viajeros, relaciones, cartas y memorias."

41. These complaints are detailed in *Correspondencia de la ciudad de Buenos Aires con los reyes de España*, ed. Roberto Levillier.

42. Emilio A. Coni, *El gaucho: Argentina, Brazil, Uruguay*.

43. These issues are discussed in detail by Molina, *Experiencias comerciales*; Canabrava, *Comércio português*, 92–118; Levillier, *Correspondencia*. See also Mario Rodriguez, "The Genesis of Economic Attitudes in the Rio de la Plata"; Manuel V. Figueredo and Enrique de Gandía, "Hernandarias de Saavedra"; Jack A. Dabbs, "Manuel de Frías and Rio-Platine Free Trade."

44. Cf. Rubio, *Exploración*, 650–60; Torre Revello, "Los gobernadores," 473.

45. Facsimiles of petitions from Buenos Aires to the court appear in Levillier, *Correspondencia*. Typical was the complaint of Diego Rodríguez de Valdés in May 1599, who alleged that isolation had produced "tanta hambre y necesidad de todas las cosas necesarias para la vida humana y sustento della, que perecieron muchas personas por falta de medicinas. . . . En esta ciudad no

hay vino para poder decir misa, ni cera, ni aceite . . . ni hierro, ni acero" [such hunger and want for everything necessary to human life and its sustenance, that many people perished for lack of medicine. . . . In this city there is neither wine with which to say Mass, nor wax, nor oil . . . nor iron, nor steel] (435).

46. These issues are widely discussed by Canabrava, Rodriguez, Figueredo and Gandía, and Dabbs; see note 43.

47. For population in the seventeenth century, see Comadrán Ruiz, *Evolución demográfica*, 44ff. A friendly critic chides my account of the seventeenth-century depression, commenting that it fails to establish whether it was linked to an "Atlantic" depression or was simply due to regional causes. Of course, both play a part and the two are impossible to separate. The depression has also recently become the subject of broader academic debate. See John J. TePaske and Herbert S. Klein, "The Seventeenth-Century Decline in New Spain"; also the selection of commentaries in *PP*, no. 97 (Nov. 1982).

48. For Potosí, see Bakewell, "Registered Silver Production"; Nicolás Sánchez Albornoz, *El indio en el alto Perú a fines del siglo XVII*.

49. Parry, *Spanish Sea-borne Empire*, 251–91; Geoffrey J. Walker, *Spanish Politics and Imperial Trade, 1700–1785*, 5–20.

50. Cf. Acarete du Biscay, "Voyage up the Rio de la Plata, and from thence by Land to Peru and His observations on It."

51. Estimates based on figures from Canabrava, *Comércio português*, 149–54.

52. The classic study of the slave trade, which includes seventeenth-century data, is Elena F. S. de Studer, *La trata de negros en el Rio de la Plata durante el siglo XVIII*. See also Canabrava, *Comércio português*, 150ff.; Comadrán Ruiz, *Evolución demográfica*, 38.

53. See Molina, *Experiencias comerciales*; José Torre Revello, "Los navíos de registro en el Rio de la Plata, 1595–1700."

54. Alfred J. Tapson, "Indian Warfare on the Pampas During the Colonial Period"; José Torre Revello, "Buenos Aires de antaño."

55. Acarete du Biscay "Voyage," 18.

56. Torre Revello, "Los gobernadores" and "Buenos Aires de antaño;" R. Lafuente Machain, *Buenos Aires en el siglo XVII*.

57. The most detailed discussion of this period is Sierra, *Historia* 2:172 passim; see also notes 54 and 56.

58. For information on the interior see Sierra, *Historia* 2:322–416; Garzón Maceda, *Economía de Tucumán*; Guillermo Furlong Cárdiff, *Nacimiento de la filosofía en el Rio de la Plata*; Aníbal Verdaguer, "La región del Cuyo hasta la creación del virreinato del Rio de la Plata"; Manuel Lizondo Borda, "El Tucumán de los siglos XVII y XVIII." Commenting on Córdoba, Acarete du Biscay declared, "The Inhabitants are Rich in Gold and Silver, which they get by the Trade they have for mules, with which they furnish Peru and other parts" ("Voyage," 31).

59. For the Calchaquí wars see Sierra, *Historia* 2:260–79; Rubio, *Ex-*

384 Notes to Pages 34–44

ploración, 750–73; Teresa Poissek Prebisch, *La rebelión de Pedro Bohórquez, el Inca del Tucumán, 1656–1659.*

60. Sierra, *Historia* 2:172ff.; José Torre Revello, *Esteco y Concepción del Bermejo.*

61. For the Jesuit missions see Magnus Mörner, *The Political and Economic Activities of the Jesuits in the La Plata Region*; Guillermo Furlong Cárdiff, *Misiones y sus pueblos de Guaraníes*; Furlong Cárdiff, "Las misiones jesuíticas"; Rubio, *Exploración*, 586–607.

CHAPTER II

1. The major European wars of the eighteenth century were: the War of the Spanish Succession (1702–1714), The War of the Austrian Succession (1740–1748; called the War of Jenkins' Ear in 1739), The Seven Years' War (1756–1763), the War of American Independence (1776–1783), the Wars of the French Revolution (1793–1795 and 1796–1801), and the Napoleonic wars (1804–1815).

2. For the origins of Côlonia do Sacramento, see Mario Rodriguez, "Dom Pedro de Braganza and Colonia do Sacramento"; Fernand de Almeida, "A Côlonia do Sacramento na epoca da soccessão de Espanha"; Julián María Rubio, *Exploración y conquista del Rio de la Plata*, 691–720; H. E. S. Fisher, *The Portugal Trade: A Study of Anglo-Portuguese Commerce, 1700–1770*, 33–47; Vicente D. Sierra, *Historia de la Argentina* 2:455–501.

3. Cf. Rubio, *Exploración*, 710–14; Sierra, *Historia* 2:463–80.

4. Cf. Rubio, *Exploración*, 715–24; Sierra, *Historia* 2:480–506.

5. Cf. Fisher, *Portugal Trade*, 33–47; Jean O. McLachlan, *Trade and Peace with Old Spain, 1667–1750*, 80–83.

6. For the second capture of Colonia, see Sierra, *Historia* 3:27.

7. For the later history of Colonia, see Sierra, *Historia* 3:80, 112, 360ff.; Sergio Villalobos R., *El comercio y la crisis colonial*; 48–49.

8. For the slave trade with the French Guinea Company, see Elena F. S. de Studer, *La trata de negros en el Rio de la Plata en el siglo XVIII*, 103–13; Villalobos, *Comercio*, 28.

9. For the activities of the South Sea Company in Buenos Aires, see Studer, *Trata de negros*, 202–40; José Torre Revello, *La sociedad colonial*, 83–86; Villalobos, *Comercio*, 40–44; Sierra, *Historia* 3:52–127.

10. For society in Buenos Aires in the early eighteenth century, see Jorge Comadrán Ruiz, *Evolución demográfica argentina durante el período hispano, 1539–1810*, 44; Hernán Asdrúbal Silva, "Pulperías, tendejones, sastres y zapateros"; Bartolomé Mitre, *Historia de Belgrano* 1:95–108; Ricardo Rodríguez Molas, "El negro en el Rio de la Plata"; Torre Revello, *Sociedad colonial*, 83–86; Lyman L. Johnson, "The Silversmiths of Buenos Aires."

11. The growth of the *navíos de registro* followed changes in the organization of Spanish commerce in the early eighteenth century, beginning with the *Proyecto de galeones* of 1718. See Villalobos, *Comercio*, 16–20, 67–77;

John Lynch, *Spanish Colonial Administration 1782–1810*, 8–10; Geoffrey J. Walker, *Spanish Politics and Imperial Trade, 1700–1785*, 108–216.

12. Cf. Villalobos, *Comercio*, 69–85; Studer, *Trata de negros*, 239–42. Some further data appear in Susan Socolow Migden, "Economic Activities of the Porteño Merchants."

13. For the growth of Buenos Aires as a military center, see Guillermo Céspedes del Castillo, *Lima y Buenos Aires*, 102–33.

14. For the *vaquerías* see Hernán Asdrúbal Silva, "El cabildo, el abasto de carne, y la ganadería"; Horacio C. E. Giberti, *Historia económica de la ganadería argentina*, 33–50; Sierra, *Historia* 3:46-91.

15. For the early *estancias* see Silva, "El cabildo"; Giberti, *Historia económica*, 33–49.

16. Cf. Roberto H. Marfany, "Fronteras con los indios en el sud y fundación de los pueblos"; Amílcar Razori, *Historia de la ciudad argentina* 2:9–86; Emilio Ravignani, "Crecimiento de la población en Buenos Aires y su campaña."

17. Members of this group are best known as *gauchos*, a term not widely used until the early nineteenth century. See Ricardo Rodríguez Molas, *Historia social del gaucho*, 29–159; Torre Revello, *Sociedad colonial*, 132–46; Emilio A. Coni, "Contribución a la historia del gaucho."

18. For farming around Buenos Aires, see Hernán Asdrúbal Silva, "El trigo en una sociedad colonial"; Tulio Halperín Donghi, *Politics, Economics, and Society in Argentina in the Revolutionary Period*, 20–29; Torre Revello, *Sociedad colonial*, 97–146.

19. For the growth of the missions, see Guillermo Furlong Cárdiff, *Misiones y sus pueblos de Guaraníes*; Comadrán Ruiz, *Evolución demográfica*, 58–61.

20. On the *comunero* movement in Paraguay, see Adalberto Lopez, *The Revolt of the Comuneros, 1721–1735*; Cayetano Bruno, *Historia de la iglesia en la Argentina* 4:221 et passim; Julio César Chávez, "La revolución paraguaya de los comuneros."

21. These events are described by Sierra, *Historia* 3:216–58.

22. Cf. Magnus Mörner, *The Expulsion of the Jesuits from Latin America*; Sierra, *Historia* 3:327–50.

23. Cf. Sierra, *Historia* 3:350; Lynch, *Spanish Colonial Administration*, 187–93.

24. Quoted by Bruno, *Historia*, 379. See also Manuel Lizondo Borda, "El Tucumán de los siglos XVII y XVIII."

25. On Potosí in the eighteenth century, see Rose Marie Buechler, *The Mining Society of Potosí*, Enrique Tandeter, "Forced and Free Labour in Late Colonial Potosí"; D. A. Brading, "Las minas del plata en el Perú y México colonial"; Enrique Tandeter, "Acumulación interna y explotación colonial en el Alto Perú" and "Mining Rent and Social Structure in Potosí in the Second Half of the Eighteenth Century."

26. Nicolás Sánchez Albornoz, "La saca de mulas de Salta al Perú, 1778–1808." The mule trade was disrupted for a time during the Tupac Amaru

rebellion in Peru in 1780. See Edberto Oscar Acevedo, "Repercusión de la sublevación de Tupac Amaru en Tucumán." For a chronological record of developments in the interior, see Sierra, *Historia* 2:508–60, 3:132–72.

27. On ethnic and population issues in the interior, see Emiliano Endrek, *El mestizaje en Córdoba*, Endrek, *El mestizaje en Tucumán*, Jorge Comadrán Ruiz, "Nacimiento y desarrollo de los núcleos urbanos y del poblamiento de la campaña del país de Cuyo durante la época hispana, 1551–1810"; Comadrán Ruiz, *Evolución demográfica*, 46–61, 86–95.

28. For the *comunero* movements in the interior and related issues, see Sierra, *Historia* 3:266–76; Ricardo Zorraquín Becú, *La organización política argentina en el período hispánico*, 283–93; Lizondo Borda, "El Tucumán," 389–419; Edberto Oscar Acevedo, *La gobernación del Tucumán en el virreinato del Rio de la Plata, 1776–1783*; Acevedo, "La Rioja hace dos siglos."

29. Cf. Comadrán Ruiz, *Evolución demográfica*, 46–61, 86–95.

30. See the classic contemporary description of the cities and rural areas of the interior: Concolorcorvo, *El lazarillo de ciegos caminantes desde Buenos Aires a Lima, 1773*.

31. On manufacturing in the interior, see Pedro S. Martínez Constanzo, *Las industrias durante el virreinato;* Halperín Donghi, *Politics,* 4–22, 32–39; Concolorcorvo, *Lazarillo,* 68–180; Sánchez Albornoz, "La saca de mulas."

32. Halperín Donghi, *Politics,* 38.

33. On elites and castes, see Endrek, *Mestizaje en Córdoba;* Carlos Sempat Assadourián, "Integración y desintegración regional en el espacio colonial."

34. This brief discussion of the Bourbon reforms is based on Richard Herr, *The Eighteenth-Century Revolution in Spain;* Manfred Kossok, *El virreinato del Rio de la Plata;* Ricardo H. Levene, *Investigaciones acerca de la historia económica del Rio de la Plata;* Emilio Ravignani, "El virreinato del Rio de la Plata."

35. See Lynch, *Colonial Administration;* Sierra, *Historia* 3:463–69.

36. See Céspedes del Castillo, *Lima y Buenos Aires,* 99 ff. for a detailed discussion of projects to remove Buenos Aires from the jurisdiction of Lima. On Anglo-Spanish international rivalries, see Octavio Gil Munilla, *El Rio de la Plata en la política internacional*.

37. Cf. Enrique M. Barba, *Don Pedro de Cevallos;* Céspedes del Castillo, *Lima y Buenos Aires,* 120–37; Zorraquín Becú, *Organización Política,* 249–87; Horacio William Bliss, *Del virreinato a Rosas: Ensayo de la historia económica argentina, 1776–1829;* Carlos E. Corona Baratech, "Notas para un estudio de la sociedad en el Rio de la Plata durante el virreinato."

38. Cf. Lynch, *Colonial Administration;* Edberto Oscar Acevedo, "Significación histórica del régimen de intendencias en Salta y Tucumán."

39. Figures on trade and revenues are based mostly on the research of Ricardo H. Levene: *Investigaciones* 2:68–85; "Riquezas, industrias, y comercio durante el virreinato"; also "Introducción"; see also Bliss, *Del virreinato a Rosas,* 24–30. Doubts as to the accuracy of Levene's figures have been expressed recently: see Herbert S. Klein, "Las finanzas del virreinato del Rio de la Plata en 1790."

40. Cf. Sierra, *Historia* 3:480; Socolow Migden, "Economic Activities" and *Kinship and Commerce*; Germán O. E. Tjarks, *El consulado de Buenos Aires y sus proyecciones en la historia del Rio de la Plata*.

41. For data on society in Buenos Aires, see Comadrán Ruiz, *Evolución demográfica*, 83–86; José Luis Moreno, "La estructura social de Buenos Aires en el año 1778"; Johnson, "Silversmiths of Buenos Aires"; Halperín Donghi, *Politics*, 48–66; Enrique M. Barba, *La organización del trabajo en el Buenos Aires colonial*; José M. Mariluz Urquijo, *El virreinato del Rio de la Plata en la época del Marquis de Avilés (1799–1801)*.

42. On rural society see Levene, "Riquezas"; César B. Pérez Colman, *Historia de Entre Rios*; Corona Baratech, "Notas," 90–114.

43. For revenues see note 39.

44. Cf. Studer, *Trata de negros*, 247–51.

45. For the rise of the independent merchants and trade issues during the 1790s, see Manuel José de Lavardén, *Nuevo aspecto del comercio en el Rio de la Plata*; Juan Carlos Garavaglia, "Comercio colonial: Expansión y crisis"; Enrique Wedevoy, *La evolución económica rioplatense a fines del siglo XVIII y principios del siglo XIX a la luz de la historia del seguro*; Socolow Migden, "Economic Activities," 274–80; Tjarks, *Consulado de Buenos Aires* 1:292–428; R. A. Humphreys and J. Lynch, *The Origins of the Latin American Revolutions, 1808–26*, 88–89; Sierra, *Historia* 3:540–56; Villalobos, *Comercio*, 99–124; Pedro S. Martínez Constanzo, *Historia económica de Mendoza durante el virreinato, 1776–1810*, 66.

46. Commercial depression in the 1790s is discussed by Levene, *Investigaciones* 2:252–56.

47. Martínez Constanzo, *Historia económica*, 148-57; Sierra, *Historia* 3:531-38; Lynch, *Colonial Administration*, 169-80; Halperín Donghi, *Politics*, 6-19.

48. The effect of monetary contraction in the interior is discussed by Levene, *Investigaciones* 2:193–211.

49. For trading conditions in the 1790s, see Sierra, *Historia* 5:531-38; Studer, *Trata de negros*, 247–351; Villalobos, *Comercio*, 99-127.

50. Levene, "Riquezas," 394–400; Studer, *Trata de negros*, 282–302. A pretext employed by the monopoly merchants in 1793 to oppose the liberalization of trade was that Crown *cédulas* had authorized the exports only of "fruits" (*frutos*), and that cattle goods were not fruit. The view which finally prevailed, however, was that "fruits" was meant generically to embrace all raw material exports.

51. For the growth of Belgrano's group and its principal ideas, see de Lavardén, *Nuevo aspecto del comercio*; Juan H. Vieytes, *Antecedentes económicos de la revolución de mayo*; Manuel Fernández López, "Los primeros economistas argentinos"; Bartolomé Mitre, *Historia del Belgrano*; Sergio Bagú, *Mariano Moreno*; Ricardo H. Levene, "Significación histórica de la obra económica de Manuel Belgrano y Mariano Moreno"; Leoncio Gianello, "La influencia del pensamiento de Belgrano en la gesta revolucionaria de mayo"; Enrique de Gandía, "Belgrano, Mitre y Alberdi."

52. Cf. Tulio Halperín Donghi, *Guerra y finanzas en los orígenes del estado argentino, 1790–1850*, 26–76.

53. On the British invasions see John Street, *La influencia británica en la independencia de las provincias del Rio de la Plata, con especial referencia al período comprendido entre 1806 y 1816;* John Lynch, *The Spanish American Revolutions, 1808–1826,* 41–64; R. A. Humphreys, *Liberation in South America, 1806–1827: The Career of James Paroissien* (London, 1952); Miguel Ángel Scenna, *Las brevas maduras;* José Luis Molinari, "Los indios y los negros durante las invasiones inglesas al Rio de la Plata en 1806 y 1807"; Joaquín Pérez, "Las rivalidades coloniales y la independencia de América, 1793–1815"; Mitre, *Historia* 1:127–214; H. S. Ferns, *Britain and Argentina in the Nineteenth Century,* 17–52.

54. For political events in 1806–1807, see Halperín Donghi, *Politics,* 114–135; Halperín Donghi, "Revolutionary Militarization in Buenos Aires, 1806–15."

55. Cf. Street, *Influencia británica,* 251–97.

56. Viz. Halperín Donghi, *Politics,* 135–56; Mitre, *Historia* 1:260–93; Street, *Influencia británica,* 374–88.

57. Bagú, *Mariano Moreno,* 24–63; Levene "Belgrano y Moreno" Miguel Ángel Scenna, "Mariano Moreno"; Ernesto J. Fitte, "Los comerciantes ingleses en vísperas de la Revolución de Mayo"; Villalobos, *Comercio,* 245–58; Halperín Donghi, *Guerra y finanzas,* 85–92.

58. For the events of 1810, see Ricardo H. Levene, "Los sucesos de mayo"; Lynch, *Spanish American Revolutions,* 51–57; Mitre, *Historia* 1:312–90.

CHAPTER III

1. See Ricardo Caillet-Bois, "La revolución en el virreinato."

2. Cf. Juan Carlos Bassi, "La expedición libertadora al Alto Perú"; Leopoldo R. Ornstein, "La expedición libertadora al Paraguay."

3. For Moreno's role, see Ricardo H. Levene, "La obra orgánica de la revolución"; Jorge Abelardo Ramos, *Revolución y contrarevolución en la Argentina,* 25–33; Miguel Ángel Scenna, "Mariano Moreno."

4. Cf. Bassi, "Expedición libertadora." Commercial and economic breakdown in the interior are defined in John Lynch, *The Spanish American Revolutions, 1808–1826,* 65–69; Tulio Halperín Donghi, *Politics, Economics, and Society in Argentina in the Revolutionary Period,* 65–73. On finance during the wars, see Tulio Halperín Donghi, *Guerra y finanzas en los orígenes del estado argentino, 1790–1850,* 119.

5. Cf. Ornstein, "Expedición libertadora"; Lynch, *Spanish American Revolutions,* 104–7.

6. For details of the rise of Artigas, see Lynch, *Spanish American Revolutions,* 89–92; John Street, *Artigas and the Emancipation of Uruguay,* 65–128; Street, *Gran Bretaña y la independencia del Rio de la Plata,* 169–220; Blanca París de Oddone, "Artigas, un caudillo revolucionario"; Roberto Etchepareborda, "Política luso-rioplatense 1810–1812."

7. Cf. Emilio Loza, "Yatusta, Tucumán y Salta"; Lynch, *Spanish American Revolutions*, 62–63; Halperín Donghi, *Politics*, 242–46.

8. For the birth of Federalism in the littoral, see José Luis Busaniche, *Estanislao López y el federalismo argentino.*

9. For politics under the First Triumvirate, see Ricardo H. Levene, "El congreso general de las provincias y la conspiración del 18 de diciembre"; Levene, "Las juntas provinciales creadas por el reglamento del 10 de febrero de 1811 y los orígenes del federalismo argentino"; Levene, "Formación del triunvirato"; Juan Canter, "El año XII, las asambleas generales y la revolución del 8 de octubre"; Canter, "La asamblea constituyente."

10. On constitutional monarchy and Queen Carlota, see Roberto Etchepareborda, "Manuel Belgrano y los proyectos carlotinos frente al arribo del nuevo virrey del Rio de la Plata"; Antonio Ramos, "La política de Portugal y la independencia del Paraguay." For Rivadavia's proposed reforms see Sergio Bagú, *El plan económico del grupo rivadaviano, 1811–1827: su sentido y sus contradicciones, sus proyecciones sociales, sus enemigos;* Lynch, *Spanish American Revolutions*, 60–62.

11. Cf. Canter, "El año XII" 693-740.

12. For the enactments of the Second Triumvirate, see Canter, "El año XII."

13. Cf. Street, *Artigas*, 163–244.

14. Cf. Emilio Loza, "La guerra terrestre 1814–15"; Héctor R. Ratto, "La campaña naval contra el poder realista de Montevideo."

15. Street, *Artigas*, 163–244.

16. Cf. Juan Canter, "La revolución de abril de 1815 y la organización del nuevo directorio."

17. Cf. Ricardo Caillet-Bois, "El directorio, las provincias de la unión y el Congreso de Tucumán." On issues of constitutional monarchy and diplomatic relations, see Mario Belgrano, "La política externa con los estados de Europa (1813–16)"; Belgrano, "La santa alianza"; Carlos A. Pueyrredón, "Gestiones diplomáticas en América."

18. For Pueyrredón, see Lynch, *Spanish American Revolutions*, 67–68; José R. López Rosas, *Entre la monarquía y la república*, 230–311.

19. For the second Portuguese invasion of the east bank and the fall of Artigas, see Street, *Artigas*, 279–328.

20. For the Constitution of 1819 and the events of 1820, see López Rosas, *Entre monarquía y república*, 311–56; Andrés M. Carretero, *Anarquía y caudillismo;* Ricardo Levene, "La anarquía de 1820 en Buenos Aires."

21. For further discussion of these issues, see Halperín Donghi, *Politics*, 76–93. Relating some of these events fifty years afterwards Bartolomé Mitre declared "No era una revolución social . . . era una disolución sin plan, sin objeto, operada por los instintos brutales de las multitudes. . . . Al frente de este elemento se pusieron caudillos oscuros, carácteres viriles fortalecidos en las fátigas campestres, acostumbrados al desorden y a la sangre; sin nociones morales, rebeldes a la disciplina de la vida civil. . . . Artigas fué su en-

carnación: imagen y semejanza de la democracia semi-bárbara" [It was not a social revolution . . . it was simply a dissolution with neither a plan nor an object, accomplished by the brutal instincts of mobs. . . . At the head of such groups obscure *caudillos* appeared, men of virile character strengthened by rural tasks and pursuits, men accustomed to disorder and blood; men lacking notions of morality, rebellious to the discipline of civic living. . . . Artigas was the incarnation of such men: the very image of the semibarbarous democracy.] (*Historia de Belgrano* 2:258). See also Rubén H. Zorrilla, *Extracción social de los caudillos*; Rodolfo Puiggrós, *Los caudillos de la revolución de mayo*; Luis C. Alen Lascano, *Juan Felipe Ibarra y el federalismo del norte*; Felix Luna, *Los caudillos*; Luis Alberto Romero, *La feliz experiencia*, 78–140.

22. For commentaries see José M. Mariluz Urquijo, *Estado e industria, 1810–1862*, 25–50; Mariluz Urquijo, "La mano de obra en la industria porteña, 1810–35"; Marta B. Goldburg, "La población negra y mulata de la ciudad de Buenos Aires"; George Reid Andrews, *The Afro-Argentines of Buenos Aires, 1800–1900*.

23. Among numerous discussions of the role of British merchants in Buenos Aires after 1810, see Halperín Donghi, *Politics*, 81–99; Miron P. Burgin, *The Economic Base of Argentine Federalism*, 14–23; Vera Blinn Reber, *British Mercantile Houses in Buenos Aires, 1810–1880*; D. C. M. Platt, *Latin America and British Trade, 1806–1914*; H. S. Ferns, *Britain and Argentina in the Nineteenth Century*; Leandro Gutiérrez, "Los comerciantes ingleses en el Rio de la Plata."

24. For the *saladeros* and the rise of the cattle-ranching elites, see Alfredo J. Montoya, *Historia de los saladeros argentinos*; Montoya, *La ganadería y la industria de salazón de carnes en el período 1810–1862*; Tulio Halperín Donghi, "La expansión ganadera en la campaña de Buenos Aires (1810–1852)"; Horacio C. E. Giberti, *Historia económica de la ganadería argentina*, 2d ed. (Buenos Aires, 1961), 61–85; Jonathan C. Brown, *A Socio-economic History of Argentina, 1776–1860*, 107–82; Esteban Echeverría, "El matadero.".

25. Political events in the early 1820s and the Indian frontier wars are discussed by Halperín Donghi, "Expansión ganadera," 88–93; Montoya, *Historia de los saladeros*, 62–70; Andrés M. Carretero, *Los Anchorena: Política y negocios en el siglo XIX*; Burgin, *Economic Base*, 21–29.

26. For general accounts of Rivadavia's career, see Lynch, *Spanish American Revolutions*, 71–101; Burgin, *Economic Base*, 53–107; Bagú, *Plan económico*; Ferns, *Britain and Argentina*, 60–199; Antonio Sagarna, "El gobierno de Martín Rodríguez y las reformas de Rivadavia: Las reformas políticas"; Ricardo Piccirilli, "Las reformas económicas-financieras, culturales, militares y eclesiásticas del gobierno de Martín Rodríguez y el ministro Rivadavia"; Romero, *Feliz experiencia*, 195–248. For rural legislation in the 1820s, see Ricardo Rodríguez Molsas, *Historia social del gaucho*, 183–200.

27. The classic study of emphyteusis is Jacinto Oddone, *La burguesía terrateniente argentina*, 57–70. See also Carretero, *Los Anchorena*; Halperín Donghi, "Expansión ganadera"; Burgin, *Economic Base*, 97–105.

28. Cf. Ferns, *Britain and Argentina*, 100–110.

29. For the Baring loan, see Ferns, *Britain and Argentina*, 103–54; Ernesto J. Fitte, *Historia de un empréstito*; Samuel E. Amaral, "El empréstito Baring y la crisis de 1826."

30. The Constitution of 1826 and reactions to it are dealt with by Emilio Ravignani, "El congreso nacional de 1824–27: la convención nacional de 1828–29."

31. Cf. Ravignani, "El congreso nacional," 131–85; Ferns, *Britain and Argentina*, 175–85. For a contemporary account by British observers, see the British Packet, *De Rivadavia a Rosas, 1826–1832*; Halperín Donghi, *Guerra y finanzas*, 154–66.

32. On the creation of Uruguay, see Ferns, *Britain and Argentina*, 199.

33. Cf. Ravignani, "El congreso nacional," 188–206; Andrés M. Carretero, *Dorrego*; Carretero, *La llegada de Rosas al poder*; Julio Godio, *Unitarios y federales*; Ricardo H. Levene, "La sublevación del 1 de diciembre de 1828 y los gobiernos de Lavalle y Viamonte"; John Lynch, *Argentine Dictator*, 30–46.

34. For an introduction to the historiographical controversies on Rosas, see Emilio Ravignani, *Rosas: Interpretación real y moderna*; José Luis Busaniche, *Juan Manuel de Rosas*; Mario Guillermo Saraví, *La suma del poder*; Roberto Etchepareborda, *Rosas: controvertida historiografía*; John Lynch, *Argentine Dictator*.

35. For Rosas's background and early career, see Lynch, *Argentine Dictator*, chaps. 1 and 2.

36. For the style of the Rosas regime, see Burgin, *Economic Base*, 158–63, 283–84; Ferns, *Britain and Argentina*, 210–14; Halperín Donghi, *Guerra y finanzas*, 170–72. The fullest account of Rosas's attitudes toward politics and power appear in Lynch, *Argentine Dictator*, 155–62, 349–54.

37. For the war against Paz, see Gorosteguí de Torres, *Historia integral* 1: 85–93; British Packet, *Rivadavia a Rosas*, 300–356.

38. Cf. Gorosteguí de Torres, *Historia integral* 1: 77–78.

39. Cf. Saraví, *Suma del poder*, for a detailed description; see also Lynch, *Argentine Dictator*, 177–86, 201–46.

40. Cf. Burgin, *Economic Base*, 276–78; Jonathan C. Brown, "Dynamics and Autonomy of a Traditional Marketing System."

41. Cf. Burgin, *Economic Base*, 184–204.

42. Cf. Burgin, *Economic Base*, 251–54; Oddone, *Burguesía terrateniente*, 70 passim; Lynch, *Argentine Dictator*, 51–88.

43. Cf. Juan Carlos Nicolau, *Industria argentina y aduana 1835–1854*; José M. Mariluz Urquijo, "Protección y librecambio durante el período 1820–35"; Saraví, *Suma del poder*, 69–73; Burgin, *Economic Base*, 221–41; Lynch, *Argentine Dictator*, 145–48.

44. On the background to the French blockade, see John F. Cady, *La intervención extranjera en el Río de la Plata, 1838–50*, 12–53; Ferns, *Britain and Argentina*, 246–49.

45. Halperín Donghi, *Guerra y finanzas*, 221–24; Lynch, *Argentine Dictator*, 205–6.

46. Halperín Donghi, *Guerra y finanzas*, 231–41.

47. Cf. Cady, *Intervención extranjera*, 53–110; Burgin, *Economic Base*, 243–46; Blinn Reber, *British Mercantile Houses*, 14–20; Saraví, *Suma del poder*, 122–78.

48. Cf. Ferns, *Britain and Argentina*, 252–77; Cady, *Intervención extranjera*, 117–76.

49. For the fall of Rosas see José María Rosa, *La caída de Rosas*; Beatriz Bosch, *Urquiza y su tiempo*; Etchepareborda, *Rosas*, 218–40; Nicolau, *Industria argentina*, 107–22; Halperín Donghi, *Guerra y finanzas*, 241–48; Lynch, *Argentine Dictator*, 308–27.

50. For a general view of social conditions during the period, see S. Samuel Trífolo, *La Argentina vista por viajeros ingleses, 1810–1860*; Richard W. Slatta, "Rural Criminality and Social Conflict in Nineteenth-Century Buenos Aires Province."

51. Cf. Burgin, *Economic Base*, 125–48.

52. The most complete description of economic life in the provinces is Jean Antoine Victor Martin de Moussy, *Description géographique et statistique de la Confédération Argentine*. For Patagonia see Charles Darwin, *Journal of Researches into the Geology, Natural History of the Various Countries Visited During the Voyage of HMS Beagle Around the World*; Carl C. Taylor, *Rural Life in Argentina*, 130–39; Romero, *Feliz experiencia*, 48–70; Brown, *Socio-economic History*, 99–105.

53. Among numerous studies of the anti-Rosas intellectuals the best introduction is José Luis Romero, *A History of Argentine Political Thought*, 136–53. See also Tulio Halperín Donghi, *Proyecto y construcción de una nación*.

54. Among the studies of the city of Buneos Aires in the early nineteenth century are Mariluz Urquijo, *Estado e industria*; Brown, "Dynamics and Autonomy"; Trífolo, *Argentina vista por viajeros*; Un inglés, *Cinco años en Buenos Aires*.

55. For the province of Buenos Aires, see Burgin, *Economic Base*, 257–61; Romero, *Felix experiencia*, 163–80; Halperín Donghi, "Expansión ganadera," 98–109. For a contemporary description, see William McCann, *Two Thousand Miles Ride Through the Argentine Provinces*; Martin de Moussy, *Description géographique* 3:50–75.

56. For the littoral provinces see Martin de Moussy, *Description géographique* 3:97–111, 183–93.

CHAPTER IV

1. These themes are explored in H. S. Ferns, *Britain and Argentina in the Nineteenth Century*, 420 et passim; Ronald Robinson, "Non-European Foundations of European Imperialism," 117–42. For a contemporary survey of social and economic change in this period, see M. G. Mulhall and E. T. Mulhall, *Handbook of the River Plate*.

2. For the *Acuerdo de San Nicolás*, see James R. Scobie, *La lucha por la consolidación nacional*, 28–47.

3. Cf. Scobie, *Consolidación nacional*, 28–29; Andrés Fontana, "Alianzas y organización nacional en la Argentina, 1852–1862," *Estudios Sociales*, Centro de Estudio de Estado y Sociedad, no. 7 (Buenos Aires, 1977); Oscar Oszlak, *La formación del estado argentino*, 59–72.

4. For the economic policies of the confederation, see Ferns, *Britain and Argentina*, 291–301; Scobie, *Consolidación nacional*, 123–30; Beatriz Bosch, *Urquiza y su tiempo*, 319–32; Bosch, "Las provincias del interior en 1856"; Oreste Carlos Ares, "Urquiza y la administración económica-financiera-contable en el Ejército Nacional."

5. For Pavón and preceding events, see Scobie, *Consolidación nacional*, 63–66, 183–354; Ferns, *Britain and Argentina*, 299–302; William H. Jeffrey, *Mitre and Argentina*; Urbano de la Vega, *El general Mitre*; Carlos Heras, "El nacionalismo de Mitre a través de la revolución del 11 de septiembre de 1852"; Bosch, *Urquiza*, 471–567; Carlos A. Segrete, "El presidente Mitre y sus relaciones con los Taboada"; Oszlak, *Formación del estado*, 79–82.

6. For different aspects of the 1862 settlement, see José A. Craviotto, "Mitre y la minería"; Ricardo M. Ortiz, *Historia económica de la Argentina, 1860–1930* 1:81–87; F. J. McLynn, "General Urquiza and the Politics of Argentina, 1861–70."

7. For the constitution of 1853, see Joaquín V. González, *Manual de la constitución argentina*; Juan B. Alberdi, *Bases y puntos de partida para la organización política de la República Argentina*; Luis Liachovitsky, "Lectura de Alberdi"; R. J. Cárcano, *Urquiza y Alberdi: intimidades de una política*; Carlos R. Melo, "La ideología federal de las provincias argentinas entre 1853 y 1880."

8. Cf. Oszlak, *Formación del estado*, 92–94.

9. For a survey of Mitre's presidency, see Ricardo H. Levene, "Presidencia de Mitre."

10. For "El Chacho" see Segrete, "Mitre y los Taboada"; McLynn, "General Urquiza," 94–100; Fermín Chávez, *El Chacho: Ángel Vicente Peñaloza, general de la confederación*; León Pomer, *Cinco años de guerra civil en la Argentina*, 221–52.

11. On Varela see Pomer, *Cinco años*, 27–76; Ernesto J. Fitte, "Horas finales de la insurrección de Felipe Varela."

12. For the background to the Paraguayan war, see Gilbert Phelps, *Tragedy of Paraguay*; León Pomer, *La guerra del Paraguay ¡Gran negocio!*, 35–72.

13. For economic aspects of the war with Paraguay, see Pomer, *Guerra del Paraguay*; McLynn, "General Urquiza," 128–231; Efraín de Cardozo, "Urquiza y la guerra del Paraguay."

14. For politics toward 1880, see Thomas F. McGann, *Argentina, the United States, and the Inter-American System, 1880–1914*, 6–51; Carlos R. Melo, "El año 1877 y los destinos políticos argentinos"; Melo, "La frustración de la conciliación de los partidos."

15. Concerning Sarmiento, see Alberto Palcos, "Presidencia de Sarmiento"; F. J. McLynn, "The Argentine Presidential Election of 1868." See also Alison Bunkley, *Life of Sarmiento*.

16. Mitre's rebellion in 1874 has not been the subject of a complete,

detailed study; see Carlos Heras, "Presidencia de Avellaneda"; José C. Chiaramonte, *Nacionalismo y liberalismo económico, 1860–1880*, 108–11.

17. For aspects of the Tejedor rebellion and the federalization measure, see Heras, "Avellaneda," 261–68; Melo, "Año 1877" and "La frustración."

18. For overviews on economic growth, see Ernesto Tornquist and Co., *The Economic Development of the Argentine Republic in the Last Fifty Years*; Vicente Vásquez-Presedo, *Estadísticas históricas argentinas*; Guido Di Tella and Manuel Zymelman, *Las etapas del desarrollo económico argentino*, 181–229; Sergio Bagú, "La estructuración económica en la etapa formativa de la Argentina moderna"; Haydée Gorosteguí de Torres, "Aspectos económicos de la organización nacional." On population growth see Zulma Recchini de Lattes and Alfredo E. Lattes, *La población de Argentina*. As specialists will be aware, during the late nineteenth and early twentieth centuries Argentine currency was measured in both gold pesos and paper pesos: the former were usually used for international accounts, the latter for domestic. Until the introduction of the Conversion Board in 1899, both measures varied over time against gold and gold-backed currencies, while the gold peso–to–paper peso ratio is simply a measure of the gold premium, i.e., the extent to which the paper peso had undergone depreciation or appreciation against a standard gold measure. In 1899 this ratio was fixed at 0.44 gold peso = 1 paper peso, or 1 gold peso = 2.27 paper pesos.

19. For the saladeros and the traditional cattle industries, see Alfredo J. Montoya, *Historia de los saladeros argentinos*; Horacio C. E. Giberti, *Historia de la ganadería argentina*, 152–55; Manuel E. Macchi, *Urquiza, el saladerista*; Simon G. Hanson, *Argentine Meat and the British Market*, 104.

20. For the early growth of wool, see Jonathan C. Brown, *A Socio-economic History of Argentina, 1776–1860*, 64–138; Juan Carlos Korol and Hilda Sábato, *Cómo fue la inmigración irlandesa en Argentina*; Chiaramonte, *Nacionalismo y liberalismo*, 35–45; Giberti, *Historia de ganadería*, 140–47; Ortiz, *Historia económica*, 57–67, 89–91.

21. For social conditions spawned by the wool boom, see Korol and Sábato, *Inmigración irlandesa*, 69–122.

22. Ibid., 75–76.

23. For general aspects of the growth of agriculture, see James R. Scobie, *Revolution on the Pampas: A Social History of Argentine Wheat, 1860–1910*; Mark C. Jefferson, *Peopling the Argentine Pampas*; Fernando Enrique Barba, "El desarrollo agro-pecuario de la provincia de Buenos Aires (1880–1920)"; Ezequiel Gallo, Jr., "Santa Fe en la segunda mitad del siglo XIX"; Roberto Cortés Conde, "La expansión territorial en la Argentina"; Ernesto Tornquist, *Economic Development*, 27–30.

24. On the agricultural colonies, see Jefferson, *Peopling the Pampas*; Gastón Gori, *Inmigración y colonización en la Argentina*; Ortiz vol. 1, *Historia económica*, 70–72, 97–101; Scobie, *Revolution*, 33–56.

25. Concerning Santa Fe, see Gallo, "Santa Fe"; Gallo, "The Cereal Boom and Changes in the Social and Political Structures of Santa Fe, Argentina"; Scobie, *Revolution*, 33–36, 200.

26. For land alienations see Miguel Ángel Cárcano, *El régimen de la tierra pública, 1810–1916*; Gori, *Inmigración*, 54; Ortiz, *Historia económica*, 255–67; Roberto Cortés Conde and Ezequiel Gallo, Jr., *La formación de la Argentina moderna*, 57–75.

27. For land legislation after 1853, see Jacinto Oddone, *La burguesía terrateniente argentina*; 120–35; Ortiz, *Historia económica*, 101–16; Roberto Cortés Conde, *El progreso argentino*, 55–66.

28. For land credit issues and *cédulas*, see Ferns, *Britain and Argentina*, 370–76; Ortiz, *Historia económica*, 134–40.

29. For land tenure issues, see Cárcano, *Tierra pública*, 82–116; Gori, *Inmigración*, 51–70; Carl C. Taylor, *Rural Life in Argentina*, 170–201; Cortés Conde, *Progreso argentino*, chaps. 1–4. A recent important overview is Carl E. Solberg, "Peopling the Prairies and the Pampas."

30. For immigration see Vásquez-Presedo, *Estadísticas históricas*, 15–20; Manuel Bejerano, "Inmigrantes y estructuras tradicionales in Buenos Aires, 1854–1930," in Di Tella and Halperín Donghi, *Fragmentos de poder*, 75–150; Recchini de Lattes and Lattes, *Población de Argentina*, 59–66; República Argentina, *Resumen estadístico del movimiento migratorio en la República Argentina, 1857–1924*.

31. For the incentives to immigration, see Gori, *Inmigración*, 83–88. As yet no study has been based on comparative international wage data.

32. On the conflicts between natives and immigrants, see Roberto Etchepareborda, "La estructura socio-política argentina y la generación del ochenta"; Bejerano, "Inmigrantes." There is no complete study on this issue for the provinces of Buenos Aires or Santa Fe; see, however, Mark D. Szuchman, *Mobility and Integration in Urban Argentina*, 88–153.

33. For Buenos Aires see James R. Scobie, *Buenos Aires*; Roberto Cortés Conde, "Problemas del crecimiento industrial, 1870–1914"; Donna J. Guy, "The Other Side of Business Imperialism"; Richard M. Morse, "Primacia, regionalización, dependencia."

34. For the beginnings of British investment, see Vera Blinn Reber, *British Mercantile Houses in Buenos Aires, 1810–1880*, 117–40; Ferns, *Britain and Argentina*, 327–58; D. C. M. Platt, *Latin America and British Trade, 1806–1914*, 68–104.

35. Cf. Ferns, *Britain and Argentina*, 327–58.

36. Cf. C. A. Jones, "British Financial Institutions in Argentina, 1860–1914."

37. For the Western and Central railroads, see Colin M. Lewis, "The British-Owned Argentine Railways, 1857–1947," 7–18; Winthrop R. Wright, *British-Owned Railways in Argentina*; Paul B. Goodwin, "The Central Argentine Railway and the Economic Development of Argentina, 1854–1881"; Ferns, *Britain and Argentina*, 344–51.

38. For the Buenos Aires Great Southern Railway, see Lewis, "British-Owned Argentine Railways," 18–22, 39–56; Ferns, *Britain and Argentina*, 351–54.

39. For a nationalist interpretation of conflicts over railroads, see Raúl Scalabrini Ortíz, *Historia de los ferrocarriles argentinos*.

40. For the depression of the mid 1870s, see Ferns, *Britain and Argentina*, 340–83; Di Tella and Zymelman, *Desarrollo económico*, 181–99; Chiaramonte, *Nacionalismo y liberalismo*, 94–108.

41. Cf. Ezequiel Gallo, Jr., "El gobierno de Santa Fe vs. el Banco de Londres y Rio de la Plata, 1876."

42. For the protectionist debates of the 1870s, see Chiaramonte, *Nacionalismo y liberalismo*, 47–70; Chiaramonte, "La crisis de 1866 y el proteccionismo argentino de la década del '70"; Dardo Cúneo, "La burguesía industrial oligárquica, 1875–1930"; Donna J. Guy, "Carlos Pellegrini and the Politics of Domestic Industry, 1873–1906"; Guillermo Gasío and María C. San Román, *La conquista del progreso, 1874–1880*, 67–73.

43. For the development of sugar, see Emilio Schleh, *Noticias históricas sobre el azúcar*; Gustavo Giménez Zapiola, "El interior argentino y el 'desarrollo hacia afuera'"; Jorge Balán, "La cuestión regional en la Argentina: burguesías del interior y el mercado interno en el desarrollo agroexportador"; Donna J. Guy, "Politics and the Sugar Industry in Tucumán, Argentina, 1870–1900"; Guy, "Tucumán Sugar Politics and the Generation of Eighty."

44. For sugar production see Schleh, *Azúcar*, 207–68; Guy, "La política azucarera y la generación del ochenta," 511–15.

45. For social issues relating to sugar, see Giménez Zapiola, "Interior argentino," 106–8; José Panettieri, *Los trabajadores*, 97–103.

46. Mendoza has received less attention than Tucumán; for a brief survey, see Balán, "Cuestión regional en Argentina."

47. For statistical overviews of the 1880s, see Ernesto Tornquist, *Economic Development*; Vásquez-Presedo, *Estadísticas históricas*; Di Tella and Zymelman, *Desarrollo económico*, 181–229.

48. For British trade in the 1880s, see Ferns, *Britain and Argentina*, 371–72; Ortiz vol. 1, *Historia económica*, 307.

49. For the "Conquest of the Desert," see Glynn Williams and Julia Garlant, "The Impact of the Conquest of the Desert upon the Tehuelche of Chubut"; Cortés Conde and Gallo, *Formación de Argentina*, 51; Ortiz vol. 1, *Historia económica*, 163–65; Scobie, *Revolution*, 276; Gasío and San Román, *Conquista del progreso*, 120–29.

50. For Roca's early career, see José Arce, *Roca, 1843–1914*; Natalio Botana, *El orden conservador*, 33–35.

51. For summaries of Roca's measures during the early 1880s, see Oscar E. Cornblit, Ezequiel Gallo, and Alfredo A. O'Connell, "La generación del ochenta y su proyecto"; Cortés Conde and Gallo, *Formación de Argentina*, 87.

52. For the general policies of Juárez Celman, see J. H. Williams, *Argentine International Trade under Inconvertible Paper Money, 1880–1900*; Ortiz vol. 1, *Historia económica*, 292–307; Ferns, *Britain and Argentina*, 446–52; A. G. Ford, *The Gold Standard, 1880–1914*.

53. Cf. Williams, *Argentine Trade*, 56–79; Ford, *Gold Standard*, 100–137.

54. Cf. Williams, *Argentine Trade*, 56–79.

55. Cf. Williams, *Argentine Trade*, 79–95; Ferns, *Britain and Argentina*, 439–58; A. G. Ford, "Argentina and the Baring Crisis of 1890."

56. For the redistributive results of government financial policies and the depression, see Ford, *Gold Standard*, 119–25; Roberto Cortés Conde, "Trends in Real Wages in Argentina, 1880–1910."

57. For the revolution of 1890, see Luis V. Sommi, *La revolución argentina del '90*; Roberto Etchepareborda, *La revolución argentina del noventa*; Gabriel Del Mazo, *El radicalismo*.

CHAPTER V

1. For further commentaries on economic conditions during the early 1890s, see John H. Williams, *Argentine International Trade under Inconvertible Paper Money, 1880–1900*, 95–140; H. S. Ferns, *Britain and Argentina in the Nineteenth Century*, 439–58; A. G. Ford, *The Gold Standard 1880–1914*, 119–40; Guido Di Tella and Manuel Zymelman, *Las etapas del desarrollo económico argentino*, 208–21; Laura Randall, *An Economic History of Argentina in the Twentieth Century*, 49–56.

2. For the growth of wheat farming, see James R. Scobie, *Revolution on the Pampas*; Fernando Enrique Barba, "El desarrollo de la provincia de Buenos Aires (1880–1930)"; Di Tella and Zymelman, *Desarrollo económico*, 236–40; Roberto Cortés Conde, *El progreso argentino*, 99–106.

3. For the Conversion Law of 1899, see Williams, *Argentine Trade*, 156.

4. Among the numerous statistical summaries of this period, see Ernesto Tornquist and Co., *The Economic Development of the Argentine Republic in the Last Fifty Years*; Carlos F. Diaz Alejandro, *Essays in the Economic History of the Argentine Republic*, chap. 1; Di Tella and Zymelman, *Desarrollo económico*, 202–93; Ricardo M. Ortiz, *Historia económica de la Argentina, 1860–1930*, vol. 2; Roberto Cortés Conde and Ezequiel Gallo, Jr., *La formación de la Argentina moderna*; Jaime Fuchs, *Argentina*.

5. On population growth see República Argentina, *Tercer Censo Nacional, 1914*; Juan C. Elizaga, "La evolución de la población argentina en los últimos 100 años"; Zulma Recchini de Lattes, "El proceso de urbanización en la Argentina."

6. Cf. Recchini de Lattes, "Proceso de urbanización"; Gustavo Beyhaut et al., "Los inmigrantes en el sistema ocupacional argentina"; Guy Bourdé, *Urbanisation et immigration en Amérique Latine*; Oscar E. Cornblit, "Inmigrantes y empresarios en la política argentina"; Carl Solberg, *Immigration and Nationalism in Argentina and Chile, 1890–1914*.

7. For foreign trade see Ford, *Gold Standard*, 154–80; Di Tella and Zymelman, *Desarrollo económico*, 202–93; Williams, *Argentine Trade*, 148–229.

8. For railroads see Winthrop R. Wright, *British-Owned Railways in Argentina*, 47–88; A. E. Bunge, *Ferrocarriles argentinos*.

9. For foreign investment see Ferns, *Britain and Argentina*, 493; Pedro Skupch, "El deterioro y fin de la hegemonía británica sobre la economía argentina, 1914–1947," 5–23; C. A. Jones, "British Financial Institutions in Argentina, 1860–1914."

10. A statistical summary of the broader aspects of change in this period is presented by Ernesto Tornquist, *Economic Development*.

11. For changes on the land, see Simon G. Hanson, *Argentine Meat and the British Market*, 83–119; also Barba, "Desarrollo de Buenos Aires," 299–301; Cortés Conde, *Progreso argentino*, 180–84.

12. Hanson, *Argentine Meat*, 119–208; Peter H. Smith, *Politics and Beef in Argentina*.

13. Cf. Reginald Lloyd, ed., *Twentieth-Century Impressions of Argentina*.

14. For Buenos Aires see James R. Scobie, *Buenos Aires*.

15. Cf. Jorge Federico Sábato, "Notas sobre la formación de la clase dominante en la Argentina moderna," 92–96.

16. The structure of the middle class is discussed by Cornblit, "Inmigrantes y empresarios"; David Rock, *Politics in Argentina, 1890–1930*, 18–24.

17. Cf. Rock, *Politics*, 68–69; José Panettieri, *Los trabajadores*; Hobart A. Spalding, Jr., *La clase trabajadora argentina*; Spalding, *Organized Labor in Latin America*, 1–47.

18. On housing see Scobie, *Buenos Aires*, 147–56; Oscar Yujnovsky, "Políticas de viviendas en la ciudad de Buenos Aires."

19. Cf. Spalding, *Clase trabajadora*; Francis Korn, *Buenos Aires*; Roberto Cortés Conde, "Trends in Real Wages in Argentina, 1880–1910." A major contemporary source for social conditions is *Boletín del Departamento Nacional del Trabajo*.

20. Alejandro E. Bunge, *La economía argentina*, 1:104–23.

21. Cf. Díaz Alejandro, *Essays in Economic History*, 152–58; Roberto Cortés Conde, "Patrones de asentamiento y explotación agropecuaria en los nuevos territorios argentinos, 1890–1910"; Sergio Bagú, "La estructuración económica en la etapa formativa de la Argentina moderna."

22. Cf. Scobie, *Revolution*; Carl Solberg, "Agrarian Unrest and Agrarian Policy in Argentina, 1912–1930"; Ortiz, *Historia económica* 2:53–91; Carl C. Taylor, *Rural Life in Argentina*, 8–20, 142–227; Joseph S. Tulchin, "El crédito agrario en la Argentina, 1910–1926."

23. For Patagonia see Lloyd, *Twentieth-Century Impressions*, 780–820; Pierre Denis, *The Argentine Republic*.

24. Cf. Lloyd, *Twentieth-Century Impressions*, 255–68; Denis, *Argentine Republic*, 101–16.

25. For Cuyo see Lloyd, *Twentieth-Century Impressions*, 204–11; Denis, *Argentine Republic*, 79–81.

26. Lloyd, *Twentieth-Century Impressions*, 346. See also Gustavo Giménez Zapiola, "El interior argentino y el 'desarrollo hacia afuera'"; Donna J. Guy, "The Rural Working Class in Nineteenth-Century Argentina."

27. For further discussion see Lloyd, *Twentieth-Century Impressions*; Denis, *Argentine Republic*; also Alberto B. Martinez and Maurice Lewandowski, *The Argentine in the Twentieth Century*; W. H. Koebel, *Argentina*; John Foster Fraser, *The Amazing Argentine*; Alejandro E. Bunge, *Las industrias del norte argentino*; Juan Bialet Massé, *Los obreros a principios del siglo*; Juan Carlos Agulla, *Eclipse of an Aristocracy*.

28. For manufacturing see Jorge Schvarzer, "Algunos rasgos del desarrollo industrial de Buenos Aires"; Adolfo Dorfman, *Historia de la industria argentina*; Roberto Cortés Conde, "Problemas del crecimiento industrial, 1870–1914"; Eduardo F. Jorge, *Industria y concentración económica*; Lucio Geller, "El crecimiento industrial argentino hasta 1914 y la teoría del bien primario exportable."

29. For politics in this period, see Rock, *Politics*, 41–47; Ezequiel Gallo, Jr., *Farmers in Revolt*.

30. Cf. Natalio R. Botana, *El orden conservador*.

31. Cf. Rock, *Politics*, 47–55.

32. For anarchism see Diego Abad de Santillán, *La FORA, ideología y trayectoria*; Iaacov Oveid, "El trasfondo histórico de la ley 4144 de residencia."

33. Cf. Richard J. Walter, *The Socialist Party of Argentina, 1890–1930*.

34. For politics between 1900 and 1910, see Botana, *Orden conservador*, 217–316; Rock, *Politics*, 34–39.

35. Cf. Natalio R. Botana, "La reforma política de 1912"; Oscar Cornblit, "La opción conservadora en la política argentina"; Carlos Ibarguren, *La historia que he vivido*, 226–313; Ezequiel Gallo, Jr. and Silvia Sigal, "La formación de los partidos políticos contemporáneos."

36. The foregoing compendium is based on Diaz Alejandro, *Essays in Economic History*, 209–16; Vernon L. Phelps, *The International Economic Position of Argentina*, 102–41; Ortiz, *Historia económica*, vol. 2.

37. The cycles are best followed in Di Tella and Zymelman, *Desarrollo económico*, 295–420; Ernesto Tornquist and Co., *Business Conditions in Argentina*; Harold J. Peters, *The Foreign Debt of the Argentine Republic*; Alejandro E. Bunge, *Los problemas económicos del presente*.

38. Figures on public accounts quoted in Rock, *Politics*, 224; see also Ortiz, *Historia económica* 2:11–86.

39. Cf. Ian Rutledge, "Plantations and Peasants in Northern Argentina: The Sugar Cane Industry of Salta and Jujuy, 1930–43."

40. For farming in the interior, see Taylor, *Rural Life*, 304–34; Fuchs, *Argentina*, 217–24; Ortiz, *Historia económica* 2:131–48.

41. For indices of manufacturing output, see Di Tella and Zymelman, *Desarrollo económico*, 309, 391–93. See also Javier Villanueva, "El orígen de la industrialización argentina;" Jorge, *Industria*, 43–105.

42. Cf. Jorge Fodor and Arturo O'Connell, "La Argentina y la economía atlántica en la primera mitad del siglo veinte"; Skupch, "Deterioro y fin"; Phelps, *International Economic Position*, 102–64.

43. For additional commentaries see Rock, *Politics*, 107–24; Peter H.

Smith, "Los radicales argentinos y la defensa de los intereses ganaderos"; Roberto Etchepareborda, *Yrigoyen y el congreso;* Rodolfo Moreno, *Intervenciones federales en las provincias.*

44. Quoted in Hebé Clementi, *Juventud y política en la Argentina,* 48.

45. For *"La Reforma"* see Richard J. Walter, *Student Politics in Argentina,* 5–83; Joseph S. Tulchin, "La reforma universitaria."

46. Cf. Rock, *Politics,* 129–31.

47. Ibid., 125–56; Paul B. Goodwin, *Los ferrocarriles británicos y la U.C.R.,* 1916–1930.

48. Rock, *Politics,* 157–200. See also Hugo del Campo, "La Semana Trágica." For events in Patagonia in 1920–1922, see Osvaldo Bayer, *La Patagonia rebelde.*

49. Army issues are discussed at length by Alain Rouquié, *Poder militar y sociedad política en la Argentina* 1:69–145.

50. For details on the later stages of Yrigoyen's first government, see Rock, *Politics,* 190–217.

51. Cf. Smith, *Politics and Beef,* 83–112; Hanson, *Argentine Meat,* 218–30; Oscar E. Colman, "Luchas interburguesas en el agro argentino."

52. For additional data on the tariff issue, see Bunge, *Economía argentina* 3:83–101, 184 et passim; Randall, *Economic History,* 122–25; Diaz Alejandro, *Essays in Economic History,* 212–86; Jorge, *Industria,* 52–77; Carl Solberg, "Tariffs and Politics in Argentina, 1916–1930"; Phelps, *International Economic Position,* 238; Peters, *Foreign Debt,* 50–100.

53. For the salient events of Alvear's administration, see Rock, *Politics,* 218–40; Raúl A. Molina, *Presidencia de Marcelo T. de Alvear;* Carl Solberg, *Oil and Nationalism in Argentina,* 76–111. Changes in the conservative movement in the 1920s can be traced in Marysa Navarro Gerassi, *Los nacionalistas;* see also Rouquié, *Poder militar* 1:182–85.

54. Cf. Solberg, *Oil and Nationalism,* 1–50; Arturo Frondizi, *Petróleo y política,* 45–65.

55. Marcos Kaplan, "Política del petróleo en la primera presidencia de Hipólito Yrigoyen, 1916–22."

56. Solberg, *Oil and Nationalism,* 51–155; Frondizi, *Petróleo y política,* 125–75.

57. Cf. Roberto Etchepareborda, ed., *Hipólito Yrigoyen;* Rock, *Politics,* 235–40; Solberg, *Oil and Nationalism,* 116–29.

58. Cf. Roger Gravil, "Anglo–U.S. Trade Rivalry in Argentina and the D'Abernon Mission of 1929"; Fodor and O'Connell, "Economía atlántica"; Solberg, *Oil and Nationalism,* 113–16.

59. Cf. Celso Rodríguez, *Lencinas y Cantoni,* 158 et passim.

60. Cf. Gravil, "Anglo–U.S. Trade Rivalry."

61. For the coming of the depression, see Di Tella and Zymelman, *Desarrollo económico,* 380–420; Solberg, *Oil and Nationalism,* 149–53; Rock, *Politics,* 252–56; Javier Villanueva, "Economic Development."

62. For further details on the background to revolution, see Robert A. Potash, *The Army and Politics in Argentina, 1928–1945*, 38–58; Roberto Etchepareborda, "Breves anotaciones sobre la revolución del 6 de septiembre de 1930"; Peter H. Smith, "The Breakdown of Democracy in Argentina, 1916–30"; Rock, *Politics*, 257–64; Rouquié, *Poder militar* 1:194–212.

CHAPTER VI

1. For further discussion see David Rock, *Politics in Argentina, 1890–1930*, 252–64; Peter H. Smith, "The Breakdown of Democracy in Argentina, 1916–30"; Anne L. Potter, "The Failure of Democracy in Argentina, 1916–1930."

2. For a detailed description of the coup, see Robert A. Potash, *The Army and Politics in Argentina, 1928–1945*, 38–58; Alberto Ciria, *Parties and Power in Modern Argentina*, 6–11; *La crisis de 1930*; Felix J. Weil, *Argentine Riddle*, 38–41; Ysabel Rennie, *The Argentine Republic*, 219–228.

3. Cf. Marysa Navarro Gerassi, *Los nacionalistas*; Carlos Ibarguren, *La historia que he vivido*, 381–86; Potash, *Army and Politics*, 43–46.

4. Cf. Potash, *Army and Politics*, 43–46.

5. Cf. John W. White, *Argentina: the Life Story of a Nation*, 148–61; Rennie, *Argentine Republic*, 225–28.

6. For descriptions of ballot-rigging practices, see Weil, *Argentine Riddle*, 67; Antonio J. Cayró, "El fraude patriótico."

7. Ciria, *Parties and Power*, 118–23; Weil, *Argentine Riddle*, 5–6; White, *Argentina*, 161–62.

8. Cf. Enrique Díaz Araujo, *La conspiración del '43*, 143–77; Ciria, *Parties and Power*, 19–53. Politics during the 1930s is reviewed in Alain Rouquié, *Poder militar y sociedad política en la Argentina* 1:230–71.

9. Cf. Weil, *Argentine Riddle*, 4–6; Peter G. Snow, *El radicalismo argentino*, 83–100; White, *Argentina*, 123–25.

10. For oil in the 1930s, see Arturo Frondizi, *Petróleo y política*, 270–367; Carl Solberg, *Oil and Nationalism in Argentina*, 157–62; Laura Randall, *An Economic History of Argentina in the Twentieth Century*, 202–15.

11. Weil, *Argentine Riddle*, 3.

12. Cf. Guido Di Tella and Manuel Zymelman, *Las etapas del desarrollo económico argentino*, 380–420. On population see Zulma Recchini de Lattes and Alfredo E. Lattes, *La población de Argentina*.

13. On foreign investment and foreign debt, see Harold J. Peters, *The Foreign Debt of the Argentine Republic*; Vernon L. Phelps, *The International Economic Position of Argentina*, 117–18.

14. Cf. Maria Elena Deligiannis, Stella Maris Martínez, and Mabel Alcira Saiz, "Política económica."

15. Cf. Phelps, *International Economic Position*, 63–85.

16. Deligiannis, Martínez, and Saiz, "Política económica," 47; Weil, *Argentine Riddle*, 142.

17. Exchange control is discussed by Virgil Salera, *Exchange Control and the Argentine Market*, 96–151; Weil, *Argentine Riddle*, 136–63; White, *Argentina*, 207–17; Phelps, *International Economic Position*, 65–74; Roger Gravil, "State Intervention in Argentina's Export Trade Between the Wars."

18. Randall, *Economic History*, 57–73; Deligiannis, Martínez, and Saiz, "Política económica," 31–32.

19. For the Roca-Runciman treaty see Daniel Drosdoff, *El gobierno de las vacas, 1933–1956*; Rennie, *Argentine Republic*, 235–48; White, *Argentina*, 203–13, 342–45; Phelps, *International Economic Position*, 207–11; Salera, *Exchange Control*, 69–95, 152–64; Jorge Fodor and Arturo O'Connell, "La Argentina y la economía atlántica en la primera mitad del siglo veinte," 52–65.

20. These themes are discussed at length in Rennie, *Argentine Republic*, 235–39; White, *Argentina*, 203–10.

21. Cf. White, *Argentina*, 217–19; Salera, *Exchange Control*, 149.

22. Fodor and O'Connell, "Economía atlántica," 54–55.

23. Cf. Pedro Skupch, "Las consecuencias de la competencia del automotor sobre la hegemonía económica británica en la Argentina, 1919–33"; Potash, *Army and Politics*, 86.

24. Cf. Peter H. Smith, *Politics and Beef in Argentina*; 170–95; Drosdoff, *Gobierno de vacas*, 53–92; Rennie, *Argentine Republic*, 252–55; Weil, *Argentine Riddle*, 116–19; Gravil, "State Intervention," 148–59.

25. Cf. Raúl García Heras, "Notas sobre la situación de las empresas de trasportes de capital británico en Argentina a comienzos de los años 30s."

26. Cf. Hebé Clementi, *Juventud y política en la Argentina*, 96.

27. Cf. Navarro Gerassi, *Nacionalistas*, 81–194; Arturo Jauretche, *FORJA y la década infame*; Rennie, *Argentine Republic*, 260–73; Potash, *Army and Politics*, 101. See also Rodolfo Irazusta, *La Argentina y el imperialismo británico"*; Raúl Scalabrini Ortíz, *Política británica en el Rio de la Plata*; Rouquié, *Poder militar* 1:262ff.

28. For Ortiz see Potash, *Army and Politics*, 106–37; Rennie, *Argentine Republic*, 286–88; Ronald H. Dolkart, "The Provinces."

29. Cf. Phelps, *International Economic Position*, 93–101; Di Tella and Zymelman, *Desarrollo económico*, 421–55.

30. These figures were compiled from several sources: see Carlos F. Diaz Alejandro, *Essays in the Economic History of the Argentine Republic*, 208–76; Javier Villanueva, "El orígen de la industrialización argentina"; Di Tella and Zymelman, *Desarrollo económico*, 109–14, 393–97, 433–37, 474–77; Weil, *Argentine Riddle*, 73–76, 135–96, 256–62; Rennie, *Argentine Republic*, 317–31; White, *Argentina*, 293–96; Adolfo Dorfman, *Historia de la industria argentina*; Arturo Luis Goetz, "Concentración y desconcentración de la industria argentina, 1930–60"; Thomas C. Cochran and Ruben Reina, *Entrepreneurship in Argentine Culture*.

31. Cf. Eduardo F. Jorge, *Industria y concentración económica*; Villanueva, "Orígen de industrialización," 465–71.

32. On textiles see Wythe, "Manufacturing"; Dorfman, *Industria argentina*, 372–80; Jorge, *Industria y concentración*, 35–37; Jaime Fuchs, *Argentina*, 226–34, 260–70.

33. For migration statistics see Alfredo E. Lattes, "La dinámica de la población rural en la Argentina entre 1870 y 1970"; Gino Germani, "El surgimiento del peronismo."

34. For wartime changes in land use see Darrell F. Fienup, Russell H. Brannon, and Frank A. Fender, *The Agricultural Development of Argentina*, 13 et passim; Diaz Alejandro, *Essays in Economic History*, 76, 478; Daniel Slutsky, "Aspectos sociales del desarrollo rural."

35. Cf. Weil, *Argentine Riddle*, 76–80, 107–10; Alison M. MacEwan, "The Invisible Proletariat."

36. The classic study on land in this period is Carl C. Taylor, *Rural Life in Argentina*.

37. For political aspects of industrial growth before 1940, see Javier Lindenboim, "El empresariado industrial argentino y sus organizaciones gremiales entre 1930 y 1946"; Weil, *Argentine Riddle*, 133–48, 175 passim; Miguel Murmis and Juan Carlos Portantiero, "Crecimiento industrial y alianza de clases en la Argentina (1930–1940)"; Gary W. Wynia, *Argentina in the Post-War Era*, 29–40.

38. Cf. Di Tella and Zymelman, *Desarrollo económico*, 456–91; Weil, *Argentine Riddle*, 155–57.

39. These adaptations and others may be followed in contemporary press reports; see, for example, *Review of the River Plate*, 1940–1942.

40. For the Pinedo Plan see "El plan de reactivación económica ante el Honorable Senado"; Weil, *Argentine Riddle*, 164–71; Murmis and Portantiero, "Crecimiento industrial," 29–41; Mario Rapoport, "La política británica en la Argentina a comienzos de la década de 1940."

41. Cf. Weil, *Argentine Riddle*, 167–68; Potash, *Army and Politics*, 146; Murmis and Portantiero, "Crecimiento industrial," 37–41.

42. On the blocked balances see Rapoport, "Política británica"; Fodor and O'Connell, "Economía atlántica."

43. For discussions of commercial links with the United States see "Plan de reactivación económica"; Mario Rapoport, *Gran Bretaña, Estados Unidos y las clases dirigentes argentinas, 1940–1945*, 78–145, 246.

44. On U.S.–Argentine commerce in the 1930s see Phelps, *International Economic Position*, 104–11; Salera, *Exchange Control*, 165–79; Rennie, *Argentine Republic*, 46–47; White, *Argentina*, 216–18.

45. Cf. Weil, *Argentine Riddle*, 10–15; Michael J. Francis, *The Limits of Hegemony*, 49–65; C. A. MacDonald, "The Politics of Intervention." The same issues are also discussed in detail by R. A. Humphreys, *Latin America and the Second World War*, vol. 1: *1939–1942*, 148–58; Carlos Escudé, *Gran Bretaña,*

Estados Unidos, y la declinación argentina, 1942–1949, 27–84; Rapoport, *Gran Bretaña*, 38–43.

46. White recognized the link between diplomacy and trade: "Winning the friendship of Argentina . . . is largely a matter of trade and economics" (*Argentina*, 21).

47. For the treaty of 1941, see Francis, *Limits of Hegemony*, 64–72; Humphreys, *Latin America*, 158.

48. Cf. White, *Argentina*, 178; Rennie, *Argentine Republic*, 268.

49. Cf. Francis, *Limits of Hegemony*, 51–68.

50. For the Army's role in manufacturing, see Marta Panaia and Ricardo Lesser, "Las estrategias militares frente al proceso de industrialización (1943–1947)."

51. Cf. Rennie, *Argentine Republic*, 289–98; Potash, *Army and Politics*, 151–79.

52. Cf. Francis, *Limits of Hegemony*, 151–76; Rennie, *Argentine Republic*, 268–76; Weil, *Argentine Riddle*, 64–99. The Rio conference of early 1942 is discussed in some detail by Humphreys, *Latin America*, 165–81.

53. British attitudes toward neutrality are discussed in Sir David Kelly, *The Ruling Few, or the Human Background to Diplomacy*, 287–314; Francis, *Limits of Hegemony*, 179–81; Rapoport, "Política británica"; see also Mario Rapoport, *Gran Bretaña*.

54. For the background to the 1943 coup, see Potash, *Army and Politics*, 191–234; Weil, *Argentine Riddle*, 43–69, 123–89; Rennie, *Argentine Republic*, 304–94; Francis, *Limits of Hegemony*, 194–210; Díaz Araujo, *Conspiración del '43*; Rapoport, *Gran Bretaña*, 37–62.

55. Cf. Díaz Araujo, *Conspiración del '43*, 55–60; Rennie, *Argentine Republic*, 344–47; Potash, *Army and Politics*, 201–5. See also Rouquié, *Poder militar* 2:17–28.

56. Cf. Rennie, *Argentine Republic*, 344–48; Díaz Araujo, *Conspiración del '43*, 204–9; Francis, *Limits of Hegemony*, 196–203.

57. Francis, *Limits of Hegemony*, 203–5; Rennie, *Argentine Republic*, 353–56.

58. Cf. Escudé, *Gran Bretaña*, 262–64.

59. Cf. Weil, *Argentine Riddle*, 45–55; Rennie, *Argentine Republic*, 340–78.

60. Francis, *Limits of Hegemony*, 206–13; Potash, *Army and Politics*, 229–34.

61. Cf. Panaia and Lesser, "Estrategias militares."

62. Fienup, Brannon, and Fender, *Agricultural Development*, 308–29; Randall, *Economic History*, 141; Weil, *Argentine Riddle*, 53–69.

63. For Perón's background see Weil, *Argentine Riddle*, 46–47; Potash, *Army and Politics*, 227–38; Robert J. Alexander, 17–29.

64. Cf. Potash, *Army and Politics*, 238–51.

65. These events have been described on numerous occasions. For a useful chronology see Lawrence Stickell, "Peronist Politics with Labor, 1943"; also Louise M. Doyon, "Organised Labour and Perón, 1943–55," 177–82; Doyon, "El movimiento sindical bajo el peronismo"; Walter Little, "Political

Integration In Peronist Argentina, 1943–1955"; Little, "The Popular Origins of Peronism"; Little, "La organización obrera y el estado peronista"; Samuel L. Baily, *Labor, Nationalism, and Politics in Argentina*, 71–96; Eldon Kenworthy, "The Formation of the Peronist Coalition"; Rouquié, *Poder militar* 2:43–51; Hiroschi Matsushita, *Movimiento obrero argentino, 1930–1945*, 263–73.

66. For labor in the 1930s and early 1940s, see Germani, "Surgimiento del peronismo"; Miguel Murmis and Juan Carlos Portantiero, "El movimiento obrero en los orígenes del peronismo"; Ricardo Gaudio and Jorge Pilone, "Estado y relaciones obrero-patronales en los orígenes de la negociación colectiva en Argentina"; Matsushita, *Movimiento obrero*, 68–240.

67. Cf. Matsushita, *Movimiento obrero*, 245–60.

68. Quoted in Ignacio Llorente, "Alianzas políticas en el surgimiento del peronismo," 275; translation mine.

69. Quoted in Darío Cantón, "El ejército en 1930," 11; translation mine.

70. For an excellent discussion of corporatist doctrine, see Alfred Stepan, *The State and Society*, 29–78.

71. Cf. Escudé, *Gran Bretaña*, 148–55.

72. For American policies at the end of the war, see Francis, *Limits of Hegemony*, 230–40; Cordell Hull, *The Memoirs* 2:1390–1419; Mario Rapoport, "La política de Estados Unidos en Argentina en tiempos de la segunda guerra mundial, 1943–1945"; Rapoport, "Las relaciones anglo-argentinas"; Escudé, *Gran Bretaña*, 174.

73. The events of 1945 are discussed in Baily, *Labor, Nationalism, and Politics*, 71–96; Felix Luna, *El '45*; Llorenti, "Alianzas políticas," 276–81; Díaz Araujo, *Conspiración del '43*, 293–307; Potash, *Army and Politics*, 239–82; Alain Rouquié, *Pouvoir militaire et societé politique en République Argentine*, 362–83; Rouquié, *Poder militar* 2:56–71.

74. For a detailed analysis of the 1946 election, see Mora y Araujo and Llorente, *Voto peronista*; Darío Cantón, *Elecciones y partidos políticos en la Argentina*, 224 et passim. The best analysis of Braden's role is in MacDonald, "Politics of Intervention," 386–90.

CHAPTER VII

1. Among apologias for the Perón regime see Antonio Cafiero, *Cinco años después*, especially 377, 383. For wages and income distribution, see United Nations, Economic Commission for Latin America (ECLA), *The Distribution of Income in Argentina*; José César Villaroel, "Política de ingresos, 1946–55"; Bertram Silverman, "Labor and Left-Fascism," 293.

2. This transition is traced by Samuel E. Baily, *Labor, Nationalism, and Politics in Argentina*, 97 et passim.

3. On sovereignty see Cafiero, *Cinco años después*, 60, 285, 329.

4. For imports of consumer goods see Carlos F. Diaz Alejandro, *Essays in the Economic History of the Argentine Republic*, 225–60.

5. For a favorable view of *justicialismo*, see Cafiero, *Cinco años después*, 369–76.

6. On manufacturing see Maria Elena Deligiannis and Stella Maris Martínez, "Política bancaria y financiera, 1946–55"; Jaime Fuchs, *Argentina*, 314; Ricardo Sidicaro, "L'état peroniste," 287–93.

7. The classic critique is United Nations, Comisión Económica para América Latina (CEPAL), *El desarrollo económico de la Argentina*; see also James W. Foley, "The Balance of Payments and Imports Substituting Industrialization in Argentina, 1945–1961"; Laura Randall, *An Economic History of Argentina in the Twentieth Century*, 158–59.

8. These changes are described in abundant detail in United Nations, CEPAL, *Desarrollo económico*.

9. These and numerous similar criticisms appear in a vast volume of anti-Peronist literature issued after 1955; see, for example, Armando Alonso Piñeiro, *La dictadura peronista*.

10. Cf. Eldon Kenworthy, "The Formation of the Peronist Coalition," 174–80; Kenworthy, "Did the New Industrialists Play a Significant Role in the Formation of Perón's Coalition, 1943–46?"

11. On exports of manufactured goods, see David Felix, "Industrial Structure, Industrial Exporting, and Economic Policy: An Analysis of Recent Argentine Experience," 295.

12. Cf. U.S. Department of State, *Foreign Relations of the United States, 1946* 11:254–76; also *Foreign Relations, 1948* 9:280; Rita Ana Giacalone, "From Bad Neighbors to Reluctant Partners."

13. Felix, *Industrial Structure*, 295; Diaz Alejandro, *Essays in Economic History*, 263.

14. For discussions on policy evaluations, see Cafiero, *Cinco años después*, 64 et passim; Hugh M. Schwartz, "The Argentine Experience with Industrial Credit and Protection" 1:19–30; Harry Raymond Woltman, "The Decline of Argentina's Agricultural Trade," 185–94; Jorge Fodor, "Perón's Policies for Agricultural Exports, 1946–1948"; Alfredo Gómez Morales, *Política económica peronista*.

15. Cf. Alberto Ciria, *Perón y el justicialismo*, 175; Peter Waldmann, *El peronismo, 1943–1955*, 73–74.

16. For the growth of government economic controls, see Deligiannis and Martínez, "Política bancaria," 20; Randall, *Economic History*, 73–76.

17. On the IAPI see Cafiero, *Cinco años después*, 216; Pedro S. Martínez Constanzo, *La nueva Argentina, 1946–1955* 2:13–15; Gary W. Wynia, *Argentina in the Post-War Era: Politics and Economic Policy Making in a Divided Society*, 47.

18. On reserves see Villaroel, "Política de ingresos," 4; Martínez Constanzo, *Nueva Argentina* 2:16.

19. For U.S. relations see Giacalone, "Bad Neighbors," 72–92.

20. On the first five-year plan, see Deligiannis and Martínez, "Política bancaria," 11–16; Cafiero, *Cinco años después*, 106, 187.

21. For economic growth between 1946 and 1949, see Guido Di Tella and Manuel Zymelman, *Las etapas del desarrollo económico argentino*, 502–17; Oscar Altimir, Horacio Santamaría, and Juan Sourrouille, "Los instrumentos de promoción industrial en la postguerra"; Randall, *Economic History*, 139–47; Diaz Alejandro, *Essays in Economic History*, 70–76, 206–56; Schwartz, "Argentine Experience" 1:43 et passim; Richard D. Mallon and Juan Sourrouille, *Economic Policy Making in a Conflict Society*, 9–14; Jorge Katz, "Una interpretación de largo plazo del crecimiento industrial argentino." For a statistical summary see Thomas E. Skidmore, "The Politics of Economic Stabilization in Post-War Latin America," 160–62.

22. For the state sector see Randall, *Economic History*, 138.

23. On nationalization see Cafiero, *Cinco años después*, 60; Eprime Eshag and Rosemary Thorp, "Las políticas económicas ortodoxas de Perón a Guido, 1953–1963," 74–75; Di Tella and Zymelman, *Desarrollo económico*, 513.

24. On railroad nationalization see Nicholas Bowen, "The End of British Economic Hegemony in Argentina"; Pedro Skupch, "El deterioro y fin de la hegemonía británica sobre la economía argentina, 1914–1947," 40–66; Martínez Constanzo, *Nueva Argentina* 2:28–75; Randall, *Economic History*, 188–89; C. A. MacDonald, "U.S.–British Relations with Argentina 1946–50"; Carlos Escudé, *Gran Bretaña, Estados Unidos, y la declinación argentina, 1942–1949*, 310–13.

25. Cf. U.S. Dept. of State, *Foreign Relations, 1947* 8:281–91.

26. These issues are outlined by Ciria, *Perón y justicialismo*, 173–78; Louise M. Doyon, "Organised Labour and Perón, 1943–55," 358–62.

27. On government-military relations see Robert A. Potash, *The Army and Politics in Argentina, 1945–1962*, 10–50; Marvin Goldwert, *Democracy, Militarism, and Nationalism in Argentina, 1930–1966*, 101–19; Kenworthy, "Peronist Coalition," 254–58; Waldmann, *Peronismo*, 138–40; Alain Rouquié, *Poder militar y sociedad política en la Argentina* 2:78.

28. For the *laborista* purge see Carlos F. Fayt, *Naturaleza del peronismo*, 138–56; Ciria, *Perón y justicialismo*, 48–49; Walter Little, "La organización obrera y el estado peronista"; Little, "The Popular Origins of Peronism"; Doyon, "Organised Labour," 398–402.

29. Cf. Juan Carlos Torre, "La caída de Luis Gay"; Doyon, "Organised Labour," 413–16; Alberto Belloni, *Del anarquismo al peronismo*, 57–63.

30. On unions see Silverman, "Labor and Left-Fascism," 211; Little, "Organización obrera," 331–76; Eldon Kenworthy, "The Function of a Little-Known Case in Theory Formation, or What Peronism Wasn't," 33–35; Louise M. Doyon, "Conflictos obreros durante el régimen peronista (1946–1955)"; Doyon, "El movimiento sindical bajo el peronismo"; Baily, *Labor, Nationalism, and Politics*, 84–97; Roberto Carri, *Sindicatos y poder en la Argentina*, 28–80. For social change in this period, see Gino Germani, *La estructura social de la Argen-*

tina; Horacio A. Torres, "El mapa social de Buenos Aires en 1943, 1947 y 1960"; Juan José Llach, "Estructura ocupacional y dinámica del empleo en la Argentina", 539–93.

31. Cf. Little, "Organización obrera"; E. Spencer Willhofer, "Peronism in Argentina"; Kenworthy, "Peronist Coalition," 233; Carri, *Sindicatos y poder,* 28–80.

32. For different aspects of this debate see Ciria, *Perón y justicialismo,* 25, 96; Fayt, *Naturaleza del peronismo,* 157 et passim; Waldmann, *Peronismo;* Silvio Frondizi, *La realidad argentina: Ensayo de interpretación sociológica,* 144–88; Kenworthy, "What Peronism Wasn't"; Mónica Peralta Ramos, "Peronism and Dependency"; Sidicaro, "Etat peroniste"; K. H. Silvert, "Liderazgo político y debilidad institucional en la Argentina"; Francisco Weffort, "Clases populares y desarrollo social"; Walter Little, "Party and State in Peronist Argentina"; Gino Germani, Torcuato S. Di Tella, Octavio Ianni, *Populismo y contradicciones de clase en Latinoamérica.*

33. On Eva Perón see J. M. Taylor, *Eva Perón. The Myths of a Woman;* Ciria, *Perón y justicialismo,* 112–120; J. Otelo Borroni and Roberto Vacca, *Eva Perón;* George Blanksten, *Perón's Argentina;* 98–107.

34. On the Constitution of 1949, see Cafiero, *Cinco años después,* 380–83; Potash, *Army and Politics, 1945–1962,* 90–102; Martínez Constanzo, *Nueva Argentina* 1:124–50; Ciria, *Perón y justicialismo,* 142; Fayt, *Naturaleza del peronismo,* 240.

35. On imports from 1946, see Cafiero, *Cinco años después,* 55; Villaroel, "Política de ingresos," 4–11; Di Tella and Zymelman, *Desarrollo económico,* 497–509; Martínez Constanzo, *Nueva Argentina* 2:16–18; Frondizi, *Realidad argentina,* 144–50.

36. On commerce see Fodor, "Perón's Policies," 135–61.

37. For trade with Britain see Skupch, "Deterioro y fin," 40–66.

38. This is reported by Frondizi, *Realidad argentina,* 180–81; Randall, *Economic History,* 101; Escudé, *Gran Bretaña,* 325–27.

39. U.S. Dept. of State, *Foreign Relations, 1948* 9:285.

40. Ibid.

41. Ibid., 290.

42. U.S. Dept. of State, *Foreign Relations, 1949* 2:473–81.

43. For Marshall Plan sales and market sales in grains, see Cafiero, *Cinco años después,* 296; Diaz Alejandro, *Essays in Economic History,* 201; Louis Rodriguez, "A Comparison: U.S. Economic Relations with Argentina and Brazil, 1947–1960," 100–102, 173.

44. U.S. Dept. of State, *Foreign Relations, 1949* 2:506.

45. On the meat deal with Britain, see Martínez Constanzo, *Nueva Argentina* 2:116; Colin Lewis, "Anglo-Argentine Trade, 1945–60," 120–22; Randall, *Economic History,* 231–34.

46. On terms of trade see Villaroel, "Política de ingresos," 21; Miguel Teubal, "Policy and Performance of Agriculture in Economic Development:

The Case of Argentina," 123; Eshag and Thorp, "Políticas económicas ortodoxas," 79.

47. Among numerous discussions on this issue see Mario Berenbau, "El desarrollo de la agricultura argentina"; Di Tella and Zymelman, *Desarrollo económico*, 496–97; Darrell F. Fienup, Russell H. Brannon, and Frank A. Fender, *The Agricultural Development of Argentina*, 15–84, 303–51; Mallon and Sourrouille, *Economic Policy Making*, 42–43; Randall, *Economic History*, 96–101.

48. Cf. Diaz Alejandro, *Essays in Economic History*, 147–206; Fienup, Brannon, and Fender, *Agricultural Development*, 187–308.

49. Fienup, Brannon, and Fender, *Agricultural Development*, 67–73; Javier Villanueva, "The Inflationary Process in Argentina," 6–10; Lewis, "Anglo-Argentine Trade," 121–29.

50. On oil and coal see Frondizi, *Realidad argentina*, 155, 202; Randall, *Economic History*, 204–10; Diaz Alejandro, *Essays in Economic History*, 245.

51. For figures on 1948–1952, see Di Tella and Zymelman, *Desarrollo económico*, 492–524; Cafiero, *Cinco años después*, 296–320; Villaroel, "Política de ingresos," 7–25; Skidmore, "Politics of Economic Stabilization," 160.

52. For policies in 1949–1952, see Di Tella and Zymelman, *Desarrollo económico*, 492–524; Eshag and Thorp, "Políticas económicas ortodoxas," 79–82; Wynia, *Argentina in the Post-War Era*, 68–70; Randall, *Economic History*, 102ff.

53. Giacalone, "Bad Neighbors," 217–80.

54. Deligiannis and Martínez, "Política bancaria," 18–20; Cafiero, *Cinco años después*, 66; Randall, *Economic History*, 189–203.

55. U.S. Dept. of State, *Foreign Relations, 1948* 9:290.

56. Ibid.

57. Labor trends are discussed in Doyon,"Organised Labour," 478–526; Little, "Organización obrera," 360–76.

58. On repression and the use of the police in 1949–1951, see Potash, *Army and Politics, 1945–1962*, 102; Blanksten, *Perón's Argentina*, 369 et passim; Milcíades Peña, *Masas, caudillos, elites*, 101–4; Rouquié, *Poder militar* 2:89.

59. Eva Perón, *La razón de mi vida* (Buenos Aires, 1951).

60. The atmosphere of 1949–1952 is described in Ciria, *Perón y justicialismo*, 117–37. See also Juan Domingo Perón, *Conducción política*; Perón, *La fuerza es el derecho de las bestias*; Alain Rouquié, *Pouvoir militaire et societé politique en République Argentine*, 389–416.

61. For the election of 1951 see Darío Cantón, *Elecciones y partidos políticos en la Argentina*, 273; Cantón, *Materiales para el estudio de la sociología política en la Argentina* 1:140–48; Walter Little, "Electoral Aspects of Peronism, 1946–1954."

62. On the Menéndez rebellion see Potash, *Army and Politics, 1945–1962*, 108–136.

63. Blanksten, *Perón's Argentina*, vii.

64. On the death of Eva Perón, see Ciria, *Perón y justicialismo*, 190; Potash, *Army and Politics, 1945–1962*, 156–59; Peña, *Masas, caudillos, elites*, 108–10.

65. For the second five-year plan, see Cafiero, *Cinco años después*, 320–28; Potash, *Army and Politics, 1945–1962*, 144–47; Martínez Constanzo, *Nueva Argentina* 2:126–36; Woltman, "Decline of Agricultural Trade," 245–59; Eshag and Thorp, "Políticas económicas ortodoxas," 81–85; Pablo Gerchunoff and Juan J. Llach, "Capitalismo industrial, desarrollo asociado y distribución de ingreso entre los dos gobiernos peronistas," 3–5; Doyon, "Organised Labour," 539–49; Wynia, *Argentina in the Post-War Era*, 70–80; Altimir, Santamaría, and Sourrouille, "Promoción industrial," 894–901.

66. For attempts to develop industrial exports, see Ciria, *Perón y justicialismo*, 164; John T. Deiner, "ATLAS."

67. On foreign investments in the early 1950s, see Waldo Ansaldi, "Córdoba: De la protoindustria a la gran industria dependiente, 1946–1954"; *Primera Plana*, 2 Aug. 1966, 64–69; Martínez Constanzo, *Nueva Argentina* 2:137–48.

68. Cf. Villanueva, "Inflationary Process," 183.

69. On the effects of devaluation, see Foley, "Balance of Payments"; John H. Ohly, "Some Effects of Export Policy on the Short-run Distribution of Real Income in Post–World War II Argentina."

70. On economic performance in 1952–1955, see Eshag and Thorp, "Políticas económicas ortodoxas," 82; Wynia, *Argentina in the Post-War Era*, 71–73; Skidmore, "Politics of Economic Stabilization," 160–62; Gerchunoff and Llach, "Capitalismo industrial," 9–15.

71. For descriptions of the economy around 1955 see United Nations CEPAL, *Desarrollo económico*; Fuchs, *Desarrollo capitalista*, 276–423; Randall, *Economic History*, 158–59, 189–204.

72. Land issues are discussed in Fienup, Brannon, and Fender, *Agricultural Development*, 94–98; Fuchs, *Desarrollo capitalista*, 283–88.

73. Potash, *Army and Politics, 1945–1962*, 151–56.

74. On strikes in 1954 see Doyon, "Organised Labour," 580–601; Daniel James, "Rationalisation and Working-Class Response."

75. On political attitudes among manufacturers, see Doyon, "Organised Labour," 608–19; Kenworthy, "New Industrialists," 15–28; Randall, *Economic History*, 158–59; Peña, *Masas, caudillos, elites*, 114–16; Peralta Ramos, "Peronism and Dependency," 82–92.

76. For the "Organized Community" see Doyon, "Organised Labour," 526–31.

77. On the Church issue see Potash, *Army and Politics, 1945–1962*, 166–88; Hugo Gambini, *El peronismo y la iglesia*; Martínez Constanzo, *Nueva Argentina* 2:165–94; Sidicaro, "Etat peroniste," 356–61; Peña, *Masas, caudillos, elites*, 121–25; Robert McGeagh, "Catholicism and Socio-political Change in Argentina, 1943–1973," 166 et passim.

78. For commentaries on the 1955 revolution, see Potash, *Army and Politics, 1945–1962*, 188–202; Goldwert, *Democracy, Militarism, and Nationalism*, 130–36; Julio Godio, *La caída de Perón*; Martínez Constanzo, *Nueva Argentina*

2:235–303; Arthur P. Whitaker, *Argentine Upheaval*; Juan Carlos Torre and Santiago Senén González, *Ejército y sindicatos*.

CHAPTER VIII

1. On education and housing see República Argentina, Poder Ejecutivo Nacional, *Plan trienal para la reconstrucción y la liberación nacional*, 362; Martin Segrera, *Argentina, superpoblada*, 164.

2. On economic growth rates see Carlos F. Diaz Alejandro, *Essays on the Economic History of the Argentine Republic*, 127–29.

3. Ibid., 146–50; Juan José Llach, "Estructura ocupacional y dinámica del empleo en la Argentina"; Sergio Bagú, "Población, recursos nacionales y neoarcaísmo organizativo en la economía latinoamericana del siglo XX."

4. For agricultural marketing issues see the annual publications of the Bolsa de Cereales, *Número estadístico* and *Memorias e informes de la Comisión Directiva de la Bolsa de Cereales*; for meat, see *Junta Nacional de Carnes, Reseñas*; Ronaldo J. Bohtlingk, *Mercados de Europa para carnes argentinas*; Carlos García Martínez and Rafael Olarra Jiménez, "Una nueva política para la exportación de carnes"; José Alfredo Martínez de Hoz, Jr., "Los cereales argentinos y el mercado común europeo"; Theodore W. Schultz, "Competition for the Food and Grain Markets in the World"; Ernesto S. Liboreiro, "Effects of the European Common Market's Agricultural Policies on Argentine Exports of Beef." On LAFTA see FIAT, Oficina de estudios para la colaboración económica internacional, *Mercado ALALC*; "¿Qué gana la Argentina con la ALALC?"

5. For an example of agricultural trends in the interior, see Lucio G. Reca, "Precios y áreas sembradas con algodón en la provincia del Chaco, 1938–1968."

6. Agricultural issues are discussed at length by Diaz Alejandro, *Essays in Economic History*, 170 et passim; Richard D. Mallon and Juan Sourrouille, *Economic Policy Making in a Conflict Society*; 36–66; Roberto Risso Patrón, *El agro y la cooperación internacional*; Jorge Federico Sábato, "La pampa pródiga," 19–34, 89.

7. On land taxation see Horacio Giberti, "Renta potencial y productividad agraria"; Martín Piñeiro, "El impuesto a la tierra."

8. On land reform see Vicente Pellegrini, *Teoría y realidad de la reforma agraria*; Solon L. Barraclough, ed., *Agrarian Structures of Latin America*, 59–82.

9. On agricultural financing and technology, see Horacio Giberti, "Uso racional de los factores directos de la producción agraria"; Guillermo Flichman, "Modelo sobre la asignación de recursos en sector agropecuario"; Lucio G. Reca, "Ingresos, tecnología y desarrollo del sector agropecuario"; Enrique R. Zeni, *El destino de la agricultura argentina*; Edith Scheinkerman de Obschatko, "Factores limitantes al cambio tecnólogico en el sector agropecuario."

10. *Latin America: Economic Report*, 17 Nov. 1978.

11. For analyses of domestic manufacturing, see Diaz Alejandro, *Essays in Economic History*, 223–74; Mallon and Sourrouille, *Economic Policy Making*, 67–92; Cheryl Ann Cook, "Macroeconomic Development and Public Policy in Argentina, 1930–1965"; José Adolfo Datas-Panero, "Import Substitution Industrialization"; Guido Di Tella, "Criterios para una política de desarrollo industrial"; Mario S. Brodersohn, comp., *Estrategias de industrialización para la Argentina*; Jorge Abot et al., "El poder económico en la Argentina"; Jorge M. Katz, "Características estructurales del crecimiento industrial argentino, 1946–1961"; Beatriz Schmukler, "Relaciones actuales de producción en industrias tradicionales no capitalistas"; Jorge Schvarzer, "Empresas públicas y desarrollo industrial en la Argentina." For the growth of the Argentine automobile industry, see *Primera Plana*, 2 Aug. 1966.

12. On exports of manufactured goods, see John R. Erikson, "La exportación de manufacturas en la Argentina"; A. B. Ribas et al., "Análisis de las dificultades internas que obstaculizan las exportaciones no tradicionales." On exports after 1976 see Ricardo Ferucci, Alberto Barbero, and Mario Rapoport, "El sector industrial argentino."

13. For a general sketch of stabilization plans, see Eprime Eshag and Rosemary Thorp, "Las políticas económicas ortodoxas de Perón a Guido, 1953–1963."

14. For analyses of devaluation see Stephen F. Overturf, "A Short-run Balance of Payments Model"; Huntley H. Biggs, "Devaluation, Inflation, and Relative Price Changes for Agricultural Exports"; Mallon and Sourrouille, *Economic Policy Making*, 93–99.

15. For the "beef cycle" see Gustavo A. Nores, "Quarterly Structure of the Argentine Beef Cattle Economy, 1960–1970."

16. Cf. Overturf, "Balance of Payments"; Biggs, "Devaluation."

17. For estimates and calculations on investment by multinationals, see Simón Guerberoff, "Un análisis de la performance del segmento industrial estable y su impacto en el modelo de crecimiento económico argentino (1949–1967)"; Abot et al., "Poder económico."

18. For further data see Oscar Braun, *El desarrollo de la capital monopolista en la Argentina*; Jorge Schvarzer, "Las empresas más grandes en la Argentina"; Guillermo Martorell, *Las inversiones extranjeras en la Argentina*; Juan V. Sourrouille, "La presencia y el comportamiento de las empresas en el sector industrial argentino."

19. Cf. Braun, *Capital monopolista*; Pedro F. Paz, "Dependencia y desnacionalización de la industria interna"; Horacio Ciafardini, "Imperialismo y dependencia"; Rogelio García Lupo, *Mercenarios y monopolios en la Argentina de Onganía a Lanusse*.

20. For foreign-debt issues see Percy D. Warner III, "The Impact of the Service on the Foreign Debt on the Monetary Structure"; Clarence V. Zuvekas, Jr., "Argentine Economic Policies under the Frondizi Government." Foreign-debt issues in the early 1980s are discussed in numerous press reports in September 1982.

21. For commentaries on resources in Argentina see United Nations, Comisión Económica para América Latina (CEPAL), *El desarrollo económico de la Argentina* 2:129; Bagú, "Población"; John E. Hutchison, Francis S. Urban, and John C. Dunmore, "Argentina."

22. For urbanization and migration see Alfredo L. Lattes, "La dinámica de la población rural en la Argentina"; Alejandro E. Rofman and Luis A. Romero, *Sistema socioeconómico y estructura regional en la Argentina.*

23. For further discussion see República Argentina, Presidencia de la Nación Argentina, Consejo Nacional de Desarrollo, *Plan nacional de desarrollo*; República Argentina, Presidencia de la Nación, Secretaría del Consejo Nacional del Desarrollo, *Plan nacional de desarrollo, 1970–1974.*

24. Cf. Llach, "Estructura ocupacional," 548–49; Segrera, *Argentina, superpoblada*, 85–97.

25. On unemployment see Diaz Alejandro, *Essays in Economic History*, 130–33; Juan Carlos de Pablo, "Sobre la distribución funcional del ingreso"; José Nun, "Superpoblación relativa, ejército industrial de reserva y masa marginal."

26. Social analysis of contemporary Argentina is disappointingly thin. On elites see José Luis de Imaz, *Los que mandan*; Imaz, "El poder de las terratenientes."

27. On social structure see Gino Germani, *La estructura social de la Argentina*; Germani, *Política y sociedad en una época de transición*; Jorge Graciarena, *Poder y clases sociales de América Latina*; Zulma Recchini de Lattes, "La participación feminina en la Argentina desde la segunda guerra hasta 1970"; Catalina H. Wainerman and Marysa Navarro, "El trabajo de la mujer en la Argentina."

28. For general accounts of post-1955 politics see Gary W. Wynia, *Argentina in the Post-War Era*; Guillermo O'Donnell, "Un 'juego imposible'"; Antonio Castagno, *Tendencias y grupos políticos en la realidad argentina*; Donald C. Hodges, *Argentina, 1943–1976*; David Rock, "The Survival and Restoration of Peronism."

29. On Lonardi see Arthur P. Whitaker, *Argentine Upheaval"*; Robert A. Potash, *The Army and Politics in Argentina, 1945–1962*, 215–25; Marcelo Cavarozzi, "Sindicatos y política en Argentina, 1955–58"; Juan Carlos Torre and Santiago Senén González, *Ejército y sindicatos.*

30. For the assault on Peronism, see Wynia, *Argentina in the Post-War Era*, 144–59; Postash, *Army and Politics, 1945–1962*, 225–31; Cavarozzi, "Sindicatos y política."

31. On the Prebisch Plan see Wynia, *Argentina in the Post-War Era*, 48–54; Prebisch's analysis is detailed in United Nations, CEPAL, *Desarrollo económico.*

32. On union responses to the *Revolución Libertadora*, see Cavarozzi, "Sindicatos y política"; Torre and Senén González, *Ejército y sindicatos*; Juan Carlos Torre, "Sindicatos y clase obrera en la Argentina post-peronista"; Torre, "El proceso interno de los sindicatos en la Argentina."

33. For economic policy under Aramburu see Mallon and Sourrouille,

Economic Policy Making, 14–19; Eshag and Thorp, "Políticas económicas ortodoxas," 84–92.

34. For the 1958 election see Potash, *Army and Politics, 1945–1962*, 262–74.

35. For Frondizi's policies see ibid., 274–88.

36. For the Stabilization Plan of 1959, see Wynia, *Argentina in the Post-War Era*, 99–107; Potash, *Army and Politics, 1945–1962*, 274–326; Aldo Ferrer, "Devaluación, redistribución de ingresos y el proceso de desarticulación industrial en la Argentina"; M. S. Brodersohn, "Estrategias de estabilización y expansión en la Argentina, 1959–67"; Eshag and Thorp, "Políticas económicas ortodoxas," 93–98; Zuvekas, "Policies under Frondizi," 68 et passim.

37. For these political issues see Potash, *Army and Politics, 1945–1962*, 299–317; Alain Rouquié, *Poder militar y sociedad política en la Argentina* 2:153–74.

38. For *desarrollismo* see Zuvekas, "Policies under Frondizi," 6–12; Wynia, *Argentina in the Post-War Era*, 90–95. Frondizi and Frigerio each issued numerous publications examining various facets of their policies; see, for example, Arturo Frondizi, *El problema agrario argentino*; Rogelio Frigerio, *Nacionalismo, potencias industriales y subdesarrollo*.

39. For economic trends in 1960 and 1961, see Zuvekas, "Policies under Frondizi," 94–112; Wynia, *Argentina in the Post-War Era*, 102–4.

40. Zuvekas, "Policies under Frondizi," 135–231; Wynia, *Argentina in the Post-War Era*, 91–105.

41. For the fall of Frondizi, see Potash, *Army and Politics, 1945–1962*, 336–70.

42. For the economy in 1962–1963, see Zuvekas, "Policies under Frondizi," 125–38; Brodersohn, "Estrategias de estabilización," 45–59; Eshag and Thorp, "Políticas económicas ortodoxas," 109–23.

43. Cf. Wynia, *Argentina in the Post-War Era*, 122–25.

44. For some light on these still obscure military conflicts see Potash, *Army and Politics, 1945–1962*, 378; Rouquié, *Poder militar* 2:194–213.

45. For politics in 1962–1963 see Castagno, *Tendencias y grupos políticos*, 6–9; Wynia, *Argentina in the Post-War Era*, 107–11.

46. The course of the Illia administration is described in Wynia, *Argentina in the Post-War Era*, 112–29; Zuvekas, "Policies under Frondizi," 197–204.

47. The 1966 coup has not yet been the subject of an ordered description. The fullest account is Rouquié, *Poder militar* 2:225–53; see also *Primera Plana*, Nov. 1965–June 1966.

48. The early stages of Onganía's regime are described in Wynia, *Argentina in the Post-War Era*, 169–84; Darío Cantón, *La política de los militares argentinos, 1900–1971*, 65–84. The most detailed account of 1966–1970 is Guillermo O'Donnell, *El estado burocrático-autoritario*.

49. Quoted in *La Razón*, 16 Feb. 1969. For a detailed analysis of the Krieger Vasena Plan, see Juan C. de Pablo, *Política anti-inflacionaria en la Argentina, 1967–1970*, O'Donnell, *Estado burocrático-autoritario*, chap. 3.

50. Issues of political control are discussed in detail by O'Donnell, *Estado burocrático-autoritario*, chap. 3.

51. This account of the *cordobazo* is based primarily on press reports. The quotations are from *Primera Plana*, 25 Mar. 1969; translation mine. See also Francisco J. Delich, *Crisis y protesta social*; Horacio González Trejo, *Argentina*.

52. For economic issues in 1969–1970, see O'Donnell, *Estado burocrático-autoritario*, chap. 6; Rogelio Frigerio, "El problema de la carne, los frigoríficos y la crisis general de la economía argentina"; Oscar Braun and Ricardo Kesselman, "Argentina 1971."

53. The growth of radical organizations in 1969-1970 may be followed in *Primera Plana*. See also the popular periodical *Los Libros* (Buenos Aires), which devoted several issues to foreign investment and SITRAC–SITRAM; also O'Donnell, *Estado burocrático-autoritario*, chap. 5.

54. For the kidnap and death of Aramburu see O'Donnell, *Estado burocrático-autoritario*, chap. 6. The incident was subsequently described by the guerrillas; see *La Causa Peronista*, 3 Sept. 1974.

55. On the guerrilla groups see Richard Gillespie, "Armed Struggle in Argentina"; Gillespie, *Soldiers of Perón*; Hodges, *Argentina, 1943–1976*, viii–x, 54–57; John William Cooke, *La lucha por la liberación nacional*.

56. These incidents are detailed in press reports from April through December 1970; see *La Prensa*, *La Nación*, and *Clarín*, for example.

57. For the fall of Onganía, see O'Donnell, *Estado burocrático-autoritario*, chap. 5.

58. For Levingston see ibid., chap. 6; Wynia, *Argentina in the Post-War Era*, 190. On Levingston's economic policy, see República Argentina, Secretarías del Consejo Nacional de Desarrollo y del Consejo Nacional de Seguridad, *Plan nacional de desarrollo y seguridad*.

59. For politics under Lanusse see Wynia, *Argentina in the Post-War Era*, 190–92; Hodges, *Argentina, 1943–1976*, 56–85; Alejandro Lanusse, *Mi testimonio*.

60. Among the best accounts of Peronism after 1955 are "Porque se dividen los peronistas"; Daniel James, "Unions and Politics: The Development of Peronist Trade Unionism, 1955–1966."

61. For the growth of Peronism in 1972–1973, see Wynia, *Argentina in the Post-War Era*, 192–205; David Rock, "Repression and Revolt in Argentina"; Hodges, *Argentina, 1943–1976*, 108–19; James, "Unions and Politics."

62. For the elections of 1973, see Peter H. Smith and Manuel Mora y Araujo, "Peronismo y desarrollo"; Héctor J. Cámpora, *La revolución peronista*.

63. For politics from March through November 1973, See Rock, "Repression and Revolt"; Hodges, *Argentina, 1943–1976*, 110–15.

64. For the Social Compact and Perón's program in 1973–1974, see Wynia, *Argentina in the Post-War Era*, 215–21; Victor Testa, "Aspectos económicos de la coyuntura actual (1973–1975)"; Carlos Ábalo, "Aldo Ferrer y el dilema económico de la Argentina"; República Argentina, *Plan trienal*; Guido Di Tella, *Perón-Perón, 1973–1976*, 93–128, 153–91.

65. Cf. Rock, "Repression and Revolt"; Hodges, *Argentina, 1943–1976*, 108–10.

66. For the guerrilla war and the growth of repression, see Gillespie, "Armed Struggle"; Organization of American States, Inter-American Commission on Human Rights, *Report on the Situation of Human Rights in Argentina.*

67. On the economy in 1974–1975 see Wynia, *Argentina in the Post-War Era*, 221; Testa, "Aspectos"; Di Tella, *Perón-Perón*, 196–255.

68. On the *rodrigazo* see Wynia, *Argentina in the Post-War Era*, 224; Di Tella, *Perón-Perón*, 269–92.

69. For politics from late 1975 to the coup of March 1976, see Hodges, *Argentina, 1943–1976*, 168 et passim; Juan Carlos Torre, "Sindicatos y trabajadores bajo el último gobierno peronista."

70. For the last phase of the guerrilla war, see Gillespie, "Armed Struggle"; Organization of American States, *Report on Human Rights.*

71. *Latin America: Political Report*, 6 Jan. 1978.

72. For economic management between 1976 and 1978, see Maria Elena Deligiannis, "La política financiera a partir de junio de 1977"; Stella Maris Martínez, Sector energético"; Roberto Frenkel and Guillermo O'Donnell, "Los programas de estabilización convenidos con el FMI y sus impactos internos"; Jorge Schvarzer, "Martínez de Hoz," 31–37.

73. On neoliberalism see Adolfo Canitrot, "La disciplina como objectivo de la política económica"; Guillermo O'Donnell, "Estado y alianzas en la Argentina"; Roberto Frenkel, "Decisiones de precio en alta inflación."

74. For estimates on the decline of manufacturing after 1976, see Canitrot, "Disciplina," 16–18; Ferucci, Barbero, and Rapoport, "Sector industrial."

75. This sketch of factional conflicts in the Junta is based on selected readings in *Latin America: Economic Report*, Jan. 1977–Dec. 1979.

76. This imbalance was foreseen as a possibility by observers as early as December 1977: "Martínez de Hoz's policy of building up the overseas debt has been helped by the favorable trade balances, though the figures also suggest that the slightest weakness in the trade balance could jeopardise the overall balance of payments" (*Latin America: Political Report*, 2 Dec. 1977). By October 1979 there were reports of a "growing feeling that the peso is being kept overvalued to stimulate the inflow of short-term speculative funds" (ibid., 26 Oct. 1979). See Schvarzer, "Martínez de Hoz," 50–77.

77. See *Latin America Weekly Report*, 26 Sept. 1980, 24 Oct. 1980, 3 Apr. 1981; Jorge Schvarzer, "Argentina, 1976–1981," 5–6, 23–31.

78. Ibid., 5 June 1981.

79. Ibid., 8 Jan. 1982.

80. Ibid., 22 Dec. 1981; 1 Jan., 8 Jan., 12 Feb. 1982.

81. Ibid., 5 Mar. 1982.

82. Argentine government assessments of the pending Falklands invasion were reported in subsequent commissions of inquiry; cf. *Guardian* (London), 28 Sept. 1982.

Glossary of Spanish Terms

acuerdo. ["agreement"] Political deal between leading politicians, in the late nineteenth and early twentieth centuries.

Aduana Seca. Customs line established by Spain in Córdoba in 1618 intended to break commercial links between Buenos Aires and Upper Peru.

aforo. Appraised value of imports on which customs duties are based.

aguardiente. Liqueur reminiscent of brandy, usually associated with San Juan province.

aguinaldo. ["Christmas box"] Wage bonus introduced by Perón, usually a year-end extra month's wage.

alcabala. Colonial sales tax.

alguacil mayor. Colonial city official with special duties for revenues.

almojarifazgo. Colonial tax on imports.

Antipersonalistas. Radical party opponents of Yrigoyen in the 1920s.

apertura. ["opening"] Effort at political liberalization made by contemporary Argentine military governments.

arribada forzosa. ["putting into port by stress"] Early colonial maritime legal convention allowing normally unauthorized foreign ships to invoke storm damage at sea to enter Spanish American ports—frequently so as to engage in illegal trade.

arroba. Archaic Spanish weight roughly equal to twenty-five pounds.

asiento. ["seat"] A slave-trading franchise.

Azules. ["Blues"] Army faction of the early 1960s.

bandeirante. Member of the seventeenth-century pack of bandit slave-raiders based in São Paulo.

Beneméritos. Early–seventeenth-century political faction in Buenos Aires that supported Paraguayan cattle interests.

417

Blancos. ["Whites"] Uruguayan rural political party.

blandengues. The rural militia in the River Plate in the late eighteenth and early nineteenth centuries.

boleadoras. Triangular weighted lasso used to trap animals.

cabecitas negras. ["little black heads"] Vulgar term used in Buenos Aires for rural migrants from the interior.

Cabildo. Central authority of the Spanish colonial city.

Cabildo abierto. Assembly of Spanish colonial citizens (*vecinos*).

capitulación. Sixteenth-century contract extended by the Spanish crown to explorers and *conquistadores.*

Casa Rosada. ["Pink House"] Government House in Buenos Aires.

caudillo. ["leader"] Early–nineteenth-century regional warlord.

La Causa. ["The Cause"] Yrigoyen's epithet for the Radical Party.

cédula. (1) Written royal directive to the colonies; (2) a land bond in the latter nineteenth century.

chaqueño. Inhabitant of the Chaco region.

chacra. A small farm.

china. Gaucho woman.

Colorados. ["Reds"] (1) Urban-based political party in Uruguay; (2) a military faction in Argentina in the early 1960s.

Colorados del Monte. Rosas's rural militia in the 1820s.

comerciantes. ["merchants"] Colonial merchants who dominated trade with Spain in the late eighteenth century.

comercio libre. ["free trade"] Neomercantilist Spanish trade system of the late eighteenth century.

comprar a quien nos compra. ["Buy from those who buy from us"] A slogan adopted by the Argentine Rural Society in the late 1920s to support a deliberate policy to purchase British imports.

comuneros. Eighteenth-century urban rebels who opposed economic and political centralization.

La Comunidad Organizada. ["The Organized Community"] Perón's corporatist system of the early 1950s.

conchabo. ["hiring bond"] The formal bonding of peons to *estancias* in eighteenth-century Buenos Aires.

Concordancia. Argentina's ruling party between 1930 and 1943, created by Agustín P. Justo.

Confederados. An early–seventeenth-century political faction in Buenos Aires that supported Portuguese traders.

confirmación real. The Spanish crown's acknowledgment of real estate ownership.

consulado. Eighteenth-century municipal chamber of commerce.

contribución del comercio. Tax on merchants during the wars of independence.

cordobazo. The great urban riot in Córdoba in May 1969.

corregidor. Hapsburg colonial official entrusted with guardianship of Indian communities.

correntino. Inhabitant of Corrientes.

criador. Cattle breeder, in contrast with *invernador,* cattle fattener.

curato. Ecclesiastical parish embracing a community of Indians.

desacato. ["disrespect"] Form of repressive control used in contemporary Argentina to prevent public criticism of government.

desarrollismo. ["developmentalism"] Economic development strategy of the early 1960s associated with Arturo Frondizi.

desarrollo hacia adentro. ["inward-led development"] Strategy for economic growth centered on expansion of the domestic market.

descamisado. ["shirtless"] Working-class follower of Perón.

diezmo. Ecclesiastical tithe.

doctrina. In Colonial Argentina, an Indian community administered by ecclesiastics.

encomienda. ["charge," "commission," "care," "protection"] System of trusteeship that placed Indians under Spanish overlords.

entrada. ["entrance"] Invasion of Indian territories by Spanish expeditions.

entreguismo. [from *entregar,* "to hand over," "to surrender"] Contemporary Argentine nationalists' term denoting a willingness to foster foreign economic penetration.

estado de compromiso. ["compromise state"] Modern Latin American social scientists' term denoting a system of government that tries to mediate and balance competing class interests.

estancia. ["estate"] Large pampas ranch.

fanega. Archaic Spanish measure of weight; of variable dimension in different periods, but usually around two hundred pounds.

financiera (casa financiera). ["financial house"] Type of credit bank in Argentina chartered in the late 1970s.

frigorífico. Meat-packing plants using freezing and chilling techniques.

Fuerzas Vivas. ["leading interests"] The economic aristocracy, a term especially common between 1890 and 1950.

gente perdida. ["lost people"] A seventeenth-century term for the free *gauchos* in the pampas.

Gran Asado Nacional. ["Great National Barbecue"] A pun on Lanusse's *Gran Acuerdo Nacional* ["Great National Agreement"] used to satirize the public barbecues of the Galtieri period.

hacienda. Large farm based on agriculture and peasant production.

interpelación. Constitutional procedure, with French antecedents, that allows the lower chamber of Congress to summon ministers to public sessions for questioning.

ingenio. Sugar mill.

intervención federal. Dissolution of a provincial government by the central government, and subsequent direct rule from Buenos Aires.

intransigentes. ["intransigents"] Faction of the Radical party formed in 1930s in opposition to electoral malfeasance.

invernador. Cattle fattener, in contrast with *criador,* cattle breeder.

junta. (1) Board or committee, as in *Junta de Algodón,* the Cotton Board of the 1930s; (2) military government coalition.

legua. Colonial measure of distance; somewhat variable, but standardly 2.6 miles.

El Líder. Hispanicized form of *leader;* popular title for Perón in the 1940s.

llaneros. ["plainsmen"] Plains inhabitants, particularly those of the province of La Rioja.

logia. Military cabal, such as the GOU (usually, *Grupo de Oficiales Unidos*) of 1943.

macucina. A debased money of the eighteenth century used among lower orders.

mayorazgo. Entailed landed estate inherited through primogeniture.

Mazorca. Irregular police force used by Rosas.

mediería. Share-cropping contract that allows a half-share of the crop to a tenant.

mercader. Eighteenth-century retail merchant.

minifundio. Small peasant farm, with the connotation of below-subsistence resources.

mita. Rotationary forced-labor draft used in mining and commercial agriculture in colonial Tucumán and Cuyo.

moneda de la tierra. Commodity, most commonly cotton, used as quasi-money in early colonial Argentina.

Montonera. Rural bandit of the mid nineteenth century.

navíos de registro. Spanish ships sailing singly and specially chartered by the Crown.

obraje. Textile workshop employing forced Indian labor.

peonía. Parcel of land set aside for agriculture.

personería gremial. A labor association, or *gremio,* enjoying full legal status.

política criolla. ["creole politics"] The Argentine Socialist Party's term to denote other political parties with a strong traditional bent.

privatización. Equivalent to English *privatization;* the alienation of public companies to private capital.

procurador. Eighteenth-century Jesuit merchant.

pulperías. Rural store or canteen in the pampas.

quintal. Archaic Spanish weight, about one hundred pounds.

rancho. A peasant smallholding.

real. A colonial monetary unit, eight of which equaled one peso.

reducción. Indian reservation.

La Reforma. University reform movement inaugurated in Córdoba in 1918.

El Régimen. ["The Regime"] Yrigoyen's term for the conservative governments before 1912.

reintegro. ["drawback"] Reimbursement to an exporter of costs incurred in importing raw materials.

repartimiento. Labor draft of Indians administered by the colonial authorities.

retenciones. Modern tax on agricultural exports.

Revolución Libertadora. ["the Liberating Revolution"] The rebellion that overthrew Perón in 1955.

rodrigazo. The general strike following Celestino Rodrigo's austerity program in mid 1975.

saladero. Early nineteenth-century meat-salting plant.

setembristas. Supporters of the revolt in Buenos Aires against Urquiza in September 1852.

sindicalismo clasista. ["class syndicalism"] A trade-union movement of the early 1970s led by SITRAC–SITRAM.

situaciones. Late–nineteenth-century Argentine term to denote ruling cliques in the provinces.

suerte de estancia. A land measure widely used on the pampas, 1.0 by 1.5 leagues.

La Tercera Posición. ["the Third Position"] Perón's doctrine of international nonalignment.

terciaría. Share-cropping agreement that granted a third share to tenants.

toldería. Indian encampment in the pampas or Patagonia.

trasvasamiento generacional. ["intergenerational supersedence"] Perón's expression in the early 1970s hinting at the imminent advent of a new generation of leaders in the Peronist movement.

unicato. One-man rule, a pejorative expression for Juárez Celman's regime.

unidad básica. ["basic unit"] The smallest unit of Peronist party organization.

vago. ["vagrant"] Eighteenth-century term for free *gaucho.*

vaquería. Cattle roundup in the pampas in the seventeenth and early eighteenth centuries.

vecino. ["neighbor"] Colonial term for a city inhabitant having full rights of citizenship.

veda. ["ban," "prohibition"] Contemporary Argentine system of food rationing by prohibition of sale of certain commodities on specified days of the week.

verticalismo. Perón's system of authoritarian control over the trade unions.

viborazo. ["explosion of vipers"] Popular name for the Córdoba riot of February 1971.

villas de emergencia. ["emergency communities"] Bureaucratic euphemism for the shantytowns of Buenos Aires; the more popular expression is *villas miserias* ("poor towns").

yanacona. Indian uprooted from his community and subject to forced labor, in the sixteenth and seventeenth centuries.

Select Bibliography

Material for this book was assembled from the following libraries: in Britain the Library of University College, London and Senate House, University of London; University of Cambridge Library; the library of St. Antony's College, University of Oxford; in Argentina the Biblioteca Nacional and the library of the Academia Nacional de la Historia; in the United States, the libraries of the University of California at Santa Barbara and Los Angeles. I wish to record my debt to librarians in all these institutions for their assistance in locating rare materials.

This bibliography is not comprehensive, but rather represents the material I consulted while preparing this book. I have not noted numerous newspaper and other documentary materials that I consulted for the twentieth century, since the bulk are mentioned in my earlier studies. Most doctoral dissertations I cite were obtained from University Microfilms International thanks to generous financial assistance from the library at the University of California, Santa Barbara.

Journals are abbreviated as follows:

AEA	*Anuario de Estudios Americanos*
BANH	*Boletín de la Academia Nacional de Historia*
BJHNA	*Boletín de la Junta de Historia y Numismática Americana*
CP	*Comparative Politics*
DE	*Desarrollo Económico*
E	*Económica*
HAHR	*Hispanic American Historical Review*
IAEA	*Inter-American Economic Affairs*
IE	*Investigaciones y Ensayos*
JDA	*Journal of Developing Areas*

423

JGS	*Jahrbuch für Geschichte von Staat, Wirtschaft und Gesellschaft Lateinamerikas*
JISWA	*Journal of Interamerican Studies and World Affairs*
JLAS	*Journal of Latin American Studies*
JPE	*Journal of Political Economy*
LAP	*Latin American Perspectives*
LARR	*Latin American Research Review*
OEP	*Oxford Economic Papers*
NS	*New Scholar*
PP	*Past and Present*
RBC	*Revista de la Bolsa de Cereales*
RE	*Revista de Economía*
REBPC	*Revista de Economía, Banco Provincial de Córdoba*
RHA	*Revista de Historia de America*
RLEUR	*Revista Latinoamericana de Estudios Urbanos-Regionales*
RLS	*Revista Latinoamericana de Sociología*
RPS	*Revista Paraguaya de Sociología*
TA	*The Americas*
TH	*Todo es Historia*

Abad de Santillán, Diego. *La FORA, ideología y trayectoria.* 2d ed. Buenos Aires: Proyección, 1971.

———. *Historia argentina.* 5 vols. Buenos Aires: Tipográfica Editora Argentina, 1965–1971.

Ábalo, Carlos. "Aldo Ferrer y el dilema económico de la Argentina." *DE* 18, no. 71 (Oct.-Dec. 1978):439–50.

Abot, Jorge, Mónica Abramzou, Miriam Chorne, Eduardo Fariña, Miguel Khavisse, Juan C. Torre, Elsa Cimillo, Edgardo Lifschitz, Juana Piotrkowowski. "El poder económico en la Argentina." *Cuadernos del CICSO.* Buenos Aires: Centro de Investigaciones en Ciencias Sociales, 1973.

Acevedo, Edberto Oscar. *La gobernación del Tucumán en el virreinato del Rio de la Plata, 1776–1783.* Seville, 1957.

———. "Repercusión de la sublevación de Tupac Amaru en Tucumán." *RHA,* nos. 49–50 (1960):85–119.

———. "La Rioja hace dos siglos." *IE,* no. 5 (July-Dec. 1968):191–213.

———. "Significación histórica del régimen de intendencias en Salta y Tucumán." *BANH* 33 (1960):119–42.

Agulla, Juan Carlos. *Eclipse of an Aristocracy: An investigation of the Ruling Elites of Córdoba.* Translated by Betty Crouse. N.p.: University of Alabama Press, 1976.

Alberdi, Juan B. *Bases y puntos de partida para la organización política de la República Argentina.* 5th ed. Buenos Aires: Rosso, 1960.

Alen Lascano, Luis C. *Juan Felipe Ibarra y el federalismo del norte*. Buenos Aires, 1968.

Alexander, Robert J. *Juan Domingo Perón*. Boulder, Colo.: Westview Press, 1979.

Almeida, Fernand de. "A Colônia do Sacramento na epoca da soccessão de Espanha." Ph.D. diss., University of Coimbra, 1973.

Alonso Piñeiro, Armando. *La dictadura peronista*. Buenos Aires: Prestigio, 1955.

Altimir, Oscar, Horacio Santamaría, and Juan Sourrouille. "Los instrumentos de promoción industrial en la postguerra." *DE* 7, no. 25 (Apr.-June 1967):893–918.

Amaral, Samuel E. "El empréstito Baring y la crisis de 1826." Ph.D. diss., University of La Plata, 1976.

Andrews, George Reid. *The Afro-Argentines of Buenos Aires, 1800–1900*. Madison: University of Wisconsin Press, 1980.

Ansaldi, Waldo. "Córdoba: De la protoindustria a la gran industria dependiente, 1946–1954." *Estudios e Investigaciones*, 20–32. Buenos Aires: Fundación para el Estudio de los Problemas Argentinos, 1979.

Arce, José. *Roca, 1843–1914: su vida, su obra*. Buenos Aires: Museo Roca, 1960.

Arenas Luque, Fermín V. *El fundador de Córdoba: Don Jerónimo Luis de Cabrera y sus descendientes*. Buenos Aires: La Facultad, 1939.

Ares, Oreste Carlos. "Urquiza y la administración económica-financiera-contable en el Ejército Nacional." *IE*, no. 10 (Jan.–June 1971):379–86.

Asdrúbal Silva, Hernán. "El cabildo, el abasto de carne, y la ganadería: Buenos Aires en la primera mitad del siglo XVIII." *IE*, no. 3 (July-Dec. 1967):393–462.

———. "Pulperías, tendejones, sastres y zapateros: Buenos Aires en la primera mitad del siglo XVIII." *AEA* 26 (1969):471–506.

———. "El trigo en una sociedad colonial: Buenos Aires en la primera mitad del siglo XVIII." *IE*, no. 5 (July -Dec. 1968):375–406.

Azara, Felix de. *Descripción e historia del Paraguay y del Rio de la Plata*. Buenos Aires: Bajel, 1943.

Bagú, Sergio. "La estructuración económica en la etapa formativa de la Argentina moderna." *DE* 1, no. 2 (July-Sept. 1961):113–28.

———. *Mariano Moreno*. Montevideo: Biblioteca de Marcha, 1971.

———. *El plan económico del grupo rivadaviano, 1811–1827: Su sentido y sus contradicciones, sus proyecciones sociales, sus enemigos*. Rosario: Universidad Nacional del Litoral, 1966.

———. "Población, recursos nacionales y neoarcaísmo organizativo en la economía latinoamericana del siglo XX." In *Ensayos sobre el desarrollo económico de México y América Latina (1500–1975)*, edited by E. Florescano, 405–25. Mexico: Siglo XXI, 1975.

Baily, Samuel L. *Labor, Nationalism, and Politics in Argentina*. New Brunswick: Rutgers University Press, 1967.

Bakewell, Peter. "Registered Silver Production in the Potosí District, 1550–1735." *JGS* 12 (1975):67–103.

Balán, Jorge. "La cuestión regional en la Argentina: burguesías del interior y el mercado interno en el desarrollo agroexportador." *DE* 18, no. 69 (Mar.-June 1978):48–87.

Barba, Enrique. *Don Pedro de Cevallos: gobernador de Buenos Aires y virrey del Rio de la Plata.* La Plata: Coni, 1937.

————. *La organización del trabajo en el Buenos Aires colonial.* La Plata: Universidad de La Plata, 1944.

Barba, Fernando Enrique. "El desarrollo agro-pecuario de la provincia de Buenos Aires (1880–1920)." *IE*, no. 17 (July-Dec. 1974):291–310.

Barraclough, Solon L., ed. *Agrarian Structures of Latin America: A Resumé of the CIDA Land Tenure Studies of Argentina, Brazil, Chile, Colombia, Ecuador, Guatemala, Peru.* Lexington, Mass.: Lexington Books, 1973.

Bassi, Juan Carlos. "La expedición libertadora al Alto Perú." In *Historia de la Nación Argentina*, edited by Ricardo H. Levene, 5:pt. 2, 241–72. Buenos Aires: Universidad de Buenos Aires, 1940.

Bayer, Osvaldo. *La Patagonia rebelde.* Buenos Aires: Nueva Imagen, 1980.

Bejerano, Manuel. "Inmigrantes y estructuras tradicionales en Buenos Aires, 1854–1930." In *Los fragmentos del poder*, edited by Torcuato S. Di Tella and Tulio Halperín Donghi, 75–150. Buenos Aires: Jorge Álvarez, 1968.

Belgrano, Mario. "La política externa con los estados de Europa (1813–16)." In *Historia de la Nación Argentina*, edited by Ricardo H. Levene, 6:pt. 1, 577–611. Buenos Aires: Universidad de Buenos Aires, 1944.

————. "La santa alianza. Los comisionados al exterior." In *Historia de la Nación Argentina*, edited by Ricardo H. Levene, 6:pt. 1, 949-1001. Buenos Aires: Universidad de Buenos Aires, 1944.

Belloni, Alberto. *Del anarquismo al peronismo.* Buenos Aires: A. Peña Lillo, 1960.

Berenbau, Mario. "El desarrollo de la agricultura argentina." *DE* 1, no. 1 (Apr.-June 1961):116–22.

Beyhaut, Gustavo, R. Cortés Conde, H. Gorosteguí, and Susana Torrado. "Los inmigrantes en el sistema ocupacional argentina." In *Argentina: sociedad de masas*, edited by Torcuato S. Di Tella, Gino Germani, and Jorge Graciarena, 85–123. Buenos Aires: Editorial de la Universidad de Buenos Aires, 1965.

Bialet Massé, Juan. *El estado de las clases obreras argentinas a comienzos del siglo.* 2d ed. Córdoba: Universidad Nacional de Córdoba, 1968.

Biggs, Huntley J. "Devaluation, Inflation, and Relative Price Changes for Agricultural Exports: Argentina, 1959–1967." Ph.D. diss., Vanderbilt University, 1970.

Blanksten, George. *Perón's Argentina.* Chicago: University of Chicago Press, 1953.

Blinn Reber, Vera. *British Mercantile Houses in Buenos Aires, 1810–1880.* Harvard Studies in Business History, no. 29. Cambridge, Mass.: Harvard University Press, 1979.

Bliss, Horacio William. *Del virreinato a Rosas: ensayo de la historia económica argentina, 1776–1829.* Tucumán: Richardet, 1958.

Bohtlingk, Ronaldo J. *Mercados de Europa para carnes argentinas.* Buenos Aires, 1965.

Borroni, J. Otelo, and Roberto Vacca. *Eva Perón.* Buenos Aires: Centro Editor de America Latina, 1971.

Bosch, Beatriz. "Las provincias del interior en 1856." *IE,* no. 13 (July-Dec. 1972):319–32.

———. *Urquiza y su tiempo* 2d ed. Buenos Aires: Raigal, 1970.

Botana, Natalio R. *El orden conservador: la política argentina entre 1880 y 1916.* Buenos Aires: Sudamericana, 1977.

———. "La reforma política de 1912." In *El regimen oligárquico: materiales para el estudio de la realidad argentina (hasta 1930),* edited by Gustavo Giménez Zapiola, 232–45. Buenos Aires: Amorrortu, 1975.

Bourdé, Guy. *Urbanisation et immigration en Amérique Latine: Buenos Aires (XIXe et XXe siècles).* Paris: Aubier, 1974.

Bowen, Nicholas. "The End of British Economic Hegemony in Argentina: Messersmith and the Eady-Miranda Treaty." *IAEA* 28, no. 14 (Spring 1975):3–24.

Brading, D. A. "Las minas del plata en el Perú y México colonial: un estudio comparativo." *De* 11, no. 41 (Apr.-June 1971):101–11.

Braun, Oscar. *El desarrollo de la capital monopolista en la Argentina.* Buenos Aires: Tiempo Contemporáneo, 1970.

Braun, Oscar, and Ricardo Kesselman. "Argentina 1971: estancamiento estructural y crisis de coyuntura." Buenos Aires. Mimeo.

British Packet, The. *De Rivadavia a Rosas, 1826–1832.* Buenos Aires: Solar Hachette, 1976.

Brodersohn, M. S. "Estrategias de estabilización y expansión en la Argentina: 1959–67." In *Los planes de estabilización en la Argentina,* edited by A. Ferrer, M. S. Brodersohn, E. Eshag, and R. Thorp, 32–63. Buenos Aires: Paidós, 1969.

———, comp. *Estrategias de industrialización para la Argentina.* Buenos Aires: Instituto Torcuato Di Tella, 1970.

Brown, Jonathan C. "Dynamics and Autonomy of a Traditional Marketing System: Buenos Aires 1810–1860." *HAHR* 51, no. 4 (Nov. 1976):605–29.

———. *A Socio-economic History of Argentina, 1776–1860.* Cambridge: Cambridge University Press, 1979.

Bruno, Cayetano. *Historia de la iglesia en la Argentina.* 7 vols. Buenos Aires: Don Bosco, 1966–1971.

Buechler, Rose Marie. *The Mining Society of Potosí.* Syracuse: Syracuse University Press, 1980.

Bunge, Alejandro E. *La economía argentina.* 4 vols. Buenos Aires: Agencia general de librerías y publicaciones, 1928–1930.

———. *Ferrocarriles argentinos.* Buenos Aires: Imprenta Mercateli, 1917.

————. *Las industrias del norte argentino*. Buenos Aires, 1922.

————. *Los problemas económicos del presente*. Buenos Aires, 1917.

Bunkley, Alison. *Life of Sarmiento*. Princeton: Princeton University Press, 1952.

Burgin, Miron P. *The Economic Base of Argentine Federalism*. Cambridge, Mass.: Harvard University Press, 1946.

Busaniche, José Luis. *Estampas del pasado argentino*. Buenos Aires: Solar Hachette, 1971.

————. *Estanislao López y el federalismo argentino*. 2d ed. Buenos Aires: Librería Cervantes, 1927.

————. *Juan Manuel de Rosas*. Buenos Aires: Theoría, 1967.

Caballero Martín, Angel S. *Las corrientes conquistadoras en el Rio de la Plata*. Santa Fe: Universidad de Santa Fe, 1943.

Cady, John F. *La intervención extranjera en el Rio de la Plata, 1838–1850*. Buenos Aires, 1943.

Cafiero, Antonio. *Cinco años después*. Buenos Aires, 1961.

Caillet-Bois, Ricardo. "El directorio, las provincias de la unión y el Congreso de Tucumán." In *Historia de la Nación Argentina*, edited by Ricardo H. Levene, 6:pt. 1, 859–947. Buenos Aires: Universidad de Buenos Aires, 1944.

————. "La revolución en el virreinato." In *Historia de la Nación Argentina*, edited by Ricardo H. Levene, 5:pt. 2, 93–240. Buenos Aires: Universidad de Buenos Aires, 1940.

Cámpora, Héctor J. *La revolución peronista*. Buenos Aires: Editorial de la Universidad de Buenos Aires, 1973.

Canabrava, Alicia Piffer de. *Comércio português no Rio da Prata, 1580–1640*. São Paulo: Universidade de São Paulo, 1944.

Canals Frau, Salvador. *Las poblaciones indígenas de la Argentina: su origen, su pasado, su presente*. Buenos Aires: Sudamericana, 1952.

Canitrot, Adolfo. "La disciplina como objectivo de la política económica: Un ensayo sobre el programa económico del gobierno argentino desde 1976." *Estudios CEDES* 2, no. 6. Buenos Aires, Centro de Estudios de Estado y Sociedad, 1979.

Canter, Juan. "El año XII, las asambleas generales y la revolución del 8 de octubre." In *Historia de la Nación Argentina*, edited by Ricardo H. Levene, 5:pt. 2, 587–755. Buenos Aires: Universidad de Buenos Aires, 1940.

————. "La asamblea constituyente." In *Historia de la Nación Argentina*, edited by Ricardo H. Levene, 6:pt. 1, 3–336. Buenos Aires: Universidad de Buenos Aires, 1944.

————. "La revolución de abril de 1815 y la organización del nuevo directorio." In *Historia de la Nación Argentina*, edited by Ricardo H. Levene, 6:pt. 1, 337–409. Buenos Aires: Universidad de Buenos Aires, 1944.

Cantón, Darío. "El ejército en 1930: el antes y el después." In *Historia integral argentina*, edited by Haydée Gorosteguí de Torres, 7:7–28. Buenos Aires: Centro Editor de Américana Latina, 1970.

————. *Elecciones y partidos políticos en la Argentina*. Buenos Aires: Siglo XXI, 1973.

————. *Materiales para el estudio de la sociología política en la Argentina.* 2 vols. Buenos Aires: Instituto Torcuato Di Tella, 1969.

————. *La política de los militares argentinos, 1900–1971.* Buenos Aires: Siglo XXI, 1971.

Caras y Caretas (Buenos Aires), illustrated weekly.

Cárcano, Miguel Ángel. *El régimen de la tierra pública, 1810–1916.* 2d ed. Buenos Aires: La Facultad, 1925.

Cárcano, R. J. *Urquiza y Alberdi: Intimidades de una política.* Buenos Aires: La Facultad, 1938.

Cardozo, Efraín de. "Asunción del Paraguay." In *Historia de la Nación Argentina*, edited by Ricardo H. Levene, 3:235–74. Buenos Aires: Universidad de Buenos Aires, 1937.

————. "Urquiza y la guerra del Paraguay," *IE*, no. 2 (1968):141–65.

Carretero, Andres M. *Anarquía y caudillismo: la crisis institucional de 1820.* Buenos Aires: Pannedille, 1971.

————. *Los Anchorena: política y negocios en el siglo XIX.* Buenos Aires: Octava Década, 1970.

————. *Dorrego.* Buenos Aires: Pampa y Cielo, 1968.

————. *La llegada de Rosas al poder.* Buenos Aires: Pannedille, 1971.

Carri, Roberto. *Sindicatos y poder en la Argentina.* Buenos Aires: Sudestada, 1967.

Castagno, Antonio. *Tendencias y grupos políticos en la realidad argentina.* Buenos Aires: Editorial de la Universidad de Buenos Aires, 1971.

Cavarozzi, Marcelo. "Sindicatos y política en Argentina, 1955–58." *Estudios CEDES* 2, no. 1. Buenos Aires: Centro de Estudios de Estado y Sociedad, 1979.

Cayró, Antonio J. "El fraude patriótico." In *Historia integral argentina*, edited by Haydée Gorosteguí de Torres, 7:173–96. Buenos Aires: Centro Editor de América Latina, 1970.

Cervera, Manuel M. *Historia de la ciudad y provincia de Santa Fe, 1573–1853.* Santa Fe: La Unión, 1907.

Céspedes del Castillo, Guillermo. *Lima y Buenos Aires.* Seville, 1947.

Charnay, Desiré. *A travers la Pampa et la Cordillère.* Paris, 1876.

Chaunu, H., and P. Chaunu. *Seville et l'Atlantique*, 8 vols. Paris: A. Colin, 1955–59.

Chávez, Fermín. *El Chacho: Ángel Vicente Peñaloza, general de la confederación.* 3d ed. Buenos Aires: Theoría, 1974.

Chávez, Julio César. "La revolución paraguaya de los comuneros." *BANH* 32 (1961):155–64.

Chiaramonte, José C. "La crisis de 1866 y el proteccionismo argentino de la década del '70." In *Los fragmentos del poder*, edited by Torcuato S. Di Tella and Tulio Halperín Donghi, 171–215. Buenos Aires: Jorge Álvarez, 1968.

————. *Nacionalismo y liberalismo económico, 1860–1880.* Buenos Aires: Solar Hachette, 1971.

Ciafardini, Horacio. "Imperialismo y dependencia: notas para la interpretación de la historia de la dependencia en América Latina." Buenos Aires. Mimeo.

Ciria, Alberto. *Parties and Power in Modern Argentina.* Translated by Carlos A. Astiz and Mary F. McCarthy. Albany: State University of New York Press, 1974.

———. *Perón y el justicialismo.* Buenos Aires: Siglo XXI, 1972.

Clark, Colin. *The Economics of 1960.* London: Macmillan, 1942.

Clementi, Hebé. *Juventud y política en la Argentina.* Buenos Aires: Siglo Veinte, 1983.

Cobb, Gwendolin B. "Supply and Transportation for the Potosí Mines, 1545–1640," *HAHR* 29 (1949):25–45.

Cochran, Thomas C., and Ruben Reina. *Entrepreneurship in Argentine Culture.* Philadelphia: University of Pennsylvania Press, 1962.

Colman, Oscar E. "Luchas interburguesas en el agro argentino: la crisis de la carne en el '20." *Cuadernos del CICSO.* Buenos Aires: Centro de Investigaciones en Ciencias Sociales, 1973.

Comadrán Ruiz, Jorge. *Evolución demográfica argentina durante el período hispano, 1535–1810.* Buenos Aires: Editorial de la Universidad de Buenos Aires, 1969.

———. "Nacimiento y desarrollo de los núcleos urbanos y del poblamiento de la campaña del país de Cuyo durante la época hispana, 1551–1810." *AEA* 19 (1962):145–246.

Concolorcovo. *El lazarillo de ciegos caminantes desde Buenos Aires a Lima, 1773.* Buenos Aires: Austral, 1942.

Coni, Emilio A. "La agricultura, ganadería e industrias hasta el virreinato." In *Historia de la Nación Argentina,* edited by Ricardo H. Levene, 4:358–69. Buenos Aires: Universidad de Buenos Aires, 1940.

———. "Contribución a la historia del gaucho." *BJHNA* 9 (1936):85–105.

———. *El gaucho: Argentina, Brazil, Uruguay.* Buenos Aires: Sudamericana, 1945.

———. *Síntesis de la economía argentina.* Buenos Aires, 1930.

Cook, Cheryl Ann. "Macroeconomic Development and Public Policy in Argentina, 1930–1965." Ph.D. diss., Yale University, 1976.

Cooke, John William. *La lucha por la liberación nacional.* Buenos Aires: Papiro, 1971.

Cornblit, Oscar E. "Inmigrantes y empresarios en la política argentina." In *Los fragmentos del poder,* edited by Torcuato S. Di Tella and Tulio Halperín Donghi, 389–438. Buenos Aires: Jorge Álvarez, 1969.

———. "La opción conservadora en la política argentina." *DE* 14, no. 56 (Jan.-Mar. 1975):599–640.

Cornblit, Oscar E., Ezequiel Gallo, Jr., and Alfredo A. O'Connell. "La generación del ochenta y su proyecto—antecedentes y consecuencias." In *Argentina: sociedad de masas,* edited by Torcuato S. Di Tella, Gino Germani, and Jorge Graciarena, 18–59. Buenos Aires: Editorial de la Universidad de Buenos Aires, 1965.

Cornejo, Atilio. "El virrey Toledo y las fundaciones de Gonzalo de Abreu en el valle de Salta." *IE* 2 (Jan.-June 1967):49-67.

Corona Baratech, Carlos E. "Notas para un estudio de la sociedad en el Rio de la Plata durante el virreinato." *AEA* 8 (1951):59–167.

Cortés Conde, Roberto. "La expansión territorial en la Argentina." *DE* 8, no. 29 (Apr.-June 1968):3–30.

———. "Patrones de asentamiento y explotación agropecuaria en los nuevos territorios argentinos." In *El régimen oligárquico: materiales para el estudio de la realidad argentina (hasta 1930)*, edited by Gustavo Giménez Zapiola, 142–55. Buenos Aires: Amorrortu, 1975.

———. "Problemas del crecimiento industrial, 1870–1914." In *Argentina: sociedad de masas*, edited by Torcuato S. Di Tella, Gino Germani, and Jorge Graciarena, 59–81. Buenos Aires: Editorial de la Universidad de Buenos Aires, 1965.

———. *El progreso argentino: La formación del mercado nacional, 1880–1910.* Buenos Aires: Sudamericana, 1979.

———. "Trends in real wages in Argentina, 1880–1910." *Working Papers*, no. 26. Cambridge: University of Cambridge, Centre of Latin American Studies, 1976.

Cortés Conde, Roberto, and Ezequiel Gallo, Jr. *La formación de la Argentina moderna.* Buenos Aires: Paidós, 1967.

Craviotto, José A. "La minería durante la conquista." *BANH* 33 (1962):727–43.

———. "Mitre y la minería. *BANH* 24 (1963):268–85.

La crisis de 1930. *Revista de Historia*, no. 3 (1958).

Cúneo, Dardo. "La burguesía industrial oligárquica, 1875–1930." in *El régimen oligárquico: materiales para el estudio de la realidad argentina (hasta 1930)*, edited by Gustavo Giménez Zapiola, 201–16. Buenos Aires: Amorrortu, 1975.

Dabbs, Jack A. "Manuel de Frías and Rio-Platine Free Trade." *RHA*, nos. 47–48 (1959):377–406.

Darwin, Charles. *Journal of Researches into the Geology, Natural History of the Various Countries Visited During the Voyage of HMS Beagle Around the World.* London: J. M. Dent and Sons, 1912.

Datas-Panero, José Adolfo. "Import Substitution Industrialization: The Argentine Experience." Ph.D. diss., American University, 1970.

Deiner, John T. "ATLAS: A Labor Instrument of Argentine Expansionism under Perón." Ph.D. diss., Rutgers University, 1969.

Del Campo, Hugo. "La Semana Trágica." *Polémica* (Centro Editor de América Latina, Buenos Aires) no. 53 (1971).

Deligiannis, Maria Elena. "La política financiera a partir de junto de 1977." *Documento de Trabajo*, no. 22. Buenos Aires: Fundación para el Estudio de los Problemas Argentinos, 1979.

Deligiannis, Maria Elena, and Stella Maris Martínez. "Política bancaria y financiera, 1946–55." *Documento de Trabajo*, no. 13. Buenos Aires: Fundación para el Estudio de los Problemas Argentinos, 1978.

Deligiannis, Maria Elena, Stella Maris Martínez, and Mabel Alcira Saiz. "Política económica—financiera (desde 1920 hasta 1940)." *Documento de Trabajo*, no 9. Buenos Aires: Fundación para el Estudio de los Problemas Argentinos, 1978.

Delich, Francisco J. *Crisis y protesta social: Córdoba, mayo de 1969.* Buenos Aires: Signos, 1970.

Del Mazo, Gabriel. *El radicalismo: ensayo sobre su historia y doctrina*. Vol. 1, *Desde los orígenes hasta la conquista de la República representativa y primer gobierno radical*. Buenos Aires: Gure, 1957.

Denis, Pierre. *The Argentine Republic: Its Development and Progress*. Translated by Joseph McCabe. London: T. Fisher Unwin, 1922.

Diaz Alejandro, Carlos F. *Essays on the Economic History of the Argentine Republic*. New Haven: Yale University Press, 1970.

Díaz Araujo, Erique. *La conspiración del '43*. Buenos Aires: La Bastilla, 1971.

Di Tella, Guido. "Criterios para una política de desarrollo industrial." *DE* 7, no. 27 (Oct.-Dec. 1967):233–60.

———. *Perón–Perón, 1973–1976*. Buenos Aires: Sudamericana, 1983.

Di Tella, Guido, and Manuel Zymelman. *Las etapas del desarrollo económico argentino*. Buenos Aires: Editorial de la Universidad de Buenos Aires, 1967.

Di Tella, Torcuato S., Gino Germani, and Jorge Graciarena. *Argentina: sociedad de Masas*. Buenos Aires: Editorial de la Universidad de Buenos Aires, 1965.

Di Tella, Torcuato S., and Tulio Halperín Donghi. *Los fragmentos del poder*. Buenos Aires: Jorge Álvarez, 1969.

Documentos para la historia argentina. Vol. 5. Buenos Aires: Compañía Sudamericana de Billetes de Banco, 1915.

Documentos para la historia argentina. Vol. 10. Buenos Aires: Compañía Sudamericana de Billetes de Banco, 1940.

Dolkart, Ronald H. "The Provinces." In *Prologue to Perón: Argentina in Depression and War*, edited by Mark Falcoff and Ronald H. Dolkart, 164–95. Berkeley: University of California Press, 1975.

Dominguez, Luis L., ed. and trans. *The Conquest of the River Plate*. London: Hakluyt Society, 1891.

Dorfman, Adolfo. *Historia de la industria argentina*. 2d ed. Buenos Aires: Solar Hachette, 1970.

Doyon, Louise M. "Conflictos obreros durante el régimen peronista (1946–1955)." *DE* 17, no. 67 (Oct.-Dec. 1977):437–74.

———. "El movimiento sindical bajo el peronismo." *DE* 15, no. 57 (Apr.-June 1975):151–63.

———. "Organised Labour and Perón, 1943–55: A study in the Conflictual Dynamics of the Peronist Movement". Ph. D. diss., University of Toronto, 1978.

Drosdoff, Daniel. *El gobierno de las vacas, 1933–1956: Tratado Roca-Runciman*. Buenos Aires: La Bastilla, 1972.

Du Biscay, Acarete. "Voyage up the Rio de la Plata, and from thence by Land to Peru and His Observations on It." In *Voyages and Discoveries in South America*, edited and translated by Christopher D'Acugna. London: S. Buckley, 1698.

Echagüe, Juan Pablo. "Los orígenes de San Juan: los Huarpes, la conquista y la colonización." *BANH* 18 (1945):163–75.

Echeverría, Esteban. "El matadero." Translated by Ángel Flores. In *History of Latin American Civilization: Sources and Interpretations*, edited by Lewis Hanke, 2:70–76. London: Methuen, 1969.

Elizaga, Juan C. "La evolución de la población argentina en los últimos 100 años." *DE* 12, no. 48 (Jan.-Mar. 1973):795–806.

Endrek, Emiliano. *El mestizaje en Córdoba: siglos XVIII y principios del XIX.* Córdoba: Universidad Nacional de Córdoba, 1966.

———. *El mestizaje en Tucumán.* Córdoba: Universidad Nacional de Córdoba, 1967.

Erikson, John R. "La exportación de manufacturas en la Argentina." *DE* 9, no. 36 (Jan.-Mar. 1970):555–80.

Ernesto Tornquist and Co. *Business Conditions in Argentina.* Buenos Aires: Tornquist, 1913–1922.

———. *The Economic Development of the Argentine Republic in the Last Fifty Years.* Buenos Aires: Tornquist, 1919.

Escudé, Carlos. *Gran Bretaña, Estados Unidos, y la declinación argentina, 1942–1949.* Buenos Aires: Belgrano, 1983.

Eshag, Eprime, and Rosemary Thorp. "Las políticas económicas ortodoxas de Perón a Guido, 1953–1963: Consecuencias económicas y sociales." In *Los planes de estabilización en la Argentina,* compiled by A. Ferrer, M. S. Brodersohn, E. Eshag. R.Thorp, 64–132. Buenos Aires: Paidós, 1969.

Etchepareborda, Roberto. "Breves anotaciones sobre la revolución del 6 de septiembre de 1930." *IE,* no. 8 (Jan.-June 1970):55–104.

———. "La estructura socio-política argentina y la generación del ochenta." *LARR* 13, no. 1 (1978):127–35.

———. "Manuel Belgrano y los proyectos carlotinos frente al arribo de nuevo virrey del Rio de la Plata." *IE* 9 (1970):219–44.

———. "Política luso-rioplatense 1810–1812: Fin de las pretensiones de la Infanta Carlota Joaquina en la regencia del Rio de la Plata y primera invasión portuguesa a la Banda Oriental." *BANH* 32 (1961):54–83.

———. *La revolución argentina del noventa.* Buenos Aires: Raigal, 1966.

———. *Rosas: Controvertida historiografía.* Buenos Aires: Pleamar, 1972.

———. *Yrigoyen y el congreso.* Buenos Aires: Raigal, 1956.

———, ed. *Hipólito Yrigoyen: Pueblo y gobierno.* Vol. 12. Buenos Aires: Raigal, 1951.

Falcoff, Mark, and Ronald H. Dolkart. *Prologue to Perón: Argentina in Depression and War.* Berkeley: University of California Press, 1975.

Fayt, Carlos F. *Naturaleza del peronismo.* Buenos Aires: Pannedille, 1967.

Felix, David. "Industrial Structure, Industrial Exporting, and Economic Policy: An Analysis of Recent Argentine Experience." In *Fiscal Policy for Industrialization and Development in Latin America,* edited by David T. Geithman, 293–339. Gainesville: University of Florida Press, 1971.

Ferguson, J. Halcro. *The River Plate Republics: Argentina, Paraguay, Uruguay.* New York: Time Inc., 1965.

Fernández López, Manuel. "Los primeros economistas argentinos." *Polémica* (Centro Editor de América Latina, Buenos Aires) no. 1 (1970).

Ferns, H. S. *Britain and Argentina in the Nineteenth Century.* Oxford: Oxford University Press, 1960.

Ferrer, Aldo. "Devaluación, redistribución de ingresos y el proceso de desarticulatión industrial en la Argentina." In *Los planes de estabilización en la Argentina*, compiled by A. Ferrer, M. S. Brodersohn, E. Eshag, and R. Thorp, 13–30. Buenos Aires: Paidós, 1969.

Ferrer, Aldo, M. S. Brodersohn, E. Eshag, and R. Thorp. *Los planes de establización en la Argentina*. Buenos Aires: Paidós, 1969.

Ferucci, Ricardo, Alberto Barbero, and Mario Rapoport. "El sector industrial argentino: análisis estructural y situación actual." *Documento de Trabajo*, no. 23. Buenos Aires: Fundación para el Estudio de los Problemas Argentinos, 1980.

FIAT, Oficina de estudios para la colaboración economica international. *Mercado ALALC; Fundamentos macroeconómicos para su evaluación*. Buenos Aires: FIAT, 1971.

Fienup, Darrell F., Russell H. Brannon, and Frank A. Fender. *The Agricultural Development of Argentina: A Policy and Development Perspective*. New York: Praeger, 1969.

———. *El desarrollo agropecuario argentino y sus perspectivas*. Buenos Aires: Instituto Torcuato Di Tella, 1972.

Figueredo, Manuel V., and Enrique de Gandía. "Hernandarias de Saavedra." In *Historia de la Nación Argentina*, edited by Ricardo H. Levene, 3:421–57. Buenos Aires: Universidad de Buenos Aires, 1937.

Fisher H. E. S. *The Portugal Trade: A study of Anglo-Portuguese Commerce, 1700–1770*. London: Athlone Press, 1971.

Fitte, Ernesto J. "Los comerciantes inglesas en vísperas de la Revolución de Mayo." *IE*, no. 2 (1967):69–139.

———. *Hambre y desnudeces en la conquista del Rio de la Plata*. Buenos Aires: Emecé, 1971.

———. *Historia de un empréstito*. Buenos Aires: Emecé, 1962.

———. "Horas finales de la insurrección de Felipe Varela." *IE*, no. 17 (July-Dec. 1974):115–39.

Flichman, Guillermo. "Modelo sobre la asignación de recursos en sector agropecuario." *DE* 10, nos. 39–40 (Jan.-Mar. 1971):375–94.

Fodor, Jorge. "Perón's Policies for Agricultural Exports, 1946–1948: Dogmatism or Common Sense?" In *Argentina in the Twentieth Century*, edited by David Rock, 135–61. London and Pittsburgh: Duckworth, 1975.

Fodor, Jorge, and Arturo O'Connell. "La Argentina y la economía atlántica en la primera mitad del siglo veinte." *DE* 13, no. 49 (Apr.-June 1973):1–67.

Foley, James W. "The Balance of Payments and Import Substituting Industrialization in Argentina, 1945–1961." Ph.D. diss., Michigan State University, 1969.

Fontana, Andrés. "Alianzas y organización nacional en la Argentina, 1852–1862." *Estudios Sociales*, no. 7. Buenos Aires: Centro de Estudios de Estado y Sociedad, 1979.

Ford, A. G. "Argentina and the Baring Crisis of 1890." *OEP* 8 (1956):127–50.

———. *The Gold Standard, 1880–1914: Britain and Argentina*. Oxford: Oxford University Press, 1962.

Francis, Michael J. *The Limits of Hegemony: U. S. Relations with Argentina and Chile During World War II*. Notre Dame: University of Notre Dame Press, 1977.

Fraser, John Foster. *The Amazing Argentine*. London: Cassell, 1914.

Frenkel, Roberto. "Decisiones de precio en alta inflación." *DE* 19, no. 79 (Oct.-Dec. 1979):291–330.

Frenkel, Roberto, and Guillermo O'Donnell. "Los programas de estabilización convenidos con el FMI y sus impactos internos." *Estudios CEDES* 1, no. 1. Buenos Aires: Centro de Estudios de Estado y Sociedad, 1978.

Frigerio, Rogelio. *Nacionalismo, potencias industriales y subdesarrollo*. Buenos Aires: Concordancia, 1961.

――――. "El problema de la carne, los frigoríficos y la crisis general de la economía argentina." *RE* (second quarter, 1970).

Frondizi, Arturo. *Petróleo y política: Contribución al estudio de la historia económica argentina y las relaciones entre el imperialismo y la vida política nacional*. Buenos Aires: Raigal, 1955.

――――. *El problema agrario argentino*. Buenos Aires: Desarrollo, 1965.

Frondizi, Silvio. *La realidad argentina: Ensayo de interpretación sociológica*. Buenos Aires: Praxis, 1955.

Fuchs, Jaime. *Argentina: su desarrollo capitalista*. Buenos Aires: Cartago, 1965.

Furlong Cárdiff, Guillermo. *Historia social y cultural del Rio de la Plata, 1536–1810: el trasplante social*. Buenos Aires: Tipográfica Editora Argentina, 1969.

――――. "Las misiones jesuíticas." In *Historia de la Nación Argentina*, edited by Ricardo H. Levene, 3:595–622. Buenos Aires: Universidad de Buenos Aires, 1937.

――――. *Misiones y sus pueblos de Guaraníes*. Buenos Aires, 1962.

――――. *Nacimiento de la filosofía en el Rio de la Plata*. Buenos Aires: G. Kraft, 1952.

Gallo, Ezequiel, Jr. "The Cereal Boom and Changes in the Social and Political Structures of Santa Fe, Argentina." London. Mimeo.

――――. *Farmers in Revolt: The Revolutions of 1893 in the Province of Santa Fe, Argentina*. London: Athlone Press, 1976.

――――. "El gobierno de Santa Fe vs. el Banco de Londres y Rio de la Plata, 1876." *Documentos de Trabajo*. Buenos Aires: Instituto Torcuato Di Tella, 1972.

――――. "Santa Fe en la segunda mitad del siglo XIX: transformaciones en su estructura regional." In *Los fragmentos del poder*, edited by Torcuato S. Di Tella and Tulio Halperín Donghi, 243–73. Buenos Aires: Jorge Álvarez, 1969.

Gallo, Ezequiel, Jr., and Silvia Sigal. "La formación de los partidos políticos contemporáneos—La U.C.R. (1891–1916)." In *Argentina: sociedad de masas*, edited by Torcuato S. Di Tella, Gino Germani, and Jorge Graciarena, 124–76. Buenos Aires: Editorial de la Universidad de Buenos Aires, 1965.

Gambini, Hugo. *El peronismo y la iglesia*. Buenos Aires: Brújula, 1971.

Gandía, Enrique de. "Belgrano, Mitre, y Alberdi." *IE*, no. 8 (1970):1–52.

――――. *Francisco de Alfaro y la condición social de los indios*. Buenos Aires: El Ateneo, 1939.

――――. "La primera fundación de Buenos Aires." In *Historia de la Nación Argentina*, edited by Ricardo H. Levene, 3:179–234. Buenos Aires: Universidad de Buenos Aires, 1937.

———. "La segunda fundación de Buenos Aires." In *Historia de la Nación Argentina*, edited by Ricardo H. Levene, 3:275–314. Buenos Aires: Universidad de Buenos Aires, 1937.

Garavaglia, Juan Carlos. "Comercio colonial: expansión y crisis." *Polémica* (Centro Editor de América Latina, Buenos Aires) no. 1 (1970).

García Heras, Raúl. "Notas sobre la situación de las empresas de trasportes de capital británico en Argentina a comienzos de los años 30s." *Documento de Trabajo*, no. 15. Buenos Aires: Fundación para el Estudio de los Problemas Argentinos, 1979.

García Lupo, Rogelio. *Mercenarios y monopolios en la Argentina de Onganía a Lanusse*. Buenos Aires: Achával Solo, 1972.

García Martínez, Carlos, and Rafael Olarra Jiménez. "Una nueva política para la exportación de carnes." Buenos Aires: Instituto Argentino de la Industria Exportadora de Carnes, 1970.

Garzón Maceda, Ceferino. *Economía del Tucumán: economía natural, economía monetaria, siglos XVI, XVII, XVIII*. Córdoba: Universidad de Córdoba, 1968.

Gasío, Guillermo, and María C. San Román. *La conquista del progreso, 1874–1880*. Buenos Aires: La Bastilla, 1977.

Gaudio, Ricardo, and Jorge Pilone. "Estado y relaciones obrero-patronales en los orígenes de la negociación colectiva en Argentina." *CEDES, Estudios Sociales*, no. 5. Buenos Aires: Centro de Estudios de Estado y Sociedad, 1976.

Geller, Lucio. "El crecimiento industrial argentino hasta 1914 y la teoría del bien primario exportable." In *El régimen oligárquico: materiales para el estudio de la realidad argentina (hasta 1930)*, edited by Gustavo Giménez Zapiola, 156–200. Buenos Aires: Amorrortu, 1975.

Gente y la actualidad. 25 de mayo de 1973–24 de marzo de 1976. Fotos. Hechos. Testimonios de 1035 dramáticos días. 4th ed. Buenos Aires: Atlántida, 1976.

Gerchunoff, Pablo, and Juan J. Llach. "Capitalismo industrial, desarrollo asociado y distribución de ingreso entre los dos gobiernos peronistas: 1950–1973." *DE* 15, no. 57 (Apr.-June 1975):3–54.

Germani, Gino. *La estructura social de la Argentina*. Buenos Aires: Raigal, 1955.

———. *Política y sociedad en una época de transición*. Buenos Aires: Paidós, 1967.

———. "El surgimiento del peronismo: el rol de los obreros y de los migrantes internos." In *El voto peronista: Ensayos de sociología electoral argentina*, edited by Manuel Mora y Araujo, and Ignacio Llorente, 87–164. Buenos Aires: Sudamericana, 1980.

Germani, Gino, Torcuato S. Di Tella, and Octavio Ianni. *Populismo y contradicciones de clase en Latinoamérica*. Mexico City: Era, 1973.

Giacalone, Rita Ana. "From Bad Neighbors to Reluctant Partners: Argentina and the United States, 1946–1950." Ph.D. diss., Indiana University, 1979.

Gianello, Leoncio. "La influencia del pensamiento de Belgrano en la gesta revolucionaria de mayo." *IE*, no. 8 (1970):171–91.

Giberti, Horacio C. E. *Historia económica de la ganadería argentina*. 2d ed. Buenos Aires: Raigal, 1961.

————. "Renta potencial y productividad agraria." *REBPC* 15, no. 21 (1969).

————. "Uso racional de los factores directos de la producción agraria." *DE* 6, no. 21 (Apr.-June 1966):17–56.

Gibson, Herbert. *The History and Present State of the Sheep-Breeding Industry of the Argentine Republic.* Buenos Aires: Ravenscroft and Mills, 1893.

Gillespie, Richard. "Armed Struggle in Argentina." Oxford. Mimeo.

————.*Soldiers of Perón: Argentina's Montoneros.* Oxford: Clarendon Press, 1982.

Gil Munilla, Octavio. *El Rio de la Plata en la política internacional: génesis del virreinato.* Seville: Escuela de Estudios Hispano-Americanos de Sevilla, 1949.

Giménez Zapiola, Gustavo. "El interior argentino y el 'desarrollo hacia afuera': el caso de Tucumán." In *El régimen oligárquico: materiales para el estudio de la realidad argentina (hasta 1930),* edited by Gustavo Giménez Zapiola, 72–155. Buenos Aires: Amorrortu, 1975.

————, ed. *El régimen oligárquico: materiales para el estudio de la realidad argentina (hasta 1930),* Buenos Aires: Amorrortu, 1975.

Godio, Julio. *La caída de Perón: De junio a septiembre de 1955.* Buenos Aires: Gránica, 1973.

————, ed. *Unitarios y federales.* Buenos Aires: Gránica, 1974.

Goetz, Arturo Luis. "Concentración y desconcentración de la industria argentina, 1930–60." *DE* 15, no. 66 (Jan.-Mar. 1976):507–48.

Goldburg, Marta B. "La población negra y mulata de la ciudad de Buenos Aires." *DE* 16, no. 66 (Apr.-June 1976):75–99.

Goldwert, Marvin. *Democracy, Militarism, and Nationalism in Argentina, 1930–1966.* Austin: University of Texas Press, 1972.

Gómez Morales, Alfredo. *Política económica peronista.* Buenos Aires: Escuela Superior Peronista, 1951.

González, Alberto, and José A. Pérez. *Argentina indígena: vísperas de la conquista.* Buenos Aires: Paidós, 1972.

González, Joaquín V. *Manual de la constitución argentina.* Buenos Aires, n.d.

González Trejo, Horacio. *Argentina: tiempo de violencia.* Buenos Aires: C. Pérez, 1969.

Goodwin, Paul B. "The Central Argentine Railway and the Economic Development of Argentina, 1854–1881." *HAHR* 57, no. 4 (Nov. 1977):613–32.

————. *Los ferrocarriles británicos y la U.C.R., 1916–1930.* Buenos Aires: La Bastilla, 1974.

Gori, Gastón. *Inmigración y colonización en la Argentina.* Buenos Aires: Editorial de la Universidad de Buenos Aires, 1964.

Gorosteguí de Torres, Haydée. "Aspectos económicos de la organización nacional." In *Los fragmentos del poder,* edited by Torcuato S. Di Tella and Tulio Halperín Donghi, 151–70. Buenos Aires: Jorge Álvarez, 1968.

————, ed. *Historia integral argentina.* 7 vols. Buenos Aires: Centro Editor de América Latina, 1970.

Graciarena, Jorge. *Poder y clases sociales de América Latina.* Buenos Aires: Paidós, 1971.

Gravil, Roger. "Anglo–U.S. Trade Rivalry in Argentina and the D'Abernon Mission of 1929." In *Argentina in the Twentieth Century*, edited by David Rock, 41–65. London and Pittsburgh: Duckworth, 1975.

––––––. "State Intervention in Argentina's Export Trade between the Wars." *JLAS* 2, pt. 1 (1970):147–73.

Guerberoff, Simón. "Un análisis de la performance del segmento industrial estable y su impacto en el modelo de crecimiento económico argentino (1949–1967)." *DE* 16, no. 64 (Jan.-Mar. 1977):467–504.

Gutiérrez, Leandro. "Los comerciantes ingleses en el Rio de la Plata." In *Historia integral argentina*, edited by Haydée Gorosteguí de Torres, 1:178–96. Buenos Aires: Centro Editor de América Latina, 1970.

Guy, Donna J. "Carlos Pellegrini and the Politics of Domestic Industry, 1873–1906." University of Arizona. Mimeo.

––––––. "The Other Side of Business Imperialism: The World of the Argentine Entrepreneur, 1870–1914." University of Arizona. Mimeo.

––––––. "La política azucarera." *See* Guy, "Tucumán Sugar Politics."

––––––. "Politics and the Sugar Industry in Tucumán, Argentina, 1870–1900." Ph.D. diss., Indiana University, 1973.

––––––. "The Rural Working Class in Nineteenth-Century Argentina: Forced Plantation Labor in Tucumán." *LARR* 13, no. 1 (1978):135–45.

––––––. "Tucumán Sugar Politics and the Generation of Eighty." *TA* 32, no. 4 (Apr. 1976): 566–84. Also published in Spanish, as "La política azucarera y la generación del ochenta," *DE* 16, no. 64 (Jan.-Mar. 1977): 505–22.

Halperín Donghi, Tulio. "La expansión ganadera en la campaña de Buenos Aires (1810–1852)." *DE* 1, nos. 1–2 (Apr.-Sept. 1963):57–110.

––––––. *Guerra y finanzas en los orígenes del estado argentino, 1790–1850.* Buenos Aires: Belgrano, 1982.

––––––. *Politics, Economics, and Society in Argentina in the Revolutionary Period.* Cambridge: Cambridge University Press, 1975.

––––––. *Proyecto y construcción de una nación: Argentina, 1846–1880.* Caracas: Biblioteca Ayacucho, 1980.

––––––. "Revolutionary Militarization in Buenos Aires, 1806–15." *PP*, no. 40 (July 1968):84–107.

Hanke, Lewis. *The Spanish Struggle for Justice in the Conquest of America.* Philadelphia: University of Pennsylvania Press, 1949.

Hanson, Simon G. *Argentine Meat and the British Market: Chapters in the History of the Argentine Meat Industry.* Stanford: Stanford University Press, 1938.

Heras, Carlos. "El nacionalismo de Mitre a través de la revolución del 11 de septiembre de 1852." *BANH* 16 (1942):120–45.

––––––. "Presidencia de Avellaneda." In *Historia argentina contemporánea*, Academia Nacional de la Historia, 1:149–60. Buenos Aires, El Ateneo, 1963.

Herr, Richard. *The Eighteenth-Century Revolution in Spain.* Princeton: Princeton University Press, 1958.

Hodges, Donald C. *Argentina, 1943–1976: The National Revolution and Resistance.* Albuquerque: University of New Mexico Press, 1976.

Hudson, William Henry. *Far Away and Long Ago: A History of My Early Life.* New York: Dutton, 1918.

Hull, Cordell. *The Memoirs*. 2 vols. New York: Macmillan, 1948.

Humphreys, R. A. *Latin America and the Second World War*. 2 vols. London: Athlone Press, 1981–1982.

—————. *Liberation in South America, 1806–1827: The Career of James Paroissien*. London: Athlone Press, 1952.

Humphreys, R. A., and J. Lynch, eds. *The Origins of Latin American Revolutions, 1808–1826*. New York: Knopf, 1965.

Hutchison, John E., Francis S. Urban, and John C. Dunmore. "Argentina: Growth potential of the Grain and Livestock Sectors." *Foreign Agricultural Economic Report*, no. 78. Washington, D.C.: U.S. Department of Agriculture, 1972.

Ibarguren, Carlos. *La historia que he vivido*. 2d ed. Buenos Aires: Editorial de la Universidad de Buenos Aires, 1969.

Ibarra Grasso, Dick. *Argentina indígena y prehistoria americana*. Buenos Aires: Editora Tipográfica Argentina, 1967.

Imaz, José Luis de. *Los que mandan*. Buenos Aires: Editorial de la Universidad de Buenos Aires, 1968.

—————. "El poder de los terratenientes: el caso de la Argentina." In *Reforma agraria en la América Latina*, edited by Oscar Delgado, 269–89. Mexico City, 1965.

Un inglés [pseud.]. *Cinco años en Buenos Aires*. Buenos Aires, 1943.

Irazusta, Rodolfo. *La Argentina y el imperialismo británico: los eslabones de una cadena, 1806–1833*. Buenos Aires, 1934.

James, Daniel. "Rationalisation and Working-Class Response: The Extent and Limits of Factory Floor Activity in Argentina." *JLAS* 13, no. 2 (Nov. 1981):375–402.

—————. "Unions and Politics: The Development of Peronist Trade Unionism, 1955–1966." Ph.D. diss., University of London, 1975.

Jara, Álvaro. *Importación de trabajadores indígenas en siglo XVII*. Santiago: Universidad de Chile, 1958.

Jauretche, Arturo. *FORJA y la década infame*. Buenos Aires: Coyoacán, 1962.

Jefferson, Mark C. *Peopling the Argentine Pampas*. New York: American Geographical Society, 1926.

Jeffrey, William H. *Mitre and Argentina*. New York: Library Publishers, 1952.

Johnson, Lyman L. "The Silversmiths of Buenos Aires: A Case Study in the Failure of Corporate Social Organizations." *JLAS* 8, no. 2 (Nov. 1976):181–213.

Jones, C. A. "British Financial Institutions in Argentina, 1860–1914." Ph.D. diss., University of Cambridge, 1973.

Jorge, Eduardo F. *Industria y concentración economica*. Buenos Aires: Siglo XXI, 1971.

Kaplan, Marcos. "Política del petróleo en la primera presidencia de Hipólito Yrigoyen, 1916–22." *DE* 12, no. 45 (Apr.-June 1972):3–24.

Katz, Jorge M. "Características estructurales del crecimiento industrial argentino, 1946–1961." *DE* 7, no. 26 (July-Sept. 1967):59–76.

—————. "Una interpretación de largo plazo del crecimiento industrial argentino." *DE* 8, no. 32 (Jan.-Mar. 1969):511–41.

Kelly, Sir David. *The Ruling Few, or the Human Background to Diplomacy.* London: Hollis and Canter, 1953.

Kenworthy, Eldon. "Did the New Industrialists Play a Significant Role in the Formation of Perón's Coalition, 1943–46?" In *New Perspectives on Modern Argentina*, edited by Alberto Ciria, 15–28. Bloomington: Indiana University Press, 1972.

————. "The Formation of the Peronist Coalition." Ph.D. diss., Yale University, 1970.

————. "The Function of a Little-Known Case in Theory Formation, or What Peronism Wasn't." *CP* 6, no. 1 (Oct. 1973):1–35.

Klein, Herbert S. "Las finanzas del virreinato del Rio de la Plata en 1790." *DE* 13, no. 50 (July-Sept. 1973):369–400.

Koebel, W. H. *Argentina: Past and Present.* London: Adam and Charles Black, 1914.

Korn, Francis. *Buenos Aires: Los huéspedes del '20.* Buenos Aires: Sudamericana, 1974.

Korol, Juan Carlos, and Hilda Sábato. *Cómo fue la inmigración irlandesa en Argentina.* Buenos Aires: Plus Ultra, 1981.

Kossok, Manfred. *El virreinato del Rio de la Plata.* Buenos Aires: La Pléyade, 1959.

Lafuente Machain, R. *Buenos Aires en el siglo XVII.* Buenos Aires, 1944.

Lanusse, Alejandro. *Mi testimonio.* Buenos Aires: Lasserre, 1977.

La Razón (Buenos Aires), 1969 (daily).

Latin America: Economic Report (London), 1976–1982 (weekly).

Latin America: Political Report (London), 1976–1982 (weekly).

Lattes, Alfredo E. "La dinámica de la población rural en la Argentina." *Cuadernos del CENEP*, No. 9. Buenos Aires: Centro de Estudios de Población, 1979.

————. "La dinámica de la población rural en la Argentina entre 1870 y 1970." *CENEP: Documento de Trabajo.* Buenos Aires: Centro de Estudios de Población, 1978.

Lattes, Alfredo E., and Ruth Sautu, "Inmigración, cambio demográfico y desarrollo industrial en la Argentina." *Cuadernos del CENEP*, no. 5. Buenos Aires: Centro de Estudios de Población, 1978.

Lavardén, Manuel José de. *Nuevo aspecto del comercio en el Rio de la Plata.* Buenos Aires: Raigal, 1955.

Levene, Ricardo H. "La anarquía de 1820 en Buenos Aires." In *Historia de la Nación Argentina*, edited by Ricardo H. Levene, 6:pt. 2, 287–342. Buenos Aires: Universidad de Buenos Aires, 1947.

————. "El congreso general de las provincias y la conspiración del 18 de diciembre." In *Historia de la Nación Argentina*, edited by Ricardo H. Levene, 5:pt. 2, 419–69. Buenos Aires: Universidad de Buenos Aires, 1940.

————. "Formación del triunvirato." In *Historia de la Nación Argentina*, edited by Ricardo H. Levene, 5:pt. 2, 539–89. Buenos Aires: Universidad de Buenos Aires, 1940.

————. "Introducción." *Documentos para la historia argentina*, 5:i–cxvi. Buenos Aires: Compañía Sudamericana de Billetes de Banco, 1915.

———. *Investigaciones acerca de la historia económica del Rio de la Plata.* Vol. 2. La Plata: Universidad de La Plata, 1928.

———. "Las juntas provinciales creadas por el reglamento del 10 de febrero de 1811 y los orígenes del federalismo argentino." In *Historia de la Nación Argentina,* edited by Ricardo H. Levene, 5:pt. 2, 471–97. Buenos Aires: Universidad de Buenos Aires, 1940.

———. "La obra orgánica de la revolución." In *Historia de la Nación Argentina,* edited by Ricardo H. Levene, 5:pt. 2, 349–417. Buenos Aires: Universidad de Buenos Aires, 1940.

———. "Presidencia de Mitre." In *Historia argentina contemporánea,* Academia Nacional de la Historia, 1:5–64. Buenos Aires, Universidad de Buenos Aires, 1963.

———. "Riquezas, industrias, y comercio durante el virreinato." In *Historia de la Nación Argentina,* edited by Ricardo H. Levene, 4:373–429. Buenos Aires: Universidad de Buenos Aires, 1938.

———. "Significación histórica de la obra económica de Manuel Belgrano y Mariano Moreno." In *Historia de la Nación Argentina,* edited by Ricardo H. Levene, 5:pt. 1, 672–701. Buenos Aires: Universidad de Buenos Aires, 1940.

———. "La sublevación del 1 de diciembre de 1828 y los gobiernos de Lavalle y Viamonte." In *Historia de la Nación Argentina,* edited by Ricardo H. Levene, 7:pt. 1, 277–344. Buenos Aires: Universidad de Buenos Aires, 1949.

———. "Los sucesos de mayo." In *Historia de la Nación Argentina,* edited by Ricardo H. Levene, 5:pt. 2, 9–52. Buenos Aires: Universidad de Buenos Aires, 1940.

———, ed. *Historia de la Nación Argentina.* Vols. 2–7. Buenos Aires: Universidad de Buenos Aires, 1937–1947.

Levillier, Roberto. "Conquista y organización del Tucumán." In *Historia de la Nación Argentina,* edited by Ricardo H. Levene, 3:331–88. Buenos Aires: Universidad de Buenos Aires, 1937.

———. "Enfrentamiento de las corrientes pobladoras del Tucumán y del Rio de la Plata." *BANH* 28 (1958):653–68.

———. *Nueva crónica de la conquista de Tucumán.* Vol. 1. Buenos Aires: Editorial Nosotros, 1926.

———, ed. *Correspondencia de la ciudad de Buenos Aires con los reyes de España.* Vol. 1, *1588–1615.* Buenos Aires: Municipalidad de Buenos Aires, 1916.

Lewis, Colin, "Anglo-Argentine Trade, 1945–65." In *Argentina in the Twentieth Century,* edited by David Rock, 114–34. London and Pittsburgh, 1975.

———. "The British-Owned Argentine Railways, 1857–1947." Ph.D. diss., Exeter University, 1974.

Liachovitsky, Luis. "Lectura de Alberdi." *DE* 12, no. 46 (July–Sept. 1972): 279–304.

Liboreiro, Ernesto S. "Effects of the European Common Market's Agricultural Policies on Argentine Exports of Beef." Michigan State University. Mimeo.

Lindenboim, Javier. "El empresariado industrial argentino y sus organizaciones gremiales entre 1930 y 1946." *DE* 16, no. 62 (July-Sept. 1976): 163-201.

Little, Walter. "Electoral Aspects of Peronism, 1946–1954." *JISWA* 15, no. 3 Aug. 1973):267–84.

———. "La organización obrera y el estado peronista." *DE* 19, no. 75 (Oct.-Dec. 1979):331–76.

———. "Party and State in Peronist Argentina." *HAHR* 53, no. 4 (Nov. 1973): 644–62.

———. "Political Integration in Peronist Argentina, 1943–1955." Ph.D. diss., University of Cambridge, 1971.

———. "The Popular Origins of Peronism." In *Argentina in the Twentieth Century*, edited by David Rock, 162–78. London and Pittsburgh: Duckworth, 1975.

Lizondo Borda, Manuel. *El descubrimiento de Tucumán: el paisaje de Almagro, la entrada de Rojas, el itinerario de Matienzo.* Tucumán, 1943.

———. "El Tucumán de los siglos XVII y XVIII." In *Historia de la Nación Argentina*, edited by Ricardo H. Levene, 3:389–418. Buenos Aires: Universidad de Buenos Aires, 1937.

———. "El Tucumán indígena del siglo XVI: Diaguitas, Lules y Tonocotes." *BJHNA* 10 (1937):73-94.

Llach, Juan José. "Estructura ocupacional y dinámica del empleo en la Argentina: Sus peculiaridades, 1947–1970." *DE* 17, no. 68 (Jan.-Mar. 1978): 539–93.

Llorente, Ignacio. "Alianzas políticas en el surgimiento del peronismo: El caso de la provincia de Buenos Aires." In *El voto peronista: ensayos de sociología electoral argentina*, edited by Manuel Mora y Araujo and Ignacio Llorente, 269–310. Buenos Aires: Sudamericana, 1980.

Lloyd, Reginald, ed. *Twentieth-Century Impressions of Argentina.* London: Lloyd's Bank, 1911.

Lockhart, James. *Spanish Peru: A Colonial Society.* Madison: University of Wisconsin Press, 1968.

Lopez, Adalberto. *The Revolt of the Comuneros, 1721–1735: A Study in the Colonial History of Paraguay.* Cambridge, Mass.: Harvard University Press, 1976.

López Rosas, José R. *Entre la monarquía y la república.* Buenos Aires: La Bastilla, 1976.

Loza, Emilio. "La guerra terrestre 1814–15." In *Historia de la Nación Argentina*, edited by Ricardo H. Levene, 6:pt. 1, 723–76. Buenos Aires: Universidad de Buenos Aires, 1944.

———. "Yatusta, Tucumán y Salta." In *Historia de la Nación Argentina*, edited by Ricardo H. Levene, 6:pt. 1, 777–833. Buenos Aires: Universidad de Buenos Aires, 1944.

Luna, Felix. *Los caudillos.* Buenos Aires: Jorge Álvarez, 1966.

———. *El '45.* Buenos Aires: Sudamericana, 1971.

Lynch, John. *Argentine Dictator: Juan Manuel de Rosas, 1829–1852.* Oxford: Oxford University Press, 1981.

———. *The Spanish American Revolutions, 1808–1826.* New York: Norton, 1973.

————. *Spanish Colonial Administration, 1782–1810: The Intendant System in the Viceroyalty of the River Plate.* London: Athlone Press, 1958.

McCann, William. *Two Thousand Miles Ride Through the Argentine Provinces.* London: Smith, Elder and Co., 1853.

Macchi, Manuel E. *Urquiza, el saladerista.* Buenos Aires: Macchi, 1971.

MacDonald, C. A. "The Politics of Intervention: The United States and Argentina, 1941–1946." *JLAS* 12, pt. 2 (Nov. 1980):365–96.

————. "U.S.–British Relations with Argentina, 1946–50." Oxford University. Mimeo.

MacEwan, Alison M. "The Invisible Proletariat." *Working Paper.* University of Essex, 1973.

McGann, Thomas F. *Argentina, the United States, and the Inter-American System, 1880–1914.* Cambridge, Mass.: Harvard University Press, 1957.

McGeagh, Robert. "Catholicism and Socio-political Change in Argentina, 1943–1973." Ph.D. diss., University of New Mexico, 1974.

McLachlan, Jean O. *Trade and Peace with Old Spain, 1667–1750.* Cambridge: Cambridge University Press, 1940.

McLynn, F. J. "The Argentine Presidential Election of 1868." *JLAS* 11, pt. 2 (Nov. 1979):303–23.

————. "General Urquiza and the Politics of Argentina, 1861–70." Ph.D. diss., University of London, 1975.

Mallon, Richard D., and Juan Sourrouille. *Economic Policy Making in a Conflict Society: The Argentine Case.* Cambridge, Mass.: Harvard University Press, 1975.

Marfany, Roberto H. "Fronteras con los indios en el sud y fundación de los pueblos." In *Historia de la Nación Argentina,* edited by Ricardo H. Levene, 4:443–80. Buenos Aires: Universidad de Buenos Aires, 1940.

Mariluz Urquijo, José M. *Estado e industria, 1810–1862.* Buenos Aires: Macchi, 1969.

————. "La mano de obra en la industria porteña, 1810–35." *BANH* 36 (1964): 583–622.

————. "Protección y librecambio durante el período 1820–35." *BANH* 34 (1962):697–717.

————. *El virreinato del Rio de la Plata en la época del Marquís de Avilés (1799–1801).* Buenos Aires: Academia Nacional de la Historia, 1964.

Martin de Moussy, Jean Antoine Victor. *Description géographique et statistique de la Confédération Argentine.* 4 vols. Paris: Firmin Didot, 1860–1873.

Martinez, Alberto B., and Maurice Lewandowski. *The Argentine in the Twentieth Century.* London: T. Fisher and Unwin, 1911.

Martínez, Stella Maris. "Sector energético: evolución reciente y Plan Energético Nacional." *Documento de Trabajo,* no. 21. Buenos Aires: Fundación para el Estudio de los Problemas Argentinos, 1979.

Martínez Constanzo, Pedro S. *Historia económica de Mendoza durante el virreinato, 1776–1810.* Madrid: Universidad Nacional de Cuyo, 1961.

————. *Las industrias durante el virreinato.* Buenos Aires: Editorial de la Universidad de Buenos Aires, 1969.

————. *La nueva Argentina, 1946–1955.* 2 vols. Buenos Aires: La Bastilla, 1975.

Martínez de Hoz, José Alfredo, Jr. "Los cereales argentinos y el mercado común europeo." *RBC: Número Estadístico,* 1962.

Martorell, Guillermo. *Las inversiones extranjeras en la Argentina.* Buenos Aires: Galerna, 1969.

Matsushita, Hiroschi. *Movimiento obrero argentino, 1930–1945: sus proyecciones en la historia del peronismo.* Buenos Aires: Siglo Veinte, 1983.

Melo, Carlos R. "El año 1877 y los destinos políticos argentinos." *BANH* 32 (1962):549–63.

————. "La frustración de la conciliación de los partidos." *BANH* 34 (1963): 673–95.

————. "La ideología federal de las provincias argentinas entre 1853 y 1880." *BANH* 29 (1958):173–203.

Mérida, José Luis. "La sociedad paraguaya hacia 1625." *AEA* 28 (1971):57–81.

Migden, Susan Socolow. *See* Socolow Migden.

Mitre, Bartolomé. *Historia del Belgrano.* 4 vols. Buenos Aires: Estrada, 1947.

Molina, Raúl A. *Presidencia de Marcelo T. de Alvear.* Buenos Aires: El Ateneo, 1965.

————. *Las primeras experiencias comerciales del Plata.* Buenos Aires, 1956.

Molinari, Diego Luis. *La representación de los hacendados de Mariano Moreno: su ninguna influencia en la vida economica del país y en los sucesos de mayo de 1810.* Buenos Aires: Coni Hermanos, 1914.

Molinari, José Luis. "Los indios y los negros durante las invasiones inglesas al Rio de la Plata en 1806 y 1807." *BANH* 34 (1963):639–73.

Montoya, Alfredo J. *La ganadería y la industria de salazón de carnes en el período 1810–1862.* Buenos Aires: El Coloquio, 1971.

————. *Historia de los saladeros argentinos,* Buenos Aires: Raigal, 1956.

Mora y Araujo, Manuel, and Ignacio Llorente. *El voto peronista: ensayos de sociología electoral argentina.* Buenos Aires: Sudamericana, 1980.

Moreno, Jose Luis. "La estructura social de Buenos Aires en el año 1778." In *América colonial: Población y economía,* Universidad Nacional del Litoral, 151–70. Rosario: Universidad Nacional del Litoral, 1965.

Moreno, Rodolfo. *Intervenciones federales en las provincias.* Buenos Aires: Cámara de Diputados, 1924.

Mörner, Magnus. *The Expulsion of the Jesuits from Latin America.* New York: Knopf, 1965.

————. *The Political and Economic Activities of the Jesuits in the La Plata Region.* Stockholm: Institute of Ibero-American Studies, 1953.

Morse, Richard M. "Primacia, regionalización, dependencia: enfoques sobre las ciudades latinoamericanas en el desarrollo nacional." *DE,* 11, no. 41 (Apr.-June 1971):55–86.

Mulhall, M. G., and E. T. Mulhall. *Handbook of the River Plate.* Buenos Aires: Trübner and Co., 1885.

Murmis, Miguel, and Juan Carlos Portantiero. "Crecimiento industrial y alianza de clases en la Argentina (1930–1940)." In *Estudios sobre los orígenes del peronismo,* compiled by Miguel Murmis and Juan Carlos Portantiero, 1: 3–58. Buenos Aires: Siglo XXI, 1971.

————. "El movimiento obrero en los orígenes del peronismo." In *Estudios sobre los orígenes del peronismo,* compiled by Miguel Murmis and Juan Carlos Portantiero, 1:59–129. Buenos Aires, Siglo XXI, 1971.

———, comps. *Estudios sobre los orígenes del peronismo.* 2 vols. Buenos Aires: Siglo XXI, 1971–1973.

Navarro Gerassi, Marysa. *Los nacionalistas.* Buenos Aires: Jorge Álvarez, 1968.

Nicholls, Madeline W. "Colonial Tucumán." *HAHR* 18 (1938):461–85.

Nicolau, Juan Carlos. *Industria argentina y aduana, 1835–1854.* Buenos Aires: Devenir, 1975.

Nores, Gustavo A. "Quarterly Structure of the Argentine Beef Cattle Economy, 1960–1970." Ph.D. diss., Purdue University, 1973.

Nun, José. "Superpoblación relativa, ejército industrial de reserva y masa marginal." *RLS* 2 (1969): 178-236.

Oddone, Jacinto. *La burguesía terrateniente argentina: Buenos Aires colonial, Capital Federal, Provincia de Buenos Aires, Provincia de Entre Ríos, Territorios Nacionales.* 4th ed. Buenos Aires: Libera, 1975.

O'Donnell, Guillermo. *El estado burocrático-autoritario.* Buenos Aires, 1981.

———. "Estado y alianzas en la Argentina." *DE* 16, no. 64 (Jan.-Mar. 1977): 523–44.

———. "Un 'juego imposible': Competición y coaliciones entre partidos políticos, 1955–66." *Documento de Trabajo.* Buenos Aires: Instituto Torcuato Di Tella, 1972.

Ohly, John H. "Some Effects of Export Policy on the Short-run Distribution of Real Income in post-World War II Argentina." Ph.D. diss., Boston University, 1975.

Olmos, Ramón Rosa. *Historia de Catamarca.* Catamarca, 1957.

Organization of American States, Inter-American Commission on Human Rights. *Report on the Situation of Human Rights in Argentina.* Washington, D.C.: General Secretariat Organization of American States, 1980.

Ornstein, Leopoldo R. "La expedición libertadora al Paraguay." In *Historia de la Nación Argentina,* edited by Ricardo H. Levene, 5: pt. 2, 273-304. Buenos Aires: Universidad de Buenos Aires, 1940.

Ortiz, Ricardo M. *Historia económica de la Argentina, 1860–1930.* 2 vols. Buenos Aires: Raigal, 1955.

Oszlak, Oscar. *La formación del estado argentino.* Buenos Aires: Belgrano, 1982.

Oveid, Iaacov. "El trasfondo histórico de la ley 4144 de residencia." *DE* 16, no. 61 (Apr.-June 1976):123–48.

Overturf, Stephen F. "A Short-run Balance of Payments Model: Argentina." Ph.D. diss., Rice University, 1976.

Pablo, Juan C. de. *Política anti-inflacionaria en la Argentina, 1967–1970.* Buenos Aires: Amorrortu, 1970.

———. "Sobre la distribución funcional del ingreso." *DE* 16, no. 64 (Jan.-Mar. 1977):555–69.

Palcos, Alberto. "Presidencia de Sarmiento." In *Historia argentina contemporánea,* Academia Nacional de la Historia, 1:89–148. Buenos Aires: El Ateneo. 1963.

Panaia, Marta, and Ricardo Lesser. "Las estrategias militares frente al proceso de industrialización (1943–1947)." In *Estudios sobre los orígenes del per-*

onismo, compiled by Miguel Murmis and Juan Carlos Portantiero, 2:83–164. Buenos Aires: Siglo XXI, 1973.

Panettieri, José. *Los trabajadores*. Buenos Aires: Jorge Álvarez, 1968.

París de Oddone, Blanca. "Artigas, un caudillo revolucionario." In *Historia integral argentina*, edited by Haydée Gorosteguí de Torres, 1:150–68. Buenos Aires: Centro Editorial de América Latina, 1970.

Parry, J. H. *The Spanish Sea-borne Empire*. London: Hutchinson, 1966.

Paz, Pedro F. "Dependencia y desnacionalización de la industria interna." Buenos Aires. Mimeo.

Pellegrini, Vicente. *Teoría y realidad de la reforma agraria*. Buenos Aires: Sudamericana, 1963.

Peña, Milcíades. *Masas, caudillos, elites*. Buenos Aires: Fichas, 1971.

Peralta Ramos, Mónica. "Peronism and Dependency." *LAP* 1, no. 3 (Fall 1974):82–92.

Pérez, Joaquín. "Las rivalidades coloniales y la independencia de América, 1793–1815." *BANH* 46 (1973):57–173.

Pérez Colman, César B. *Historia de Entre Rios*. Vol. 1. Paraná Entre Rios: Imprenta de la provincia, 1936.

Perón, Eva. *La razón de mi vida*. Buenos Aires: Peuser, 1951.

Perón, Juan Domingo. *Conducción política*. Buenos Aires: Freeland, 1971.

———. *La fuerza es el derecho de las bestias*. Montevideo, 1958.

Peters, Harold J. *The Foreign Debt of the Argentine Republic*. Baltimore: Johns Hopkins University Press, 1934.

Peterson, Harold F. *Argentina and the United States, 1810–1960*. Albany: State University of New York, 1964.

Phelps, Gilbert. *Tragedy of Paraguay*. New York: C. Knight, 1975.

Phelps, Vernon L. *The International Economic Position of Argentina*. Philadelphia: University of Pennsylvania Press, 1938.

Piccirrilli, Ricardo. "Las reformas económicas-financieras, culturales, militares y eclesiásticas del gobierno de Martín Rodríguez y el ministro Rivadavia." In *Historia de la Nación Argentina*, edited by Ricardo H. Levene, 6:pt. 2, 357–520. Buenos Aires: Universidad de Buenos Aires, 1947.

Piñeiro, Martín. "El impuesto a la tierra: su impacto potencial sobre la producción agropecuaria." *E* 16, no. 3 (Sept.-Dec. 1970):313–28.

"El plan de reactivación económica ante el Honorable Senado." *DE* 19, no. 75 (Oct.-Dec. 1979):403–26.

Platt, D. C. M. *Latin America and British Trade, 1806–1914*. London: Adam and Charles Black, 1972.

Poissek Prebisch, Teresa. *La rebelión de Pedro Bohórquez, el Inca del Tucumán, 1656–1659*. Buenos Aires: Juárez, 1976.

Pomer, León. *Cinco años de guerra civil en la Argentina*. Buenos Aires: Amorrortu, 1977.

———. *La guerra del Paraguay ¡Gran negocio!* Buenos Aires: Caldén, 1968.

"Porque se dividen los peronistas." *Cuarto Poder*. Buenos Aires, 1972.

Potash, Robert A. *The Army and Politics in Argentina, 1928–1945: Yrigoyen to Perón*. Stanford: Stanford University Press, 1969.

―――. *The Army and Politics in Argentina, 1945–1962: Perón to Frondizi*. Stanford: Stanford University Press, 1980.

Potter, Anne L. "The Failure of Democracy in Argentina, 1916–1930: an Institutional Perspective." *JLAS* 13, pt. 1 (May 1981):83–109.

Primera Plana (Buenos Aires), 1966–1970 (weekly).

Pueyrredón, Carlos A. "Gestiones diplomáticas en América." In *Historia de la Nación Argentina*, edited by Ricardo H. Levene, 6:pt. 1, 613–721. Buenos Aires: Universidad de Buenos Aires, 1944.

Puiggrós, Rodolfo. *Los caudillos de la revolución de mayo: Del plan de Moreno al tratado del Pilar*. Buenos Aires: Editorial Problemas, 1942.

Pyle, Jean. "A Re-examination of Aboriginal Population Estimates for Argentina." In *The Native Population of the Americas in 1492*, edited by William M. Denevan, 181–204. Madison: University of Wisconsin Press, 1976.

"¿Qué gana la Argentina con la ALALC?" *Veritas* 15 Nov. 1971.

Ramos, Antonio. "La política de Portugal y la independencia del Paraguay." *JGS* 10 (1973):251–97.

Ramos, Jorge Abelardo. *Revolución y contrarevolución en la Argentina: Historia de la Argentina en el siglo XIX*. 4th ed. Vol 1. *Las masas y las lanzas, 1810–1862*. Buenos Aires: Editorial del Mar Dulce, 1976.

Randall, Laura. *An Economic History of Argentina in the Twentieth Century*. New York: Columbia University Press, 1978.

Rapoport, Mario. *Gran Bretaña, Estados Unidos y las clases dirigentes argentinas: 1940–1945*. Buenos Aires: Belgrano, 1981.

―――. "La política británica en la Argentina a comienzos de la década de 1940." *DE* 16, no. 62 (July-Sept. 1976):203–28.

―――. "La política de Estados Unidos en Argentina en tiempos de la segunda guerra mundial, 1943–1945." *Estudios e Investigaciones* 1, no. 2. Buenos Aires: Fundación para el Estudio de los Problemas Argentinos, 1978.

―――. "Las relaciones anglo-argentinas: aspectos políticos y económicos: la experiencia del gobierno militar, 1943-1945." *Documento de Trabajo*, no. 20. Buenos Aires: Fundación para el Estudio de los Problemas Argentinos, 1979.

Ratier, Hugo. *El cabecita negra*. Buenos Aires: Centro Editor de América Latina, 1971.

Ratto, Héctor R. "La campaña naval contra el poder realista de Montevideo." In *Historia de la Nación Argentina*, edited by Ricardo H. Levene, 6:pt. 1, 801–58. Buenos Aires: Universidad de Buenos Aires, 1944.

Ravignani, Emilio. "El congreso nacional de 1824–27: la convención nacional de 1828–29: inconstitución y régimen de los pactos." In *Historia de la Nación Argentina*, edited by Ricardo H. Levene, 7:pt. 1, 3–209. Buenos Aires: Universidad de Buenos Aires, 1949.

―――. "Crecimiento de la población en Buenos Aires y su campaña." In *Documentos para la historia argentina*, 10:I-XXII. (Buenos Aires: Penetenciaría Nacional, 1940).

―――. *Rosas: interpretación real y moderna*. Buenos Aires: Pleamar, 1970.

———. "El virreinato del Rio de la Plata." In *Historia de la Nación Argentina*, edited by Ricardo H. Levene, 4:27–326. Buenos Aires: Universidad de Buenos Aires, 1938.

Razori, Amílcar. *Historia de la ciudad argentina*. 2 vols. Buenos Aires: López, 1945.

Reber, Vera Blinn. *See* Blinn Reber.

Reca, Lucio G. "Ingresos, tecnología y desarrollo del sector agropecuario." *IDIH*, no. 253 (Jan. 1969).

———. "Precios y áreas sembradas con algodón en la provincia del Chaco. 1938–1968." *DE* 9, no. 35 (Oct.-Dec. 1969):387–98.

Recchini de Lattes, Zulma. "La participación feminina en la Argentina desde la segunda guerra hasta 1970." *CENEP: Documento de Trabajo*. Buenos Aires: Centro de Estudios de Población, 1980.

———. "El proceso de urbanización en la Argentina: distribución, crecimiento y algunas características de la población urbana." *DE* 12, no. 48 (Jan.-Mar. 1973):867–86.

Recchini de Lattes, Zulma, and Alfredo E. Lattes. *La población de Argentina*. Buenos Aires: Zlotopioro, 1975.

Rennie, Ysabel. *The Argentine Republic*. New York: MacMillan, 1945.

República Argentina. *Resumen estadístico del movimiento migratorio en la República Argentina, 1857–1924*. Buenos Aires: Ministerio de Agricultura, 1925.

———. *Tercer censo nacional, 1914*. 5 vols. Buenos Aires, 1915–1917.

———. Bolsa de Cereales. *Memorias e informes del Consejo Directivo de la Bolsa de Cereales*. Buenos Aires: Bolsa de Cereales, 1950–1970 (annual).

———. *Número Estadístico*. Buenos Aires: Bolsa de Cereales, 1950–1970 (annual).

———. Departamento Nacional del Trabajo. *Boletín del Departamento Nacional del Trabajo*. Buenos Aires, 1907–1928.

———. Dirección General de Estadística de la Nación. *Extracto estadístico de la República Argentina correspondiente al año 1915*. Buenos Aires, 1916.

———. Junta Nacional de Carnes. *Reseñas*. Buenos Aires: Junta Nacional de Carnes, 1950–1970 (annual).

———. Poder Ejecutivo Nacional. *Plan trienal para la reconstrucción y la liberación nacional*. Buenos Aires, 1973.

———. Presidencia de la Nación, Consejo Nacional de Desarrollo. *Plan nacional de desarrollo*. Buenos Aires, 1965.

———. Presidencia de la Nación, Secretaria del Consejo Nacional del Desarrollo. *Plan nacional de desarrollo, 1970–1974*. Buenos Aires, 1970.

———. Secretarías del Consejo Nacional de Desarrollo y del Consejo Nacional de Seguridad. *Plan nacional de desarrollo y seguridad*. Buenos Aires, 1971.

Revista Popular (Buenos Aires) 1910–1921 (weekly).

Ribas, A. B., F. F. Johansen, N. A. Belozercovsky, and F. García Martínez. "Análisis de las dificultades internas que obstaculizan las exportaciones no tradicionales." *FIEL*, no. 4 (1970).

Risso Patrón, Roberto. *El agro y la cooperación internacional.* Buenos Aires, 1963.

Robertson, J. P., and W. P. Robertson. *Letters on South America.* 3 vols. London: J. Murray, 1843.

Robinson, Ronald. "Non-European Foundations of European Imperialism: Sketch for a Theory of Collaboration." In *Studies in the Theories of Imperialism,* edited by Roger Owen and Bob Sutcliffe, 117–42. London: Macmillan, 1972.

Rock, David. *Politics in Argentina, 1890–1930: The Rise and Fall of Radicalism.* Cambridge: Cambridge University Press, 1975.

———. "Repression and Revolt in Argentina." *NS* 7, nos. 1–2 (1973):105–20.

———. "The Survival and Restoration of Peronism." In *Argentina in the Twentieth Century,* edited by David Rock, 179–222. London and Pittsburgh: Duckworth, 1975.

———, ed. *Argentina in the Twentieth Century.* London and Pittsburgh: Duckworth, 1975.

Rodríguez, Celso. *Lencinas y Cantoni: El populismo cuyano en tiempos de Yrigoyen.* Buenos Aires: Belgrano, 1979.

———. "Regionalism, Populism, and Federalism in Argentina, 1916–1930." Ph.D. diss., University of Massachusetts, 1974.

Rodriguez, Louis, "A Comparison: U.S. Economic Relations with Argentina and Brazil, 1947–1960." Ph.D. diss., Louisiana State University, 1963.

Rodriguez, Mario. "Dom Pedro de Braganza and Colonia do Sacramento." *HAHR* 38 (1958):179–208.

———. "The Genesis of Economic Attitudes in the Rio de la Plata." *HAHR* 36 (1956):171–89.

Rodríguez Molas, Ricardo. *Historia social del gaucho.* Buenos Aires: Marú, 1968.

———. "El negro en el Rio de la Plata." *Polémica* (Centro Editor de América Latina, Buenos Aires) no. 2 (1970).

Rofman, Alejandro E., and Luis A. Romero. *Sistema socioeconómico y estructura regional en la Argentina.* Buenos Aires: Amorrortu, 1974.

Romero, José Luis. *A History of Argentine Political Thought.* Translated by Thomas H. McGann. Stanford: Stanford University Press, 1968.

Romero, Luis Alberto. *La feliz experiencia.* Buenos Aires: La Bastilla, 1976.

Rosa, José María. *La caída de Rosas.* Buenos Aires: Plus Ultra, 1968.

Rouquié, Alain. *Poder militar y sociedad política en la Argentina.* 2 vols. Translated by Arturo Iglesias Echegaray. Buenos Aires: Emecé, 7th ed. 1983.

———. *Pouvoir militaire et societé politique en République Argentine.* Paris: Presses de la Fondation Nationale des Sciences Politiques, 1978.

Rubio, Julían María. *Exploración y conquista del Rio de la Plata: Siglos XVI y XVII* Barcelona: Salvat, 1953.

Rutledge, Ian. "Plantations and Peasants in Northern Argentina: The Sugar Cane Industry of Salta and Jujuy, 1930–43." In *Argentina in the Twentieth Century,* edited by David Rock, 88–113. London and Pittsburgh: Duckworth, 1975.

Sábato, Jorge Federico. "Notas sobre la formación de la clase dominante en la Argentina moderna." Buenos Aires: Centro de Investigaciones Sociales Sobre el Estado y la Administración. Mimeo.

———. "La pamı̨ a pródiga: Claves de una frustración." *CISEA: Ensayos y Tesis.* Buenos Aires: Centro de Investigaciones Sociales sobre el Estado y la Administración, 1982.

Sagarna, Antonio. "El gobierno de Martín Rodríguez y las reformas de Rivadavia: Las reformas políticas." In *Historia de la Nación Argentina,* edited by Ricardo H. Levene, 6:pt. 2, 343–66. Buenos Aires: Universidad de Buenos Aires, 1947.

Salera, Virgil. *Exchange Control and the Argentine Market.* 1941. Reprint. New York: Columbia University Press, 1968.

Sánchez Albornoz, Nicolás. *El indio en el alto Perú a fines del siglo XVII.* Lima, 1973.

———. "La saca de mulas de Salta al Perú, 1778–1808." In *America colonial: población y economía,* Universidad Nacional del Litoral, 261–323. Rosario: Universidad Nacional del Litoral, 1965.

Saraví, Mario Guillermo. *La suma del poder.* Buenos Aires: La Bastilla, 1976.

Scalabrini Ortiz, Raúl. *Historia de los ferrocarriles argentinos.* 4th ed. Buenos Aires: Reconquista, 1940.

———. *Política británica en el Rio de la Plata.* Buenos Aires: F. Blanco, 1957.

Scenna, Miguel Ángel. *Las brevas maduras.* Buenos Aires: La Bastilla, 1974.

———. "Mariano Moreno" *TH,* no. 35 (Mar. 1970):8–29.

Scheinkerman de Obschatko, Edith. "Factores limitantes al cambio tecnólogico en el sector agropecuario." *Número Estadístico.* Buenos Aires: Banco Ganadero Argentino, 1971.

Schleh, Emilio. *Noticias históricas sobre el azúcar.* Buenos Aires: Centro Azucarero Argentino, 1945.

Schmidtmeyer, Peter. *Travels in Chili, over the Andes, in the year 1820 and 1821, with some sketches of the production and agriculture.* London: S. McDowall, 1824.

Schmukler, Beatriz. "Relaciones actuales de producción en industrias tradicionales no capitalistas." *Estudios Sociales,* no. 6. Buenos Aires: Centro de Estudios de Estado y Sociedad, 1977.

Schultz, Theodore W. "Competition for the Food and Grain Markets in the World." *Agricultural Paper,* no. 69. Department of Economics, University of Chicago, n.d.

Schvarzer, Jorge. "Algunos rasgos del desarrollo industrial de Buenos Aires." Mimeo.

———. "Argentina, 1976–1981: El endeudamiento externo como pivote de la especulación financiera." *Cuadernos del Bimestre,* no. 1. Buenos Aires: Centro de Investigaciones Sociales sobre el Estado y la Administración, 1983.

———. "Las empresas más grandes en la Argentine: Una evaluación." *DE* 17, no. 66 (July-Sept. 1977):319–38.

———. "Empresas públicas y desarrollo industrial en la Argentina." *Documento de Trabajo.* Buenos Aires: Centro de Investigaciones Sociales sobre el Estado y la Administración, 1979.

————. "Martínez de Hoz: La lógica política de la política económica." *CISEA: Ensayos y Tesis*, no. 4. Buenos Aires: Centro de Investigaciones Sociales sobre el Estado y la Administración, 1983.

Schwartz, Hugh M. "The Argentine Experience with Industrial Credit and Protection." Ph.D. diss., Yale University, 1967.

Scobie, James R. *Buenos Aires: Plaza to Suburb, 1870–1910*. New York: Oxford University Press, 1974.

————, *La lucha por la consolidación nacional*. Buenos Aires: Academia Nacional de la Historia, 1964.

————. *Revolution on the Pampas: A Social History of Argentine Wheat, 1860–1910*. Austin, University of Texas Press, 1964.

Segrera, Martin. *Argentina, superpoblada*. Buenos Aires, 1976.

Segrete, Carlos A. "El presidente Mitre y sus relaciones con los Taboada." *IE*, no. 11 (July-Dec. 1971):231–68.

Sempat Assadourián, Carlos. "Integración y desintegración regional en el espacio colonial: un enfoque histórico." *RLEUR* 2, no. 4 (Mar. 1972):11–24.

————. "Sobre un elemento de la economía colonial: producción y circulación de mercancías en el interior de conjunto regional." *RLEUR* 3, no. 8 (Dec. 1973):135–93.

————. *El tráfico de esclavos en Córdoba, 1588–1610*. Córdoba: Universidad de Córdoba, 1965.

Sempat Assadourián, Carlos, Guillermo Beato, and José C. Chiaramonte. *Argentina: de la conquista a la independencia*. Buenos Aires: Paidós, 1972.

Serrano, Antonio. *Los pueblos y culturas indígenas del litoral*. Santa Fe: Castellví, 1955.

Service, Elman R. "The Encomienda in Paraguay," *HAHR* 31 (1951):230–52.

Shtrajov, Alexey. "Trasplante de las instituciones españolas al Rio de la Plata en los siglos XVI y XVII." *AEA* 28 (1971):479–87.

Sidicaro, Ricardo. "L'état péroniste: État et classes sociales en Argentine, 1943–1955." Ph.D. diss., University of Paris, 1977.

Sierra, Vicente D. *Historia de la Argentina*. 2d ed. Vols. 1-3. Buenos Aires: Científica Argentina, 1967.

Silverman, Bertram. "Labor and Left-fascism: A Case Study of Peronist Labor Policy." Ph. D. diss., Columbia University, 1967.

Silvert, K. H. "Liderazgo político y debilidad institucional en la Argentina." *DE* 1, no. 2 (July-Sept. 1961):155–82.

Skidmore, Thomas E. "The Politics of Economic Stabilization in Post-War Latin America." In *Authoritarianism and Corporatism in Latin America*, edited by James M. Malloy, 149–90. Pittsburgh: University of Pittsburgh Press, 1977.

Skupch, Pedro. "Las consecuencias de la competencia del automotor sobre la hegemonía económica británica en la Argentina, 1919–33." Buenos Aires: Instituto de Investigaciones Económicas, Universidad de Buenos Aires. Mimeo.

————. "El deterioro y fin de la hegemonía británica sobre la economía argentina, 1914–1947." In *Estudios sobre los orígenes del peronismo*, compiled by

Miguel Murmis and Juan Carlos Portantiero, 2:1–81. Buenos Aires: Siglo XXI, 1973.

Slatta, Richard W. "Rural criminality and social conflict in nineteenth-century Buenos Aires province." *HAHR* 60, no. 3 (Aug. 1980):450–72.

Slutsky, Daniel. "Aspectos sociales del desarrollo rural." *DE* 8, no. 29 (Apr.-June 1968):95–136.

Smith, Peter H. "The Breakdown of Democracy in Argentina, 1916–30." In *The Breakdown of Democratic Regimes: Latin America*, edited by Juan J. Linz and Alfred Stepan, 3–25. Baltimore: Johns Hopkins Press, 1978.

———. *Politics and Beef in Argentina: Patterns of Conflict and Change.* New York: Columbia University Press, 1969.

———. "Los radicales argentinos y la defensa de los intereses ganaderos." *DE* 7, no. 25 (Apr.-June 1967):795–829.

Smith, Peter H. and Manuel Mora y Araujo. "Peronismo y desarrollo: Las elecciones de 1973." In *El voto peronista: ensayos de sociología electoral argentina*, edited by Manuel Mora y Araujo and Ignacio Llorente, 441–72. Buenos Aires: Sudamericana, 1980.

Snow, Peter G. *El radicalismo argentino.* Translated by Ana Noboa de Dufaux. Buenos Aires: Francisco de Aguirre, 1972.

Socolow Migden, Susan. "Economic Activities of the Porteño Merchants: The Viceregal Period." *HAHR* 35, no. 1 (Feb. 1975):1–24.

———. *Kinship and Commerce: The Merchants of Viceregal Buenos Aires.* Cambridge: Cambridge University Press, 1977.

Solberg, Carl. "Agrarian Unrest and Agrarian Policy in Argentina, 1912–1930." *JISWA* 13 (1971):15–55.

———. *Immigration and Nationalism in Argentina and Chile, 1890–1914.* Austin: University of Texas Press, 1970.

———. *Oil and Nationalism in Argentina.* Stanford: Stanford University Press, 1979.

———. "Peopling the Prairies and the Pampas: The Impact of Immigration on Argentine and Canadian Agrarian Development, 1870-1930." *JISWA* 24, no. 2 (May 1982):131–61.

———. "Tariffs and politics in Argentina, 1916–1930." *HAHR* 53, no 2 (May 1973):260–84.

Sommi, Luis V. *La revolución argentina del '90.* Buenos Aires: Gonzalo Pineda, 1972.

Sourrouille, Juan V. "La presencia y el comportamiento de las empresas en el sector industrial argentino." *Estudios CEDES* 1, no. 2. Buenos Aires: Centro de Estudios y Sociedad, 1978.

Spalding, Hobart A., Jr. *La clase trabajadora argentina: documentos para su historia, 1890–1916.* Buenos Aires: Galerna, 1970.

———. *Organized Labor in Latin America: Historical Case-Studies of Workers in Dependent Societies.* New York: New York University Press, 1977.

Stepan, Alfred. *The State and Society: Peru in Comparative Perspective.* New Haven: Yale University Press, 1978.

Stickell, Lawrence. "Peronist Politics with Labor, 1943." In *New Perspectives on*

Modern Argentina, edited by Alberto Ciria, 29–48. Bloomington: Indiana University Press, 1972.

Street, John. *Artigas and the Emancipation of Uruguay.* Cambridge: Cambridge University Press, 1959.

———. *Gran Bretaña y la independencia del Rio de la Plata.* Buenos Aires: Paidós, 1967.

———. *La influencia británica en la independencia de las provincias del Rio de la Plata, con especial referencia al período comprendido entre 1806 y 1816.* Montevideo, 1956.

Studer, Elena F. S. de. *La trata de negros en el Rio de la Plata durante el siglo XVIII.* Buenos Aires: Universidad de Buenos Aires, 1958.

Susnik, Branislava. *El indio colonial del Paraguay.* Asunción: Museo Etnográfico "Andrés Barbero," 1965.

Szuchman, Mark D. *Mobility and Integration in Urban Argentina: Córdoba in the Liberal Era.* Austin: University of Texas Press, 1980.

Tandeter, Enrique. "Acumulación interna y explotación colonial en el Alto Perú." University of London. Mimeo.

———. "Forced and Free Labour in Late Colonial Potosí," *PP,* no. 93 (Nov. 1981):98–136.

———. "Mining Rent and Social Structure in Potosí in the Second Half of the Eighteenth Century." University of London. Mimeo.

Tapson, Alfred J. "Indian Warfare on the Pampas During the Colonial Period." *HAHR* 42 (1962):1–28.

Taylor, Carl C. *Rural Life in Argentina.* Baton Rouge: State University of Louisiana Press, 1948.

Taylor, J. M. *Eva Perón. The Myths of a Woman.* Chicago: University of Chicago Press, 1979.

TePaske, John J., and Herbert S. Klein. "The Seventeenth-Century Decline in New Spain: Myth or Reality." *PP,* no. 90 (Feb. 1981):116–35.

Testa, Victor. "Aspectos económicos de la coyuntura actual (1973–1975)." *Cuadernos del CISCO.* Buenos Aires: Centro de Investigaciones en Ciencias Sociales, 1975.

Teubal, Miguel. "Policy and Performance of Agriculture in Economic Development: The Case of Argentina." Ph. D. diss., University of California at Berkeley, 1976.

Tjarks, Germán O. E. *El consulado de Buenos Aires y sus proyecciones en la historia del Rio de la Plata.* 2 vols. Buenos Aires: Universidad de Buenos Aires, Facultad de Filosofía y Letras, 1962.

Torre, Juan Carlos. "La caída de Luis Gay." *TH,* no. 89 (1971):81–93.

———. "El proceso interno de los sindicatos en la Argentina." *Documento de Trabajo.* Buenos Aires: Instituto Torcuato Di Tella, 1971.

———. "Sindicatos y clase obrera en la Argentina post-peronista." *RLS* 1 (1968):108–44.

———. "Sindicatos y trabajadores bajo el último gobierno peronista." Oxford University. Mimeo.

Torre, Juan Carlos, and Santiago Senén González. *Ejército y sindicatos—los sesenta días de Lonardi*. Buenos Aires: Galerna, 1969.

Torre Revello, José. "Buenos Aires de antaño." *BANH* 17 (1944):185–95.

———. *Esteco y Concepción del Bermejo: dos ciudades desaparecidas*. Buenos Aires: Peuser, 1943.

———. "Los gobernadores de Buenos Aires (1617–1777)." In *Historia de la Nación Argentina*, edited by Ricardo H. Levene, 3:459–525. Buenos Aires: Universidad de Buenos Aires, 1937.

———. "Los navíos de registro en el Rio de la Plata, 1595–1700." *BANH* 34 (1963):529–59.

———. *La sociedad colonial*. Buenos Aires: Pannedille, 1970.

———. "Viajeros, relaciones, cartas y memorias." In *Historia de la Nación Argentina*, edited by Ricardo H. Levene, 4:545–85. Buenos Aires: Universidad de Buenos Aires, 1938.

Torres, Horacio A. "El mapa social de Buenos Aires en 1943, 1947 y 1960: Buenos Aires y los modelos urbanos." *DE* 18, no. 70 (July-Sept. 1978): 163–204.

Trífolo, S. Samuel. *La Argentina vista por viajeros ingleses, 1810–1860*. Buenos Aires: Raigal, 1959.

Tulchin, Joseph S. "El crédito agrario en la Argentina, 1910-1926." *DE* 18, no. 71 (Oct.-Dec. 1978):381–409.

———. "La reforma universitaria—Córdoba 1918." *Criterio* (June 1970).

United Nations, Comisión Económica para América Latina (CEPAL). *El desarrollo económico de la Argentina*. 4 vols. Mexico City: United Nations, CEPAL, 1959.

———. Economic Commission for Latin America (ECLA). *The Distribution of Income in Argentina*. New York: United Nations, ECLA, 1969.

U.S. Department of State. *Foreign Relations of the United States: 1946*. Vol. 11, *The American Republics*. Washington, D.C., 1969.

———. *Foreign Relations of the United States: 1948*. Vol. 9, *The American Republics*. Washington, D.C., 1971.

———. *Foreign Relations of the United States: 1949*. Vol. 2, *The American Republics*. Washington, D.C., 1973.

Urien, Carlos M. *Geografía argentina*. Buenos Aires: Penetenciaría Nacional, 1905.

Vásquez-Presedo, Vicente. *Estadísticas históricas argentinas, 1875-1914*. Buenos Aires, 1971.

Vega, Urbano de la. *El general Mitre: historia, contribución al estudio de la organización nacional y a la historia militar del país*. Buenos Aires, 1960.

Verdaguer, Aníbal. "La región de Cuyo hasta la creación del virreinato del Rio de la Plata." In *Historia de la Nación Argentina*, edited by Ricardo H. Levene, 3:527–39. Buenos Aires: Universidad de Buenos Aires, 1937.

Vieytes, Juan H. *Antecedentes económicos de la revolución de mayo*. Buenos Aires: Raigal, 1956.

Vilar, Pierre. *A History of Gold and Money, 1450–1620*. London: New Left Review, 1976.

Villalobos R., Sergio. *El comercio y la crisis colonial: un mito de la independencia.* Santiago: Universidad de Chile, 1968.

Villamarin, Juan A., and Judith E. Villamarin. *Indian Labor in Mainland Spanish America.* Newark: University of Delaware Press, 1975.

Villanueva, Javier. "Economic Development." In *Prologue to Perón: Argentina in Depression and War, 1930–1943,* edited by Mark Falcoff and Ronald H. Dolkart, 57–67. Berkeley: University of California Press, 1976.

———. "The Inflationary Process in Argentina." Ph.D. diss., Columbia University, 1964.

———. "El orígen de la industrialización argentina." *DE* 12, no. 47 (Oct.-Dec. 1972):451–76.

Villar, Daniel. *El cordobazo.* Buenos Aires: Centro Editor de América Latina, 1971.

Villaroel, José César. "Política de ingresos, 1946–55." *Documento de Trabajo,* no. 19. Buenos Aires: Fundación para el Estudio de los Problemas Argentinos, 1979.

Wainerman, Catalina H., and Marysa Navarro. "El trabajo de la mujer en la Argentina: un análisis preliminar de las ideas dominantes en las primeras décadas del siglo XX." *CENEP: Documento de Trabajo.* Buenos Aires: Centro de Estudios de Población, 1979.

Waldmann, Peter. *El peronismo, 1943–1955.* Buenos Aires: Sudamericana, 1981.

Walker, Geoffrey J. *Spanish Politics and Imperial Trade, 1700–1785.* Bloomington: Indiana University Press, 1979.

Wallerstein, Immanuel. *The Modern World System: Capitalist Agriculture and the Origins of the European World Economy in the Sixteenth Century.* New York: Academic Press, 1974.

Walter, Richard J. *The Socialist Party of Argentina, 1890–1930.* Austin: University of Texas Press, 1977.

———. *Student Politics in Argentina: The University Reform and Its Effects, 1918–1964.* New York: Basic Books, 1968.

Warner, Percy D., III. "The Impact of the Service on the Foreign Debt on the Monetary Structure: Argentina, 1955–1965." Ph.D. diss., Michigan State University, 1970.

Wedevoy, Enrique. *La evolución económica rioplatense a fines del siglo XVIII y principios del siglo XIX a la luz de la historia del seguro.* La Plata: Universidad de La Plata, 1967.

Weffort, Francisco. "Clases populares y desarrollo social." *RPS* 5, no. 13 (Dec. 1968):62–159.

Weil, Felix J. *Argentine Riddle.* New York: John Day, 1944.

Whitaker, Arthur P. *Argentine Upheaval: Perón's Fall and the New Regime.* London: Atlantic Press, 1956.

White, John W. *Argentina: The Life Story of a Nation.* New York: Viking Press, 1942.

Willhofer, E. Spencer, "Peronism in Argentina: The Social Bases of the First Regime, 1946-1955." *JDA* 11 (Apr. 1977):335–56.

Williams, Glynn, and Julia Garlant. "The Impact of the Conquest of the Desert upon the Tehuelche of Chubut—From Hunters and Gatherers to Peasants." British Society for Latin American Studies. Mimeo.

Williams, J. H. *Argentine International Trade under Inconvertible Paper Money, 1880–1900.* Cambridge, Mass.: Harvard University Press, 1920.

Woltman, Harry Raymond. "The Decline of Argentina's Agricultural Trade: Problems and Policies, 1929–54." Ph.D. diss., Stanford University, 1959.

Wright, Winthrop R. *British-Owned Railways in Argentina: Their Effect on Economic Nationalism* (Austin: University of Texas Press, 1974).

Wynia, Gary W. *Argentina in the Post-War Era: Politics and Economic Policy making in a Divided Society.* Albuquerque: University of New Mexico Press, 1978.

Yrigoyen, Hipólito. *Pueblo y gobierno.* Edited by Roberto Etchepareborda. Vol. 12. Buenos Aires: Raigal, 1951.

Yujnovsky, Oscar. "Políticas de viviendas en la ciudad de Buenos Aires." *DE* 14, no. 54 (July-Sept. 1974):327–71.

Zeni, Enrique R. *El destino de la agricultura argentina.* Buenos Aires: La Pléyade, 1972.

Zorraquín Becú, Ricardo. "Migraciones indígenas en la época colonial." *BANH* 38 (1965):317–24.

———. *La organización política argentina en el período hispánico.* Buenos Aires: Librería del Plata, 1959.

Zorrilla, Rubén H. *Extracción social de los caudillos.* Buenos Aires: La Pléyade, 1972.

Zuvekas, Clarence V., Jr. "Argentine Economic Policies under the Frondizi Government." Ph.D. diss., Washington University, 1967.

Index

457

Compositor: Interactive Composition Corporation
Text: Linotron 202 Palatino
Display: ITC Novarese Medium
Printer: Braun-Brumfield, Inc.
Binder: Braun-Brumfield, Inc.